Marriage, Couple, and Family Therapy

THEORY, SKILLS, ASSESSMENT, AND APPLICATION

Bassim Hamadeh, CEO and Publisher
Leah Sheets , Project Editor
Jess Estrella , Senior Graphic Designer
Alexa Lucido, Licensing Coordinator
Natalie Piccotti, Senior Marketing Manager
Kassie Graves, Vice President of Editorial
Jamie Giganti, Director of Academic Publishing

Cover image copyright © 2014 by iStockphoto LP/KeithBishop.

Printed in the United States of America

ISBN: 978-1-5165-1035-1 (pbk) / 978-1-5165-1036-8 (br)

Marriage, Couple, and Family Therapy

THEORY, SKILLS, ASSESSMENT, AND APPLICATION

Brandé Flamez and Janet Hicks

Brief Contents

Extended Contents

PART III   The Schools and Models of Family Therapy

Preface

Marriage, Couple, and Family Therapy: Theory, Skills, Assessment, and Application provides a foundational basis for counselors working with couples and families. Whether you are working specifically with couples and families, in a school, private practice, or an agency setting, this text covers all the bases from theory to practical application. As an added bonus, current issues such as immigration, diverse family structures, the impact of grief and illness on the family, and parental and adolescent influences on family development are covered from a systemic, empathic, and multicultural perspective. Readers will find the case presentations, guided practice activities, and expert reflections that accompany each chapter interesting, relevant, and helpful.

The aim of *Marriage, Couple, and Family Therapy: Theory, Skills, Assessment, and Application* is to provide readers with a strong foundation in marriage and family therapy (MFT) history, theory, and clinical assessment that will allow them to develop the skills and competencies needed to become effective, ethical counseling practitioners in today's diverse society. Currently, there are no textbooks on the market that have a section dedicated specifically to the role of assessment within introduction books for marriage and family counseling.

This text thoroughly prepares students by infusing the role of assessment with the theoretical knowledge and skills deemed important by national boards, organizations, and accrediting bodies. The National Association of Regulatory Boards in Marriage and Family Therapy determine specific knowledge areas are necessary for those seeking to become licensed clinicians. These topics consists of major models and theories of MFT and clinical, research, and ethical topics. The Council for the Accreditation of Counseling and Related Programs Assessment (CACREP, 2016) also aligns with the American Association for Marital and Family Therapy (AAMFT, 2014) and has established skills, practice, and knowledge domains. Each have identified the importance of having knowledge related to assessment.

Marriage and family therapy cannot adequately assist clients without proper assessment. For this reason, this text focuses on and views assessment as an integral part of the counseling process. As part of the holistic counseling process, therapists are taught to gather and integrate information about an individual from multiple sources using multiple methods to positively impact the counseling process (Watson & Flamez, 2014, Drummond & Jones, 2016). Once this assessment process begins, therapists and clients begin to see the numerous benefits of assessment in all aspects of counseling practice from rapport building, problem identification, diagnosis, treatment planning, assessing treatment efficacy, and evaluating client outcomes. Highlighting the importance of sound assessment in the practice of counseling, previous authors have contended that it is imperative for counselors, working in a variety of clinical settings, to develop refined assessment skills (Whiston, 2016). Thus we have an entire section dedicated to assessment.

To further meet these goals our textbook is divided into four main sections. The first section will cover the history and conceptual frameworks of marriage and family counseling. The next section will focus on research, intake, assessment, and progress evaluation. The third section covers all the major schools and models of family therapy, including: transgenerational family therapies, strategic and Milan, structural, behavioral and cognitive behavioral, solution-focused, narrative, family psychoeducation and enrichment, and integrative models. The textbook comes to an end by covering special issues within marriage and family therapy such as nonnuclear families, influences on parental functioning on the family, and child and adolescent influences on the family. Each chapter includes the following:

- **Learning Objectives** based on the COAMFTE and CACREP standards.
- 4–5 **Guided Practice Exercises**, which include mini case studies, tables, charts, and activities.
- **Reflections from the Contributor's Chair**, in which authors share how they apply and use the material in their practice.
- Rich **Case Presentations** to demonstrate the applied practice of the content
- **Keystones**, which contain bulleted main summary points.
- **Additional Resources**, including readings, websites, and videos for additional study.

In addition, each chapter is written by experts in our field who have been recognized nationally for their publications and leadership related to marriage and couples therapy. Students introduced to the topics in this text have the unique and unusual advantage of exposure to not only expert knowledge but also to their personal reflections, strategies, and unique case presentations. Where else can students hear so many personal reflections and stories, and even read advice from so many top counselors in the field?

While this book covers multiple aspects of family therapy and includes up-to-date research, we realize that this text alone cannot adequately address all the issues one may come across when working with couples and families. However, we hope that exposure to the rich, substantive, and interesting material not only increases learning but encourages students to question, research, and discuss other possibilities. As discussed in this text, questions lead to research, which leads to improved client services and outcomes. We hope you enjoy reading the many differing views and strategies in the text as much as we did!

Acknowledgments

Completing a project of this scope would not have been accomplished without the perseverance, dedication, hard work, and wonderful contributions of the contributing authors. To each of you, I extend my sincere appreciation for helping create an introduction marriage and family text that introduces the role of assessment in working with couples and families.

To my family and friends, especially my parents, Rosemary and John, I thank you for your love and support during the many hours spent on this project. Your love and encouragement is one of the greatest gifts a daughter could ever ask for.

A special thank-you to my friend and coeditor, Dr. Janet Hicks, for all your hard work and the many laughs we shared during this journey. I am grateful for our friendship.

I would like to thank those at Cognella Inc. who helped turn my vision into reality, especially my editor Kassie Graves. Your support, patience, and encouragement are invaluable, and this book would not have been possible without your involvement and your continued support. Finally, I would like to give a warm thank you to Leah Sheets, my associate editor, for her helpful and enthusiastic responses.

Each and every one of you has my sincere appreciation and gratitude.

—Brandé Flamez

I would like to thank the authors who dedicated their time and talents to making this text possible. Thanks to your perseverance and countless hours, this work is now a reality. I would also like to thank Brandé Flamez for her professionalism and tireless work ethic. You inspire me! Your enthusiasm and energy are contagious, and I can't think of a better partner for this vision. Finally, I would like to thank my husband, Matt, for his support and encouragement throughout this process. I feel blessed to have your unconditional support and love in this and every venture.

—Janet Hicks

About the Editors

Brandé Flamez, PhD, LPC, NCC, is a licensed professional counselor and clinical professor in the Counseling and Special Populations department at Lamar University. Dr. Flamez is also the CEO and founder of the nonprofit SALT (Serving and Learning Together) World Inc., which provides donations and volunteer services to developing countries. Her clinical background includes working with children, adolescents, and families in community-based and private counseling settings. In addition, Dr. Flamez helped design an outpatient program for court-referred adolescents. Dr. Flamez is active in the counseling profession. She has served on the American Counseling Association (ACA) Governing Council for the International Association of Marriage and Family Counselors (IAMFC), ACA Finance Committee, ACA Investment Committee, and chaired the ACA Publications Committee. She is also the past president for the Association for Humanistic Counselors (AHC) and currently serves as the president for IAMFC and co-chairs the Bylaws/Ethics Committee for AHC.

Dr. Flamez is on the editorial board for the *Family Journal*. She has presented numerous times at the nationally and internationally level and coauthored several book chapters and articles. Dr. Flamez is the coauthor of the assessment textbook *Counseling Assessment and Evaluation: Fundamentals of Applied Practice*, coauthor of the dissertation book *A Counselor's Guide to the Dissertation Process: Where to Start & How to Finish*, the coeditor for *Diagnosing Children and Adolescents: A Guide for Mental Health Practitioners* (Wiley) and the upcoming supervision book *Practical Approaches to Clinical Supervision Across Settings*. She is the recipient of numerous national awards, including the 2017 Dr. Judy Lewis Counselors for Social Justice Award, 2015 Counselor Educator Advocacy Award, 2014 ACA Kitty Cole Human Rights Award, 2012 ACA Gilbert and Kathleen Wrenn Award for a Caring and Humanitarian Person, and the 2012 IAMFC Distinguished Mentor Award.

Janet Froeschle Hicks, PhD, LPC, is a licensed professional counselor and certified school counselor who currently serves as professor and director of Mental Health Counseling at Belmont University in Nashville, Tennessee. She was inducted into the American Counseling Association Fellows in 2015 and is listed as an expert on the *Psychology Today* website, where she authors a professional child- and family-focused blog entitled *Raising Parents*. She has served as a media expert at national and state levels on topics related to child, adolescent, and family counseling and serves professionally through many volunteer activities. For example, Dr. Hicks served as Special Events chair for the International Association of Marriage and Family Counselors, Research Committee co-chair for the Texas Counseling Association, and currently serves as By-Laws Committee chair for the Tennessee Counseling Association.

Dr. Hicks has researched and written over 50 publications and presented numerous times on topics related to child, adolescent, family, and school counseling. She currently serves as a reviewer for the *Journal of Women and Minorities in Engineering*, and her work has appeared in journals such as *Professional School Counseling, Journal of Creativity in Mental Health, Middle School Journal, Journal of School Counseling, Family Journal,* and *International Journal of Play Therapy,* among others. In addition, her work has been demonstrated in invited presentations at the American Counseling Association Conference & Expo as well as in *Counseling Today* articles. She has received numerous awards, including induction into the 2015 ACA Fellows, 2008 and 2009 High Plains Counseling Association Outstanding Counselor Award, the 2010–2011 Texas Tech University Hemphill Wells New Professor Excellence in Teaching Award, and 2014 Barney Rushing Outstanding College Research Award.

List of Contributors

Mary B. Ballard, PhD, LPC, is a professor and core faculty member in the Master of Science Counseling Program at Southeastern Louisiana University, where she serves as program coordinator. She specializes in school counseling, addiction counseling, and school-based family issues. Her scholarly interests include children and adolescent issues that affect school success, transgenerational family influences, aging, and family addiction dynamics.

Rebecca Pender Baum, PhD, LPCC, NCC, is a core faculty member and clinical coordinator for the counseling program at Murray State University. She completed her masters of science in education in 2008 with a specialization in marriage, couple, and family counseling. She specializes in providing counseling services for individuals, couples, and families using structural and strategic principles while integrating play and sand tray therapy. In addition, she currently provides clinical supervision to graduate students and postgraduates working toward their license in counseling. Her research interests include counseling supervision, creativity in counseling, and crisis and trauma counseling.

Esther Benoit, PhD, LPC, NCC, is a core faculty member in the Marriage, Couples, and Family Counseling Program and assessment coordinator for the School of Counseling at Walden University. She specializes in providing counseling services for couples and families, using structural, experiential, and cognitive-based approaches. Her research interests include military families, counselor education and supervision, and moral development.

Stephan Berry, PhD, LPC, is assistant professor and school counseling coordinator at Troy State University. He received his PhD in counselor education and supervision from Texas Tech University. He is a licensed professional counselor and supervisor with experience in both the clinical mental health and school settings.

Hannah Bowers, PhD, LMFT, is an assistant professor of school counseling at Florida Atlantic University. She has been working with children and families for the past 7 years, as both a marriage and family therapist and a school counselor. Her research thus far has focused on investigating school counseling programs and interventions that are aligned with the ASCA national model. She advocates for the school counseling profession and engages the entirety of the school system. She was recently selected as an emerging leader for the Association of Humanistic Counseling and promoted to associate editor for the *Journal of Humanistic Counseling.*

Loretta J. Bradley, PhD, LPC-S, LMFT-S, NCC, is a former president of ACA, ACES, IAMFC, and Texas AADA. She is a frequent presenter at national, regional, state, and international conferences, and she has many publications in couples counseling. She is a fellow of the ACA. She has received research awards from ACA, ACES, and the British Association for Counseling and Psychotherapy. Her research endeavors include ethical issues/dilemmas in family and couples counseling, supervision, professional wills, and multicultural/social justice issues for couple and family counselors.

Rochelle Cade, PhD, LPC-S, is an assistant professor in the Graduate Counseling Department at the University of Mary Hardin–Baylor. She received her bachelor's degree in psychology, master's degree in community counseling, and PhD in counselor education from Texas A&M University–Corpus Christi. She is a licensed professional counselor-supervisor with clinical experience in assessment, individual, and group counseling in criminal justice settings. Dr. Cade is active in the International Association of Marriage and Family Counselors (IAMFC). She is a former editorial assistant and current editorial board member for the *Family Journal.*

Tracy Calley, PhD, has been teaching within higher education since 2004 and is a lecturer within the Professional Counseling Program at Texas State University. She is the clinic coordinator for two university-based counseling clinics that serve individuals, families, and couples within the community. In addition, she is the practicum and internship coordinator for her program and works to ensure students are placed at quality sites. Her scholarly interests include counselor supervision models, sleep–wake disorders in adolescents, and utilizing creativity in counseling.

Brian S. Canfield, Ed.D., LPC-S, LMFT-S, is a licensed psychologist who specializes in marriage counseling and couples therapy. He holds appointment as professor of clinical mental health counseling at Florida Atlantic University. He has presented to professional groups throughout the United States and internationally on marriage and family therapy practice. He is a past president of the International Association of Marriage and Family Counselors and a fellow and past president of the American Counseling Association.

Angela M. Catena, PhD, LMHC, is a clinical assistant professor at Arizona State University (ASU) in the Counseling and Counseling Psychology program. She teaches core clinical courses and supervises students during their practicum at ASU's Counselor Training Center. She has been supervising counselors-in-training for 4 years. Additionally, her clinical work has included women who have experienced various forms of trauma, providing both individual and family counseling.

Abby Dougherty, PhD, NCC, LPC, is an assistant clinical professor and the counseling curriculum coordinator for the Creative Art Therapies and Counseling Program at Drexel University. She is the president-elect for the Greater Philadelphia Area Counseling Association and has provided college counseling at several Philadelphia area colleges. She loves to learn and produce scholarship on relational-cultural theory and using mindfulness and contemplative tools in counselor education.

Adriana Dyurich, M.S., LPC-intern, is a licensed professional counselor intern and doctoral candidate in Counselor Education at Texas A&M University–Corpus Christi. Her research concentrates on issues related to women and children, perinatal depression, academic success, pain management, and motivation. She has presented and written on the use of dialectical behavior therapy and narrative therapy. In addition to her regular academic studies, she has training in acceptance and commitment therapy, trauma-focused CBT, and play therapy.

Laura Fazio-Griffith, PhD, LPC-S, LMFT, NCC, registered play therapist-supervisor, is an associate professor and core faculty member in the Master of Science Counseling Program at Southeastern Louisiana University, where she coordinates the Marriage, Couple, and Family Counseling, and Play Therapy Programs. Her research interests include clinical supervision, play therapy, and couples, family, and adolescent counseling.

Joshua Francis, PhD, LPCC-S, LICDC-CS (Ohio), has over 20 years of clinical counseling experience working in community mental health, hospitals, schools, and private practice. He has owned and operated a private counseling and consultation practice and is an assistant professor of clinical mental health counseling at Wright State University in Dayton, Ohio. His clinical specialties and areas of research include child and adolescent mental health, marriage and family therapy, high-conflict divorce, trauma, counselor ethics, counselor wellness, evolutionary/primal mental health, and process/behavioral addictions.

Perry C. Francis, Ed.D., LPC, NCC, ACS, is a professor of counseling at Eastern Michigan University and the coordinator of the counseling training clinic in the College of Education Clinical Suite. He teaches in the counseling program; sees individuals, couples, and families in the clinic; and is an active member of the American Counseling Association. He was also the chair of the American Counseling Association Code of Ethics Revision task force that created the 2014 ACA Code of Ethics. He writes and presents in the area of ethics and practice in the counseling profession.

Melissa Gaa, PhD, LPC, is currently assistant professor of counselor education at Tarleton State University. She is a licensed professional counselor in Texas. She is cofaculty advisor for the Chi Sigma Iota chapter at Tarleton State University. Her areas of research include lesbian, gay, bisexual, and transgender issues, feminist counseling, ethics in counseling, and training programs in counseling. She has previously worked with both families and individuals in community agencies and private practice.

Sarah H. Golden, MA, LPC, NCC, DCC, ACS, received her master of arts degree in counselor education from Western Michigan University and completed her undergraduate work at Hope College. She is currently working on her doctorate in counselor education and supervision at Walden University. Sarah provides counseling services for youth ages 5–21 and enjoys working with diverse populations both in urban and rural environments. She is currently working with youth and families in a blended learning charter school environment and is developing a counseling program that meets the needs of students who receive in-person and online education focusing on positive mental health, crisis counseling, family support, and academic support. Her professional and research interests include working with marginalized populations, consultation, crisis intervention, program development, virtual counseling, and multicultural counseling.

Laura R. Haddock, PhD, LPC-S, NCC, ACS, is a core faculty member in the Mental Health Counseling Program at Walden University. She has been a counselor educator since 2002, supported by more than 25 years as a mental health clinician. Her clinical practice includes work with a variety of populations, with particular focus on women's issues. She is an active counseling professional and has served on the Mississippi Licensed Professional Counselors Board of Examiners and the executive boards for Mississippi Counseling Association and Mississippi Licensed Professional Counselors Association. Her scholarly interests include counseling supervision, counselor wellness and secondary trauma, spirituality, crisis response, and cultural identity.

Melinda Haley, PhD, is a licensed psychologist in New Mexico and works as a counselor educator and core faculty member in the Counselor Education and Supervision doctoral program at Walden University. She has written numerous book chapters and journal articles on diverse topics related to counseling. She has extensive clinical experience working with adults, adolescents, children, inmates, domestic violence offenders, and culturally diverse populations in the areas of assessment, diagnosis, treatment planning, crisis management, and intervention.

Brooks B. Hanks, PhD, LCPC, is a core faculty member at Walden University in the Clinical Mental Health Counseling Program. Dr. Bastian Hanks's scholarly interests include child sexual abuse, vicarious trauma, and mental health accessibility. Clinically, Dr. Bastian Hanks has been working with children who have been sexually abused and their families since 2005. She also works as a forensic interviewer and victim advocate.

Kathryn Helmers, MA, attained her MA degree in English at the University of Denver and her MA in counseling at Belmont University. She has presented on topics related to family therapy, and her research interests are animal assisted therapy and pastoral care. She currently serves on the Tennessee Counseling Association's By-Laws Committee.

Bret Hendricks, EdD, LPC-supervisor, is professor and coordinator of the Counseling Education Program at Texas Tech University. His research interests include ethics in counseling and wellness strategies for counselors. He is a past president of the International Association of Marriage and Family Counselors and the Texas Counseling Association. He is a frequent speaker at regional, national, and international conferences and has served on the editorial boards of two national journals.

Katherine M. Hermann-Turner, PhD, PLPC, NCC, is an assistant professor in the Department of Counselor Education at the University of Louisiana–Lafayette. She is an active counselor educator engaging in scholarship and service at the university and national level, including a leadership role with the Association for Adult Development and Aging and service on several editorial boards. Her current research interests include the impact of meal preparation on couples and families, neurological benefits of mindfulness practices, integration of Web 2.0 teaching techniques into higher education, and relational cultural theory.

K. Michelle Hunnicutt Hollenbaugh, PhD, LPC-S, is an associate professor in the Department of Counseling and Educational Psychology at Texas A&M University–Corpus Christi. She specializes in dialectical behavior therapy and evidence-based practices with adults and adolescents. She has several years of experience teaching and engaging in standardized assessment.

Lynn Jennings, PhD, LPC-S, LSOTP, is counselor and owner of Jennings and Associates Counseling Services in Amarillo, Texas. She graduated with her PhD in counselor education and supervision from Texas Tech University and her master's degree in counseling from West Texas A&M University.

Stephen Jennings, PhD, LPC-S, LSOTP, is counselor and owner of Jennings and Associates Counseling Services in Amarillo, Texas. He graduated with his PhD in counselor education and supervision from Texas Tech University and his master's degree in counseling from West Texas A&M University.

Tom Knowles-Bagwell, DDiv, LPT, is an associate professor of counseling and associate director of the Mental Health Counseling Program at Belmont University. He is a graduate of Vanderbilt Divinity School with both the master of divinity and doctor of ministry degrees. He is licensed as a clinical pastoral therapist in Tennessee and is an ordained minister in the Christian Church (Disciples of Christ). In addition, Tom is certified as a diplomate in the American Association of Pastoral Counselors and is a certified sexual addiction therapist through the International Institute for Trauma and Addiction Professionals.

Reshelle C. Marino, PhD, LPC-S, NCC, is an assistant professor and core faculty member in the Master of Science Counseling Program at Southeastern Louisiana University, where she coordinates the School Counseling Program. She specializes in school counseling and providing clinical counseling services to children, adolescents, and families. Her scholarly interests include counseling supervision, multicultural issues, and legal and ethical issues in counseling.

Cheryl A. Mark, PhD, LPC, NCC, is an assistant professor at Colorado Christian University, teaching master's counseling students. She is the 2017–2019 Board Member at Large for the International Association of Marriage and Family Counselors and also serves on the Emerging Leaders Committee. She is a presenter at state, national, and international conferences. She specializes in working with trauma, is a neurofeedback practitioner, and is certified in eye movement desensitization and reprocessing therapy. Her research interests include attachment, self-disclosure, and marital intimacy in couples, specifically in military couples.

Mary G. Mayorga, PhD, LPC, is an associate professor and clinical coordinator of the Mental Health Counseling Program at Belmont University in Nashville, Tennessee. She obtained her PhD at Texas A&M University–Corpus Christi in counselor education in 2005. She has a master's degree in counseling from Texas Southern University and a bachelor's degree in sociology from Texas A&M University–Corpus Christi. She has certification as a licensed professional counselor, national certified counselor, certified chemical dependency counselor, and certified anger resolution therapist.

Michael Moyer, LPC-S, is an associate professor of counseling at the University of Texas–San Antonio (UTSA). His primary research interests include nonsuicidal self-injury, ethical decision making, and school counselor education. Since 2004 he has authored/coauthored 17 journal articles; delivered over 30 presentations at regional, state, and national conferences; and been recognized for his contributions to the profession. In 2008 he was the recipient of both the Texas Counseling Association's research and professional writing awards and was a corecipient of the 2014 Chi Sigma Iota national research award. In addition to his work at UTSA, he maintains a small private practice and specializes in treating nonsuicidal self-injury.

Robika Modak Mylroie, PhD, is a distance clinical professor in the Department of Counseling and Special Populations at Lamar University. She received her bachelor's degree in psychology from Millsaps College and her master's and PhD in counseling from Mississippi State University. She was a school counselor in the middle school setting for several years, as well as a licensed professional counselor in Mississippi. Her current research interests include childhood obesity's impact on personal, social, and academic growth in children and adolescents; animal-assisted therapy; and yoga in therapy with women who have experienced trauma.

Rebecca D. Goodrich-Rodriguez, PhD, LPC, is a clinical manager of case management in the managed care market and an adjunct instructor in the department of Clinical Mental Health Counseling at South University. She has worked in disease management, as a therapist for the U.S. Air Force, and as a counselor at a women's shelter, where she worked with children and families. She has published articles on insomnia and supervision and contributed to book chapters on gestalt therapy and technology in counselor education. Her other research interests include ethics, motivational interviewing, and case management.

Leslie Neyland-Brown, PhD, LPC, NCC, is an assistant professor at Wright State University, where she currently serves as the school counseling graduate program director. As a dually licensed counselor in the state of Ohio, she has years of experience working with children and adolescents in both the school and clinical setting. Her research interests include supervision, multicultural issues, and school counselor training.

Marvarene Oliver, EdD, LMFT-S, LPC-S, is a professor in the Department of Counseling and Educational Psychology at Texas A&M University–Corpus Christi. She is the coordinator of the marriage, couple, and family counseling emphasis and clinical coordinator for the master's and doctoral programs. She provided counseling and psychotherapy to individuals, couples, and families for over 3 decades and supervises postdegree individuals seeking licensure as professional counselors and marriage and family therapists. She is a clinical fellow and approved supervisor in the American Association for Marriage and Family Therapy.

Samir H. Patel, PhD, LMHC, is a core faculty member and program coordinator of the counseling program at Murray State University. Clinically, he is grounded in humanistic counseling and specialized in providing community-based counseling to children and families and counseling services to adolescents in residential treatment facilities. His teaching and scholarship focus on wellness within a multicultural, social justice framework.

Torey Portrie-Bethke, PhD, NCC, is a core faculty member in the Clinical Mental Health Counseling Program at Walden University. She specializes in providing counseling services for children, adolescents, and families, using experiential methods such as adventure-based counseling, play therapy, and sand play. Her scholarly interests include counseling supervision, adventure-based counseling, online counselor education, childhood sexual abuse, vicarious trauma, and experiential teaching.

Cassandra Riedy earned her MA in medical ethics from the University of Virginia in 2011 and her BA from Georgetown University in 2009. She is currently completing her MA in mental health counseling at Belmont University in Nashville, Tennessee, and graduates in 2018. She has written articles and presented on topics related to cross-generational counseling and social justice. She served on both the Tennessee Counseling Association's By-Laws and Human Rights Committees.

Derek L. Robertson, PhD, LPC-S, is an assistant professor of counselor education at the University of Texas–San Antonio. His counseling work focused on children in the foster care system as well as immigrant, LGBT, and military families. His research interests include promoting cognitive complexity through in-depth intercultural experiences, multicultural counseling best practices, and the effects of social media on psychological wellbeing and relationships.

Jarryn J. Robinson, PhD candidate, LMFT associate, is a student in counselor education and supervision at the University of Texas at San Antonio. She is currently a licensed marriage and family therapist associate in Texas and actively works in drug recovery and mental health relapse prevention. She is interested in multicultural and social justice issues in mental health and higher education.

Mark Scholl, PhD., LMHC (New York), is an associate professor in the Department of Counseling at Wake Forest University. He is an active member in the American College Counseling Association and in the Association for Humanistic Counseling. He is an associate editor for the *Journal of College Counseling* and is a past two-term editor of the *Journal of Humanistic Counseling*. For four years he has provided career support services to members of the ex-offender population in Greenville and Winston-Salem, North Carolina. In 2012 he was awarded the Joseph Hollis Publication Award. He is a past president of the Association for Humanistic Counseling (AHC) and began a term as the AHC's ACA Governing Council Representative in July 2017.

Stephanie K. Scott, PhD, LMHC, is a core faculty member of the Marriage, Couple, and Family Counseling program at Walden University. She specializes in adolescent and family counseling, focusing most of her clinical work on mood disorders, trauma, and systemic patterns of abuse. She has worked with adolescents, couples, and families for almost 20 years and has developed interventions based in creativity and metaphor. Her academic focus lies predominantly in human development and clinical skills training, and she has published research in these areas as well as in counselor education.

Lauren Shure, PhD, LMHC, is currently an assistant professor of counseling at Barry University. She has an MEd and EdS in marriage and family counseling and a PhD in counselor education. Her professional interests include multicultural training and supervision, crisis training and intervention, and best practices in counseling and counselor education.

Quinn K. Smelser, MA, NCC, LPC, RPT, is a doctoral student in counseling at George Washington University and a licensed professional counselor in Texas working on transferring licensure to the Washington, D.C., area. She is also a registered play therapist and national certified counselor. Quinn earned her master's degree in counseling from Texas State University and currently works as a therapist for children and families who have experienced trauma, working at the Gil Institute for Trauma Recovery and Education under the supervision of Dr. Eliana Gil, LMFT, RPT-S.

Lee A. Teufel-Prida, **PhD, LPCC, LMHC, NCC,** is a clinical assistant professor and assistant director of training at Counseling@Northwestern at the Family Institute at Northwestern University. She specializes in clinical training, supervision, and counseling children. Her current research focuses on children and families. Specifically, her interest centers on advocating for children with neurodevelopmental disorders and how counselors and counselor educators may best increase services and initiatives for children and families impacted by neurodevelopmental disorders.

Baylea Wagener, MS, LPC-intern, is a doctoral student in the Counselor Education program at the University of Texas A&M–Corpus Christi and a crime victim counselor with the Corpus Christi Police Department. Her professional focus is in providing individual, family, or group counseling services, specializing in treatment for trauma and abuse as well as clinical mental health issues. Her scholarly interests include complex trauma, posttraumatic growth, vicarious trauma, counselor supervision, and interpersonal neurobiology.

Mike Walsh, PhD, LPC, CRC, has been an assistant professor of neuropsychiatry and behavioral science in the University of South Carolina School of Medicine's Rehabilitation Counseling Program since 2009. In addition to his work as a counselor educator, he has been active in the national counseling arena, having served two terms as president of the Association for Humanistic Counseling, and has served as a member of the American Counseling Association's Governing Council. He also served on the ACA Ethics Committee from 2010 to 2013 and again from 2014 to 2017, and was the cochair in 2011. Mike has authored and delivered well over 150 local and national presentations and trainings. He is active in private practice, working with both individuals and families. He uses family therapy in his clinical work and has coauthored several book chapters on humanistic and experiential approaches to family therapy work.

Elizabeth Ann Wardle, PhD, LPC-S, RN, is a Clinical Mental Health Counselor who graduated from Texas A & M University—Corpus Christi with a Ph.D. in Counselor Education, in addition to being a Registered Nurse She has taught at Del Mar College, the

University of Houston—Victoria, and Texas A & M University—Kingsville. She has provided supervision for Licensed Professional Counselor Interns. Her academic experience also includes grant writing and civic engagement projects, in addition to professional presentations at the local, regional, state, national and international level. She has published articles in professional journals that address utilizing technology, non-traditional students, wellness and burnout. Her research, as well as teaching interests also include psychopharmacology, service learning and experiential learning. She has served as faculty advisor for Chi Sigma Iota, and president of the Gulf Coast Counseling Association.

Kathy Ybañez-Llorente, PhD, LPC-S, is an associate professor in the Professional Counseling Program at Texas State University. She specializes in providing counseling services to children, adolescents, and families in a variety of settings, including private practice, community counseling agencies, foster care/state contract settings, and inpatient psychiatric settings. Her scholarly interests include clinical supervision, multicultural issues in supervision, professional identity, ethical practice, professional licensure, and advocacy.

Anthony Zazzarino, MA, LPC, ACS, CPRP, is a lecturer at Rutgers University, Department of Psychiatric Rehabilitation and Counseling Professions. He also provides individual clinical supervision to associate counselors and provides group counseling to adolescents at an intensive outpatient program. His research interests include sexual minorities, serious mental illness, counselor preparation, and clinical supervision.

PART I

History and Conceptual Framework

CHAPTER 1

Family Therapy: Concepts, Context, and Criteria

Stephanie K. Scott and Lee A. Teufel-Prida

"In every conceivable manner, the family is link to our past,
bridge to our future."

—Alex Haley

As you embark on studying family therapy, there is no doubt you will realize that each family is unique. You will learn that there are a variety of approaches, techniques, and interventions; there is no "one-size-fits-all" approach; and there are many ways of offering help. As a professional it is important to have a fundamental understanding of the key concepts in family therapy.

Family therapy can trace its origins to the groundbreaking work of Alfred Adler a century ago. Though Adler's work focused on the wellness of individuals, he recognized early on the significant role the family of origin played in an individual's development and mental health. Early in his career, Adler was mentored by Sigmund Freud, but he soon departed from the strict views of Freud. This departure from the traditional psychoan-alytical theory of the time was significant in Adler's early work in family therapy. Adler rejected what he saw as a myopic focus on sexual themes and an overemphasis on the power of the unconscious. While he recognized these considerations as influential, Adler asserted that the more relevant aspect was how these manifested in relational dynamics. He gave value to the social context of individuals, noting direct ties between family experiences in early life and identity and worldview in adulthood. In many ways, Adler was a systemic therapist before systems theory was widely known. Adler's foundation in the field of family therapy, combined with the popularity of general systems theory (GST) in the mid-20th century, laid the groundwork for what would eventually become family systems therapy and eventually simply family therapy. The field has evolved exponentially over the past 50 years, with a variety of theoretical approaches and empirically supported interventions to support its efficacy. In this chapter, we provide an overview of these theories and their application.

Before we embark on a review of key theories, we want to ensure that you have a firm understanding of the underpinnings of family therapy. Thus, in this chapter, we will review these fundamentals—including concepts, constructs, and considerations. We will also discuss some of the advantages and challenges to systems-focused counseling and provide some perspective from real-life clinical experiences with family work.

LEARNING OBJECTIVES

After reading this chapter, you will be able to do the following:

- Understand key concepts in the study of family therapy.
- Recognize the roots and common themes across family therapy disciplines.
- Determine the appropriateness of systems-focused interventions.
- Integrate cultural considerations and adaptations into systems-focused interventions.
- Compare and evaluate the strengths and barriers in clinical work with families.

KEY CONCEPTS

Though each systemic theory will have some unique elements and foci, there are many concepts that are common across disciplines. In this section, we will discuss some of those universal concepts, including relevance and application.

General Systems Theory

GST was first proposed by Ludwig von Bertalanffy in the early to mid-20th century. Sometimes referred to as a "general theory of systems," Bertalanffy's ideas forever changed the way researchers viewed and organized ideas about their respective fields. His theory shifted traditional focus from components or pieces to relationships and mutual influences. At the core of GST are the ideas that "a) circumstances and events can be evaluated and understood through analysis of dynamic interactions among influential elements, and b) all systems have shared patterns that reveal key characteristics of that system" (Scott, 2015, p. 129). The expanding popularity of GST during the 20th century significantly impacted the field of psychotherapy by transferring focus from individuals to relationships. GST was the foundation for the rapidly evolving **family systems theory**

example

Family Systems Theory [handwritten]

REL & ENV [handwritten]

in which individuals were viewed within the context of their systemic relationships. This **ecological perspective** helped further advances in clinical mental health by actively integrating the role of both relationships and environment on the health and wellness of individuals (Magnavita, 2012). For the first time, the existing connections, bonds, and associations were considered vital to the treatment equation, in turn supporting the view that relationships themselves are often the "client." Guided Practice Exercise 1.1 asks you to consider the rationale for viewing relationships instead of individuals as the major focus in counseling.

healthy vs. unhealth [handwritten]

GUIDED PRACTICE EXERCISE 1.1

In family therapy, the relationship, rather than the individual, is seen as the client and each individual is viewed as being part of the family system. Why do you think this viewpoint became prevalent in family therapy? What might happen if family therapists viewed only one person in a relationship as the client? How would focusing on the relationship as client help each individual separately?

determine what is unhealthy in the REL. & then each person's role in that unhealthiness [handwritten]

Cybernetics

Cybernetics is the study of self-regulation in systems (Smith-Acuna, 2010). The concept—applicable across disciplines and fields—provides an understanding of the processes, limitations, and mechanisms by which systems maintain themselves. A simple example of this can be seen in the temperature regulation common in modern-day households. The temperature is set by the home owner on a thermostat. The thermostat monitors the internal temperature of the home, alternately turning on heating or cooling elements to keep the temperature inside consistent. The temperature system in the home, therefore, monitors and controls itself through a **feedback loop**. The feedback loop is an essential part of the communication necessary to maintain a **homeostasis**—or steady equilibrium—in the environmental temperature. In social systems, there are "rules" that regulate acceptable behaviors within the system; such rules "which are often implicit, serve as the system's thermostat" (Smith-Acuna, 2010, p. 69). If the behaviors deviate from the established rules, the system will respond with feedback to reestablish the system's homeostasis.

Feedback loops in couple and family relationships—as with many other types of self-regulating systems—can be **positive** or **negative**. These terms are not reflective of the relative impact of the feedback, but rather the mechanism of action. **Positive feedback loops** encourage the increase of a particular behavior to maintain equilibrium, while negative feedback loops discourage certain behaviors. Either way, the system strives to maintain its homeostasis, which has been established by history and habit and is often separate from the health or wellness of the system.

In studying the cybernetics of human systems, early researchers discovered that while systems do have an overall tendency to maintain homeostasis over time, the variations in practices and the inefficacy of some feedback loops do not always support

this is where codependency is birth - attempts to avoid negative [handwritten] this. Punishments, guilt, and shame are common negative feedback processes in family systems, and though designed to provide regulation to the system, they may prove to be both ineffective and destructive. For example, an adolescent who breaks household rules by staying out all night may find himself or herself on the receiving end of parental anger and punishment. This reaction is designed to bring the child back to the acceptable behavior of the system. However, the consequence may be rejected by the adolescent, who instead responds with his or her own anger and a rebellion toward the parents' efforts. The conflict escalates, with the system experiencing a "runaway effect" in which the feedback loops fail, resulting in the system's extended *disequilibrium*—perhaps even necessitating intervention or outside assistance. Still, it is important for couple and family counselors to recognize that systems are disposed toward homeostasis, regardless of whether such is healthy or unhealthy, and are generally resistant to change without concerted and collaborative efforts of all within the system (Scott, 2015).

Everyone working on it.

The reality and regularity of runaway feedback loops in couple and family systems helped better explain not only the observed variations in system dynamics, but also the recognition of different levels of change. For example, in the situation above, the adolescent accepting parental consequences and changing his or her behavior to conform to the parents' rules would be an example of **first-order change**. Such changes are more simplistic and most easily recognized by system members; they also can have a more immediate impact on restoring homeostasis to the system. A **second-order change** for this system might be a change in the behaviors concerning the rules and system regulation—such as a family meeting to discuss parents' feelings of worry as well as the teenager's desire to have more freedom. It is important to note that couple and family therapists work with both levels of change within the system, being careful not to impose values or personal judgment on system members, but rather to focus their efforts on promoting a healthy homeostasis in which all members flourish.

Functionalism

In simplest terms, **functionalism** provides an answer to the question "what purpose does this serve?" Most often applied to behaviors, this concept may also apply to overarching patterns, smaller pieces, unique characteristics, or even circumstances within a system. Functionalism became an important element in the evolution of couple and family therapy, as researchers sought to better comprehend the complexities and influences in systems. Using a functionalist perspective provided another dimension to the role and function of certain traits, behaviors, or characteristics (Morgan, 2014). For example, in the family system described above, it might be argued that the adolescent's behavior serves a purpose; perhaps he or she is trying to assert independence as he or she moves closer to adulthood. Alternatively, perhaps the parents have a high-conflict relationship and frequently fight, which the teen finds stressful. By creating a conflict in the form of rebellion, the teen forces the parents to unite in their reaction—thereby easing (temporarily) the tension in the parental relationship.

Practical?

Key things to consider

Functionalism can sometimes be limiting or restrictive, as it often relies heavily on assumptions. Considerations of gender roles, motivations, dyadic influence, and culturally driven forces, for example, are given great weight in functionalism, though they may vary widely from one system to the next. Still, functionalism validates the potential importance of these considerations and should not be overlooked. In fact, it could be argued that functionalism is an essential aspect of family systems theory and clinical work, as it adds a depth to the understanding of problems themselves.

Structuralism *Functionalism*

Structural Theory

Just as functionalism helps explain the role of conflicts and behaviors, **structuralism** helps to explain *the position* of these relative to the system and its members (Morgan, 2014). Furthermore, structuralism provides a deeper understanding of suprasystems and subsystems that influence family dynamics and patterns. According to the structural theory of family systems, clear and consistent boundaries are essential elements of healthy dynamics. Boundaries that are too weak, too strong, or simply unclear can contribute to the system becoming dysfunctional. In this view, the key to positive change in structuralism is to improve the position of the individual relative to the system; this is done through the clarification and adjustment of relational bonds. A structurally focused counselor considers how the systemic relationships impact the etiology and resolution of the presenting issues. Let's turn to Guided Practice Exercise 1.2 and consider how structuralism might affect family behaviors.

GUIDED PRACTICE EXERCISE 1.2

Assume a teen has unclear or enmeshed boundaries with her mother in the family system. This same teen stayed out past curfew, and both parents decided to enforce boundaries together. How do you suppose this teen will react to each parent? Will the enmeshment cause more defiance toward the mother? Do you think this would affect the nature of conflict in the family system?

"enmeshment" overly stifled kids by parents no autonomy

Structuralism was the foundation of Salvador Minuchin's work in the 1970s and arguably had the greatest impact on the advancement of family therapy. However, it is also true that structuralism is inseparable from functionalism in a practical sense. Thus, from a foundational perspective, it is often best to consider these core concepts together as "structural-functionalism," wherein issues, behaviors, conflicts, and other systemic attributes are considered for their purpose, role, and impact on system members—and vice versa. Critics of this view have argued that how one interprets the relative importance of these components changes over time, generally as a function of sociohistorical forces (Dickerson, 2010). You will learn more about structuralism in Chapters 2 and 11. This **poststructuralist** view emphasizes the importance of a broader epistemology relating to systems theory, and a move toward **critical realism,** which provides a truly integrative epistemological perspective (Pocock, 2015). Such deliberations are relevant to the budding family clinician because they assist in the comprehensive understanding of the very theories that guide clinical practice, as well as how to adapt and integrate these to best meet clients' needs.

Family

Thus far we have discussed the system of the family in rather abstract terms—but what defines a "family"? How do you define your family? It is not sufficient to understand how the family system operates; we must also describe the system in more concrete terms. Historically, **family** has consisted of individuals related by blood, marriage, or adoption. Other definitions have included those with economic interdependency, such as sharing a common household. More contemporary views have included those with emotional or psychological interdependency, such as domestic partners or those in long-standing committed relationships. In addition, systemic function can help define family—such as economic support, child rearing, companionship, and safety. With such varied and contextual definitions, it is important for clinicians to consider how the family system defines itself. In simplest terms, if the system members consider themselves "family," they should be viewed as such.

Even with such broad and potentially abstract terms, there are some commonalities across differing definitions of "family." For example, there is often a shared past and an expectation of a shared future. The family unit also generally includes economic connections, such as the rearing and support of any young within the system. Contextually, families also experience common effects of environment, such as cultural influences. Most importantly, there is an identity attached to the membership in the family and a commitment to maintaining that identity over time. Guided Practice Exercise 1.3 notes examples of simple and complex relationships; which do you consider family?

GUIDED PRACTICE EXERCISE 1.3

Consider the examples below—which do you consider "families" and why?

- A husband and wife and their children
- Divorced parents of grown children
- A 45-year-old single woman, her live-in boyfriend, and her adult daughter
- A 38-year-old single man and his cat, Zeus
- A lesbian couple and their biological children
- Two 27-year-old female best friends who have cohabited since college
- Two adult brothers living together
- Two grandparents raising their grandchild
- A widow and her deceased husband's niece's partner
- A gay couple and their adopted daughter
- A newly married couple in their 50s and their adult children from previous marriages

GOALS of FAMILY THERAPY

A single adult man and his two young children

An 80-year-old woman and her lifelong best friend

- A 30-year-old single woman, her live-in partner, and her divorced parents
- A professional football team

For further discussion: What cultural and socioenvironmental influences affect your definition of family? How can ensure that you honor the constructs and definitions of your clients?

Question on intake "Who does your family include?"

Family Life Cycle

Stage based view

The concept of **family life cycle** evolved from a developmental perspective that asserted that families change over time in predictable ways. Though grounded in traditional definitions of family, family life cycle constructs can often be applied to less traditional, more contemporary family systems. At the core of this stage-based view are several key elements: first, that family life cycle stages are marked by the addition or subtraction of family members; second, that the developmental stages of individuals within the system impact the stages of the system; and third, that socioenvironmental influences impact the family life cycle. The purpose of this framework was to help clinicians identify and understand the developmental tasks associated with the family life cycle, as well the complex interactions between individual and systemic development. A more detailed discussion of family life cycle is provided in Chapter 3 of this text.

Family Therapy

Family therapy is a clinical approach to mental health treatment wherein the family is the primary focus, rather than the individuals who make up the family. The system itself is the "client" in family therapy, with the treatment focus being the relationships, interactions, and overall dynamics that support systemic functioning. Family therapy acknowledges the systemic influences of homeostasis and equilibrium as being powerful forces that demand attention if change and growth are to be permanent. That is, family therapy acknowledges that without change in the system, there is unlikely to be lasting change in any members of the system. Therefore, unlike individual psychotherapy, the focus of treatment in family therapy is communication, conflict resolution, and relational dynamics rather than insight, self-awareness, and personal growth (Walrond-Skinner, 2014). That is not to say that family members participating together in therapy do not experience insight, self-awareness, and personal growth, but rather that these facets occur as a consequence of family therapy rather than as the major treatment focus. Methods, interventions, and theoretical orientations in family therapy have evolved considerably over the past 50 years, the details and specifics of which are described in detail in subsequent chapters. Professional identity issues and considerations related to distinctions between family "therapy" and "counseling" have also been mentioned in the literature and are discussed in detail in Chapter 5.

Differentiation

The development of the concept of **differentiation** is widely attributed to Murray _
(1978). You will learn more about Bowen in Chapters 2 and 9. Though his roots were
firmly planted in psychoanalytic theory, Bowen was largely influenced by biology and
the processes he observed in growth and development. Bowen saw a metaphoric correlation between undifferentiated cellular masses and the psychological fusion observed
in family systems. He coined the phrase **undifferentiated family ego mass** to describe
the unified emotionally driven behaviors observed in relational systems (Bowen, 1978).
From Bowen's work emerged the term *differentiation*, whose use is not limited to
Bowenian family therapy but has found a home across disciplines. Differentiation—in
simplest terms—is the relative degree to which individuals develop their own identity
separate from their systemic origin. Furthermore, differentiation is reflected in and
impacted by **boundaries** within systems, which in turn are evidenced by rules, patterns
of communication, and relational dynamics.

Differentiation has been found to be directly correlated with psychological well-being
(Krycak, Murdock, & Marszalek, 2012; Skowron, Stanley, & Shapiro, 2009). Furthermore,
the correlation persists across both individualistic and collectivist cultures, though variations are noted in contextual environmental influences (Chung & Gale, 2009; Lohan &
Gupta, 2016). An awareness of the impact of differentiation is essential to the systemic
practitioner, as it provides insight into the individual's ability to balance intimacy and
autonomy in relationships. Moreover, it helps provide a deeper understanding of the self,
as well as the self in relation to others (Ross & Murdock, 2014).

Attachment

If **differentiation** can be viewed as a contextually driven assessment of security in
individual identity, then **attachment** can be viewed as the experiential foundation on
which that identity is based. Research focusing on the characteristics of attachment
bonds between parents and children was brought to the forefront by the work of John
Bowlby (1958) and later expanded on by Mary Ainsworth (Ainsworth & Bell, 1970).
Both researchers recognized patterns in the way parents interacted with their children,
noting that the mother–child dyad was especially impactful. Further, they noted that
these interactional patterns directly affected the developing child's sense of security and
autonomy. This in turn has an ongoing impact on cognitive and social development. In
fact, poor attachment in childhood can have an impact that lasts throughout the life
span.

The study of attachment—including its development, modification, persistence, and
impact—can be a professional specialization for the systemic counselor. Interest in this
essential concept of systems-based counseling may even lead to adopting the empirically based attachment-based family therapy as one's primary theoretical orientation
(Diamond, Russon, & Levy, 2016). However, at this juncture and for better understanding
of topics discussed in this text, a foundational understanding of attachment will suffice.
Table 1.1 shows a comparison of children and adults' attachment styles.

Table 1.1: A comparison of children's and adults' attachment styles

Children	Adults	Relational traits
Secure	Secure	Confident, adapts easily
Anxious	Preoccupied	Clingy, needy
Avoidant	Dismissing	Indifferent, detached

Note the correlations between the observed emotional behaviors. To understand the impact of these attachment patterns, systemic counselors should recognize that all human beings are driven to attach to others and that they desire security in those attachments. Clinical interventions designed to enhance the quality of attachment styles—and repair weaknesses where they might exist—will have a direct positive impact on both relational dynamics and individual identity (Diamond et al., 2016; Fraley, 2010; Johnson, 2009).

Triangulation

The concept of **triangulation** is another that was originally associated with Murray Bowen and his theory of family systems therapy but is now integrated across multiple theoretical orientations. Triangulation is simply the formation of a three-person system, which Bowen (1978) believed was the smallest stable relationship structure. He asserted that while dyads are the initial structural building block in systems, external stressors create tension and anxiety in the dyad, which responds by brining another person into it—thus creating the triad or triangle. The energy flow across the triangle impacts the relational dynamics of individuals involved. That is, changes in attention, support, and connection in dyads within the triad alter the way the entire system functions. The alliances formed by shifts in the system's energy may be transient or permanent; regardless, they are associated with increased anxiety and conflict (Bowen, 1978). For example, a mother may complain to her teenage daughter about her husband (the child's father), perhaps sharing that she's frustrated about his lack of attentiveness or engagement in the family system. Whether she is aware of it or not, she has triangulated the child by creating a situation in which the child must react with support and empathy, but in opposition to her father. This can create anxiety for the child and form an alliance with the mother in a manner that was previously absent. The change in the energy flow of this triad can give rise to further conflict and stress across the system. Triangles and triangulation will be discussed in more detail in subsequent chapters.

Narratives

Thus far we have looked at some of the concepts within couple and family therapy that help describe the framework of the system and its members. **Narratives,** by contrast, focus on how the family members view themselves—including their individual, systemic, and social roles. Narratives are stories, constructs, and beliefs that individuals develop over time and which determine the way they derive meaning (Logan, Jackson, Teufel-Prida, & Wirick, 2015). Based in social constructionism, narratives are essential to how people define their realities and experience events. For example, in the family above in which the mother has triangulated the daughter due to conflict with her husband, a key element to the mother's stress lies in her own narrative of what marriage is "supposed to be." She has an expectation of behavior in her husband and a belief about how much time he should spend with her and the family. Her constructs are a result of her environmental influences and experiences throughout her life, and they form the basis for her marital narrative. Her narrative is not "right" or "wrong"—it just *is*. Similarly, her husband has his own narrative about marriage and probably does not view his behavior as problematic. If this couple were to seek clinical support for their marital troubles, an early step for the counselor would be to understand how their individual narratives affect their interpretations of the presenting issues and the relationship itself.

Narratives are critical elements in couple and family therapy, as they exist on both the individual and systemic levels, impacting perceptions and behaviors. Regardless of one's theoretical orientation, counselors must understand the sociocultural influences that affect their clients' experiences and worldview. Further, they need to recognize the role of narratives not only in the experience of current issues, but also in the revision and construct of a new reality.

Identified Patient

Couple and family counselors may see multiple issues relating to differentiation, attachment, and narratives in presenting family systems. However—more often than not—a single family member is considered the **identified patient**. This designation is twofold. First, the identified patient in the family is the one whom the system has determined is "the sick one." The system presents this person as needing the clinician's help to "get better," preferably with little or no change to the homeostasis of the system itself. "Identified patient" is a concept associated with projection, scapegoating—even active participation and collusion—depending on the theoretical orientation of the clinician. However, regardless of the underpinnings of treatment, the concept has a prominent role in couple and family work, as it is vital to understanding the structure and dynamics of the system, as well as the deeper pathologies present.

The external symptoms evident in the identified patient are viewed by the system as the focus of treatment; however, a couple and family counselor sees these symptoms as manifestations of internal issues within the system itself. That is, this individual is simply the "member expressing a disturbance existing in the entire family" (Gurman & Kniskern, 2013, p. 365). Thus, the clinician views **the family** as the patient. Treatment focus is on relational dynamics and dysfunctional family patterns, rather than on a single member's specific behaviors. It is not uncommon for family systems to cling to the notion that one individual is "the problem" to be defensive in considering a more systemic view. However, with support, empathy, psychoeducation, and a nonjudgmental approach to examining issues, couple and family counselors can help shift the family paradigm to a more systemic treatment view.

The second facet of the "identified patient" concept may initially sound contradictory to the first one but is a reality of contemporary clinical work. Though a couple and family counselor views the relationships as the focus and the system itself as the patient or client, the realities of managed care and third-party payers require one family member to literally be the identified patient—if only for reimbursement purposes. This may put the clinician at odds with his or her theoretical orientation and perhaps even undermine the progress true systemic work can do; however, the need for this designation is a pragmatic one. Clinicians can mitigate the potential negatives by educating clients on policies and procedures and keeping focus on the support and improvement of the system.

FAMILY THERAPY INDICATORS

Deciding whether family therapy or individual therapy is indicated is a multifaceted decision for therapists. In reality, both family therapy and individual therapy are important. The individual personality matters, as evidenced by years of evidenced-based research substantiating the importance of individual psychotherapy (Shechtman, 2016), as well as family therapy that asserts that the family is the natural unit for change. Therapists must consider if family therapy, individual therapy, or both family and individual therapy is warranted. In addition, there are specific indications for when family therapy is most appropriate. Similarly, family therapy must consider aspects of culture, diversity, and what therapeutic adaptations may need to be employed for treatment success.

When Is Family Therapy Warranted?

You are probably wondering, "How do I know when family therapy is appropriate or necessary?" "Is this a family or systemic issue?" "Would it be better addressed in individual counseling?" Often there is no clear answer when trying to determine whether it is "necessary" or "better" to use a systemic approach to treatment, and ultimately the answer will be associated with the therapist's theoretical orientation. Therapists who ascribe to or practice one of the following will believe family therapy is warranted in most situations, if not all: structural family therapy, strategic family therapy, and intergenerational family therapy. Family therapy may be best as an additional therapy or cotherapy in situations of individual psychological factors, such as a person diagnosed with schizophrenia, and larger social systems that are not able to be addressed within the context of family systems.

The question remains: When is family therapy warranted? A major premise of family therapy is that most problems originate in families and can be solved within families. Systemic interventions alone or as cotherapy are considered effective for sleep, feeding, and attachment problems in infancy; child abuse and neglect; conduct problems (specifically, child behavioral problems, attention-deficit/hyperactivity disorder, delinquency, and drug abuse); emotional problems (specifically, anxiety, depression, grief, bipolar disorder, and suicidality); eating disorders; and somatic problems (specifically, enuresis, encopresis, abdominal pain, and issues associated with controlling asthma and diabetes; Carr, 2014).

Individual Versus Family Therapy

The most obvious difference between individual and family therapy is who the identified client is. In individual counseling, the identified client is the individual, and in family therapy the identified client is the family. Many times, the difference between individual and family therapy is the focus of the therapy in a given session. In individual therapy, the focus is on the individual. In family therapy, the focus is more complex and can change. There are several people in the room during family therapy. If an individual is having an issue and is in family therapy, his or her issue may be the focus, but the family members are also there working to learn and assist in resolving the given issue with the individual. Also, family therapy can focus on issues of many family members and an issue that the entire family is addressing. It is important to recognize that family therapy typically works to alter the way an entire family system operates. Additionally, family therapy may be a variety of interactions between couples, parents and child(ren), entire families, and/or extended families.

More specifically, individual therapy tends to focus on psychopathology, individual coping, and problem solving. Often the therapist makes assessments of individuals against prescribed norms and works to address the root cause of the person's discomfort. In most of the individual therapeutic models, the therapist remains objective to discover the individual's emotions, cognitions, and/or disruptive behaviors. The therapist then employs a variety of interventions to improve the individual client.

Family therapy is about process. The family therapist is expected to focus on the various transactions, interactions, and exchanges that occur between persons in the family therapy session. Family therapy "involves seeing the purpose and systemic logic in what often appear to be paradoxical processes" (Bitter, 2014, p. 21).

Just as there are differences between family therapy and individual therapy, there are also similarities. Both family therapy and individual therapy can be brief, crisis or trauma focused, and treatment goal orientated. It is often the case that families and individuals enter therapy to address a certain issue or need. Both individual and family therapy serve to improve psychological wellness and often are used as adjunctive services to medical care, legal involvement, or grief and loss.

Cultural Considerations and Adaptations

Cultural and subcultural factors are an inherent part of family. Attitudes, values, and belief systems and more specifically how families define health, wellness, and mental health are associated with one's culture. The determinations of what is an identified issue or treatment goal for therapy and the types of interventions that are appropriate for the family are all made within the context of a specific family or group's attitudes, values, and beliefs. For example, in some intrafamilial systems, the prevailing attitude and belief regarding physical child and spouse abuse may be that these are private family matters, with neither warranting nor requiring intervention or therapy by persons outside the family.

An additional example of how therapy goals are influenced by family attitudes, values, and beliefs is whether to vaccinate a child. While the scientific evidence supports that vaccination is safe and effective, many parents make the decision based on their religious and own personal research to not vaccinate. Outside the United States, in developing countries, other cultures are often eager to vaccinate their children and do not understand the "option" to not vaccinate. Therapists working with families often must navigate diverse issues and integrate the family's value system into the dialogue of the family sessions. Navigating conflicting attitudes, values, and beliefs that you might have as a therapist while in session with a family is common challenge. Yet given the opportunity to work with the family, a family therapist will be able to approach a given goal from a variety of ways. There are multiple advantages and challenges in family therapy.

Advantages

Strengths. A systemic approach offers the opportunity to look at an issue from multiple vantage points. The systemic approach unto itself as an epistemological concept is a strength; it is unlike any other approach. As an approach, the systemic way of thinking and doing therapy challenged the "traditional" and linear cause-and-effect way of approaching therapy. Hence, the theoretical underpinnings and concepts of the approach are strengths of the systemic approach.

For example, the systemic approach would invite a family to therapy and include all perspectives in the therapeutic dialogue, and the family in conjunction with the therapist would identify areas of concern and areas that would be addressed in therapy. In individual therapy, there is often an identified "issue," and the client seeks to address that specific goal in therapy. In family systems work, there are multiple areas or systems that can be addressed that are associated with the family and just as many ways to reach a potential goal.

Specifically, psychotherapy is dominated by approaches that are individualistic in orientation, and the systemic approach offers equality in the multiple avenues to goal achievement. Thus, **equifinality** is strength of the systemic approach—equifinality being the idea that in a system, an identified goal can be reached by a variety of ways, and thus a therapist can focus on an issue within the familial system that seems to make sense.

CASE PRESENTATION 1.1: THE CASE OF LIU YANG AND BEN

Liu Yang is a Chinese American mother to a 13-month-old boy named Tai. Liu Yang is married to a multiracial man named Ben who was born in United States. Liu Yang and Ben live in a progressive area of the country, and Liu Yang is responsible for caring for Tai while Ben earns the money for the family. Ben works out of the home and earns a very comfortable living. Liu Yang and Ben enter family counseling due to concern over Tai's development (he is small for his age, and there is a family history of autism). Liu Yang is still breast-feeding Tai, and Ben disagrees with this practice. Also, Tai is sleeping in Liu Yang and Ben's bed at night. Tai has co-slept since he was born. Liu Yang believes in co-sleeping, whereas Ben does they should continue to co-sleep. In addition to disagreements about co-sleeping, Ben and Liu like to have another baby.

As the family therapist of Liu Yang, Ben, and Tai, you note that there is an identified goal of growing the family and assessing the development of Tai. Other potential issues in therapy may center on multicultur-alism, gender roles, value systems, and specifically the parenting practice of co-sleeping. A strength of the systems approach is that there are an equal number of ways to potentially reach the goals that Liu Yang and Ben hope to accomplish in therapy. The therapist could address Liu Yang's value system, as it is associated with her parenting practice of co-sleeping, or Ben's gender role or the multicultural and Chinese view of young male development or the potential life cycle impact of a new child. All approaches being equal would result in systemic change.

Viewing families as a system involves recognizing the various relationships between and within the family and the inherent power, behaviors, emotions, thoughts, values, and attitudes associated with the family system. The lens of a systemic approach requires a certain "systems intelligence" by which a clinician can understand and approach a clinical familial case from the standpoint of balancing between parts, content, context, and reci-procity (Sweeney & Sterman, 2007, p. 286). This "systems intelligence" is ultimately a more contemporary version of thinking about the interweavings of life, family, and problems versus the historical or organismic version of systems whereby organisms thrive or die in accordance with their openness or closeness to their environments (Bertalanffy, 1934, 1968). Ultimately, a key strength of a systemic approach is how a therapist conceptualizes the family in its entirety (wholeness) versus its individual pieces or parts.

In addition to the conceptual, albeit theoretical, strengths of equifinality and whole-ness, multiple strengths of the systemic approach lie in the application of the approach in couple and family interventions. The systemic approach is unmatched in its ability to comprehend the complexities of family life. Similarly, in systems work a therapist under-stands and recognizes reciprocity. We are all interconnected. If an aspect of the system is changed, other systems are affected. Therapists working with the systems approach are aware of reciprocity between systems, thus strengthening their therapeutic interventions accordingly. Similarly, a systems therapist can conceptualize change, observe patterns and trends, make connections, deal with physical or symbolic ambiguity of system boundaries, and address aspects of perspective and time in therapy (Stanton & Welsh, 2012).

Benefits. According to Bitter, Long, and Young (2010), "Modern system therapists tend to want as many members of the family as possible in the room—often including friends and other members from the family's community" (p. 19). There is an inherent respect for diversity and multiculturalism in a systemic approach. The systems counselor works to include, not exclude. The benefit of systems work is to address diverse family makeup and emerging forms of family in a way that is inclusive, not exclusive. Also, the systems counselor works to address interdependence and issues of influence and sub-jectivity that are common in the discussions of race, socioeconomic status, gender, age, sexual orientation, creed, and culture.

Beneficial to the systemic approach is the specific focus on process and crossing boundaries between systems. This approach allows for an effective client-centered experience that is based in theory and interventions (Patterson & Sexton, 2013). Rooted in process and function, the systemic approach is beneficial due to common family therapy techniques. For example, the technique joining (Haley, 1976; Minuchin, 1974) provides both structure and support for a family. By joining with a family, the therapist forms a therapeutic alliance with the family—meeting, greeting, and forming a bond in a quick but relaxed way.

Many times, clinicians using a systemic approach find that they have "more ideas about how to proceed" and clients were "better engaged" in the process of therapy (Fredman, 2014, p. 2). In a systemic approach, there is a collaborative environment. Thus, the systemic therapist works together with various systems to provide the benefit of unity and goal orientation.

Challenges

Common issues. Conceptualizing a family from a systemic approach is rich with strengths and benefits, but also laden with challenges and potential risks or barriers. Mechanistic models of systems have focused on a historical model of a family, thus excluding a contemporary definition of family and the changing view of family. In addition, traditional systemic approaches may not account for the complex interaction of factors in problem origination, continuation, or change in a contemporary family system.

While the systemic approach is strong in its willingness to "include" and consider multiple perspectives, a common issue within this approach that should continue to be addressed is multiculturalism and diversity. The roles of families and couples—how to define roles in a family and the ambiguity of who is an "outsider"—remain complex. In addition, the systemic approach must continue to work to include multiple perspectives by addressing the changing landscape of family and partnership. Similarly, issues of culture and gender are a challenge that the systems approach theoretically is posed to address, yet in the therapeutic process a common issue emerges of whether the systems approach accounts for contemporary understandings of culture and gender. This is considering that in the early years of family therapy, issues of gender and culture were virtually ignored. Many of the predominant theoretical orientations under the systems approach umbrella are likely to often reflect the dominant value system and ignore the effects of oppression.

Barriers. The systems therapist must be able to establish a relationship with multiple individuals (Stanton & Welsh, 2012). There are challenges to establishing relationships and connections with multiple people. One member of the family might connect with the therapist versus another who may not, or some members of the family may or may not be able to attend all sessions. The potential barriers to connect revolve around issues of client and therapist transference and countertransference.

In addition, the establishment of a strong relationship with the family system can be threatened if the counselor overemphasizes details, making everyone happy, verbal expression, coming to an early or too easy resolution, and dealing with one member of the family (Kalima, 2005). Similarly, there may be issues related to counselor underemphasis. Underemphasizing structure, showing care and concern, engaging family members in the therapeutic process, and letting the family work on its problems are also common barriers for family counselors (Kalima, 2005).

Issues common to therapeutic process of other approaches are also common to the systemic approach. Legal and ethical issues may arise with changing couple, family, and individual systems. The therapist would have barriers of communication and limitations of confidentiality with multiple persons. With each change in formation—couple to family, for example—the ethics of changing the relationship, informed consent, and confidentiality would need to be addressed. Similarly, termination is more complex for the systemic therapist due to the varying needs of the different people involved.

Common issues. Common issues in family therapy mirror barriers in family therapy. In addition, family therapy involves more than one person, and not all family members may show up for a given session. Client no-show or one family member being unavailable for a session is a common issue in family therapy. Families have busy schedules, and it is difficult to find a time that works for everyone's schedule. Therapists may view no-shows for therapy and difficulty finding a time for sessions as a form of client resistance, another common issue in family therapy.

Resistance can take many forms in families. Some family members might be silent, while others will avoid talking about the issue presented for therapy. Beyond resistance, some common issues are beyond client control. Family therapy may or may not be covered by insurance. Family therapy could be needed but not offered at the agency where the client is receiving services for individual therapy. If family therapy isn't readily available or if insurance doesn't cover family therapy, this may deter the person from pursuing familial treatment. Part IV of the textbook is dedicated to special issues. You will have the opportunity to read about these in more detail in Chapters 18 to 20.

Table 1.2: **Advantages and Challenges of a Systemic Approach**

Systemic Principle	Advantage or Challenge
Equifinality	Advantage
Wholeness	Advantage
Comprehending complexity	Advantage
Reciprocity	Advantage
Conceptualizing change	Advantage
Observing patterns and trends	Advantage
Making connections	Advantage

Systemic Principle	Advantage or Challenge
Dealing with ambiguity	Advantage
Multiculturalism	Advantage and Challenge
Diversity	Advantage and Challenge
Establishing multiple relationships	Challenge
Legal issues	Challenge
Ethical issues	Challenge

SUMMARY

Family therapy is a systemic approach to counseling that focuses on relationships between individuals. While it does not discount individual influences and perspectives, it does emphasize the relational dynamics of the system, as well as how these dynamics in turn affect the system members. Family systems theory has its underpinnings in general systems theory and cybernetics. Key assumptions include the system's tendency toward homeostasis and the resistance to change due to the equilibrium of the system. In addition, the theory recognizes the role of conflicts and behaviors, as well as their relative position within the system.

In this chapter, we reviewed some of the basics foundational concepts found in family therapy, including basic definitions of "family." Families can be defined by legal criteria, relationships, or both. The most important element in identifying a family is how the family system members define themselves; cultural and experiential influences play a significant role in the development of these constructs. Though every family is unique, there are some common elements to the experiences of the family system. All families go through a life cycle of sorts, wherein the developmental processes of the individual members affect the identity of the system. Family members also experience important developmental catalysts such as differentiation and attachment, both of which directly impact the identity development both of the individuals within the system and of the system itself. These concepts will be discussed in more detail in Chapter 3 of this text.

Family therapy can be used as a primary clinical approach or as an adjunct to individual treatment. When doing family therapy, the family itself is the "client," although for billing and reimbursement reasons, usually one individual system member needs to be the *identified* client. This can sometimes create its own challenges to the process, though generally it can be managed by the clinician. Many advantages to family therapy generally outweigh the challenges, including the engagement and involvement of the entire system. The primary strength in a systems approach is the recognition of interconnectedness and the inherent dynamic influences that exist. It is an inclusive, adaptable, culturally sensitive approach to addressing issues.

KEYSTONES

Among the key points addressed in this chapter are:

- Family therapy is a systemic approach to counseling that focuses on relationships between individuals.
- Family systems theory recognizes the role of conflicts and behaviors, as well as their relative position within the system.
- Families can be defined in many terms. The most important element in identifying a family is how the family system members define themselves.
- Family therapy can be used as a primary clinical approach or as an adjunct to individual treatment.
- In family therapy, the family itself is the "client," and the relationships in the system are the focus of treatment.

REFLECTIONS FROM THE CONTRIBUTOR'S CHAIR

I remember very clearly the day I realized I was a systems therapist. I was in my master's program, which was designed to support my licensure as an Licensed Mental Health Counselor in Florida. It was my second term in the program, and I was taking a theories course. I found it all terribly fascinating, but I was left with this nagging feeling that there was *more*. For example, while I could clearly see the correlations between negative cognitions and affect, I could not deny the influence of day-to-day interactions in relationships and how these in turn affect individuals. I was also starting to figure out that my niche in the field was going to be working with adolescents, so having a firm base in family systems was essential.

Interestingly, after nearly 20 years in the field, I see elements of systems influences all around me. That is, understanding these concepts has not only helped my clinical work, it has also helped me better understand relational dynamics in extended social systems, the workplace, my community—even society as a whole. We are all interconnected. We influence those around us, and they influence us in return. Recognizing and respecting these dynamics, and learning how to positively impact them, has been key to both my professional success and my personal happiness.—Stephanie K. Scott

ADDITIONAL RESOURCES

The following resources provide additional information relating to the chapter topics.

Useful Websites

- American Association for Marriage and Family Therapy (AAMFT) http://www.aamft.org/iMIS15/AAMFT/

This website provides information about the AAMFT, including licensing, career, ethical codes, state resources, and more.

- American Family Therapy Academy
  https://afta.org/

This website provides information on the oldest family therapy academy in the United States, including education conferences, seminars, publications, and additional resources.

- Association of Marital and Family Therapy Regulatory Boards
  https://www.amftrb.org/

This website provides information for those interested in the marriage and family therapy field anywhere in the United States. Links to different licensure boards, as well as related groups and associations, are organized and listed by state.

- International Association of Marriage and Family Counselors (IAMFC)
  http://www.iamfconline.org/

This website provides information about the IAMFC, including ethical codes and standards, publications, resources, and more.

REFERENCES

Ainsworth, M. D. S., & Bell, S. M. (1970). Attachment, exploration, and separation: Illustrated by the behavior of one-year-olds in a strange situation. *Child Development, 41*, 49–67.

Bertalanffy, L. (1934). *Modern theories of development: An introduction to theoretical biology.* Oxford: Oxford University Press.

Bertalanffy, L. (1968). *General systems theory: Foundations, development, and application.* New York: Braziller.

Bitter, R. J. (2014). *Theory and practice of family therapy and counseling.* Belmont, CA: Brooks/Cole.

Bitter, J. R., Long, L. L., & Young, M. E. (2010). *Theory and practice of family therapy and counseling.* Mason, OH: Cengage Learning.

Bowen, M. (1978). *Family therapy in clinical practice.* New York: Aronson.

Bowlby, J. (1958). The nature of the child's tie to his mother. *International Journal of Psychoanalysis, 39*, 350–371.

Carr, A. (2014). The evidence base for family therapy and systemic interventions for child-focused problems. *Journal of Family Therapy, 36*(2), 107–157.

Diamond, G., Russon, J., & Levy, S. (2016). Attachment-based family therapy: A review of the empirical support. *Family Process, 55*(3), 595–610.

Dickerson, V. C. (2010). Positioning oneself within an epistemology: Refining our thinking about integrative approaches. *Family Process, 49*(3), 349–368.

Fraley, R. C. (2010). A brief overview of adult attachment theory and research. Retrieved from https://internal.psychology.illinois.edu/~rcfraley/attachment.htm

Fredman, G. (2014). Weaving networks of hope with families, practitioners and communities: Inspirations from systemic and narrative approaches. *Australian and New Zealand Journal of Family Therapy, 35,* 54–57.

Gurman, A. S., & Kniskern, D. P. (2013). *Handbook of family therapy.* New York: Routledge.

Haley, J, (1976). Development of a theory: A history of a research project. In C. E. Sluzki & D. C. Ransom (Eds.), *Double-bind: The foundation of the communication approach to the family* (pp. 59–104). New York: Grune & Straton.

Johnson, S. M. (2009). Attachment theory and emotionally-focused therapy for individuals and couples. In J. H. Obegi & E. Berant (Eds.), *Attachment theory and research in clinical work with adults* (pp. 410–433). New York: Guilford Press.

Kalima, I. (2005). The technique of "redirection" in couple therapy. *Family Journal: Counseling and Therapy for Couples and Families, 13,* 199–200.

Krycak, R. C., Murdock, N. L., & Marszalek, J. M. (2012). Differentiation of self, stress, and emotional support as predictors of psychological distress. *Contemporary Family Therapy, 34*(4), 495–515.

Logan, C. R., Jackson, A. H., Teufel-Prida, L. A., & Wirick, D. M. (2015). Counseling couples using life cycle and narrative therapy lenses. In D. Capuzzi and M. D. Stauffer (Eds.), *Foundations of couples, marriage and family counseling* (pp. 241–358). Hoboken, NJ: Wiley.

Lohan, A., & Gupta, R. (2016). Relationship between differentiation of self and marital adjustment in Indian couples. *Journal of Psychosocial Research, 11*(1), 139–146.

Magnavita, J. J. (2012). Advancing clinical science using system theory as the framework for expanding family psychology with unified psychotherapy. *Couple and Family Psychology: Research and Practice, 1*(1), 3–13.

Minuchin, S. (1974). *Families and family therapy.* Cambridge, MA: Harvard University Press.

Morgan, D. H. (2014). *Social theory and the family.* New York: Routledge.

Patterson, T., & Sexton, T. (2013). Bridging conceptual frameworks: A systemic heuristic for understanding family diversity. *Couple and Family Psychology: Research and Practice, 2*(4), 237–245.

Pocock, D. (2015). A philosophy of practice for systemic psychotherapy: The case for critical realism. *Journal of Family Therapy, 37,* 167–183.

Ross, A. S., & Murdock, N. L. (2014). Differentiation of self and well-being: The moderating effect of self-construal. *Contemporary Family Therapy, 36*(4), 485–496.

Scott, S. K. (2015). Psychodynamic therapies: Approaches and applications. In D. Capuzzi & M. D. Stauffer (Eds.), *Foundations of couples, marriage and family counseling* (pp. 129–158). Hoboken, NJ: Wiley.

Shechtman, Z. (2016). Why do people prefer individual therapy over group therapy? *International Journal of Group Psychotherapy, 66*(4), 571–591.

Skowron, E. A., Stanley, K. L., & Shapiro, M. D. (2009). A longitudinal perspective on differentiation of self, interpersonal and psychological well-being in young adulthood. *Contemporary Family Therapy, 31*(1), 3–18.

Smith-Acuna, S. (2010). *Systems theory in action: Applications to individual, couple, and family therapy.* Hoboken, NJ: Wiley.

Stanton, M., & Welsh, R. (2012). Systemic thinking in couple and family psychology research and practice. *Couple and Family Psychology: Research and Practice, 1,* 14–30.

Sweeney, L. B., & Sterman, J. D. (2007). Thinking about systems: Student and teacher conceptions of natural and societal systems. *System Dynamics Review, 23*(2), 285–312.

Walrond-Skinner, S. (2014). *Family therapy: The treatment of natural systems.* New York: Routledge.

CHAPTER 2

History and Development of Family Therapy

Melinda Haley, Rebecca D. Goodrich-Rodriguez, Sarah H. Golden, and Anthony Zazzarino

"It is now clear to me that the family is a microcosm of the world. To understand the world, we can study the family: issues such as power, intimacy, autonomy, trust, and communication skills are vital parts underlying how we live in the world. To change the world is to change the family."

—Virginia Satir

As Virginia Satir, who is one of the leaders and developers of marriage, couple, and family therapy (MCFT) that you will read about in this chapter, states in the quote above, we can understand our world by seeking to understand our families, and through our understanding we can effect change. I think that is also true of the MCFT profession. By understanding our profession and knowing our past and how we arrived at this place in time, we can continue to grow and perfect this profession. By learning from our past endeavors and understanding what has and has not worked, we can continue to perfect the methods by which we help couples and families. To add to what Satir stated, my own opinion is that healthy couples and families form the foundation for a healthy society. In this chapter, you will have an opportunity to learn about those individuals who came before us in this profession and how they formed the foundation on which our profession rests today. You will also learn about the organizations and historical events that occurred and how the MCFT profession has developed around the world. In understanding this unique past, it will help guide you, as you become the leaders of tomorrow.

—Melinda Haley

A s discussed in Chapter 1, the profession of marriage and family therapy has an extensive history, beginning in the early 1900s when Alfred Adler began the child guidance movement. From that time to the present, a series of important individuals have served as advocates, activists, and social change agents to develop the profession into the great benefit it is today for millions of individuals around the world (Schmidt, 2015). Over time this profession has been referred to as marriage and family counseling, marriage and family therapy, and marriage, couple, and family therapy or counseling. We will talk more about this in Chapter 5. However, in this chapter and throughout the remaining chapters, we will refer to this profession as marriage, couple, and family therapy to remain consistent in our terminology as well as to be inclusive of all people who live in systems with others, regardless of their familial or relationship status. In this chapter, we will also discuss the major events, individuals, and organizations that have helped shape the marriage, couple, and family therapy profession as we know it today.

LEARNING OBJECTIVES

After reading this chapter, you will be able to do the following:

- Describe the major events that have shaped the profession of marriage, couple, and family therapy from the 1930s to the present.
- Discuss the contributions of key individuals who helped develop this profession.
- Discuss the significance and importance of various organizations that have sought to serve, protect, foster, and standardize the profession (e.g., AAMFT, CACREP).
- Describe the requirements needed to become a licensed marriage, couple, and family therapist.
- Discuss the origins of evidenced-based practice and the biopsychosocial perspective.

KEY CONCEPTS

Family therapy evolved thoughout the 20th century. The following sections discuss this evolution including key players who helped develop many of the concepts used today.

1900s–EARLY 1950s

In this section, we will discuss the origins of the marriage, couple, and family therapy (MCFT) profession starting with the influence of the social work movement, to Alfred Adler's child guidance movement, to the development of the first family counseling centers by Rudolf Dreikurs. We will highlight important events and discuss the influence and contributions of major individuals who helped guide the development of the profession.

The Social Work Movement's Influence

Before there were formalized MCFT practices, the professional social work movement sought to provide support for the disruptive influences of urbanization and industrialization on family living (Bowen, 2015). The idea behind the professional social work movement was that families needed a more formal and organized approach to help adjust to and cope with the changes and challenges of industrialization. Collectively, the Charity Organization Society and the settlement house movement began to challenge the individualist view of people experiencing problems. Instead, there was a shift to view the challenges within the confines of the family unit, the community, and the social, political, and economic environments (Bowen, 2015; McFadden, 2014).

The Charity Organization Society began its quest to build relationships with poor urban families, to help support their needs by providing in-home support (Richmond, 1917). Mary Richmond (1917), the director of organization, shifted the charity's focus to incorporate a more systemic approach that emphasized the need for supportive counseling for individuals within the family unit. Though the Charity Organization Society did attempt to care for the concerns of the entire family, the settlement house movement placed a greater focus on the family unit (Bowen, 2015; McFadden, 2014).

The Child Guidance Movement

Initiated by Alfred Adler in the early 1900s in Vienna, the child guidance movement began the early research on the treatment of children to prevent the development of mental problems (Mansager, 2015). According to Adler, the behavioral problems of a child were related to the social context in which the behaviors occurred and in which the child may be trying to overcome feelings of inferiority (Mansager, 2015; Rasheed, Rasheed, & Marley, 2011). Therefore, Adler established that there was a need to study both the social and family dynamics that could impact the child (Mansager, 2015; Rasheed et al., 2011).

Meanwhile, in the United States in the 1920s, Rudolf Dreikurs, Adler's associate, founded the family counseling centers. The family counseling centers were an extension of Adler's child guidance approach that emphasized the importance of the social context related to the child's behaviors. Therefore, the child guidance movement in the United States emphasized a team approach, which focused on treating the whole family in the clinic (Abrams, 2015).

The Groves Conference

The Groves Conference of 1934 was cofounded by Professor Ernest Groves and extended the earlier work from the social work movement to help support the foundation of marriage, couple, and family therapy (Hamon & Smith, 2014). Groves was one of the first academicians to offer a marriage and family course (Groves Conference, 2016). The major focus of the Groves Conference was to begin the development of theory and empirical research in relationship to marriage, couple, and family counselors and to develop the profession (Groves Conference, 2016).

The New York Meetings

Around the same time as Groves was developing the Groves Conference, Dr. Robert Dickerson was forming a series of meetings in New York during the winter of 1931. These meetings would help support the formation and development of the MCFT profession (Cole & Cole, 2012). Dickerson collaborated with other important pioneers in the field that spanned the Northeast: Emily Mudd from Philadelphia; Lester Dearborn from Boston; and Drs. Abraham and Hannah Stone, Dr. Valerie Parker, and Dr. Robert Laidlaw from New York (Cole & Cole, 2012).

Emily Mudd and Lester Dearborn would be the linkage between the Groves Conference and the New York meetings, thus bridging the two major forces of the MCFT field together during this time. As a direct result of the connection, the group of academicians and physicians founded the American Association of Marriage Counseling (AAMC) in 1942, which changed its name to the American Association for Marriage and Family Therapy (AAMFT) in 1979 (Cole & Cole, 2012). *now AAMFT*

First Institutes of Professional Marriage, Couples, and Family Counseling (1930s)

During the 1930s, marriage, couple, and family therapy continued to grow across the country. As the conversations increased regarding the need to support and treat families, the first two institutes opened in the United States, each on opposite coasts (Popenoe, 1975). In 1930 Paul Popenoe opened the first marriage counseling center, the American Institute of Family Relations, in Los Angeles, California (Popenoe, 1975). Researchers have identified Popenoe (1975) as the individual who brought the term *marriage counseling* to the forefront of discussion.

Meanwhile, just two years later, in 1932, Abraham and Hannah Stone opened their institute in the New York Labor Temple (McGeorge, Carlson, & Wetchler, 2015). As the need for education and training support for marriage, couples, and family therapy grew, Emily Mudd opened a third center, the Marriage Council of Philadelphia, in 1932 (McGeorge et al., 2015). Distinctly different from the other two institutes, Mudd's institute was the first of its kind to focus on the need for research to enhance the profession (McGeorge et al., 2015).

Following the development from the Groves Conference and the New York meetings, the AAMC accredited three institutes in the United States: the Marriage Council of Philadelphia, the Menninger Foundation, and the Merrill–Palmer Institute (Cole & Cole, 2012). Over time, these institutes have continued to grow across the country. In 1969 the Family Institute of Chicago opened to offer courses and supervision to therapists who had an understanding that in addition to the relationship between the therapist and client, there was a critical need to explore the family as well (Rampage, 2014). Throughout the 1960s and 1970s, more family institutes continued to open across the country to help the development of marriage, couple, and family therapists, or MCFTs (Rampage, 2014).

Kurt Lewin and Small Group Dynamics

Some of the earliest ideas throughout the institutes and meetings of marriage, couples, and family therapy are connected to Kurt Lewin's (1947) work on group dynamics. Through his work on field theory, Lewin influenced MCFTs to recognize that the whole of a group was greater than the sum of its parts (Erickson, 2015; Lewin, 1946). By exploring the entire family unit, MCFTs could emphasize Lewin's notion that change can occur more readily than exploring each person separately.

Lewin's emphasis shifted the focus in marriage, couple, and family therapy, whereas therapists began to put greater emphasis on the ways families discuss their problems instead of focusing on the specificity of the problems. Furthermore, MCFTs needed to gain competence in group dynamics to fully understand and work effectively with the family unit (Erickson, 2015; Rasheed et al., 2011). Ultimately, Lewin's work began the major shift of examining the interrelated parts of the family system (Rasheed et al., 2011).

Nathan Ackerman

Nathan Ackerman is often thought of as the father of family therapy (Weinstein, 2013). Ackerman was one of the first therapists to work with the whole family. In 1938 he illuminated the importance of viewing the family as a single unit, instead of multiple individual aspects. While Ackerman understood that the family might appear to be united, he also believed that each member of the unit might have opposing views that can create conflict (McGeorge et al., 2015). Therefore, for the first time, MCFTs would work with the entire family at the same time (McGeorge et al., 2015).

Through his emphasis on the intrapsychic phenomena, Ackerman utilized his personality to help families identify new ways of relating (McGeorge et al., 2015). His work continued to resonate with his students; specifically, Salvador Minuchin, who utilized the Ackerman's foundation to articulate structural family therapy (McGeorge et al., 2015). Ackerman went on to establish the Family Institute in New York City in 1960 to enhance the training and supervision of MCFTs; it would change its name to the Ackerman Institute in 1971 (Rampage, 2014).

Frieda Fromm-Reichmann

Building on the works of Ackerman, Frieda Fromm-Reichmann published an article entitled, *Notes on the Development of Treatment of Schizophrenia by Psychoanalytic Psychotherapy,* in the 1940s, in which she explored the mother–child dynamic and its impact on the onset of schizophrenia (Fromm-Reichmann, 1948; Johnston, 2013). She coined the term *schizophrenogenic mother* to connect the attributes of a mother with the onset of schizophrenia in the child (Fromm-Reichmann, 1948). Fromm-Reichmann's term *schizophrenogenic mother* would be one of the most disapproved of in early marriage, couple, and family research, and researchers would later discredit it (Harrington, 2012).

Though researchers discredited the schizophrenogenic mother, Fromm-Reichmann was one of the first people to assert the relationship between members of the family unit and the importance of exploring the impact of interactions of the members in a family (Johnston, 2013). Fromm-Reichmann's work would lay the foundation for future MCFTs to explore the interaction between mother and son. Fromm-Reichmann's work caught the interest of Murray Bowen, who would later go on to research and implement Bowen systems theory (Bowen, 1978).

Theodore Lidz

Everyone plays a role.

When Fromm-Reichmann highlighted the mother's impact on her child's development, Theodore Lidz took notice and began to question the severity of such an impact (Lidz, Parker, & Cornelison, 1956). Instead, Lidz emphasized the role of the father's influence on the child, further suggesting the role each member plays in the family unit (Lidz et al., 1956). However, Lidz elaborated on his initial thoughts and hypothesized that the interaction between the parents could impact the child's behavior (Lidz et al., 1956; McGeorge et al., 2015).

mom dad kid

Therefore, Lidz's work further explored the connection between mother and father and the marital relationship's contribution to the development of the child (or children); specifically, Lidz highlighted marital schism and marital skew (Lidz et al., 1956). Within the family unit, a marital schism exists when the parents are focusing on their problems. Therefore, the parents have internal conflict and compete for their child's attention without assessing the needs of the child. Meanwhile, in a marital skew, children are torn between parents as one parent dominates and the other is more passive (Lidz & Lidz, 1949). *schism skew*

John Bowlby

ATTACHMENT

John Bowlby's work at the Tavistock Clinic on the core human need for attachment further supported the premise of MCFTs that parental interaction can impact a child's behavior (Bowlby, 1949). Marriage, couple, and family therapists often use attachment theory as a foundation to explore processes related to parental influences on a child's future relationships (Hall, 2015). Bowlby urged that the importance of the family unit was to be a secure base from which the child could explore his or her environment and suggested that MCFTs should assess for this during therapy (Schwartz, 2015). See Chapter 1 for more discussion about attachment theory.

Don Jackson

Strategic family therapy

In 1954 Don Jackson, who was one of the members of a group participating in the study of schizophrenia also known as the Palo Alto Group, began to lay the foundation for strategic family therapy (Rampage, 2014). Jackson and his group wanted to gain a greater understanding of how feedback loops control information-processing systems (Breulin

& Jacobsen, 2014). Therefore, those in the group explored cybernetics to guide their research studying family communication patterns of people diagnosed with schizophrenia. Cybernetics emphasized systems theory and highlighted the importance of exploring behaviors together so that MCFTs could gain a deeper understanding of how individual family member behaviors affected each family member (Hale & Frusha, 2016; Phipps, 2014). See Chapter 1 for more information on cybernetics, first-order change, and second-order change.

MID-1950s TO MID-1960s

The 1950s and 1960s were considered pivotal decades in the emergence of the MCFT profession. The 1950s yielded a framework from which family therapy became rooted in connectedness, and collaboration of professionals as a newly growing profession began to transpire (Lebow & Sexton, 2016). The cultivation of a new perspective changed how mental health providers perceived treatment, thus integrating a more holistic, inclusive perspective giving attention to a systemic foundation. The development of family therapy was evident in the work and collaboration of researchers such as Gregory Bateson, who was a contributor to evidence-based practices and studies of the dynamics of families (Lebow & Sexton, 2016). Additionally, during this time frame, individuals such as John Bell and other mental health professionals, including Jay Haley, Don Jackson, and John Weakland, contributed to family therapy through utilizing the dynamic of family group therapy and studies of patients diagnosed with schizophrenia (Lebow & Sexton, 2016).

Major Contributors

In this section, we will discuss the major contributors to MCFT for this time period. These will include the contributions of John Bell and John Weakland. We will also discuss some of the major theories or discoveries that helped shape how practitioners worked with families, including the double bind.

John Bell. Bell (1913–1995) was a practicing psychologist in the 1950s who began to shape the dynamics of traditional therapy when he began working with families on his own accord, independently contributing to the family therapy movement (Bell, 1983). Initially, his work with families emerged from an identified gap in the appropriateness of adult therapies with adolescents (Bell, 1983). The framework that shaped his approach included a view of family as a unit for problems; therefore, Bell's premise was that the interactions and problems of the individual may be related to communal or family contexts, rather than solely an individualistic perspective (Bell, 1962, 1983).

John Weakland. Along with Bateson, Jackson, and Haley, Weakland was a contributor to the research study and subsequent article, *Toward a Theory of Schizophrenia* (Bateson, Jackson, Haley, & Weakland, 1956; Weakland, 1960). In addition to this, Weakland was also instrumental in developing family-oriented brief therapy and made other substantial contributions to many of Gregory Bateson's projects (Ray, 2015; Ray & Schlanger, 2012). Further, Weakland (2010) suggested that due to the interactive context in relationships, a behavioral change may result in the disruption of a pattern, thus ultimately impacting the entire unit.

Double Bind

The double bind theory was influential in a variety of ways, as it set a foundation for a deeper level of understanding of families and communicative interactions. From an anthropological framework, Bateson led this research and other projects that heavily influenced family therapy (Lawley, 2013). *Toward a Theory of Schizophrenia* was a pivotal research publication (Bateson et al., 1956). The study on schizophrenia yielded the groundwork for research studies pertaining to communication within the family unit (Mental Research Institute [MRI], n.d.c). This study led Bateson and contributors Jackson, Haley, and Weakland to broach the concept of the double bind theory, which ultimately pioneered a multifaceted examination of communication while drawing from the concept of cybernetics (Bateson et al., 1956; MRI, n.d.c).

The double bind theory is a concept that was derived from an examination of patients diagnosed with schizophrenia and a research focus to examine the communication styles between the patient, familial, and systemic contexts of the family unit (Bateson et al., 1956). From the communication standpoint, a double bind occurs when there are regularly present and occurring incompatible and opposing messages given to an individual (Bateson, Jackson, Haley, & Weakland, 1963). The overall message received by a person yields a conflict in the individual's reality, thus creating conflict and incongruence (Bateson et al., 1963). Thus, Bateson, Jackson, Haley, and Weakland were instrumental in laying the groundwork for studies that were fruitful in comprehension of the process communication in the dynamics of the family unit (MRI, n.d.a). For a list of important people who were integral in the development of the MCFT profession in the United States, please review Table 2.1.

Study Centers

The research on the double bind did more than study communication patterns in the family context. The key contributors were instrumental in launching training and continued research. Founded in 1958, the Mental Research Institute (MRI) of Palo Alto was developed in response to the studies led by Bateson and his team (Institute Gregory Bateson, 2015b; MRI, n.d.b). Don Jackson gave a lecture at the VA hospital in 1954 on family homeostasis and Gregory Bateson was in the audience. This fortuitous meeting resulted in a collaboration that led to the formation of the Mental Research Institute (MRI, n.d.b).

The key members involved in the beginnings of the MRI include key founder and director Jackson, as well as Weakland, Fisch, and Watziawick (Institute Gregory Bateson, 2015a; MRI, n.d.b). Bateson also contributed by serving as a consultant with the MRI (n.d.b). Other key contributors included Virginia Satir, Jay Haley, and Jules Riskin (MRI, n.d.a).

Mental Research Instit.

The contributing members of the MRI have been influential in contributing to research pertaining to the study of family systems and the individual within the family unit (Jackson, 1965). Through the MRI, researchers have been able to contribute to over 60 projects in areas of family and family specializations, family and medical concerns, culture as related to family and communities, and mental disorders (MRI, n.d.a). Today the MRI continues to provide mental health counseling services to individuals and families, conducts research, and provides education and training (MRI, n.d.a). Let's turn for a minute to our Guided Practice Exercise 2.1 and explore the MRI website.

GUIDED PRACTICE EXERCISE 2.1

Please go to the MRI's web page at http://mri.org/. Read the descriptions related to strategic family therapy and brief family therapy, both of which are offered at the MRI clinic. If you were going to avail yourself of therapy at this clinic, which approach would most appeal to you? What intrigues you about the approach you chose?

International Family Therapy

The advent of family therapy was also seen on global scale. As early as the 1950s, mental health hospitals in India began to incorporate families into the therapeutic process. One of the first examples of this was the vital contributions by Vidya Sagar, who influenced how families were treated in therapy while working at the Amritsar Mental Hospital (Chadda & Deb, 2013). This trend continued into the 1960s, and during this time there was an increase in families being treated within programs (Chadda & Deb, 2013). Following similar trends, family therapy became more visible in England as independent practitioners such as Robin Skynner and John Howells began to work with the family within a social context and in practices such as translating group work and applying those techniques with the family unit (Stanton, Harway, & Vetere, 2013). In the early 1960s family therapy was also emerging in Mexico, as Raymundo Macias brought the concept of family therapy to the educational setting through teaching (Kaslow, 2000). Also in the 1950s and 1960s, the presence of family therapy was also seen in South Africa, Yugoslavia, and Argentina (Hill & Perkel, 2014; Kaslow, 2000).

MID-1960s TO MID-1970s

Though formalized family therapy initially emerged in the United States in the late 1940s and early 1950s, there was an explosion in the use of family therapy in the 1960s that continued over the next few decades (Gladding, 2014; Lev, 2015). Beginning in the 1960s, a more robust transition from individual counseling to family systems–based counseling was observed.

In 1965, family services programs affiliated with church organizations were emerging in major cities such as Philadelphia, New York, Boston, and Buffalo (Gladding, 2014).

What goes wrong

During all this, the focus of marriage, couples, and family (MCF) counseling shifted to more systemic or circular approach, in which family therapists placed emphasis on problem patterns and behaviors, belief systems, and predisposing factors within the family system; a practice that required multiple active participants rather than just individuals (Lambert, Skinner, & Friedlander, 2012). During this period, general systems theory founded by Ludwig von Bertalanffy served as the foundation for most family therapy models (Gladding, 2014).

family of origins

Review of Family Therapists From the 1950s

Several family therapists played significant roles in the development and progression of the practice of family therapy, both in the decade before and the decade after the 1960s (Gladding, 2014). Though Bateson, Bowen, Erickson, Ackerman, and Jackson made their primary contributions in the 1950s, each therapist also continued to influence other family therapists into the 1960s and beyond.

1950

Gregory Bateson. Bateson was the father of Batesonian therapy. As previously mentioned, Bateson was closely connected with Jay Haley, who was a therapist and influential leader in the 1960s (Gladding, 2014). Though Bateson emerged in the 1950s, his work continued into the early 1960s until his group disbanded in 1962, though his work was continued at the MRI in Palo, Alto, California (Gladding, 2014). Bateson also served on the editorial board of the *Family Process* journal and published *Steps to an Ecology of Mind* in 1972. Bateson's last book, *Angels Fear*, though based on his work, was written and published by his daughter in 1987 (Beels, 2011).

Murray Bowen. Bowen was a psychiatrist and family therapist and was the father of Bowen family systems theory, or simply Bowenian family therapy (Kott, 2014; Bowen Center for the Study of the Family, 2017). The Bowenian approach to family therapy involves awareness of expectations of family members (MacKay, 2012). Bowen's family systems therapy, and its focus on triangular relationships, is considered to be one of the most comprehensive additions to marriage and family therapy (Berg-Cross & Worthy, 2013). Bowen was an integral component of the family therapy movement (Kott, 2014).

expectation

Milton Erickson. Erickson was a strategic family therapist specializing in psychiatry and hypnosis at the University of Wisconsin. Erickson founded the American Society of Clinical Hypnosis ("Milton Hyland Erickson," 2011; Milton H. Erickson Foundation, n.d.). Erickson was credited with creating strategic family therapy and was responsible for creating the paradox, reframing, and going with resistance techniques (Nash, 2012). Erickson's work served as a precursor for Jay Haley and other strategic family therapists (Gladding, 2014).

Nathan Ackerman. Ackerman was one of the pioneers in involving young children in the family therapy process (Weinstein, 2013). Ackerman's approach to family therapy involved incorporating cultural mores of the era in his practice and as a means to affirm widely accepted social practices. Ackerman founded *Family Process*, the first family therapy journal, in 1961 in collaboration with Don Jackson. Ackerman headed up the Family Institute of New York, also known as the Ackerman Institute for the

Family, in the late 1960s (Ackerman Institute for the Family, 2014; Gladding, 2014). One of his most recognized works is *Treating the Troubled Family*, published in 1966.

Donald (Don) Jackson. Jackson was a cofounder of *Family Process*. Jackson founded the MRI in Palo Alto, California, in 1958 and served as the institute's first director. He is considered the founder of interactional theory and conjoint family therapy. Jackson's family therapy focus was on family homeostasis, with the goal of stability seeking, and focuses on the reparation of the "problematic" family member. Jackson's identification of therapeutic double binds, or multilevel messages, was one of the most prolific additions to marriage and family therapy (Charny, 2014; Ray, Stivers, & Brasher, 2011).

Family Therapists From the 1960s

Preceded and aided by the continued work of Gregory Bateson, Murray Bowen, Milton Erickson, Nathan Ackerman, Don Jackson, and others, some of the most influential individuals credited with the continued rise of family therapy during the 1960s included Jay Haley, Salvador Minuchin, Virginia Satir, and Carl Whitaker (Gladding, 2014; Lev, 2015). We will detail those contributions in further detail in the following paragraphs. For a list of important events that helped shape the MCFT profession, please review table 2.2.

Table 2.1 Important people in the development of MCFT in the United States

Ackerman, Nathan	Haley, Jay
Adler, Alfred	Hare-Mustin, Rachel
Baker Miller, Jean	Jackson, Don
Bateson, Gregory	Lewin, Kurt
Bell, John	Lidz, Theodore
Bertalanffy, Ludwig von	Minuchin, Salvador
Bowen, Murry	Mudd, Emily
Bowlby, John	Popenoe, Paul
Dearborn, Lester	Richmond, Mary
Dickerson, Robert	Riskin, Jules
Dreikurs, Rudolf	Satir, Virginia
Erickson, Milton	Stone, Abraham and Hannah
Fromm-Reichmann, Frieda	Weakland, John
Gilligan, Carol	Whitaker, Carl

Table 2.2 Important events in the development of MCFT in the United States

The social work profession's response to the needs of families during industrialization re: the Charity Organization Society and the settlement house movement

The child guidance movement

The Groves Conference

The New York meetings

The development of professional organizations and centers devoted to the practice of the MCFT profession

The development of cybernetics and systems theory, including the double bind, family homeostasis, and Kurt Lewin's small group dynamics

The recognition of MCFTs as mental health professionals eligible for specialized training in family therapy as well as federal grants, solidified by the Public Health Service Act, Title III, Section 303 (d)(1)

The influence of the feminist movement

The development of licensure, program accreditation, and a code of ethics

The development of study centers such as the MRI and the Institute for Family Studies in Milan, Italy

The emergence of evidence-based practice and the biopsychosocial approach

The spread of MCF therapy worldwide

Jay Haley. Haley was a member of the MRI in Palo Alto, California, along with other family theoreticians such as John Bell, Virginia Satir, and Gregory Bateson (Beels, 2011; Bloom, 2015). Haley's primary contributions stemmed from Milton Erickson's work, as did many strategic family therapists of this time (Beels, 2011; Bloom 2015). One of Haley's early writings on family therapy, *Strategies of Psychotherapy*, had several chapters dedicated to family therapy that discussed the shift from individual counseling to relationship counseling, and the logical next step, which was family counseling. Haley (1963) explored therapeutic paradoxes present in family therapy. As part of his work as a strategic family therapist, Haley conducted family therapy in Philadelphia at the Child Guidance Clinic under Salvador Minuchin (Gladding, 2014).

Salvador Minuchin. Minuchin developed structural family therapy, in which the therapist strives to understand the rules within the family system by becoming directly involved and helping the family identify and explore alternative ways of relating and developing healthier patterns of interaction with one another (Norfleet, 2014). Minuchin wrote several books, the most famous among them being *Families and Family Therapy* and *Psychosomatic Families* (Gladding, 2014). Though he officially retired in 1996, he continues to be involved in family therapy and publish with peers and students (Stagner, 2012; Wylie, 2013). One of his latest publications is *The Craft of Family Therapy* (Minuchin, Reiter, & Borda, 2013).

Virginia Satir. Satir was responsible for the development of Satir Transformational Systemic Therapy, or simply Satir therapy (Banmen & Maki-Banmen, 2014). Satir's model, sometimes referred to as Satir family reconstruction, is a form of therapy that emphasizes the use of self of the therapist (Novak, 2012). Reportedly, Satir saw her first family of clients in 1951 and spent four decades honing her unique approach to family therapy (Banmen & Maki-Banmen, 2014). Satir, a social worker with her own practice in Chicago, was the only woman among the numerous family therapy founders, which contributed to her impact on the family therapy field (Gladding, 2014). Perhaps her most famous work, *Conjoint Family Therapy*, was published in 1964 (Gladding, 2014). Satir taught courses at the MRI, and in 1976 she began the Satir Family Camp, which was a training camp targeted at educating family therapists (Banmen & Maki-Banmen, 2014).

Carl Whitaker. Whitaker's approach was known as symbolic-experiential family therapy, which was sometimes known for implementation of outlandish techniques in session but also included experience and symbolism as its main tenets (Cag & Acar, 2015). Whitaker was a large proponent of cotherapy and live supervision. He became chair of the department of psychiatry at Emory University in 1946 and coauthored *The Roots of Psychotherapy*. Whitaker contributed to the literature on family therapy with *The Involvement of the Professional Therapist* (Whitaker, Warkentin, & Malone, 1959) and published works such as *I Had to Learn Because I Wasn't Being Taught* (Whitaker, 1990).

International Family Therapy in the 1960s

During the 1960s, family therapy was also experiencing a renaissance of sorts internationally. While there is limited research on the introduction of family therapy in Mexico, Nathan Ackerman traveled to the country in the 1960s to help pioneer family therapy in the region (de Millán, 2015). Raymundo Macias, who was credited as being the first lecturer to focus on family therapy at the National University of Mexico, prompted the establishment of graduate programs in family therapy at Mexican universities, leading to higher rates of family-focused therapy in the 1970s and beyond (Kaslow, 2000).

In the United Kingdom, there were family therapy pioneers parallel to those in the United States, among them Robin Skynner, John Howells, and John Byng-Hall (Kaslow, 2000). This collective group of family therapists' approach to therapy began because of group psychotherapy and eventually shifted to conceptualizing families as their own groups (Kaslow, 2000). Though first introduced in the 1920s, it was during the 1960s that marriage, couple, and family practice became more widely utilized, and the United Kingdom began establishing institutions dedicated to this form of therapy, with the London Institute of Family Therapy and the Family Therapy Project among them (Stratton & Lask, 2013).

Family Therapy Legacy of the 1960s

During the 1960s several institutions devoted to family therapy were founded, some of which still exist today. The MRI in Palo Alto, the Family Institute in New York, the Albert Einstein College of Medicine in New York, the Child Guidance Clinic in Philadelphia, the Family Institute of Philadelphia, the Boston Family Institute, and the Institute for Family Studies in Milan, Italy (Gladding, 2014). Additionally, many publications named after these early family therapists, or stemming from the family therapy movement of the 1960s, are still in print today; *Satir Journal* and *Family Process* are two examples among many (Maki-Banmen, 2012; Novak, 2012). Furthermore, 1963 was also the year the first licensure law, sanctioned by the state of California, regulated family counselors as a separate mental health entity (Gladding, 2014).

[handwritten margin note: 1963 ca = Licensing]

Family Therapy in the 1970s

The family therapy movement in the 1970s was very much an extension of the progress in the 1960s, only with a larger audience and a stronger influence. Despite this, another shift in the 1970s was also taking place. Up to this time, women in family therapy were disregarded and historically viewed in traditional gender roles (Lebow, 2014). The feminist movement, discussed later in this section, aimed to challenge that tradition.

In the first part of the 1970s, few novel family therapists or family theories emerged. Rather, the work of Haley, Minuchin, Satir, and Whitaker were developing into more widely distributed and used forms of therapy. Furthermore, the focus of the first part of the 1970s was more on organizational change and establishment, rather than on new treatment modalities (Lebow, 2014). During this decade, theories that had been developed in the previous years were refined and utilized more widely, the practice of which was facilitated by workshops, presentations, and publications (Lebow, 2014).

In the 1970s there were significant increases in membership of many previously established family therapy organizations, including the AAMFT and the American Family Therapy Academy (Gladding, 2014). New divisions of organizations devoted to family therapy also emerged during this time, such as divisions of the American Psychological Association's Division of Family Psychology and the International Association of Marriage and Family Counselors (IAMFC), which later became an American Counseling Association division. Additionally, the *Journal of Marital and Family Therapy* published its first issue in 1974 (Gladding, 2014).

International Therapy in the 1970s

Brazil was introduced to family therapy in the 1970s as an alternative to psychoanalysis, prompted by psychiatrists with disdain for the current system, such as Lindemberg Rocha in Rio de Janeiro. Rocha was director of the Family Sector of the Pedro Ernesto Hospital at the State University of Rio de Janeiro, where he was instrumental in promoting the teaching and use of family therapy and the eventual development of programs specifying education and training in family therapy in the 1980s and beyond (Picon, 2012).

In Germany the development of family therapy paralleled that of the United States in that psychoanalysts also played an important part in introducing and advocating for a systems approach. Virginia Satir was known to have participated in workshops and conferences, and she was an influential force in the training of family therapists in Germany (Retzlaff, 2013).

Mara Selvini-Palazzoli is credited with engineering the Milan systemic approach in the early 1970s (Gladding, 2014; Luciano et al., 2012). Selvini-Palazzoli was a psychoanalytic therapist and head of the Milan Group in Milan, Italy. She emphasized a circular approach with triadic questioning and was responsible for the expansion of strategic family therapy (Gladding, 2014).

In the 1970s Scandinavia experienced interest in family therapy (Jensen, 2013), facilitated by Hans Jurgen Holm, medical director of an inpatient psychiatric facility near Oslo, Norway. Holm and his colleagues initiated the first family-centered form of therapy in the region, offering families extended stays in the cottages on the facility grounds. From Norway the family therapy movement spread into Finland, Sweden, and Estonia, where workshops and trainings based on the work of Haley and strategic family therapy were the primary influence (Jensen, 2013), Additionally, publications focusing on family therapy began to appear in the area in the 1970s; the *Norwegian Journal of Family Therapy* was the most notable at the time (Jensen, 2013).

Though family therapy was initially introduced to South Africa in the 1960s, it was not until the 1970s that the practice of marriage, couple, and family therapy became publicized at the South African Congress of Psychiatry. This was followed by workshops and symposia conducted by Donald Bloch at the University of the Witwatersrand and the University of Cape Town (Hill & Perkel, 2014; Kaslow, 2000).

Family therapy first emerged in South Korea in the 1970s via practitioners who studied in other countries and brought the practice back home (Lee et al., 2013). From that initial introduction, an initiative for training, education, credentials, and the incorporation of family therapy in various settings was witnessed.

In the 1970s, family systems therapy in Yugoslavia was introduced (Kaslow, 2000). The family and social network therapy of alcoholism was pioneered by psychiatrist Branko Gacic, Dr. Pavel Kastel, and social worker Jovica Potrebic in 1973 at the Institute for Mental Health. The approach instituted by these therapists viewed alcoholism as a multigenerational family problem that required participation from multiple family members (Kaslow, 2000). Let's turn our attention to Guided Practice Exercise 2.2 in order to practice reviewing international literature.

GUIDED PRACTICE EXERCISE 2.2

Choose any country other than the United States. Do a brief literature review and find five articles or book chapters related to the history of the MCFT profession in your chosen country. What were the similarities and differences in the development of the MCFT profession between the United States and your chosen country? What surprised you regarding what you read?

LATE 1970s TO MID-1980s FEMINISTS

During the latter part of the 1970s, the feminist movement was born, which sparked a never-before-seen emphasis on female-centered approaches in family therapy (Gladding, 2014). This signified the beginning of the feminist theory stronghold led by activists such as Rachel Hare-Mustin, Jean Baker Miller, Carol Gilligan, and other strong female leaders of the time who imagined an egalitarian and gender-equal form of family therapy (Gladding, 2014; Lebow, 2014). Because of this, many, but not all, of the family therapists emerging during this time were connected to, or influenced by, feminist approaches.

Rachel Hare-Mustin. Hare-Mustin published "A Feminist Approach to Family Therapy" in 1978 in the *Family Process* journal, an article which has been credited with challenging the historical approach to family therapy and facilitating the feminist approach to family therapy (Gladding, 2014). Among her other publications echoing feminist themes include "Resource Collaboration, Feminist Therapy, and Models" (Hare-Mustin, 1984), and "Family Change and Gender Differences: Implications for Theory and Practice" (Hare-Mustin, 1988).

Jean Baker Miller. Miller was the first director of the Stone Center for Developmental Services and Studies at Wellesley College and published *Psychoanalysis and Women* in 1973 and *Toward a New Psychology of Women* in 1976 (Jordan, 2011; Vermes, 2017). Miller's involvement in feminist family therapy was prompted by witnessing her clients' involvement in feminist groups. The crux of Miller's approach emphasized a woman's experience and the impact of relationships in human growth from a female perspective. Though Miller died in 2006, the Jean Baker Miller Training Institute at the Stone Center was dedicated in memoriam to her (Jordan, 2011; Stewart, 2007).

Carol Gilligan. Gilligan experienced reservations about the male-centered approaches to therapy (Women's Intellectual Contributions, n.d.). Gilligan published perhaps her most famous work in 1982, *In a Different Voice: Psychological Theory and Women's Development* in which she outlined her observations on traditional approaches to development (Gilligan, 1993; Women's Intellectual Contributions, n.d.). Gilligan is also a founding member of the collaborative Harvard Project on Women's Psychology and Girls' Development (Gilligan, 1992). While not primarily a family therapist, Gilligan's work has influenced the incorporation of feminist undertones in many forms of family therapy practiced today.

Family Therapy in the 1980s

In the 1980s, family therapy continued its upward projection in terms of attention, practice, research, organizational membership, and publications (Gladding, 2014). During the 1980s a heavier focus on research was emphasized, as evidenced by the *Journal of Marriage and Family* and *Journal of Family Issues*, both publishing about research methodology within family therapy. Perhaps, most importantly, it was also during this decade that family therapists became recognized as mental health professionals eligible for specialized training in family therapy as well as federal grants, solidified by the Public Health Service

Act, Title III, Section 303 (d)(1) (Gladding, 2014). It was also during the 1980s that multisystemic therapy was developed. This is a collective combination of approaches from the behavioral, cognitive, and other family therapies designed to address both familial and interpersonal aspects of treatment. Practitioners used this as a community approach for adolescents at risk and juveniles with antisocial tendencies (Gladding, 2014).

International Family Therapy in the 1980s

Family therapy continued to expand in international markets during this time. Argentina embraced marriage, couple, and family therapy in the 1980s in response to the focus on family and marriage counseling in other countries. The Argentine Systemic Federation was created in the mid-1980s, and training centers dedicated to MCFT approaches were founded and embraced (Herscovici, González, Label, Vega, & Chong Garcia, 2013).

Marriage, couple, and family therapy in China did not begin to emerge until the early 1980s. Even then, the utilization of systemic forms of therapy were slow to be incorporated, and training was limited (Deng, Lin, Lan, & Fang, 2013). Though the desire to learn about family systems was present, it was not until the 1990s that family therapy began to thrive in terms of training, the foundation of family therapy-oriented organizations emerged, and in the 2000s, publications targeting family therapy began circulation (Deng et al., 2013). For a list of important organizations that have helped guide the MCFT profession, please review Table 2.3.

Table 2.3 **Important organizations in the development of MCFT in the United States**

American Association for Marriage and Family Therapy

American Association of Marriage Counseling

American Family Therapy Academy

American Psychological Association's Division of Family Psychology International

Association of Marital and Family Therapy Regulatory Board

Commission on Accreditation for Marriage and Family Therapy Education

Council for Accreditation of Counseling and Related Educational Programs

International Association of Marriage and Family Counselors

Palo Alto Group and the Mental Research Institute

MID-1980s TO PRESENT

Through growth and development, MCFT history has become common practice among practitioners throughout the world (International Association of Marriage and Family Counselors [IAMFC], 2016). According to the AAMFT (2017), "Since 1970 there has been a 50-fold increase in the number of marriage and family therapists. At any given time, they are treating over 1.8 million people" (para 10). Overall in the United States, there has been an impending growth in the specialty of marriage, couples, and family therapy, which examine the levels of competency among professionals and have attended to common trends in licensing statewide (Gladding, 2014). The focus has evolved from competency and training to a heightened cognition of the need for evidence-based practices as the profession has continued to advance in a culmination of effectual and ... 2014). We will discuss evidenced-based practice later

... as evolved in the United States as a known and regulated ... 2014b), between 1986 and 2009, there has been an in- ... rofession through licensure or credentialing. During ... from 11 states that required licensure to practice to all ..., 2014b). Currently, both the state licensing boards ... to provide standards and structure in the MCFT ... has evolved, state licensure boards have taken on ... rnance of licensing and regulation (West, Hinton,

... uring ethical practice, as evidenced by the devel- ... s code of ethics. The AAMFT's code of ethics (AAMFT, 2015) attends to numerous facets of the MCFT profession and is effectual in guiding the decision-making processes in application to clients, conduct, and working with the individual or group, and helping the practitioner avoid harm to the client, couple, or family. These ethical codes attend to areas that include mandatory professional expectations, guidelines for decisions and choices, as well as ethical practice, professional standards, responsibilities, research guidelines, and conduct for supervision, education, and client relationships (AAMFT, 2015).

Through the progression of the growth, associations, and structured clinics, training programs began to emerge to further strengthen the profession's roots. Reinforcing these trends, the American Counseling Association incorporated a division, the IAMFC, in 1989, to help bring unification, cultural awareness and competency, and a set of standards that will help bring increased competency (IAMFC, 2015). Similarly, the IAMFC (2015) developed a certification that demonstrated a standard for training, thus increasing the accountability and integrity of the profession and division via the National Credentialing Academy. The IAMFC has just published an update to its ethical code. Ethical codes are dynamic documents that are periodically revised to address new issues that arise as we evolve as a society (e.g., social media; IAMFC, 2017).

Role of the AAMFT. As the name suggests, the American Association of Marriage and Family Therapy is the association that was created to support and promote the integrity of the field of marriage, couples, and family therapy and promotes the professional identity of MCFTs (AAMFT, 2014a; West et al., 2013). This association has been instrumental in the growth of the MCFT profession and evolutionary changes as the field has developed (West et al., 2013). The AAMFT serves as a platform for the foundation of standards, competencies, and ethical practices, while enhancing the profession with a focus on development and research to deeply root the field in evidence-based practices. The AAMFT assumes a role in the MCFT profession that advocates and promotes wellness, awareness, social justice, and advocacy as needs emerge for populations, society, and the profession and professionals based on legal and ethical components (Bordoloi, O'Brien, Edwards, & Preli, 2013).

The Commission on Accreditation for Marriage and Family Therapy Education (COAMFTE). The COAMFTE was developed to accredit graduate-level marriage, couple, and family therapy training programs and to provide program standards and competencies that must be met, thus ensuring consistency in training and development among MCFTs who seek licensure (COAMFTE, 2014). The aim of the accreditation is to encourage the practice of programmatic-based self-evaluation and educational growth to continue to ensure a graduate program's level of competency and standard of excellence in training and educating MCFT students in their professional development (COAMFTE, 2014). While the space constraints of this chapter prevent us from going into depth about these standards and competencies, a link has been provided to this document under the heading "Additional Resources" below.

Programs that are accredited by the COAMFTE (2014) are upheld by an expectation and standard that is measurable and evaluative. The COAMFTE (2014) accreditation is useful to support students, administrators, and training programs with a standard of quality in education, licensure preparation, class transferability, program consistency, level of measurable status, attention to diversity and ethical practice, and adequate preparation. Accreditation attends to standards of education, competency, ethical codes, licensure, and examination criteria (COAMFTE, 2014).

The Council for Accreditation of Counseling and Related Educational Programs (CACREP). Recognized as an independent specialty, CACREP standards have established a set criterion for competency in marriage, couples, and family counseling programs. These competencies extend beyond the core structure of counseling and into specialty-specific themes that include attention to various facets of counseling in the context of marriage, family, and couples in relation to foundations, diversity and advocacy, assessment, research, and evaluation (CACREP, 2016). These standards require that counselors demonstrate competency and knowledge in capacities such as crisis and trauma, prevention, intervention, cognition to addiction, and legal and ethical arenas (CACREP, 2016).

Additionally, MCFTs must be able to exhibit competency in human sexuality counseling, multicultural contexts and complexities, and understand the individual as part of a cyclical unit within the family or couple (CACREP, 2016). Furthermore, CACREP (2016) standards attend to the familiarization with familial dynamics as related to violence, aging, sexuality, and trauma. A competent marriage, couple, and family program should also educate on program assessment, evaluation, and research (CACREP, 2016).

Again, while length constraints prevent us from discussing these standards in detail, a link to these standards can be found under the header "Additional Resources." Let us turn our attention to Guided Practice Exercise 2.3, where we will compare the standards and competencies of the COAMFTE and CACREP.

GUIDED PRACTICE EXERCISE 2.3

Please go to the websites of the COAMFTE and CACREP (see a link to these documents under the heading "Additional Resources." Pull up both organization's documents related to the competencies and standards required by each for accreditation of MCFT programs. Compare and contrast these two documents. What similarities and differences between these two documents do you notice?

Licensing exams. Licensure standards provide a framework for which state licensing boards can measure and evaluate candidates for the counseling licenses (Association of Marital and Family Therapy Regulatory Board [AMFTRB], 2017a). To qualify for licensing, candidates must meet a variety of components, including academic course work, intern hours, and passing a licensure exam. The Association of Marital and Family Therapy Regulatory Board (AMFTRB) created an exam as a standard for cumulative measurement of knowledge to be used as a means of qualification for the Marriage and Family Therapy License (AMFTRB, 2017b). The marriage and family therapy exam is a computerized exam that consists of questions that evaluate candidates in areas pertaining to assessment, treatment, systemic therapy, crisis, ethics and standards, and treatment evaluation and termination (AMFTRB, 2017b). *need to know how to terminate.*

International Family History

As previously noted, trends in family therapy began to emerge on a global scale around the 1950s and further expanded throughout the course of the decades. Family therapy was seen in countries such as Poland and India, where hospitals began to treat individuals from family contexts (Chadda & Deb, 2013; Józefik, Barbaro, Iniewicz, & Namysłowska, 2013). In Poland this profession emerged in several contexts ranging from contributors such as Maria Orwid and team to the Family Therapy Outpatient Unit that was established 1983 (Józefik et al., 2013). Family therapy also appeared in South America., Specialized family therapy training was offered at the Psychiatry Institute of the Federal University of Rio de Janeiro (Kaslow, 2000). Further, family therapy became more visible in China during 1980s and continued to emerge as journal articles were published and family therapy became a field of study in education, particularly at the Institute of Psychology in Chinese Academy of Sciences (Deng et al., 2013). The expansion of family therapy on a global scale continues to emerge, as this specialty has become more visible, recognized, and regulated. For a list of people who are important to the development of the MCFT profession internationally, please see Table 2.4.

Table 2.4 **Important people in the development of MCFT globally**

Bloch, Donald	Orwid, Maria
Byng-Hall, John	Potrebic, Jovica
Gacic, Branko	Rocha, Lindemberg
Holm, Hans Jurgen	Selvini-Palazzoli, Mara
Howells, John	Sagar, Vidya
Kastel, Pavel	Skynner, Robin
Macias, Raymundo	

Research and Trends

As an established profession, MCFT necessitates research to further establish it from a framework of evidence-based practices (Oka & Whiting, 2013). In this vein, researchers have conducted studies on a variety of topics. An example of this includes an examination of trends in MCFT regarding supervisors who serve as gatekeepers to the profession in training (Sampson, Kelly-Trombley, Zubatsky, & Harris, 2013). Other trends include attention to areas that may need advocacy, particularly in the context of underserved populations and sociocultural differences (Bordoloi et al., 2013). You will learn more about research and trends in Chapter 6, which focuses on couples and families research.

Evidenced-based practice. Evidence-based practice was formulated in the early part of this century due to the desire of some practitioners to form clinical practices based on what the research confirmed was effective (Smith, 2014). This approach has been somewhat controversial, with some practitioners in favor of such an approach, while others prefer to rely on their own clinical expertise and experience sans official research confirmation (Fraser, Solvey, Grove, Lee, & Greene, 2012; Smith, 2014). Many such practitioners believe that their vast clinical experience and success rates are proof enough that their approach works (Dattilio, Piercy, & Davis, 2014). A part of this controversy centers on two camps: those who believe in a common factors approach to explain why therapy works, and those who propose a specific factors approach (Fraser et al., 2012). In other words, it is the specific interventions, assigned in a specific way, that explain the success of an approach (Fraser et al., 2012). However, evidence-based approaches are continuing to gain in popularity because they are favored by insurance companies and other third-party payers (Dattilio et al., 2012). The MCF profession is also advocating more research education for students currently studying to join the profession. Many in the MCFT profession are calling for better trained scholar-practitioners due to this growing call for more evidence-based practices (Dattilio et al., 2012).

A biopsychosocial perspective. Marriage, couple, and family therapists often integrate a biopsychological or biopsychosocial approach with other theories to treat mental health issues within the couple or the family (Negash & Hecker, 2010). The biopsychological approach was developed by Engel (1977). This model was adopted *bio · psychological*

by the MCF profession due to many MCF therapists' collaborations with the medical community within the field of family medicine (Howe, 2011; Pereira & Smith, 2006). The biopsychological approach is a strengths-based, holistic model that recognizes that human beings are biological, social, and psychological entities (Miller, Christenson, Glunz, & Cobb, 2016). Therefore, more than just the psychological wellness of an individual, couple, or family is considered. This approach is also very adaptable to many different cultures, because it considers the cultural relativism of the individual, or the family, across the age span (Howe, 2011).

strengths-based

SUMMARY

In this chapter, we discussed the origins and development of the marriage, couples, and family counseling profession from its earliest influences through the child guidance and social work movements to current-day developments such as recognizing and honoring the importance of couple relationships that do not fall neatly into a "married" package; hence the gradual shift from referring to marriage and family therapy to marriage, couple, and family therapy. In Chapter 3 you will learn more about the core principles and paradigms in the MCFT profession.

KEYSTONES

Among the key points addressed in this chapter are:

- Many individuals have made substantial contributions to the development of the marriage, couple, and family counseling profession, including but not limited to Nathan Ackerman, Gregory Bateson, John Bell, Murray Bowen, John Bowlby, Milton Erikson, Frieda Fromm-Reichmann, Carol Gilligan, Jay Haley, Rachel Hare-Mustin, Don Jackson, Kurt Lewin, Theodore Lidz, Jean Baker Miller, Salvador Minuchin, Virginia Satir, Mara Selvini-Palazzoli, Carl Whitaker, and John Weakland. Each brought unique contributions related to theory or process that has led the profession to how it is practiced today.

- There have been many key events that have helped shape the profession, such as the Groves Conference, the New York meetings, Kurt Lewin's small group dynamics, the influence of the social work profession, the development of family systems theory, and the spread of marriage, couples, and family therapy worldwide.

- While the early development of the profession was mostly led by men, during the 1970s and with the influence of the feminist movement, many prominent women made substantial contributions to how marriage, couples, and family therapy is practiced today. The 1970s has been viewed as a boom time for the development of MCFTs, and since then there has been a proliferation of practitioners in this profession (Schmidt, 2015).

- The MCFT profession is regulated by several organizations (e.g., AAMFT, COAMFTE, CACREP) that have set competencies and standards for the training of practitioners and who help oversee the professional development graduate-level educational and training programs. Currently all 50 US states require those wishing to practice MCFT to be licensed through their respective states boards.

- The MCFT profession is moving more toward evidenced-based practices and incorporating a biopsychosocial lens to the work practitioners do with couples and families.

REFLECTIONS FROM THE CONTRIBUTOR'S CHAIR
Melinda Haley

I have found that it is always important to understand the history of a profession to understand its progression and development and to where it is headed in theory and in practice. As an educator, I have found no greater pleasure than to engage in scholarship with my current and former students. Collaborating on this chapter was truly a labor of love, and it is thrilling to realize that soon, my students will be mentoring their own students in scholarship. The MCFT profession has progressed and grown in much the same way, with one generation mentoring the next; and we too pass on the torch of knowledge, discovery, and passion to those of you reading this chapter, who will go on to participate in the wellness of individuals, couples, and families. Enjoy your journey of discovery!

ADDITIONAL RESOURCES
The following resources provide additional information relating to the chapter topics.

Useful Websites

- American Association for Marriage and Family Therapy
  http://www.aamft.org/iMIS15/AAMFT/

This website provides information about the profession of MCFT, building your career, when conferences will be held, and how to find a therapist or a supervisor.

- Association of Marital and Family Therapy Regulatory Boards: State Licensure Comparison Chart
  https://www.amftrb.org/pdf/2009_amftrb_natllicensurecomparison.pdf

This website provides information regarding the requirements for licensure within each state.

- Commission on Accreditation for Marriage and Family Education: Accreditation Standards
  https://www.aamft.org/imis15/Documents/Accreditation_Standards_Version_11.pdf

This website provides the accreditation standards for the COAMFTE.

- Council for Accreditation of Counseling and Related Educational Programs: 2016 CACREP Standards
  http://www.cacrep.org/for-programs/2016-cacrep-standards/

This website provides the accreditation standards for CACREP.

READINGS

American Association of Marriage and Family Therapy. (2015). *Code of ethics.* Retrieved from http://www.aamft.org/iMIS15/AAMFT/Content/Legal_Ethics/Code_of_Ethics.aspx

This publication is a guideline for how to practice the profession of MCFT ethically and honorably within the United States. This document includes topics such as how to honor the public trust, the need to engage in social change and advocacy, how and when to seek consultation and engage in ethical decision making and resolve complaints.

Aponte, H. J., & Kissil, K. (2016). *The person of the therapist training model: Mastering the use of self.* New York: Routledge.

The authors of this edited book discuss different models of how to use yourself as a therapeutic tool to help families and couples.

Thornton, A. (2009). Historical and cross-cultural perspectives on marriage. In E. H. Peters (Ed.), *Marriage and family: Perspectives and complexities* (pp. 3–32). New York: Columbia University Press.

The author of this chapter discusses the history of marriage and family throughout time as well as from the perspective of different cultures.

International Association of Marriage and Family Counselors. (2017). *IAMFC code of ethics.* Alexandria, VA: Author.

This document provides the most updated ethical code governing the profession of MCFT worldwide.

VIDEOS

https://www.youtube.com/watch?v=QRBjvCxeBeg&list=PLaByyx03ueSpAJpJxQ3JZTNXL_UGVtmBJ

This video will give you an overview on systemic therapies, particularly those of the MRI and the Milan approach.

https://www.youtube.com/watch?v=31EgvvbXS6M

This video will provide you with an overview of the benefits of marriage, couples, and family therapy.

REFERENCES

Abrams, M. S. (2015). Coming together to move apart: Family therapy for enhancing adolescent development. *American Journal of Psychotherapy, 69*(3), 285–299.

Ackerman Institute for the Family. (2014). Our history. Retrieved from https://www.ackerman.org/our-history

American Association for Marriage and Family Therapy. (2014a). About AAMFT. Retrieved from http://www.aamft.org/iMIS15/AAMFT/Content/About_AAMFT/Qualifications.aspx

American Association for Marriage and Family Therapy. (2014b). MFT licensing boards. Retrieved from https://www.aamft.org/iMIS15/AAMFT/Content/Directories/MFT_Licensing_Boards.aspx?hkey=2f66f29c-ca16-4a58-8fff-30d176311f87

American Association for Marriage and Family Therapy. (2015). Code of ethics. Retrieved from http://www.aamft.org/iMIS15/AAMFT/Content/Legal_Ethics/Code_of_Ethics.aspx

American Association for Marriage and Family Therapy. (2017). About marriage and family therapists. Retrieved from http://www.aamft.org/iMIS15/AAMFT/Content/About_AAMFT/About_Marriage_and_Family_Therapists.aspx

Association of Marital and Family Therapy Regulatory Board. (2017a). Policy statement. Retrieved from https://www.amftrb.org/stateboards.cfm

Association of Marital and Family Therapy Regulatory Board. (2017b). The purpose of the examination. Retrieved from https://www.amftrb.org/exam.cfm

Banmen, J., & Maki-Banmen, K. (2014). What has become of Virginia Satir's therapy model since she left us in 1988? *Journal of Family Psychotherapy, 25*(2), 117–131. doi:10.1080/08975353.2014.909706

Bateson, G., Jackson, D. D., Haley, J., & Weakland, J. (1956). Toward a theory of schizophrenia. *Behavioral Science, 1*(4), 251–264.

Bateson, G., Jackson, D. D., Haley, J., & Weakland, J. H. (1963). A note on the double bind—1962. *Family Process, 2*(1), 154–161.

Beels, C. (2011). *Family process, 1962–1969. Family Process, 50*(1), 4–11. doi:10.1111/j.1545-5300.2010.01342.x

Bell, J. E. (1962). Recent advances in family group therapy. *Journal of Child Psychology and Psychiatry, 3*, 1–15. doi:10.1111/j.1469-7610.1962.tb02034.x

Bell, J. E. (1983). Family group therapy. In S. Sherman & B. Wolman (Eds.), *Handbook of family and marital therapy* (pp. 231–245). New York: Springer.

Berg-Cross, L., & Worthy, G. (2013). The contemporary utility of Bowen's original works. *Psyccritiques, 58*(42). doi:10.1037/a0034387

Bloom, P. B. (2015). Comment on the special issues: Jay Douglas Haley. *International Journal of Clinical and Experimental Hypnosis, 63*(4), 376–379. doi:10.1080/00207144.2015.1062688

Bordoloi, S. D., O'Brien, N., Edwards, L. L., & Preli, R. (2013). Creating an inclusive and thriving profession: Why the American Association of Marriage and Family Therapy (AAMFT) needs to advocate for same-sex marriage. *Journal of Feminist Family Therapy: An International Forum, 25*(1), 41–55. doi:10.1080/08952833.2013.755082

Bowen, E. (2015). Community practice in the bulldozer's shadow: The history and legacy of social work in urban renewal. *Journal of Community Practice, 23*, 164–181. doi:10.1080/10705422.2015.1027460

Bowen, M. (1978). *Family therapy in clinical practice.* New York: Aronson.

Bowen Center for the Study of the Family. (2017). About Murray Bowen. Retrieved from https://www.the-bowencenter.org/theory/about-murray-bowen

Bowlby, J. P. (1949). The study and reduction of group tensions in the family. *Human Relations, 2*, 123–138.

Breulin, D. C., & Jacobsen, E. (2014). Putting the "family" back into family therapy. *Family Process, 53*(3), 462–475. doi:10.1111/famp.12083

Cag, P., & Acar, N. V. (2015). A view of the symbolic-experiential family therapy of Carl Whitaker through movie analysis. *Educational Sciences: Theory and Practice, 15*(3), 575–586. doi:10.12738/estp.2015.3.2477

Chadda, R. K., & Deb, K. S. (2013). Indian family systems, collectivistic society and psychotherapy. *Indian Journal of Psychiatry, 55*(Suppl 2), S299–S309. doi:10.4103/0019-5545.105555. Retrieved from http://www.ncbi.nlm.nih.gov/pmc/articles/PMC3705700

Charny, I. W. (2014). Recovering the lost art of naturalistic family therapy: Retrospective and prospective. *Journal of Family Psychotherapy, 25*, 99–116. doi:10.1080/08975353.2014.909705

Cole, C. L., & Cole, A. L. (2012). The initiation of marriage and family therapy. In. R. H. Rubin & B. H. Settles (Eds.), *The Groves conference on marriage and family: History and impact on family science* (pp. 63–86). Ann Arbor: Michigan.

Commission on Accreditation for Marriage and Family Therapy. (2014). About accreditation. Retrieved from http://www.coamfte.org/iMIS15/COAMFTE/Accreditation/Value%20of%20Accreditation.aspx

Council for Accreditation of Counseling and Related Educational Programs. (2016). 2016 CACREP standards. Retrieved from http://www.cacrep.org/for-programs/2016-cacrep-standards

Dattilio, F. M., Piercy, F. P., & Davis, S. D. (2014). The divide between "evidenced-based" approaches and practitioners of traditional theories of family therapy. *Journal of Marital and Family Therapy, 40*(1), 5–16. doi:10.1111/jmft.12032

de Millán, S. G. (2015). Development of Latin-American societies in the IFPS. *International Forum of Psychoanalysis, 23*(2), 104–110. doi:10.1080/0803706X.2013.870352

Deng, L., Lin, X., Lan, J., & Fang, X. (2013). Family therapy in China. *Contemporary Family Therapy: An International Journal, 35*(2), 420–436. doi:10.1007/s10591-013-9273-3

Engel, G. L. (1977). The need of a new medical model: A challenge for biomedicine. *Science, 196*(4286), 129–136.

Erickson, P. (2015). *The world the game theorists made.* Chicago: University of Chicago Press.

Fraser, J. S., Solovey, A. D., Grove, D., Lee, M. Y., & Greene, G. J. (2012). Integrative families and systems treatment: A middle path toward integrating common and specific factors in evidence-based family therapy. *Journal of Marital and Family Therapy, 38*(3), 515–528. doi:10.1111/j.1752-0606.2011.00228.x

Fromm-Reichmann, F. (1948). Notes on the development of treatment of schizophrenics by psychoanalytic psychotherapy. *Psychiatry, 11*(3), 263–274.

Gilligan, C. (1992). Changing psychology. *Psyccritiques, 37*(7), 657–658. doi:10.1037/032331

Gilligan, C. (1993). *In a different voice: Psychological theory and women's development.* Cambridge, MA: Harvard University Press.

Gladding, S. (2014). *Family therapy: History, theory, and practice* (6th ed.). Upper Saddle River, NJ: Pearson.

Groves Conference. (2016). About. Retrieved from http://www.grovesconference.org/about.html

Hale, D., & Frusha, C. V. (2016). MRI brief therapy: A tried and true systemic approach. *Journal of Systemic Therapies, 35*(2), 14–24. doi:10.1521/jsyt.2016.35.2.14

Haley, J. (1963). *Strategies of psychotherapy.* New York: Grune and Stratton. doi:10.1037/14324-007

Hall, S. S. (2015). Working models of marriage: An application of attachment theory. *Marriage & Family Review, 51*(8), 713–729. doi:10.1090/01494929.2015.1068252

Hamon, R. R., & Smith, S. R. (2014). The discipline of family science and the continuing need for innovation. *Family Relations, 63*(3), 309–322.

Hare-Mustin, R. T. (1984). Resource collaboration, feminist therapy, and models. *American Psychologist, 39*(2), 185. doi:10.1037/0003-066X.39.2.185

Hare-Mustin, R. T. (1988). Family change and gender differences: Implications for theory and practice. *Family Relations: An Interdisciplinary Journal of Applied Family Studies, 37*(1), 36–41. doi:10.2307/584427

Harrington, A. (2012). The art of medicine: The fall of the schizophrenogenic mother. *Lancet, 379*(9823), 1292–1293.

Herscovici, C. R., González, S. C., Label, H., Vega, R. Z., & Chong García, N. C. (2013). Development and practice of the systems paradigm in Argentina, Chile and Peru. *Contemporary Family Therapy: An International Journal, 35*(2), 200–211. doi:10.1007/s10591-013-9241-y

Hill, A., & Perkel, A. (2014). Couple work in South Africa: A historical overview from Cape Town. *Psycho-Analytic Psychotherapy in South Africa, 22*(1), 106–117.

Howe, T. R. (2011). *Marriages and families in the 21st century: A bioecological approach.* Hoboken, NJ: Wiley-Blackwell.

Institute Gregory Bateson. (2015a). FAQ training. Retrieved from http://www.igb-mri.com/faq.php

Institute Gregory Bateson. (2015b). The Palo Alto Group. Retrieved from http://www.igb-mri.ch

International Association of Marriage and Family Counselors. (2015). Excellence in couples and family counseling. Retrieved from http://www.iamfconline.org

International Association of Marriage and Family Counselors. (2016). About IAMFC. Retrieved from http://www.iamfconline.org/public/-3.cfm

International Association of Marriage and Family Counselors. (2017). *IAMFC code of ethics.* Alexandria, VA: Author.

Jackson, D. D. (1965). The study of the family. *Family Process, 4,* 1–20. doi:10.1111/j.1545-5300.1965.00001.x

Jensen, P. (2013). Family therapy in Norway: Past and present. *Contemporary Family Therapy: An International Journal, 35*(2), 288–295. doi:10.1007/s10591-013-9254-6

Johnston, J. (2013). The host of the schizophrenogenic mother. *American Medical Association Journal of Ethics, 15*(9), 801–805.

Jordan, J. V. (2011). The Stone Center and relational–cultural theory. In J. C. Norcross, G. R. VandenBos, & D. K. Freedheim (Eds.), *History of psychotherapy: Continuity and change* (2nd ed., pp. 357–362). Washington, DC: American Psychological Association. doi:10.1037/12353-012

Józefik, B., de Barbaro, B., Iniewicz, G., & Namysłowska, I. (2013). Family therapy in Poland: Development and current perspectives. *Contemporary Family Therapy, 35*(2), 308–318. doi:10.1007/s10591-013-9257-3

Kaslow, F. W. (2000). History of family therapy: Evolution outside of the U.S.A. *Journal of Family Psychotherapy, 11*(4), 1–35.

Kott, K. (2014). Applying Bowen theory to work systems. *OD Practitioner, 46*(3), 76–82.

Lambert, J. E., Skinner, A. H., & Friedlander, M. L. (2012). Problematic within-family alliances in conjoint family therapy: A close look at five cases. *Journal of Marital and Family Therapy, 38*(2), 417–428. doi:10.1111/j.1752-0606.2010.00212.x

Lawley, J. (2013). What are double binds? Retrieved from http://www.cleanlanguage.co.uk/articles/blogs/87/What-are-Double-Binds.html

Lebow, J. (2014). *Couple and family therapy: An integrative map of the territory.* Washington, DC: American Psychological Association. doi:10.1037/14255-001

Lebow, J., & Sexton, T. L. (2016). The evolution of family and couple therapy. In T. L. Sexton & J. Lebow (Eds.), *Handbook of family therapy* (pp. 1–10). New York: Routledge.

Lee, S. H., Chun, Y. J., Chung, H., Shin, S. I., Lee, I., Lee, D. S., & Choi, Y. S. (2013). The profession of family therapy in South Korea: Current status and future directions. *Contemporary Family Therapy: An International Journal, 35*(2), 388–399. doi:10.1007/s10591-013-9270-6

Lev, A. I. (2015). Family therapy. In *GLBTQ Social Sciences*, pp. 1–4. Retrieved from http://tigrisinstitute. com/wp-content/uploads/2014/10/glbtq-encyclopedia-family-therapy.pdf

Lewin, K. (1946). Behavior as a function of the total situation. In L. Carmichael (Ed.), *Manual of child psychology* (pp. 791–844). New York: Wiley.

Lewin, K. (1947). Frontiers in group dynamics: Concept, method and reality in social science; social equilibria and social change. *Human Relations, 1*(5), 5–41. doi:10.1177/001872674700100103.

Lidz, R. W., & Lidz, T. (1949). The family environment of schizophrenic patients. *American Journal of Psychiatry, 106*(5), 332–345.

Lidz, T., Parker, B., & Cornelison, A. (1956). The role of the father in the family environment of the schizophrenic patient. *American Journal of Psychiatry, 113*(2), 126–132.

Luciano, M., Sampogna, G., del Vecchio, V., Giacco, D., Mul, A., de Rosa, C., & Maj, M. (2012). The family in Italy: Cultural changes and implications for treatment. *International Review of Psychiatry, 24*(2), 149–156. doi:10.3109/09540261.2012.656306

MacKay, L. (2012). Trauma and Bowen family systems theory: Working with adults who were abused as children. *Australian and New Zealand Journal of Family Therapy, 33*(3), 232–241. doi:10.1017/aft.2012.28

Maki-Banmen, K. (2012). Personal alchemy: The art of Satir family reconstruction. *Satir Journal, 5*(1), 71–73.

Mansager, E. (2015). Review of the collected clinical works of Alfred Adler. *Journal of Individual Psychology, 71*(3), 337–358.

McFadden, J. J. (2014). Disciplining the "Frankenstein of Pauperism": The early years of charity organization case recording, 1877–1907. *Social Service Review, 88*(3), 469–492.

McGeorge, C. R., Carlson, T. S., & Wetchler, J. L. (2015). The history of marriage and family therapy. In J. L. Wetchler & L. L. Hecker (Eds.), *An introduction to marriage and family therapy* (2nd ed., pp. 3–40). New York: Routledge.

Mental Research Institute. (n.d.a). About us. Retrieved from http://mri.org/about

Mental Research Institute. (n.d.b). Don D Jackson. Retrieved from http://mri.org/don-d-jackson

Mental Research Institute. (n.d.c). Gregory Bateson. Retrieved from http://mri.org/gregory-bateson

Milton Hyland Erickson. (2011). *Hutchinson's biography database*. Abingdon, UK: Research Machines, Helicon.

Miller, A. L., Christenson, J. D., Glunz, A. P., & Cobb, K. F. (2016). Readiness for change: Involving the family with adolescents in residential settings. *Contemporary Family Therapy, 38*, 86–96. doi:10.1007/s10591-016-9376-8

Milton H. Erickson Foundation. (n.d.). *Biography of Milton H. Erickson*. Retrieved from

https://www.erickson-foundation.org/biography

Minuchin, S., Reiter, M. D., & Borda, C. (2013). The craft of family therapy. *Psychotherapy Networker Magazine, 37*(5), 22.

Nash, M. (2012). Foundations of clinical hypnosis. In M. Nash & A. Barnier (Eds.), *The Oxford handbook of hypnosis: Theory, research and practice* (pp. 487–502). New York: Oxford University Press.

Negash, S. M., & Hecker, L. L. (2010). Ethical issues endemic to couple and family therapy. In L. Hecker (Ed.), *Ethics and professional issues in couple and family therapy* (pp. 225–242). New York: Routledge.

Norfleet, M. A. (2014). A different style of therapy. *Psyccritiques, 59*(33). doi:10.1037/a0036870

Novak, S. (2012). An example of the use of self in Satir-based family therapy. *Satir Journal, 5*(1), 21–33.

Oka, M., & Whiting, J. (2013). Bridging the clinician/researcher gap with systemic research: The case for process research, dyadic, and sequential analysis. *Journal of Marital and Family Therapy, 39*(1), 17–27. doi:10.1111/j.1752-0606.2012.00339.x

Pereira, M. G., & Smith, T. E. (2006). Evolution of the biopsychosocial model in the practice of family therapy. *International Journal of Clinical and Health Psychology, 6*(2), 455–467.

Phipps, W. D. (2014). Introduction to the special issue on the state of the art in systems family therapy. *Journal of Family Psychotherapy, 25*(2), 87–91. doi:10.1080/08975353.2014.909703

Picon, F. (2012). Family therapy in Brazil: Current status. *International Review of Psychiatry, 24*(2), 81–85. doi:10.3109/09540261.2012.655714

Popenoe, P. (1975). Foreword. In American Institute of Family Relations (Ed.), *Techniques of marriage and family counseling* (Vol. 4). Los Angeles: American Institute of Family Relations.

Rampage, C. (2014). The role of family institutes in promotion the practice of family therapy. *Family Process, 53*(3), 489–499. doi:10.1111/famp.12074

Rasheed, J. M., Rasheed, M. N., & Marley, J. A. (2011). *Family therapy: Models and techniques*. Thousand Oaks, CA: Sage.

Ray, W. A. (2015). Theory and practice of systemic therapy: A re-introduction to Jackson and Weakland's conjoint family therapy. *Journal of Systemic Therapies, 34*(4), 29–32.

Ray, W. A., & Schlanger, K. (2012). John H. Weakland: An interview in retrospect. *Journal of Systemic Therapies, 31*(1), 53–73. doi:10.1521/jsyt.2012.31.1.53

Ray, W. A., Stivers, R. J., & Brasher, C. (2011). Through the eyes of Don D. Jackson M.D. *Journal of Systemic Therapies, 30*(1), 38–58.

Retzlaff, R. (2013). Development of family therapy and systemic therapy in Germany. *Contemporary Family Therapy: An International Journal, 35*(2), 349–363. doi:10.1007/s10591-013-9267-1

Richmond, M. (1917). *Social diagnosis*. New York: Sage.

Sampson, J. M., Kelly-Trombley, H. M., Zubatsky, M., & Harris, S. M. (2013). Breaking up is hard to do: Dismissing students from MFT programs. *American Journal of Family Therapy, 41*(1), 26–33. doi:10.1080/01926187.2011.628205

Schmidt, C. (2015). Professional settings and career choices. In V. Sangganjanavanich & C. Reynolds (Eds.), *Introduction to professional counseling* (pp. 72–104). Los Angeles: Sage.

Schwartz, J. (2015). The unacknowledged history of John Bowlby's attachment theory. *British Journal of Psychotherapy, 31*(2), 251–266.

Smith, S. M. (2014). What does this mean for graduate education in marriage and family therapy? Commentary on "The divide between 'evidenced-based' approaches and practitioners of traditional theories of family therapy." *Journal of Marriage and Family Therapy, 40*(1), 17–19.

Stagner, B. H. (2012). Salvador Minuchin, family therapy pioneer. *Psyccritiques, 57*(39). doi:10.1037/a0030078

Stanton, M., Harway, M., & Vetere, A. (2013). Education in family psychology. In J. H. Bray & M. Stanton (Eds.), *Handbook of family psychology* (pp. 129–145). Chichester, UK: Blackwell.

Stewart, A. J. (2007). Growth is the great gift: Jean Baker Miller, 1927–2006. *Women's Review of Books, 1*, 30–31.

Stratton, P., & Lask, J. (2013). The development of systemic family therapy for changing times in the United Kingdom. *Contemporary Family Therapy: An International Journal, 35*(2), 257–274. doi:10.1007/s10591-013-9252-8

Vermes, C. (2017). The individualism impasse in counselling psychology. *Counselling Psychology Review, 32*(1), 44–53.

Weakland, J. (1960). The "double-bind" hypothesis of schizophrenia and three-party interaction. In J. H. Weakland & D. D. Jackson (Eds.), *The etiology of schizophrenia* (pp. 373–388). Oxford: Basic Books. doi:10.1037/10605-013

Weakland, J. (2010). "Family therapy" with individuals. *Journal of Systemic Therapies, 29*(4), 40–48. doi:10.1521/jsyt.2010.29.4.40

Weinstein, D. (2013). The pathological family: Postwar America and the rise of family therapy. London: Cornell University Press.

West, C., Hinton, W. J., Grames, H., & Adams, M. A. (2013). Marriage and family therapy: Examining the impact of licensure on an evolving profession. *Journal of Marital and Family Therapy, 39*(1), 112–126. doi:10.1111/jmft.12010

Whitaker, C. A. (1990). I had to learn because I wasn't being taught. *Contemporary Family Therapy: An International Journal, 12*(3), 181.

Whitaker, C. A., Warkentin, J., & Malone, T. P. (1959). The involvement of the professional therapist. In A. Burton (Ed.), *Case studies in counseling and psychotherapy* (pp. 218–256). Oxford: Prentice Hall. doi:10.1037/10575-009

Women's Intellectual Contributions to the Study of Mind and Society. (n.d.). Carol Gilligan. Retrieved from http://www2.webster.edu/~woolflm/gilligan.html

Wylie, M. S. (2013). The therapist's most important tool. *Psychotherapy Networker Magazine, 37*(5), 48–50.

CHAPTER 3

Principles and Paradigms in Family Therapy

Stephanie K. Scott

"We must take care of our families wherever we find them."

—Elizabeth Gilbert

In Chapter 1, we discussed common terms used in family therapy, as well as the indicators for, and strengths and weakness of, family systems treatment. Chapter 2 gave you an overview of the history and evolution of family therapy theories and methods, including the core competencies and standards. In this chapter, let's take these ideas one step further and focus on core principles that have developed from these underpinnings.

Family therapy includes a broad spectrum of theoretical orientations and approaches; however, these theoretical lenses have shared constructs. These constructs not only provide common language to the field but also help define consistency and validity in treatment. Furthermore, collective paradigms used in family systems work provide perspective to the systems counselor *and* to the client families by helping lend clarity to presenting issues, relational dynamics, and system functionality.

LEARNING OBJECTIVES

After reading this chapter, you will be able to do the following:

- Understand core principles of clinical work with families.
- Recognize the framework of family structure, dynamics, and relational processes.
- Recognize key transitional experiences common to family life cycle stages.
- Apply concepts of family wellness, resiliency, and cultural influence.
- Understand the role of the therapist in family systems work.

THERAPEUTIC PROCESSES AND KEY CONCEPTS

The specific interventions and emphases utilized in systemic work with families can vary significantly, depending on the theoretical orientation of the clinician. However, there are many paradigms and principles that are common across disciplines. In this section, we will discuss the most prominent of these, including function, significance, and purpose.

FAMILY DYNAMICS

The underpinning of effective clinical work with couples and families lies in the recognition of the system as the "client." The interactions of individuals across the system—or **family dynamics**—are the primary focus of treatment (Walrond-Skinner, 2014). Specific goals and interventions will be determined by family dynamics, and progress will be assessed by how the system grows and evolves together. That is, family dynamics are a prominent element of treatment, from assessment through termination.

Family dynamics have been found to play an important role in not only in the health of the system itself, but also in the health and behaviors of the individual members. For example, individuals with healthy family dynamics may be at less risk for depression and self-injurious behavior (Fei, Xiang, Shuo, Qilun, & Hodge, 2016; Gatta, Miscioscia, Sisti, Comis, & Battistella, 2017), as well as financial and ethical risk taking (Kennison, Wood, Byrd-Craven, & Downing, 2016). Furthermore, strong sibling bonds have been found to buffer the adjustment challenges associated with foster placement, thus decreasing the likelihood for placement change (Waid, Kothari, Bank, & McBeath, 2016). Conversely, negative family dynamics are associated with secondary risk factors, including family violence and addiction (Levy & Brekke, 2016).

Certainly, the associations between family dynamics and the individual system members' health are not simply causal, but reciprocal and bidirectional. In addition, consideration needs to be given for environmental and cultural influences, as these can also affect dynamics. Just as the relational interactions can affect how the system members adapt to their environments, they can also impact how system members experience acculturation and cultural expression (Lazarevic, 2016; Smokowski, Rose, Bacallao, Cotter, & Evans, 2017). A primary explanation for how this influence is manifested, and why it is bidirectional in nature, lies in the relative interconnectedness of the system.

Interconnectedness. A fundamental construct to clinical work with couples and families is the recognition that the relational system is dependent on the interactions between its members. Furthermore, counselors must also recognize the role of suprasystems and subsystems that may apply, and the influences these can have on the functionality of the core system. It is the **interconnectedness** of individuals across the various levels of systems that makes them vulnerable to each other. Consider the adolescent whose parents have recently separated and who has been acting out in school. A systems therapist would look not only at how the stress of marital discord may be affecting the adolescent's behavior, but also how the adolescent's behavior may affect the marital dyad. That is, while it is very possible that the teenager's behavior in school is an indirect result of stress at home, it is also possible that the behavior serves a secondary gain, such as forcing the parents to unite to address their child's issues. In other words, relationships across the system affect all the system members directly or indirectly; the individual members, in turn, affect the relationships within the system.

It is also of note that interconnectedness is not limited to the system itself. In addition to **subsystems**—or relational systems within the family system—families are affected by the *suprasystems* to which they belong. These include next-level environmental contexts that also exert bidirectional influence, such as work, school, neighborhoods, religious affiliation, culture, and society. Guided Practice Exercise 3.1 notes the role of poverty in the social suprasystem. *Outside of home relationships*

GUIDED PRACTICE EXERCISE 3.1

Poverty is one example of a characteristic present in the social suprasystem. Remember the family described previously in this chapter? Consider how the addition of poverty as a systemic factor might shift the context and perspective of the system. What kind of strain might low socioeconomic status be on the marital dyad? What if the parents were separated but still living together because they could not afford to live separately, thus continuing to expose their child to the conflicts that often accompany separation? It is not possible to fully understand the family dynamics without also considering the system within context of its environment. How might you begin to address these considerations as the system's counselor?

When considering the interconnectedness of a family system, it is essential to recognize the influence of culture. What is "normal" is not nearly as relevant as what *works* for a family system. For example, in the United States, the predominant culture is considered individualistic in that we emphasize independence and personal responsibility. This is not to say that we are not interconnected with families, friends, and the larger society, but our definition of what this means can be significantly different from that seen in more collectivist cultures. What works for one family system may be very different from what works for another; similarly, dynamics that are problematic in one systemic context may be functional and supportive in another. The systemic counselor needs to view interconnectedness as relative trait to be assessed through a cultural *and* functional lens. The cultural lens affects the way members of a system view their relational dynamics, roles within the system, and responsibility for each other.

Systems thinking tells us that it is not possible to change one part of the system without changing the system itself. It is the interconnectedness of the system that drives its functionality, whether healthy or unhealthy. Interconnectedness also helps frame the process of change and gives perspective to the need to address multiple perspectives simultaneously.

Communication patterns. Perhaps the most observable and consistent way families display their dynamics lies in their **communication patterns.** These are essentially the verbal and nonverbal ways in which the individual members of the system convey information using the system's established sequences of interaction. For example, the adolescent described previously may be scolded at home for acting out in school, which may then lead to a confrontation that fuels even more acting out. For the systems therapist, it is the pattern, not the behavior, that is the focus of treatment.

The primary differences in how communication patterns are addressed in family therapy lie in the theoretical orientation of the systems therapist. A psychodynamic family therapist might focus on the system members' beliefs about self in relation to the system, and how this in turn impacts communication. A strategic family therapist might focus on how members of the system reacted when the conflict arose and what purpose the negative communication served. A structural family therapist might focus on the observed communication pattern as being indicative of poor boundaries or unclear hierarchies within the system. Regardless of the theoretical orientation, the communication patterns inform the practitioner about the dynamics within the system, as well as starting points to address core issues. In all cases a fundamental goal of treatment is improvement of communication patterns across the system.

FAMILY GEOMETRY

Family geometry refers to the "shapes" observed in the types of interactions and processes in systems; these may be linear, circular, or triangular in nature. Family geometry is built on family dynamics and the responses to stressors on the system and its members. Furthermore, the types of geometric patterns observed within a system will directly impact the family structure and its resiliency.

Linear processes. Linear processes are a "cause-and-effect" way of looking at issues in a system. Simply put, in a linear approach, effort is made to identify the cause of the problem, then to create and implement a solution. This is the traditional approach to individual therapy, in which the focus is on the one person participating in treatment. While linear processes are deemphasized in systemic work, their influence is still of note.

First, it is important to recognize the existence of objectifiable facts and their impact. For example, the sudden and traumatic loss of a family member will undoubtedly impact the individuals in the family system. In a linear model, loss leads to grief; the "solution," therefore, is found in identifying and implementing coping skills. This would be considered a **first-order change** in systemic work—not the focus of treatment, but a step in the process.

Another reason for the inclusion of linear processes in systemic work lies in the recognition that they are the precursors to **circular causality**. That is, before we can understand the patterns and feedback loops of a system, we must first acknowledge the processes that create them. As such, linear processes can be viewed as the building blocks of circular causality and may vary across the system, depending on the perspectives and influences of the system members.

Circular causality. Circular causality takes linear thinking to the next level, recognizing that cause and effect are both continuous and mutually dynamic. In this view, an event elicits a reaction, which elicits another event, which elicits another reaction, and so on. As applied to clinical work with families, this view acknowledges the role of relationships and interactions on the problems systems face. For example, in the case of loss described above, circular causality would look at the influence of the relationships with the deceased on the expression of grief, as well as how system members' expressions of grief impact each other. Treatment focus would be on the complex associations of these factors and seek *second-order change* to the system as applied to relationships and interaction patterns.

Circular causality is an essential element of family geometry and of understanding systems treatment. Too often, individuals seek a quick and easy "cure" for their problems, not recognizing that without change to the system, the same problem or a similar one is likely to occur. Circular causality forces people to recognize not only the multidimensional aspects of presenting issues, but also their own participation in the problem. Furthermore, its emphasis on the cycle of action and reaction can give hope where linear processes fail: You do not have to "solve" the original problem to have symptom relief, as the "solution" lies in altering the circle.

Triangles. The construct of **triangles** in family geometry is credited to Murray Bowen (1978); however, it has become one of the core concepts that not only has persisted but crosses theoretical orientations and disciplines. Prior to Bowen's research, much of the focus of clinical work with families tended toward addressing one dyad within the system at a time. Bowen, however, recognized that dyads broke down when stress was introduced; one or both parties would reach out for support from a person outside the dyad, creating a relationship *triangle*. This observation was so pervasive in his research that Bowen (1978) concluded that three people is the smallest stable unit of a relationship. Triangulation can stabilize a relationship, but it can also breed further conflict as the precipitating stressor tends to go unresolved. Consider, for example, a couple experiencing marital conflict. The woman complains to her mother about how horrible her husband is to live with, creating a triangle in the system. Though the woman may feel some relief from venting to her mother, the mother is now drawn into the conflict, which remains unresolved. In addition, new conflict may arise if the mother now feels pressured to "take sides" or perhaps even change her behavior toward her son-in-law.

The dynamics of triangles are such that they result in one person being "out" at any given moment in time (Papero, 2015). In healthy family geometry, the person on the "outside" remains consistent and aligns with boundaries appropriate to the relationships affected. In dysfunctional family geometry, this is not the case. Instead, the triangles not only do not align with system roles and boundaries, but may also shift without notice. Triangles can also highlight the **alliances** and **coalitions** that exist in the system, both of which can either strengthen or weaken the relational dynamics. For example, in the case of the couple with marital conflict, the triangle already exists and its "activation" may be inevitable. However, the type of response by the parties involved reflects the general health of the system.

It is important to recognize that triangles are not inherently problematic, but more of a fact in family geometry. It is the way triangles are activated and manifest that impacts the functionality of the system. Furthermore, counselors may find themselves *triangulated* while working with couples and families. Again, this is not in itself problematic, but it needs to be addressed as part of the therapeutic process. Open communication by all parties as to how the triangulation occurred, how it felt, and what purpose it served can become part of the therapeutic process. In fact, triangulation with the systemic counselor may serve to help clients better understand their tendency to activate triangles within their system and provide the counselor with a here-and-now example with which to role-play healthier interactions (Titelman, 2014). Case Presentation 3.1 shows some of the essentials of family geometry.

CASE PRESENTATION 3.1: THE STEVENS FAMILY

The Stevens family is composed of parents Tim and Alexandra, both in their 40s, and adolescent sons Jay (16) and Cam (13). Jay has been caught drinking several times by Alexandra, who has grounded him each time. Jay sneaks out of the house when his parents are asleep and continues to use alcohol whenever the opportunity arises. Alexandra has told Tim that she thinks Jay may have a serious problem, to which Tim responded, "He's just being a teenage boy. He'll grow out of it." Jay has also elicited the help of his younger brother in covering for him in case his parents discover that he is still drinking. Alexandra found out about Jay's nighttime escapes and the fact that Cam was trying to cover for him. This resulted in a major confrontation between Alexandra and her two sons. Tim came home in the middle of it and immediately asked his shouting wife to calm down and tell him what was going on. Alexandra was too angry to speak, feeling unsupported by her husband, and went into the couple's bedroom to cool off. Tim took his two sons into the garage, where they often worked on projects together, jokingly saying. "Mom's mad again … let's go to the man-cave."

1.   What linear processes can you identify in this system?
2.   What evidence do you see of circular causality?
3.   What triangles are there in this interaction?

4. What additional information might you want to gather to better understand the geometry of this system and its impact?

FAMILY STRUCTURE

As noted previously, the family structure has its underpinnings in the geometry of the system. This is because the framework of family structure—namely, power, boundaries, and hierarchies—are themselves built on and maintained by the types of processes within the system. Family structure is generally a consistent construct; however, it may temporarily shift on occasion, such as in reaction to a stressor. Family systems tend to return to a balanced structure in their homeostasis; in fact, a system's structural elements are critical to both the integrity and flexibility of the system and directly affect its resiliency.

Family structure is often illuminated in the construction of a **family genogram**, in which essential structural elements of the system are identified. These elements include both the members of the system—the "family" as they define themselves—and their relationships. Family structure can also be discerned through observations of dynamics within the system, with the power, boundaries, and hierarchies becoming clear as the members interact. In other words, family structure is both the physical composition of the system and the rules that govern its functionality.

Power. The concept of **power** in family systems is simply the relative ability to assert one's desire, whether such is **autonomous** or **relational**. Autonomy is an important element of development and is essential to individuals' ability to be independent and self-governing. Autonomous power is nurtured through parent–child dyads in youth and reinforced by relational dynamics of adulthood. Relational power is the relative influence people have on each other's decision making and can impact both relationship quality and individuals' ongoing self-concept. Thus, power in systems is an important element to understand when assessing family structure.

Power in systems is a complex concept based primarily in the intersection of roles, responsibilities, and resources. For example, in a family system composed of parents and children, the bulk of the power within the family lies with the parents, who determine the rules of the household and provide for their children. As children age, power shifts as they develop more autonomy and independence. Power dynamics in families shape the relationship patterns, and vice versa—it is a recursive process which directly impacts the system structure and functionality (Papero, 2015). Power within the marital relationship may be a unique consideration, or an element of the power dynamics across the family system. Marital power is generally reflective of both the contribution and resources of the couple; this includes decision making, influence, self-perception, and relationship role.

Regardless of whether the systemic power is familial or marital, power is almost self-defined by the way in which it is manifested and used across the system. For example, coercive power is based on the ability to forcibly influence another person through psychological or physical intimidation. This can manifest as physical punishment of a child or the threat thereof. It can also be observed in intimate partner violence, or the threat of withholding attention or love. The groundbreaking work of social scientists French and Raven (1959) identified six main types of power observed in social systems: coercive, reward, expert, informational, referent, and legitimate. Decades of research on the existence, persistence, and impact of these types of power have served to further validate the researchers' work, with additional focus being on *how* these power bases are used within systems. For example, Raven (1992) noted that the use of different power bases within a relational dynamic is influenced not only by context and circumstance but also by the individual's comfort level with a power base, as well as his or her own experience with efficacy in manipulating the power in question. Szinovacz (2013) recognized this as well, adding that power in any relational dynamic is an "emergent phenomenon" (p. 676) impacting both the relationship itself and future behaviors. This is a more dynamic and complex view of power dynamics and may better account for some of the ancillary influences of environment and culture.

Systems counselors need to be aware of both personal and social power within systems and how each is expressed, supported, or restricted. Power is generally observable through interactions of the system and may be significantly impacted by cultural constructs and influences. As such, counselors should focus on how power *works or doesn't work* within the system itself, rather than take a purely objective or textbook approach to evaluation.

Boundaries. **Boundaries** as applied to family systems work refers to the lines or limits of interaction between members of the system. Boundaries are applicable to subsystems (i.e., dyads or triads), the primary system itself, and suprasystems to which the members belong. The attention given to boundaries and their functionality in clinical systems work, however, generally focuses on those observed within the client family (the system and its subsystems). In fact, across theoretical orientations, a frequent goal in family work is clarifying boundaries in systems and helping system members understand how boundaries help manage *proximity* and *hierarchy*.

In a healthy family system, boundaries are neither too rigid nor too soft, neither too open nor too closed. Extremes in boundaries can lead to relationships becoming enmeshed or disengaged—either of which is problematic for long-term systemic health and consistent family structure. A common metaphor in describing boundaries is to view them as like a cellular membrane: For a cell to maintain its health, nutrients must be able to pass through the membrane. If the membrane is *impermeable*—or too rigid—the cell cannot receive nutrition. If the membrane is *open*—or too soft—the cell cannot maintain its structure. Thus, a balance of structure and permeability is ideal for a membrane to support long-term health of the cell.

For families, rigid boundaries may cause relationships to be *disengaged*, as a lack of nurturing adversely affects the quality of the relationship. In such cases, the individuals in the relationship have firm roles but lack sufficient emotional, psychological, or physical interaction to sustain a healthy relationship. By contrast, soft boundaries may cause relationships to be *enmeshed,* creating unclear roles within the relationship. In these cases, the interactions within the relationship blur the lines between the individuals. Neither of these extremes is desirable and will often directly or indirectly create conflicts within the system. Let's now look at Figure 3.1, which illustrates the continuum of relational boundaries and their outcomes.

Figure 3.1 **Boundaries in Family Systems**

Rigid	Clear & Balanced	Diffuse
Disengaged	Healthy	Enmeshed

Adapted from: Salvador Minuchin, Families and Family Therapy, pp. 53-54. Copyright © 1974 by Harvard University Press.

It is also important to note, however, that though extremes in boundaries often adversely impact the system, there can also be benefits. For example, disengaged parent–child boundaries may lack attention or interaction but may also foster independence and autonomy. Enmeshed parent–child boundaries may create psychological or emotional dependence but may also convey unconditional love and support. When these positive elements are present, it can be comforting to families to see what they are *doing right*, even if there are some elements that need to change. This is the essence of a wellness approach to revising boundaries in a system and to helping families recognize the positive aspects of their relationships that they wish to preserve.

Boundaries in family systems tend to present in complementary, reciprocal patterns. That is, where there is a disengaged boundary, there is also usually an enmeshed one. An example of this may be seen in the "workaholic" parent who is enmeshed with his or her career but disengaged at home. Another example could be the parent who is enmeshed with his or her children but disengaged with his or her partner. Further, the system may display a reciprocal pattern—such as would apply to a family whose external boundary with society was rigid and closed but displayed diffuse and open boundaries within the family. Recognizing these patterns helps families better understand the compensation that may be taking place across the system and gives them a starting point to finding a healthier equilibrium in their relational dynamics.

Clear, healthy boundaries are important to the health of the family system. However, systems counselors also need to be aware of the impact of culture and circumstance when assessing system boundaries. What may appear as disengaged in one cultural context may be clear and healthy in another. Similarly, temporary circumstances may cause certain boundaries to appear enmeshed, when in fact the dynamic is supportive and functional. While this may be confusing to a systems counselor, it is more reflective of the importance of context of the system. Understanding how and why system members display the types of boundaries they do is as important as the boundaries themselves.

Hierarchies. Hierarchies in family systems are maintained by both the power and boundaries of the system. They reflect the way leadership and control are manifested within the system, as well as how these may evolve over time as the system grows and changes. For example, parental authority is an essential component of *generational hierarchy* and is maintained by the power and boundaries exhibited in the parent–child dynamics. *Sibling hierarchy* is also common in family systems in which children are of varying ages. This hierarchy is often expressed as older children having caretaking responsibilities over younger siblings. While such behaviors can be helpful to the overall family system, they can also be problematic if clear boundaries are not established and maintained. **Marital hierarchy** may also exist in the system, such as when partners have significantly different roles that may in turn yield varying levels of power and influence in the system. For example, more traditional family structures often include one individual as the "head" of the family. This individual usually assumes a primary leadership role as provider and decision maker in the family. Contemporary family systems tend more toward *egalitarianism,* with partners in the couple or marital relationship being at the top of the hierarchy together. All types of hierarchies are strongly influenced by cultural and environmental factors.

Hierarchies function to preserve the overall structure and functionality of the system and are static when the system is in homeostasis. However, they may change over time as the system moves through its life cycle. One common change often observed in families is the lessening parental authority and influence as children move into adulthood. Over time, parents often move from being leaders of their children to being guides and confidants when the children are fully into adulthood and may themselves be the leaders of their own families. Changes in generational hierarchy are highly impacted by the influences of culture, as well as by the boundaries that exist within the system.

Hierarchies can also change temporarily in response to stress or trauma. In such cases, the **incongruent hierarchy** may create conflict the family system, even though it is serving as a coping mechanism in response to the stressor. Incongruence in hierarchies can be a sign of resiliency and cohesion when short term but become problematic in family structure and dynamics if maintained for too long. Figure 3.2 illustrates the change in hierarchy of the Freeman family following the father's diagnosis of a terminal illness. In this family the father was no longer able to work, and the mother became his full-time caretaker. Because the father's needs were high, the mother was not able to work outside the home nor tend to the daily needs of the children. The oldest daughter, who was 17, got a job to help subsidize the family's finances and assumed much of the caretaking of her younger siblings, ages 15 and 13. While this response was indicative of resiliency and support across the system, it also shifted the hierarchy, creating conflicts between the oldest daughter and her siblings. In addition, this shift elevated the daughter to a more parental role in the hierarchy, making her less receptive to the leadership and authority of her mother.

when older kids are left in charge...

Hierarchy

Figure 3.2 Hierarchy of the Freeman Family

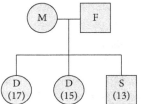

Before illness: Congruent hierarchy

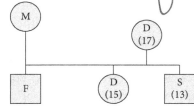

After illness: Incongruent hierarchy

In comparing the differences in the hierarchies before and after the onset of the father's illness, several significant themes emerge. The most obvious is the shift in power within the system. The father has become fully dependent on the mother for his care and no longer has active power within the hierarchy. The mother has moved into the primary leadership role in the hierarchy, though most of her time and attention is centered on the father and his care. The mother and daughter have created an **executive subsystem** that reflects their cooperative efforts to support the family. This has put the 17-year-old daughter in a position of leadership and responsibility in the system—a new role that can be stressful and that is not generally age appropriate for a teen. In addition, the elevation of the 17-year-old to a position of authority over her siblings, who are only a few years younger, has its own inherent conflicts; she is not their "parent" but has assumed a significant portion of their daily caretaking. Furthermore, though the 17-year-old is partnered with the mother in a leadership subsystem, she is not equal to the mother—there remains a hierarchy within this system that can confuse roles and expectations. The multiple changes in the hierarchy of this system can catalyze significant conflicts as the members not only try to maintain family cohesion, but also negotiate their new positions and dynamics. On a positive side, this family shows strong resiliency and cohesion, as they adapted to the circumstances as they thought would best maintain the integrity of the system. The illustrated hierarchy of the family system helps highlight these considerations, which can be helpful to facilitate understanding, communication, and conflict resolution in the system.

Hierarchies are also important from the perspective of problem identification and change. While the most effective family work will involve all system members, if the members at the top of the hierarchy are not invested in change, there is little likelihood of lasting success. In addition, it is important for families to understand the function and role of the hierarchies within their system, as well as the alliances and coalitions that either reinforce or undermine the structural integrity of the family. Systems counselors will address hierarchies with an emphasis that reflects their specific theoretical orientation, though all have the common goal of improving functional dynamics of the system.

FAMILY LIFE CYCLE

[handwritten: Family Life Cycle Theory]

It has been noted that family hierarchy can vary over time as system members grow and evolve. This change is a natural progression as families experience different developmental challenges and tasks throughout the family life cycle. The **family life cycle** is a theoretical construction describing the establishment, sustainment, modification, and closure of marital and family relations. Family life cycle theory is based on a multistage model, generally including between six and eight stages, described in a linear progression. In addition to identifying the system's developmental tasks, family life cycle theory helps provide context to the presenting issues in the system. Guided Practice Exercise 3.2 considers the intersection of developmental and family life cycle issues.

GUIDED PRACTICE EXERCISES 3.2

[handwritten: what changed]

Consider a family system in which there is an adolescent who is "acting out." As the counselor, you would want to know how the parent(s) have—or have not—adjusted parenting from the way the child was parented in younger years. Why is this important to know? Also, since it is not uncommon for stress to be associated with the transition stages of a family life cycle, this would be a consideration as well for all system members. How might family transition stages be affecting this adolescent's behavior?

[handwritten: which is 50% of marriages]

Though family life cycle theory has been highly researched and validated, its linear format is restrictive and does not account for variations of family development, including those that occur because of divorce or trauma. However, family life cycle theory still provides a solid framework for understanding some of the influences impacting the system. Furthermore, cross-referencing family life cycle stages with individual developmental theory—such as psychosocial-based or cultural identity theories—can help shed further light on the challenges, conflicts, and desired developmental outcomes impacting members of a family system.

Duvall's stages. The foundation of family life cycle theory is widely credited to sociologist Evelyn Duvall (1977), whose pioneering research in from the 1940s through the 1960s led to the identification of distinct stages through which families move over time. Table 3.1 provides a summary of each stage and the associated developmental tasks according to Duvall's model.

[handwritten: cycle created in a time of no divorce.]

Table 3.1 **Duvall's family life cycle stages**

Level	Developmental task
Newly married or childless couples	Adjusting to married life and partner's family system Considering future parenting

[handwritten: family of origin ?]

(handwritten note: can be in multiple stages)

②	**Couples with children under 2½ years**	Adjusting to parenting Creating a new satisfying parental and family system
③	**Couples with children 2½–6 years**	Changing family structures and learning methods to aid in the positive development of young children Managing lack of privacy and the fatigue that accompanies parenting
④	**Couples with children 6–13 years**	Helping children adapt to and achieve in school Adapting to increasing parental responsibility
⑤	**Couples with adolescents aged 13–20**	Finding nonparental societal roles *(handwritten: find other identity outside home.)*
⑥	**Couples of young adults (first child gone to last child leaving home)**	Launching young adults with adequate support in socially accepted ways Reestablishing the couple's relationship
⑦	**Middle-aged/empty-nest parents**	Securing stable relationships with parents, children, and grandchildren
⑧	**Aging couples from retirement to death**	Settling into the retirement role and lifestyle Coping with deaths of friends, family, and spouse Adjusting to life without a partner

Source: Evelyn Ruth Millis Duvall, "Duvall's Family Life Cycle Stages," Marriage and Family Development. Copyright © 1977 by Lippincott Williams & Wilkins Inc..

(handwritten margin note: similar to Erik Erikson)

Duvall's research—like so much other family- and systems-focused work in the 20th century—was based primarily on data gathered from traditional, nuclear families, which was the predominant family structure of the era. However, the potential limitations of this do not detract from the valuable insights the model offers. Families that experience divorce, remarriage, trauma, or other unexpected changes to their life cycle may not fit neatly into specific stages in Duvall's theory, but the developmental tasks noted often do still apply. Furthermore, recognizing the possibility for families to be in multiple stages concurrently can lend insight into the complex stressors on the system and its members.

Taking a slightly different perspective but still building on Duvall's work, Barnhill and Longo (1978) proposed that the developmental tasks identified by Duvall represented *transitions* the family system was experiencing. They also contended that families—like individuals—can become "stuck" at a critical transition point and fail to move forward in their development. Furthermore, they asserted that a significant portion of stress and conflict within the system arises from such unsuccessful transitions and negotiations (Barnhill & Longo, 1978). In fact, anxiety and stress in general are highest when the system moves from one stage to another, even when it does so smoothly. Haley (1979) concurred with this perspective, adding that presenting symptomology in one or more system members can be traced to a disruption in normal family development.

Consider, for example, you are working with a couple who have three adult children. The youngest child has recently left home for college, making the couple officially "empty nesters." Some of the life cycle–related issues this couple may be experiencing include negotiating how much help and support to give newly launched children and refocusing their attentions on the marital relationship. These concerns may be at the forefront of their presenting issues or merely the backdrop. Regardless, it is important to consider the contextual influences of where this couple is in the family life cycle. In addition, the older grown children in this family system may also be in part of an additional family life cycle, which can in turn have influence on your client couple. Figure 3.3 shows a representation of how family life cycle stages overlap in this hypothetical family system. While the counselor's primary focus in this case would be the 55-year-old couple, what their adult children are experiencing may also be relevant to clinical work with this couple, as the adult children are still part of the client couple's family system.

Figure 3.3 Overlapping of family life cycles

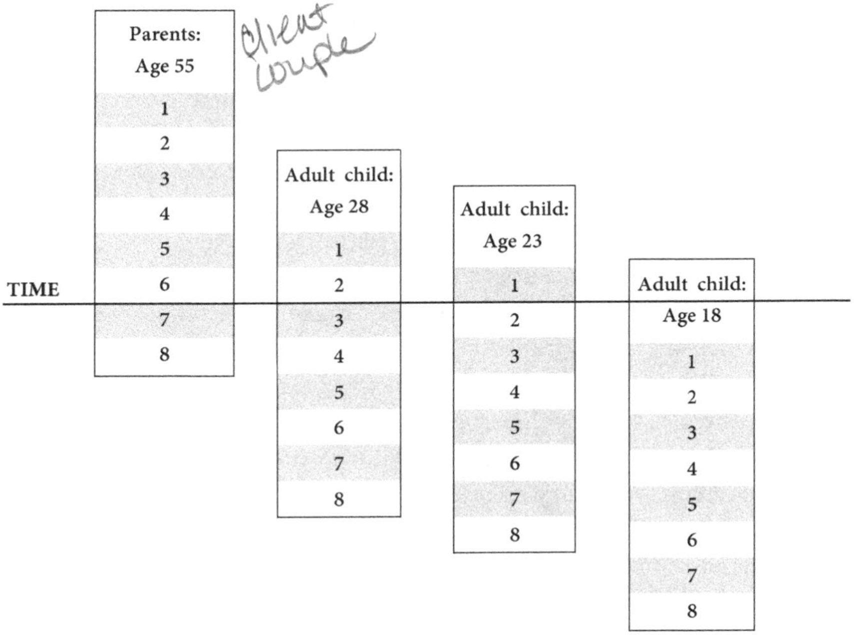

Another important point that becomes apparent in viewing overlapping family life cycles is the lack of language available for the adult child who is not yet married. In the case of this family, it could be said that the youngest child is in "stage 0" of his own family life cycle, as he is neither married nor partnered. According to Duvall's theory, family life cycle begins when a couple gets married. However, contemporary couples are not necessarily bound by such a restrictive view. It is not uncommon for young adults to be single and on their own for quite some time before marrying—if they even choose to marry. It is also not uncommon for young adults to live together before marriage or to have children together without the legality of marriage. Therefore, it may be necessary to take some liberties with identifying family life cycle stage using Duvall's theory.

Constricting rules and limiting definitions are common criticisms of linear stage theories of family life cycle. Traditional stage theories tend to bound by restrictive terms, putting many contemporary families outside the boundaries of these theories; this might imply that these families are "abnormal," when such may not be the case at all. Experiences common to contemporary families such as divorce and remarriage must be considered and represented in the family life cycle. Furthermore, the experience of partners whose family life cycle stages occur "out of order"—such as having children before marriage—is difficult to represent using a fully linear stage theory. Lastly, traditional stage theories do not reflect the influences of diversity in families; there is a general lack of representation for the variations experienced by racial, ethnic, and sexual minority families.

Beyond Duvall. Despite criticisms and identified weaknesses, linear stage theories such as that proposed by Duvall were the first to offer a common language to the experience of a family life cycle and to begin to recognize that families do often have some common experiences that help contextualize issues. This recognition, combined with the acknowledged limitations of purely linear family life cycle theory, prompted researchers to expand their understanding of family life cycle into a more three-dimensional, evolving concept. Carter and McGoldrick (1980) were among the first to pioneer a **multigenerational framework** for family life cycle and to include considerations for divorce and remarriage. Subsequent iterations of their theory included the integration of socioeconomic, racial and ethnic, and sexual orientation influences (Carter & McGoldrick, 1999). Carter and McGoldrick based their theory on a streamlined version of Duvall's work, with a foundation of six key stages across the family life cycle. However, they also integrated the emotional processes associated with these stages, identifying them as foundational principle on which successful transitions were dependent. Furthermore, they recognized the multidimensional influences in the overlapping family life cycles of multiple generations and how these can impact life stage transitions (Carter & McGoldrick, 1999).

Injecting systems theory into stage theory to better represent family life cycle became popular in the late 20th century as researchers sought to integrate more complex influences into their understanding of the family life cycle. That is, they recognized that the family's experiences and dynamics directly impacted the family life cycle, and vice versa. Breunlin's (1991) oscillation theory was among the first to also integrate both systemic and subsystemic influence into the family life cycle. He viewed families as a combination of individuals *and* relationships, and asserted that *both* experienced development across the family life cycle. According to this theory, family life cycle is not experienced in discreet shifts across stages, but rather as continuous movement and flow that is significantly dependent on family functioning. That is, though events do occur that can move families across stages, it is the response to events and resulting functionality that determines healthy stage transition. Family systems can move back and forth across stages from a **functional** perspective as they respond to change in a successful or unsuccessful manner.

Cultural influences. Regardless of which family life cycle model a systems counselor uses as a foundation, there is a consistent message of "common" family experiences at different stages. It is vital for the counselor to also consider the impact of cultural influences on how "common" is defined for the client family. The lived experience of stages, transitions, adaptations, and oscillations is substantially influenced by the cultural traditions to which the system is bound. Different cultures may experience the family life cycle in ways which are common, functional, and healthy within the context of their own culture yet very different from that of the dominant culture. Examples of these can include the following (Felicov, 2016):

Collectivistic cultural family difference

- A longer state of interdependence between parents and children
- A more relaxed attitude about children's achievement of self-reliance skills
- An absence of an independent living situation for young unmarried adults
- An absence of an empty-nest syndrome or a middle-age crisis *(Because kids aren't leaving!)*
- An absence or delay of refocusing on the marital relationship and issues
- A continuous involvement, status, and usefulness of elders in the family

In addition, cultural influence on family life cycle may be impacted by the level of acculturation and assimilation across the system. For example, if adult children have been raised in the dominant culture and have a superior knowledge of the languages and customs compared to their parents, they may remain living at home—either by choice or obligation—to assist their parents.

Systems counselors must be cognizant of their own cultural bias and expectations and how these can influence their view of the life cycle of their client family. To truly understand a family in context means to understand it from the vantage point of its members—at least to the greatest degree allowed as an empathetic outsider. A systems counselor should focus on what the family considers normal, how their lived experience of transitions either works or doesn't work for family members, and how their unique family life cycle relates to the presenting issues, tensions, and challenges they are facing at the time of treatment.

Age–stage influences. In addition to the consideration for *how* families transition across the life cycle from a functional and relational perspective is the significance of developmental stages on the experience of the family life cycle. That is, it is important to recognize that the relative psychosocial stages and their associated conflicts and stressors can impact the family life cycle. For example, families in which the parents are very young will experience the stressors of parenthood differently than those in which the parents are older. Younger adults who are just at the beginning of Erikson's *intimacy versus isolation* stage may be less experienced in relationships and have fewer coping skills for the inherent challenges of partnering and parenthood. Thus, the primary family life cycle task of establishing a satisfying home for both parents and children may be more difficult for younger parents than for older ones. Younger parents may also be less established in careers, resulting in less comfortable financial circumstances than those experienced

Erik Erikson

by older parents, who are more likely to have gainful, consistent employment; the stress of financial insecurity can have a significant impact on marital satisfaction. Conversely, younger parents may be better equipped to cope with the physical demands of parenting, including greater activity and decreased sleep. These differing traits that are tied to both physical age and psychosocial development can directly affect the way individuals experience family life cycle challenges and transitions.

Another example of age–stage influences on family life cycle can be seen in families in which the ages of children are far apart. The developmental needs of young children are quite different from those of older children, which causes families to straddle multiple life cycle stages simultaneously. This can make parenting particularly challenging, as well as put a strain on the marital relationship. Consider, for example, a family system in which there are two adolescents, ages 15 and 17. At this point in their development, the teenagers are likely to have at least some autonomy and to be preparing to transition into their adult years. The parents are likely to have adapted their parenting style to encourage differentiation and individuation in their children and have both time and opportunity to focus more energy on the marital relationship and their personal interests. The addition of a newborn into this system would change the dynamic considerably. The parents would need to revert to an earlier stage in their family life cycle, as they now must focus on the demands of parenting an infant.

Age–stage influences can also give perspective to the types of pressures from outside the system that can influence relational dynamics. Work–family conflict, for example, tends to be greater when children are younger, declines as children age, and is lowest incidence during the empty-nest phase (Allen & Finklestein, 2014). This change is due in part to the different demands of family life, depending on children's ages. Younger children require greater supervision and guidance during their early development; thus, parents need to allocate more time during younger years. This can pose significant pressure on working parents. However, as priorities evolve throughout the life span, working adults are generally able to better manage their work–life balance and minimize conflicts between these (Demerouti, Peters, & Van der Heijden, 2012).

Just as developmental age can affect the experience of family life cycle stages, the opposite is also true. Family life cycle transitions, oscillations, and related challenges can also impact the individual development of family members. For example, the experience of the last child launching from home might elicit a period self-reflection and evaluation in a parent, as he or she adjusts his or her identity and self-concept as the definition of parenting has changed. Perhaps the experience of the empty nest catalyzes a premature transition into the *ego integrity versus despair* stage of psychosocial development. In other words, it may be possible for a dysfunctional family life cycle stage transition to adversely impact psychosocial development of the individual. Research has shown that the *contextual variables* of the individuals in the system—including demographics, social constructs, expectations, and relational dynamics—can significantly impact the personal experiences of stage transitions (Bouchard, 2014).

Of course, family life cycle stages can also have a positive impact on individual development. The experiencing of partnering—whether through marriage or other formal commitment—can help individuals actualize their ideals of love and relationships, as well as learn how to live them realistically. Becoming a parent may also impact individual's identity and self-concept, whether partnered or single. Being invested in a family system and committed to its longevity can give people a sense of purpose and achievement, which are essential developmental tasks. Thus, daily life cycle experiences and transitions can help people move through healthy psychosocial development.

FAMILY WELLNESS

Family wellness is a concept describing the functionality, mutual support, and strength of a family system. It recognizes the uniqueness of each system and highlights the resources and potentials of its members. Family wellness, therefore, is contextual by nature and adapts easily across cultural and other demographical variables. A **family wellness model** emerged in the 1980s based largely on the work of Virginia Morgan Scott and George Doub (Hernandez, 2013) and was a multidisciplinary lens through which to understand family psychological health. Furthermore, the model—while not intended to be a separate systemic theory—provided a framework for psychoeducation and clinical interventions. As Hernandez (2013) explains:

> *Every psychotherapist has his or her own conceptualization of why people are the way they are, why they behave the way they do, and what it takes for people to become ill, dysfunctional, or inauthentic. Similarly, each mental health professional has an idea of what it takes for people to get better, do well, or achieve their potential. The therapeutic orientation of every clinician forms the basis for his or her therapeutic worldview and provides the guide for assessment, treatment planning, and intervention. The Family Wellness model has never sought to become yet another school of psychotherapy. Instead, Family Wellness seeks to translate complex thought from existing psychosocial theory into direct and everyday language that becomes accessible when people need it most: when they are in crisis. (p. xiv)*

The takeaway from this description of the family wellness model is the idea that family wellness is predicated on an understanding of the family itself—what works within the system, the strengths of the system and its individual members, and how the system impacts the greater society. The focus of family wellness is strength, competence, self-management, and a recognition that the system is emboldened with potential and resources.

Furthermore, this lens not only promotes positive behaviors in daily interactions but asserts that healthy systems can handle challenges before they evolve into major conflicts.

The concept of family wellness and the model that it gave rise to have their underpinnings in the quality of relational dynamics across the system. Specifically, communication and commitment to the system and its members are the core focus. As such, in a family wellness perspective, a key role for the systems counselor is facilitating the development of these two core areas from a strength-based, nonpathological perspective. This focus may seem at odds sometimes with the medical view of crises and challenges people face, and the need for clinicians to identify pathology in one individual within the system for third-party payer reimbursement. Such is a reality of clinical practice; however, clinicians can still use this framework as the lens through which to conceptualize their goals for the family counseling components of treatment.

In its early years, the concept of family wellness was seen as paramount to individual and personal empowerment. Rather than viewing individuals as weak or unwell, this view assumed that all individuals had their unique gifts and competencies, but the realization of these is in some way hampered by destructive familial relationships and interactions. Over the years, this problem-focused view shifted to one that is more solution-focused, with an emphasis on what *works* in the system. Family wellness, then, has become a complement to individual wellness, as well as a stand-alone model for supporting systems. To focus on strengths, counselors identify *exceptions* to problems and conflicts, which are invariably extant but often hidden under the weight and force of presenting issues. Such a focus highlights systems resources and potential, empowering its growth and resilience.

Family resilience. No overview of family wellness is complete without at least a brief consideration of family resilience and its impact. **Family resilience** differs from family wellness in that it is an outcome or result of a healthy family system. Walsh (2003) defined family resilience as "the ability to withstand and rebound from disruptive life challenges" and hinges on "positive adaptation" (p. 1) to circumstances involving substantial difficulty. The efficacy of family resilience hinges on the system's ability to react to trials and conflicts in a manner that fosters growth and development of the system (Hays, Snow, & Pusateri, 2015). Therefore, in many ways it is not only directly related to family wellness but also a direct function of it.

Family resilience is also interwoven and interdependent with family life cycle. As has been noted earlier, family life cycle stages are punctuated by transitions that can cause stress to the family system. The ability to adapt and move through these transitions with relative ease is indicative of the system's resilience. Similarly, successful transitions further reinforce resiliency patterns and behaviors that in turn strengthen the system for future challenges. Conversely, legacies from unsuccessful transitions and resulting perceptions of loss can impede the system's future adaptation, thus adversely impacting its overall resiliency (Walsh, 2003).

Considerations of a family's resilience are essential to all stages of the clinical process, including assessment, treatment planning, interventions, and termination. Walsh (2016) described three key domains of family resilience:

- Shared belief systems—Characterized by making meaning from adversity, maintaining a positive outlook, and having transcendence and spirituality.
- Organizational processes—Characterized by flexibility and connectedness in the system, as well as an ability to mobilize social and economic resources.
- Communication/problem-solving processes—Characterized by clarity and open emotional sharing, and a collaborative problem-solving style. (p. 620)

Regardless of the clinician's theoretical orientation, this strength-based perspective of family functioning can lend insights into how the family responds to stress, utilizes its resources, and adapts to challenges based on assessments across these domains. Furthermore, these crucial elements in family functioning enhance understanding of the system in context. A family resilience view "recognizes the diversity of families, their varied situational challenges, and the viability of many pathways in resilience" (Walsh, 2016, p. 622). It is an ecosystemic perspective that highlights not only collaboration within the system to enhance competence and functionality but also collaboration with the clinician, who serves as a catalyst for growth across resiliency domains.

A family resilience model (FRM) has evolved that builds on extant research into the operationalizing of resiliency characteristics, taking the foundational work of Walsh and others a step further. The FRM identifies the core elements of resilience as risk, protection, vulnerabilities, and adaptation (Henry, Morris, & Harrist, 2015), noting the dynamic interaction between these and **family adaptive systems** (which include emotion, control, meaning maintenance, and stress response). The FRM represents a next-level view in the integration of family resilience into clinical application as it integrates the complex dynamics present in systems, as well as the evolving adaptations and experiential outcomes throughout the life cycle. In more simple terms, the FRM helps account for the impact of narratives on current adaption needs in the system, as well as how these may evolve over time. The role of narratives and evolving systems beliefs on family resiliency has been established as a key to adaptation. In fact, Saltzman, Pynoos, Lester, Layne, and Beardless (2013) specifically noted that "family narratives can help to bridge intra-familial estrangements and re-engage communication and support processes that have been undermined by stress, trauma, or loss" (p. 294). To the systems counselor, this highlights the importance of communication and constructs in fostering resilience and cocreating narratives that further support a family's adaptive strategies.

FAMILY CULTURE

As we now have a cursory understanding of the influence of narratives in family functioning, it is important to explore to role of **family culture** in establishing and promoting those narratives. Family culture—in its most broad sense—is a collection of beliefs, constructs, rituals, and customs in which the system exists. It is the result of the cumulative effects of multigenerational influences, including extended ancestry and current family of origin. Family culture can also be influenced by surrounding community and larger society as whole, as these, too, impact family identity. Figure 3.4 illustrates the levels of systemic influences on family culture. Family culture can impede resiliency and change as well as support it, depending on the nature of the associated narratives and behaviors. Family rituals, for example, have been found to support family cohesiveness and positively impact resiliency (Wolin & Bennett, 1984). Family beliefs and expectations can influence the identities and pathways of individuals within the system, including personal endeavors such as sports participation, education and career paths, and courtship behaviors (Ajami, Rasmi, & Abudabbeh, 2015; Chhuon & Hudley, 2008; Wheeler, 2011). These facets of family culture contribute to both the family identity and the identities of the individual system members.

Figure 3.4 Levels of cultural systems

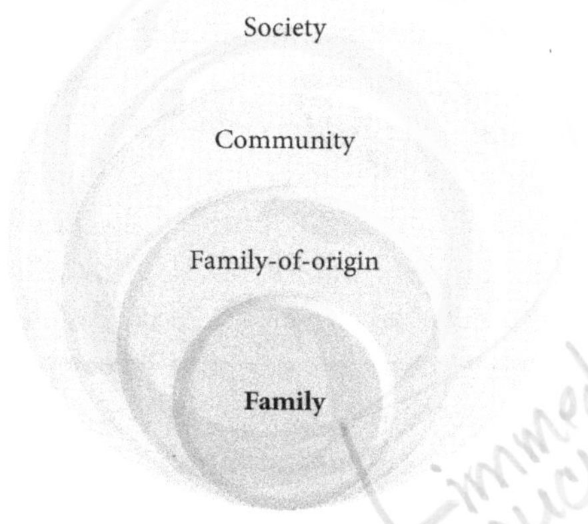

Society

Community

Family-of-origin

Family

The influence of family culture is most readily illustrated in the narratives by which system members define themselves and their roles, both within the system and the immediate environment. For example, family culture has a significant impact on constructs associated with gender role and gender-normed behaviors. In families in which more traditional male and female roles are emphasized, the systems counselor may observe the females in the system take a more submissive role in family dynamics and decision making. While this may contradict the counselor's own beliefs and tendencies, it is essential to view the family through a lens of functionality related to their family culture. To maintain a culturally sensitive awareness of the impact of family culture, systems counselors should consider the cultural contexts when conceptualizing the system and the presenting issues and devise interventions that are consistent with the family culture.

Systems counselors must be aware of how past experiences define family narratives, maintain family culture, and influence interpretations of future events. While narratives are certainly open to constant assessment and revision, they also tend to have persistent elements that can be resistant to change. The narrative elements of family culture can distort views of events or relationships for better or worse, stretching realities until they fit the family plotline. Consider, for example, the family who comes to counseling as part of the treatment of a member with substance abuse issues. The family has expectations of the process before they walk in the door; they also have defined roles within the system that maintain the dysfunction. Changing the system often means changing the narrative elements of the culture in which they are embedded.

Thus far we have been considering family culture and family-of-origin culture interchangeably; they are related concepts, but not synonymous. For clarity's sake, "family culture" is the immediate narrative elements of a single-family system (the client family, for example), while "family-of-origin culture" is that which is rooted in ancestry. Understandably, there is often substantial overlap between these concepts. However, where there are differences, there may be added conflict. That is, in systems in which the family culture differs significantly from the family-of-origin culture, there are likely to be added stressors and conflict. Similarly, there can be significant differences between family culture, family-of-origin culture, and the culture of the larger society. Again, it is in the differences, not similarities, that most conflicts will be rooted. In addressing these, a systems therapist is likely to find common themes across levels of culture.

To illustrate this point, consider the narratives and associated family culture in an African American client family. A significant aspect of the family culture is rooted in the reality that they exist in a dominant culture that persistently devalues them, both as individuals and as a cohesive system. Personal worth, safety, opportunity, even freedom itself may be defined very differently for this system than for a family whose culture is part of the majority. In fact, the destructive narratives that may exist in this family culture are likely versions of those that are pervasive in the larger society.

This is not to say that the impact of family culture is always negative; the opposite is true. However, counselors are remiss if they do not recognize the role and impact of persistent constructs and narratives that are imposed from the larger society, as these can be most resistant to change. Still, family culture can empower and strengthen the system and can contribute directly to resiliency and efficacy (Kao & Caldwell, 2015).

CLINICAL APPLICATIONS AND CHALLENGES

Thus far we have been examining the processes and concepts in clinical work with family systems. These core constructs are common across disciplines and theoretical orientations; the differences are seen in the way these principles are operationalized, prioritized, and emphasized. To the systems therapist—whether working with a couple or a family—the focus of treatment lies in the processes and dynamics of the system itself. Rather than focusing on the internalized aspects of these influences, as the individual counselor might, the systems counselor focuses on the externalized elements and how these influence the presenting issues. By working with the system, the counselor seeks to effect long-lasting change through coordinated effort and recognition of the complex contributory forces.

Therapist Role in Systemic Process

In simplest terms, the therapist is a catalyst for change; this is true whether referring to individual or systemic counseling. When working with couples and families, the counselor uses the same foundational skills used in individual counseling—such as building empathy and rapport, reflecting feeling, challenging, validating, and exploring deeper meaning—but must do so equally for all members of the system. This is a fundamental aspect of establishing and maintaining the engagement of family members in the treatment process. **Engagement**—which is reflective of the level of involvement and motivation of the systems members—can vary substantially even within a single system. Consider, for example, the client family composed of a single mother and two adolescent daughters, neither of whom want to be in family therapy. The counselor would likely have to work a bit harder to engage the daughters than the mother—but he or she must also be cautious not to alienate the mother by appearing to "take sides" with the daughters. Rapport and empathy can sometimes take a bit longer to develop in systems counseling, as the relational dynamics impact the counselor's process.

Other variations seen in a counselor's role in the systemic process are tied primarily to the theoretical orientation with which the counselor aligns. The common theoretical underpinning of family systems counseling lies in one essential principle: *Individuals are inseparable from the systems that they influence and that influence them.* Though there are many different theoretical orientations within family systems therapy, each one is either firmly entrenched in—or is a combination of—structural, strategic, or intergenerational therapy. In each type, the counselor has a somewhat different role and approach to treatment. These are discussed in more detail in Part III of the textbook, which focuses on the various schools and models in family therapy.

Structural family therapies. In a structural theoretical orientation, the counselor focuses on the relationships, behaviors, and patterns across the family system. Specific attention is given to the hierarchies that exist in the system, the structure and composition of the overall system and subsystems that exist, and the nature of the system's boundaries. The structurally oriented counselor takes a challenging and directive role in treatment, as he or she facilitates the restructuring or the systems boundaries and roles to a healthier equilibrium.

Strategic family therapies. In a strategic theoretical orientation, the counselor focuses on the family's core processes, such as communication and problem-solving patterns. Specific attention is given to the metaphors that exist within the symptoms—that is, what they represent, such as the motivation for power or love. The strategic counselor has an active and directive role in this orientation as well and often encourages second-order changes to the system; these might include new views, rules, or perspectives of both the presenting issues and the system itself. Strategic family counselors often use reframes, conflict-resolution techniques, and parental coaching to help achieve these goals.

Intergenerational family therapies. With intergenerational family therapies, the counselor often takes a directive role; however, he or she is also often part of the process itself. The counselor develops a relationship with the overall system but also nurtures connections with each individual member of the system. The counselor is also aware of the importance of role modeling healthy interactions and promoting cohesiveness, often serving as a catalyst for attachment within the system. In this theoretical orientation, attention is also given to normalizing issues, increasing differentiation, and recognizing external influences. The counselor's consideration of the multigenerational effects on individual and family behaviors is essential to this group of therapies.

Almost any problem or challenge humans encounter can be treated with systems therapy—either alone or in conjunction with individual treatment. In fact, the more closely tied to relationships a presenting issue is, the more impact systems treatment is likely to have. The counselor's purpose is to help family members recognize the system's role in presenting issues and how the strengths of the system can be used to promote individual healing and overall systemic wellness.

RESISTANCE

Another important role of the systems counselor is addressing and confronting resistance in treatment. **Resistance** may present in negative engagement, adherence, or compliance, all of which are common issues in individual treatment as well. These resistance behaviors often present as people fear change or unfamiliar situations; uncertainty can be far more intimidating than dysfunctional family patterns. Children, for example, will often display resistance through passively oppositional behavior, through active disengagement, or by exerting their independence (O'Reilly & Parker, 2013). In systems work, the underlying fears and resulting externalized behaviors are magnified by the multiple members of the system and by the consideration that disrupting the system may be both difficult and painful. Furthermore, resistance can be contagious; family members who are otherwise engaged may be less motivated by the resistance of other system members. The best approach for the system counselor is to recognize and normalize the observed behaviors and validate the underlying fears in the family members.

Such an approach is also recommended for another type of common resistance issue: violation of privacy. Of course, a system's counselor does not set out to "violate" anything, but families may feel very threatened by the intrusion of an outsider. In systems work, there is an additional layer of vulnerability to the process; not only are the clients being asked to bare their souls, they are exposing themselves to each other and the system to the counselor. There is often a fear of being judged by the therapist or by other systems members (Frankel & Levitt, 2009; O'Reilly & Parker, 2013). Systems members may resist engagement in the clinical process until they decide that it is safe to do so and worth the gamble. In fact, one might consider family resistance as a protecting function and reframe it as such when it is encountered.

THE ROLE OF THE SYMPTOM

It is interesting to note that family members identified as the "problem" within a system are often given less leeway when it comes to displaying resistance (O'Reilly & Parker, 2013). This observation can give insight into the role and function of the symptom in family systems work. Often the **symptom** is the presenting issue that motivates the family for treatment; however, it is very rarely the core issue and the focus of systemic intervention. For example, a couple in counseling desiring to heal from infidelity may believe initially the infidelity itself it the problem—when in fact it is a manifestation of the problem, or a *symptom*. As such, the symptoms observed give clues as to what is happening behind the proverbial curtain and help the counselor explore more deeply to identify underlying problems.

Sometimes, families may use the symptom as a tool for resistance by continually shifting focus back to the surface reason they came to treatment. It is important for the systems counselor to delicately and empathetically validate their perspective, while also educating the members as to the role of systemic patterns and processes in the perpetuation of the symptoms. For example, it would be important for the couple mentioned above to understand that while infidelity is a very serious symptom, it is directly related to deeper problems within the marital relationship.

Lastly, it can also be helpful for counselors to recognize—and provide psychoeducation to the system members—that symptoms may serve the purpose of *derailing* focus from underlying problems. For example, the rebellious teenager who stays out all night and abuses alcohol may be doing so in part to shift the parents' focus from their own marital problems. Of course, such ties are not always present, but exploration of them is warranted, as symptoms may serve an adaptive process in a system. Changing them to more functional behaviors is an important goal, but the potential short-term repercussions as the system adapts should be acknowledged.

SUMMARY

In this chapter, we explored some of the popular principles and paradigms in family therapy theory. Probably the most common of all focus areas in systemic interventions is family dynamics. Specifically, the elements of interconnectedness and communication patterns highlight both strengths within the system and areas that need improvement. Therefore, family dynamics can be both a protective factor and a risk factor, depending on the nature of the relationship. Family dynamics also indicate the relative strength of the system and convey strength in the family geometry. Family structure develops from the geometry of the system and its internal processes. These processes include power, boundaries, and hierarchies, which together form the framework of the system.

In addition to having common structural elements, all families have common life cycle elements that impact the system members' identities, health, and wellness. Family life cycle is a theoretical construction describing the establishment, sustainment, modification, and closure of marital and family relations. Traditional models were more rigid and stage oriented, while contemporary models are more complex and dynamic. Family life cycle helps both clinicians and their clients understand the relative transitional challenges associated with a family's development over time. Family wellness is a concept describing the functionality, support, strength, and resiliency of the system, and it highlights the resources and potentials of its members. Family wellness, therefore, is contextual by nature and adapts easily across cultural and other demographical variables. Family culture is a collection of beliefs, constructs, rituals, and customs in which the system exists. It is the result of the cumulative effects of multigenerational influences, including extended ancestry and current family of origin. All three of these elements—family life cycle, family wellness, and family culture—are interwoven and intimately connected.

KEYSTONES

Among the key points addressed in this chapter are:

- *Family geometry* is an umbrella term given to the shapes observed in family systems. These include linear processes, triangles, and circular causality.
- Family geometry is built on family dynamics and gives indications of the nuances of family structure and resiliency potential.
- Family structure can be visually represented to include composition of the system as well as the rules that govern its functionality.
- Understanding a family's life cycle stage can place important developmental considerations in context.
- Systems counselors must recognize that individuals are inseparable from the systems that influence them and must therefore view the entire system as the client.
- While the specific clinical methods will vary somewhat across theoretical orientations, all systems counselors will utilize common processes and principles during treatment.

REFLECTION FROM THE CONTRIBUTOR'S CHAIR

I am a very visual person. Drawing things out helps me analyze and better understand the subject matter. I have found the tools discussed in this section to be invaluable to my clinical work. In fact, I often use them not only to provide me with perspective but also to share insights I have gained with the client family. Of course, genograms are a common tool to share with clients, but even beyond that, I have used drawings to help families better understand the subsystems that exist, patterns of power and hierarchy, boundary issues, structural dynamics, and even overlapping life cycle issues. I have found that applying the principles to visual representations invariably provides clarity to families. I have had many "a-ha!" moments with couples and families when we talk about the different forces within the system and how they impact presenting issues.

ADDITIONAL RESOURCES

The following resources provide additional information relating to the chapter topics.

Useful Websites

- Family Therapy Resources
  http://www.familytherapyresources.net/

This website is a service of the American Association for Marriage and Family Therapy. Designed for both therapists and consumers, it provides links to a variety of resources, including books, articles, audio tapes, and more.

- GenoPro
  http://www.genopro.com/

This website provides software to help you create your own family tree or genogram. Free trial and purchase products are available.

- International Family Therapy Association (IFTA)
  http://www.ifta-familytherapy.org/

This website is dedicated to the IFTA and provides a variety of resources, including links to their publications, standards, accreditation information, and more.

- Tools & Techniques for Family Therapy
  https://www.psychotherapy.net/data/uploads/511942daefe54.pdf

This handy PDF gives some wonderful descriptions of common tools and techniques used across theoretical orientations.

REFERENCES

Ajami, J., Rasmi, S., & Abudabbeh, N. (2015). Marriage and family: Traditions and practices throughout the life cycle. In M. A. Amer & G. H. Awad (Eds.), *Handbook of Arab American Psychology* (pp. 103–116). New York: Routledge.

Allen, T. D., & Finklestein, L. M. (2014). Work-family conflict among members of full-time dual-earner couples: An examination of family life stage, gender, and age. *Journal of Occupational Health Psychology, 19*(3), 376–384.

Barnhill, L. R., & Longo, D. (1978). Fixation and regression in the family life cycle. *Family Process, 17*(4), 469–478.

Bouchard, G. (2014). How do parents react when their children leave home? An integrative review. *Journal of Adult Development, 21*, 69–79.

Bowen, M. (1978). *Family therapy in clinical practice.* New York: Aronson.

Breunlin, D. (1991). Oscillation theory and family development. In C. J. Falicov (Ed.), *Family transitions: Continuity and change over the life cycle* (pp. 133–156). New York: Guilford Press.

Carter, E., & McGoldrick, M. (1980). *The family life cycle: A framework for family therapy*. New York: Gardner Press.

Carter, E., & McGoldrick, M. (1999). Overview: The expanded family life cycle—individual, family, and social perspectives. In E. Carter & M. McGoldrick (Eds.), *The expanded family life cycle: Individual, family and social perspectives* (pp. 1–26). Needham Heights, MA: Allyn & Bacon.

Chhuon, V., & Hudley, C. (2008). Factors supporting Cambodian American students' successful adjustment into the university. *Journal of College Student Development, 49*(1), 15–30.

Demerouti, E., Peeters, M. C. W., & Van der Heijden, B. I. J. M. (2012). Work–family interface from a life and career stage perspective: The role of demands and resources. *International Journal of Psychology, 47*, 241–258.

Duvall, E. (1977). *Marriage and family development* (5th ed.). Philadelphia: Lippincott.

Fei, S., Xiang, G., Shuo, G., Qilun, L., & Hodge, D. R. (2016). Depressive symptoms among older Chinese Americans: Examining the role of acculturation and family dynamics, *Journals of Gerontology: Social Sciences*, gbw038. doi:10.1093/geronb/gbw038

Felicov, C. J. (2016). The multiculturalism and diversity of families. In T. L. Sexton & J. Lebow (Eds.), *Handbook of family therapy* (pp. 66–85). New York: Routledge.

Frankel, Z., & Levitt, H. (2009). Clients' experiences of disengaged moments in psychotherapy: A grounded theory analysis. *Journal of Contemporary Psychotherapy, 39*, 171–186.

French, J. R. P., & Raven, B. H. (1959). The basis of social power. In D. P. Cartwright (Ed.), *Studies in social power* (pp. 150–167). Ann Arbor: University of Michigan Press.

Gatta, M., Miscioscia, M., Sisti, M., Comis, I., & Battistella, P. A. (2017). Interactive family dynamics and non-suicidal self-injury in psychiatric adolescent patients. *Frontiers in Psychology, 8*(46), 1–5. doi:10.3389/fpsyg.2017.00046

Haley, J. (1979). *Leaving home: Therapy with disturbed young people*. New York: Grune & Stratton.

Hays, D. G., Snow, K. C., & Pusateri, C. G. (2015). Violence, abuse, and trauma in family therapy. In D. Capuzzi & M. D. Stauffer (Eds.), *Foundations of couples, marriage and family counseling* (pp. 419–447). Hoboken, NJ: Wiley.

Henry, C. S., Morris, A. S., & Harrist, A. W. (2015). Family resilience: Moving into the third wave. *Family Relations, 64*, 22–43.

Hernandez, J. L. (2013). *Family wellness skills: Quick assessment and practical interventions for the mental health professional*. New York: Norton.

Kao, T. A., & Caldwell, C. H. (2015). Family efficacy within ethnically diverse families: A qualitative study. *Family Process, 56*(1), 217–233.

Kennison, S. M., Wood, E. E., Byrd-Craven, J., & Downing, M. L. (2016). Financial and ethical risk-taking by young adults: A role for family dynamics during childhood. *Cogent Economics & Finance, 4*, 1232225. doi:10.1080/23322039.2016.1232225

Lazarevic, V. (2016). Effects of cultural brokering on individual well-being and family dynamics among immigrant youth. *Journal of Adolescence, 55*, 77–87.

Levy, A. J., & Brekke, J. S. (2016). Spouse battering and chemical dependency: Dynamics, treatment, and service delivery. In R. Potter-Efron, P. Potter-Efron, & B. Carruth (Eds.), *Aggression, family violence, and chemical dependency* (pp. 81–98). New York: Routledge.

O'Reilly, M., & Parker, N. (2013). You can take a horse to water but you can't make it drink: Exploring children's engagement and resistance in therapy. *Contemporary Family Therapy, 35*, 491–507.

Papero, D. V. (2015). The family emotional system. In R. J. Noone & D. V. Papero (Eds.), *The family emotional system: An integrative concept for theory, science, and practice* (pp. 15–28). London: Lexington.

Raven, B. H. (1992). A power/interaction model of personal influence: French and Raven thirty years later. *Journal of Social Behavior & Personality, 7*(2), 217–244.

Saltzman, W. R., Pynoos, R. S., Lester, P., Layne, C. M., & Beardslee, W. R. (2013). Enhancing family resilience through family narrative co-construction. *Clinical Child and Family Psychology Review, 16*, 294–310.

Szinovacz, M. E. (2013). Family power. In S. K. Steinmetz & M. B. Sussman (Eds.), *Handbook of marriage and the family* (pp. 651–694). New York: Plenum Press.

Smokowski, P. R., Rose, R. A., Bacallao, M., Cotter, K. L, & Evans, C. B. R. (2017). Family dynamics and aggressive behavior in Latino adolescents. *Cultural Diversity and Ethnic Minority Psychology, 23*(1), 81–90. doi:10.1037/cdp0000080

Titelman, P. (2014). The concept of differentiation of self in Bowen theory. In P. Titleman (Ed.), *Differentiation of self: Bowen family systems theory perspectives* (pp. 3–64). New York: Routledge.

Waid, J., Kothari, B. H., Bank, L., & McBeath, B. (2016). Foster care placement change: The role of family dynamics and household composition. *Children and Youth Services Review, 68*, 44–50.

Walrond-Skinner, S. (2014). *Family therapy: The treatment of natural systems.* New York: Routledge.

Walsh, F. (2003). Family resilience: A framework for clinical practice. *Family Process, 42*(1), 1–18.

Walsh, F. (2016). Applying a family resilience framework to training, practice, and research: Mastering the art of the possible. *Family Process, 55*(4), 616–632.

Wheeler, S. (2011). The significance of family culture for sports participation. *International Review for the Sociology of Sport, 47*(2), 235–252.

Wolin, S. J., & Bennett, L. A. (1984). Family rituals. *Family Process, 23*(3), 401–420.

CHAPTER 4

Ethical, Legal, and Professional Issues in Marriage, Couples, and Family Counseling

Perry C. Francis

> *"A code of ethics is a reflection of our profession's values and moral principles. Creating and promoting a code of ethics communicates our commitment to the service of others and a promise to place clients first. It is one of the hallmarks of a profession."*
>
> —Perry C. Francis

The creation of a code of ethics is one of the most important stepping stones toward professionalism for an organization. It is considered a "hallmark of professionalism" (Gorman & Sandefur, 2011, p. 279) and communicates the profession's commitment to protect the welfare of its clients and an orientation of service to others (Francis & Dugger, 2014). In a larger sense, it is a statement of the collective values, beliefs, and moral principles that guide the actions of the provider and demonstrates that the needs and concerns of clients are of primary concern over and above the needs, values, and interests of the individual member of that profession (DeMitchell, Hebert, & Phan, 2011; Hancock, 2014). For the mental health profession, a code of ethics also establishes norms and expectations to minimize risk to clients (Corey, Corey, Corey, & Callanan, 2015; Remley & Herlihy, 2014) and provide a "professional ethical identity" to those who are seeking to enter the ranks of mental health providers (Handelsman, Gottlieb, & Knapp, 2005, p. 59). This development or training is part of acculturating our students to the expectations of the profession.

Each of the mental health professions (counseling, social work, and psychology) have their own code of ethics, while many of the specialties either have their own code of ethics (e.g., school counselors; American School Counselor Association, 2016) or guidelines that offer direction on how to apply the profession's code to the specialty's current code (e.g., forensic psychologist; Martindale & Gould, 2013). The profession of marriage, couple, and family therapists (henceforth called family therapists) is no different. There is a code of ethics for the profession that is promulgated by the American Association for Marriage and Family Therapy (AAMFT, 2015), as well as specific training standards (COAMFTE, 2016). Additionally, there is a division (specialty) of the American Counseling Association (ACA) whose primary function is marriage and family counseling, the International Association of Marriage and Family Counselors (IAMFC, 2017), and has developed its own code of ethics that serves as a supplement to the ACA Code of Ethics (ACA, 2014). There are also specific education and training standards within the standards of the Council for Accreditation of Counseling and Related Educational Programs (CACREP, 2016) that govern the accreditation of counselor education programs, including marriage and family counseling. Using these codes of ethics and training standards as our guides, this chapter will review the common ethical issues that arise in the practice of family therapy.

LEARNING OBJECTIVES

After reading this chapter, you will be able to do the following:

- Have a clearer understanding of the various codes of ethics guiding the practice of marriage, couple, and family therapy.
- Understand the ethical concepts supporting the practice of marriage, couples, and family therapy.
- Gain a greater awareness of the common ethical issues facing marriage, couples, and family therapists.
- Understand and articulate how professional and personal values impact the practice of marriage, couple, and family counseling.
- Understand the ethics that guide the use of technology, social media, and electronic measures in the provision of marriage, couple, and family therapy.

KEY CONCEPTS

Codes of ethics provide a foundation for working with clients in marriage, couple, and family counseling. The next sections offer basic understanding of these ethical codes and discuss training, competency, and other issues faced regularly when counseling families and couples.

TRAINING AND COMPETENCY

AAMFT Code of Ethics, Standard III

> *Marriage and family therapists maintain high standards and professional competence and integrity.*

IAMFC Code of Ethics, Section C (preamble)

> *Couple and family counselors actively seek training, ongoing supervision and/or consultation, and continuing education directly related to couples and family counseling, including the ethical standards of couple and family counseling.*

While there are formal training programs that specifically focus on educating family therapists (i.e., COAMFTE, CACREP), more often than not, most non–family therapy counselor education programs only provided one or two courses in family therapy and very little clinical practice and supervision focused on family counseling in their practicum and internship sites (Levitt, 2004; Margolin, 2008). Practitioners like Sam (Case Presentation 4.1) who were educated in other counseling specialties are often providing services beyond their formal competence when offering comprehensive family therapy (Corey et al., 2015). Counselors wishing to add the specialty of family therapy to their practice are required, according to the ACA Code of Ethics (ACA, 2014), to follow a certain path to achieve an appropriate level of competence prior to independent practice. For example, the ACA Code of Ethics clearly states: "Counselors practice in specialty areas new to them only after appropriate education, training, and supervised experience. While developing skills in new specialty areas, counselors take steps to ensure the competence of their work and protect others from possible harm" (ACA, 2014, C.2.b).

CASE PRESENTATION 4.1: THE CASE OF SAM

Sam has been a professional counselor for 5 years. After graduating from a CACREP clinical mental health program, he immediately went to work at a counseling center associated with a large church that had a strong family ministry focus. He has always been interested in couple and family work since taking the one required class in his graduate counseling program. Unfortunately, no other classes were offered in family counseling, so he had to make do with periodic continuing education classes and sporadic consultation. Sam is one of three counselors in the center, and his practice has primarily been focused on working with older teens, individuals, and clients struggling with addiction issues. The one counselor whose practice was mainly focused on couple and family has recently moved to a new agency, and the pastoral staff need someone to refer couples and families to until they can fill the vacant position. The departing counselor who provided sporadic consultation to Sam when he saw couples or families suggested Sam could fill in until a new counselor is hired and offered to provide consultation should Sam feel he was "in over his head." Sam likes the idea and readily agrees to see the couples and families referred from the pastoral staff.

1. Does Sam have the education and experience necessary to provide competent services to couples and families?

2. Sam has a willing consultant in the departing therapist. Should Sam seek more regular supervision if he begins seeing couples and families?

3. What additional training or supervision should Sam obtain, if any?

Levitt (2004) noted comprehensive training goes beyond two or three courses in family therapy as part of a larger counselor education program. It includes the infusion of issues specific to family counseling and development throughout the entire curriculum that addresses the treatment of not just an individual within the family unit, but the treatment of the entire family unit. This requires a shift from conceptualizing the issues as the problem of one individual to seeing the issues as a product of system dysfunction (Southern, Smith, & Oliver, 2005). Therefore, courses must address not only individual development but the development of the family unit and the impact each person in the family has on the other. Additionally, supervised experience in practicum and internship must provide the opportunity to learn not only from individual clients but from couples and families who present themselves for services (Margolin, 2008).

Whether competence is earned in an educational program specifically addressing family therapy and postgraduate supervision or added as a new specialty through additional education, supervision, and practice, it must be maintained through a planned program of continuing education. Knowledge in the specialty of family counseling, just like that in all mental health fields, is always evolving. Additionally, graduate training programs, even when focused on the specialty of family counseling, can only provide so much information. Continuing education and periodic consultation is expected of all mental health providers to maintain, advance, and improve their practice of counseling (AAMFT, 2015; IAMFC, 2017; ACA, 2014). Workshops, seminars, webinars, and other forms of continuing education provide an effective means of exposing family therapists to information that may not have been covered during graduate training or new information that has developed since graduate school (Levitt, 2004; Remley & Herlihy, 2014; Welfel, 2013)

WHO IS THE CLIENT?

In Chapter 1, we discussed who is the *client*. Let us now turn our attention to how the various ethical codes address this issue.

AAMFT Code of Ethics, Standard I:

> *Marriage and family therapists advance the welfare of families and individuals and make reasonable efforts to find the appropriate balance between conflicting goals within the family system.*

IAMFC Code of Ethics, Section A (preamble):

> *Couple and family counselors advocate for the family as a whole system while considering the uniqueness of each family member. Couple and family counselors use systems perspectives and theories as they practice counseling.*

ACA 2014 Code of Ethics, B.4.b:

> *In couple and family counseling, counselors clearly define who is considered "the client" and discuss expectations and limitations of confidentiality. Counselors seek agreement and document in writing such agreement among all involved parties regarding the confidentiality of information. In the absence of an agreement to the contrary, the couple or family is considered to be the client.*

Most professional counselors are trained to conceptualize clients as individuals and to spend little or no time focusing on the influence that the family, community, or society has on the development and maintenance of dysfunction or mental health issue (Watts, Nelson, Bruhn, & Nichter, 2011). As discussed in Chapters 1 and 3, family therapists operate from a different perspective in that they view the system as the client. As you can see in Case Presentation 4.2, viewing each individual in a family as a *client* presents the family therapist with competing needs and goals for therapy.

CASE PRESENTATION 4.2: THE ALEXEI FAMILY

The Alexei family—Amid (45), Seva (42), Natasha (16), and Nicholas (16)—have completed two sessions with Steve Ruppert, a family counselor suggested to them by Nicholas's school counselor. The family emigrated to the United States from Ukraine 10 years ago. Amid found work as an engineer, and

Seva works as a registered nurse. The traditions and values of their country of origin as well as their Muslim religious roots are important to the parents, but not so much to the twins. The family moved into an area of the state with a large Ukrainian population and support system. Family counseling was suggested due to the systemic nature of the issues presented to the school counselor. Nick and Natasha are reluctant participants in counseling and have been fighting with their parents about the rules of the family. Each wants more freedom to live like many of their friends, including dating, musical choices, and career and educational opportunities, among other issues. The conflict has put a strain on the family and the parent's marital relationship, as Seva is also expressing a need for more independence within the marital system.

The goals of the parents are to maintain the traditions of the family and culture, and the goals of the twins are to develop a more American identity and freedom from their parent's supervision. Additionally, Seva has asked for a private session so she can express her own frustration about Amid without confronting him directly. She has hinted that she may be developing feelings for a coworker at the hospital where she works.

1. Who is the client in this case?
2. As Steve works with the family, whose goals should he focus on?
3. How should Steve handle the request for a private session with Seva?

The system (family) is a made up of interconnected persons who have a relationship with each other over time and influence each other's behavior. The view of the problem with one member of the system changes from an intrapersonal focus to one of an interpersonal focus that shifts the creation and maintenance of the presenting issue from the individual to the system (Goldenberg & Goldenberg, 2013). This view of the system as the client has ethical and legal implications for how the family therapist approaches several issues, including informed consent, confidentiality, seeing individuals apart from the family, goal setting, and holding secrets (Hill & Crews, 2005).

INFORMED CONSENT

AAMFT (Standard 1.2), IAMFC (Standards A & B), & ACA (Standard A.2.) each address the necessity of providing information to the client or system to ensure each person has the opportunity to freely decide if he or she wants to enter into a counseling relationship. The major difference in family counseling is that there is generally more than one participant in the counseling process. It is incumbent on the therapist to present the information in a manner that is both developmentally appropriate and culturally sensitive. While minors may not have the legal right to sign the informed consent, it is nonetheless important to ensure that younger members of the family have a basic understanding of the process of counseling and their rights. It is also important to document, in writing, each individual's right to confidentiality. While the family therapist views the system as the client, the law treats all members of the family as individuals, each having distinct rights and responsibilities (Goldenberg & Goldenberg, 2013; Remley & Herlihy, 2014).

Remley and Herlihy (2014) point out that family therapists will want to be prepared to answer the following questions for themselves and the family as they work through the consent process:

- Who gives consent for the family?
- Who in the family is seeking counseling, and are there reluctant participants? Can family members who feel pressured to join in the counseling process give truly free consent?
- What happens when one of the adults in the family refuses to give consent for family counseling?
- How capable are potential participants, particularly children, of understanding what they are getting into?
- How can counselors adequately address the reality that there will be changes in the family system, as well as in individual members, because of counseling? (p. 252)

LIMITS TO CONFIDENTIALITY

The ethics of all major mental health providers includes the requirement for confidentiality for services to be effective. Yet confidentiality has its limits, both ethically and legally. This is no different in family counseling. The system (couple or family) needs to be informed about the limits to confidentiality so that the family can feel safe sharing information and to ensure that, should the need arise (e.g., issues of child or elder abuse, suicide, or harm to others), appropriate interventions can be made, including the disclosure of confidential information to the proper authorities or other identified people who may be at risk of harm. These limits are determined by state law, and it is incumbent on you to know and understand these boundaries. Prior to any disclosure, it is always a good practice to consult with another counseling professional and/or utilize an ethical decision-making model. Additionally, a clear record of your decision to break confidentiality must be noted in the client record, including your rationale for the decision.

CONFIDENTIALITY AND SECRETS

Whether the counseling modality is an individual, families, or groups, the only person that the therapist can guarantee will maintain confidentiality is the therapist him- or herself. As more and more people are added to the consultation room, the challenges to confidentiality increase dramatically (Kliest & Bitter, 2013). The family therapist, as part of the informed consent process, needs to impress on the clients that confidentiality can only be ensured if all members respect each other's right to confidentiality. This helps create a safe place where all members of the family can participate without fear of issues being shared with others outside the system. Additionally, it models a sense of respect for the process of counseling and the therapeutic bond between the therapist and the family.

On occasion, a person within the family may ask for an individual session, or the therapist may determine that one member of the system needs a session alone. Prior to such issues arising, the therapist will want to review as part of the initial informed consent, and again as necessary during the course of therapy, the policy on managing and maintaining information that is shared during an individual session (Margolin, 2008). The IAMFC Code of Ethics (2017) states: "Couple and family counselors do not participate in keeping secrets for or from clients and maintain professional relationships with clients, refraining from multiple relationships with clients involving business and social contacts, whenever possible" (preamble, p. 1). An additional section addresses the adult individuals in the system concerning confidentiality:

> *Each person who is legally competent and deemed an "adult" must be provided a confidentiality agreement with the couple and family counselor(s). The agreement must be time limited, consistent with legal statutes. The parameters of confidentiality must be agreed upon by the client and counselor. (IAMFC, 2017, B.2., p. 3)*

An example of when such issues arise and complicate couples therapy is the disclosure by one member of a couple of an ongoing affair or past infidelity in an individual session. This disclosure by a client who refuses to bring it up in the couple's session and does not give the therapist permission to share it in session places the therapist in a compromised position of knowing information that impacts the couple's ability to deal with pertinent issues.

Remley and Herlihy (2014) offered three different positions on how to deal with secrets:

- Secrets are kept and individual confidentiality is maintained. By taking this stance, the therapist "will be more likely to obtain honest and complete information" (p. 258).
- No secrets are kept. Secrets impede the progress of family therapy. Only by refusing to keep secrets can the therapist remain independent (untriangulated) and continue providing appropriate services to all parties involved.
- The therapist exercises professional judgment and decides when to divulge or maintain the confidence for the greatest benefit of the entire system. This position requires experienced professional judgment.

Whatever policy a therapist adopts, if an individual client refuses to reveal information that puts the therapist in the position of appearing to collude against other members of the family or otherwise promotes, contributes, or maintains the dysfunction in the family system and interferes with the goals of the counseling itself, the therapist can terminate treatment and refer the clients to another therapist.

CONFIDENTIALITY AND MINORS

As a family therapist, there may be times when you work with children apart from their parents or guardians. This presents not only treatment issues but legal and ethical issues as well. The most salient for this chapter is the limits to confidentiality (Sartor, McHenry, & McHenry, 2017). As part of the informed consent process, especially when working with minors, you will need to decide the boundaries you will follow during treatment. Depending on the age of the minor(s) involved, these limits to confidentiality become fluid.

There are four basic positions you may take:

- Providing complete confidentiality to the minor(s) and limited to no information to the parents or guardians.
- Limited confidentiality that requires the minor(s) to waive, prior to disclosure, the right to know what will be revealed.
- Informed forced consent whereby the therapist only informs the minor(s) what will be disclosed prior to the disclosure.
- No confidentiality is guaranteed to the minor(s) (Sartor et al., 2017).

Whatever the decision made, all parties need to be fully informed prior to the commencement of services.

TREATMENT PLANNING AND GOALS

A common practice as part of any initial counseling session is to inform the client of the risks and benefits of counseling. Additionally, you set initial goals and develop a treatment plan in consultation with the client family. This is an ongoing process throughout the course of therapy (see ACA Code of Ethics: Standard A.2; ACA, 2014). This takes on a greater complexity when working as a family therapist, as your focus moves from working with an individual to an entire system that may or may not be in the consultation room.

At the core of all mental health counseling ethics are the basic principles that guide our practice and professional behavior (autonomy, nonmaleficence, beneficence, justice, fidelity, and veracity). It is the concept of beneficence, "working for the good of the individual and society by promoting mental health and well-being" (ACA, 2014, p. 3) that most influences our actions at this step in family counseling. This definition of beneficence is modified in family counseling in that the family therapist is *working for the good of the system*. This creates a dilemma for family therapists in that what might be a goal for one member of the system might not be beneficial for another member of the system. Margolin (1982) used the example of "a mother's request for her child to become better behaved might ease the mother's tension, and perhaps even provide secondary benefits for the marriage, but not be advantageous to the overall development of the child" (p. 789). The family therapist seeks to ensure that the goals and treatment planning that may result in the improvement of one member of the system does not occur at the expense of any other member of the system. The family therapist seeks to promote the welfare of all members of the system through direct involvement with all members of the system. In this way family therapy is different from individual counseling in that the therapist is more aware of and assesses how the behavior each member of the system impacts other members of the system (Margolin, 1982, 2008).

INTIMATE PARTNER VIOLENCE, TREATMENT GOALS, AND SAFETY

While the family therapist works to balance the goals of treatment for all members of the system, this requirement takes a backseat to the safety of the victims of intimate partner violence (IPV). In fact, there is much controversy in using systems theory or conjoint therapy at all when IPV is part of the presenting problems (Antunes-Alves & de Stefano, 2014; Stith & McCollum, 2011; Stith, McCollum, Amanor-Boadu, & Smith, 2012). As you can see in Case Presentation 4.3, providing family or conjoint therapy to a couple working through IPV can be difficult and complex.

CASE PRESENTATION 4.3: THE CASE OF JOSE AND MARIA

José (22) and Maria (21) have been married for 3 years and have a 2-year-old daughter. José works for a large construction company, and Maria is employed at the day care center their daughter attends. They are struggling financially, due to the seasonal nature of the construction industry. When José is not working, Maria's meager income is all they have to live on. Maria was referred to Manny Gonzales, a family counselor, by the family pastor, due to problems she expressed to the pastor about her marriage. Maria was tentative during the initial session, describing a difficult life in their mountain community. During the summer her husband is extremely busy building condos and vacation homes. During the winter work slows to a trickle, due to the snow and cold impacting construction. The economic slowdown of the past few years has also been hard on them and the construction industry in their area. Manny notes that Maria is wearing long sleeves, even though they were meeting in the peak of the summer season. There was also a faint outline of a bruise under her left eye. When pressed for an explanation about the bruise and long sleeves, Maria breaks down in tears and speaks tentatively about José's temper. She denies any long-term physical abuse and notes that she sought help from the pastor and now Manny due to a singular physical incident between her and José. She goes on to tell Manny that while José is generally good to her and their daughter, he has a short temper and is prone to yelling a lot. Maria also has a temper when pushed to extremes. She wants help to control her own temper so things around the house are less stressful for her and their daughter.

Manny has been providing family counseling services for 18 years in the area and is well versed on the cultural elements present in the community. He also has participated in a 6-hour continuing education seminar (3 years ago) on working with issues of IPV. This is his third client family that he has seen with IPV issues. He has no supervisor but can consult with a colleague who works at the local women's shelter.

1. Should Manny proceed with providing counseling services with Maria, or should he also ask Maria to invite José to any future sessions?
2. What issues should you consider prior to proceeding with counseling services in this case?
3. Does the level of the violence impact your decision of whether to move forward with providing services in this case?
4. How would your feelings and values impact your ability to provide services?

Researchers have found that of couples who have presented themselves for family therapy, 37% to 58% have experienced male-to-female physical violence in 2008. Female-to-male physical violence has a 37% to 57% prevalence rate in the same 12-month period of the research (Jose & O'Leary, 2009). This demonstrates that violence is a common theme for couple counseling. Maas-DeSpain and Tohahl (2014) and Antunes-Alves and de Stefano (2014) advocated that family therapists be trained in how to assess for IPV and provide counseling in those situations in which the violence is mild to moderate. When violence is severe to life threatening, systemic treatment modalities are contraindicated, and an individual approach is called for (Antunes-Alves & de Stefano, 2014). Alternatively, Corey et al. (2015) stated that providing couple therapy when there is *ongoing* IPV can be dangerous to the abused and should be consider unethical unless the perpetrator has completed a course of treatment for domestic violence. Even then, a decision to engage in couples therapy needs to be considered in light of the treating faculty's assessment of the progress made by the perpetrator.

One critical issue that appears repeatedly in the literature (Antunes-Alves & de Stefano, 2014; Charlés, Thomas, & Thornton, 2005; Jose & O'Leary, 2009; Maas-DeSpain & Todahl, 2014; Remley & Herlihy, 2014; Stith & McCollum, 2011; Stith et al., 2012; Wilcoxon, Remley, & Gladding, 2007) is how power and violence in the couple's system impact the decision of whether to engage in conjoint therapy. Conjoint therapy begins with the assumption that there is a mutual problem to be solved. This can result in the perpetrator not taking responsibility for the violence and instead assigning the blame to the family system and dysfunctional relationship patterns. The implication of this is that the perpetrator or primary aggressor can now say the other person "made me do it," transfer the responsibility to the system, and lessen his or her role in the violence while maintaining control of the system. The result of this is demoralization of the victims, who feel intimidated and afraid of therapy. They do not share freely in an environment in which they are to blame, and they see the therapist as underestimating the extent of the violence and its impact on them (Meyer, 2016).

Ancillary to this is the dilemma of the family therapist's own value system and the safety and autonomy of the client (Wilcoxon et al., 2007). If the family therapist insists or encourages the victim to leave the relationship, is she or he imposing his or her own values onto the victim and thus taking away the victim's right to autonomy? Yet if the family therapist does not encourage the victim to leave an obviously dangerous situation, especially if the violence is severe or life threatening, is she or he violating the basic ethical principle of nonmaleficence (do no harm)? In any case, the issue of safety and safety planning needs to be considered.

Issues to be considered before engaging in couples counseling when IPV is evident are:

- Is the therapist trained and experienced in providing therapy to couples who have experienced IPV? If not, is the therapist seeking consultation or supervision and ongoing education?
- Is the therapist skilled in assessing for IPV?
- What is/was the level of violence?
- Is the IPV ongoing, or was it a singular event?
- Is the therapist familiar with domestic violence treatment for perpetrators?
- Has the perpetrator participated in treatment to stop the IPV?
- Will the therapist take a clear stance against violence, and if so, how will this impact the reporting of violence should it occur?
- If violence reoccurs, will the therapist terminate the sessions and refer the couple for individual counseling or seek to deal with the violence in couples counseling?
- How will the therapist deal with any power differential between members of the system?
- Will there be a safety plan in place should violence reoccur? Who is the safety plan shared with?

The purpose of highlighting these issues is not to dissuade the family therapist from providing treatment to couples who have experienced IPV. It is to demonstrate that counseling couples who have experienced IPV requires additional consideration prior to the initiation of services. The family therapist will need to obtain additional training and supervision beyond what is normally required and, even then, should consider if conjoint therapy is called for, given the specific circumstance of each presenting couple. In Chapter 19, IPV will be discussed in greater detail.

BOUNDARIES IN FAMILY THERAPY

Family therapy is wrought with complex relationships and boundaries. At times, the family therapist may be drawn to a member of the system that goes beyond the therapeutic relationship. This can manifest in many ways (e.g., sexual relations, favoritism, etc.) and be the impetus for an unhealthy response on the part of the family therapist. At the same time, maintaining rigid boundaries can also negatively impacts the therapeutic process (Barnett, 2014). Each professional association's codes of ethics address this issue in multiple ways. The common elements in each include the following:

- Sexual relationships with current or former clients is forbidden.
- Sexual relationships with family members of current or former clients is forbidden.
- Family therapists avoid nonsexual relationships that have the possibility to manipulate or exploit current or former clients (e.g., business partnerships, social situations, etc.).
- In such instances wherein social interaction may be beneficial to the client (e.g., weddings, funerals, etc.), the family therapist reviews with the clients the impact of attendance at such events and determines the risks and benefits of attendance.

If family therapists find themselves drawn into unhealthy relationships or tempted to *stretch* or *violate* boundaries, it is best to enter supervision immediately and additionally seek help through personal counseling to manage the needs that are not being met outside the consultation room.

DIAGNOSIS IN FAMILY THERAPY

IAMFC Code of Ethics, Section E:

> *Couple and family counselors use assessment procedures to promote the well-being of the client.*

ACA 2014 Code of Ethics, E.5.a:

> *Counselors take special care to provide proper diagnosis of mental disorders. Assessment techniques (including personal interviews) used to determine client care (e.g., locus of treatment, type of treatment, recommended follow-up) are carefully selected and appropriately used.*

The subject of clinical diagnosis encompasses several issues in family counseling, including philosophical and theoretical understandings about diagnosis, wellness, and individual psychopathology (Crews & Hill, 2005); the lack of relational descriptors and diagnoses beyond V codes (those codes depicting non-disease or injury related factors) in the *Diagnostic and Statistical Manual of Mental Disorders*, 5th edition (DSM-5; American Psychiatric Association, 2015; Denton & Bell, 2013); the impact family distress has on individuals and the necessity to assess family functioning as part of any intake process (Snyder & Halford, 2012; Snyder, Heyman, & Haynes, 2005); and the ethical and legal concerns about the requirement to diagnose an individual to be reimbursed by many third-party payers (Christensen & Miller, 2001; Crews & Hill, 2005; Hill & Crews, 2005). Perhaps the most salient issue beyond the philosophical and theoretical arguments is what Crews and Hill (2005) called the "ethical double bind" (p. 63) of diagnosis. In many cases, for family counseling to be paid through a third party, a diagnosis is required. Yet the diagnostic system is not relationally based. So the family therapist struggles to diagnose a family issue in a way that does the least amount of harm to one person in the system and at the same time makes counseling available to all the members of the family. But family therapists are entreated not to compromise the accuracy of any diagnosis to make it fit the *DSM-5* individual criteria for the purposes of payment, as this could constitute fraud. Look at Case Presentation 4.4 to see how the necessity of a diagnosis for an individual family member can lead to an ethical and treatment dilemma for the family and family therapist.

CASE PRESENTATION 4.4: THE CASE OF ELLEN

The Tappert family came to see Dr. Tussin because their oldest daughter, Ellen, has become increasingly deviant at home, wants to spend more time with her boyfriend and other friends rather than with the family, and has let her grades slip slightly from all As to Bs (she is in three Advanced Placement courses and is receiving college credit for these courses). Her father (Jim) is not as concerned as her mother (Kay). Kay suggests that Jim is "wrapped around the little finger of our oldest daughter" and lets Ellen get away with much more than she herself would. Kay grew up in a home with definite boundaries and roles, whereas Jim's family was less restrictive but nonetheless quite healthy. Kay is concerned that Ellen has something else going on that needs some sort of intervention that only counseling can provide.

Ellen tells Dr. Tussin that she deserves more independence than her parents, especially her mom, are willing to give her. She will be 18 in 3 months and will be going away to college in 6 months, and her grades are being impacted because she finds herself feeling angry and depressed when at home, "doing family stuff I have done since I can remember." She wants peace and more independence.

Dr. Tussin listens carefully to all that he has been told and understands the situation as a classic case of family development and teen individuation. He views the parent's actions to discipline Ellen and bring her into line with family expectations as an attempt at first-order change. He suggested a course of treatment that includes family counseling to renegotiate boundaries, expectations, and relationships as well as some parenting classes for Jim and Kay, as they have two younger children who are watching all this with rapt attention.

The Tappert family's insurance will pay for individual counseling for Ellen if Dr. Tussin can offer a suitable diagnosis. The insurance company will not pay for any issues that can be classified as a V code diagnosis or parental education, and Dr. Tussin does not see a way to provide that kind of classification. Besides, he is a family therapist, and the issues reside in the relational system, not in any one person within the system. The Tapperts are blue-collar workers of modest means, and their insurance, while better than what they had prior to the Affordable Care Act, is still minimal at best.

1. How does Dr. Tussin proceed with counseling and still get paid for his services?
2. What are the long-term implications if Dr. Tussin assigns an "adjustment disorder" diagnosis for Ellen?
3. What ethical issues should Dr. Tussin consider prior to proceeding with the Tappert family treatment?

The AAMFT Code of Ethics (AAMFT, 2015) only addresses diagnosis by noting that "marriage and family therapists do not diagnose, treat, or advise on problems outside the recognized boundaries of their competencies" (Standard 3.10, p. 5). In a related way, it is implied that family therapists diagnose as part of "forensic services which may include interviews, consultations, evaluations, reports, and assessments both formal and informal, in keeping with applicable laws and competencies" (AAMFT, 2015, Standard 7.1, p. 9), but no other guidance is provided beyond these two standards. The IAMFC Code of Ethics notes that family counseling comes from a systems orientation and that couple and family therapists "use systems perspectives and theories as they practice counseling" (IAMFC, 2017, p. 1). The IAMFC also reflects the counseling philosophy toward wellness and development. Like the AAMFT Code of Ethics, the focus is on appropriate assessments, methods, and instruments but is relatively silent on diagnosis. The code of ethics from the ACA (2014), while more individually orientated, requires counselors to take "special care" to ensure a "proper diagnosis" (p. 11) through the use of suitable procedures and assessments. Thus, modifying or otherwise changing a diagnosis without an appropriate clinical reason to make it possible for a family or individual to receive services is considered a violation of the ethics.

[handwritten margin note: Counseling is systems & theories]

VALUES IN COUPLE AND FAMILY THERAPY
AAMFT Code of Ethics, Standard 1.1:

> *Marriage and family therapists provide professional assistance to persons without discrimination on the basis of race, age, ethnicity, socioeconomic status, disability, gender, health status, religion, national origin, sexual orientation, gender identity, or relationship status.*

IAMFC Code of Ethics, Section A.1:

> *Couple and family counselors do not discriminate or con-*
> *done discrimination based on age, color, culture, disability,*
> *ethnic group, gender, race, language preference, religion,*
> *spirituality, sexual orientation, or socio-economic status.*

ACA Code of Ethics, A.2.b:

> *Counselors are aware of—and avoid imposing—their own*
> *values, attitudes, beliefs, and behaviors. Counselors respect*
> *the diversity of clients, trainees, and research participants*
> *and seek training in areas in which they are at risk of impos-*
> *ing their values onto clients, especially when the counselor's*
> *values are inconsistent with the client's goals or are discrim-*
> *inatory in nature.*

Rokeach (1973), in his classic text on human values, defined *values* as "an enduring belief that a specific mode of conduct or end-state existence is personally or socially preferable to an opposite or converse mode of conduct or end-state of being" (p. 5). The belief that personal values do not play a role in all forms of counseling has long been put to rest in the mental health community (Corey et al., 2015). Therefore, the role of the family therapist's personal values in the provision of therapy has been a subject of interest for decades, especially as these values are reflected in clinical decisions regarding sex roles, sexual identity, career issues, infidelity, and marriage (Fife & Whiting, 2007; Green, 2003; Margolin, 1982; Melito, 2003; Rosik, 2003; Welfel, 2013). Values inform the family therapist's attitudes, evaluations, decisions, and behaviors. While the terms *values* and *ethics* are frequently used interchangeably, ethics are often more concrete expectations for professional behavior, while values include the prizing of one course of action over another, judgments between degrees of worth, and the preference or expectation concerning roles and behaviors (Fife & Whiting, 2007). It is therefore very important that family therapists are aware of their own cultural and personal values and those of the profession and seek to manage how those values impact the services they provide. While family therapists are not asked to check their values at the door of the consultation room, they should have an understanding of how to manage those values and balance them with the needs and goals of the clients and the professional values and principles that provide the foundation for all mental health ethics (Fife & Whiting, 2007). Recognizing that values play an important part in how a therapist understands and implements a code of ethics, the ACA (2014) sought to clearly delineate the broad *professional* values of counseling in its 2014 Code of Ethics.

Professional values are an important way of living out an ethical commitment. The following are core professional values of the counseling profession:

DO THIS
BE THIS

- enhancing human development throughout the life span;
- honoring diversity and embracing a multicultural approach in support of the worth, dignity, potential, and uniqueness of people within their social and cultural contexts;
- promoting social justice;
- safeguarding the integrity of the counselor–client relationship; and
- practicing in a competent and ethical manner. (ACA, 2014, p. 3)

The imposition of personal values and value conflicts can arise in covert ways—for example, when a family therapist demonstrates less interest in a woman's career aspirations than a man's—or they can arise in overt ways, such as refusing to provide counseling services to an LGBT couple because the family therapist's belief and value system opposes gay relationships or same-sex marriage. In either case, the family therapist may be practicing in a discriminatory manner (Herlihy, Hermann, & Greden, 2014; Shiles, 2009). Decide for yourself how Elena, the family therapist in Case Presentation 4.5 should respond to an ethical and values dilemma present during her session with Tom and Lavar.

CASE PRESENTATION 4.5: THE CASE OF TOM AND LAVAR

Elena has been a practicing family counselor for 15 years at a large local church. She has enjoyed her work and colleagues at the church's counseling office. It is a very supportive atmosphere as all the counselors share similar backgrounds and belief systems. Yet Elena needed a change and started her own private practice so she could expand her client base to others outside of the church's community. Within 6 months, Elena's practice was thriving as she had built an excellent reputation in the larger community, especially in the areas of adoption and parenting.

Tom and Lavar sought out Elena after consulting with a few friends. They have been together since graduating college in 2002 and recently got married when their state opened marriage to lesbian and gay couples in 2012. They are considering adopting children now that both their careers are stable. The adoption process has been more stressful than they imagined and has amplified some simmering yet modest differences they have been avoiding in their relationship. They wanted to clear these issues up before adopting children.

Elena has worked with a few lesbian and gay couples in her years as a family counselor. She sought out supervision during her first experience providing couple's counseling with a lesbian couple so she could learn to manage her values concerning LGBT clients. But her concerns about a gay couple adopting and raising children were very strong. Additionally, this couple was having some problems. After meeting with Tom and Lavar for an intake session, Elena struggled with what to do next.

1. Would it be appropriate for Elena to refer Tom and Lavar to another family counselor? Why or why not?
2. Should Elena discuss her concerns with Tom and Lavar prior the continuing counseling services? If so, how might she do that?

3. Assuming that Elena is competent to provide counseling for the issues brought up by Tom and Lavar, what else might she do to ensure she is providing her clients with appropriate services?

4. How can Elena balance her values with those of the profession and the ethical obligation not to discriminate against clients?

A family therapist's perspective, which is influenced by the values of the therapist, will influence his or her conceptualization of the system's problems, who is client, and what type of interventions will be implemented. This can lead to the family therapist imposing his or her values onto the system. Consider your values about the following issues and how they might impact your professional relationship with a couple or larger family system.

- Sex and gender roles
- Cohabitation, marriage, and divorce
- Responsibility for birth control in a relationship
- Responsibility for the primary parenting and discipline within a family structure
- The roles and expectations of children within a family system
- Is a woman's affair outside the primary relationship more serious than a man's affair?
- Whose career is primary in a relationship?
- LGBT or interracial relationships and marriage
- Adoption of children by a single parent or LGBT parents

Family therapists work at being aware of their own values on these and other issues. In doing this, they practice in a way that seeks to ensure that the client's values and goals for therapy are respected. Should family therapists find they are struggling with managing or bracketing off their values, the ethics and standards of care call for the use of continuing education, consultation, and supervision to help in the provision of appropriate services (Corey et al., 2015; Kocet & Herlihy, 2014).

Family therapists who carry into the consultation room their own cultural-bound or values-bound assumptions are at risk of perpetrating what Sue and colleagues (2007) termed "racial microaggressions" (p. 271) or "brief and commonplace daily verbal, behavioral, or environmental indignities, whether intentional or unintentional, that communicate hostile, derogatory, or negative racial slights and insults toward people of color" (p. 271). While Sue and colleagues are referring primarily to racial issues, the same can be applied to personal values that are intentionally or unintentionally applied during the provision of services to a family system. These microaggressions can include small assaults, insults, or invalidations that may be perceived consciously or unconsciously by both the family therapist and members of the system and serve to invalidate, devalue, and reject the thoughts, feelings, and behaviors of a person (Johnson, 2015; Sue, 2010).

Trying to match the family therapist and clients for areas of race, culture, and values agreement is as impossible as it is impractical, as family therapists and clients will always have the potential for regions of congruence and incongruence in these and other areas. Additionally, how a family therapist approaches these differences is the subject of some debate in the counseling profession (La Roche & Maxie, 2003; Melito, 2003), as highlighted in recent court cases from other counseling specialties (*Bruff v. North Mississippi Health Services, Inc.*, 2001; *Keeton v. Anderson-Wiley et al.*, 2010; *Walden v. Center for Disease Control & Prevention*, 2012; *Ward v. Wilbanks et al.*, 2009). Fife and Whiting (2007) identified three approaches from the literature. The first approach is for family therapists to take on a values-neutral stance and suspend their own values for the duration of the therapy. As has already been stated, this has been discounted by the profession as naive and unworkable. The second approach is for family therapists to be explicit about their own values, sharing them with the clients in a way that is respectful of the clients' right to self-determination (autonomy). This requires family therapists to be aware of the power differential between clients and therapists and ensure that clients are not forced to embrace the therapists' values. This also requires a keen sensitivity for the cultural background of the client, since in some cultures, the family therapist is seen as an expert whose instructions are to be followed (Sue & Sue, 2012). The third approach involves family therapists working within the clients' value system. As the work proceeds, the family therapist helps clients challenge and change their own values as needed and requested.

One option that has been used by many mental health providers when the values conflict seems untenable is to simply refer the client to another professional (Ford & Hendrick, 2003). This view is seemingly supported by the AAMFT 2015 ethical Standard 1.10 concerning referrals, which states, "Marriage and family therapists respectfully assist persons in obtaining appropriate therapeutic services if the therapist is unable or unwilling to provide professional help" (p. 3). Yet ethical codes are to be understood within the context of the entire code and in this case must be understood in light of Standard 1.1 concerning nondiscrimination: "Marriage and family therapists provide professional assistance to persons without discrimination on the basis of race, age, ethnicity, socioeconomic status, disability, gender, health status, religion, national origin, sexual orientation, gender identity or relationship status" (AAMFT, 2015, pp. 2–3). When Standard 1.10 is not understood in the context of Standard 1.1, values-based referrals can be confusing at best, and when understood in the context of Standard 1.1, they can continue to be confusing if the family therapist believes he or she is "unable" to provide professional help, often due to a concern and confusion about competence.

This practice has been challenged in recent years as discriminatory (see ACA, 2014, A.11.b; Francis & Dugger, 2014; Herlihy et al., 2014; Kocet & Herlihy, 2014; Shiles, 2009). Shiles (2009) points out that referrals have been made for various reasons, including differing religious beliefs, cultural backgrounds, and sexual orientation. The profession's reasoning for making such referrals include: (a) it is a common practice within the profession, (b) the sense that referring a client avoids the counselor's possibly harming the client due to a lack of competence, and (c) a lack of reflection on the practice by the profession. Shiles offers eight questions to determine the appropriateness of a client referral:

- Based on both my training and professional experience, do I feel competent to work with this client?
- Can I be respectful of my client's beliefs related to their presenting concern?
- How might my reaction to this client differ from my reaction to a client with a similar presenting concern, but with different demographic variables?
- Can I expand my competence regarding this issue through reading, supervision, or other professional activities?
- Am I willing to work at expanding my competence, and if not, why?
- Is this an area that the APA regards as essential for competent practice?
- Would referring this client cause more harm than good for this client and for other clients with similar characteristics who are considering counseling?
- Have I exhausted all other options before considering this referral? (p. 153)

[handwritten margin note: discerning whether to refer or not...]

Two related themes highlighted in these questions are competence and essential knowledge for competent practice. Working with a diverse population is considered essential knowledge in the training and practice of family counselors (COAMFTE, 2016; CACREP, 2016). No counselor will ever be competent with every issue, value, culture, or race, and counselors are to recognize their boundaries of competence. That is why all three codes of ethics reinforce that all counselors are to maintain their competence to practice through education, training, and supervision, and in the case of multicultural counseling competence, to "gain knowledge, personal awareness, sensitivity, dispositions, and skills pertinent to being a culturally competent counselor in working with a diverse client population" (ACA, 2014, p. 8). Because ethical competence is enhanced through the use of ethical decision-making models, Guided Practice Exercise 4.1 asks you to find and analyze some of these models.

GUIDED PRACTICE EXERCISE 4.1

When confronted with an ethical dilemma, all mental health providers are strongly encouraged to use an ethical decision-making model. There is no one model that is universally accepted as the common standard.

Review the ethics literature to find at least two different ethical decision-making models and view them through the lens of the issues raised in this chapter (e.g., whose is the client, differences in informed consent for family therapy, confidentiality, boundaries, etc.). Using one of case studies, apply these decision-making models. What, if any, differences do you find in your decision making when viewing the dilemma through the lens of a systems model? What similarities do you find?

DISTANCE COUNSELING, TECHNOLOGY, AND SOCIAL MEDIA

Electronic technology (computers, cell phones, tablets, etc.) is ubiquitous in our world today. Cell phones have replaced landlines for the majority of 25- to 34-year-olds (Luckerson, 2014). Tablets and touch screens are quickly overtaking laptop computers in dominance on the office desk. Social media (e.g., Facebook, Twitter, Instagram, blogs, etc.) has become the world's town square, where information is shared by everyone about everything, to the benefit or determent of the person posting the information. We can now video call, via our computers, an Internet connection, and a computer program (e.g., Skype) with people around the world. Professional counselors of all types have been using the Internet to file insurance claims for many years (Pollock, 2006). Is it any wonder that counselors of all types are now using this technology to provide distance counseling services to the general public (Barnett, 2011)? This has raised an important question: How do the ethics of our profession address the use of computers, technology, and social media for counseling services? Look at Case Presentation 4.6 and decide for yourself how comfortable you would be providing professional services in the same manner as Olivia.

CASE PRESENTATION 4.6: THE CASE OF OLIVIA

Olivia, a new family counselor in your clinic who just graduated from State University's graduate program in marriage and family counseling, is never far from her mobile device, texting at a pace that makes your fingers feel tired just watching her. While supervising Olivia, you learn she has a Facebook page, a blog on health care reform, and 2,000 followers for her Twitter feed.

Olivia is a popular therapist with the younger crowd. She is frequently requested by families with teens who have been referred from the local high schools. She can connect easily with them and their parents, who enjoy having easy access to Olivia through her Facebook page and texting.

1. What concerns might you have for Olivia, yourself, and her clients?
2. What precautions should Olivia take to ensure her personal and professional boundaries do not become blurred with her clients?
3. What the threats to confidentiality can you identify, and how might she address those?

For the purposes of this section, technology-assisted services, distance professional services, or online counseling is defined as involving "the use of electronic or other means (e.g., telephones or computers) to provide services such as counseling, supervision, consultation or education" (National Board for Certified Counselors, 2012, p. 1). Social media will be understood to be "Internet-based applications used in direct and indirect social interactions" (Jordan et al., 2014, p. 105).

One of the first occurrences in a code of ethics that remotely dealt with the use of technology when providing counseling services was in 1961 by the American Personnel and Guidance Association (APGA), a predecessor body of the ACA. In its first *Ethical Standards,* the APGA (1961) states:

> *The member shall offer professional services only, through the context of a professional relationship. Thus, testing, counseling, and other services are not to be provided through the mail, by means of newspaper or magazine articles, radio or television programs, (italics added) or public performances.* (p. 207)

When the ACA, IAMFC, and AAMFT revised their ethics, each either greatly expanded a section already addressing technology (ACA and IAMFC) or created a new section to deal with this issue (AAMFT). These continual updates related to technology and other specific concepts require constant education. For this reason, Guided Practice Exercise 4.2 asks you to analyze ethical concepts mentioned in several related codes of ethics.

GUIDED PRACTICE EXERCISE 4.2

The ethics of each professional association (i.e., ACA, IAMFT, and AAMFT) vary slightly when addressing specific concepts (e.g., confidentiality) and are similar when addressing other specific concepts (e.g., boundaries). Identify at least six different ethical concepts (e.g., informed consent, confidentiality, distance counseling and social media, imposition of values, etc.) and compare and contrast the codes of ethics from each of the previously mentioned professional associations. List similarities and differences. How do these similarities and differences impact the way you provide counseling services? Consider what you might have to do differently when working with an individual as opposed to working with a family system.

COMPETENCY

Counselor education and marriage and family counseling programs do not sufficiently prepare family counselors to provide services via technology (Blumer, Hertlein, & VandenBosch, 2015). The current accreditations standards for both CACREP (2016) and COAMFTE (2016) only direct training programs to provide students information or help in developing competency concerning technology's impact on the profession and client lives. There are no mandated classes. Further, the lack of government approved training programs leaves professional associations with the tasks of developing or offering their own Internet training or certification programs (TeleMental Health Institute, 2015), developing procedures for establishing online counseling practices, and creating a standard of professional practice involving the use of technology (International Society for Mental Health Online, 2015; American Telemedicine Association, 2013). All three professional association's (ACA, AAMFT, IAMFC) codes of ethics require counselors to develop and maintain competency in the use of technology-assisted services and social media. How that competency is developed is left in the hands of the family therapist. Currently, only one state (Arkansas) requires counselors who are using technology-assisted therapy to obtain additional education and supervision (Kaplan, Wade, Conteh, & Martz, 2011).

LEGAL AND JURISDICTIONAL ISSUES

Family therapists who use technology to provide services may find themselves working with couples and families who do not reside in their state. This presents a potential problem, as family therapists may be providing services in states where they are not licensed to practice. State licensing boards are only beginning to develop laws and rules to regulate the practice of online counseling and social media, and none specifically prohibit online practice (Haberstroh, Barney, Foster, & Duffey, 2014; Kaplan et al., 2011). Yet 4 states do not allow electronic communications under their scope of practice (Maryland, New Mexico, Tennessee, and Virginia), and 10 states do allow electronic communication, but only within their own jurisdiction (Arkansas, California, Iowa, Kansas, Minnesota, Nebraska, New York, North Carolina, Ohio, and Utah; Kaplan et al., 2011). It is therefore prudent for the ethical family therapist to ensure that he or she is practicing within the law when providing services across state lines.

INFORMED CONSENT

Informed consent and disclosure statements change when services are provided through technological means. Providing the same documents to a client who is receiving counseling via the Internet does not address the inherent risks and benefits of using technology (Jordan et al., 2014). In addition to the standard information provided, the client has a right to know (a) any special credentials obtained by the family therapist to provide online services; (b) contact information other than that provided through the Internet; (c) risks and benefits of online counseling services; (d) procedures for alternate means of services should there be a technological failure; (e) response times for electronic communications; (f) procedures should an emergency arise and the family therapist is not available; (g) working through any issues that may affect delivery of services (e.g., language or cultural); (h) time zone issues; (i) social media policy; and (j) insurance issues (e.g., denial of payment for online counseling). The family therapist will also need to make arrangements for how these agreements will be delivered, reviewed, signed, and returned to the therapist, ensuring that the individuals who are present on the Internet are also the same people signing and returning the documents to the therapist.

CONFIDENTIALITY

Communication over the Internet is not as secure as one might believe. Any e-mail generated through a server that is not owned by the family therapist may be maintained for a period of time on the servers of the company providing access to the Internet (Jordan et al., 2014). It is incumbent on the family therapist to ensure that all communications (e.g., e-mail, video communication, etc.) are secure through the use of encryption technology or websites that meets legal requirements (Zur, 2014). Additionally, the storage of records through electronic means must be secure using current security software. If a family therapist works for an agency that owns its own equipment, the therapist needs to make the client aware that there may be others besides the therapist who have access to the electronic files (e.g., information and systems technologists, supervisors, etc.).

SOCIAL MEDIA AND E-MAIL

Social media (e.g., Facebook, professional websites, blogs, etc.) presents a special challenge to family therapists. Social media is a common way that many people maintain contact with and interact with family, friends, and acquaintances. Family therapists are no different. Yet family therapists who want to maintain appropriate professional boundaries with their clients will need to consistently manage the privacy settings on their social media sites. It may not be therapeutic for a client who is struggling with a substance abuse issue within the family to see pictures of the family therapist celebrating a private event with copious amounts of alcohol. It is therefore advised that a family therapist who wishes to maintain a presence on social media platforms have both a personal page that has high privacy safeguards and a professional page that only offers information concerning his or her practice. Additionally, as previously mentioned, a social media policy is necessary for both the face-to-face and distance counseling informed consent (Jordan et al., 2014) that outlines the boundaries of the professional relationship and issues such as "friending" (connecting to the social media account) the family therapist's page.

Communication with clients via e-mail or social media platforms (e.g., Facebook, blogs, chatrooms, etc.) also presents its own set of issues that will need to be addressed in the informed consent. First, issues of confidentiality need to be considered. Complaints have been filed against therapists for e-mails being sent to the wrong person and, at this time, one complaint relating to Facebook account activities in Ohio (Kaplan et al., 2011). Who sees the communication shared via a blog or social media account? What happens if a client posts a concerning communication (i.e., suicidal or homicidal ideation) in a chat room and no one is there to respond to the post? Addressing these issues prior to the initiation of counseling services is required so that both the client and family therapist know and understand the boundaries for the safety of the client and peace of mind of the therapist. These boundaries and issues even extend to techniques and interventions used within counseling sessions. Let us look at how ethics applies when using nontraditional techniques, including, but not limited to, social media, email, art, and other creative interventions as discussed in Guided Practice Exercise 4.3.

GUIDE PRACTICE EXERCISE 4.3

Family therapists use many different creative techniques and interventions such as corrective parenting, body work, or family sculpting as a part of their practice. What ethical issues must the family therapist consider when planning and implementing these techniques and interventions? Additionally, what else must the family therapist consider when using nontraditional techniques and interventions in light of the ACA Code of Ethics (2014) concerning scientific basis for treatment modalities?

SUMMARY

The practice of marriage, couple, and family therapy is more than a set of techniques. It is an identity that is reflected in the values and ethics of the profession. It involves a mind-set that requires specialized training and experience and a conceptualization that we all live within different systems that impact who our clients are, how we relate to them, and finally, how we deliver services to our clients. The codes of ethics of each organization that represent the diverse counselor population reflect this philosophy and how it is applied to the practice of family therapy. Having an in-depth knowledge not only of the code of ethics that relates to your professional identity but also of how to apply that code to your practice is necessary to provide the bests services to your clients. And remember that in the end, it is about the clients we serve and how well we serve them.

KEYSTONES

Among the key points addressed in this chapter are:

- Codes of ethics are a statement by the members of a profession about the values they hold and the public responsibility they have to the clients they serve.

- To be a competent family therapist requires specialized training and experience and an ethical mind-set that understands the complex nature of the systems our clients inhabit.

- The autonomy of the system (family) to manage itself is reflected in the requirement that we fully inform our clients about the risks, benefits, and boundaries of the services we provide.

- The values of our profession are reflected in our actions and the interventions we provide our clients, and our personal values are never imposed on the clients we serve.

- Technology is impacting all that we do personally and professionally. Be aware of how technology can be used ethically in family therapy so that the clients receive the best care.

ADDITIONAL RESOURCES

The following websites will take you to the main codes of ethics for each professional association that guides the work of family therapists.

Useful Websites

- American Association of Marriage & Family Therapy Code of Ethics
www.aamft.org/iMIS15/AAMFT/Content/Legal_Ethics/Code_of_Ethics.aspx

This website provides the AAMFT ethical codes.

- American Counseling Association 2014 Code of Ethics
www.counseling.org/knowledge-center/ethics

This website provides the ACA Code of Ethics.

- International Association of Marriage & Family Counselors Code of Ethics
www.iamfconline.org/public/department3.cfm

This website provides the IAMFC ethical codes.

- National Board of Certified Counselors (NBCC) Policy for Distance Counseling
www.nbcc.org/Assets/Ethics/NBCCPolicyRegardingPracticeofDistanceCounselingBoard.pdf

This website provides the NBCC's Policy for Distance Counseling.

- Zur Institute Index of Professional Associations Codes of Ethics related to Telemental Health
www.zurinstitute.com/ethicsoftelehealth.html

This website provides information regarding ethics related to Telemental Health.

REFERENCES

American Association for Marriage and Family Therapy. (2015). *AAMFT code of ethics.* Alexandria, VA: Author.

American Counseling Association. (2014). *2014 ACA code of ethics.* Alexandria, VA: Author.

American Personnel and Guidance Association. (1961). Ethical standards: American Personnel and Guidance Association. *Personnel and Guidance Journal, 40*(2), 206–209. doi:10.1002/j.2164-4918.1961.tb02428.x

American Psychiatric Association. (2015). *Diagnostic and statistical manual of mental disorders* (5th ed.). Washington, DC: Author.

American School Counselor Association. (2016). *Ethical standards for school counselors.* Alexandria, VA: Author.

American Telemedicine Association. (2013). *Practice guideline for video-based online mental health services.* Washington, DC: Author.

Antunes-Alves, S., & de Stefano, J. (2014). Intimate partner violence: Making the case for joint couple treatment. *Family Journal, 22*(1), 62–68. doi:10.1177/1066480713505056

Barnett, J. E. (2011). Utilizing technological innovations to enhance psychotherapy supervision, training, and outcomes. *Psychotherapy, 48*(2), 103–108. doi:10.1037/a0023381

Barnett, J. E. (2014). Sexual feelings and behaviors in the psychotherapy relationship: An ethics perspective. *Journal of Clinical Psychology, 70*(2), 170–181. doi:10.1002/jclp.22068

Blumer, M. L. C., Hertlein, K. M., & VandenBosch, M. L. (2015). Towards the development of educational core competencies for couple and family therapy technology practices. *Contemporary Family Therapy: An International Journal, 37*(2), 113–121. doi:10.1007/s10591-015-9330-1

Bruff v. North Mississippi Health Services, Inc., 244 F3rd 495 (5th Cir. 2001).

Charlés, L. L., Thomas, D., & Thornton, M. L. (2005). Overcoming bias toward same-sex couples: A case study from inside an MFT ethics classroom. *Journal of Marital and Family Therapy, 31*(3), 239–249. doi:http://dx.doi.org/10.1111/j.1752-0606.2005.tb01566.x10.1111/j.1752-0606.2005.tb01566.x

Christensen, L. L., & Miller, R. B. (2001). Marriage and family therapists evaluate managed mental health care: A qualitative inquiry. *Journal of Marital and Family Therapy, 27*(4), 509–514.

Commission on Accreditation for Marriage and Family Therapy Education. (2016). *Accreditation standards: Graduate and post-graduate marriage and family therapy programs.* Alexandria, VA: Author.

Corey, G., Corey, M. S., Corey, C., & Callanan, P. (2015). *Issues and ethics in the helping professions* (9th ed.). Stamford, CT: Cengage Learning.

Council for Accreditation of Counseling and Related Educational Programs. (2016). 2016 CACREP Standards. Retrieved from http://www.cacrep.org/wp-content/uploads/2013/12/2009-Standards.pdf

Crews, J. A., & Hill, N. R. (2005). Diagnosis in marriage and family counseling: An ethical double bind. *Family Journal, 13*(1), 63–66. doi:10.1177/1066480704269281

DeMitchell, T. A., Hebert, D. J., & Phan, L. T. (2011). The university curriculum and the constitution: Personal beliefs and professional ethics in graduate school counseling programs. *Journal of College and University Law, 39,* 303–344.

Denton, W. H., & Bell, C. (2013). DSM-5 and the family therapist: First-order change in a new millennium. *Australian and New Zealand Journal of Family Therapy, 34*(2), 147–155. doi:10.1002/anzf.1010

Fife, S. T., & Whiting, J. B. (2007). Values in family therapy practice and research: An invitation for reflection. *Contemporary Family Therapy: An International Journal, 29*(1–2), 71–86. doi:10.1007/s10591-007-9027-1

Ford, M. P., & Hendrick, S. S. (2003). Therapists' sexual values for self and clients: Implications for practice and training. *Professional Psychology: Research and Practice, 34*(1), 80–87. doi:10.1037/0735-7028.34.1.80

Francis, P. C., & Dugger, S. M. (2014). Professionalism, ethics, and value-based conflicts in counseling: An introduction to the special section. *Journal of Counseling & Development, 92*(2), 131–134. doi:10.1002/j.1556-6676.2014.00138.x

Goldenberg, H., & Goldenberg, I. (2013). *Family therapy: An overview* (8th ed.). Belmont, CA: Brooks/Cole.

Gorman, E. H., & Sandefur, R. L. (2011). "Golden age," quiescence, and revival: How the sociology of professions became the study of knowledge-based work. *Work and Occupations, 38*(3), 275–302. doi:10.1177/0730888411417565

Green, R.-J. (2003). When therapists do not want their clients to be homosexual: A response to Rosik's article. *Journal of Marital and Family Therapy, 29*(1), 29–38. doi:10.1111/j.1752-0606.2003.tb00380.x

Haberstroh, S., Barney, L., Foster, N., & Duffey, T. (2014). The ethical and legal practice of online counseling and psychotherapy: A review of mental health professions. *Journal of Technology in Human Services, 32*(3), 149–157. doi:10.1080/15228835.2013.872074

Hancock, K. A. (2014). Student beliefs, multiculturalism, and client welfare. *Psychology of Sexual Orientation and Gender Diversity, 1*(1), 4–9. doi:10.1037/sgd0000021

Handelsman, M. M., Gottlieb, M. C., & Knapp, S. (2005). Training ethical psychologists: An acculturation model. *Professional Psychology: Research and Practice, 36*(1), 59–65. doi:10.1037/0735-7028.36.1.59

Herlihy, B. J., Hermann, M. A., & Greden, L. R. (2014). Legal and ethical implications of using religious beliefs as the basis for refusing to counsel certain clients. *Journal of Counseling & Development, 92*(2), 148–153. doi:10.1002/j.1556-6676.2014.00142.x

Hill, N. R., & Crews, J. A. (2005). The application of an ethical lens to the issue of diagnosis in marriage and family counseling. *Family Journal, 13*(2), 176–180. doi:10.1177/1066480704273068

International Association of Marriage and Family Counselors. (2017). *IAMFC code of ethics.* Alexandria, VA: Author.

International Society for Mental Health Online. (2015). About ISMHO. Retrieved from http://ismho.org/ismho/about-ismho

Johnson, D. E. (2015). *The impact of microaggressions in therapy on transgender and gender-nonconforming clients: A concurrent nested design study.* Retrieved from http://ezproxy.emich.edu/login?url=http://search.proquest.com/docview/1668010416?accountid=10650

Jordan, N. A., Russell, L., Afousi, E., Chemel, T., McVicker, M., Robertson, J., & Winek, J. (2014). The ethical use of social media in marriage and family therapy: Recommendations and future directions. *Family Journal, 22*(1), 105–112. doi:10.1177/1066480713505064

Jose, A., & O'Leary, K. D. (2009). Prevalence of partner aggression in representative and clinic samples. In K. M. O'Leary & E. M. Woodin (Eds.), *Psychological and physical aggression in couples: Causes and interventions* (pp. 15–35). Washington, DC: American Psychological Association.

Kaplan, D. M., Wade, M. E., Conteh, J. A., & Martz, E. T. (2011). Legal and ethical issues surrounding the use of social media in counseling. *Counseling and Human Development, 43*(8), 1–10.

Keeton v. Anderson-Wiley et al., No. 1:10-CV-00099-JHR-WLB, 733 F. Supp. 2d 1368 (S.D. Ga. 2010).

Kliest, D., & Bitter, J. R. (2013). Virtue, ethics, and legality in family practice. In J. R. Bitter (Ed.), *Theory and practice of family therapy and counseling* (2nd ed., pp. 71–94). Belmont, CA: Brooks/Cole.

Kocet, M. M., & Herlihy, B. J. (2014). Addressing value-based conflicts within the counseling relationship: A decision-making model. *Journal of Counseling & Development, 92*(2), 180–186. doi:10.1002/j.1556-6676.2014.00146.x

La Roche, M. J., & Maxie, A. (2003). Ten considerations in addressing cultural differences in psychotherapy. *Professional Psychology: Research and Practice, 34*(2), 180–186. doi:10.1037/0735-7028.34.2.180

Levitt, D. H. (2004). Ethical responsibilities in training marriage and family counselors. *Family Journal, 12*(1), 43–46. doi: 10.1177/1066480703258704

Luckerson, V. (2014, July 8). Landline phones are getting closer to extinction. *Time*. Retrieved from http://time.com/2966515/landline-phones-cell-phones

Maas-DeSpain, A., & Todahl, J. L. (2014). Rape, sexual violence, and acquiescence in intimate relationships: Screening, assessment, and clinical decision making. *Journal of Feminist Family Therapy: An International Forum, 26*(1), 28–49. doi:10.1080/08952833.2014.875447

Margolin, G. (1982). Ethical and legal considerations in marital and family therapy. *American Psychologist, 37*(7), 788–801. doi:10.1037/0003-066X.37.7.788

Margolin, G. (2008). Ethical and legal considerations in marital and family therapy. In D. N. Bersoff (Ed.), *Ethical conflicts in psychology* (4th ed., pp. 346–353). Washington, DC: American Psychological Association.

Martindale, D. A., & Gould, J. W. (2013). Ethics in forensic practice. In R. K. Otto & I. B. Weiner (Eds.), *Handbook of psychology, Vol. 11: Forensic psychology* (2nd ed., pp. 37–61). Hoboken, NJ: Wiley.

Melito, R. (2003). Values in the role of the family therapist: Self determination and justice. *Journal of Marital and Family Therapy, 29*(1), 3–11.

Meyer, S. (2016). Still blaming the victim of intimate partner violence? Women's narratives of victim desistance and redemption when seeking support. *Theoretical Criminology, 20*(1), 75–90. doi:10.1177/1362480615585399

National Board for Certified Counselors. (2012). National Board for Certified Counselors policy regarding the provision of distance professional services. Retrieved from http://www.nbcc.org/Assets/Ethics/NBCCPolicyRegardingPracticeofDistanceCounseling Board.pdf

Pollock, S. L. (2006). Internet counseling and its feasibility for marriage and family counseling. *Family Journal, 14*(1), 65–70. doi:10.1177/1066480705282057

Remley, T. R. Jr., & Herlihy, B. (2014). *Ethical, legal, and professional issues in counseling* (4th ed.). Upper Saddle River, NJ: Pearson.

Rokeach, M. (1973). *The nature of human values*. New York: Free Press.

Rosik, C. H. (2003). Motivational, ethical, and epistemological foundations in the treatment of unwanted homoerotic attraction. *Journal of Marital and Family Therapy, 29*(1), 13–28. doi:10.1111/j.1752-0606.2003.tb00379.x

Sartor, T. A., McHenry, B., & McHenry, J. (2017). Ethics of working with children, adolescents, and their parents. In T. A. Sartor, B. McHenry, & J. McHenry (Eds.), *Ethical and legal issues in counseling children and adolescents* (pp. 5–20). New York: Routledge.

Shiles, M. (2009). Discriminatory referrals: Uncovering a potential ethical dilemma facing practitioners. *Ethics & Behavior, 19*(2), 142–155. doi:10.1080/10508420902772777

Snyder, D. K., & Halford, W. K. (2012). Evidence-based couple therapy: Current status and future directions. *Journal of Family Therapy, 34*(3), 229–249. doi:10.1111/j.1467-6427.2012.00599.x

Snyder, D. K., Heyman, R. E., & Haynes, S. N. (2005). Evidence-based approaches to assessing couple distress. *Psychological Assessment, 17*(3), 288–307. doi:10.1037/1040-3590.17.3.288

Southern, S., Smith, R. L., & Oliver, M. (2005). Marriage and family counseling: Ethics in context. *Family Journal, 13*(4), 459–466. doi:10.1177/1066480705278688

Stith, S. M., & McCollum, E. E. (2011). Conjoint treatment of couples who have experienced intimate partner violence. *Aggression and Violent Behavior, 16*(4), 312–318. doi:10.1016/j.avb.2011.04.012

Stith, S. M., McCollum, E. E., Amanor-Boadu, Y., & Smith, D. (2012). Systemic perspectives on intimate partner violence treatment. *Journal of Marital and Family Therapy, 38*(1), 220–240. doi:10.1111/j.1752-0606.2011.00245.x

Sue, D. W. (2010). *Microaggressions in everyday life: Race, gender, and sexual orientation*. Hoboken, NJ: Wiley.

Sue, D. W., & Sue, D. (2012). *Counseling the culturally diverse: Theory and practice* (6th ed.). Hoboken, NJ: Wiley.

Sue, D. W., Capodilupo, C. M., Torino, G. C., Bucceri, J. M., Holder, A. M. B., Nadal, K. L., & Esquilin, M. (2007). Racial microaggressions in everyday life: Implications for clinical practice. *American Psychologist, 62*(4), 271–286. doi:10.1037/0003-066X.62.4.271

TeleMental Health Institute. (2015). TeleMental Health Institute training options. Retrieved from http://telehealth.org/courses

Walden v. Center for Disease Control & Prevention, No. 10-11733, 669 F.3d 1277 (11th Cir. 2012).

Ward v. Wilbanks et al., No. 139, 10--CV-11237 (E.D. Mich. 2009).

Watts, R., Nelson, J., Bruhn, R., & Nichter, M. (2011). Couple and family counseling. In S. C. Nassar-McMillan & S. G. Niles (Eds.), *Developing your identity as a professional counselor: Standards, settings, and specialties*. Belmont, CA: Brooks/Cole.

Welfel, E. R. (2013). *Ethics in counseling and psychotherapy: Standards, research, and emerging issues* (5th ed.). Belmont, CA: Brooks/Cole.

Wilcoxon, S. A., Remley, T. R. Jr., & Gladding, S. T. (2007). *Ethical, legal, and professional issues in the practice of marriage and family therapy*. Upper Saddle River, NJ: Pearson.

Zur, O. (2014). Utilizing Skype and VSee to provide TeleMentalHealth, E-Counseling, or E-therapy: Reviewing the debate on Skype & HIPAA compliance and introducing the VSee option. Retrieved from http://www.zurinstitute.com/skype_telehealth.html

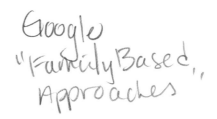

CHAPTER 5

Intercultural Family Counseling

Brian S. Canfield and Lauren A. Shure

"All relationships are "intercultural" to some extent."

—Dr. Brian S. Canfield

In Chapter 1, you learned about family therapy, but in this chapter, we would like to expand your understanding of intercultural contexts and the various types of professionals who work to assist couples and families. While the use of family-based approaches to address a wide range of client issues has gained in popularity in recent decades, there is often confusion over professional titles such as family counselor, family therapist, and family psychologist. Such confusion is understandable, since these groups of professionals provide similar services to the public. Isomorphic to this confusion, the terms *counseling* and *therapy* are increasingly used interchangeably, both in common usage and in the professional literature, to describe a professional helping relationship.

A great deal has been written in the behavioral science field about diversity and multiculturalism. Applying these concepts to counseling practice has, by and large, been an attempt to view and categorize clients based on a shared cultural demographic. Parsing humanity into groups may serve a practical purpose. However, such classifications are often problematic, leading to broad generalizations and misleading assumptions about a person, couple, or family. Regardless, the concept of cultural identity continues to play a prominent role in how we see ourselves, how others see us, and how we see others. In this chapter, we identify strategies for working with couples and families from an intercultural perspective.

We commonly self-identify, or others may identify us, as belonging to a group of people with whom we share some common qualities or attribute. Our cultural identity may stem from any number of factors, such as race, ethnicity, a common language, national origin, sexual orientation, religious affiliation, philosophical or political ideology, shared traditions and rituals. etc. The similar qualities and attributes that people share often serve to create a sense of community or shared identity; conversely, dissimilar characteristics may create divisions among people. In a broad sense, the similarities we share with others provide the foundation of our cultural identity.

From birth, we spend our formative years, if not our entire lives, within a unique context of interpersonal relationships. Though family structure and family roles vary, regardless of one's selected or imposed cultural identity, family is universal in the human experience.

Cultural awareness and competency is widely recognized as an essential and fundamental skill for establishing an effective counseling relationship. However, given the multitude of cultural groups in the world, it is not possible for any counselor to gain a meaningful understanding of all existent cultures. A challenge that counselors must face is how to best identify cultural differences and similarities that exist between the client and counselor and understand to what extent the interface of these cultural factors may enhance or potentially impede the counseling relationship. Effective intercultural counseling requires the acquisition of specific knowledge and skills that are essential in creating a productive therapeutic relationship. Critical to this task is the ability to discern those cultural traits that are critical in achieving this goal from those that may be merely incidental.

Effective counseling is not just about the client, it is about the client and the counselor working collaboratively to achieve a common goal. Since both the client and counselor bring into the counseling relationship their respective cultural orientations, it is not sufficient to merely gain an understanding of the client's culture and personal sense of cultural identity. The unique nature of the counseling relationship is coconstructed by the client and counselor.

Both client and counselor draw from their own unique context. The family rules that exert an influence on each member of the family are informed and influenced by a broader set of cultural rules. The nature and organization of the family unit may vary from culture to culture. However, the concept of family is transcultural. As such, the theories and methods of family counseling offer a means for helping people (i.e., individuals, couples, and families) address a wide range of mental health, relationship, and life-adjustment issues, regardless of cultural identity. Case Presentation 5.1 offers a look at how culture impacts the family.

CASE PRESENTATION 5.1: THE CASE OF RANA AND DEV

Rana and Dev moved to the United States following political unrest in their home country. They have three children, ages 13, 15, and 18. Dev was able to secure a visa to open a convenience grocery store. Rana decided she wanted to study to become a real estate agent. While Dev was initially supportive of Rana studying to pass her real estate licensing exam, after she passed he was hesitant and had concerns about her working outside of the home. While the two younger children also appeared to be supportive of their mother working, the eldest child, Devi, one of two sons, became defiant and resentful toward his mother and her desires to deviate from the more traditional gender and family roles he was accustomed to in their home country. Dev and Rana both became concerned about Devi, Dev stating that all would be better if Rana quit her job and stayed home with Devi, and Rana stating that Devi's problems were not about her work and were probably more related to his maladjustment to US culture. Once Rana began making money and doing well as a real estate agent, she told the family she was considering moving out of the house. Dev's appetite and sleep have been affected, as well as his mood, which has shifted to dysthymic with congruent low energy and sad affect. The clients presented with discord in their marriage, concern about their eldest son, and Dev's symptoms as described above. At the initial joining stage, the counselor asked the couple to talk about how they met and about times when they were satisfied in the relationship or times they felt the relationship was working well. The triad then began discussing how the couple came to move to the United States and what that was like for each of them. At this point, differences in perception and acculturation became evident. Rana reported being excited about moving to the United States, volunteering at her children's schools and in the community, and making friends easily. On the other hand, Dev worked long hours in his store and seldom sought out opportunities to build relationships with others or participate in activities besides with his family. Acculturation stressors proved challenging, especially in terms of how divergent their expectations for marriage and goals for the future became. Through couples counseling, the couple gained greater clarity about what they wanted from a marital relationship. Dev waned to retain a more traditional relationship with accompanying gender roles, and Rana wanted to work outside the home and have greater freedom than she felt her former life afforded her. While in many ways regrettable, this was the ultimate decision of the couple. Both members felt couples counseling provided them with greater insight into their dynamics and expectations during this impasse. They came to the realization that they had differing expectations and wanted different things from a marriage and, perhaps, from life in general. At this point attention shifted to assisting the couple and family in the dissolution of the marriage and assisting the children in adjusting to the end of their parent's marriage. Assessment for depression and discussion about a referral for individual therapy for Dev was also included during treatment.

Every problem or client concern, even problems that are biogenic in nature, have a relationship component. Therefore, it is not surprising that the theories and methods of family counseling resonate in many countries and across cultures as an increasingly preferred method for addressing client needs. Whether engaging in counseling practice in a school setting, substance abuse treatment in a residential facility, private practice, or inpatient behavioral medicine unit, the ubiquity of family across human cultures gives credence to the notion that, at least tangentially, every counselor is a family counselor.

It may be useful to consider that the practice of counseling and therapy are only the most recent manifestation of a tradition of human helping that has existed for millennia. All human societies have utilized individuals who were recognized as possessing helpful knowledge and skills for alleviating physical pain and human suffering that is often referred to as psychological distress. The names and methods of culturally indigenous helpers may bear little resemblance to contemporary counseling or psychotherapy as practiced in developed Western countries, but the purpose was essentially the same—to help people find solutions to problems and issues of concern.

Counseling, psychology, and marriage and family therapy are separate and distinct mental health professions that are recognized and regulated by law in all 50 US states. Family counseling is an area of specialization within the profession of counseling. Both the psychology specialization of family psychology and the counseling specialization of family counseling emphasize the importance of relationships and context in understanding and ameliorating a wide range of mental health, relationship, and life-adjustment issues. The profession of marriage and family therapy holds essentially the same goals and objectives.

Professionals may identify themselves primarily or exclusively as either family counselors or family therapists, title distinctions that reflect different educational, training, and credentialing paths. However, the work that family counselors and family therapists perform is essentially the same. Family counselors and family therapists typically share a relational orientation, share a growing body of common knowledge, study the same theories, read many of the same books, and employ similar intervention strategies and change techniques. The utilization of relational concepts and family-based therapeutic interventions and the ability to think and act systemically to bring about a therapeutic change are not proprietary to any single profession.

In terms of training and practice regulation, clear distinctions exist between various professional groups. However, many of these distinctions are political, rather than clinical. At a practical level, a couple or family struggling with a problem cares little about the professional identity of the helper, aside from an assurance of competency.

It is the overarching goal of this chapter is to expand cultural awareness and intercultural skills by explicating selected case examples and intervention strategies. We hope that in gaining an increased awareness of the issues presented, you will be better prepared to help couples and families.

Although much as been written about multiculturalism and the cultural identity of clients, cultural considerations have been largely overlooked when examining counseling interventions that focus on couples and families (Bitter, 2009.) Surprisingly, little has been written about the intercultural relationship that often exists between the counselor and the client couple or family. This chapter seeks to bridge that gap in the professional literature by examining aspects of intercultural relationships between family counselors and clients and presenting strategies for working more effectively with couples and families who differ from the counselor in some cultural aspect.

The concepts of intercultural counseling and systemic family therapy offer a logical and complementary fit that support the utility of family counseling as a preferred treatment modality when working with many clients who are addressing life adjustment, relationship concerns, and a wide range of mental health issues.

LEARNING OBJECTIVES

After reading this chapter, you will be able to do the following:

- Examine the counseling relationship from a relational systemic perspective.
- Expand understanding of intercultural relationships that exist in many individual and multiclient counseling relationships.

- Present key concepts of a relational systemic approach to family counseling.
- Provide a four-step protocol and specific intervention strategies for working with clients who differ from the family counselor in some cultural aspect.

KEY CONCEPTS

As summarized in the Learning Objectives above, this chapter focuses on working with diverse couples and families. The next sections discuss diversity regarding families and also focuses on intercultural therapy and considerations when working with diverse client formations.

INTERCULTURAL

FAMILIES

As discussed in previous chapters, families exist in a variety of relational structures throughout the world. All humans experience birth, relationships with others, and death. While the nature and structure of the family takes many forms, it is a fundamental social unit common to the human experience. However, the idea of the typical American family is a fiction. For example, the traditional American *nuclear family*—consisting of a first-time married couple with children, with the father as the primary wage earner and mother as a stay-at-home mom—is increasingly rare. Less than 3% of the population of the United States lives in a household that is demographically White, heterosexual, Christian Protestant, economically middle class, with married heterosexual parents and school-aged children (McGoldrick & Hardy, 2008). Let's look at Case Presentation 5.2 for an example of a modern couple facing conflicts regarding financial earnings.

CASE PRESENTATION 5.2: THE CASE OF SHANA AND REGGIE

Shana, age 35, and Reggie, age 38—married for 10 years, with no children—presented with marital dissatisfaction, noting increasing arguments and conflict. Shana worked in the field of medical equipment sales, earning an annual income more than $300,000. Reggie held a secure position with the federal government with an annual income of approximately $80,000. Shana, who is African American, came from a relatively affluent family. Her father was a medical doctor, and her mother had earned a nursing degree but worked as a stay-at-home parent throughout the marriage. Shana's siblings held professional or graduate degrees and were highly successful in their career fields. Reggie, whose family was of Cuban descent, came from a middle-class blue-collar family background. His mother worked as an office administrative assistant, and his father was a construction worker. Reggie was the first in his family to graduate from college, with a bachelor's degree in business administration. During the initial session, the counselor focused on joining with the client couple, gaining an understanding and normalizing differences between the couple's respective family of origin backgrounds. This led to a discussion of spousal role expectations. Even though Reggie earned a good income, he stated that it "just wasn't right" that his wife made so

Initial goal: join the client couple

much more than he did. This led to a conversation about gender role cultural stereotypes—allowing the couple to examine their respective marital expectations. The counselor's role was the facilitation of this discussion, not presenting any preconceived ideas regarding life roles and choices that might be deemed more appropriate to the couple. Over the course of several sessions, the couple renegotiated relationship expectations. Specific positive changes in the couple's interactions were noted that appeared to become self-reinforcing. Following two additional counseling sessions spaced several months apart, all parties agreed to terminate counseling work, with the understanding that counseling could be reinstituted as the couple deemed appropriate.

Demographics in the United States are changing rapidly. Most notable in the 2010 U.S. Census are the following trends: Out of 116.7 million households reporting in 2010, the unmarried partner population numbered 7.7 million in 2010 and grew 41 percent between 2000 and 2010, 4 times as fast as the overall household population (10 percent). For same-sex households, estimates for 2000 and 2010 showed an 80 percent increase. In 2010 less than half of all households (48 percent) were husband–wife households, down from 52 percent in 2000 and 55 percent in 1990. This is the first time that husband–wife families fell below 50 percent of all households in the United States since data on families were first tabulated in 1940.

Two thirds of all households in the United States were family households. This proportion varied considerably by race: 64 percent of homogeneous non-Hispanic White households were family households, compared with 78 percent of homogeneous Hispanic or Latino households. Households consisting of a husband–wife couple family varied as well: 29 percent of all Black or homogeneous African American households were husband–wife households, while 60 percent of Asian homogeneous households were husband–wife families. Three in 10 Black or African American family households were headed by an adult female, with no in-residence spouse or partner, 3 times as high as White family households (9.9 percent), and Asian family households (9.5 percent). Male-headed family households with no spouse present represented 5 percent of all U.S. households. Almost half of these households contained children of the male householder. Family households maintained by a female householder with no spouse present numbered 15.3 million, more than twice the number maintained by a male householder with no spouse present (5.8 million).

In addition to the diversity of families, persons from various cultural backgrounds increasingly relocate to new places that are different from their cultural community of origin. Population movements occur for a variety of reasons. For some people, relocation is temporary and voluntary—often prompted by a desire to improve economic circumstances and quality of life. For some, relocation can be a disruptive and even traumatic experience—such as the case of persons displaced by societal instability, conflict, or war. Immigrate populations—particularly first-generation adults—often encounter tremendous challenges (Esses, Deaux, Lalonde, & Brown, 2010; Fortuna & Porche, 2014; Leong, Park, & Kalibatseva, 2013.) Having been removed from familiar cultural points of reference, immigrants may feel overwhelmed by the challenges of adjusting to a new society and life in a new community. Therefore, counseling can serve as a useful aid to the acculturation process (Yakushko & Chronister, 2005).

INTERCULTURAL COUNSELING

Skilled therapists can recognize and bridge cultural differences that often exist between the counselor and client. Culturally homogenous communities exist in urban enclaves or rural communities. With rare exceptions, it is highly unlikely that counselors will practice among culturally similar people over the course of their career. Particularly in urban areas, it is inevitable that counselors will encounter clients who differ from them in some demographic cultural aspect. It is increasingly recognized that counseling in the United States, and in many other countries, is inherently an intercultural activity. It is assured that the cultural identity of a family counselor will not align with the cultural characteristics of all clients with whom the counselor works.

Increasingly, immigration is changing the cultural demographic composition of many communities and countries (United Nations, 2013.) Because of these changes, in the United States and many other countries, therapists are required to address a wide range of mental health and life adjustment issues within an intercultural context. See Case Presentation 5.2 for an example of this concept.

Recognizing the relational nature of an effective therapeutic relationship, intercultural counseling goes beyond an examination of the cultural identity of the client, additionally examining the cybernetic process of therapy between therapist and client. Recognizing and addressing the interrelationship of cultural identities is essential in building a productive counselor–client relationship. Establishing a collaborative counseling relationship requires a degree of understanding of the cultural orientation of the client and a high level of cultural self-awareness on the part of the counselor.

While single client counseling is the predominant counseling modality in many therapeutic settings, the authors note anecdotally that working with a single client is often more difficult and less productive than working with a couple or family—due to reduced access to client information and therapeutic options.

Differences between people are inevitable. Existing differences may provide an initial barrier to mutual understanding and initial familiarity, or the differences may be merely incidental to the formation of a relationship connection. Depending on the meaning attributed to cultural similarities or differences, a client may feel a connection with their counselor or feel dissimilar and less connected. The meaning attributed to differences and similarities serve to create initial impressions that either accelerate or impede the establishment of a therapeutic relationship, increasingly recognized as foundational to a successful therapeutic outcome (Duncan, Miller, Wampold, & Hubble, 2009; Wampold, 2001; Wampold et al., 1997). While cultural reference points vary and life events may be interpreted differently, all people experience similar life events and life stressors, albeit within differing cultural contexts. Though each person experiences particular life experiences that are unique, all people who live a full life span share common life experiences such as birth, childhood, relationships, stressors, loss, successes, aging, and death. Regardless of the initial sense of cultural familiarity between the counselor and client, it is incumbent on the counselor to utilize techniques and strategies to bridge perceived differences. Successful counseling is built on the nature of the relationship between the therapist and client (Duncan et al., 2003; Duncan, Miller, & Sparks, 2004; Orlinsky, Ronnestad, & Willutzki, 2004.)

INDIVIDUAL COUNSELING

The perspectives presented in this chapter view intercultural family counseling from a conceptual framework of applied cybernetics, recognizing that it is the interrelationship between the counselor and client that provides the foundation for creating therapeutic change (Becvar, Canfield, Becvar, 1997.) In considering the therapeutic utility of intercultural family counseling, it may be helpful to examine the concept of the individual person—a concept that is inherently limiting in many respects. However, traditional schools of psychology, including most current theoretical models of counseling and psychotherapy—some dating back to the early days of psychoanalysis—focus on the individual as the object of examination and the locus of treatment. While humans certainly exist as monadic biological entities, this preoccupation with the individual is, at best, incomplete and offers a confined conceptual framework for ameliorating many, if not most, client concerns. Since most psychological and relationship problems do not emerge solely within the individual, it seems logical that change strategies require interventions at a systemic level broader than the individual.

Psychologically and physically, humans are social creatures—connected to other people over the course of life. From birth until around 4 years of age, people are dependent on others for survival. The care and life-sustaining sustenance provided by another person is essential to the survival of toddlers and young children.

Beyond childhood, most people continue to live their lives interacting with others. Even the hermit monk of legend—who as an adult rejects interaction with human society—was earlier in life nurtured as an infant and instilled with the knowledge of others. Yet a preoccupation with and an emphasis on the individual remains deeply imbedded in Western philosophies and most psychological theories. The concept of the *individual* is not false, but it is incomplete. Attempting to help a couple, family, or individual client without possessing an understanding of the relational matrix in which that client is imbedded is inherently limiting.

Recognizing the relational nature in all forms of counseling and psychotherapy, the authors view *individual counseling* as inaccurate and potentially misleading. This position emerged from a realization that the most elemental form of counseling or therapy consists of a dyadic relationship, consisting of a single counselor and a single client. It is this collaboration between the therapist and client(s) that creates a therapeutic environment that facilitates desired change.

COUPLE COUNSELING

The term **couple counseling** refers to a therapeutic relationship consisting of at least one counselor and two people in an intimate dyadic relationship (e.g., marriage) engaged in a professional relationship. Couple counseling includes both legally married couples, as well individuals who are in a self-recognized relationship, though not necessarily recognized by legal authority or sanctioned by a religious entity.

FAMILY COUNSELING

Family counseling refers to a therapist(s) and two or more people—typically connected by genetic relatedness, adoption, marriage, or household proximity, and perhaps other participants—who are engaged in a professionally facilitated interaction with a therapeutic intent. The defined family may or may not share a common domicile—but all members of the family hold a current or historical relationship with one another. *home*

THEORETICAL CONSTRUCTS OF INTERCULTURAL FAMILY COUNSELING

Counseling theories abound, and almost every approach works with some clients some of the time. The fact that no counseling approach has been shown to be effective with every client in every situation will be discussed in more detail in Chapter 6. A counselor typically employs some type of theoretical or conceptual model that serves as a framework for helping clients. Unavoidably, the process of counseling is invasive. The process of counseling requires the client to enlist the help of an outsider—essentially a stranger—who becomes privy to very personal aspects of the client. Among people whose cultural values emphasize self-sufficiency or privacy, the invasive nature of counseling can be particularly challenging. Questions posed by the counselor that the client considers overly intrusive or familiar may not be welcomed or readily understood. While the benefits of counseling are well known to the culture of the counselor, counseling may seem alien to many people oriented to a different cultural tradition for addressing personal problems.

All human relationships consist of a minimum of two people. Therefore, the most elemental relationship is the **dyad** (Canfield, 2007.) For any role—such as counselor, teacher, or parent—there is a logical complementary role—such as client, student, or child. Although one role does not create the other, a logical complement exists in every relational role. For example, the role of bully does not exist in the absence of someone being bullied (Becvar et al., 1997).

Unlike traditional counseling approaches that typically view the client as the primary locus of therapeutic interest, applied cybernetics holds the view that the client and counselor cocreate a unique dyadic relationship. In joining with the family, the counselor becomes the logical complement to the client family. This coconstructed therapeutic system establishes a context in which members of that system can address various issues, including counseling goals, and the respective roles and responsibilities of the client and therapist in attaining desired goals.

Applied cybernetics provides a conceptual frame for creating a successful therapeutic relationship (Becvar et al., 2007.) This conceptual framework provides a template for counseling clients, regardless of cultural identity. Central to this approach is an understanding that the counseling relationship is coconstructed by the counselor and client (Becvar, Canfield, & Becvar, 1997).

A cybernetic perspective of counseling holds that clients are embedded in dysfunctional, but often stable, patterns of interaction. These interactive behaviors among clients serve, in part or whole, to create and maintain problem issues. By inviting the counselor to become part of the client's relational system, the counselor can work with the client to identify, disrupt, and replace undesirable interactive behaviors with more productive and useful interactive behaviors. Inherent in understanding the cybernetic nature of the counseling relationship is an awareness of the respective salient cultural qualities and issues of the counselor and client. However, it cannot be assumed that client cultural identity may be regarded as a concomitant issue in counseling.

PROFESSIONAL STANDARDS AND ETHICAL CONSIDERATIONS

Goldenberg and Goldenberg (2000) defined *culture* as "shared behaviors, meanings, symbols, and values transmitted from one generation to the next" (p.436). Increasingly, professional counseling associations recognize the importance of cultural understanding and intercultural competency for working effectively with clients. These considerations apply to all clients but are of particular importance when the client and family counselor hold different core cultural identities. The Preamble of the Code of Ethics of the ACA (2014) states: "Counseling is a professional relationship that empowers diverse individuals, families, and groups to accomplish mental health, wellness, education, and career goals" (p. 3). Core professional counseling values include: "honoring diversity and embracing a multicultural approach in support of the worth, dignity, potential, and uniqueness of people within their social and cultural contexts" (ACA, 2014, p. 3).

Family counselors have an ethical responsibility to protect the welfare of a client. To this end, professional ethics require that

> counselors actively attempt to understand the diverse cultural backgrounds of the clients they serve. Counselors also explore their own cultural identities and how these affect their values and beliefs about the counseling process.... Counselors communicate information in ways that are both developmentally and culturally appropriate. (ACA, 2014, pp. 3–4, Standard A.2.c)

Additionally, "Counselors recognize that culture affects the way clients' problems are defined and experienced. Clients' socioeconomic and cultural experiences are considered when diagnosing mental disorders" (ACA, 2014, p. 11, Standard E.5.b).

When working with a multiple client therapeutic system (e.g., a couple or family), competing agendas or priorities may become evident. Therefore, it is essential that the role of a family counselor, as a professional working on behalf of all family members, be clarified to avoid any misunderstanding.

CACREP—which is recognized by the ACA as the educational program accrediting body for the counseling profession—recognizes the importance of multicultural competency in counselor training (CACREP, 2016.) The proscribed training requires an understanding of "multicultural and pluralistic characteristics within and among diverse groups nationally and internationally" (CACREP, 2016, p. 9), as well as an understanding of the evolving and shifting trends in a multicultural society.

INTERCULTURAL FAMILY COUNSELING CONSIDERATIONS

For the culturally attuned family counselor, fundamental questions arise relating to demographic characteristics such as race, ethnicity, or group identity. To effectively serve the diversity of client families likely to be encountered in counseling practice, family counselors are called on to continuously develop multicultural competence (Canino & Inclan, 2001; Cole, Piercy, Wolfe, & West, 2014). The Multicultural and Social Justice Counseling Competencies include proficiency in understanding cultural attitudes and beliefs, knowledge, skills and actions. Each aspect of multicultural competence exists within the following domains of treatment processes: counselor self-awareness, client worldview, counseling relationships, and counseling and advocacy interventions (Ratts et al., 2016). **Attitudes and beliefs** refer to an awareness of the values, beliefs, biases, and worldviews that counselors possess about themselves and their clients. **Knowledge** refers to an understanding of sociopolitical systems and the complexities surrounding counselor and client identity development, worldviews, and the nuances of culture. **Skills** refer to counselors' abilities to modify interventions that align with the cultural identities and worldviews of clients. **Action** refers to counselors' abilities to operationalize attitudes and beliefs, knowledge, and skills into effective and competent conceptualization and treatment with clients. Let's look at Case Presentation 5.3 to see how the therapist uses knowledge, skills, and actions to help a family.

CASE PRESENTATION 5.3: THE CASE OF PRISHA, AMIR, AND SHANAYA

Prisha and Amir moved to the United States when their daughter, Shanaya, was 12 years old. Shanaya attends public school, as well as lessons at the local Hindu temple. Shanaya says she is proud of her Indian heritage and enjoys going to temple, celebrating the Hindu holidays, and learning the traditional

Respectful
Model

ways (as her mother and father call them). When she turned 16, like many of her friends at school, she wanted to begin dating. However, her parents began speaking with other local Indian families about arranging a marriage for her. When Prisha and Amir began arranging meetings through the temple with the parents of eligible sons for Shanaya, she began acting out and would leave the house when the families were coming over and not return until late in the night, sometimes ignoring calls from her parents. Her parents became increasingly worried about her when her grades began dropping, and they heard from another family at the temple that Shanaya was seen holding hands and kissing a boy in a local diner. Prisha and Amir blamed her drop in academic performance to her being "boy crazy." Shanaya's school counselor recommended that the family make an appointment to see a family therapist. The family therapist could normalize and validate for the family that Prisha and Amir wanted Shanaya to follow the traditional ways of their home country and that Shanaya wanted to date and enjoy being a teenager like many of her peers and friends from school. The therapist asked Prisha and Amir to share their story of arranged marriage and what it meant to them. Shanaya was asked to share her hopes and dreams for her future. The therapist inquired about each family member's roles and responsibilities and noted that the family was quite high functioning. The symptoms Shanaya was exhibiting appeared to be a response to the family's developmental transition, as Shanaya began moving toward adulthood and the system attempted to readjust. The therapist pointed out that each family member seemed to have a similar vision of what they wanted for the future of their family. Shanaya and her parents both discussed Shanaya getting married and having children. However, they had different ideas of how that would happen. After identifying the similarities they shared in their future visions and the many strengths of their family unit (e.g., communication, closeness, shared spirituality, etc.), the family then moved on to discuss how their family would transition to this next stage of Shanaya moving from childhood to adulthood. After weeks of discussions and speaking to other local Indian families with daughters a little older than Shanaya, the family agreed that they would begin meeting families they may want to unite with through Shanaya's marriage, and that Shanaya would be involved in this process. Each family member agreed that there was no rush, Shanaya was still young, and she would be able to spend time with these possible suitors and have the final say on who she would marry. Shanaya began meeting with families, along with Prisha, and her grades began to improve. She was thinking about college, and the family discussed the possibility of her attending a local college where she could live at home and find a suitable husband. At the beginning of treatment, Prisha and Amir identified Shanaya improving her grades and not sneaking around as goals, while Shanaya identified being allowed to be a normal teen and having some control over her life and future as therapeutic goals. Once the family came to an agreement about how Shanaya would approach finding a husband, she became reengaged in school and began planning for college, and the therapist highlighted how the family was able to work together and reach both sets of goals they developed for therapy. The family discussed what the process of therapy was like for them and what strengths and skills they used to reach their goals. Feeling empowered and having reached their treatment goals, the course of family therapy was terminated.

Many theoretical and clinical models have emerged that seek to expand the intercultural competencies of counselors. One example is the RESPECTFUL model developed by D'Andrea and Daniels (1997, 2001), which provides a framework for identifying cultural aspects of identity that inform the conceptualization and treatment process in counseling. This model posits that the intersecting aspects of identity impact all aspects and stages of the therapeutic process, from joining the family and building rapport to termination and family empowerment. While not an exhaustive list, the RESPECTFUL model cues us to consider personal identity and development contextually using the following domains: R, religious/spiritual identity; E, economic class background; S, sexual identity; P, psycho- *U. unique* logical maturity; E, ethnic/racial identity; C, chronological/developmental challenges; T, *charac!* trauma and threats to well-being; F, family background and history; U, unique physical *L = Location* characteristics; and L, location of residence and language differences. To begin building *Languey* self-awareness by reflecting on your personal identity and development, see Guided Practice Exercise 5.1.

Bible

GUIDED PRACTICE EXERCISE 5.1

Because counseling is a coconstructed relationship in which the respective experiences, attitudes, and beliefs of the counselor and client influence the counseling process, an understanding of the contributing factors that have shaped your worldview is critical. List all the influences that you feel have contributed to the shaping of your worldview (e.g., gender, race, ethnicity, sexual preference, political or philosophical view, religion, education, economic status, and age). In addition to compiling this list, note on a scale of 1 to 10 (1 being incidental, and 10 being crucial) the importance you attribute to each of these influences. What might cause you to change or modify the importance of each of these influences?

The Bible

While the importance of training culturally competent family therapists has been wide-ly noted (Gushue, Constantine, & Sciarra, 2008; Hardy & Laszloffy, 1995; Constantine, Juby, & Liang, 2001), little research has been done on counselor cultural competence in working with families (Gushue et al., 2008). Likewise, little is known about best practices in counseling families in which cultural differences (e.g., first- and second-generation immigrant families and racially/ethnically different coupled partners) impact dynamics related to client couple and family presenting concerns (Ibrahim & Schrodeder, 2009; *How* Lee, Su, & Yoshida, 2005.) Validating and normalizing the difficulty of navigating in- *to!* tercultural couple and family dynamics, as well as facilitating improved communication and compromise between family members, are techniques that have been used to assist couples and families overcome cultural conflicts in counseling (Ibrahim & Schroeder, 2009).

THE JAST MODEL

Creating an environment that allows therapeutic change to take place is the respon-sibility of the counselor. To this end, the family counselor, regardless of theoretical *be good* orientation, must strive to accomplish four essential tasks, conceptualized as the opera- *4 this* tionalization of skills and actions following the consideration and ongoing development of intercultural attitudes and beliefs and knowledge. This chapter presents a four-step process, the JAST model, for operationalizing these skills with culturally diverse client families. This process includes four essential tasks—joining, assessing, supporting, and terminating—that must take place over the course of the counseling relationship and treatment intervention process.

Joining with the Family

The process of family counseling requires that the counselor enter into the family system without being absorbed into the system. As the process of joining with the family takes place, the counselor becomes part of the emotional and relational system of the family. Family members form an initial impression of the therapist that may change or evolve over the course of therapy. As a temporary member of the family system, the counselor may utilize their role to establish connections with selected family members, strengthen or weaken alliances, and use their position as expert and outsider as a catalyst for change.

While it is important to acknowledge that the counselor enters the family and becomes a part of the family unit, it is essential for the counselor and all members of the client family to remain cognizant of the fact that the counselor is a temporary member of the family system and that the counselor's participation is time limited to a specific purpose. It is the goal of an effective counselor to exit the family (terminate counseling) at the earliest possible juncture, once desired changes have taken place.

The way joining occurs is often subtle and indirect. Upon casual observance, engaging members of the family on seemingly innocuous topics such as sports, food, or current events may seem a waste of time and a distraction from the purpose of therapy—but in actuality it can serve to establish a common connection and sense of familiarity between the counselor and client. The process of joining establishes the foundation for effective family counseling.

Conveying a sense of interest and curiosity with the family on various subjects—independent of the presenting issue or concern—serves to create an atmosphere of open communication. Once the family feels a connection and has joined with the counselor, the exploration of more delicate and difficult topics with the family is greatly enhanced. Joining comments or questions may include:

- "I noticed the Dolphins sticker on your car, have you been following the team this season?"
- "You were telling me about your date this weekend, what is your favorite food when you eat out?"
- "Like you, I love to cook—I am just not particularly good at cleaning up!"
- "How was your weekend? My weekend was uneventful, as well. I spent a lot of time doing yard work. I find gardening (or any activity you suspect you many have in common with the client) helps me cultivate patience. Who in the family has a green thumb?"

Assessing the Family Structure

An initial task of the family counselor is to gain a sense of how the family is organized and operates. This includes an exploration of relational patterns, overt and covert beliefs, cultural factors, emotional and physical health, and other internal and external influences. Considering a multitude of factors, the counselor can recognize evident strengths and areas of deficiency—which may contribute to the formation, maintenance, and potential amelioration of concerns or presenting issues. This assessment will allow the counselor to conceptualize the repetitive relational patterns within the family, setting the stage for disrupting and changing those patterns. Questions that may be useful to this process include:

- "Who oversees the family? Mom, Dad, or someone else? Has this always been the case?"
- "What strengths do you possess as a couple that has allowed you to stay married for the past 10 years?"
- "If you need something, would it be easier to ask Mom or Dad?"
- "Given the issues with which you are struggling, I'm curious why things aren't worse. How have you managed to keep things together?"
- "Who is the first person to sense tension in the family? How do they let you know this?"

Supporting the Client in Bringing About Desired Change

The task of moving from current patterns of interaction to more functional relationships belongs to the client. However, the counselor plays an active role in helping the client achieve this goal by creating a therapeutic environment that allows the family to recognize dysfunctional patterns—disrupt those patterns and replace them with more functional behaviors. This is accomplished through a variety of therapeutic techniques and intervention strategies, such as in-session conversation, questions of curiosity and provocation, goal clarification, reframing, in-session activities, and between-session assignments (Ibrahim & Schroeder, 1990; Olson, Larson, & Olson-Sigg, 2009; Ruby & Ruby, 2009.) The scope and variety of available therapeutic interventions are essentially unlimited, provided such actions are within acceptable cultural mores and ethical codes and do not cause harm the client.

Terminating and Leaving the Family Empowered

The goal of therapy is to attain desired outcomes as rapidly as possible using the least invasive means available. From the onset of counseling, termination upon accomplishment of goals should be a shared goal of the counselor and client. This might include questions such as:

- "What change would need to take place so that it would no longer be necessary for you to continue counseling?"
- "How will you know when it is time for us to end our work together?"

JAST

google
Read
example

• "If you knew we only had 2 months to work on this problem, how could you best use that time to accomplish your goals?"

In accomplishing these four essential tasks (join, assess, support, and terminate), techniques and intervention strategies that draw from a variety of systemically focused approaches to counseling are often useful when working with clients, regardless of cultural identity. These include engendering hope; sociometric techniques (i.e., genogram, sociogram, family constellation); counselor–researcher posture; defining, redefining, and reframing; exploration of historical attempted solutions; the use of open-ended and circular questions; scaling problem concerns; in-session experiential activities (e.g., sculpting); between-session assignments; and obtaining commitments for change.

Guided Practice Exercise 5.2 will give you an opportunity to conceptualize a client couple from a cybernetics perspective and practice applying the JAST model (see Case Presentation 5.2). After you complete Guided Exercise 5.2 with Case Presentation 5.2, repeat Guided Exercise 5.2 with the client family in Case Presentation 5.3.

GUIDED PRACTICE EXERCISE 5.2

Write a case conceptualization of Shana and Reggie's presenting concerns from an applied cybernetics perspective. What are their presenting concerns? How do you understand their presenting concerns from a systemic perspective? What cultural issues are central to their concerns? What intercultural family counseling techniques do you think would be most effective with them? Describe and discuss (and role play) how you would apply the JAST model in your work with the client couple.

COUNSELOR SELF-AWARENESS

Some researchers suggest that family of origin characteristics are among factors related to effectiveness as counseling professionals (Softas-Nall, Baldo, & Williams, 2001). For example, the level of support from family of origin impacted stress levels during training in one thesis study. Furthermore, some counselor trainees report experiencing changes in family relationships during training (Guy, 1987; Henry, Sims, & Spray, 1973; Owen, 1993; Truell, 2001). Thus, exploration into one's own family and family of origin can provide insights that may be helpful to the counselor-in-training.

While genograms and other sociometric techniques tools (such as family autobiographies) are useful techniques for helping client families identity recursive patterns of functioning, communication, and so on; they may also be useful in helping trainees develop insight into their own family roles.

Development as a counselor involves a process of developing psychological minded-ess. This process includes self-reflection and introspection as a counselor trainee learns rchological theories and gains an increased understanding of a person's development, vior, motivations, and relationships. Especially working with more complex relational

I have this

Constantly
reflective

systems such as a family, trainees are inevitably faced with consideration of their own professional development and personal growth as a human being as it relates to their own family of origin and cultural experiences (Lawson & Gaushell, 1988). To further explore your attitudes and beliefs and continue building cultural awareness, see Guided Practice Exercise 5.3.

GUIDED PRACTICE EXERCISE 5.3

Consider a couple you think you would easily join with and treat. Consider a couple or presenting issue that you would be challenged by. Considering your own cultural self-awareness, explain (and discuss with a partner) why you think you would be natural and challenged by each situation.

as a Christian — easy to join w/ Christian
as a Christian, difficult to join

EMERGING TRENDS

It is widely recognized that effective counseling requires an understanding and sensitivity to cultural differences. Throughout the world, there is an increase in the population percentage residing in urban areas. This trend toward urbanization tends to create a more culturally heterogeneous environment, compared to smaller and more isolated communities that tend to be more culturally homogeneous. There is need to develop and expand various counseling approaches that have broad utility across cultures. Common factors research suggests that, rather than specific theory and technique, it is the helping relationship—in which a counselor conveys genuine caring and investment in the client's welfare—that is most therapeutically impactful. Counseling approaches that utilize the therapeutic relationship within a cultural context appear promising.

ADD to PDP

a strength I have build rapport easily

SUMMARY

Family counselors have a responsibility to develop cultural awareness and competency to serve the diversity of families they are likely to encounter in their work. Culturally competent family counselors can identify and navigate cultural differences between themselves and their clients, as well as assist families with presenting concerns that may include intercultural challenges. Knowledge of every culture is not possible. By exploring personal attitudes and beliefs to develop self-awareness and recognizing when to locate relevant cultural knowledge to better understand client family processes, family counselors can ethically and competently apply the JAST model with the families they serve: (a) joining with the family, (b) assessing the family structure, (c) supporting the client in bringing about desired change, and (d) terminating and leaving the family empowered. The JAST model provides a framework for applying cybernetic principles and intercultural counseling skills and actions with client families. Now that you have a foundational knowledge of the key concepts in family therapy, we will shift our focus to the second section of the book, which is dedicated to research, intake, and assessment. But before you move on, pause to review the keystones.

KEYSTONES

Among the key points addressed in this chapter are:

- Demographics in the United States, along with the structure of U.S. families, are changing.

- Cultural awareness and competency is widely recognized as a fundamental skill for working effectively with client families.

- Even individual counseling is relational in nature. Applied cybernetics posits that a counselor and client (or client family) cocreate a unique therapeutic system to address presenting issues and work toward treatment goals.

- Many theoretical and clinical models (e.g., the RESPECTFUL model) have emerged to provide a framework for identifying cultural aspects of identity that inform the conceptualization and treatment process in counseling.

- In conjunction with the development of intercultural attitudes, beliefs, and knowledge, the JAST model (join, assess, support, and terminate with empowerment) provides a framework for accomplishing four essential tasks in family counseling.

- Exploration into one's own family and family of origin, as well as the exploration of one's own cultural identities, will assist counselors-in-training in developing effective intercultural attitudes and beliefs, as well as self-awareness.

REFLECTIONS FROM THE CONTRIBUTOR'S CHAIR
Lauren A. Shure

I spent part of 2005 working with adults and families in London, England. Even though I had previously completed a multicultural counseling course and worked with a diversity of clients and families as I pursued my master's degree in marriage and family therapy, London was where my learning curve regarding intercultural family counseling became steep. Working as part of the National Health Service serving adult clients and families, I was struck not only by the cultural differences between my client families and myself but also by the cultural differences between my client family members. I worked with families settling in from various countries within Asia, Africa, and beyond. Many of these families struggled raising children who were acculturating to British culture, while their parents often retained the values, beliefs, and worldviews of their home countries. This began a learning process for me that continues to this day and is never ending. Fortunately, I had colleagues who were from Africa, Asia, and beyond as well and could help me conceptualize and develop effective approaches to assist these families in navigating these intercultural challenges. The first step was often normalizing and validating the cultural differences within these multicultural families (join). Next, I would seek to understand the family dynamics that existed in their home countries and how these dynamics shifted after immigrating (assess). Once this was established, I worked to facilitate communication of expectations among family members and encouraged them to negotiate and clarify family roles and responsibilities (support). Lastly, once it was evident positive changes were taking place within the family, I would review that goals and objectives were met, highlight and reinforce the changes and strengths within the family unit, and exit the system (terminate). Case Presentation 5.3 is an amalgamation of some of the common presenting concerns of families I worked with in London. These days I work in Miami, Florida. I continue to work with many intercultural families and have learned to conceptualize all families and counseling relationships as intercultural. As the world becomes smaller through globalization and immigration, intercultural family counseling will become increasingly important and relevant to all family therapists. We offer you this chapter as an introduction to viewing each family and all family therapy relationships as intercultural. We hope you will enjoy this journey and see yourselves in it as both someone who comes from a family and someone who is learning to become an effective intercultural family therapist.

Brian S. Canfield

Having worked for couples and families from various cultures over the past 30 years, what has struck me is the diversity of relationships. Most textbooks on multicultural counseling present chapters that purport to generalize cultural groups—typically with a chapter on working with African American clients, Asian clients, Hispanic clients, and so on. I consider such an approach woefully inadequate for two essential reasons. First, an approach that focuses on the cultural grouping of clients invariably generalizes to a degree that provides little useful insight into various cultural groups and the uniqueness of each client. Conversely, such generalization may be misleading and potential detrimental to the counseling relationship. For example, when referring to the grouping of Hispanic clients—sixth-generation families of Mexican descent living in the Rio Grande valley of Texas are grouped with all other fellow Hispanics—including Puerto Ricans living in New York, affluent Cubans residing in southern Florida, inner-city Chicano gang members in east Los Angeles, Mexicans of Lebanese descent living in the Yucatan, graduate students from South America living in New Orleans, and migrant farmworkers in the Central Valley of California. Aside from perhaps sharing a common use of the Spanish language, these groups may hold very little in common—politically, socially, or economically. Given the existence of hundreds of separate and distinct cultural groups that exist throughout the world, I have found it impossible to gain an in-depth understanding of all cultural groups with whom I may come into contact. I have worked with clients from scores of cultural groups. I recall working with a Cambodian immigrant family. Cambodia is a unique country with a variety of cultural groups. My prior experience in working with Laotian, Thai, Malaysian, and Vietnamese families provided no real insight into the unique cultural aspects of this Cambodian family.

Second, an approach to intercultural counseling that focuses exclusively on client cultural groupings fails to examine the essential relationship that is formed between the counselor and client family. While an understanding of the cultural reference points of the client is important, I have found it to be equally important to routinely check my own cultural reference points.

Part of my job is to bridge the cultural differences that often exist between my client and me. I have found that this is best accomplished by showing genuine respect for my client and conveying a desire to be of help.

ADDITIONAL RESOURCES

The following resources provide additional information relating to the chapter topics.

Useful Websites

- American Association for Marriage and Family Therapy—www.aamft.org
- American Counseling Association—www.counseling.org
- American Mental Health Counselors Association—www.amhca.org
- Association for Counselor Education and Supervision—www.acesonlinenet
- Association for Lesbian, Gay, Bi-sexual & Transgender Issues in Counseling—www.algbtic.org
- Association for Multicultural Counseling and Development—www.multiculturalcounseling.org
- Association for Spiritual, Ethical, and Religious Values in Counseling—www.aservic.org
- International Association of Marriage and Family Counselors—www.iamfconline.org

The sources above are professional counseling association sites and offer information on multicultural counseling from numerous perspectives.

- Center for Multicultural Mental Health Research—www.multiculturalmentalhealth.org
- Center for Multilingual Multicultural Research—www.bcf.usc.edu
- Consortium for Multicultural Psychology Research—www.psychology.msu.edu/cmpr

The sources above offer current research information on topics related to multiculturalism.

- Ecohealth—www.springerlink.com

This site offers numerous books on the topic of multiculturalism.

- Improving Intercultural Competence: School Counselors in Increasingly Multicultural Schools: https://www.schoolcounselor.org/school-counselors-members/professional-development/site-based-training/improving-intercultural-competence

This site offers information for school counselors, including training and competence.

- Multicultural Parenting Resources: http://www.csun.edu/~vcpsy00h/parenthood/culture.htm
- The Multicultural Family Institute: http://multiculturalfamily.org/

The sites above offer information for parents and families.

- *The World Factbook*—www.cia.gov/library/publications/the-world-factbook
- United Nations Data—www.data.un.org
- U.S. Department of Health and Human Services—www.ncadi.samhsa.gov

The sites above offer facts and resources so counselors have accurate multicultural data.

READINGS

Family Therapy: Diverse Families—What Do Today's Families Look Like?

http://www.aamft.org/iMIS15/magazine/MarchApril2014/fscommand/SinglePageMA14.pdf

This reading offers information about family diversity from the American Association of Marital and Family Therapists.

Use of the Multicultural Genogram

http://www.healthalt.org/uploads/2/3/7/5/23750643/cultural_genogram_2.pdf

This reading illustrates how genograms may be used to assist diverse families.

Using Family Culture to Illustrate the Basics of Intercultural Interaction: An Exercise to Teach the Problems and Potential of Cross-Cultural Interaction

http://www.uwosh.edu/hst/?p=499

This reading discusses information to guide counselors with intercultural interactions.

VIDEOS

Intercultural Couples Talk About Their Relationships

https://www.youtube.com/watch?v=PzvLYhbBlYo

Reenee Singh on Intercultural Relationships

https://www.youtube.com/watch?v=h373itL6Y7w

Report on Pew Research Study on Intercultural Marriages

https://www.youtube.com/watch?v=LzAwlCSCo7s

The videos above offer current data and insight on intercultural marriages and relationships.

REFERENCES

American Counseling Association. (2014). *Code of ethics and standards of practice*. Alexandria, VA: Author.

Becvar, R., Canfield, B.., & Becvar, D. (1997). *Group work: Cybernetic, constructivist, and social constructionist perspectives*. Denver, CO: Love.

Bitter, J. R. (2009). *Theory and practice of family therapy and counseling*. Belmont, CA: Brooks/.

Canfield, B. (2007). The dyadic complexity formula. *Family Journal, 15*(2), 116–118.

Canino, I. A., & Inclan, J. E. (2001). Culture and family therapy. *Child and Adolescent Psychiatric Clinics of North America, 10*(3), 601–612.

Cole, E. M., Piercy, F., Wolfe, E. W., & West, J. M. (2014). Development of the multicultural therapy competency inventory—client version. *Contemporary Family Therapy, 36*, 462–473.

Council for Accreditation of Counseling and Related Educational Programs. (2016) Retrieved from http://www.cacrep.org/for-programs/2016-cacrep-standards/

D'Andrea, M., & Daniels, J. (1997). RESPECTFUL counseling: A new way of thinking about diversity counseling. *Counseling Today, 40*(6), 30, 31, 34.

D'Andrea, M., & Daniels, J. (2001). RESPECTFUL counseling: An integrative model for counselors. In D. Pope-Davis & H. Coleman (Eds.), *The interface of class, culture and gender in counseling* (pp. 417–466). Thousand Oaks, CA: Sage.

Duncan, B., Miller, S., & Sparks, J. (2004). *The heroic client: A revolutionary way to improve effectiveness through client directed outcome informed therapy* (Rev. ed.). San Francisco: Jossey-Bass.

Duncan, B., Miller, S., Sparks, J., Claud, D., Reynolds, L., Brown, J., & Johnson, L. (2003). The Session Rating Scale: Preliminary psychometric properties of a "working" alliance measure. *Journal of Brief Therapy, 3*, 3–12.

Duncan, B., Miller, S., Wampold, B. E., & Hubble, M. A. (2009). Heart and soul of change: Delivering what works in therapy (2nd ed.). Washington, DC: American Psychological Association.

Esses, V. M., Deaux, K., Lalonde, R. N., & Brown, R. (2010). Psychological perspectives on immigration. *Journal of Social Issues, 66*(4), 635–647.

Fortuna, L. R., & Porche, M. V. (2013, August 15). Clinical issues and challenges in treating undocumented immigrants. *Psychiatric Times*. Retrieved from http://www.psychiatrictimes.com/special-reports/clinical-issues-and-challenges-treating-undocumented-immigrants

Ibrahim, F. A., & Schroeder, D. O. (1990). Cross-cultural couples counseling: A developmental, psychoeducational intervention. *Journal of Comparative Family Studies, 21*(2), 193–205.

Lee. R. M., Su, J., & Yoshida, E. (2005). Coping with intergenerational family conflict among Asian American college students. *Journal of Counseling Psychology, 52*(3), 389–399. doi:10.1037/0022-0167.52.3.389

Leong, F., Park, Y. S., & Kalibatseva, Z. (2013). Disentangling immigrant status in mental health: Psychological protective and risk factors among Latino and Asian American immigrants. *American Journal of Orthopsychiatry, 83*(2–3), 361–371.

McGoldrick, M., & Hardy, K. V. (2008.) *Re-visioning family therapy: Race, culture, and gender in clinical practice* (2nd ed.). New York: Guilford.

Olson, D. H., Larson, P. J., & Olson-Sigg, A. (2009). Couple checkup: Tuning up relationships. *Journal of Couple & Relationship Therapy: Innovations in Clinical and Educational Interventions*, 8(2), 129–142.

Orlinsky, D. E., Rønnestad, M. H., & Willutzki, U. (2004). Fifty years of process-outcome research: Continuity and change. In M. J. Lambert (Ed.), *Bergin and Garfield's handbook of psychotherapy and behavior change* (5th ed., pp. 307–390). New York: Wiley.

Ratts, M., Singh, A., Nassar-McMillan, S., McCullough, J. R., & Butler, S. K. (2016). Multicultural and social justice counseling competencies: Guidelines for the counseling profession. *Journal of Multicultural Counseling & Development, 44*, 28–48.

Ruby, J. R., & Ruby, N. C. (2009). Improvisational acting exercises and their potential use in family counseling. *Journal of Creativity in Mental Health*, 4(2), 152–160. doi:10.1080/15401380902951945

Wampold, B. E. (2001). *The great psychotherapy debate: Models, methods, and findings*. Mahwah, NJ: Erlbaum.

Wampold, B. E., Mondin, G. W., Moody, M., Stich, F., Benson, K., & Hyun-nie, A. (1997). A meta-analysis of outcome studies comparing bona fide psychotherapies: Empirically, "all must have prizes." *Psychological Bulletin, 122*, 203–215.

Yakushko, O., & Chronister, K. M. (2005). Immigrant women and counseling: The invisible others. *Journal of Counseling and Development, 83*, 292–298.

PART II

Research, Intake, and Assessment

Couple and Family Therapy Research: Evaluating Therapy and Practice Implications

Brandé Flamez, Cheryl Mark, Torey Portrie-Bethke,
Brooks Hanks, and Janet Froeschle Hicks

*"I think that the thing I most want you to remember is that
research is a ceremony. And so is life. Everything that we
do shares in the ongoing creation of our universe."*

—Shawn Wilson

New family therapists often ponder the necessity for reading and conducting research. Shawn Wilson's statement above made us stop and remember that research is necessary to improve services and keep our profession's credibility intact. It is also a candid reminder that research and life are intertwined, just as counseling and our existence parallel one another. We hope this chapter inspires you to conduct and read research that leads to efficacious outcomes for your future clients.

Couple and family therapy is a blend of clinical practice and research, yet a gap exists between the efficacy and the effectiveness of couple and family therapy. We must close this gap, also referred to as the "scientist–practitioner gap," if change is to occur in couples and families (Halford et al., 2015; Pinsof, Goldsmith, & Latta, 2012; Sexton & Datchi, 2014). The scientist–practitioner gap is reportedly due to the challenges of research, following manuals, and the lengthy process between data collection, analysis, and the actual implementation of evidence-based practices in the counseling office (Pinsof et al., 2012). It is important to note that research does not limit clinical work; instead, it provides practitioners with efficacious choices for treatment when examining couple and family relationships; offers clients' readiness to change; screens for individual psychopathology; and assesses feedback from clients (Sexton & Datchi, 2014). To contribute to the sustainability of marriage, couple, and family therapy research, we must participate in research endeavors, specifically understanding the variables that affect change. According to Lebow (2016), the blending of research and practice advances our profession.

In approaching challenging family and couple sessions, we should not fear loss of creativity through research, because research offers reassurance and competence when working with life-threatening problems such as substance abuse, domestic violence, anorexia nervosa, and suicidal ideations. According to Hatchett (2017), the development and use of evidence-based treatments is an important standard family therapists must meet.

LEARNING OBJECTIVES

After reading this chapter, you will be able to do the following:

- Understand the history and background of couple and family counseling research.
- Explain the role of therapists in couple and family therapy research.
- Understand the role of research in effective family therapy.
- Identify various research methods in family therapy.
- Understand the efficacy and evidence-based evaluation of couple and family therapy for a variety of problems.

KEY CONCEPTS

In this chapter, we address couple and family research and provide information on many conditions that drive couples and families to seek therapy. These conditions include issues such as relational concerns, mental health problems, substance use, process addictions, behavioral problems, and medical problems. In addition, we discuss the efficacy of couple and family therapy, consider the role of ethics and culture, and look at the future of our practice.

Before we dive into the history and role of research in our profession, let's turn to Guided Practice Exercise 6.1. In this exercise, you are asked to contemplate ways to bring research into practice to help Mr. and Mrs. Wu.

HISTORY AND BACKGROUND

Background

Marriage, couple, and family therapy is a blanket term covering over 20 systemic therapies (Tan, 2011); thus, many contributors shaped the field through varied approaches. Sexton et al. (2011) support finding commonalities in treatment models and principles to assist therapists' use of effective interventions, thereby strengthening the field of couple and family counseling. Since no two families are alike, creative integration of treatment approaches, such as those mentioned later in Chapter 17, have been beneficial for meeting clients' needs. In addition, a family therapist's personal worldview and family therapy model of choice must be congruent for effective therapeutic outcomes (Carr, 2013). Let's turn our attention to Guided Practice Exercise 6.2, in which we consider how worldview can impact our work with families.

Samuel Gladding, a pioneer of creativity in the counseling profession, stated that "counseling is evidence based" (as cited in Donovan & Weigel, 2015, p. 205), and when proven theories and techniques aren't working in session, new counselors can try creative, innovative strategies. To understand what works in the therapy session and with whom, examining couple and family clinical interventions and outcomes is necessary. Fortunately, previous research by Carr (2016) inferred that two out of three couples that receive couples therapy benefit from treatment. Although the remaining third do not report any benefit from therapy, relationship distress is important to address, as it is inferred to impact mental health (Moore & Crane, 2014).

The research base will improve if current and future couple and family therapy models demonstrate how the change process works, followed by outcomes, which point to the change process itself, and how the therapeutic service is delivered (Lebow et al., 2014). Even research studying clients with ineffective outcomes may offer insight into reasons this occurs. For example, clients reporting little therapeutic progress may be impacted by issues such as limited therapist training.

Interestingly, little formal training is offered for therapists who desire to conduct couples therapy beyond that found in marriage and family therapy degree programs. Despite this, 70% of mental health care professionals reported they provide couples therapy (Lebow et al., 2012; Snyder & Halford, 2012). Consequently, the enhancement and promotion of our profession requires maintaining and developing high standards of training and education for marriage and family therapists (West, Hinton, Grames, & Adams, 2013).

Policy and Funding for Couple and Family Therapy

In the past, U.S. government large-scale research funding for mental health was limited to diagnoses found within the *DSM-IV* (American Psychiatric Association, 1994), where diagnoses were individual problems and marital distress was not classified as a disorder (Lebow et al., 2012). Today marital distress is still not categorized as a disorder, but in the updated *DSM-5* (American Psychiatric Association, 2013) the T and Z codes provide support for treatment. According to Carr (2014b), systemic therapists prefer to view problems through a systemic lens rather than through the common individual pathological approach as used in the DSM-5.

It remains to be seen if government funding of couple and family therapy research will expand. Family therapy may save taxpayer funds since it is cost-effective when compared to individual therapy (Carr, 2016; Sexton & Datchi, 2014). Further, the research indicates that many individual problems and relational concerns benefit from couples therapy (Snyder & Haford, 2012). Let's look at Guided Practice Exercise 6.3, in which we consider couples therapy and research from Germany's perspective and how that may or may not apply in the United States.

GUIDED PRACTICE EXERCISE 6.3

In Germany, cognitive behavioral therapy is paid for by the German national health care system; however, German citizens do not have access to systemic therapy (Lebow, 2013b). Have you thought about evidence-based practice as contributing to positive social change in your country? Without evidence-based practices marriage, couple, and family therapy will not join the lists of accepted treatments for insurance reimbursement. Conducting research will build empirical support for marriage, couple, and family therapy, providing greater access to members of society.

To understand the history of evidence-based treatment interventions in the mental health field, couple and family research must be juxtaposed with managed health care, policies for funding research, and whether all of what transpires in the therapy room is conducive to experimental research (Tanenbaum, 2015). Although controversy exists over evidence-based practices in the mental health field, couple and family therapists actively contribute to the scientific evaluation of therapeutic interventions to improve on evidence based practices. Let us examine the origins of family therapy research.

Family therapy research was initially influenced by psychologists who, by following a medical model of treatment, borrowed from the field of medicine and conducted random clinical trials, thereby establishing evidence-based practices in the mental health care field (Strong & Busch, 2013). Since this origin, couple and family therapy evolved from providing non-research-based practical couples therapy to a profession participating in the scientific evaluative process of therapeutic interventions and outcomes. This research resulted in evidence-based practices (Gurman & Fraenkel, 2002; as cited in Lebow et al., 2012), resulting in contributions to clinical practice, and offered evidence supporting the value of family therapy as a unique specialty (Lebow et al., 2014). Guided Practice Exercise 6.4 asks you to examine how research has influenced the therapist–client alliance.

GUIDED PRACTICE EXERCISE 6.4

Research has been influential in determining the importance the counseling alliance has on the success or failure of therapy (Norcross & Wampold, 2011). If research had not revealed this importance, how would family therapy be different today? How would this have held back the profession? What other areas has research changed family therapy over time?

Effectiveness of Couple and Family Research

Following a review of the literature, we found that most couples respond positively to therapy; however, 25% to 35% do not respond positively (Carr, 2013; Lebow et al., 2012). In addition, Gurman (2011) found that only two couples therapies have been tested with random clinical trials: behavioral couples therapy and emotion-focused therapy; however, there is not much difference among the different models of treatment and therapeutic outcomes. Still, research has not answered the important question, how does it work (Gurman, 2011)? Tan (2011) also found that behavioral couple therapy and emotion-focused therapy have the most support for their effectiveness. Integrative behavioral couple therapy was found to have better outcomes than traditional behavioral couple therapy, and nearly half of surveyed counselors reported having an eclectic theoretical orientation, pointing toward increases in integrative therapy in the future (Tan, 2011).

The therapeutic alliance is significant when discussing marriage and family therapy outcomes and effectiveness. In fact, its strength is indicative of treatment success or failure (Norcross & Wampold, 2011). It is no surprise, then, that all evidence-based couple therapies include five common alliance-based processes to assist clients that are not utilized in individual therapy. These consist of viewing the relationship with objectivity, not blaming; decreasing dysfunctional and dysregulated emotional behavior; promoting shared emotions and expressions of vulnerability; improving communication; and building on relationship strengths and resilience (Snyder & Halford, 2012).

Specific Treatment Model Research Outcomes

According to Sevier, Atkins, Doss, and Christensen (2015), research on how change takes place in therapy is necessary to link clinical work and has been slow to develop. Even though much research supports psychotherapy, there is still a gap in the literature and therefore a lack of understanding in how to apply theory and interventions in clinical process sessions (Greenman & Johnson, 2013). Science has guided the couple and family therapy movement, positioning "emotion-focused, cognitive-behavioral, and integrative behavioral couple therapy" (Lebow, 2013 p. 3) as three evidence-based theories with the most support. Through a review of the literature, including articles in the *Family Journal*, *Couple and Family Psychology: Research and Practice Journal*, *Journal of Consulting and Clinical Psychology*, *Journal of Family Therapy*, *Journal of Marriage and Family Therapy*, and *Family Process*, the current research supports the following treatment models for marriage, couple, and family therapy.

Behavioral Couple Therapy (BCT) or Traditional Behavioral Couple Therapy (TBCT)
BCT is reported to be one of the top two empirically supported models for couple therapy and it is used by 80% of couple therapists (Gurman, 2013).

Clients who do not respond to TBCT show a slow decline in constructive behaviors and an increase in negativity at the end of therapy as the most challenging issues are discussed toward the end of treatment (Sevier et al., 2015).

Research inferred that 5 years after therapy, couples experiencing infidelity had twice the divorce rate as other couples. However, couples receiving either TBCT or integrative behavioral couple therapy demonstrated no significant differences when comparing infidelity between the two groups.

Brief Strategic Family Therapy (BSFT)
BSFT is an evidence-based model of treatment, effective for substance abuse problems, as well as behavioral problems in adolescents and children (Merritts, 2016).

Cognitive Behavioral Couple Therapy (CBCT)
When couples have negative attributions and inaccurate expectations, CBCT leads to positive changes (Carr, 2013).

Emotion-Focused Couple Therapy (EFCT)

EFCT is reported to be one of the top two "empirically supported" (Johnson, 2008; as cited in Gruman, 2013, p. 124) therapies for couples.

When couples participated in EFCT, increases in expression of attachment-based needs and reduced belligerent behavior were evidenced (Carr, 2013).

Researchers inferred when there is emotional injury in couples' relationships, promoting vulnerable self-disclosures of emotions between partners contributes to healing emotional wounds providing a rationale for utilizing these disclosures in therapy (McKinnon & Greenberg, 2013).

Insight-Oriented Couple Therapy (IOCT)

Four years after completing therapy, a comparison between couples receiving IOCT and BCT showed that 38% of couples that received BCT divorced, compared to 3% of couples who received IOCT (Snyder & Halford, 2012).

Integrative Behavioral Couple Therapy (IBCT)

Early in therapy, clients focus on the most problematic challenges, and those who were nonresponsive during therapy gradually decreased their negativity over time in treatment (Sevier et al., 2015).

IBCT was found to increase tolerance of a partner's negative behaviors (Carr, 2013).

Integrated Systemic Couple Therapy (ISCT)

Integrated systemic couple therapy interrupted negative, repetitive cycles of interaction by reframing problems and assigning new meaning to cycles. At a 4-month follow-up, couples who received ISCT instead of EFCT were found to have maintained positive gains (Snyder & Halford, 2012).

For a detailed explanation of BCT, CBCT, and IBCT, please see Chapter 13. Chapter 14 provides information on solution-focused brief therapy, Chapter 15 provides an overview of narrative therapy, and Chapter 17 provides a description of IBCT and a discussion on integrative models in couple therapy.

General Findings of Marriage, Couple, and Family Research

Couple and family therapy both operate from a system's perspective, and couples function as a subsystem of the family, having separate concerns such as infidelity, separation, sexual concerns, or divorce (Lebow, 2013). Research studies provide information supporting the use of random clinical trials in marriage, couple, and family therapy models and in assessment instruments. The research provided information on which conditions benefited from couple and family therapy, the therapeutic alliance, the presenting problem, deterioration following treatment, monitoring progress and feedback, alignment of worldviews, and the benefit of these therapies for individual and relational concerns. The following research findings are indicative of the support in the literature for couple and family therapy:

Following a review of the couple and family therapy scientific evidence in 2012, couple and family therapy was found to be the "treatment of choice" for numerous relational challenges, problems with children, and adult related concerns (Carr, 2013).

Marriage and family therapy clients report the alliance with the therapist and family members is critical to resolving problems, and clients valued collaborative goal setting and the ability to provide feedback to their therapist about what is and isn't helpful (Carr, 2013).

A counselor's personal worldview and model of therapy alignment as well as the client's worldview and alignment with the model contribute to a positive therapeutic outcome (Carr, 2013).

Following an evaluation of five couple treatment models, 45% of couples with initial successful therapy outcomes experienced deterioration 2 years after treatment (Snyder & Halford, 2012).

Couple and family therapy is beneficial for addressing relationship distress as well as individual concerns including medical and psychological disorders (Carr, 2014).

Monitoring client progress improves treatment outcomes, and couples who do not benefit from therapy are identifiable because they demonstrate a lack of progress early in treatment (Pepping, Halford, & Doss, 2015).

Monitoring feedback may be a promising strategy to enhance therapy outcomes for couples (Pepping et al., 2015; Snyder & Halford, 2012).

Couples in agreement concerning the presenting problem in therapy are more likely to complete treatment and benefit from therapy, especially when treatment is brief and problem focused (Biesen & Doss, 2013).

Family Therapy for Major Mental Illness

Early in the 21st century, the U.S. Department of Health and Human Services recommended that treatment of severe mental illness adopt a nonpathologizing, "recovery orientation" (Gehart, 2012, p. 429) model of care. The research provides evidence that families contribute to the recovery process of those with a major mental illness by giving their support, providing information that is beneficial in assessment, and participating in follow-up care (Chambless, 2012; Gehart, 2012). Adoption of a non-pathologizing recovery model of care has evolved parallel to valuing and developing evidence-based treatments for severe mental illness that promote dignity, establish independence, resilience, and acknowledge the needs of the whole person (Gerhart, 2012).

Recent research in the field of neuroscience has shed light on the decades old nature versus nurture argument (Patterson & Vakili, 2013). Today we understand that the family is the setting where genes, environment, and biology intersect (Patterson & Vakili, 2013). In addition, families are where developing brains form relationships and attachment connections that shape an individual's relational template, forming negative or positive beliefs about self and other. When these environmental influences go awry during influential developmental periods in early life, individual biology combined with stressors leaves some individuals with mental health vulnerabilities, some contributing to major mental illness (Patterson & Vakili, 2013). Healing and finding recovery from mental health problems within the context of a family acknowledges the power of relationships, either detrimental or positive in the lives of both the mentally healthy and the mentally ill.

In addition, research supports family therapy as an effective treatment for a large spectrum of mental illnesses and is reported to be as effective as the use of medicine and surgery are for medical treatment (Carr, 2010). For example, family therapy is beneficial in the treatment of schizophrenia, a condition found in less than one percent of the population (Carr, 2014a). Medication is the primary treatment modality; however, family therapy is beneficial in relieving stress, which is detrimental to the disease process (Carr, 2014a). Many other disorders such as anxiety and depression also show promise when using family therapy. Guided Practice Exercise 6.5 asks you to discuss issues related to family therapy when mental illness is a component.

GUIDED PRACTICE EXERCISE 6.5

How might you encourage family members to come to a family session to support a mentally ill family member? Think through how you might discuss treatment in a way that promotes the dignity of the diagnosed client. What do you know from the research that would support your request?

Family Therapy for Depression

Hollon and Sexton (2012) referred to depression as "a major public health problem that clearly runs in families" (p. 199). Family therapy is therefore considered best practice when an adult member of a family is experiencing a depressive episode (Macfarlane, 2011). According to Sexton et al. (2011), if a person's symptoms are treated without consideration for the context in which they take place, there is a greater chance of symptom relapse. In addition, antidepressants are helpful in reducing symptoms, but they do not address underlying family concerns that may be the impetus for the depression as would occur in family therapy (Hollon & Sexton, 2012). According to Carr (2016), two randomized controlled studies found family therapy was more beneficial than individual therapy for adolescents with anorexia nervosa and was also more effective than antidepressant medication for chronically depressed adults at a 2-year follow-up.

Family Risk Factors for Depression

According to Patterson and Vakili (2013), individuals who experience chronic stress early in life and negative events in childhood are susceptible to mental illness. Researchers, applying the theory of neurosensitization, assume that brains become "sensitized or "kindled" (Patterson & Vakili, 2013, p. 28) to being depressed, creating vulnerabilities to mental illness. Additional risk factors for depression and anxiety include having a parent who suffers from a mental health disorder (Winter, Morawska, & Sanders, 2012). According to Hollon and Sexton (2012), children who live with a depressed parent are four times more likely to experience a mental health disorder, with a high risk for depression.

Family-Based Treatment for Anxiety

The following three "debilitating anxiety disorders: agoraphobia with panic disorder, obsessive-compulsive disorder (OCD) and post-traumatic stress disorder (PTSD)" (Carr, 2014a, p. 168) benefited from family therapy. Medication, specifically serotonin reuptake inhibitors, provided benefit for some; however, once medication was stopped, there was the potential for relapse (Carr, 2014a). In addition, Carr (2014a) found that some individuals cannot tolerate the negative side effects of medications. A systemic approach is, therefore, beneficial in treatment and includes engaging in therapeutic work to understand the underlying beliefs that drive anxiety (Carr, 2014a).

Panic Disorder, Agoraphobia, OCD, and PTSD

Families who have a member suffering from panic disorder and agoraphobia may contribute to the "restricted lifestyle" (Carr, 2014a, p. 169) of the diagnosed family member by helping the family member avoid anxiety producing situations which trigger panic attacks. Systemic therapy interrupts this negative relational dynamic. The research supports couple therapy, contributing to between 54% and 86% reductions in both agoraphobia and symptoms of panic disorder (Carr, 2014a). OCD, utilizing obsessive thoughts and rituals to temporarily reduce anxiety, also involves family members who inadvertently participate in ritualistic behaviors to avoid conflict (Carr, 2014a). Family therapy was found to be more effective in treating OCD than individual cognitive behavioral therapy (Carr, 2014a).

EFCT was reported to be a successful treatment for PTSD, reducing symptoms that resulted from childhood sexual abuse and military combat (Carr, 2014a). Cognitive behavioral therapy is also an efficacious treatment modality for anxiety disorders, and when combined with attachment-based family therapy leads to symptom reduction (Sprenkle, 2012). For successful treatment of anxiety disorders, both systemic therapy and medication may be necessary to alleviate symptoms.

Family-Based Treatment for Child and Adolescent Behavioral Problems

Family therapy is reported to be an evidence-based treatment model for child-focused problems (Carr, 2014a), and it is a beneficial model for working with troubled adolescents (Sexton & Datchi, 2014). According to L'Abate (2015), the most common presenting problems triggering a child's referral into therapy are the following behavioral problems: lying, temper tantrums, and sibling-rivalry. L'Abate (2015) found that once a child came in for play therapy, the child became the problem or "identified patient" (p. 180), so he realigned his work, adopting a more inclusive family systems approach. Children's problems may begin in infancy with temporary eating and sleeping problems, or there may be attachment-based problems with parents, which can lead to adjustment difficulties and serious psychological problems reaching into adulthood (Carr, 2014a). Other serious problems studied by researchers include conditions of neglect, physical abuse, and sexual abuse.

Family therapy has shown promise in treating behavioral problems in children and adolescents. Contextual problems, such as poor parenting practices, are addressed during behavioral parenting education sessions and research findings infer a positive effect on 60% to 70% of children (Carr, 2014b). Programs where fathers were involved contributed to even greater reductions of problematic behaviors (Carr, 2014b; Winter et al., 2012).

Additional problems frequently found with adolescents include: substance abuse, emotional problems, self-harming behaviors, OCD, depression, suicidality, grief, bipolar disorder, eating disorders, and other somatic and medical problems (Carr, 2014b). There is also a dearth of research on effective systemic interventions for neglect, abuse, and emotional problems in adolescents (Carr, 2014b, p. 139). What is known is that multisystemic family therapy is a beneficial treatment approach in working with adolescents who have severe emotional, psychological, and behavioral problems.

Family Therapy for Substance Use

According to the Center for Behavioral Health Statistics and Quality, an estimated 27.1 million people aged 12 or older in the United States were self-identified as current illicit drug users in 2015 (Center for Behavioral Health Statistics and Quality [CBHSQ], 2016). Approximately 1 in 10 individuals aged 12 or older used illicit drugs in 2015. During that same year, an estimated 8.8 percent of adolescents aged 12–17 were identified as having used illicit drugs. Substance use is therefore a prevalent issue impacting the family system within the United States. Goorden et al. (2016) found family therapy to be promising for treating substance use issues in adolescents. Carr (2014a) found evidence for the effectiveness of couple and family therapy for adults with substance use disorder, which affects interpersonal violence. A more recent review of the literature characterizes family therapy as being commonly accepted as one of the most effective treatment approaches with this population (Rowe, 2012). Since drug use and family relations are clearly connected, family involvement in the treatment process is imperative (Rowe, 2012).

Family Risk Factors for Substance Use

It has been widely accepted that substance use has both a genetic and environmental link (Palmer et al., 2015). Therefore, it is important to address substance use within a family context. Some environmental risk factors of substance use in relation to family functioning includes but is not limited to strained family relationships, parenting deficits, parent substance use history, parental mental health status, and relational distance (Ewing et al., 2015; Horigian et al., 2015; Rowe, 2012). Conversely, positive family relations, intact nuclear family or two-parent households, and valuing family needs over individual needs have been identified as potential protective factors for substance use (Ewing et al., 2015).

Family-Based Interventions for Adolescent Substance Use

A review of current research shows overwhelming support for family involvement in the prevention of adolescent substance use and the treatment of adolescents with substance use problems (Dixon et al., 2001; Ewing et al., 2015; Kuntsche & Kuntsche, 2016; Van Ryzin, Roseth, Fosco, Lee, & Chen, 2016). Due to the legal status of adolescents, the involvement of parents is imperative to the successful treatment of an adolescent struggling with substance use. Family-based interventions may include psychoeducation (Dixon, et al., 2001), family therapy, and family group therapy. Kuntsche and Kuntsche (2016) found that successful family-based treatment programs focus on improving parent–child communication, helping families establish more strict and consistent boundary setting against underage substance use, and assisting parents in more actively monitoring activities of the adolescent when not in the direct care of parents. Further, Van Ryzin et al. (2016) found youth-focused components, such as family relations and the adolescent's orientation to the future to be key components of successful family-based treatment programs.

Family-Based Interventions for Adult Substance Use

Many similarities exist between adolescent and adult substance use treatment. Family-based interventions for adults have also been found to be effective and supported within the research (Holland et al., 2016; Fals-Stewart, Lam, & Kelley, 2009). One significant difference between adolescent treatment and adult substance use treatment is the use of couples therapy. Fals-Stewart and colleagues asserted strong empirical support that BCT specifically is among the most effective treatment methodologies for adults with substance use problems. Further, they found that BCT participants had fewer relapses, fewer criminal charges, a decrease in intimate partner violence, and fewer substance related hospitalizations than those in the study receiving individual-based treatment (Fals-Stewart, Lam, & Kelley, 2009). Rowe (2012) stated that the involvement of family members is an important factor in getting adults with substance use problems to engage in and continue the treatment process. A review of the research literature indicated a reduction in substance use, intimate partner violence, an improvement of family and couple relationships, and improved child functioning when family-based interventions were utilized during adult substance use treatment (Rowe, 2012).

Family Therapy for Eating Disorders

Family therapy has been a proven treatment method and a crucial element for treating clients diagnosed with eating disorders (Dodge, 2016). For children and adolescents' experiencing disordered eating patterns, family therapy provides a means for enhancing the emotional connection and development of healthy parental attachments. A fundamental factor maintaining eating disorders is the clients' or families' emotional dysregulation and inability to potentially identify and communicate affective experiences resulting in emotional processing deficits (Robinson, Dolhanty, & Greenberg, 2013; Becker-Stoll & Gerlinghoff, 2004; Bydlowski et al., 2005). To best understand the family system and the dynamics in place to control affect, the family system is involved in the treatment process. The family may comprise biological parents, stepparents, grandparents, siblings, or other supports the client deems as important figures in his or her life. No single person is responsible for a child, adolescent, or person's eating disorder, and rejecting past widely held beliefs that the family or parent is to blame for the child's behaviors creates a working dynamic between the family therapist and family. This working alliance allows for a blame-free environment conducive to addressing the complexities of the illness and the challenges within the family dynamics.

Family Risk Factors for Eating Disorders

Research and clinical experience evaluating eating disorders and characteristics of family dynamics concluded that diverse characteristics, various parenting styles, and varying family backgrounds have been identified as factors contributing to the disorder (Lyke & Matsen, 2013). Therefore, not one person, dynamic, or characteristic is to blame for the manifestation of the eating disorder, and multiple contributing factors need to be examined. Lyke and Matsen (2013) postulated that specific family dysfunction is directly related to eating disorder behaviors and the family's operational process may be examined to identify the factors inherently impacting overall family wellness.

Disordered eating behaviors are generally seen in families with dysfunctional and unhealthy patterns of interacting and coping (Lyke & Matsen, 2013). Several risk factors for disordered eating were identified by Slade and Dewey (1986) through the SCANS: A screening instrument for identifying individuals at risk of developing anorexia or bulimia nervosa. The five risk factors identified for developing disordered eating were personal and social anxiety, general life dissatisfaction, weight control, adolescent identity issues, and perfectionism. Understanding and overcoming risk factors is crucial in family therapy; therefore, many therapists work from a strengths-based perspective addressing protective factors as a balancing component for disordered eating risks.

Langdon-Daly and Serpell (2017) conducted a systematic review of the literature resulting in 25 research studies based on factors influencing eating disorders. These studies identified family system protective factors guarding against the development of disordered eating and included family relationships, communication satisfaction, and resiliency (Langdon-Daly & Serpell, 2017). Other crucial events reducing disordered eating are family meals centering on healthy family interactions. These meals focus on family relationships rather than negative discussions of weight, issues with food, or other distressing family dynamics.

EFFICACY OF MARRIAGE AND COUPLES THERAPY

According to Snyder and Halford (2012), intimate partner relationships are supportive and act as a buffer for life's stressors. Only a quarter of couples experiencing difficulties seek out professional help for their relationships (Doss, Simpson, & Christensen, 2004), and according to Gottman (1999; as cited in Gutierrez, Carlson, Daire, & Young, 2017), most couples wait about 6 years before seeking help. Researchers discovered communication problems and emotional distance are two of the common reasons couples sought out therapy; however, what a couple does not disclose as problematic is also important to assess and understand so that treatment aligns with clients' expectations and needs (Doss et al., 2004). For this reason and due to loss of neutrality, potential transference, and countertransference issues, couple therapy is one of the most challenging types of therapy (Wolska, 2011). Because of the challenges of working with couples and families, which includes individual problems within the dyad as well as couple distress, counselors must be prepared with interventions that work.

Studies in the efficacy of counseling outcomes for relationships found that many couples (39% to 55%) made improvements in their relational functioning after therapy; however, 8% to 20% of couples deteriorated after treatment with a subsequent divorce rate of 3% to 38% (Biesen & Doss, 2013, p. 658). Other researchers found significant improvements between 17% and 40% with only 2% to 3 % of couples' relationships deteriorating after treatment (Biesen & Doss, 2013, p. 658). Several factors are inferred as relating to improving family outcomes. For example, researchers reported when couples agreed on the presenting problem, the treatment was shorter, couples were less likely to terminate before completion, and they benefited from therapy (Biesen & Doss, 2013). In the following section as well as in Chapters 7 and 8, we will explore in more detail how assessment also plays a role in effective couple therapy.

Assessment

Assessment was found to increase positive couple and family therapy outcomes (Snyder & Halford, 2012). For example, assessments assist clinicians in providing effective couple interventions by screening for relationship satisfaction and distress. This is especially beneficial for couples where one partner has a serious medical problem or a psychological disorder (Snyder & Halford, 2012). Since 30% of families end therapy after just three sessions, consistent monitoring of clients' shared hopes, goals, and motivation for change is necessary and contributes to a strong therapeutic alliance throughout the therapeutic process (Jurek, Janusz, Chwal, & de Barbaro, 2014).

Therapists should assess this risk of drop out by considering the following during couple counseling: therapy attendance on wife's insistence, indifference toward therapy, pessimistic attitude toward therapy, lack of belief or trust in the therapy process, a lack of bonding between partners, and pressure from one partner to discontinue therapy (Chwal et al., 2014). Positive factors to assess include: hope in therapeutic process, willingness to change, and perceiving the therapy process as able to restore the relationship (Chwal et al., 2014). Additional therapist assessment skills include the ability to assess turning points in the therapeutic process, clients' lack of accommodation to suggestions, and the ability to positively embrace and utilize emotions benefiting the therapeutic process (Chwal et al., 2014).

THE BASICS OF RESEARCH

This chapter discussed several studies implying the efficacy of couple and family therapy. How does this research occur? What types of research are used? The following section discusses a few of these methods.

As you think about the words *research method*, we want you to remember that a research method comprises the overall strategy from collecting and analyzing data. According to Creswell (2013), we can categorize research into one of three fundamental research processes: qualitative, quantitative, and mixed methods. Both quantitative and qualitative research can be broken down into several distinct types. However, for the purposes of this chapter we want you to walk away with a basic sense of these three approaches. Mostly likely you will take a research class in your program of study and there you will learn about the specific types of research that fall under the three broad categories.

It is important to remember that the type of methodology you use will depend on the research question/hypothesis (Flamez, Lenz, Balkin, & Smith, 2017). In others words, the method you select is based on the research question-not the other way around. Before we discuss both the quantitative and qualitative approach it is important to note that both kinds of research are valued and should not be seen in opposition of each other. They each represent complimentary components of the scientific method. Depending on the nature of the question, topic, or problem to be investigated one is generally more appropriate than the other. It is also important to note that the distinctions we offer you below do not completely define quantitative and qualitative approaches, but rather highlight some of the differences.

In **quantitative research**, we tend to collect and analyze numerical data so that we can explain, predict, and/or control a phenomena of interests. As Creswell (2013) noted, quantitative studies are frequently used when one wants to identify or explain relationships between several variables. In quantitative studies the researcher states the hypothesis to be examined and specifies the procedures that are needed to carry out the study. The researcher studies large samples and populations. The researcher also tries not to influence the collection of data and has little interaction with the participant. This is why you will see the use of noninteractive instruments such as paper-and-pencil or computerized assessments.

In **qualitative research** the goal is to describe the nature of things instead of examining for causes and relationships. The researcher collects, analyzes, and interprets comprehensive narrative and visual data in order to gain insight into a particular phenomenon or interest. The hypothesis and research procedures are not stated in the beginning like quantitative research, but instead in qualitative research the research problems and methods evolve as the understanding of the topic deepens. The sample size studied is smaller and tends to be individual units such as a person, family, or community in their naturalistic setting. And while quantitative researchers elect participants as randomly as possible, qualitative researchers purposely select participants. Unlike quantitative research in which the researcher has little interaction with the participant, in a qualitative study the researcher usually has extensive interaction. The researcher may also be the primary instrument for collecting data through his or her observations.

Mixed methods combine both quantitative and qualitative methods in one study (Flamez et al., 2017). The purpose of a mixed methods approach is to build on the strength of both the qualitative and quantitative approaches in order to understand a research phenomenon more fully than using just qualitative or quantitative alone. Although you may be asking yourself, "Why wouldn't everyone want to use this approach?," it is important to note that this approach requires a thorough understanding of both quantitative and qualitative approaches and one must have considerable time to implement such an approach.

ETHICS AND CULTURAL CONSIDERATIONS

As the world becomes increasingly more diverse, it becomes vitally important for couple and family counselors to achieve ethical and multicultural competence. This is true when serving as a couple and family counselor or as a researcher. Following is information detailing ethical and cultural issues that might be considered when working within the realm of couple and family counseling research.

Ethical codes written by the American Association for Marriage and Family Therapy (AAMFT) as well as the International Association of Marriage and Family Counselors (IAMFC) offer specific guidance for conducting research. For example, the IAMFC Code of Ethics (IAMFC, 2017) states that "couple and family counselors respect the rights of those who submit their research for publication and other scholarly purposes and encourage publication efforts of their colleagues to advance research in couples and family counseling" (p. 7). Ten specific points are discussed within this code, including protecting privacy and safety of participants, avoiding misleading research results, assuming credit for research only when serving as a substantial contributor, making original data available to other researchers, avoiding plagiarism, serving as a role model to student researchers, and protecting author confidentiality and research propriety (IAMFC, 2017). The AAMFT Code of Ethics (AAMFT, 2012) discusses many of the same guidelines as those mentioned above but adds some additional considerations. For example, the AAMFT code states that researchers gain institutional approval for research conducted, ensure participants are given informed consent including the right to withdraw from a study, and mentions ensuring accurate citations within publications.

Each of these codes discusses the importance of cultural sensitivity, and the AAMFT code specifically ties the concept to research. The AAMFT Code of Ethics (AAMFT, 2012) research section states, "diversity, equity, and excellence (be employed) in clinical practice, research, education, and administration." Although the IAMFC Code of Ethics does not mention diversity within the research section of the code, the importance of diversity within the profession is mentioned in other sections. For example, when discussing diversity and advocacy, the code states, "Couple and family counselors respect the dignity, worth, uniqueness, and potential of couples and families in their cultural contexts" (IAMFC, 2017, p. 10). Both codes make it clear that ethical counselor-researchers follow these codes and value those from differing cultures when conducting research.

FUTURE DIRECTIONS

Not surprisingly, much research is lacking in couple and family therapy. While offering much hope for couples and families, research on major mental illnesses such as depression and anxiety, emotional and behavioral problems among youth, substance use, eating disorders, medical issues, and sexual dysfunctions require more research if clients are to attain optimal results. Future research on these as well as emerging issues discussed as follows might reveal undiscovered methods.

The future may hold promise as researchers attain better understanding of cross-cultural counseling methods, discover efficacious approaches through neuroscience, and become more familiar with technology and its applications to counseling. As families become progressively more diverse, efforts are needed to ensure that diversity is considered between counselor and client as well as within families (Falicov, 2014). Despite an emphasis within relevant codes of ethics stressing diversity as a major consideration in counseling (AAMFT, 2012; IAMFC, 2017), West-Olatunji (as cited in Shallcross, 2013) states that most counseling research focuses on how "multicultural counseling *is* rather than how we *enact* it" (par. 11). Future research should focus on clinical practice if cross-cultural counseling is to be adequately applied in the couple and family counseling setting (Shallcross, 2013). This focus on the integration between research and clinical practice is evident not only in multicultural counseling but affects other areas as well.

Neuroscience is making broad strides in understanding phenomena occurring within the brain. Counselors are now able to view brain imaging that offers clues to human thought, emotion, and behavior (Busacca, Sikorski, & McHenry, 2015). Research on the infusion between brain imaging and specific treatment models can bridge the gap between science and counseling practice on issues ranging from addiction to affective and behavioral concerns. This infusion between research, technology, and counseling practice is an important consideration since technology is rapidly changing not only brain science but also the way couples and families communicate.

The Internet has changed the way couples and families interact with one another and within society. These interactions can lead to potential stressors such as cyberbullying, cyberdating, sexting, long-distance relationships, Internet infidelity, technological harassment, gaming disorder, and miscommunications, to name a few (Campbell, Slee, & Spears, 2013; Lenhart & Duggan, 2014; Petry & O'Brien, 2013). Advances in clinical practice can only be achieved in these areas if research and clinical practice synthesize to create efficacious treatment modalities targeting these emerging issues.

SUMMARY

Clinical practice in couple, marriage, and family counseling must be substantiated through continual research. Although couples, marriage, and family counseling are reported as effective overall (Sexton & Datchi, 2014), life-threatening situations such as abuse, eating disorders, suicide, and substance use evidence the need for continually researching and utilizing efficacious interventions (Rhodes, 2012). Further, clinicians must find ways to reach the 25% to 35% of clients who do not respond positively to current therapeutic interventions (Carr, 2013; Lebow et al., 2012). Now that you have gained an understanding of the role of effective research in family therapy, you will learn about the intake and assessment process in therapy.

KEYSTONES

Among the key points addressed in this chapter are:

- Three fundamental research processes: qualitative, quantitative, and mixed methods.
- Although research offers credence to couples and family counseling, more research is needed to improve counseling outcomes (Halford et al., 2015; Pinsof, Goldsmith, & Latta, 2012; Sexton & Datchi, 2014).
- Family therapy offers promise in treating issues such as problem behaviors in children, eating disorders, panic disorder, OCD, depression, substance use, and other mental health disorders (Carr, 2014a; Dixon et al., 2001; Ewing et al., 2015; Fals-Stewart et al., 2009; Kuntsche & Kuntsche, 2016; Lyke & Matsen, 2013; Rowe, 2012; Van Ryzin et al., 2016).
- Assessment plays a major role in improving the focus of therapy and client outcomes (Snyder & Halford, 2012). The future offers new hope with foci on emerging issues such as neuroscience, multicultural issues, mental disorders, and Internet-based phenomena.

REFLECTIONS FROM THE CONTRIBUTOR'S CHAIR
Brande Flamez

In one of my first classes as a graduate student, I remember asking myself, "Why do I need to take a research class? I want to be a licensed therapist, not a researcher." But then my eyes were opened to what it means to be a scholar-practitioner and the importance the role of research plays in establishing credibility for our profession.

For example, several of the authors in this chapter work with military families. Within our private practice we had the opportunity to provide postcombat veterans and their families with supportive care and effective treatments that address disputes and divorce. What we found is that there was inadequate research on the effects of military combat on prevalence of divorce and prevention strategies addressing relationship problems in military couples. We saw a gap in the literature in that more research was required for counselors to provide competent care to military families, specifically addressing the underlying factors that lead military couples to divorce court. As we shared throughout the chapter, research is an ongoing practice and requires you to have a thorough understanding of the gap in the literature. Thus we worked together to provide an overview of the relevant literature addressing the factors that contribute to divorce among military couples, considerations for treatment related to military culture, professional competencies, and effective treatments related to divorce and disputes within military families to our professional field. Now that we have published this information and have a strong idea of the gap in the literature we will now begin on forming our research questions that will be the basis for our next research project.

As Shawn Wilson stated, "Everything that we do shares in the ongoing creation of our universe." We hope this chapter has inspired you to be aware of the current research in our field and consider your role as a researcher as you begin your journey and marriage and family therapy.

ADDITIONAL RESOURCES

The following resources provide additional information relating to the chapter topics.

- Ackerman Institute for the Family
  http://www.ackerman.org/

The Ackerman Institute for the Family, founded in 1960, is a family therapy training institution in New York. In addition to training programs, couple and family therapy is provided on-site. The institute combines training, clinical service, and research and is a leader in the profession.

- American Association for Marriage and Family Therapy (AAMFT)
  http://www.aamft.org/iMIS15/AAMFT/Content/Legal_Ethics/
  Code_of_Ethics.apx

This site offers access to the AAMFT Code of Ethics.

- European Family Therapy Association (EFTA)
  http://www.europeanfamilytherapy.eu

The EFTA has been around for 25 years. It supports research in family therapy and is a great place to learn about what is going on in family therapy in Europe.

- International Association of Marriage and Family Counselors (IAMFC)
  http://www.iamfconline.org/public/department3.cfm

This is the official website of the IAMFC and highlights the written code of ethics.

- National Council on Family Relations
  http://www.ncfr.org/

The National Council on Family Relations is a great online site for professional resources. In addition, it publishes three scholarly journals: the *Journal of Marriage and Family*, *Journal of Family Theory and Review*, and *Family Relations: Interdisciplinary Journal of Applied Family Studies*.

REFERENCES

American Psychiatric Association. (2013). *Diagnostic and statistical manual of mental disorders* (5th ed.). Washington, DC: Author.

Becker-Stoll, F., & Gerlinghoff, M. (2004). The impact of a four-month day treatment program on alexithymia in eating disorders. *European Eating Disorders Review, 12*(3), 159–163.

Biesen, J. N., & Doss, B. D. (2013). Couples' agreement on presenting problems predicts engagement and outcomes in problem-focused couple therapy. *Journal of Family Psychology, 27*(4), 658–663. doi:10.1037/a0033422

Busacca, L. A., Sikorski, A. M., & McHenry, B. (2015). Infusing neuroscience within counselor training: A rationale for an integrally-informed model. *Journal of Counselor Practice, 6*(1), 39–55.

Bydlowski, S., Corcos, M., Jeammet, P., Paterniti, S., Berthoz, S., Laurier, C., ... & Consoli, S. M. (2005). Emotion processing deficits in eating disorders. *International Journal of Eating Disorders, 37*(4), 321–329.

Campbell, M. A., Slee, P. T., Spears, B., Butler, D., & Kift, S. (2013). Do cyberbullies suffer too? Perceptions of the harm they cause to others and to their own mental health. *School Psychology International, 34*(6), 613–629. doi:10.1177/0143034313479698

Carr, A. (2010). Ten research questions for family therapy. *Australian and New Zealand Journal of Family Therapy, 31*(2), 119–132. doi:10.1375/anft.31.2.119

Carr, A. (2013). Thematic review of family therapy journals in 2012. *Journal of Family Therapy, 35*(4), 407–426. doi:10.1111/1467-6427.12021

Carr, A. (2014a). The evidence base for couple therapy, family therapy and systemic interventions for adult-focused problems. *Journal of Family Therapy, 36*(2), 158–194. doi:10.1111/1467-6427.12033

Carr, A. (2014b). Thematic review of family therapy journals in 2013. *Journal of Family Therapy, 36*(4), 420–443. doi:10.1111/1467-6427.12061

Carr, A. (2016). How and why do family and systemic therapies work? *Australian and New Zealand Journal of Family Therapy, 37*(1), 37–55. doi:10.1002/anzf.1135

Center for Behavioral Health Statistics and Quality. (2016). Key substance use and mental health indicators in the United States: Results from the 2015 National Survey on Drug Use and Health (HHS Publication No. SMA 16-4984, NSDUH Series H-51). Retrieved from http://www.samhsa.gov/data

Chambless, D. L. (2012). Adjunctive couple and family intervention for patients with anxiety disorders. *Journal of Clinical Psychology, 68*(5), 548–560. doi:10.1002/jclp.21851

Chwal, M., Jurek, J., Janusz, B., & de Barbaro, B. (2014). Drop-out in the systemic therapy from the family's perspective. *Archives of Psychiatry and Psychotherapy, 2*, 43–49. Retrieved from http://www.kom-red-wyd-ptp.com.pl/indexen.php

Creswell, J. W. (2013). *Research design: Qualitative, quantitative, and mixed method approaches* (4th ed.). Thousand Oaks, CA: Sage.

Dixon, L., McFarlane, W. R., Lefley, H., Lucksted, A., Cohen, M., Falloon, I., ... & Sondheimer, D. (2001). Evidence-based practices for services to families of people with psychiatric disabilities. *Psychiatric Services, 52*(7), 903–910.

Dodge, E. (2016). Forty years of eating disorder-focused family therapy—the legacy of "psychosomatic families." *Advances in Eating Disorders, 4*(2), 219–227. doi:10.1080/21662630.2015.1099452

Donovan, K. A., & Weigel, D. J. (2015). Samuel T. Gladding: A consistent and creative voice in the field of marriage, couple, and family counseling. *Family Journal, 23*(2), 201–208. doi:10.1177/1066480715572980

Doss, B. D., Simpson, L. E., & Christensen, A. (2004). Why do couples seek marital therapy? *Professional Psychology: Research and Practice, 35*(6), 608–614. doi:10.1037/0735-7028.35.6.608

Ewing, B. A., Osilla, K. C., Pedersen, E. R., Hunter, S. B., Miles, J. N. V., & D'Amico, E. J. (2015). Longitudinal family effects on substance use among an at-risk adolescent sample. *Addictive Behaviors, 41*, 185–191. doi:10.1016/j.addbeh.2014.10.017

Falicov, C. J. (2014). *Latino families in therapy*. New York: Guilford.

Fals-Stewart, W., Lam, W., & Kelley, M. L. (2009). Learning sobriety together: behavioral couples therapy for alcoholism and drug abuse. *Journal of Family Therapy, 31*, 115–125. doi:10.1111/j.1467-6427.2009.00458.x

Flamez, B., Lenz, A. S., Balkin, R. S., & Smith, R. L. (2017). *A counselor's guide to the dissertation process: Where to start and how to finish*. Alexandria, VA: American Counseling Association.

Gehart, D. R. (2012). The mental health recovery movement and family therapy, part 1: Consumer-led reform of services to persons diagnosed with severe mental illness. *Journal of Marital and Family Therapy, 38*(3), 429–442. doi:10.1111/j.1752-0606.2011.00230.x

Goorden, M., Schawo, S. J., Bouwmans-Frijters, Clazien A. M., van der Schee, E., Hendriks, V. M., & Hakkaart-van Roijen, L. (2016). The cost-effectiveness of family/family-based therapy for treatment of externalizing disorders, substance use disorders and delinquency: A systematic review. *BioMed Central Psychiatry, 16*, 1–22. doi:10.1186/s12888-016-0949-8

Greenman, P. S., & Johnson, S. M. (2013). Process research on emotionally focused therapy (EFT) for couples: Linking theory to practice. *Family Process, 52*(1), 46–61. doi:10.1111/famp.12015

Gurman, A. S. (2011). Couple therapy research and the practice of couple therapy: Can we talk? *Family Process, 50*(3), 280–292. doi:10.1111/j.1545-5300.2011.01360.x

Gurman, A. S. (2013). Behavioral couple therapy: Building a secure base for therapeutic integration. *Family Process, 52*(1), 115–138. doi:10.1111/famp.12014

Gutierrez, D., Carlson, R. G., Daire, A. P., & Young, M. E. (2017). Evaluating treatment outcomes using the integrative model of brief couples counseling: A pilot study. *Family Journal, 25*(1), 5–12. doi:10.1177/1066480716678619

Halford, W. K., Pepping, C. A., & Petch, J. (2015). The gap between couple therapy research efficacy and practice effectiveness. *Journal of Marital and Family Therapy, 42*(1), 32–44. doi:10.1111/jmft.12120

Hatchett, G. T. (2017). Monitoring the counseling relationship and client progress as alternatives to prescriptive empirically supported therapies. *Journal of Mental Health Counseling, 39*(2), 104–115. doi:10.17744/mehc.39.2.02

Holland, J. M., Rozalski, V., Beckman, L., Rakhkovskaya, L. M., Klingspon, K. L., Donohue, B., ... & Gallagher-Thompson, D. (2016). Treatment preferences of older adults with substance use problems. *Clinical Gerontologist, 39*(1), 15–24. doi:10.1080/07317115.2015.1101633

Hollon, S. D., & Sexton, T. L. (2012). Determining what works in depression treatment: Translating research to relational practice using treatment guidelines. *Couple and Family Psychology: Research Practice, 1*(3), 199–212. doi:10.1037/a0029901

Horigian, V. E., Feaster, D. J., Brincks, A., Robbins, M. S., Perez, M. A., & Szapocznik, J. (2015). The effects of Brief Strategic Family Therapy (BSFT) on parent substance use and the association between parent and adolescent substance use. *Addictive Behaviors, 42*, 44–50. doi:10.1016/j.addbeh.2014.10.024

International Association of Marriage and Family Counselors. (2017). *IAMFC Code of Ethics*. Alexandria, VA: Author.

Jurek, J., Janusz, B., Chwal, M., & de Barbaro, B. (2014). Premature termination in couple therapy as a part of therapeutic process. Cross case analysis. *Archives of Psychiatry and Psychotherapy, 16*(2), 51–59. doi:10.12740/APP/26962

Kelton-Locke, S. (2016). Eating disorders, impaired mentalization, and attachment: Implications for child and adolescent family treatment. *Journal of Infant, Child, and Adolescent Psychotherapy, 15*(4), 337–356. DOI:10.1080/15289168.2016.1257239

Kuntsche, S., & Kuntsche, E. (2016). Parent-based interventions for preventing or reducing adolescent substance use-A systemic literature review. *Clinical Psychology Review, 45*, 89–101. doi:10.1016/j.cpr.2016.02.004

L'Abate, L. (2015). Highlights from 60 years of practice, research, and teaching in family therapy. *American Journal of Family Therapy, 43*(2), 180–196. doi:10.1080/01926187.2014.1002367

Langdon-Daly, J., & Serpell, L. (2017). Protective factors against disordered eating in family systems: A systematic review of research. *Journal of Eating Disorders, 5*(12), 1–15. doi:10.1186/s40337-017-0141-7

Lebow, J. (2013). Editorial: Couple therapy and family therapy. *Family Process, 52*(1), 1–4. doi:10.1111/famp.12027

Lebow, J. (2016). Editorial: Family research and the practice of family therapy. *Family Process, 55*(1), 3–6. doi:10.1111/famp.12209

Lebow, J. L., Chambers, A. L., Christensen, A., & Johnson, S. M. (2012). Research on the treatment of couple distress. *Journal of Marital and Family Therapy, 38*(1), 145–168. doi:10.1111/j.1752-0606.2011.00249.x

Lenhart, A., & Duggan, M. (2014). Couples, the Internet, and social media. Pew Research Center. Retrieved from http://www.pewinternet.org/2014/02/11/couples-the-internet-and-social-media

Macfarlane, M. M. (2011). Family centered care in adult mental health: Developing a collaborative interagency practice. *Journal of Family Psychotherapy, 22*(1), 56–73. doi:10.1080/08975353.2011.551100

McKinnon, J. M., & Greenberg, L. S. (2013). Revealing underlying vulnerable emotion in couple therapy: Impact on session and outcome. *Journal of Family Therapy, 35*(3), 303–310. doi:10.1111/1467-6427.12015

Merritts, A. (2016). A review of family therapy in residential settings. *Contemporary Family Therapy, 38*(1), 75–85. doi:10.1007/s10591-016-9378-6

Moore, A. M., & Crane, D. R. (2014). Relational diagnosis and psychotherapy treatment cost effectiveness. *Contemporary Family Therapy, 36*(2), 281–299. doi:10.1007/s10591-013-9277-z

Norcross, J. C., & Wampold, B. E. (2011). Evidence-based therapy relationships: Research conclusions and clinical practices. In J. C. Norcross (Ed.). *Psychotherapy relationships that work: Evidence-based responsiveness* (2nd ed., pp. 423–430). New York: Oxford University Press.

Palmer, R. H. C., Brick, L., Nugent, N. R., Bidwell, L. C., McGeary, J. E., Knopik, V. S., & Keller, M. C. (2015). Examining the role of common genetic variants on alcohol, tobacco, cannabis and illicit drug dependence: Genetics of vulnerability to drug dependence. *Addiction Research Report, 110*(3), 530–537. doi:10.1111/add.12815

Patterson, J. E., & Vakili, S. (2013). Relationships, environment, and the brain: How emerging research is changing what we know about the impact of families on human development. *Family Process, 53*(1), 22–32. doi:10.1111/famp.12057

Pepping, C. A., Halford, W. K., & Doss, B. D. (2015). Can we predict failure in couple therapy early enough to enhance outcome? *Behavior Research and Therapy, 65,* 60–65. doi:10.1016/j.brat.2014.12.015

Petry, N. N., & O'Brien, C. (2013). Internet gaming disorder and the DSM-5. *Addiction, 108*(7), 1186–1187.

Pinsof, W. M., Goldsmith, J. Z., & Latta, T. A. (2012). Information technology and feedback research can bridge the scientist–practitioner gap: A couple therapy example. *Couple and Family Psychology: Research and Practice, 1*(4), 253–273. doi:10.1037/a0031023

Rhodes, P. (2012). Nothing to fear? Thoughts on the history of family therapy and the potential contribution of research. *Australian and New Zealand Journal of Family Therapy, 33*(2), 171–182. doi:10.1017/aft.2012.18

Robinson, A. L., Dolhanty, J., & Greenberg, L. (2013). Emotion-Focused Family Therapy for eating disorders in children and adolescents. *Clinical Psychology and Psychotherapy 22*(1), 75–82. doi:10.1002/cpp.1861

Rowe, C. L. (2012). Family therapy for drug abuse: Review and updates 2003–2010. *Journal of Marital & Family Therapy, 38*(1), 59–81. doi:10.1111/j.1752-0606.2011.00280.x

Sevier, M., Atkins, D. C., Doss, B. D., & Christensen, A. (2015). Up and down or down and up? The process of change in constructive couple behavior during traditional and integrative behavioral couple therapy. *Journal of Marital and Family Therapy, 41*(1), 113–127. doi:10.1111/jmft.12059

Sexton, T. L., & Datchi, C. (2014). The development and evolution of family therapy research: Its impact on practice, current status, and future directions. *Family Process, 53*(3), 415–433. doi:10.1111/famp.12084

Sexton, T., Gordon, K. C., Gruman, A., Lebow, J., Holtzworth-Munroe, A., & Johnson, S. (2011). Guidelines for classifying evidence-based treatments in couple and family therapy. *Family Process, 50*(3), 377–392. doi:10.1111/j.1545-5300.2011.01363.x

Shallcross, L. (2013, September 1). Multicultural competence: A continuing pursuit. *Counseling Today.* Retrieved from http://ct.counseling.org/2013/09/multicultural-competence-a-continual-pursuit

Slade, P. D., & Dewey, M. E. (1986). Development and preliminary validation of SCANS: A screening instrument for identifying individuals at risk of developing anorexia and bulimia nervosa. *International Journal of Eating Disorders, 5*(3), 517–538.

Snyder, D. K., & Halford, W. K. (2012). Evidence-based couple therapy: Current status and future directions. *Journal of Family Therapy, 34*(3), 229–249. doi:10.1111/j.1467-6427.2012.00599.x

Sprenkle, D. H. (2012). Intervention research in couple and family therapy: A methodological and substantive review and an introduction to the special issue. *Journal of Marital and Family Therapy, 38*(1), 3–29. doi:10.1111/j.1752-0606.2011.00271.x

Strong, T., & Busch, R. (2013). DSM-5 and evidence-based family therapy? *Australian and New Zealand Journal of Family Therapy, 34*(2), 90–103. doi:10.1002/anzf.1009

Tan, S. (2011). *Counseling and psychotherapy: A Christian perspective.* Grand Rapids, MI: Baker Academic.

Tanenbaum, S. J. (2015). Evidence-based practice as mental health policy: Three controversies and a caveat. *Health Affairs, 24*(1), 163–173. doi:10.1377/hlthaff.24.1.163

Van Ryzin, M. J., Roseth, C. J., Fosco, G. M., Lee, Y., & Chen, I., (2016). A component-centered meta-analysis of family-based prevention programs for adolescent substance use. *Clinical Psychology Review, 45,* 72–80. doi:10.1016/j.cpr.2016.03.007

West, C., Hinton, W. J., Grames, H., & Adams, M. A. (2013). Marriage and family therapy: Examining the impact of licensure on an evolving profession. *Journal of Marital and Family Therapy, 39*(1), 112–126. doi:10.1111/jmft.12010

Winter, L., Morawska, A., & Sanders, M. R. (2012). The effect of behavioral family intervention knowledge of effective parenting strategies. *Journal of Family Studies, 21*(6), 881–890. doi:10.1007/s10826-011-9548-y

Wolska, M. (2011). Marital therapy/couples therapy: Indications and contraindications. *Archives of Psychiatry and Psychotherapy, 3,* 57–64. Retrieved from http:.//www.kom-red-wyd-ptp.com.pl/indexen.php

CHAPTER 7

Getting Started: Intake and Clinical Assessment in Family Therapy

Kathy Ybañez-Llorente and Quinn K. Smelser

"All great changes are preceded by chaos."

—Deepak Chopra

When first meeting families for therapy, we have learned that even the best laid plans for the intake and assessment phase of therapy will likely go awry. In these times, we are reminded that this chaos is part of the process of change. Families come to therapy because things in their lives are no longer occurring in the predictable and functional way that the family would prefer. Communication, behavioral patterns, and interactions have become chaotic and unmanageable, but this chaos will look very different for each family system. As family therapists, we can instill hope by normalizing what may feel very abnormal to a family. We try to normalize the chaos and produce change!

Families enter family therapy with well-established patterns of communication and oftentimes complex issues, from many of which they are seeking immediate relief. The initial intake and assessment process gives you an opportunity to start to gather perspectives from family members, namely the way the family is structured, and how they communicate and interact with one another. The use of assessment strategies for specific issues and areas of concern will be the first step in gathering information that allows for selecting appropriate interventions. The selected interventions will be based on a collaborative treatment plan, created to guide your work with families. After examining various facets of family relationships, one will develop a working hypothesis of what has created and sustained the presenting problem and dysfunctional patterns of interaction.

The therapist will then work to prioritize interventions to be utilized in different phases of treatment.

This chapter is divided into sections consisting of brief overviews describing how to get started with the initial assessment of families coming in for therapy, including a discussion of systemic family therapy approaches to assessment. We will also highlight four important tasks to focus on in the first interview, how to utilize a genogram in the assessment of family patterns, and specific individual issues that could impact family interaction patterns. Finally, we will examine challenges you may be faced with when assessing families, as well as how to use assessment in treatment planning and risk management.

LEARNING OBJECTIVES

After reading this chapter, you will be able to do the following:

- Describe the use of assessment from a relational and systemic perspective.
- Describe different types of informal family assessments, from interviews, to genograms, to self-report measures.
- Identify the components of a treatment plan for relational concerns.
- Name relational, career, and school-related concerns presented by clients.
- Discuss the importance of assessing for presenting problems such as substance abuse, suicide, interpersonal violence, and child abuse.
- Describe the impact of stressors such as crisis, addiction, and unemployment on marriages, couples, and families.
- Discuss cultural factors relevant to marital, couple, and family functioning.
- Utilize assessment data to conceptualize and implement treatment planning, goal setting, and intervention strategies in marital, couple, and family counseling.

KEY CONCEPTS

The importance of assessment cannot be underestimated in marriage, couple, and family counseling. The next section details the importance of assessment used in counseling. The case example that follows illustrates the complex nature and non-ending process we use when assessing clients.

CASE PRESENTATION: RAY'S PHONE CALL

Ray Taylor called the office, stating he needed to schedule a family therapy appointment. Ray states he and his family were told by a counselor this morning they needed to continue with family therapy after Gabriel was discharged from the hospital. Ray is married to Patricia, and they have two children: 17-year-old Danielle, a senior in high school, and 15-year-old Gabriel, a sophomore. Ray works for a sales company, and Patricia is a former teacher. Ray states Gabriel was caught selling ADD medication at school and was suspended. Neither Ray nor Patricia could be reached to pick up Gabriel, so Danielle was pulled out of class to take Gabriel home. Ray stated Patricia was home that day, but he doesn't understand why she didn't go get Gabriel. When Ray arrived home that evening, he heard Danielle yelling at Gabriel: "You're worthless! I am so tired of taking care of you, but we all know I'll keep doing it anyway!" Gabriel wouldn't open his door when Ray went to check on him. Later that evening, Ray heard Danielle scream after finding Gabriel with a plastic bag over his head. Gabriel was rushed to the ER and subsequently admitted to a psychiatric unit when he stated he still wanted to "be gone." The therapist asked a few more questions of Ray on the phone, but Ray was unable to answer many of them. Ray stated for the past year he has been working out of town during the week and is home on weekends, so he isn't aware of a lot going on in the house. Danielle was heard in the background, answering questions for Ray. Ray said he was glad to have Danielle because she has been his "eyes and ears at home" when he is gone. Ray stated Gabriel's behavior has been getting increasingly worse over the past 8 months, and they need to get help to address these things he is doing. He says he guesses they are all "pretty disconnected from each other, so hopefully family therapy could help" all of them. An appointment for family therapy was scheduled for the following afternoon.

Figure 7.1 details the client intake form completed by the therapist during Ray's phone call. Later in the chapter, we will see the treatment plan for this case, taking us through the initial, working, and closing phases of treatment with the Taylor family.

FAMILY THERAPY APPROACHES TO CLINICAL ASSESSMENT

As is the case with most forms of therapy, assessment evolves from the first call or meeting with a family, all the way through the termination session. The initial interview with the family allows the family therapist to collect descriptive information about why the family has sought therapy, typically an informal assessment process. Some therapists may elect to use formal assessments such as questionnaires or measures specific to family functioning (Huff, Anderson, & Edwards, 2014).

Like individual assessment, family therapists gather information about the clients they are working with according to the therapist's primary theoretical orientation. For instance, a cognitive behavioral therapist would approach the assessment phase of therapy focusing on what the family thinks of the problem, the frequency the problem occurs, the magnitude of the problem, and the length of time the problem has been occurring

| Sample Completed Family Intake Form

Date <u>1/15/2017</u>

Client Information

Client of record: <u>Ray Taylor</u>

Spouse/Partner: <u>Patricia Taylor</u>

Address: <u>1234 Main Street</u>   City: <u>Akron</u>   State: <u>Ohio</u>   Zip Code: <u>44333</u>

Phone (home): <u>(330) 555-5555</u>   Phone (cell): <u>(330) 555-6666</u>

Referral source: Akron General; Clinical Services Counselor, M. Staff; (330) 800-3000

Family members in household:

Last name	First name	DOB	Education	Employ/School	Married
Taylor	Ray	03-27-75	4 yr. Univ	Medical sales, traveling	1998
Taylor	Patricia	08-01-77	4 yr. Univ	Stay at home; former teacher	1998
Taylor	Danielle	11-21-99	12th grade	Akron High School	NA
Taylor	Gabriel	06-08-01	10th grade	Akron High School	NA

Clinical Information

Presenting problem:

Mr. Taylor stated son was recently hospitalized after suicide attempt following suspension from school. Referred by counselor to continue family therapy; Son will have own individual therapy with local LPC and follow up with psychiatrist for medication management. He thinks family disconnect started one year ago when he started to travel for work. Wife decided to leave stress filled job teaching since his income increased, but she has not found another job to occupy her time. Believes she is depressed, but she has not sought treatment. Reports Gabriel is no longer voicing suicidal ideations, stated he was just embarrassed and angry.

Previous therapy:

Name	Organization	Date	Duration
Patricia	Akron Family Center	April 2000	6 months, 1x per week

Scheduling information

Next appointment date: <u>1-16-2017</u>   Time: <u>5:00 pm</u>   Therapist: <u>June Gomez</u>

(Erford, 2014). The principle of equifinality applies to the assessment phase of family therapy in that all family therapists strive to achieve the same thing, despite each reaching this goal in different ways. All approaches assess the reason the family has come to need therapy and ideally, will see the maladaptive pattern of behavior or communication in the therapy room. Different therapists will view and conceptualize these reasons and patterns from differing theoretical lenses, developing a treatment plan and therapeutic goals based on the family's input and therapist's way of approaching clinical assessment. Family therapists also use many tools and techniques from across paradigms and theoretical backgrounds, including expressive and play therapy interventions.

In one of the first thorough reviews of existing family assessments at that time, Wilkinson (1987) concluded that family therapy assessment relies on gauging the family as a unit with all possible dyads, triads, or subunits that have formed. This reminds us that the biggest mistake family therapists make in assessment is appraising each individual in the family, rather than evaluating each member as a part of a system that is likely not functioning as well as it once did. That being said, there are often situations in which an individual or individuals in the family may have a clinical disorder and need an evaluation of their own (Wilkinson, 1987). When this is the case, the family therapist must also assess how the family system is adapting to and influencing this individual and vice versa.

Approaches to family therapy once understood families as merely "networks of individuals" (Wilkinson, 1987, p. 373) until Minuchin developed structural family therapy. This began a shift toward theories attempting to explain the structure and workings of the entire family system. Many clinicians, theorists, and researchers agree that the assessment process itself can be therapeutic for the family (Huff et al., 2014). We have found that unless we are using very formal assessments, families typically do not even realize that the first few sessions are part of the assessment phase. According to a family therapist's theoretical lens, the therapist assesses the system itself and its functional and dysfunctional organization, roles, patterns, communication styles, structure, and subsystem as a part of the assessment and rapport building phase in therapy (Bitter, 2014).

SYSTEMIC APPROACH TO ASSESSMENT

According to the American Educational Research Association (AERA), the American Psychological Association (APA), and the National Council of Measurement in Education (NCME), the term *assessment* is defined as "a process that integrates test information with information from other sources (e.g., information from other tests in the individual's social, educational, employment, health, or psychological history)" (AERA, 1999, p. 3). But how do we think of assessment when it comes to working with families? "Assessment is a complex process that involves … physiological, psychological, life cycle, and social/environmental factors influencing family function and dynamics" (Rasheed, Rasheed, & Marley, 2011, p. 336). In family therapy, this means attending to the interactions and intentions of behaviors at the systems level for all the individuals in the family. The therapist is assessing the purposeful actions of each individual and how these are interacting within the system (Bitter, 2014). Further, the therapist is beginning to formulate a conceptualization about the system's patterns, hierarchy, subsystems, and the system's process during the initial meeting (Bitter, 2014). In this systemic approach to assessment, the therapist reflects observations about the networking of the system back to the family members, as these unfold in the first session (Huff et al., 2014).

Adopting this shift in perspective to focusing on the entire family unit not only informs the therapist and family from the onset of treatment, it also shifts the focus of the problem off one member of the system and onto the patterns present in the entire family unit (Nichols & Tafuri, 2013). This alone can help alleviate pressure from family members and eliminate blaming or finger-pointing. When thinking about the problem, families can then adopt a new perspective of what is not working in their system, with the family therapist modeling a different approach than what the family might be used to (Finn & Tonsager, 1997). We have even known therapists who use a buzzer to remind families when they begin to use their old patterns of thinking and blaming family members. Additionally, intake forms, and more formal assessments such as observational ratings of behaviors and self-report questionnaires may be utilized, with the interactions that present themselves with paperwork informing the assessment process (Bitter, 2014). See Chapter 8 for a detailed discussion of observational and standardized assessments used in family therapy. As in all family therapy, the initial interview and subsequent sessions should appeal to all members of the family through engagement of the oldest member to the youngest child member.

Initial Interview

The first meeting in family therapy begins the assessment process. Similarly, the first phone call or e-mail interaction with the family is the beginning of the formation of a therapeutic relationship with the family. Establishing rapport with the family carries through the assessment phase. The initial interview with the family begins the first face-to-face rapport building as the family therapist works to clarify the problem bringing the family to therapy while also instilling hope for change. Through this process, the family therapist is largely regarded as the expert who the family might expect to immediately solve their problem (Nichols & Tafuri, 2013). With so much information needing to be gathered in this first meeting, educators and supervisors have expressed concern for new family therapists, who may be overwhelmed by the multitude of items needing to be addressed in the first meeting. Weber, McKeever, and McDaniel (1985) created a step-by-step guide for new family therapists operating under supervision that outlines twelve phases of the first interview. Each phase includes

> *specific tasks designed to accomplish the four goals: 1. Join the family, accommodating to the style of family members and creating an environment in which family members will feel supported. 2. Organize the interview so that family members will begin to gain confidence in the therapist's leadership. 3. Gather information about the problem in such a way that the family's transactions around the problem become clearer. 4. Negotiate a therapy contract, emphasizing the family's initiative in defining goals and desired changes. (Weber et al., 1985, p. 2)*

Despite the length of time since Weber at al. (1985) created their step-by-step guide, it is still highly relevant today and extremely useful to today's budding family therapists. The subsequent topics in this chapter will inform what we will look for or do in each of the phases. Let's look at the proposed phases outlined in Table 7.1 below.

Table 7.1 Beginner's Guide to the Problem-Oriented First Family Interview: A Foundation for Beginning Family Therapists

Phases of the first interview	
I. Telephoning	VII. Defining goals (5 minutes)
II. Forming hypotheses	VIII. Contracting (5 minutes)
III. The greeting (5 minutes)	IX. First interview checklist
IV. The social phase (5 minutes)	X. Revising hypotheses
V. Identifying the problem (15 minutes)	XI. Contacting the referral person
VI. Observing family patterns (15 minutes)	XII. Gathering records

Source: Timothy Weber, James E. McKeever, and Susan H. McDaniel, "Beginner's Guide to the Problem-Oriented First Family Interview," Family Process, vol. 24, no. 3. Copyright © 1985 by John Wiley & Sons, Inc.

We must also keep in mind that Weber et al. (1985) stressed the importance of utilizing the model only after one received family therapy training, and only under close supervision. Also worth noting is the fact that today's managed care environment still demands that these phases be addressed and documented within the first session. Next, we will examine four critical components that contribute to a successful initial interview. Especially during those chaotic moments in our early sessions, we remember the importance of establishing rapport, clarifying the family's problem(s), establishing our own competence and credibility, and beginning to instill hope for the change that occurs after the chaos.

Establishing Rapport

In a qualitative study of families and their therapists, Sundet (2011) highlighted the importance of collaboration in the therapeutic relationship. This emphasizes the significance of what others have called presence, joining, or the three core conditions (i.e., empathy, congruence, unconditional positive regard) outlined by Carl Rogers (Bitter, 2014). Rapport building occurs at first contact and ultimately enables the family therapist to challenge the family further along in the therapeutic relationship. Higgins-Klein (2013) described the goals of the first meeting as an opportunity for the family therapist to connect with the entire family and "provide space for the expression of each family member's positive qualities" (p. 40). Even when using formal, written assessments, Finn and Tonsager (1997) importantly discovered that therapists who utilized a therapeutic approach stayed connected to the family, collaborated on goal setting, and immediately shared assessment results were more successful in relieving distress than those therapists who treated the assessment phase as a strict informa-tion-gathering process. It is this therapeutic approach to family assessment and intake that will assist family therapists to move through the rest of the steps necessary for a successful initial interview.

Clarifying the Presenting Problem

While working to build a relationship using the basic client-centered Rogerian tools, the family therapist must still identify what brings the family to therapy. Nichols and Tafuri (2013) emphasize doing so in a "dynamic" manner and "actively investigating the possibility that the presenting complaint might be significantly influenced by the family interactions" (p. 208). An informal interview using open-ended questions can aid in facilitating this initial conversation as can more formal, self-report tools such as the McMaster Family Assessment Device, one of the first formal methods originally developed by Epstein, Baldwin, and Bishop (1983). The systems-oriented family therapist must also begin to assess and reflect how the problem has been perpetuated in both the therapist's view as well as from the perspective of all family members. As the assessment phase evolves, the family therapist will use circular causality to understand when the problem began and how it has been maintained, in that "circular thinking suggests that problems are sustained by an ongoing series of actions and reactions" (Nichols & Tafuri, 2013, p. 209).

Establishing Competence and Credibility

Working in collaboration with the family to more clearly understand their perspectives on the presenting problem while formulating a clinical conceptualization of the presen-tation, family therapists must also establish their credibility with every family member as someone who has the tools to help them. Huff et al. (2014) found that clinicians who are trained in systemic assessment and develop experiential expertise during their training as therapists feel more competent and likely present as more confident to the families they work with. Displaying a license to practice as well as a framed degree builds a therapist's credibility as well. Higgins-Klein (2013) emphasized interactions with case managers, doctors, judicial workers, and other potential members of a family clinical service team. When the family therapist works as a leader in the clinical team role, this also enhances a therapist's competence and credibility.

Instilling Hope for Change

As mentioned above, Finn and Tonsager's (1997) important study demonstrated the power in creating a therapeutic assessment phase rather than merely gathering information from the family. Sharing assessment results as well as initiating rapport can alleviate some of the stress being experienced in the family (Finn & Tonsager, 1997). By joining with the family, assessing in a therapeutic manner, and speaking of the problem as inherent to the system rather than to an individual within the system, the systems-oriented, family therapist can instill hope into the family dynamic from a more objective perspective (Bitter, 2014).

Indeed, some families with children may improve tremendously as the assessment phase of treatment progresses beyond the initial interview (Gil, 2016).

Genogram

Given that family therapists assess the problem from a systemic point of view, the family genogram is essential in mapping demographic information, current patterns of relationships, family of origin history, as well as relational history within the family. Nearly all family therapy theoretical orientations include some version of the genogram. Platt and Skowron (2013) defined a genogram as

> *a pictorial diagram of a family using data gathered during a semi-structured interview to assess for various elements of family functioning, such as conflict, cutoff, enmeshment, and other family relationship patterns. A genogram resembles a "family tree," however, the information gathered includes both the simple structure of the family and the emotional patterns and processes present in the nuclear and extended family system. (p. 35)*

Case Presentation 7.1 details the case of an immigrant family from Ecuador. From the first phone call to the termination session, it is always important that the family therapist be sensitive to cultural diversity and differing ideas of family. We will discuss these further in this chapter, but pay attention to what stereotypes and biases may come up for you while reading this case. We all have biases. It is important that we continually build our own awareness of them.

CASE PRESENTATION 7.1: THE GENOGRAM

Creating a genogram: An immigrant family from Ecuador comes to your trauma-informed, private practice with concerns about their teenager (14-year-old Anna), who has previously disclosed sexual abuse by her mom's ex-boyfriend. As you begin your informal assessment with the family in your first meeting, you come to understand that the teenage girl's aunt is her primary caregiver in the United States and that her mother has been deported back to Ecuador. The girl's aunt has custodial rights to the child and is helping her assimilate into U.S. culture as well as into her family. In your office are Anna, her aunt (Laura), who is holding an infant (age 10 months, named Cristina), and a 10-year-old male child (Mario).

You decide to begin the assessment with a genogram of the family to begin to understand their system, as well as to provide a visual for the current patterns of interaction in the family. The early stages of the genogram you draw on a dry erase board can be seen in Figure 7.2.

Figure 7.2 Anna's genogram

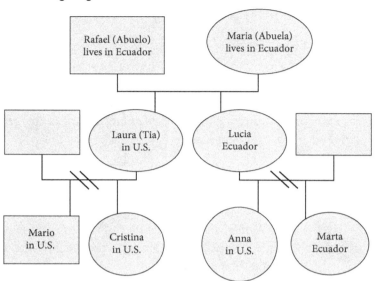

The family genogram is an outstanding tool to begin to understand the culture of the family. Figure 7.2 depicts how to start the genogram of Anna's family. There are many kinds of symbols, lines, shapes, and patterns you can use to create a genogram. Usually, females are depicted with a circle and males with a square. There are also many genogram symbols that use other shapes to acknowledge the continuum and fluidity of gender and sexual identifications. Similarly, termination in relationships is denoted by some sort of break in line connections or double lines perpendicular to the line connecting the two persons, as we see in Figure 7.2.

The genogram is a formal and informal assessment tool that provides an extensive collaboration opportunity for the family and the therapist to begin to tackle the presenting problem, while also considering the transgenerational impact of family communication patterns. Each family's genogram can be tailored to include additional factors impacting the family, such as spirituality, culture, and sex and sexuality (Belous, Timm, Chee, & Whitehead, 2012).

Genogram Development

In Chapters 1–3, you learned that in 1978, family systems therapist Murray Bowen was the first to introduce the genogram for mental health purposes. Developing a family's genogram may take several sessions, should be a process, and should be referred to throughout treatment. Oftentimes, talking about intergenerational conflicts can be difficult for families, though it can be tremendously helpful to the family in shifting to a systemic perspective (Higgins-Klein, 2013). There are many variables, family members, relationships, and patterns a family therapist might be interested in collecting data on according to their theoretical orientation. Similarly, there are many different approaches to gathering this information. Some of these are more structured interviews and some might rely on the genogram more as an intervention tool (Platt & Skowron, 2013; Belous et al., 2012). With the flexibility to create a genogram over multiple sessions, it is important to have a writing space large enough that can be either saved or re-created to revisit each session (i.e., dry erase board and markers, butcher paper, and markers). Guided Practice Exercise 7.1 below challenges you to create your own family genogram. The website provided will show you various ways to create genograms with the differing symbols mentioned in your reading. This exercise is meant to help you develop your own awareness about the thoughts, feelings, and emotions that might arise for a family while creating a genogram.

GUIDED PRACTICE EXERCISE 7.1

Prior to class, go to the following website: http://www.genograms.org/create.html . Review the pages detailing components of genograms, communication patterns, and clues that will help you understand relationship patterns. Click on "Create Your Own" to learn how to construct your family's genogram. After completing your own genogram, take a while to examine it and then write down what you learned about yourself and your family in relation to the clues described: relevant dates; gender beliefs and values: family secrets; losses; themes regarding family core values and beliefs; cultural heritage; family boundaries—external and internal. How have these clues impacted your immediate family, as well as your relationships with others?

Family of Origin Information

Most often, family therapists aim to gather information about at least three generations within the family genogram: one generation of grandparents, parents, and children. Of course, this will look different for the varying family constellations who seek therapy. It is important to collect as much information as each family member knows and is willing to share about their respective families of origin (Higgins-Klein, 2013). You should keep in mind that clients might be comfortable sharing more information as therapy progresses. As much as one is able, therapists must assess intergenerational trauma history, mental illness, relationship status, gender and sexual orientation identity, as well as current relational dynamics between family of origin and the family in therapy. These patterns can be depicted within the genogram (Higgins-Klein, 2013; Platt & Skowron, 2013; Belous et al., 2012.). For families that are more receptive to, or in need of a more experiential creation of a genogram, the family floor plan tool (Coppersmith, 1980) can be utilized. Highly creative and innovative for its time, the activity in Table 7.2 below will take a client through a series of instructions that can help re-create memories, rules, or family ideas that may have been lost, but that still impact a family's functioning today. As a future family therapist, this would be a helpful exercise for you to experience as well! Take out a piece of paper and create your Family Floor Plan.

Table 7.2 The Family Floor Plan Tool

Participants are asked to draw a floor plan of the house they lived in as a child. As participants are drawing, the trainer slowly interjects the following directions and questions:

1. As you draw, note the mood of each room for you.

2. Let yourself recall the smells, sounds, colors, and people in this house.

3. Was there a particular room where people gathered?

4. When extended family visited, where did they go?

5. Were there rooms you could not enter?

6. Did you have a special place in this house?

7. Let yourself be aware of how issues of closeness and distance, privacy or the lack of privacy were experienced in this house.

8. What was the place of this house in the neighborhood in which it stood? Did it fit or not?

9. Let yourself recall a typical event that occurred in this house; let yourself hear typical words that were spoken by family members.

Source: Evan Coppersmith, "The Family Floor Plan Tool," Journal of Marital and Family Therapy, vol. 6, no. 2, pp. 142. Copyright © 1980 by John Wiley & Sons, Inc.

Relationship History Information

A genogram provides a launching point to begin to assess relational patterns and dynamics within generations of the family system. Relationship history is portrayed in the lines connecting individuals within a genogram and indicates whether relationships are healthy, intact, cutoff, or problematic as indicated by the kinds of lines used. For less verbal clients, therapists may ask clients to draw faces associated with how they feel about certain family members, or do so via play or sand tray genograms as developed by Gil (2016). Many therapists also depict attachment-style histories, enmeshments, differentiations of self, and volatile or supportive relationships via the connecting lines of a genogram (Bitter, 2014). In Case Presentation 7.2, we learn more about Anna's family. The dialogue shows us what kind of information might come up for the family while creating their genogram. In all our work, the genogram is completed over many sessions because so much therapeutic content arises out of it. Guided Practice Exercise 7.1 challenged you to create your own genogram. How vulnerable was that experience for you? Did something similar happen in your thought processes like what develops in the case presentation below?

CASE PRESENTATION 7.2: THE CASE OF ANNA, LAURA, AND MARIO

Culturally competent assessment in family therapy: As you draw the genogram and get to know Anna's family from Ecuador, you learn about their heritage and what brought the family to the United States. You also have questions about why the family has had to separate.

Anna: I don't get to see my mom anymore except when we have enough money to go to Ecuador.

Therapist: I'm hearing some sadness in your voice as you say that.

Laura: Yes, it's been really hard on all of us, especially Anna since her mother left. Anna is not used to the United States like we are.

Mario: Don't cry, Anna.

Therapist: Anna, I have never been to Ecuador and want to hear more about your experience. Help me understand more about the differences between being here and being there.

Anna (through tears and smiles)**:** Here I go from school to home, and don't get to spend much time outside. We live on a big farm in Ecuador. My *abuelo* has a lot of chickens and a horse that I used to ride every day.

Mario: And I got to ride it once, too.

Therapist: That sounds exciting, tell me more.

Laura: My parents are farmers. They sent me and my sister to the United States to live with our cousins when we were going to junior high school just like Anna. They knew it would be hard for all of us, but they wanted better opportunities for us, and that wasn't going to happen in Ecuador. I miss them and try to visit whenever we have enough money. I want Mario to know them, too.

Anna: It's expensive for my Tia Laura to let me go visit. But the social workers said my mom didn't take care of me right so she had to leave or would be deported.

ASSESSING INDIVIDUAL ISSUES

In addition to collecting information about family structure, it is equally important to understand how problems experienced by individuals affect the family system. Ensuring you are asking questions related to specific problems like drug and alcohol use, stress and work-related issues, gender issues, and systems of support will allow the initial interview to shed light into areas that might otherwise remain dark. Again, from a systems perspective, the goal is not to place blame on any one person within the family, but it is to uncover how actions and reactions work to sustain the presenting problem. Let's explore the importance of these individual issues on family functioning.

Drug and Alcohol Use

Drug and alcohol use continue to be a problem in our country, with increasing numbers of adults abusing both over-the-counter medications and controlled classes of prescription medication. In the 2015 national survey on drug use and health, more than 4.5 million people received substance abuse treatment for alcohol and/or illicit drugs (CBHSQ, 2016). With numbers this pronounced, chances are high that marriage and family therapists will come across clients for whom alcohol or drugs are an issue needing to be discussed in therapy. Longstanding researchers in the field of intimate partner violence, Leonard and Quigley (2017) examined 30 years of research and concluded, "while neither a necessary nor a sufficient cause, excessive alcohol use does contribute to the occurrence of partner violence and that contribution is approximately equal to other contributing causes such as gender roles, anger and marital functioning" (p. 7). Laslett, Jiang, and Room (2017) emphasized "the effects of heavy drinking upon intimate partners (IP)—including partners, ex-partners or boyfriends/girlfriends—extend to poor performance of one's role, ignoring partners' needs, disregard for their feelings, serious arguments, verbal abuse, and physical and sexual harm" (p. 72). Given the high prevalence of clients affected by substance use disorders, Cox, Ketner, and Blow (2013) recommended that therapists make substance abuse assessment a standard practice for all clients, understand the impact of substance use on relationships and consider treatment modalities such as BCT, which "treats the substance-abusing individual and spouse concurrently to strengthen support for abstinence, reduce relapse, improve couple communication skills, increase positive regard for the relationship, and increase relationship-strengthening activities" (p. 167). An easily used objective measure to screen for alcohol/substance dependence is the Substance Abuse Subtle Screening Inventory (SASSI); it can be administered by paper/pencil or electronically. This formal yet easy measure is also helpful to determine if the client is ready for change (Laux, Piazza, Salyers, & Roseman, 2012). Walker (2017) found that "for individuals for whom alcohol played a role in their IPV, changing attitudes and their use of alcohol were described as important in the process of desistance" (p. 134), highlighting treatment focused areas for these families.

Stress and Work-Related Issues

Families experiencing significant stressors can pose unique challenges for family therapists in that a stressor for one family may not have the same impact upon another. We will look at examples of family stressors, including the reframing of a stressor borne from a bad economy. While experiencing poverty, unemployment, and homelessness can create punishing levels of stress for families, consequences can sometimes be exceedingly more difficult for another group less frequently studied: low-income mothers. Ellerbe et al. (2011) evaluated a program designed to help low-income mothers overcome barriers to self-sufficiency and found that by incorporating assessment, pretreatment services, intensive case management, and follow-up services, many of the participants experienced significantly fewer obstacles. Comprehensive assessments completed by master's level clinicians allowed for early identification of stressors and a customized service plan to reduce barriers to self-sufficiency and family stability. Similarly, flexibility in family therapy assessment and intervention approaches facilitated Ellenwood and Jenkins's (2007) model of assisting chronically ill members and their families in building support systems and remaining connected to each other during a difficult time. Families dealing with chronic illnesses represent another large population that may not always be addressed, but for whom family therapy interventions are critical to facilitate family functioning.

Additional factors that can negatively impact family relationships are work-place demands and work-life conflicts. When the culture of some companies is to work through vacations and illness, many employees feel pressured to spend increasing numbers of hours at work, reducing the amount of time in nonwork activities like time with family, time spent sleeping, or time spent in recreation. Interestingly, Barnes, Bhave, Lefter, and Wagner (2016) found that "during economic booms, employees work more and therefore spend less time with family, sleeping, and recreating … (and) in recessionary economies, employees spend less time working and therefore more time with family, sleeping, and recreating" (p. 235). This is not what one would expect during a recession but is a helpful reframe for an otherwise stressful time!

Gender Issues

As members of today's society, we realize that we have all been socialized with specific gender roles and norms, their impact evidenced daily with ongoing stories of sexism and oppression. These same norms have the potential to negatively impact clients receiving family therapy. Awareness of personal biases and preconceived ideas is an ongoing ethical duty, to minimize the possibility of family therapists imposing their values and beliefs on their clients. Examining male experiences in counseling, Clayton (2015) noted the power of socialization and stated that men "can recite a litany of subtle messages, shamings, beatings, humiliations, and rejections that have communicated to us that we are to be creatures not of feeling and connection but of cold rationality and rugged independence" (p. 96). Stressing the role of family therapists working from a systemic perspective naturally being in a place to assess often overlooked fathers' experiencing of paternal peripartum depression, Freitas and Fox (2015) suggest they "use their practice as a form of social intervention … building relationships and providing resources, family therapists can do their part in not only educating other providers, but by bridging the gap between detection and treatment through direct referrals" (p. 422). According to McGoldrick (2016), "therapists need to be active educators in therapy, helping women realize that they are not alone, encouraging them to network to diminish their isolation, and empowering them to join forces to change the way society operates" (p. 51). Knudson-Martin et al. (2015) developed seven competencies and requisite skills needed to address gender and power in couples counseling: "Competency 1: Identify enactments of cultural discourse; 2: Attune to underlying socio cultural emotion; 3: Identify relational power dynamics; 4: Facilitate relational safety; 5: Foster mutual attunement; 6: Create relationship model based on equality; 7: Facilitate shared relational responsibility" (p. 208). With skills and competencies such as these, gender equality in therapy may soon be on the horizon.

Sources of Support

Social support networks, such as family, extended family, school, church, and friends, all work to lessen the impact of stressors on the family. Assessing support structures in the lives of families can be eye opening for a family. Some families believe they have all the support they need, but when asked about a specific type of support, they may not be able to name anyone. Relying on different people across a supportive network can ensure no one person is relied upon too heavily for support. Lack of support could exacerbate stressors, making it difficult to manage new structures in the face of change and stress. As more is learned about the clients in session, the family therapist may recommend groups in the community to increase support to more than one person in the family. Groups like AA, Al-Anon, and Alateen are helpful support groups for strength during alcohol abuse recovery. Other sources of support for families can come through educational materials offered to or recommended by the family therapist. Imagine two loving parents having significant differences in parenting styles, creating confusion for children, but at their core, a strength they have is love for the family. Helping parents get on the same page with a mutually agreed up on style of parenting could be helpful for all children involved. What types of recommendations would you have for a client seeking cultural or religious support?

ASSESSING INTERACTION PATTERNS

Understanding the way families interact with each other is key to being successful in showing respect to the family when you join with them and accommodate their communication style (Rasheed et al., 2011). In a first session, you should introduce yourself to each family member by name, but start with the parents or caregivers when starting to find out their perspectives on what has brought them to family therapy. Respecting the established hierarchy of the family enables you to build trust with the members, start to build rapport, and become part of their interaction during the session. In future sessions, there will be time for you to join with each family member, conveying empathy and understanding of their opinion.

Family life cycle. To better understand common developmental features of families, you learned in Chapter 3 that Monica McGoldrick and Betty Carter (McGoldrick, Preto, & Carter, 2016) developed the family life cycle model to describe the developmental stages a family system goes through as it evolves and grows. Let's take a closer look. Figure 7.3 provides a visual representation of this updated model, showing the progression of a family moving from one stage to the next. Each stage also has a series of developmental tasks that a family may be faced with resolving. If a family is responsive to each stage's new needs and concerns, individuals in the family system will successfully move with the system to the next stage of family development. Just as with life, movement through the stages is not always linear, and with the addition of a family member through birth or remarriage, the family can find itself navigating previously experienced stages and tasks. Where do you find yourself in this family life cycle? Where would you place your family of origin?

Figure 7.3: Source: Monica McGoldrick, Betty Carter, and Nydia Garcia-Preto, "Family Life Cycle Phases," Expanding Family Life Cycle: Individual, Family, and Social Perspectives. Copyright © 2016 by Pearson Education, Inc.

Figure 7.3 Family Life Cycle Phases (McGoldrick, Garcia Preto, Carter, 2016)

Emerging Young Adults	Couple Formation	Families with Young Children	Families with Adolescents	Launching Children; Moving on in Midlife	Families in Late Middle Age	Families Nearing the End of Life

Family structure. Structure refers to the people who belong to the couple or family unit, how they interact with each other within the system, how they cope with changes, how close or distant members are, and how flexible the system is when changing rules, hierarchy, roles, problem solving, or resolving conflict. Interactional information can be gained by the family therapist by watching how affect is demonstrated toward others, who speaks first, who doesn't speak at all, who speaks for everyone, and who does (or doesn't) allow that to happen. Keep in mind that you will be stepping into a system that existed prior to your working with them. Your task at the first session is to assess how the family is structured, how they communicate and relate to one another, and what strengths the family brings to therapy. Let's look at family functioning from the perspective of communication styles below.

Communication patterns. Communication patterns within the family structure will often be evident from the first point of contact with the family, and become more apparent in the first few assessment sessions of treatment. Many families will have developed a dysfunctional communication style, evidenced by family members who speak for other members, members who do not allow for opposing viewpoints, members who blame others, and members who may be entirely disengaged (Bitter, 2014).

It is rare that a family who is communicating well will decide to come to therapy. Bitter (2014) describes Virginia Satir's four patterns of defensive communication: placating or using pleasing behaviors, blaming, becoming super reasonable, or introducing irrelevant information to distract from conversation. Triangulation can occur in family communication patterns as well, where a dyad engages a third member of the family to lessen anxious and negative emotions within the dyad (Bitter, 2014). Let's explore a couple of ways that dysfunctional communication patterns can show up in families.

Disengagement. There are times when communication is completely shut-off and family members become estranged or disengaged from others. As discussed in Chapters 1–3, Bowen (1978) argued that disengagement or emotional cut-off was a form of enmeshment in that the family member maintained a level of emotional intensity to actively not engage with that person. "The possibility of repeating certain behaviors in interpersonal relations is particularly likely if family members, especially between generations, are characteristically either emotionally overinvolved (i.e., fused) with each other or emotionally cut off (psychologically or physically) from each other" (Gladding, 2015, p. 239).Taking the time to determine if disengagement if serving a purpose, or if it is the family's regular way of relating to each other will help you move forward in the assessment process and help the family better understand the impact of their communication patterns on each other.

Parentification. Family therapists may see many role reversals occurring within a family (Higgins-Klein, 2013), potentially contributing to dysfunctional communication patterns within a family system and the resulting disengagement of family members who no longer perform their prior responsibilities. Parentification is one type of role reversal in which a child takes on the role of caregiver for siblings or another adult, oftentimes leading to strained relationships. Parentification can be considered a "family process in which children sense the vulnerabilities of their parent and the needs in their family and try to act in response to these needs in an active way … involving experiential and behavioral aspects in both children and parents" (Van Parys, Bonnewyn, Hooghe, De Mol, & Rober, 2015, p. 523).

While it is difficult to assess in the first few sessions, over time, the family therapist may notice a pattern of triangulation with a child, inappropriate caregiving by a child, inappropriate seeking of care from a child, inappropriate seeking of care from one parent by another, and other signs that family members are fulfilling potentially precarious roles (Higgins-Klein, 2013). This phenomenon has been seen in children dealing with a parent diagnosed with depression: a circular experience of the child worrying about and caring for the parent, and the parent anguished over the role the child has taken on (Van Parys & Rober, 2013). Van Parys et al. (2015) found that children had a difficult time understanding the experience, but suggested the family therapist could be beneficial in "helping the adolescent to find support outside of the family, reflect on his or her own identity, deal with his or her own emotions, take some distance (psychologically and physically), and find an appropriate way to express one's emotions" (p. 534). Keeping this in mind, parental roles and roles for children vary across cultures, so family therapists are cautioned against pathologically describing something that may be inherent and accepted within a particular cultural context (Khafi, Yates, & Luthar, 2014).

Intimate Partner Violence

In Chapter 4 we focused on the ethical and legal concerns around intimate partner violence (IPV). Here let's take a closer look at assessing for violence within relationships. Assessing for IPV is a critical component in the intake process and cannot be overlooked. Despite its pervasiveness, Froerer, Lucas, and Brown (2012) found that only 1 in 5 couples were assessed for domestic violence, despite violence indicators being noted by clients in clinical intake documents. Questions of how therapists are trained to assess and treat domestic violence is important, but beyond the scope of this chapter. Family violence can range from covert messages of intimidation and control, to overt actions of violence. Living with this on a day-to-day basis may lead to a family who avoids conflict and problem-solving, to minimize the possibility of being harmed. Understanding the consequences of leaving an abusive relationship is important for those working with abused partners: "fear of the partner's action/reaction to leaving; inability to cope with effects lowered self-esteem; aloneness and isolation from family and possibly children; fear of not being able to support oneself" (Rasheed et al., 2011, p. 441). For many of these reasons, couple and family therapy is contraindicated when IPV is a current issue, and individual counseling should be offered instead.

Family Strengths

Exploring family interaction patterns allows for a better understanding of the system, and can provide insight into psychological well-being across one's life (Fuller-Iglesias, Webster, & Antonucci, 2015). Fuller-Iglesias et al. (2015) found that a family support network comprised of family members and good friends serves as a protective factor until after middle age when a change in the composition of the support group can lead to lowered psychological well-being. Ungar (2015) created a map detailing family resilience, naming patterns that both served as protective factors (post-traumatic growth), as well as those that would not be expected (avoidant, maladaptive), but equally serve a protective purpose. How families support each other during times of change is an important part to assess at the beginning of family therapy, and could be information you use to instill hope for change with the family.

CHALLENGES TO ASSESSMENT

In any therapy session, there can be challenges and unforeseen events that unfold. A therapist comes to weekly sessions with a plan for the family, but that is completely derailed when the family comes in with a crisis. The same is true of assessment. While a family therapist has either formal or informal assessment strategies scheduled for a session, many challenges often arise. Families attend therapy to resolve issues causing them enough of disturbance that they have reached out for help. This means that families are likely attending their first sessions with extensive conflict and pain. They likely feel chaos in their lives. These presenting problems alone can pose a challenge in therapy and assessment. You will want to keep in mind that one or more family members may be very reluctant, angry, or even unwilling to attend therapy. Similarly, a family may not be ready for therapy. In all cases, your job as the family therapist is to assess each family member as well as the functioning of the family system.

Determining Readiness for Family Therapy

Higgins-Klein (2013) detailed the concept of "high-functioning" and "low-function-ing" (p. 131) families. A family that is functioning well enough will likely never be seen in therapy. If they do come to therapy, we find that they have usually already identified the problem and attempted to solve it in many ways, albeit maybe not as successfully as they hoped. On the contrary, a lower functioning family may never attend therapy, but may have enormous challenges and maladaptive functioning. In this case, a family may not be ready for family therapy, until individual members of the family are worked with to understand their own behavior in the context of their family. A family that is really struggling may not be ready to sit together in a room until certain dyads' or individuals' needs are met in a few individual sessions.

Bradford (2012) created an instrument measuring readiness for change in couple therapy, based on the seminal transtheoretical model of change put forth by Prochaska and Norcross. In the assessment phase of therapy, family clinicians should be looking at the following phases to gauge where each member of the family is in relation to readiness for change: precontemplation, contemplation, preparation, action, maintenance, and termination (Prochaska & Norcross, 2001). Family therapists may use formal or informal measures, including instruments such as the one outlined by Bradford (2012) to assess readiness for change. An individual in therapy who is not ready for change will likely not be successful in the therapy, an essential piece of information to be gathered before starting family therapy. Let's turn our attention to Guided Practice Exercise 7.2, in which you will consider a recent transition in your own life. How did you experience these phases of change?

GUIDED PRACTICE EXERCISE 7.2

Prochaska and Norcross's (2001) stages of change are precontemplation, contemplation, preparation, action, maintenance, and termination. In a journal or on another sheet of paper, write down a major life change you have experienced within the past couple of years. It may be a decision to apply for a new job, change geographic locations, or even your decision to become a family therapist. Thinking back to that experience, at which stage of change did you start? Map out the stages of change and write down what you would have been thinking, feeling, and doing in each stage. What would have helped you to move from one stage to the next?

In instances of abuse and trauma, determining readiness for family therapy is paramount. For example, an adolescent who has disclosed sexual abuse should be worked with individually and be ready to speak to the trauma in family therapy before the adolescent is thrown into a family session. Further, Gil (2016) stressed the importance of assessing how the family handled a disclosure of abuse before working through the trauma in family therapy. Parents may not understand the impact of trauma and abuse, so providing resources to them would be critical. See "Additional Resources" at the end of this chapter for examples.

Unwilling Family Member

There may be many instances where a family member is unwilling to attend family therapy, but this does not mean that the therapy cannot begin. A family member who is unwilling to attend sessions tells the family therapist quite a bit about the functioning of that individual member as well as the family unit having to work without that member.

In research on couples therapy, many authors suggest that males are more often hesitant or unwilling to attend family therapy than are females for a variety of factors including gender expectation norms (Doss, Mitchell, Georgia, Biesen, & Rowe, 2015). The reasons a family member is refusing to either attend or participate in therapy may shed light onto a greater systemic issue in the family's maladaptive functioning. Guided Practice Exercise 7.3 provides you with a short vignette describing a blended family having difficulty coming together. Given the description, what might the family dynamics look like in the first family therapy session? How would you manage the family members in this therapy session?

GUIDED PRACTICE EXERCISE 7.3

Barbara and Jim met 6 months ago in a support group for widowed partners. They each have one child and are both close to the same age, so when they moved in together last month, they assumed all would easily come together. Both families find themselves very busy with full-time work, children's schoolwork, and extracurricular activities. Relationally, there are problems: Barbara's and Jim's children do not get along and do not want to share their parents. Both children create physical barriers between Barbara and Jim anytime they can, leaving the parents little time to spend together. What area of assessment would you focus on with this blended family?

Culturally Competent Family Therapy

The preamble to the ACA Code of Ethics (ACA, 2014) states that counselors must "[embrace] a multicultural approach in support of the worth, dignity, potential and uniqueness of people within their social and cultural contexts" (p. 3). As with any therapy, a consideration for cultural diversity, intersectionality, and inclusion must always be in the mind of the therapist. Not only must family therapists work to understand the cultural heritage of the family, they must also respect the family's culture. Of interest to culturally competent family therapists, Ellenwood, Snyders, Poignon, and Roberts (2006) created a tool to expand on traditional diagnostic interviews to assess cultural influences on family functioning, highlighting ways to interview and assess from a multicultural lens, especially in the case of migrant or immigrant families. After exploring the experiences of black clients in marriage and family therapy, Awosan, Sandberg, and Hall (2011) asserted that "lessening the burden of cultural mistrust among Black clients in their attempt to seek and maintain therapeutic services becomes a paramount responsibility for mental health service providers, particularly White therapists" (p. 155).

Equally important to cultural competence as a family therapist is an awareness of one's own privilege and how systems of oppression are engrained in society, experienced at a greater level for some families than others. Hardiman, Jackson, and Griffin (2013) outlined a conceptual map of oppression and highlight how attitudes and behaviors systematically drive conscious and unconscious oppression at an individual level, either intentionally or unintentionally. From these attitudes and beliefs, people in power "codify oppression in laws, policies, practices, and norms" thereby enforcing institutional oppression (Hardiman et al., 2013, p. 28). As their family therapist, you should be aware of and assess the cultural experience and experiences of oppression with family members as well as the family as a system in a larger societal system. Case Presentation 7.3 presents the case of a Chinese family presenting for family therapy, in which the parents and children hold differing views. How would you ensure you are assessing and balancing these views equally in family therapy?

CASE PRESENTATION 7.3: DIFFERING GENERATIONAL VIEWS

Cheng and Jun, a Chinese couple, present for family therapy with their 12-year-old daughter, Liang, and Song, their 10-year-old son. Cheng works full time for a technology company, and Jun works part time for a book store. The parents report increasing levels of conflict and disobedience from the children. The children state their parents are too hard on them and don't support them in the way they should. Cheng and Jun do everything they can for their children and sacrifice a lot to provide Liang and Song with educational opportunities they never had.

USING ASSESSMENT IN TREATMENT PLANNING

The process of assessment helps us to determine which issues are most important to address in therapy. Assessment helps the family therapist to hypothesize what has created problems facing the family, and to conceptualize a plan of treatment for this family. You also need to make sure you are working collaboratively with the family to know and keep in mind what the goals of the family are. As in the case of the Gabriel's family, his father indicated that the family was seeking help to address Gabriel's defiant attitude and recent suicide attempt. From the therapist's perspective, marital conflict between Ray and Patricia has had a significant impact on Gabriel as well as his sister, Danielle. If the therapist chooses to focus on the marital issues before addressing Gabriel's issues, the family may feel like their stated concerns are not being addressed and may end treatment prematurely. In this section, we will look at treatment planning for Gabriel's family from the initial phase of treatment, to the working phase of treatment, and through the closing phase of treatment. Reminders for each section will precede Gabriel's family's treatment plan.

Diagnosis. Depending on the theoretical approach taken by the family therapist, the focus of diagnosis may be on the types of family boundaries, as is the case for structural family therapists. Understanding interrelationships becomes key so the therapist knows how to modify family member interactions. Diagnosis leads to us thinking of DSM-5, but it focuses more on individually diagnosed disorders (more often reimbursed by insurance companies) and only includes a brief focus on a few relational codes (not reimbursed by third-party payers). Relational codes generally used by family therapists include parent–child relational problems, partner relational problems, and sibling relational problems (Flamez & Sheperis, 2015).

Treatment plan. Soon after meeting with the family for the first time, the family therapist will complete a treatment plan, providing a road map for family therapy. Typical features in the treatment plan include a list of the following: identified problems, long term goals, short term goals (also called objectives), therapeutic interventions to be utilized, and a diagnosis. Treatment plans should always be tailored to each specific family, even if problems this family is facing sound just like the problems of another family you are treating. Incorporated into each treatment plan are the existing strengths of the family, which can vary greatly from family to family. Treatment plans will also vary based on the theoretical orientation of the family therapist.

Initial phase of treatment. The initial phase of treatment can be completed anywhere from the first session, up to the third session. The difference in time can vary based on how easy it is for the family and the therapist to achieve the following goals: development of the therapeutic relationship, assessment of the primary problem, goal setting, and completion of early referrals for adjunct services. Based on the case study presented at the beginning of the chapter, goals/objectives and selected interventions will be listed for each phase.

Goal 1. Join with family and accommodate to family rules, patterns, and structure.

    a.   Understand family members' feelings and reflect empathy to all members.

    b.   Track and maintain family communication style while matching and acknowledging family hierarchy and rules.

Goal 2. Assess family's structure and boundaries and determine goals.

    a.   Ask about each individual's perspective of the problem, family structure, and interaction.

    b.   Identify structural patterns by observing spontaneous family interactions.

It was important in this phase to honor each person's perspective and hear how they each had been impacted over the past year. Ray's change in employment caused a significant shift in hierarchy, structure, and boundaries of the family members, much to everyone's frustration.

Working phase of treatment. The working phase of therapy happens over two or more sessions. Goals in this phase will answer questions asked of the family in the initial phase: What are your hopes for us meeting together? Do you already have ideas about how to best achieve these goals? This phase is where most of the interventions are implemented, moving between the therapist's focus on the therapy process or content of the sessions.

Rasheed et al. (2011) cautioned that in this phase, the therapist should "remain firm in his or her selection of theory and technique(s) to be used to avoid moving around from problem area to problem area" (p. 343), even if the family is inclined to address another problem they would like to see resolved. For novice therapists, it is tempting to go where the family goes, but the role of the therapist also calls for leadership skills, slowing the family down in the therapy process. Knowing that significant change takes time, Rasheed et al. also stressed that "it is important to be patient with the theory, technique, and problem area selected, and to give them time to work" (p. 344).

Goal 1. Reestablish the parental subsystem; adjust generational hierarchy; strengthen parental coalition.

    a.   Present affective intensity statements to assist in highlighting parent–child hierarchical power imbalance, particularly between Ray and Danielle, and between Patricia and Gabriel.

    b.   Unbalance the system by taking the least dominant family member's side (Gabriel) to assist in increasing his position in the family.

Goal 2. Develop clear boundaries between all subsystems.

    a.   Challenge family assumptions associated with relational boundaries.

    b.   Initiate boundary-making techniques, such as having clients arrange chairs to challenge current hierarchy, coalitions, and boundaries.

Challenging established boundaries remained the primary focus during this phase, as the family structure had shifted to Danielle and Ray being in charge over the past year. Danielle's parenting of Gabriel had increased in the past 4 months, as Patricia involved herself less and less in the parenting of her son. Patricia disclosed that she was feeling depressed and believed that was what allowed her to let her daughter take over parenting responsibilities. Gabriel admitted to acting out to take the focus off his mother, whom he started to check in on daily when he saw her less involved in his care. Ray learned that he didn't need Danielle to continue to be his "eyes and ears" but could instead form a coalition with his wife to reinforce rules and boundaries with their children.

Closing phase of treatment. The closing phase of treatment can occur during the last 2 weeks of therapy. Goals during this phase include pointing out and solidifying gains made by the family, developing strategies for managing future issues, discussing long-term goals, and providing referrals for ongoing sources of support.

Goal 1. Develop strategies for managing future boundary issues.

    a.   Use enactments to role-play situations of concern for each family member.

    b. Increase competence by transferring new skills and behaviors to other relationships.

Goal 2. Establish and solidify newly established family norms and structures.

    a. Reinforce competence by focusing on what was learned and accomplished by the family.

    b. Positively reframe structural alterations to assist in introducing each member's role.

The Taylor family made great strides in restructuring their family and adopting new rules of engagement. Each person continued to be heard and engaged with each other well when concerns were brought up regarding how the family was going to maintain these gains, despite Ray's employment situation not changing. Each person expressed feeling reassured of their role, and parents were firmly in charge. Referrals to community resources were made for individual therapy for Patricia and for weekly support groups for adolescent boys for Gabriel.

    Writing useful client goals and therapeutic tasks. In today's age of accountability, therapists must be able to show that a treatment plan's accompanying goals are being reached. This is also important information for the family to know, so they know whether they are moving toward problem resolution or not. Goal setting should be a "collaborative process between therapist and the family ... giving the family power of its (therapeutic) fate is also an empowering process ... (and) may also serve to decrease the amount of resistance in families" (Rasheed et al., 2011, p. 339). Families may first have broad ideas of what they would like to be different, so much so that you would have a difficult time measuring the goal. By helping them operationalize the goal, you get them to define it according to specific behaviors they would like to see. We can use this information to create goals or objectives that are specific, observable, and measurable, preferred characteristics when selecting goals for therapy. According to Berman (2015), "these goals will assist in charting treatment progress, instill hope for change, and help the clinician plan treatment sessions" (p. 7). Short-term objectives and therapeutic interventions (tasks) should be those that have shown to be effective with populations in evidence-based treatments (EBTs). When selecting interventions, Dattilio and Jongsma (2015) remind us that in "common problems faced by families (e.g., geographic relocation) which no studies have specifically focused on, an EBT, such as behaviorally based parenting techniques or problem-solving skills, can be utilized to help the family through that particular challenge" (p. 3).

    Risk management. Assessing for safety and crisis issues is critical while the treatment plan is being created. Short-term objectives may be put in place, ensuring safety factors and actions are being addressed on a weekly basis. Taking steps to eliminate or minimize risk factors will increase family stability and safety, facilitating ongoing family therapy. Since we don't always know when issues of safety will arise, you can attach safety plans to the treatment plan as an addendum, if needed.

Suicide and homicide assessment. Assessing for danger to self or others is an ethical mandate that family therapists should be prepared to navigate. Whether in an individual or family session, the therapist should remain calm and strive to understand the client's feelings and perspective. What is the message behind this threat? To determine the need for immediate intervention (hospitalization or law enforcement) or ongoing assessment (with family support), the lethality of the suicide or homicide plan should be determined: how extensive is the client's plan? How effective is the method of self-injury to cause harm? Has the client thought through steps that would prevent recue? The higher each of these are rated, the more immediate the need for immediate intervention (consult your state laws regarding duty to warn requirements). At each stage, you will want to make every effort to include a supportive network made up of spouses/partners, immediate and extended family members, friends, and case workers to gain a commitment to ongoing treatment.

Child and elder/dependent abuse. Family therapists need to be aware of indicators of abuse. In many states, mental health providers are considered mandated reporters of abuse against children, elders, and vulnerable adults, making it an important topic starting with the informed consent process. Since this is an exception to confidentiality, families need to understand the steps the family therapist would have to make to protect the family. Explaining the process also gives the therapist a chance to reframe the purpose of protective services organizations, focusing on how these organizations help families with resources like parenting, counseling, safety plans, and child care as the family works to protect these vulnerable populations. Therapists may also empower clients to make the call reporting abuse, allowing the client to engage with social services directly, and then serving as support for the family through therapy. At no time does this mean the therapist is delegating the report to the family, and all steps should be documented in the client's file accordingly. Case Presentation 7.4 provides us with a look at a family who are receiving mandated services through their state's child protective services. If you were the family's family therapist, what would be the first areas you would work to understand about the family? What treatment goals would you discuss with the family?

CASE PRESENTATION 7.4: THE CASE OF SEAN AND MARY

One year ago, Sean and Mary lost custody of their three children (ages 9, 6, and 2) after Sean lost his job and they were not able to maintain a household with proper living conditions. The children were removed after the two younger children were found wandering the neighborhood without clothing to protect them from the cold. Mary states that she was able to get a couple of hours of work that day, so she asked a neighbor to watch the children. The babysitter fell asleep, and the children wandered outside. Sean was not home, because he was out looking for work. Social services picked up the children and deemed the house unsafe, putting the children in foster care until the parents could provide appropriate living conditions. Sean and Mary completed the state's required safety plan, but now that the children have been returned, there has been a lot of arguing between all the family members, especially the children.

Safety plan components. For those clients currently or recently in any type of crisis situations, therapists can assist clients with the creation of safety plans. In the case of a client crisis, the therapist will work with the client to create a safety plan to include answers to the following: warning signs a crisis is developing; internal coping strategies; settings that can help provide distraction; people who can be approached for help; agencies to be contacted during the crisis; and listed last is the clinician. In the case of someone whose safety is threatened, such as someone experiencing domestic violence, the client can work with the therapist to create a safety plan, outlining the steps one would take when deciding to leave the relationship. Creating a viable safety plan is skill that is developed through practice. For this reason, Guided Practice Exercise 7.4 directs you to a Safety Planning Guide for Clinicians that you should use for practice. Read through the guide and then work with a classmate, taking turns role-playing scenarios where safety planning is critical to client treatment.

GUIDED PRACTICE EXERCISE 7.4

The Suicide Prevention Resource Center provides a Safety Planning Guide for clinicians. Go to the following link, download the safety plan guide, and practice filling it out with a fellow student. The more practice you have discussing safety plans, the easier it will be when faced with a client who needs your assistance to document a sound plan to keep them http://www.sprc.org/resources-programs/safety-planning-guide-quick-guide-clinicians

Additional risk factors. Families support each other through developmental stages, changes, and tasks, as well as other stressors from the environment. The number of additional risk factors facing a family can be numerous, but your job as a family therapist will be limited to helping the family to examine the stressor and develop a goal to minimize its negative impact on the family. Areas of risk such as self-harm without suicidal intent, eating disorders, chronic medical illness, poverty, homelessness, unemployment, and educational difficulties are all things that a family therapist may be called on to address with a family.

COMMUNICATING WITH OTHER PROFESSIONALS

Because families do not exist in a vacuum but interact with many different systems, it is important that family therapists be prepared to work with the many agents in these systems. It is in the best interest of a family therapist to be "willing to collaborate with a range of people in the wider community" (Higgins-Klein, 2013, p. 30). This means a family therapist might work with the child's school, family case worker, psychiatrist, psychologist, social worker, professional counselor, religious leader, and other service provider involved in the family's life. Despite involving many signed releases of information, this cooperative approach allows you to get the best picture of the family functioning and the functioning of its systemic parts. At times, family therapists may have little time to contact all the necessary parties or might be hesitant to act as the case manager for the family. However, the family therapist must realize these other professionals are a part of the family's and the therapist's team and all team members play crucial roles for the family to be successful in therapy (Higgins-Klein, 2013).

SUMMARY

We looked at how to start working with families, from conducting a brief intake and conducting clinical assessment sessions, to best techniques for learning about their needs and concerns. Collaborative interventions such as a genogram can help the family therapist assess family structure and communication patterns, in addition to highlighting individual issues that could impact family interaction patterns. Knowing in advance the challenges you may face when conducting assessment sessions can head off interruptions and facilitate your gaining enough information to create not only a hypothesis relating to the family's presenting problem but also a treatment plan to guide your work with the family. Now that we have discussed the intake process, we will take a closer look at the role of assessment and evaluating outcomes in Chapter 8. The keystones below highlight the takeaway points before you proceed to Chapter 8.

KEYSTONES

Among the key points addressed in this chapter are:

- Assessment begins at first contact with the family, as each encounter gives the family therapist more data by which to begin to develop an idea of the maladaptive patterns that have developed within the family system.
- Assessment is a therapeutic intervention by which the family learns more about how they interact.
- The treatment plan includes culturally competent approaches to identifying goals, short-term and long-term objectives, and implementing therapeutic interventions.
- The family therapist should advocate for the family by communicating with other professionals and working with the larger contextual problems influencing the family.

REFLECTIONS FROM THE CONTRIBUTOR'S CHAIR
Kathy Ybanez-Llorente & Quinn K. Smelser

Remembering all these aspects of assessment through the first few sessions of family therapy can be overwhelming and exhausting for the beginner therapist. Equally, when a seasoned family therapist encounters a difficult case, anxieties about being sure to cover everything abound. To give us a sort of blueprint, we begin building a genogram with every individual and family seen. This gives a starting point for assessment and can be done via play therapy, sand tray, expressive arts, and talking, so it is appropriate for even the youngest member of the family. In addition to having the family fill out formal assessment measures gauging impact of trauma, we also spend a great deal of time normalizing issues the family brings to counseling. More and more, we find ourselves introducing neurobiology research as well as assessing attachment relationships in the family. Discussing brain development, attachment security, and maladaptive patterns that are fostered often help families feel more normal as they begin therapy. It also helps us build competence and credibility when working with the families. Working extensively with clients in crisis has helped to increase our ability to connect with clients quickly, convey empathy while assessing lethality, and listening for things like protective factors and reasons for living that may be difficult to hear through the pain. Families can be incredibly supportive structures—sometimes they just need to be shown how.

ADDITIONAL RESOURCES
The following resources provide additional information relating to the chapter topics.

PLAY AND EXPRESSIVE TECHNIQUES FOR FAMILY ASSESSMENT WITH CHILDREN AND ADOLESCENTS

Readings
These books provide descriptions of interactive techniques that can be utilized in family assessment when children and adolescents are participating.

Gil, E. (2016). *Play in family therapy*. New York: Guilford Press.

Higgins-Klein, D. (2013). *Mindfulness-based play-family therapy*. New York: Norton.

Lowenstein, L. (2008; 2010; 2011). *Assessment and treatment activities for children, adolescents, and families: Practitioners share their most effective techniques*. 3 Vols. Ontario: Champion Press.

Useful Website
- Creative Family Therapy Technique
  http://www.lianalowenstein.com/articleFamilyTherapy.pdf

This online article describes many play-oriented techniques and art-based approaches that can be utilized in family therapy to encourage positive relational interactions.

TRAUMA ASSESSMENT AND INTERVENTIONS

Readings

Courtois, C. A., & Ford, J. D. (2013). *Treatment of complex trauma: A sequenced, relationship-based approach.* New York: Guilford Press.

Perry, B. D., & Szalavitz, M. (2006). *The boy who was raised as a dog: And other stories from a child psychiatrist's notebook. What traumatized children can teach us about loss, love, and healing.* New York: Basic Books.

Van der Kolk, B. (2014). *The body keeps the score: Brain, mind, and body in the healing of trauma.* New York: Penguin Books.

The above books provide understanding of the impact of trauma on individuals and families.

Useful Websites

- Child Trauma Academy, Neurosequential Model of Trauma Treatment
  http://www.childtrauma.org
- Circle of Security Assessment
  http://theattachmentclinic.org/services.html
- National Child Traumatic Stress Network Guidelines for effective interventions and assessments
  http://nctsn.org/training-guidelines
- Whole Brain Child
  http://www.drdansiegel.com/resources/

These websites provide more information on trauma-based treatment for children and adolescents. With increasing numbers of people reporting adverse childhood experiences, practitioners will be best served with up-to-date treatment options regarding trauma.

PARENTING AND ATTACHMENT RESOURCES

Readings

Dinkmeyer, D., McKay, G. D., & Dinkmeyer, D. (2008). *Parenting young children: Systematic training for effective parenting (STEP) of children under six.* Coral Springs, FL: Step.

Faber, A., & Mazlish, E. (2012). *How to talk so kids will listen and listen so kids will talk.* New York: Scribner.

Kline, F., & Fay, J. (2006). *Parenting with love and logic.* Colorado Springs: Pinon Press.

Siegal, D. J. (2012). *The whole brain child: 12 revolutionary strategies to nurture your child's developing mind.* New York: Bantam Books.

The above websites and books provide parenting instruction and recommendations, key to minimizing parent–child conflicts by forming boundaries and rules within a home.

Useful Website
- ZERO TO THREE
  https://www.zerotothree.org

This site helps build family engagement and connection.

Readings
Bailey, B. A. (2000). *I love you rituals.* New York: HarperCollins.

Bany-Winters, L. (2006). *Family fun nights: 140 activities the whole family will enjoy.* Chicago: Chicago Review Press.

These books provide a series of games and activities that parents and other family members can use to engage the whole family, with few materials needed.

Useful Website
- Jesuit Social Services
  http://www.strongbonds.jss.org.au/workers/default.html

This website provides resources for parents and caregivers for adolescents, as well as treatment recommendations and resources for mental health professionals working with adolescents and their families.

REFERENCES
American Counseling Association. (2014). *ACA code of ethics.* Alexandria, VA: Author.

American Educational Research Association, American Psychological Association, National Council on Measurement in Education [AERA/APA/NCME]. (1999). Standards for educational and psychological testing. Washington, DC: American Psychological Association.

Awosan, C. I., Sandberg, J. G., & Hall, C. A. (2011). Understanding the experience of Black clients in marriage and family therapy. *Journal of Marital & Family Therapy, 37*(2), 153–168. doi:10.1111/j.1752-0606.2009.00166.x

Barnes, C. M., Bhave, D. P, Lefter, A. M., & Wagner, D. T. (2016). The benefits of bad economies: Business cycles and time-based work-life conflict. *Journal of Occupational Health Psychology, 21*(2), 235–249. doi:10.1037/a0039896

Belous, C. K., Timm, T. M., Chee, G., & Whitehead, M. R. (2012). Revisiting the sexual genogram. *American Journal of Family Therapy, 40*(4), 281–296. doi:10.1080/01926187.2011.627317

Berman. P. S. (2015). *Case conceptualization and treatment planning: Integrating theory with clinical practice* (3rd ed.). Thousand Oaks, CA: Sage.

Bitter, J. R. (2014). *Theory and practice of family therapy and counseling* (2nd ed.). Belmont, CA: Brooks/ Cole.

Bowen, M. (1978). *Family therapy in clinical practice.* New York: Aronson.

Bradford, K. (2012). Assessing readiness for couple therapy: The stages of relationship change questionnaire. *Journal of Marital & Family Therapy, 38*(3), 486–501. doi:10.1111/j.1752-0606.2010.00211.x

Center for Behavioral Health Statistics and Quality. (2016). *2015 national survey on drug use and health: Detailed tables.* Rockville, MD: Substance Abuse and Mental Health Services Administration.

Clayton, R. E. (2015). Men in the triangle: Grief, inhibition, and defense. *Journal of College Student Psychotherapy, 29,* 94–110. doi:10.1080/87568225.2015.1008361

Coppersmith, E. (1980). The Family Floor Plan: A tool for training, assessment and intervention in family therapy. *Journal of Marital & Family Therapy, 6*(2), 141–145. doi:10.1111/j.1752-0606.1980.tb01298.x

Cox, R. B., Ketner, J. S., & Blow, A. J. (2013). Working with couples and substance abuse: Recommendations for clinical practice. *American Journal of Family Therapy, 41*(2), 160–172. doi:10.1080/01926187.2012.6 70608

Dattilio, F. M., & Jongsma, A. E. (2015). *The family therapy treatment planner* (2nd ed.). New York: Wiley.

Doss, B. D., Mitchell, A., Georgia, E. J., Biesen, J. N., & Rowe, L. S. (2015). Improvements in closeness, communication, and psychological distress mediate effects of couple therapy for veterans. *Journal of Consulting and Clinical Psychology, 83*(2), 405–415. doi:10.1037/a0038541

Ellenwood, A. E., & Jenkins, J. E. (2007). Unbalancing the effects of chronic illness: Non-traditional family therapy assessment and intervention approach. *American Journal of Family Therapy, 35,* 265–277. doi:10.1080/01926180600968431

Ellenwood, A. E., Snyders, R., Poignon, J., & Roberts, A. (2006). Expanding the traditional diagnostic interview: Gathering migration history via a cultural diagnostic interview. *Journal of Family Psychotherapy, 17*(2), 51–65. doi:10.1300/J085v17n02_04

Ellerbe, T., Carlton, E. L., Ramlow, B. E., Leukefeld, C. G., Delaney, M., & Staton-Tindall, M. (2011). Helping low-income mothers overcome multiple barriers to self-sufficiency: Strategies and implications for human services professionals. *Families in Society: The Journal of Contemporary Social Services, 92*(3), 289–294. doi:10.16061044-3894.4137

Epstein, N. B., Baldwin, L. M., & Bishop, D. S. (1983). The McMaster Family Assessment Device. *Journal of Marital and Family Therapy, 9,* 171–180. doi:10.1111/j.1752-0606.1983 .tb01497.x

Erford, B. T. (2014). *40 Techniques every counselor should know.* Upper Saddle River, NJ: Merrill.

Finn, S. E., & Tonsager, M. E. (1997). Information-gathering and therapeutic models of assessment: Complementary paradigms. *Psychological Assessment, 9*(4), 374–385. doi:10.1037/ 1040-3590.9.4.374

Flamez, B., & Sheperis, C. J. (Eds.). (2015). *Diagnosing and treating children and adolescents: A guide for mental health professionals.* Hoboken, NJ: Wiley.

Freitas, C. J., & Fox, C. A. (2015). Fathers matter: Family therapy's role in the treatment of paternal peripartum depression. *Contemporary Family Therapy, 37*(4), 417–425. doi:10.1007/s10591-015-9347-5

Froerer, A. S., Lucas, B. M., & Brown, T. B. (2012). Current practices of intimate partner violence assessment among marriage and family therapy trainees at a university clinic. *Journal of Couple & Relationship Therapy, 11*(1), 16–32. doi:10.1080/15332691.2012.639702

Fuller-Iglesias, H. R., Webster, N. J., & Antonucci, T. C. (2015). The complex nature of family support across the life span: Implications for psychological well-being. *Developmental Psychology, 51*(3), 277–288. doi:10.1037/a0038665

Gil, E. (2016). *Play in family therapy* (2nd ed.). New York: Guilford Press.

Gladding, S. T. (2015). *Family therapy: History, theory, and practice* (6th ed.). Hoboken, NJ: Pearson.

Hardiman, R., Jackson, B. W., & Griffin, P. (2013). Conceptual frameworks. In M. Adams, W. J. Blumenfield, C. Castaneda, H. W. Hackman, M. L. Peters, & X. Zuniga (Eds.), *Readings for diversity and social justice* (3rd ed., pp. 26–35). New York: Routledge.

Higgins-Klein, D. (2013). *Mindfulness-based play-family therapy*. New York: Norton.

Huff, S. C., Anderson, S. R., & Edwards, L. L. (2014). Training marriage and family therapists in formal assessment: Contributions to students' familiarity, attitude, and confidence. *Journal of Family Psychotherapy, 25*(4), 300–315. doi:10.1080/08975353.2014.977673

Khafi, T. Y., Yates, T. M., & Luthar, S. S. (2014). Ethnic differences in the developmental significance of parentification. *Family Process, 53*(2), 267–287. doi:10.1111/famp.12072

Knudson-Martin, C., Huenergardt, D., Lafontant, K., Bishop, L., Schaepper, J., & Wells, M. (2015). Competencies for addressing gender and power in couple therapy: A socio emotional approach. *Journal of Marital & Family Therapy, 41*(2), 421–437. doi:10.1111/jmft.12068

Laux, J. M., Piazza, N. J., Salyers, K., & Roseman, C. P. (2012). The Substance Abuse Subtle Screening Inventory-3 and stages of change: A screening validity study. *Journal of Addictions & Offender Counseling, 33*(2), 82–92. doi:10.1002/j.2161-1874.2012.00006.x

Laslett, A., Jiang, H., & Room, R. (2017). Alcohol's involvement in an array of harms to intimate partners. *Drug and Alcohol Review, 36*(1), 72–79. doi:10.1111/dar.12435

Leonard, K. E., & Quigley, B. M. (2017). Thirty years of research show alcohol to be a cause of intimate partner violence: Future research needs to identify who to treat and how to treat them. *Drug and Alcohol Review, 36*(1), 7–9. doi:10.1111/dar.12434

McGoldrick, M. (2016). Women and the family life cycle. In M. McGoldrick, N. G. Preto, & B. Carter (Eds.), *Expanding family life cycle: Individual, family, and social perspectives* (5th ed., pp. 45–62). Boston: Pearson.

McGoldrick, M., Preto, N. G., & Carter, B. (2016). The life cycle in its changing context. In M. McGoldrick, N. G. Preto, & B. Carter (Eds.), *Expanding family life cycle: Individual, family, and social perspectives* (5th ed., pp. 1–44). Boston: Pearson.

Nichols, M., & Tafuri, S. (2013). Techniques of structural family assessment: A qualitative analysis of how experts promote a systemic perspective. *Family Process, 52*(2), 207–215. doi:10.1111/famp.12025

Platt, L. F., & Skowron, E. A. (2013). The family genogram interview: Reliability and validity of a new interview protocol. *Family Journal: Counseling and Therapy for Couples and Families, 21*(1), 35–45. doi:10.1177/1066480712456817

Prochaska, J. O., & Norcross, J. C. (2001). Stages of change. *Psychotherapy, 38*(4), 443–448. doi:10.1037/0033-3204.38.4.443

Rasheed, J. M., Rasheed, M. N., & Marley, J. A. (2011). *Family therapy: Models and techniques*. Thousand Oaks, CA: Sage.

Sundet, R. (2011). Collaboration: Family and therapist perspectives of helpful therapy. *Journal of Marital and Family Therapy, 37*(2), 236–249. doi:10.1111/j.1752-0606.2009.00157.x

Ungar, M. (2015). Varied patterns of family resilience in challenging contexts. *Journal of Marital and Family Therapy, 42*(1), 19–31. doi:10.1111/jmft.12124

Van Parys, H., Bonnewyn, A., Hooghe, A., De Mol, J., & Rober, P. (2015). Toward understanding the child's experience in the process of parentification: Young adults' reflections on growing up with a depressed parent. *Journal of Marital and Family Therapy, 41*(4), 522–536. doi:10.1111/jmft.12087

Van Parys, H., & Rober, P. (2013). Trying to comfort the parent: A qualitative study of children dealing with parental depression. *Journal of Marital and Family Therapy, 39*(3), 330–345. doi:10.1111/j.1752-0606.2012.00304.x

Walker, K. (2017). The role of alcohol as men desist from physical intimate partner violence. *Drug and Alcohol Review, 36*(1), 134–142. doi:10.1111/dar.12445

Weber, T., McKeever, J. E., & McDaniel, S. H. (1985). A beginner's guide to the problem-oriented first family interview. *Family Process, 24*(3), 357–364. doi:10.1111/j.1545-5300.1985.00357.x

Wilkinson, I. (1987). Family assessment: A review. *Journal of Family Therapy, 9*(4), 367–380. doi:10.1046/j..1987.00289.x

Gathering Information to Help Families Change: Assessment in Marriage and Family Counseling

K. Michelle Hunnicutt Hollenbaugh, Baylea Wagener,
Janet Froeschle Hicks, and Brandé Flamez

"My family is my strength and my weakness."

—Aishwarya Rai Bachchan

In our work counseling families, we have found that every family has their own unique strengths and weaknesses, and these attributes unequivocally alter each individual within the system—for better or worse! In the previous chapter, we covered the initial interview and assessment, as well as treatment planning. Though assessment is obviously important in the beginning, it is crucial to engage in assessment practices throughout the counseling relationship to evaluate whether the couple or family has made any improvements or changes based on the treatment plan (Sperry, 2012). In Chapter 8 we will cover activities you can engage in as a therapist, to evaluate this plan. It will include formal, structured assessments, as well as qualitative assessments and structured interviews. Finally, to align with the evaluation of progress in treatment, we will discuss formats for progress notes as they relate to treating families.

Marriage and family assessment is far more complicated than individual assessment. The therapist must assess the dynamics between all of the family members and the social context in which the relationships exist (Carlson, Krumholz, & Snyder 2013). Relationship satisfaction can change frequently, and families can be at different individual developmental levels, which can affect responses on a formalized assessment (Whiston, 2016). Different types of assessment are also important, as they can help give the therapist a bigger picture of the clinical issues from different perspectives (Carlson et al., 2013). As many therapists approach families from a systems perspective, marriage and family assessment is assessing the system (Whiston, 2016).

LEARNING OBJECTIVES

After reading this chapter, you will be able to do the following:

- Understand the importance of assessment to measure progress in marriage and family therapy.
- Identify important aspects of reliability and validity in marriage and family assessments.
- Describe popular assessments used when working with couples and families.
- Identify individual assessments used in marriage and family, including those used to address specific issues like sexual dysfunction and domestic violence.
- Discuss the cultural and ethical issues related to assessment in marriage and family therapy.

KEY CONCEPTS

Chapter 7 communicated the importance of intake assessment and information gathering when working with families. This chapter expands on the importance of assessment by illustrating how assessment impacts goals, treatment plans, and the change process. Let us start by discussing client progress based on assessment, baseline establishment, notes, measurements, and treatment plans.

EVALUATING THE PLAN

Assessments

Therapists often use assessment during the treatment planning process to establish a baseline upon which to measure the client's progress. When developing the treatment plan, the therapist may identify a construct related to the client's goals that can be measured through an assessment. For example, if a client or family wanted to improve their ability to communicate, the therapist would consider assessments that evaluate communication. The therapist could administer this assessment at various points throughout the course of treatment. Changes in the assessment outcomes would indicate progress toward the overall goal, stagnation, or regression from the goal.

Progress Notes

Progress notes are created by the therapist during treatment in order to track and monitor family progress as it relates to their overall goal. While assessments may be administered periodically across treatment, progress notes are kept for each session. As you work at various agencies, you may find that the structure of progress notes may vary with each site, but the overall intention is to document any steps taken or made toward achieving the family's goal and identify a plan for continued progress. By reviewing progress notes, therapists may be able to determine if an assessment is needed by comparing the family's past and present status. While assessments may indicate where a family stands at a given moment, therapists may identify barriers to treatment, or trends in behaviors through reviewing progress notes over a period of time.

Considerations for Choosing Marriage and Family Assessments

There are several factors to consider when choosing assessments for couples and families. Assessments are developed meticulously; however, it is the responsibility of the user to assess whether assessments are appropriate for his or her client. This includes evaluation of the reliability, validity, norming group, and administrator qualifications.

Reliability and Validity

Once the therapist has established that he or she is qualified to administer the chosen assessment, he or she must then assess the reliability and the validity of the assessment. **Reliability** refers to the consistency of the measure—in other words, if this assessment was given to the same individual or family several times, how likely is it that they would attain same score at each administration? There are several ways researchers establish the reliability of an instrument, however this most often includes the calculation of a statistic called the **coefficient alpha** (AERA, APA, & NCME, 2014). This statistic calculates the extent to which the scores on the instrument are related to each other: the higher the statistic, the more related the scores are to each other and the better the reliability. Researchers may also calculate the **test–retest reliability**. This is a similar statistic that indicates how much an individual's scores are related when they take the assessment more than once. Again, the higher the statistic, the more related they are, and the higher the reliability. Though some researchers have stated a reliability coefficient of .70 or higher is acceptable, others argue lower or higher scores will suffice. Regardless, as a therapist evaluating a psychometric assessment, it will important for you to consider all of the different types of reliability evidence and decide whether it is sufficient (Watson & Flamez, 2014).

    Validity refers to how accurately the instrument measures what it intends to measure. There are several types of validity that can be reported by the instrument developer in the manual; however, **construct validity** is considered the most important type of validity and includes many aspects, including statistical analysis (Watson & Flamez, 2014). When evaluating the validity evidence for an instrument, therapists should review the manual for several different types of validation evidence related to construct validity—including (but not limited to) **concurrent validity** (how much responses on the instrument are related to other, similar measurements); internal structure validity (how much the items are related to each other); **criterion validity** (how much the instrument is related to other, related variables); and **predictive validity** (how much the instrument predicts what it claims to measure). Let's take a look at Guided Practice Exercise 8.1 and review the reported reliability and validity evidence in various assessments.

GUIDED PRACTICE EXERCISE 8.1

You will notice there is brief information included regarding the reliability and validity of the assessments listed in this chapter. Though this information is by no means exhaustive, it does give an idea of the evidence the researchers have provided. Take a moment and review these statistics. What do you notice? Are there some assessments that seem to have more evidence than others?

Norming Groups

When some instruments are created, they are administered to a large group of individuals to assess what the average scores are for certain individuals. This is called the **norming group** for any given test. It is important for therapists to evaluate the norming group before using the assessment—basically, was this instrument normed on individuals or families that are similar to the clients it will be used for? It is important to not only evaluate age, and gender, but also ethnicity, socioeconomic status, and level of education. As with many formalized assessments, one of the major challenges of working with assessments for families is the lack of diversity in the norming samples (Whiston, 2016).

Administrator Qualifications

The first thing the therapist needs to consider is whether he or she is qualified to administer the test. The companies that publish the tests set different qualification classifications; however, tests usually are classified into three general different groups:

- Level A: Administration of an assessment at this level solely requires the manual.
- Level B: This level of test requires a master's degree that includes specific assessment-related training.
- Level C: The highest level of test, an assessment at this level requires a master's degree and specific training in the assessment, or a PhD.

Qualitative Assessments

Recall from Chapter 6 that qualitative assessments include the observational methods as well as coding of conversations between family members. These assessments are sometimes standardized, and other times are not. Therapists should use qualitative assessment in conjunction with other approaches in order to gather information regarding the family and choose the best treatment plan. Regardless of the intervention used, therapists can use a qualitative approach by observing the family when they enter the session, and noting where each family member sits, their nonverbal communication, and who initiates discussion in the family. They can also make observations about whether family members interrupt each other, or dominate the discussion (Duffy & Chenail, 2012).

Family Sculpting

Generated from experiential family therapy, family sculpting involves physically moving the family members into positions based on their relationships in the family (Faddis & Cobb, 2016). One family member is chosen to commence the sculpting (often a child or adolescent) and then others are invited to give their perspective. Sculpting the family includes physically moving them, but also facial expressions, gestures, and positions as well. This helps the therapist and the family members have a visual representation of the relationships and emotional affect of the family. They can be asked to pick a specific historical moment for the family, or how the relationships are currently (Faddis & Cobb, 2016). This method emerged in the 1960s with several publications regarding this topic through the 1990s; however, there is little current research on this technique. You will learn more about family sculpting in Chapter 12.

Recursive Frame Analysis

Recursive frame analysis was originated by Keeney in 1987. This qualitative approach to assessment involves the analysis of the family's conversations to identify the themes that emerge. In this type of analysis, these themes are called **frames**. Frames can then be grouped into galleries of themes that seem related, and then museums of related galleries. The therapist can analyze the semantics of what is said, or how each individual contributes to the conversation. Sequentially, or, who contributes first, and how they alternate between frames and galleries, and finally, pragmatic, or how much the individual is present in the conversation at all (Chenail & Duffy, 2011. Though qualitative analysis can be very time consuming, the outcome can be extremely helpful for the therapist to not only understand the themes that continue to emerge for the family, but also each member's approach to that theme (Duffy & Chenail, 2012). Chapter 7 discusses qualitative assessment methods in greater detail.

Observational Assessments

Beavers Interactional Scales

The Beaver Interactional Scales has two scales: the Interactional Competence Scale (12 subscales: overt power, parental coalition, closeness, mythology, goal-directed negotiation, clarity of expression, responsibility, permeability, range of feelings, mood and tone, unresolvable conflict, and empathy); and the Interactional Style Scale (7 subscales: dependency needs, adult conflict, physical proximity, social presentation, expression of looseness, aggressive/hostile expression, types of feelings). The administrator watches a 10-minute segment of the family conversing and then rates their interactions on a Likert scale. The scales are based on the Beavers systems model, which includes family competence on a scale from optimal to severely dysfunctional, and family style on a scale from internalizing to externalizing. Authors provide evidence for interrater reliability (.85 and above) and concurrent validity with the Self-Report Family Inventory, or SFI (though this is also derived from the Beavers systems model) and the McMaster model. Benefits of these scales are that they well researched and free to use (Hampson & Beavers, 2012).

McMaster Model Clinical Rating Scale

Based on the McMaster Model of Family Functioning, the clinical rating scale (CRS) measures overall family functioning and includes six subscales—problem solving, communication, roles, affective responsiveness, affective involvement, and behavior control—based on observation or detailed family interview. This assessment is also Likert scaled and includes the sibling self-report scale (Family Assessment Device) and structured interview (McMaster Structured Interview for Family Functioning). Researchers recommend conducting the clinical interview first, then administering the CRS. Test–retest reliability coefficients are considered acceptable, as is interrater reliability (between .68 and .87). The researchers provide evidence for concurrent validity citing high correlations with the Family Assessment Device, and discriminant validity in identifying functional versus dysfunctional families (Hampson & Beavers, 2012).

Family Task Interview

The Family Task Interview (FTI) is designed to facilitate clinically relevant interaction among family members (Kinston & Loader, 1988). This multiple task interview can be administered by a prerecorded audiotape as an interview may pose as a distraction to the family. The interview itself asks families to perform basic tasks which facilitate interaction between family members. When using the FTI, therapists should consider applicability, length, task complexity as well as variety and number, and the interview atmosphere (Kinston & Loader, 1988). The family's size and age of the children should influence the type of tasks chosen. Tasks may also be modified based on special needs of the family members. When determining the length of the interview, therapist should give consideration to the age of the children. Long stretches of time may not be well suited for smaller children. Tasks that are overly complicated may interfere with the standardization of the interview, as this may require more intervention from the administrating therapist. By using a fixed time limit, the administrating therapist can determine the number of tasks given by the length of time it should take to complete each task. The atmosphere of the FTI should be supportive and safe. The structure of the interview should follow an introduction, tasks instructions, and conclusion format. Each instruction should be given twice. Examples of task could be items such as pattern recognition through card sorting, building a tower with blocks, discussing likes and dislikes, or planning something together (Kinston & Loader, 1988).

CRS for the Circumplex Model of Marital and Family Systems

Developed by Olson & Killorin, (1984, three rating scales are included in the CRS that align with the Circumplex Model: cohesion, flexibility, and communicating. Family system type is related to the Circumplex Model (see Figure 8.1). The CRS is for use after a family observation or a semistructured interview based on the Circumplex Model. The Family Adaptability and Cohesion Evaluation Scale (FACES) is also related to the Circumplex Model and more popular than the CRS (Hampson & Beavers, 2005). A circumplex is a graphical depiction of a set of related variables that is circular and displays the variables as if they are on a continuum on several axes. Therefore, the Circumplex Model of Couples and Families includes levels of cohesion and flexibility on continuums. Communication is a facilitating dimension and not included graphically. For cohesion, families can be disengaged, separated, connected, or enmeshed. Flexibility includes chaotic, flexible, structured, and rigid (Olson, 1995. Both cohesion and flexibility are curvilinear, meaning it is not necessarily best for the family to score low or high on these scales, but instead, right in the middle (Hampson & Beavers, 2012). These combinations can lead to families that are balanced, mid-range, or unbalanced. Authors encourage users to use this observer assessment in conjunction with the Circumplex Assessment Package for a full gestalt of the family relationships. The authors provide reliability evidence in the form of alpha coefficients .94 and above, and test–retest coefficients ranging from .75 to .86. Statistical analysis regarding validity shows the CRS is highly related with the circumplex theory; more so, in fact than the self-report instruments (FACES) (Thomas & Olson, 1993).

STANDARDIZED ASSESSMENTS

GUIDED PRACTICE EXERCISE 8.2

The Mental Measurements Yearbook (MMY) was originally published in 1938 and is now in its 17th edition. This is an important assessment resource, as it includes reviews of innumerable standardized tests. The MMY is likely available through your university library. Search the database for some of the assessments listed here to find more complete psychometric information, as well as the reviewers' opinions regarding this information.

There are innumerable standardized assessments for families and couples, however we will only include some of the most pertinent here. See Guided Practice Exercise 8.2 to learn more about standardized assessments for families, and where to find them.

Figure 8.1 The Circumplex Model

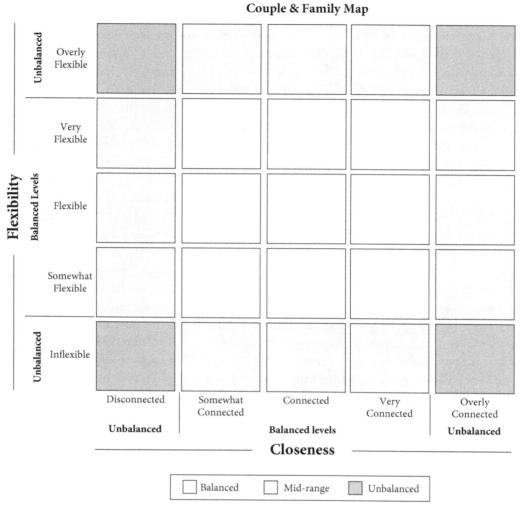

Source: David Olson, "Circumplex Model from Faces IV and the Circumplex Model: A Validation Study," Journal of Marital and Family Therapy, vol. 3, pp. 75. Copyright © 1995 by John Wiley & Sons, Inc. Reprinted with permission.

ASSESSMENT IN PREMARITAL COUNSELING

PREPARE/ENRICH. One of the most popular assessments for premarital counseling, this program originated in 1978 (Olson, Olson, & Larson, 2012) and includes several assessments and psychoeducational approaches for couples in different phases of their relationships. The most recent version, titled the "customized version," was published in 2009 and is offered online. In this version, developers report there are numerous possible verities of assessments that can be administered, as each one is customized for the needs of the couple. The previous (non-online) version of PREPARE includes three different assessments—premarital couples, premarital couples with children, and cohabitating premarital couples. Similarly, ENRICH is an assessment administered for married couples, and also includes an assessment for couples over 50. Both PREPARE and ENRICH include core scales—idealistic distortion, communication, conflict resolution, partner style and habits, financial management, leisure activities, family and friends, roles/responsibilities, spiritual believes, child and parenting, sexual relationship, forgiveness, marriage/relationship expectations, and character traits. The assessments also include scales measuring relationship dynamics (assertiveness, self-confidence, avoidance, and partner dominance) as well as personality factors (socialization, openness to change, organization, cooperation with others, and emotion regulation). Due to the fact the assessment includes implementation of psychoeducational interventions, administrators are required to engage in training before using the assessments (Olson et al., 2012). The developers provide ample evidence regarding the reliability and validity of the assessment; however, it should be noted that others have expressed concern about the lack of detail provided regarding the norming group.

COUPLE AND MARITAL ASSESSMENT

Assessing Specific Problems and Stressors

Derogatis Interview for Sexual Functioning (DISF). Designed to assess individual current sexual functioning, The DISF is the shorter, interview version of the Derogatis Sexual Functioning Inventory, which contains 254 items and can take 45 to 60 minutes to administer (Derogatis, Lopez, & Zinzeletta, 1988). The DISF, however, includes 25 Likert-scaled questions and can be utilized via interview or self-report and takes 15 to 20 minutes to complete (Derogatis, 1997). It includes five scales: sexual cognition/fantasy, sexual arousal, sexual behavior/experience, orgasm, and drive/relationship. Though there are gender-specific versions, there is also a version that is gender neutral that the researchers consider suitable for use with straight and gay, lesbian, bisexual, transgender, and intersex (GLBTI) individuals (Derogatis, 1997). Coefficient alpha scores range from .74 to .80, with test–retest coefficients ranging from .81 to .90. Derogatis (1997) established discriminant validity in a study in which the instrument accurately discriminated between individuals who were considered dysfunctional and those who were not.

Revised Conflict Tactics Scale (CTS2). The CTS2 (Straus, Hamby, Boney-McCoy, & Sugarman, 1996) is a widely used instrument used to measure domestic violence and abuse between couples. The assessment includes 78 Likert-scaled questions regarding the frequency of related behaviors for the individual and his or her partner. The scale is divided into five subscales: negotiation, physical assault, injury, psychological aggression, and sexual coercion. Coefficient alpha scores range from .79 to .95 for all scales and evidence of construct validity with high correlations with actual abusive behaviors and situations in relationships (Straus et al., 1996).

Assessing the Quality of the Relationship

Locke–Wallace Marital Adjustment Test. This assessment was developed by Locke and Wallace and clearly has been around for a long time; however, researchers still mention it in discussions regarding assessments of marital satisfaction. In fact, 11 items in the Dyadic Adjustment Scale were taken directly from this instrument (Bagarozzi & Sperry, 2012). This 15-item instrument assesses marital adjustment, which they define as "an accommodation of partners to each other at a given time" p. 138 (Bagarozzi & Sperry, 2012). The evidence of psychometric properties of this instrument are a bit lacking; however, at the time it was created, it was the first of its kind due to its brevity—other marital satisfaction inventories were hundreds of questions long (Fredman & Sherman, 1987). Others contend that items are out of date and were normed on stereotypical couples during the 1960s. So why bother mentioning this instrument at all? It remains popular, and an update on the psychometric properties in the 1990s showed it continues to have some merit (Freeston & Pléchaty, 1997).

Dyadic Adjustment Scale (DAS; Spanier, 1989. This scale has been used in over 1,000 studies (Sperry, 2012). Though researchers and clinicians alike use the scale to measure marital satisfaction, others contend that relationship adjustment is a different construct than marital satisfaction and the DAS therefore should be used for this purpose with caution (Ward, Lundberg, Zabriskie, Berrett, 2009). The instrument contains four subscales—dyadic consensus, dyadic satisfaction, affectional expression, and dyadic cohesion—in addition to the total dyadic adjustment score. There are significant limitations regarding the diversity of the norming group; however, it continues to be a widely used quick assessment of relationship "adjustment" (e.g., satisfaction). A significant amount of research has been conducting using this scale, and other, shorter versions have been created as well (Graham, Liu, & Jeziorski,, 2006). The most popular of these shortened versions is the Revised Dyadic Adjustment Scale (Busby, Crane, Arson, & Christensen, 1995). Researchers report a coefficient alpha of .73 and above for all scales and evidence of concurrent and predictive validity with the Marital Adjustment Scale.

Marital Satisfaction Inventory, Revised (MSI-R). Developed by Snyder (1997), this instrument includes 13 scales: global distress, affective communication, problem-solving communication, aggression, time together, disagreement about finances, sexual dissatisfaction, role orientation, family history of distress, dissatisfaction with children, conflict over child rearing, inconsistency, and conventialization. This instrument can be used throughout treatment for assessment of movement toward treatment goals (Snyder, 1997). Researchers cite adequate divergent validity, as the instrument can accurately identify distressed couples versus nondistressed couples, and convergent validity with high correlations with other similar instruments. Coefficient alpha scores range between .70 and .93 for all scales. See Case Presentation 8.1 for an example of when you might use the MSR-I.

CASE PRESENTATION 8.1: THE CASE OF STACY, TERRY, AND TYLER

Stacy and Terry have recently started counseling due to conflicts in their marriage after their oldest son, Tyler, has been in trouble at school. Tyler has been skipping school, failing classes, and even was recently caught vandalizing school property. They inform Chris, their counselor, that they have experienced a variety of problems such as arguing about finances, frustrations over how to discipline Tyler, or agreeing on solutions to simple problems around their home. Chris decides to use the MSI-R in order to establish a baseline for goal progress within the relationship. From this assessment, Chris is able to gain a better understanding of the dynamics within Stacy and Terry's marriage.

FAMILY ASSESSMENT INSTRUMENTS

Systematic Clinical Outcome Routine Evaluation

The Systematic Clinical Outcome Routine Evaluation (SCORE 15) was developed from the original SCORE 40, which was developed to measure how family members engage in lifestyle activities and manage their relationships. The SCORE 15 only contains 15 items (compared to 40) and can be used as an ongoing evaluation of clinical outcomes of families in therapy. It includes three subscales: strengths and adaptability, overwhelmed by difficulties, and disrupted communication. Researchers report coefficient alpha of .89, with high validity when correlated with the original assessment (Stratton et al., 2014). This instrument is optimal for use, due to the fact that administration and scoring is quick, and it can be accessed free of charge via the association for family therapy's website (http://www.aft.org.uk).

Family Adaptability and Cohesion Evaluation Scale IV

The Family Adaptability and Cohesion Evaluation Scale IV (FACES-IV) is the corresponding self-report measure to the CRS (see above under observational assessments) and measures family cohesion and flexibility, again via the Circumplex Model (see Figure 8.1). Researchers contend the goal is to have a balanced level of cohesion and flexibility, as an unbalanced level (too much, or too little) can lead to problems in family functioning. Previous editions of the FACES (I, II, and III) and the CRS have been used in over 1,000 studies to measure family dynamics (Olson, 2011). The FACES is completed by one or more family members and contains 42 Likert-scaled items regarding the family dynamics. The FACES includes 6 scales, 2 balanced scales (cohesion and flexibility), and 4 unbalanced scales unbalanced levels of cohesion (disengaged and enmeshed) and flexibility (rigid and chaotic). The FACES has adequate internal consistency with coefficient alpha scores ranging from .77 to .89. Content validity was established via experts in the field, and concurrent validity has been established with high correlations with the SFI (Hampson & Beavers, 1996), Family

Assessment Device (Epstein, Baldwin, & Bishop, 1983), and the Family Satisfaction Scale (Olson, 1995).

Family Assessment Measure

The Family Assessment Measure (FAM-III) includes three scales—the general scale measures the overall health of the family (50 questions), the self-rating scale measures one's own functioning in the family (42 questions), and the dyadic relationship scale measures specific relationships between two family members (Skinner, Steinhauer, & Sitarenios, 2000). Though others have expressed concern that administration of the full assessment that includes all dyadic pairs in the family can be quite time consuming (Skinner, Steinhauer, & Santa Barbara, 1995), a short version of the scales, which includes 14 items each, is also included. Others have expressed concern regarding the norming sample, as the assessment was normed on a predominantly White population. The FAM-III is based on the Process Model of Family Functioning. The basis of this model is that the goal of the family is to accomplish tasks. Role performance, communication, affective expression, involvement, and values and norms all play an essential role in the accomplishment of these tasks (Skinner et al., 2000). Coefficient alpha for all scales range from .86 to .93 for all scales, and good test–retest reliabilities range from .56 to .66. Researchers also established discriminant validity between clinical and nonclinical samples and construct validity with correlations with several other self-report family assessment scales (Skinner et al., 2000).

Family Environment Scale, 4th Edition

The Family Environment Scale, 4th edition, was developed to assess the social environment and contains 90 true/false items (Moos & Moos, 2009). It contains four forms—real (how the individual perceives the family environment currently), ideal (how the individual wishes the family was), expectations (how the individual thinks the family should be), children (30-item pictorial adaptation). There are 10 subscales included on each scale, under three dimensions: relationship (cohesion, expressiveness, conflict); personal growth (independence, achievement orientation, intellectual–cultural orientation, active-recreational orientation, moral–religious emphasis); and systems maintenance and change (organization, and control). Seven family types emerge from the results: independence oriented, achievement oriented, intellectual–cultural oriented, moral–religious oriented, support oriented, conflicted oriented, and disorganized. These types can help clinicians develop treatment plans and families ultimately understand their relationships and environments (Moos & Moos, 2009). Coefficient alpha scores range from .61 to .78 with test–retest reliabilities from .68 to.86 after 2 months. Discriminant validity was established comparing normal and distressed families, and construct validity with other, similar assessments (Moos & Moos, 2009).

PARENTING ASSESSMENTS

Researchers cite parenting approaches as one of the major factors in behavioral problems in children and adolescents (Pastorelli et al., 2016). Further, dysfunctional parenting approaches may be difficult to identify without a formal method of assessment the adults' approaches to parenting in the family. There are innumerable assessments of parenting beliefs and behaviors, though only three pertinent assessments will be briefly discussed here.

The Adult–Adolescent Parenting Inventory-2

The Adult–Adolescent Parenting Inventory-2 (AAPI-2) is widely used, contains 40 items, and was developed to assess parenting styles specifically related to adolescents (Conners, Whiteside-Mansell, Deere, Ledet, & Edwards, 2006). It has five scales, based on attitudes of abusive parents: inappropriate expectations of children, parental lack of empathy toward children's needs, strong belief in the use of corporal punishment as a means of discipline, reversing parent–child role responsibilities, and oppressing children's power and independence. The AAPI-2 was normed on over 1,400 adults and adolescents and includes two forms, A and B. Researchers have found convergent validity between the AAPI-2 and other similar assessments, including the Parental Discipline Methods Interview (Baydar, Reid, & Webster Stratton, 2003). Coefficient alpha scores range from .50 to .79 for the scales, a value of .85 for the total score (Conners et al., 2006).

The Alabama Parenting Questionnaire

The Alabama Parenting Questionnaire (Frick, 1991) is a 42-item Likert-scaled instrument developed to assess parenting practices and includes 5 scales that assess constructs specifically related to behavior problems in children and adolescents—parental involvement, positive parenting, poor monitoring/supervision, inconsistent discipline, and corporal punishment. The instrument includes a child and parent version, which can be administered in person or over the phone. Coefficient alpha scores are fair for both self-report versions and range from .55 to .77. Construct validity continues to be established; however, studies have found the assessment has discriminant validity and correctly identifies families with problems with parenting and children with conduct disorders (Blader, 2004).

The Parenting Scale

The Parenting Scale was developed to measure dysfunctional parenting approaches (Arnold, O'Leary, Wolff, & Acker, 1993). The 30-item, Likert-scaled, parent self-report instrument includes three scales considered important in approaching discipline—laxness, overreactivity, and verbosity. Construct validity was established via comparing observations and ratings on the three scales with actual responses, and convergent validity was established with high correlations with responses on the Child Behavior Checklist (Achenbach, Edelbrock, & Howell, 1987). Coefficient alpha scores for the scales range from .63 to .84 (Arnold et al., 1993). It should be noted that though the Parenting Scale is widely used, follow-up studies have not found evidence to support the verbosity scale but have found sufficient evidence to support the laxness and overreactivity scale (Lorber, Xu, Slep, Bulling, & O'Leary, 2014).

INDIVIDUAL ASSESSMENTS

Myers–Briggs Type Indicator

The Myers–Briggs Type Indicator (MBTI; Myers, McCaulley, Quenk, & Hammer, 1998) is an extremely popular assessment based on Jungian theory and used to measure personality traits on four dichotomous traits—extroversion-introversion, sensing-intuition, thinking-feeling, and judging-perceiving. Respondents complete the 70-item forced-answer questionnaire and then receive a four-letter personality type based on their responses (Myers et al., 1998). Though the MBTI is historically used in personality and career assessment, marriage and family therapists have found the MBTI useful, as knowledge of individual personality characteristics can help couples and family members understand each other, without labeling traits or preferences as positive or negative (Whiston, 2016). See Case Presentation 8.2 for an example of how to use this assessment with families.

CASE PRESENTATION 8.2: THE CASE OF JIMMY, LIZ, AND CASADY

For 2 months Jimmy, Liz, and their 14-year-old daughter, Casady, have been attending family counseling sessions with Tina, a marriage and family therapist in their community. Throughout the duration of their time in counseling, Casady has stated she feels like her parents hardly know her. Jimmy and Liz have both described complications with work that often keep them away from home or working late hours. As a result, Casady spends much of her time outside of school with her grandmother. Liz has admitted she feels embarrassed for not knowing what Casady's interests are and feels Casady is often distant when they are together. Jimmy expresses that interactions with Casady can be awkward at times and states it's almost like talking to a stranger. Upon hearing these disconnections in the family dynamic, Tina decides to incorporate the MBTI assessment to help the family begin to understand characteristics of each other's individual personality and how those may work together in the family unit.

Minnesota Multiphasic Personality Inventory-2

The Minnesota Multiphasic Personality Inventory-2 (MMPI-2; Butcher, Dahlstrom, Graham, Tellegen, & Kraemmer, 1989) is another extremely popular personality assessment; however, it is much more complicated to score and interpret than the MBTI. The MMPI-2 includes 567 true/false items and has 7 validity scales in addition to numerous clinical scales. Again, this personality assessment can help couples and families understand each other's personalities and how they may be contributing to issues within the system. However, recently two scales were added to the MMPI-2 that specifically measure family dynamics: the Family Problem Scale and the Marital Distress Scale (Nurse &

Sperry, 2012. The MMPI-2 is a level-three test; therefore, therapists will need specific training on this assessment before being considered qualified to use it.

CULTURAL AND ETHICAL CONSIDERATIONS

Cultural Considerations

The IAMFC Code of Ethics (IAMFC, 2017) insists counselors refrain from using biased and prejudiced assessments. This means counselors must consider the cultural and ethnic background of the family one is working with when conducting assessments with couples and families. As mentioned earlier, one first must be aware of the diversity (or often, lack thereof) of the norming group used to validate the instrument. The therapist should be aware of his or her own attitudes and beliefs, knowledge, and skills, and those of his or her client, which will play an integral part in their interactions during sessions (Ratts, Singh, Nassar-McMillan, Butler, & McCullough, 2016).

The Association for Assessment and Research in Counseling (AARC; previously the Association for Assessment in Counseling and Education) is a division of the American Counseling Association and developed the Association for Assessment in Counseling and Education's Standards for Multicultural Assessment (2012) currently in its fourth edition. In these standards, the AARC Task Force delineates competencies, including advocacy, selection, administration and scoring, interpretation, and training related to assessment. Therapists are encouraged to review the entire document, which can be found at the following link: http://aarc-counseling.org/assets/cms/uploads/files/AACE-AMCD.pdf.

Considerations for GLBTI couples and families. Special considerations should be taken for families that include GLBTI couples, as there are many unique issues that members of this population struggle with. Members of the GLBTI community often suffer harassment and abuse from others. This may or may not include family members and loved ones who have severed ties with them after they have disclosed their sexual orientation (termed "coming out"). When solely conducting marriage and couple therapy, the therapist may wish to include an unstandardized approach to his or her initial assessment and address each individual's views and opinions regarding their lifestyle and past experiences that may be affecting their relationship today. Many assessments may not be applicable for families with GLBTI couples, especially assessments that are gender specific when discussing parental relationships (Wetchler & Bigner, 2012).

Ethical Considerations

As discussed in Chapter 4, in addition to cultural considerations, therapists should pay attention to any ethical dilemmas related to assessment with couples and families. All therapists are ethically bound to choose the appropriate tests for their clients, administer, score, and interpret them appropriately, as well as report the results in an ethical manner that clearly communicates the strengths and limitations of the assessment (Watson & Flamez, 2014). There are several resources that can be helpful regarding this matter;

for example, the IAMFC Code of Ethics (IAMFC, 2017) includes a section regarding assessment, which highlights the importance of beneficence in assessing families and interpreting assessment results in the context of other available information on the client. Below we have listed several more relevant ethical codes related to assessing families. See Guided Practice Exercise 8.3 to familiarize yourself with these resources further.

- The American Counseling Association (ACA) Code of Ethics
  http://www.counseling.org/resources/aca-code-of-ethics.pdf
- The Responsibilities of Users of Standardized Tests
  http://aac.ncat.edu/Resources/documents/RUST2003%20v11%20 Final.pdf
- Standards for Assessment in Marriage and Family Counseling
  http://aarc-counseling.org/assets/cms/uploads/files/AACE-IAMFC.pdf

GUIDED PRACTICE EXERCISE 8.3

Follow the links for the listed ethical codes and standards. When comparing and contrasting the different lists, what do you notice? Are there some aspects that seem repetitive? Or perhaps other aspects that should be emphasized more?

EVALUATING PROGRESS

Standardized Versus Nonstandardized Assessments

A **standardized assessment** is an assessment that has been developed by experts on the topic, verified via statistical analysis and other methods to be sure it is an accurate measure of the construct it claims to measure. Conversely, a **nonstandardized** assessment is often an unstructured verbal interview conducted by the therapist that has not gone through rigorous testing. For example, "How often did you argue in the past week?" might be asked. Though this chapter highlights a significant number of standardized assessments, nonstandardized assessments are equally important. They are adaptable for the needs of the client, can be used every session, and can include aspects not covered in more formalized assessments. Further, though standardized assessments are considered more reliable and valid, they may take more time than nonstandardized assessments, and depending on the instrument may cost significantly more to administer regularly (Gehart, 2010). When considering how to evaluate progress in couple and family counseling, it may be beneficial to incorporate both standardized and nonstandardized assessments.

FINAL THOUGHTS ON OUTCOME

A therapist may use these assessment methods throughout the course of treatment to monitor or check progress. By comparing assessment outcomes across the course of treatment, the therapist is able to understand how the family may be progressing based on the construct measured in the assessment. Assessment outcomes may indicate a range of changes in the family such as slow progress, no progress, or even regression at times. Therapists can use assessment outcomes to gain valuable insight into the family's progress outside of the counseling session.

Writing Progress Notes

Similar to working with individuals, as mentioned in Chapter 4, your ability to document what happened during a couples or family session via a progress note is crucial. Though your site will often have a specific format you will be required to follow, it is helpful to be aware of the aspects that will be crucial in your documentation. Progress notes include several aspects, including the interventions used and client response, future plans, therapist observations and clinical opinions, and detailed accounts of any crisis situations (Gehart, 2005).

Though there are several note formats used by therapists. One of the most popular is SOAP, which stands for **subjective, objective, assessment, and plan**. **Subjective** includes the information the family shared during the session. **Objective** includes the therapist's perspectives and what he or she observed in session with the family. **Assessment** is the section where the therapist takes the information from the subjective and objective sections and gives his or her clinical opinion. Finally, **plan** includes any future activities by the therapist or the couple or family. This includes the day and time of the next appointment, any homework or changes to the treatment plan, and any plans for next the session (Cameron & Turtle-Song, 2002).

It should be noted that **progress notes** are different from **psychotherapy notes**. Progress notes are the actual, official documentation you will use at your site, whereas psychotherapy notes are your personal notes that you keep regarding the clients and the sessions. These notes are often kept separate from progress notes and rarely shared with others (Gehart, 2010). See Figures 8.2 and 8.3 for examples of what progress notes might look like.

CASE PRESENTATION: THE TAYLOR FAMILY

Let's use the example of the Taylor family, from Chapter 7. Imagine they are still in the initial phase of treatment, and you want to work on goal 2 from their treatment plan: **assess family's structure and boundaries and determine goals.** At the beginning of the session, you explain what the SCORE 15 is and the purpose of the assessment. You then ask each of them to sit down and complete it independently. After each family member completes the SCORE 15, you review and discuss their responses together, to elicit further conversation and gather more details regarding their interactions and boundaries. Patricia and Ray are both saddened and surprised to find that Gabriel scored the family so high (indicating lower healthy functioning) on several items, especially the question "It feels miserable to be in our family." They are able to communicate their love for him and Danielle in session, and all family members leave the session committed to treatment goals. See Figure 8.2 for a sample progress note from this session that includes the results of the SCORE 15. Figure 8.3 illustrates an all-purpose case note that includes common insurance and agency requirements. Figure 8.4 shows a sample treatment plan demonstrating the initial, working, and closing phases of treatment.

Figure 8.2 **Sample SOAP Case Note**

Client Name: Ray Taylor

Date: 6/1/2017

Start Time: 18:00   End Time: 18:50

Subjective Information: Family arrived on time to session. Counselor explained and then administered the *SCORE15* assessment. The family reviewed results together and processed the implications of those results.

Objective Information: Ray and Patricia have gained insight into the personal struggles of their children, as evidenced by their shock and sadness while discussing the *SCORE15* assessment. All family members became tearful at times, and counselor joined with the family to facilitate re-establishment of relationships.

Assessment: All family members are motivated for treatment, and completing the *SCORE15* was a successful intervention in increasing awareness and cohesion in the family.

Plan: Family will engage in one "family game night" over the next week, during which they all commit to refraining from use of electronic devices.

SCORE 15 Overall Scores:

Ray Taylor: 35

Patricia Taylor: 26

Danielle Taylor: 39

Gabriel Taylor: 52

Figure 8.3 **Sample All-Purpose Case Note**

Symptoms	Duration/Frequency Since Last Visit	Progress Setback ... Initial ... Goal
Suicide attempt/son	Attending individual sessions/Taking medications	−5......1.......5......10 This Week: 7
School suspension/son	No reports or issues this week	−5......1.......5......10 This Week: 8
Depression/wife	Daily	−5......1.......5......10 This Week: 1
Family disconnect	Daily	−5......1.......5......10 This Week: 1
Wife past work stress and current unemployment	Completed homework each day	−5......1.......5......10 This Week: 2
Anger of son	No reports or outbursts this week	−5......1.......5......10 This Week: 8

Client: Ray Taylor

Date: 6/1/2017   Time: 18:00   Session Length: 50 minutes   Billing Code: Family-50 min.

Explanatory Notes: *Score 15* results reviewed and discussed.

Interventions/Homework: Family will engage in one "family game night" over the next week, during which they all commit to refraining from use of electronic devices.

Client Response/Feedback: All state they are motivated to improve family cohesion.

Plan: Continue with Treatment Plan

Next Session: 6/8/2017 9 A.M.

Crisis Issues: Son denies suicide ideation after last attempt and is seeing an LPC and psychiatrist for monitoring, assistance, and medication.

Figure 8.4 **Clinical Treatment Plan Example**

Therapist: June Gonzalez   Client: Ray Taylor

Theory: Bowenian

Primary Configuration: Family

Medications: Son/Prozac

Contextual Factors considered: Age, Gender, Family Dynamics, Economic, and Trauma

Describe plan relationship to contextual factors: Son's suicide attempt and wife's employment issues impact family cohesion.

Initial Phase of Treatment

1A. Initial Therapeutic Tasks

    Assessment

TT1: Develop therapeutic relationship with family.

Intervention: Rogerian empathy and paraphrasing integrated with Bowenian techniques

Intervention: Introductions to instill hierarchies

TT2: Assess family dynamics

Intervention: *Score 15* administration and discussion

Intervention: *Family Assessment Device* and discussion to clarify presenting problem

Intervention: Genogram developed by family

Goals: Improve family awareness of disconnect; Gain Family agreement with goal

Goal 1. Join with family and accommodate to family rules, patterns, and structure.

    a. Understand family members' feelings and reflect empathy to all members.

    b. Track and maintain family communication style while matching and acknowledging family hierarchy and rules.

Goal 2. Assess family's structure and boundaries and determine goals.

    a. Ask about each individual's perspective of the problem, family structure, and interaction.

    b. Identify structural patterns by observing spontaneous family interactions.

Referrals and Crisis: Son's referral to LPC and psychiatrist for medication, school issues, anger, and suicide ideation; Wife's referral to employment counselor

1. B. Initial Client Goals

    1. Increase amount of time family spends together to reduce family tension and Sustain lack of tension for 3 weeks with no more than 3 family outbursts.

Working Phase of Treatment

II.A. Working Therapeutic Tasks

Monitor Progress toward Goals

Intervention: Family Game Night Once Twice Per Week for 3 Weeks

Monitor Relationship

Intervention: Assess family functioning using the *McMaster Model Clinical Relationship Scale;*
Discuss results

II.B. Client Goals for Working Phase

Assessment/Monitoring: Observationally assess for Satir's four patterns of defensive communication as well as for triangulation, enmeshment, and disengagement

Goal 1. Reestablish the parental subsystem; adjust generational hierarchy; strengthen parental coalition.

  a. Present affective intensity statements to assist in highlighting parent/child hierarchical power imbalance, particularly between Ray and Danielle, and between Patricia and Gabriel.
  b. Unbalance the system by taking the least dominant family member's side (Gabriel) to assist in increasing his position in the family.

Goal 2. Develop clear boundaries between all subsystems.

  a. Challenge family assumptions associated with relational boundaries.
  b. Initiate boundary-making techniques, such as having clients arrange chairs to challenge current hierarchy, coalitions, and boundaries.

Goal 3. Improve family communication and reduce negative behavior patterns.
Increase positive dialogue and reduce negative outbursts for 3 weeks with no more than 2 occurrences where yelling is exhibited by members.

Closing Phase of Treatment

Termination Plan: After 3 weeks of successful family interactions, treatment is terminated. Aftercare is available and scheduled bi-monthly for 6 months after termination. After 6 months, care is available by appointment if needed.

Closing Client Goals:
Goal 1. Develop strategies for managing future boundary issues.

  a. Use enactments to role play situations of concern for each family member.
  b. Increase competence by transferring new skills and behaviors to other relationships.

Goal 2. Establish and solidify newly established family norms and structures.

  a. Reinforce competence by focusing on what was learned and accomplished by the family.

Figure 8.4 Clinical Treatment Plan Example *(continued)*

> b. Positively reframe structural alterations to assist in introducing each member's role.
>
> Intervention: Retake the *Score 15, McMaster Model Clinical Relationship Scale,* discuss improved findings as well as family self-reports.
>
> Treatment plan discussed with client on 6/1/2017.
> Client agrees with plan but concerned about termination. Aftercare options discussed to ease family anxiety.

SUMMARY

In this chapter, we discussed the role of assessment in the marriage and family counseling process. We reviewed the importance of evaluating assessment characteristics such as reliability, validity, norming group, and administrator qualifications. We examined various qualitative, observational, and standardized assessments, as well as how these are incorporate into couple, marital, and family therapy. We also discussed the importance of documentation and writing case notes.

KEYSTONES

Among the key points addressed in this chapter are:

- Marriage and family assessment is much more complicated than the assessment of individuals, as one is evaluating the interrelated systems that exist between family members. Assessment should continue throughout the counseling relationship to measure progress.
- Therapists should consider the user qualifications, norming groups, validity, and reliability of a standardized assessment before use.
- Qualitative assessments can include simply observing the family's interactions or can be standardized.
- Observational assessments are assessments the clinician completes during or after observation of the family.
- Self-report assessments are completed by one or more family members and can be used to evaluate marital satisfaction, family functioning, parenting, and individual characteristics.

- Cultural and ethical considerations related to assessment are important when working with families.
- Progress notes are important legal documents, though the structure may vary by site.

REFLECTIONS FROM THE CONTRIBUTOR'S CHAIR

Baylea Wagener

In the field of counseling, I believe we often view assessment as a rigorous process involving standardized test materials and hours analyzing the results. However, in my practice, I have found I frequently use nonstandardized assessment methods in family counseling without realizing it. Any time I am working with a family, I use observational assessment to evaluate how family members interact with one another. I employ simple interview questions such as "How often does this happen?" or "How would you rate this behavior on a scale of 1-10?" I may incorporate standardized methods by completing individual assessments with family members to better understand how they fit in the family unit as a whole. Completing assessments early on in treatment also allows me to establish a baseline for progress in the future. When I use standardized methods of assessment with clients, I explain prior to administration how the assessment can be used to better inform the client's treatment plan. When possible, I try to ease any client anxiety about assessment by explaining that assessment can be similar to a casual conversation, as opposed to a clinical interview.

ADDITIONAL RESOURCES

The following resources provide additional information relating to the chapter topics.

Useful Websites

- Association for Assessment and Research in Counseling
  http://www.aarc-counseling.org

This website provides information on assessment standards and other resources relevant to assessment in counseling.

- Association for Family Therapy
  http://www.aft.org.uk

In addition to resources for counseling families, this website also provides access to the SCORE 15.

- California Evidence-Based Clearing House for Child Welfare
  http://www.cebc4cw.org/

This website is an excellent resource for practicing clinicians who need information regarding specific assessments or interventions. There are a variety of family-based assessments provided, as well for individuals.

- International Association of Marriage and Family Therapists
  http:///www.iamfconline.org

This website provides information regarding trainings and resources for counseling families and couples.

Readings

Corcoran, K., & Fischer, J. (2013). *Measures for clinical practice and research. Volume 1: Couples, family and children.* New York: Oxford University Press.

Thomlison, B. (2015). *Family assessment handbook: An introduction and practical guide to family assessment.* Boston: Cengage Learning.

This handbook is useful for those preparing to work with families. Readers will learn more about how to conduct an assessment to determine case interventions.

Williams, L., Edwards, T., Patterson, J., & Chamow, L. (2011). *Essential assessment skills for couple and family therapists.* New York: Guilford Press.

This text provides clinicians with ways to incorporate assessment into therapy with couples and families. Authors also provide strategies for understanding family functioning.

REFERENCES

Achenbach, T. M., Edelbrock, C., & Howell, C. T. (1987). Empirically based assessment of the behavior/ emotion problems of 2- and 3-year old children. *Journal of Abnormal Child Psychology, 15*, 629–650.

American Educational Research Association, American Psychological Association, & National Council on Measurement in Education. (2014). *Standards for educational and psychological testing.* Washington, DC: American Educational Research Association.

Arnold, D. S., O'Leary, S. G., Wolff, L. S., & Acker, M. M. (1993). The Parenting Scale: A measure of dysfunctional parenting in discipline situations. *Psychological Assessment, 5*(2), 137–144.

Association for Assessment in Counseling and Education. (2012). Standards for Multicultural Assessment. Retrieved from http://aarc-counseling.org/assets/cms/uploads/files/AACE-AMCD.pdf.

Bagarozzi, D. A., & Sperry, L. (2012). Couples assessment strategies and inventories. In L. Sperry (Ed.), *Family assessment* (pp. 137–162). New York: Routledge.

Baydar, N., Reid, M. J., & Webster-Stratton, C. (2003). The role of mental health factors and program engagement in the effectiveness of a preventive parenting program for Head Start mothers. Child Development, 74, 1433–1453.

Blader, J. C. (2004). Symptom, family, and service predictors of children's psychiatric rehospitalization within one year of discharge. *Journal of the American Academy of Children & Adolescent Psychiatry, 43,* 440–451.

Busby, D. M., Crane, D. R., Larson, J. H., & Christensen, C. (1995). A revision of the Dyadic Adjustment Scale for use with distressed and nondistressed couples: Construct hierarchy and multidimensional scales. *Journal of Marital and Family Therapy, 21*(3), 289–308. doi:10.1111/j.1752-0606.1995.tb00163.x

Butcher, J. N., Dahlstrom, W. G., Graham, J. R., Tellegen, A., & Kraemmer, B. (1989). *Minnesota Multiphasic Personality Inventory-2 (MMPI-2): Manual for administration and scoring.* Minneapolis: University of Minnesota Press.

Cameron, S., & Turtle-Song I. (2002). Learning to write case notes using the SOAP format. *Journal of Counseling and Development, 80*, 286–292.

Carlson, C., Krumholz, L. S., & Snyder, D. K. (2013). Assessment in marriage and family counseling. In K. F. Geisinger (Ed.), *APA handbook of testing and assessment in psychology, Vol. 2* (pp. 569–586). Washington, DC: American Psychological Association

Chenail, R. J., & Duffy, M. (2011). Utilizing Microsoft Office to produce and present recursive frame analysis findings. *Qualitative Report, 16*(1), 292–307. Retrieved from http://www.nova.edu/ssss/QR/QR16-1/rfa.pdf

Conners, N. A., Whiteside-Mansell, L., Deere, D., Ledet, T., & Edwards, M. C. (2006). Measuring the potential for child maltreatment: The reliability and validity of the Adult Adolescent Parenting Inventory-2. *Child Abuse & Neglect, 30*(1), 39–53. doi:10.1016/j.chiabu.2005.08.011

Derogatis, L. R. (1997). The Derogatis Interview for Sexual Functioning (DISF/DISF-SR): An introductory report. *Journal of Sex & Marital Therapy, 23*, 291–304.

Derogatis, L. R., Lopez, M. C., & Zinzeletta, E. M. (1988). Clinical applications of the DSFI in the assessment of sexual dysfunctions. In R. A. Brown & J. R. Fields (Eds.), *Treatment of sexual problems in individual and couple therapy* (pp. 167–186). Great Neck, NY: PMA.

Duffy, M., & Chenail, R. J. (2012). Qualitative assessment. In L. Sperry (Ed.), *Family assessment: Contemporary and cutting-edge strategies* (2nd ed., pp. 17–52). New York: Routledge.

Epstein, N. B., Baldwin, L., & Bishop, D. (1983). The McMaster Family Assessment Device. *Journal of Marital and Family Therapy, 9*, 213–228.

Faddis, T. J., & Cobb, K. F. (2016). Family therapy techniques in residential settings: Family sculptures and reflecting teams. *Contemporary Family Therapy: An International Journal, 38*(1), 43–51. doi:10.1007/s10591-015-9373-3

Fredman, N., & Sherman, T. (1987). Handbook of measurements for marriage and family therapy. New York: Brunner/Mazel.

Freeston, M. H., & Pléchaty, M. (1997). Reconsiderations of the Locke-Wallace Marital Adjustment Test: Is it still relevant for the 1990s? *Psychological Reports, 81*(2), 419–434. doi:10.2466/PR0.81.6.419-434

Frick, P. J. (1991). The Alabama Parenting Questionnaire. Unpublished rating scale, University of Alabama.

Gehart, D. (2010). *Mastering competencies in family therapy: A practical approach to theories and clinical case documentation* (5th ed.). Belmont, CA: Brooks/Cole.

Graham, J. M., Liu, Y. J., & Jeziorski, J. L. (2006). The Dyadic Adjustment Scale: A reliability generalization meta-analysis. *Journal of Marriage and Family, 68*, 701–171.

Kinston, W., & Loader, P. (1988). The Family Task Interview: A tool for clinical research in family interaction. *Journal of Marital and Family Therapy, 14*, 67–87.

Lorber, M. F., Xu, S., Slep, A. M. S., Bulling, L., & O'Leary, S. G. (2014). A new look at the psychometrics of the Parenting Scale through the lens of item response theory. *Journal of Clinical Child & Adolescent Psychology, 43*(4), 613–626. doi:10.1080/15374416.2014.900717

Moos, R. H., & Moos, B. S. (2009). *Family Environment Scale manual and sample set: Development, applications, and research* (4th Ed.) Menlo Park, CA: Mind Garden.

Myers, I. B., McCaulley, J. H., Quenk, N. L., & Hammer, A. L. (1998). *MBTI manual: A guide to the development and use of the Myers-Briggs Type Indicator.* Palo Alto, CA: CPP.

Nurse, R., & Sperry, L. (2012). Standardized assessment. In L. Sperry (Ed.), *Family assessment: Contemporary and cutting edge strategies* (2nd ed., pp. 53–82). New York: Routledge.

Olson, D. H. (1995). *Family Satisfaction Scale.* Minneapolis: Life Innovations.

Olson, D. H. (2011). FACES IV and the Circumplex Model: Validation study. *Journal of Marital and Family Therapy, 37,* 64–80. doi10:1111/j.1752-0606.2009.00175.x

Olson, D. H., & Killorin, E. (1984). *Clinical rating scale for the circumplex model.* St. Paul, MN: University of Minnesota, Family Social Sciences.

Olson, D. H., Olson, A. K., & Larson, P. J. (2012). PREPARE-ENRICH program: Overview and new discoveries about couples. *Journal of Family & Community Ministries, 25,* 30–44.

Pastorelli, C., Lansford, J. E., Kanacri, B. P. L., Malone, P. S., Di Giunta, L., Bacchini, D., & Sorbring, E. (2016). Positive parenting and children's prosocial behavior in eight countries. *Journal of Child Psychology and Psychiatry, 57*(7), 824–834. doi:10.1111/jcpp.12477

Ratts, M. J., Singh, A. A., Nassar-McMillan, S., Butler, S. K., & McCullough, J. R. (2016). Multicultural and Social Justice Counseling Competencies: Guidelines for the counseling profession. *Journal of Multicultural Counseling and Development, 44*(1), 28–48. doi:10.1002/jmcd.12035

Skinner, H., Steinhauer, P., & Santa Barbara, J. (1995). Family Assessment Measure (FAM III). Multi Health Systems. Retrieved from https://prezi.com/ohzk5gwkdzjo/family-assessment-measure-fam-iii/

Skinner, H., Steinhauer, P., & Sitarenios, G. (2000). Family Assessment Measure (FAM) and Process Model of Family Functioning. *Journal of Family Therapy, 22*(2), 190–210. doi:10.1111/1467-6427.00146

Snyder, D. K. (1997). *Marital satisfaction inventory—Revised.* Los Angeles, CA: Western Psychological Services.

Spanier, G. B.(1989). *Manual for the Dyadic Adjustment Scale.* North Tonowanda, NY: Multi-Health Systems.

Sperry, L. (Ed.). (2012). *Family assessment: Contemporary and cutting-edge strategies* (2nd ed.). New York: Routledge.

Stratton, P., Lask, J., Bland, J., Nowtony, E., Evans, C., Singh, R., … & Peppiatt, A. (2014). Detecting therapeutic improvement early in therapy: Validation of the SCORE-15 index of family functioning and change. *Journal of Family Therapy, 36,* 3–19. doi:10.1111/1467-6427.12022

Straus, M. A., Hamby, S. L., Boney-McCoy, S., & Sugarman, D. B. (1996). The revised Conflict Tactics Scales (CTS2): Development and preliminary psychometric data. *Journal of Family Issues, 17*(3), 283–316. doi:10.1177/019251396017003001

Thomas, V. & Olson, D.H. (1993). Problem families and the Circumplex Model: observational assessment using the Clinical Rating Scale (CRS). Journal of Marital & Family Therapy, 19, 159–175.

Ward, P. J., Lundberg, N. R., Zabriskie, R. B., & Berrett, K. (2009). Measuring marital satisfaction: A comparison of the Revised Dyadic Adjustment Scale and the Satisfaction with Married Life Scale. *Marriage & Family Review, 45*(4), 412–429. doi:10.1080/01494920902828219

Watson, J., & Flamez, B. (2014). *Counseling assessment and evaluation: Fundamentals of applied practice.* Los Angeles, CA: Sage.

Wetchler, J. L., & Bigner, J. J. (2012). *Handbook of LGBT-affirmative couple and family therapy.* New York: Routledge.

Whiston, S. C. (2016). *Principles and applications of assessment in counseling* (5th ed.). Boston: Cengage.

PART III

The Schools and Models of Family Therapy

CHAPTER 9

Transgenerational Family Therapies

Mary Ballard, Laura-Fazio Griffith, and Reshelle Marino

"You have inherited a lifetime of tribulation. Everybody has
inherited it. Take it over, make the most of it, and when you have
decided you know the right way, do the best you can with it."

—Murray Bowen

Families are complicated. Each member represents generations of deeply entrenched values and beliefs that may or may not find a harmonious union when joining with others. As therapists, we have walked with those experiencing the "tribulation" of all things family. And we have seen the healing power of relationships when families work to discover and understand each other in new ways. To "do the best you can with it" is a lofty goal indeed, and one that we feel privileged to promote.

In the previous chapters, you focused on research, intake, and assessment. In the next section of this book, we will focus on the schools and models of family therapy. Especially in this chapter, we will discuss transgenerational family therapy, which offers a framework for examining the interactions of families across generations and therefore often explains current or future family problems. For example, current family problems are often the result of unhealthy thoughts and behavioral patterns spanning three or more generations. Understanding how the family responded to these crises and stressors in the past can provide insight into current familial struggles. Since this unresolved conflict can remain for generations and result in severe family dysfunction, understanding these entrenched or enmeshed patterns of behavior is an important contribution in resolving immediate concerns. Therefore, the major goal of transgenerational family therapy is to break the cycle of dysfunction through an awareness of unhealthy ways of relating that have been passed from generation to generation.

LEARNING OBJECTIVES

After reading this chapter, you will be able to do the following:

- Identify the major concepts that define transgenerational family therapy.
- Identify the early pioneers of transgenerational family therapy.
- Discuss methods of assessing and treating the family using transgenerational family therapy.
- Identify the intervention strategies of transgenerational family therapy.
- Discuss the role of the transgenerational family therapist.
- Apply the theories and intervention strategies of transgenerational family therapy to actual case studies.

PROFILE OF MAIN FIGURES

The major figures most commonly associated with transgenerational family therapy include Murray Bowen (1978), Ivan Boszormenyi-Nagy (Boszormenyi-Nagy & Krasner, 1986), and James Framo (1982). The tenants of each of these theories are discussed in greater detail in this chapter.

MURRAY BOWEN

Credited as the father of family systems theory, Bowen was a World War II psychiatrist who, after the war, began his work studying families diagnosed with schizophrenia and their mothers at the Menninger Clinic. He continued his work with families after moving to the National Institute of Mental Health (NIMH), where he conducted his landmark study in 1954 by hospitalizing schizophrenics and their families. The findings of this research resulted in the development of his major concept of differentiation of self, which is discussed in greater length later in this chapter. After leaving the NIMH, he continued his career at Georgetown University in Washington, D.C., where he spent 30 years refining much of his family systems theory. Perhaps his most controversial moment came in 1967, while presenting his new theoretical constructs and intervention strategies at a conference. His presentation involved a great deal of self-disclosure about his own family as well as his personal journey of self-differentiation. Since therapist self-disclosure was not very popular at the time, his actions led to heated debates among clinicians. His thoughts about this lecture and his personal discoveries are noted in his seminal article titled "On Differentiation of Self," which was published in *Family Therapy in Clinical Practice* (Bowen, 1978).

IVAN BOSZORMENYI-NAGY

A contemporary of Bowen and a student of Virginia Satir, Boszormenyi-Nagy authored contextual family therapy, which goes beyond the examination of generational patterns of behavior to further explore relational fairness and trustworthiness in family relationships. Boszormenyi-Nagy founded the Family Center at the Eastern Pennsylvania Psychiatric Center in 1957 and worked at the site for 20 years. He believed that families were bound across generations by the concepts of loyalty and relational ethics. He believed these concepts to be the "glue" that held families together. He served an additional 20 years as chief of Family Therapy in the Department of Psychiatry at Hahnemann University, now Drexel University. He also served as professor emeritus in the program of Marriage and Family Therapy at Drexel. He was a founding member of the American Family Therapy Academy and the Institute for Contextual Growth, where he and his wife conducted training programs in contextual family therapy. His seminal work, *Invisible Loyalties*, with Geraldine Spark (1973), had a tremendous impact on family therapists throughout the world.

JAMES FRAMO

Trained as a clinical psychologist, Framo worked at the Eastern Pennsylvania Psychiatric Institute from 1956 to 1969. In 1960 he accepted a position as professor of psychology at Thomas Jefferson University and later at Temple University. He retired in 1999 from the United States International University in San Diego. He also served as chief of the Family Therapy Unit at the Jefferson Community Mental Health Clinic in Philadelphia from 1969 to 1973. Along with Boszormenyi-Nagy, he was a founding member of the American Family Therapy Association. Framo combined object relations and intergenerational theories and the techniques of conjoint marital and family therapy in his work with families. He was most interested in working with the client's family of origin to address presenting problems (Framo, 1976). Armed with this insight, he felt individuals, couples, and families could avoid old relational pitfalls and begin to relate in more positive and productive ways.

As you can see, transgenerational family therapists offer unique approaches for working within the family system yet have much in common. For example, they believe generational history to be key when improving family system issues, and therefore individual pathology is seen as unimportant. Let us look more closely at some of the key concepts of these major family theorists.

KEY CONCEPTS

Bowen Family Theory

Bowen believed that families should be viewed as a single unit and not as individual members with unrelated problems. His early observations of his own family, as well as others, cemented his views on the transgenerational nature of issues that present within the family system. Eight underlying concepts define Bowen family theory:

1. Differentiation of self

2. Triangles

3. Nuclear family emotional process

4. Family projection process

5. Multigenerational transmission process

6. Emotional cutoff

7. Sibling position

8. Societal emotional process

Differentiation of self. Differentiation of self is the hallmark or flagship of Bowen's theory. The notion of differentiation of self involves the ability to maintain a strong sense of self, while balancing emotional reactivity to the emotional system inherent within families. A differentiated self is accomplished by being a productive member of the family system, while holding onto personal beliefs, values, and opinions. Differentiated individuals take into consideration the advice of others, but ultimately make decisions that are independent of other systems in their lives. Differentiation of self is a process that evolves over time and involves an individual's family, social networks, relationships, and work environment. Ultimately, it is the ability to separate thoughts from feelings, self from others, and togetherness from individuality the makes one differentiated (Gladding, 2014). Similarly, Bowen believed that a differentiation of thinking from emotion involves biology, physiology, and mental processing. Decisions about behavior are made through a cognitive thinking process, instead of reacting quickly and intensely to an emotional system. The ultimate goal is to develop a balance between thinking and feeling and to avoid irrational and emotional reacting, which allows for sound decision making.

In the absence of differentiation, relationships become fused (Bowen, 1978). Bowen defined fusion as the tendency to be so emotionally attached to another that a sense of self and appropriate relational boundaries are lost. Once this happens the intellectual and emotional systems within the family become blurred (see Case Presentation 9.1). Bowen believed that family members ultimately strive for a balance between meeting their needs for intimacy and autonomy. Without autonomy, however, family members are less likely to think independently, thus making them more apt to adopt the ideas and opinions of others. Differentiation of self is not possible without the presence of autonomy.

Bowen espoused that all family members are searching for intimacy within the family system. Intimacy is the healthy, emotional connection that allows family members to feel loved and complete. The development of intimate relationships in families is a natural process in fulfilling needs for human connection and interaction. However, when these needs become unhealthy and overbearing, and family members begin to lose their autonomy, Bowen warned of the development of fusion anxiety. Fusion anxiety causes family members to emotionally react when presented with stress. Bowen believed that the entire family system is susceptible to developing symptoms related to fusion anxiety when encountering severe stressful events. However, a family member with a higher level of self-differentiation will experience less symptomology and be better equipped to cope with the stressful events, as opposed to a family member who is fused with others. The more differentiated a family member is the more likely he or she is to stop and think about a situation before impulsively making decisions as a reaction to someone or something (Nelson, 2003).

Bowen stated that levels of differentiation exist on a scale from 0 (no differentiation) to 100 (complete differentiation). Although we are all on this continuum and differentiate depending on life experiences, Bowen focused on life events that are a catalyst for self-differentiation. He felt most problems resulted from emotional rather than cognitive reactions. Even though we are constantly exposed to others' views, as we learn from our life experiences, we become more autonomous and less dependent on others for guidance. Bowen encouraged family members to think under emotional pressures and make decisions that concomitantly balanced the intellectual and emotional parts of self.

Triangles. As discussed in the earlier chapters of this text, a triangle is a three-person relationship system that exists in all families and social groups for the purpose of temporarily alleviating stress. According to Bowen, when the tension becomes too great between two family members, one member of the dyad, usually the one who is the most unhappy, will "triangle in" a third person in an attempt to relieve anxiety and stabilize the troubled relationship. As part of the assessment process, the therapist can observe if triangles exist, when they detriangulate, and when they reform throughout the family system. Since triangles are typically very stable and can tolerate more stress than a dyad, the family members may reject the therapist's attempts to convey to the family members when it is noticed. Triangles, or the lack thereof, can be an assessment tool for family members themselves. The therapist could ask the family members to verbalize when they notice triangles forming, and then can work to address the root issue rather than attempt to alleviate the tension. Triangles only offer temporary relief, because the original problem that created the stress is typically not addressed. Most triangles are loosely formed and fluid during less stressful times. This would be a good time for a therapist to bring the awareness to the family members. If the family is flexible and displays a balance of mild and rigid triangulation, it will cope effectively when faced with life stressors. However, when the family is under extreme stress, the triangle may become very rigid and dysfunctional. If the family establishes a pattern of rigid triangulation depending on someone or something to alleviate the stress, then more severe problems develop. The therapist can utilize the concept of triangulation and formulate therapeutic goals for the family based on the level of rigidity in the system.

Nuclear family emotional process. This process describes the single generation relationships between members of a nuclear family. Bowen felt the nuclear family was the most basic unit in society and that, over time, chronic stress and anxiety were inevitable. He defined four common patterns of behavior that governed how families react to these stressors: marital conflict, dysfunction of a spouse, impairment of children, and emotional distancing.

Marital conflict. The less differentiated and more fused couples are the more likely they are to react emotionally as anxiety levels increase in the family. In the face of conflict, each spouse attempts to control the other by projecting his or her anxiety onto the other. In the absence of a spouse who is willing to give in or accommodate the other, marital conflict occurs.

Dysfunction of a spouse. As the marital conflict intensifies, the more accommodating spouse may acquiesce in an attempt to preserve the harmony of the relationship. However, this spouse may continue to harbor resentment that leads to more stress and anxiety, which can result in the development of physical, mental and emotional symptoms.

Impairment of one or more children. If the parents focus their anxieties on one or more children, symptoms will develop in those children. Children mirror back with equal intensity the same level of focus or attention being exhibited by the parents. This causes children to be hypersensitive to the needs, anxieties and expectations of parents, which undermines their ability to differentiate. These children may experience physical, emotional and/or social consequences.

Emotional distancing. To reduce the intensity of a relationship, family members will distance themselves emotionally from one another for a period of time. However, this behavior is problematic if the family member completely isolates from the rest of the family.

Multigenerational transmission process. When examining a multigenerational family, it is common to observe that some branches of the family tree are more differentiated than others. This process occurs gradually from one generation to the next. The process begins when one sibling experiences a high level of differentiation, while the other sibling experiences a low level of differentiation. Because we tend to partner with people who share our same level of differentiation, the highly differentiated sibling will marry someone equally differentiated (Kerr, 2003). The two will then parent a highly differentiated child who will transmit this pattern of behavior to the next generation. The less differentiated sibling, however, will marry someone who is also not well differentiated, leaving them to parent a poorly differentiated child who will also transmit this behavior pattern to the next generation. For example, on a highly differentiated branch of the family tree you may observe a family that is more educated, physically healthy, and financially successful. The poorly differentiated branch might involve family members who participate in criminal activity, do not value education, and engage in domestic violence.

Emotional cutoff. Some family members attempt to resolve family conflict by cutting themselves off from any significant family interactions. These members adopt the belief that the family is of no influence and may even go as far as moving to another part of the country. They may even stop speaking to other family members entirely. However, this emotional cutoff is not productive, but clearly a sign that the family is in control. Bowen encouraged family members to face their anxiety and work on family issues rather than cutting themselves off.

Sibling position. Bowen incorporated the work of Walter Toman (1976), a German psychologist, in his theory on sibling position. Bowen posited that birth order often predicts the characteristics and behaviors of family members. For example, first-born siblings tend to be rule oriented and will gravitate toward leadership positions, while youngest siblings adopt a more relaxed and carefree role (Shah & Jadav, 2016). The family system role adopted greatly influences the interaction and behavior patterns between members. Bowen felt that sibling positioning offered much insight into the success or failure of a marriage (Bowen, 1978).

Societal emotional process. Societal behavior is often governed by one's emotional system, which can serve to promote both progressive and regressive societal periods. Just as in the family, attempts to alleviate systemic societal problems can fall short, leaving leaders to struggle for short-term, ineffective solutions. This period of regression leads to a less differentiated society where members can no longer share in mutual problem-solving behavior. Only chaos and confusion exist when mutual respect and a cooperative spirit are lost. To alleviate societal stress and anxiety, short-term, feel-good solutions are adopted at the expense of discovering real answers to society's problems

CASE PRESENTATION 9.1: THE CASE OF BECKY, MACK, AND EVAN

Ashton and her mother, Becky, make an appointment to see Evan, a marriage and family therapist. Ashton, a 17-year-old high school senior, tells Evan that she often feels too depressed and anxious to go to school. Ashton's mother says she's "tried everything" to help her daughter, but now recognizes she needs professional help. As a transgenerational therapist, Evan begins his assessment by asking questions to learn more about the presenting problem in the context of the broader family. He then follows with the completion of a three-generational genogram. He learns that Ashton and her older brother have had a tumultuous relationship with their father, Mack, ever since a nasty divorce almost a decade ago. Even after all these years, Becky and Mack remain enmeshed by continuing their bitter quarrels about everything from money to visitation arrangements. The genogram reveals generational patterns of emotional cutoff, over involvement and triangulation in the families of both parents. Becky was overinvolved with her mother and emotionally cutoff from her father, while just the opposite was true for Mack, who was overinvolved with his mother, but emotionally cutoff from his father. Evan quickly discovers that Ashton has been triangulated into her parent's troubles to the point she has become the symptom bearer for the family. Since Ashton is the most vulnerable member of the family, the family projection process is at work in her, as she is viewed by her family as the member who "has a problem." In continuing the generational pattern of behavior, she is emotionally cutoff from her father and overly involved with her mother. She has a low level of self-differentiation and responds emotionally to the stressors in the family. Acting as a coach or a guide, Evan's goal is to have Ashton detriangulate and move to a healthier level of self-differentiation. He would also invite the entire family to participate in the counseling process.

As you can see, Bowen focused on the differentiation of self and the dissolution of dysfunctional triangles as major goals for working within the family system. Therapists working within this framework must view their families within the context of the family unit and the multigenerational web of that existence. Another theorist, Boszormenyi-Nagy, also viewed family relationships as major factors in family therapy. Let us examine his concepts including the intriguing concept of relational ethics.

IVAN BOSZORMENYI-NAGY AND CONTEXTUAL FAMILY THERAPY

Boszormenyi-Nagy's contextual family therapy revolves around the concept of relational ethics to promote the emotional healing of families (Boszormenyi-Nagy, 1987). The consequences from a lack of trust and caring in a family can be severe and passed from generation to generation. These intergenerational conflicts are what usually bring individuals, couples, and families to counseling. Boszormenyi-Nagy developed several tenets that are unique to a contextual family therapy approach. Case Presentation 9.2 provides you with an overview of how these tenets work together to assist the therapeutic process.

Loyalty. Family members will show preference to other members when there is an indebtedness of earned merit. This favored stance is referred to as loyalty. As trustworthiness grows between family members, deepening levels of commitment or loyalties will develop. If loyalties developed in the family of origin conflict with those of the nuclear family, split loyalties will emerge creating stress and anxiety. Sometimes invisible loyalties exist between unlikely family members, such as a child and an abusive parent. An example might include a child who is scapegoated and symptomatic. Split loyalties occur when a child is pressured to display loyalty to only one parent.

Parentification. Parentification is a reversal of roles between the parent and child. These children are forced into adult roles in order to meet the physical and/or emotional needs of the parents. Although most if not all children assume adult responsibilities from time to time, these children do so habitually without any support. Such a compromise in the natural development of children influences all other current and future relationships.

Legacies. The spoken, unspoken, conscious, or unconscious expectations that family members have for each other are called legacies. They are handed down from generation to generation and keep track of what is given out of obligation and what is owed based on current or past actions in the family. Boszormenyi-Nagy described how people believe that they owe it to their families to uphold these legacies, even if they are destructive. An example would be an abused child who continues as an adult to abuse the next generation. An unconscious, invisible loyalty exists to 'pay the debt off' to the next generation. Boszormenyi-Nagy went on to describe merit, which is to be earned by considering and supporting the interests of others in the family (Boszormenyi-Nagy, 1987). When children exonerate their parents for past failures, they understand them in a multigenerational perspective, which earns them merit.

Revolving slate. This concept describes the transgenerational transmission of injustices and destructive entitlements. Parents with unresolved family of origin issues pursue their entitlement from their children. This, however, deprives children of their entitlement. This creates a vicious cycle whereby the children now experience the same injustices and destructive entitlements as their parents received in the family of origin.

Family ledger. The family ledger is similar to a bank ledger. It is a balance sheet of obligations and indebtedness. Simply stated, it keeps an account of what is due and what is owed in the family. All family members are obligated to give and entitled to receive. But when ledgers appear unbalanced in the face of life cycle changes, family functioning is negatively affected. Overtime, imbalances in the family ledger can lead to stagnation or the lack of an autonomous and trustworthy relationship. When there is an imbalance of entitlement and obligation, relationships stagnate and people develop symptomatic ways of fulfilling family legacies. Unless interrupted, transgenerational patterns of entitlement and indebtedness will continue.

Entitlement. A major concept of contextual therapy, entitlements are what family members are due at birth. Children are entitled to trustworthy parenting, and parents are entitled to loyal children. As time goes on, the family ledger measures the degree of earned entitlement based upon the obligations made and met. Entitlements can become destructive and be passed from generation to generation. For example, children not receiving trustworthy parenting can become angry adults who project their anger onto their spouses and children.

Dimensions of relational reality. Boszormenyi-Nagy outlined four dimensions to assist in understanding the relationships between family members: facts of life, individual psychology, transactional patterns, and relational ethics.

Facts of life. This dimension includes the facts surrounding the unchanging life events that occur in the family, such as birth, death, marriage, divorce, physical and mental illnesses, and natural and human-made events. These facts influence current and future relationships of all family members.

Individual psychology. In terms of contextual family therapy, individual psychology is the way in which a family member takes external information and processes it internally, such as thoughts, dreams, aspirations, intellectual ability, and emotions. Boszormenyi-Nagy believed this is a key factor in explaining how family members relate to one another. It provides the therapist with subjective information about how family members view themselves and how they may relate to others.

Transactional patterns. The interactions between individuals in relationships that develop over time, as well as over multiple generations, are called transactional patterns. These patterns offer insight into the relational indebtedness, legacies, and entitlements that have developed and come to represent fair and just relatedness over time.

Relational ethics. The final dimension noted by Boszormenyi-Nagy is relational ethics. This dimension is the theoretical cornerstone of contextual family therapy. This concept describes a fundamental way of interacting with others that requires a balance of ethical consideration for the interests of others as well as self.

CASE PRESENTATION 9.2: THE CASE OF JOSE AND HANNA

Robert, a contextual family therapist, meets with Jose and Hanna for couple counseling closed that Hanna has started drinking excessively, and Jose works long hours to avoid ... however, does not work outside the home and suspects Jose is having an affair and not working late as he claims. They have been married 4 years. Robert notes their lack of trust, problems in communicating with one another, and strained family of origin relationships. Robert works with the couple to (a) help them reach an ethical balance in their relationship based on fairness and the recognition of obligations and entitlements, (b) eliminate Hanna's excessive drinking, (c) find ways to restore a sense of loyalty to each one's family of origin, and (d) restore trust in the relationship. After spending time exploring their current and past transgenerational patterns of behavior, Jose and Hanna recognize they are repeating many of the destructive behaviors they learned in their families of origin. Robert encourages them to settle old family accounts in order for trust and fairness to flourish in their own relationship. Jose and Hanna continue to work on identifying shared entitlements and obligations, which allow them to agree on what is fair in their relationship. Jose expressed that he is entitled to expect Hanna not to drink excessively, to be responsible with money, and to treat him with kindness. Hanna agrees he deserves this and feels she is entitled to his honesty, presence, and kindness, to which Jose also agrees. Robert works with the couple to establish a concrete plan to balance debts in the relationship.

JAMES FRAMO AND OBJECT RELATIONS THERAPY

Framo's approach to therapy focuses on understanding how unconscious motives originating in the family of origin influence current relationships. Family members are encouraged to correct their reactive thoughts and behaviors as related to their relationships in their family or origin, which subsequently allows for healthier nuclear family relationships (Framo, 1992).

Transgenerational projection, introjects, and splitting. An important concept of Framo's theory is that of transgenerational projective identification and introjects. Beginning in infancy, children experience their parents as having good and bad characteristics. For example, the parent (external object) of a child being potty trained may become upset and yell (bad), and then change the diaper (good). Because the children cannot control or change their outer reality, they attempt to make sense of it and control their pain and confusion by internalizing the bad parts of the external object (parents). The internalized object is referred to as the introject, which is now a component of the personality as an unconscious object or "split." Introjection is the psychological representation of the external object (parents). The emotional relationship between children and their parents is now based upon introjection and not on reality. The children then develop into adults and unconsciously place specific introjects, or unowned parts of themselves, onto their spouses or children, rather than resolve them within the family of origin. This process is entrenched and influences all other current and future relationships. This is why Framo has couples explore and begin to let go of damaging introjects that were established in childhood.

According to Framo, there are four categories that describe how adults typically relate to their family of origin: overinvolved, superficially involved, uninvolved, and appropriately involved. Overinvolved adults lack appropriate boundaries and resist making friends or social commitments outside the family. Superficially involved adults maintain the appearance of closeness, but their contact with the family is primarily continued out of a sense of obligation or duty. The uninvolved adults assert that they are no longer connected to their family. However, their emotional ties are still strong, and the family is still very much in control of the thoughts and behaviors of the adult. Lastly, the appropriately involved adult displays a health connection to the family of origin. This adult is able to balance the needs of his or her spouse and children with that of the family of origin (Gehart & Tuttle, 2003).

In working with couples, Framo helps them understand the power of introjection and splits, and encourages them to invite members from their family of origin to participate. The involvement of extended family members provides the therapist with a more complete historical picture of the family. This additional information is used to further understand the projective identification process at work in the family and the presence of bad or negative introjections. Helping adult children begin to see their parents as they really are and not introjected pieces and parts is important to restoring healthy marital relationship.

Framo also used couples' groups as a therapeutic technique to bring about awareness and change (Boszormenyi-Nagy & Framo, 1965). In the group with multiple couples, important feedback is shared by group members once they have observed the interaction of each couple. With multiple group members providing feedback, couples are less likely to project their introjections. He also encouraged the use of a cotherapist to deter the entanglement of the therapist into the couple's unresolved object relations issues.

PREMISES OF THE THEORY

Each theory consists of uniques premises. The following sections detail unique distinctions between each theory.

Bowen Family Theory

Bowen did not believe in diagnostic labels. He focused on alleviating anxiety within the family system through the process of self-differentiation as a means of eliminating the current symptoms exhibited by the family. His research with families diagnosed with schizophrenia revealed that family systems operate on a continuum of emotional fusion and differentiation. He also observed that individual family members operate along this same continuum. Bowen defined the ongoing struggle to achieve a healthy balance between satisfying personal needs with those of the family as the differentiation of self, which is the cornerstone of his family systems theory. Simply stated, the higher the level of differentiation, the healthier the family. Differentiated families allow members to maintain their individuality while actively participating in the family system. Low levels of differentiation result in members being fused, emotionally reactive, stressed, and anxious. Bowen theorized that the mentally ill suffer from poor differentiation and thus become the symptom bearers for the entire family. Therefore, his treatment involved the hospitalization of the entire family to treat the whole emotional system.

Bowen differentiated between the basic self and the pseudoself. He described the basic self as constant and able to handle life events, while the pseudoself fluctuates according to stress levels in intimate and emotional situations. The pseudoself is usually less differentiated in emotional situations. The basic self is thought to develop from the nuclear family projection process, which involves the transmission of parents' immaturity and lack of differentiation to their children. The pseudoself can be adapted in different situations, and our personality and level of maturity can appear more in control depending on the situation and level of emotionality involved in the varied situations. For example, one person may appear more differentiated, or emotionally stable in a new relationship than the other. The stability is attributed to pseudo differentiation.

Boszormenyi-Nagy and Contextual Family Therapy

I like this— makes sense

Boszormenyi-Nagy's contextual family therapy is an intergenerational approach that is an outgrowth of both individual and classical family therapy. The influence of past relationships on current family functioning, as well as the need for family members to achieve a healthy balance of separation and togetherness, are the underlying concepts of this approach (Boszormenyi-Nagy & Ulrich, 1981). With the concept of relational ethics as the foundation for his approach, Boszormenyi-Nagy strongly emphasized the need for ethical principles to guide the interpersonal give and take that goes on between family members. It is the perceived fairness of this give and take process that sets the stage for the establishment of trustworthiness. The concepts of relational fairness and trustworthiness anchor family relationships as family ledgers keep track of debts that are paid and earned. Balanced ledgers give way to balanced relationships in which family members are free to individuate. Loyalties and legacies must also be mediated from generation to generation to preserve healthy family functioning. Because family members are often unaware of the motives behind their behaviors, contextual therapy examines patterns of behavior in families and the meaning that is ascribed to them. He believed marital dysfunction results from ledger imbalances over multiple generations. For example, a lack of intimacy is likely a result of a loyalty to parents rather than a lack of communication skills. Boszormenyi-Nagy believed that families become stagnant not because they are pathological or dysfunctional, but because the ethical considerations for one another are broken.

James Framo and Object Relations Therapy

Framo's approach to therapy requires families to examine and correct troublesome family of origin relationships in order to understand and address immediate or current problems in the family. His intergenerational approach draws heavily from Ronald Fairbairn's (1954) approach to object relations therapy, which broadened it by suggesting that people form relationships out of the need to be in a relationship, not just out of an instinctual drive (Fairbairn, 1954). This expanded view provides a framework for considering the behaviors of the individual within the larger context of the family.

Object relations therapy is based on impressions of internalized images of self and others that occur in early parent–child interactions and affect a person's way of conceptualizing and interacting with other people. Framo's concept of working with couples and families began with complete parental understanding, not just remembering the good, bad, and neutral introjects (Framo, 1972). He would then focus on conjoint and group marital therapy, and then transition to working with the whole family through weekend marathon sessions.

ROLE OF THE THERAPIST

Transgenerational family therapists do not subscribe to a particular set of skills or techniques. Their role in therapy centers on being a coach, guide and teacher in helping family members understand the transgenerational nature of the presenting problem. Transgenerational family therapists focus on the promotion of differentiation (in regard to self/family and intellect/emotion; Kolbert, Crothers, & Field, 2013). Therefore, they must also spend time in therapy working on their own family of origin issues before working with families. An effective transgenerational family therapist will exhibit high levels of differentiation (Friedman, 1991). In order to effectively work with families, the therapists must first undergo an emotional change through their own personal transgenerational work (Kerr, 1981). Failing to do this may delay any healthy shifts that families may experience.

The transgenerational therapist maintains a calm presence and peaceful demeanor, and remains objective and neutral at all times. Empathy, unconditional positive regard, and a true interest in the issues and problems being presented in the therapy sessions are continuously displayed. The underlying role of the therapist is to gather as much current and historical family information as possible. By asking questions, family members are required to think about and respond to many of the family dynamics that are influencing current behavior. Armed with this insight, the therapist guides or coaches the family in resolving the family-of-origin issues that are creating stress and anxiety in the family (Kerr, 2003).

The transgenerational family therapist discourages families from being consumed with emotionalism and confusion in the face of family problems. Instead, family members are instructed to rise above the emotionality of their issues and respond by remaining reasonable, neutral, and self-controlled. This type of therapy mirrors that of a Socratic dialogue, with the therapist in the role of teacher or coach. (Wylie, 1991).

Boundary and differentiation issues from a generational perspective are a concern for the transgenerational family therapist. The therapist, in the role of coach, works with the family to search for "clues" as to where the various pressures on the family have been expressed and how effectively or ineffectively the family has adapted to stress since its

inception. The transgenerational family therapist employs different techniques s
the genogram or encouraging the client to visit their family of origin. Spending time
family of origin members provides insight into the relational dynamics of the family
can assist the client in therapy (Gladding, 2015).

Transgenerational family therapists are, perhaps, the most important aspect in
facilitating the growth and resolution of generational patterns, issues, and behaviors.
The role of the therapist is extremely important and can be complex if the therapist
has not worked on his or her own generational issues and moved toward self-differentiation. The process of family therapy can have very positive outcomes if the
therapist remains calm and neutral and is aware of how important his or her role is
to the therapeutic process.

ASSESSMENT IN TRANSGENERATIONAL FAMILY THERAPIES

Family therapy tends to vary extensively in terms of the formal assessment process. The
therapist's theoretical orientation to systemic issues and transgenerational family therapy
usually drives the scope of the initial assessment. Several factors can be used during the
initial intake to provide a clear assessment of how to work with the family from a transgenerational perspective. These factors can be utilized to embark of effective treatment
for the family system.

The transgenerational family therapist believes an extended family systems assessment
process is vital to the effectiveness of therapeutic treatment. In transgenerational family
therapy, understanding your role in the family's problems, as well as how these problems
are embedded in the history of the extended family, are so important. It is this assessment
that is most critical to this approach. The therapist begins an extended family history
assessment with a description of the presenting problem. Exact dates are noted by the
therapist and later checked for the relationship to events in the extended family life cycle
(Nichols & Schwartz, 2012).

The therapist then moves to gather a history of the nuclear family. This information
may include stories about where the parents met, courtship, marriage, and childbearing.
Where the family has lived and when they moved, especially in relation to location of
the extended families, is also important information. The therapist then proceeds with
gathering a history of spouses' births and sibling positions, as well as significant facts
about their childhood and past and current functioning of their parents. The therapist
records all of this information in a genogram covering at least three generations. If the
therapist fails to provide the attention needed to the assessment process, associations that
can help clients gain perspective on their problems may be overlooked.

Presenting Problem

The presenting problem is the catalyst for families to enter into a therapeutic relationship.
The inquiry into the presenting problem is detailed and empathic. The therapist explores
the presenting problem by hearing the family's account of the problem. All members of

the family have an opportunity to express their perspective. The therapist acknowledges their description of the problem and feelings associated with it (Nichols & Schwartz, 2012). The therapist may begin with an open-ended inquiry, which is followed by detailed and specific questions to find out more about the precise nature of the problem. The family's attempts to cope and resolve the problem in their family system are also explored. Questions to ask include: What have they tried in the past? What has been helpful? What has not worked? Who, other than those present, have been involved to help or hinder with these issues? The therapist gathers specific and concrete information regarding the presenting issue in order to move forward with treatment interventions and techniques.

IDENTIFYING THE SYSTEMIC CONTEXT

The therapist must have a clear understanding of the interpersonal context of the problem. Questions to answer include: Who are the members of this family? Are there important figures in the life of the problem that are not present, and what is the nature of their input? Does the family see this input as helpful? Family therapy is an approach that views people in context (Nichols & Schwartz, 2012). The most relevant context is often the immediate/nuclear family. However it is imperative, as part of the assessment process, to derive the most important context related to the presenting problem in order to provide effective treatment.

Family History

The transgenerational family therapist relies on a detailed family history as an integral part of the assessment process. The therapist begins by encouraging the family member(s) to tell their life story. This can include: stories about where the parents met, courtship, marriage, and childbearing. The therapist will pinpoint important information such as: where the family has lived and when they moved, especially in relation to location of the extended families. Finally, the therapist then proceeds with gathering a history of spouses' births and sibling positions, as well as significant facts about their childhood and past and current functioning of their parents (Nichols & Schwartz, 2012).

Genograms. In Chapter 7 you briefly learned about the rich information a family therapist can gather using the genogram as part of the assessment process. The therapist records all of the information gathered during the assessment/initial intake into a genogram covering at least three generations. The family member(s) and the therapist use the genogram to determine the themes and patterns that may need to be addressed during the therapeutic process. The genogram will be used to assess the patterns of emotional process that has been passed down over several generations. The therapist and the family member(s) are provided with a clear understanding of the family history, relationships, and patterns. The genogram is utilized to assess the family member(s) relationships within the family system and to develop a plan to identify therapeutic work. To learn more about genograms, see Guided Practice Exercises 9.1 and 9.2.

GUIDED PRACTICE EXERCISE 9.1

Prior to class, go to the following website, http://genograms.org/. This site contains information about family interaction patterns of communication and how those patterns are manifested across three or more generations. Review all of the tabs at the top of the page (e.g., introduction, theoretical basis, etc.), paying particular attention to the "Symbols" and "Clues" tabs. Think about your family of origin. What issues come to mind that would be important to include in your family genogram? You might want to begin writing a list of significant topics that will help you with the next guided practice exercise.

GUIDED PRACTICE EXERCISE 9.2

Prior to class, go to the following website, http://www.genopro.com/. Peruse the website and all of the things it offers. If you use a PC, you can request a free 14-day trial of an online genogram-generating software at http://www.genopro.com/registration/academic/. If you would rather use your computer, you can simply use http://www.smartdraw.com or http://www.genopro.com/genogram/templates/. Create your own genogram. Include all significant details going back at least three generations. You might want to consult with a family member if you have difficulty doing so. For tips, revisit the "Create your Own" tab from the genogram website in the previous guided practice exercise. What focal points are helpful in discovering patterns and meaning in your genogram? Specifically, what issues serve as clues that can assist you in evaluating and interpreting your family genogram? Print out your genogram and come to class prepared to discuss your genogram and experience completing it. What did you learn about your family and yourself? What stood out to you? If you would rather not discuss certain topics due to the sensitive nature of this activity, you do not have to. Feel free to share what you are comfortable sharing. Always respect your classmates' stories and maintain confidentiality.

Going home again. In this exercise, the therapist encourages family members to visit their families of origin with the goal of getting to know them better. The assumption is that a greater understanding of the family will help families more clearly differentiate. Recognizing that the visit may stir volatile emotions, the therapist works with the family member(s) prior to the visits regarding coping mechanisms such as relaxation techniques.

Once the family member(s) have returned to family sessions, the therapist will discuss with the family member(s) the emotions that were elicited upon returning to their family of origin. The family member(s) will process their feelings, thoughts, and behaviors related to visiting their family of origin. The therapist will ask the family member(s) to discuss what new information they have gained from the visit. How might this new information change their perceptions and feelings about their family of origin? The therapist will encourage the family member(s) to focus on the new information that was presented during the visit and whether the visit assisted the family member(s) in reevaluating their relationships with their family of origin.

Detriangulating. Helping family members recognize and remove themselves from unhealthy triangles is a major focus of Bowen family theory. Family members learn to mselves from being "triangled in" when stress and anxiety are present in the ...n. Learning to respond rationally during these times, as opposed to reacting ...tionally, is very important. Family members learn to let others own their personal struggles without becoming overinvolved. Detriangulating is a necessary step toward the differentiation of self.

The therapist will work with the family member(s) to assist them in recognizing the catalysts for triangulation. As the family member(s) begin to recognize triangulation within their relationships, the therapist works with the triangulated family members on communication patterns and styles to move towards detriangulating. The therapist will model the use of I statements in order for the family member(s) to communicate effectively with each other regarding the triangulation, the purpose of the triangulation, and how to become detriangulated during the therapeutic sessions. The importance of recognizing thoughts, feelings, and behaviors when triangulated will be the focus of I messages. The family member(s) will develop enhanced communication skills to confront the triangulating behaviors and to change these behaviors.

Engaging in person-to-person relationships. This exercise is designed to help family members learn to communicate without triangulating. Two family members are instructed to talk to each other about the personal things going on in their lives without discussing anyone else in the family. For family members previously engaged in rigid triangles, this will be a difficult exercise.

Talking directly to the therapist. To discourage emotional reactions to the anxiety experienced in therapy, Bowen instructed family members to look at and talk to the therapist and not to each other. This approach also minimizes attempts by family members to triangulate the therapist into the issues at hand. This approach is unique to Bowen family theory.

Process questions. The goal of process questioning is to move family members toward increased levels of differentiation. The questions are designed to elicit logical or rational answers versus emotionally reactive ones. Process questions require family members to think about or observe their circumstances before responding. For example, the therapist would ask, "How do you express your opinion?" and not "What is your opinion?"

One of the primary outcomes of successful treatment with families from a transgenerational approach is that family members understand intergenerational patterns and gain insight into historical circumstances that influence ways in which they presently interact (Learner, 1983). The therapist expects that with this knowledge a focus on changing intergenerational inferences operating within the current family will occur during the treatment process (Smith, 1991). At the end of treatment, issues related to fusion and unconscious relationship patterns should be evident. Families should be able to relate at an autonomous and cognitive level, void of the destructive reactive and emotional patterns of the past (Kerr & Bowen, 1988). Greater self-differentiation should be seen during the therapeutic process among nuclear family members.

Transgenerational family therapy focuses on change within individuals and couples. The therapist does not typically see the whole family system. Instead, individuals are often targeted for treatment, even though the emphasis of this approach is systemic (Gladding, 2015). Improvement of the family system is always a goal, regardless of the number of people attending the session (Kerr, 1981). It is important to note that a family can be influenced for the better just by a change occurring in one member of the family system (Kolbert et al., 2013).

The assessment and treatment procedures utilized by therapists operating from a transgenerational approach focus primarily on past behavioral patterns to understand current problems. Families must understand and learn from these patterns or risk repeating them in the future. The approach is systemic in nature and cognitive in practice, which gives therapist and their families a concrete evaluation process as treatment progresses. Guided Practice Exercise 9.3 will give you an opportunity to conceptualize a family member's presenting problem and determine how you might approach it using transgenerational family therapy.

GUIDED PRACTICE EXERCISE 9.3

Given what you have just read about transgenerational family therapies, what family patterns can you identify in your family of origin that have been significant in your life? Specifically, what patterns have been passed down to your family from previous generations? Discuss with a partner if these patterns have been rectified, or if the behaviors have been repeated? How have these patterns positively or negatively influenced your development?

STRENGTHS AND LIMITATIONS

Provides Great info

A major strength of transgenerational family therapy is the opportunity to explore patterns of family interaction across multiple generations. This exploration provides insight and understanding into entrenched behavioral patterns that have been passed down from generation to generation. This knowledge allows family members to interrupt the generational cycle of dysfunction by choosing new behaviors and attitudes versus relying on harmful behavioral patterns of reacting. The focus on family of origin issues and their influence on current family functioning makes transgenerational family therapy very effective.

A potential weakness of transgenerational family therapy is the time, money, and commitment level needed to explore transgenerational issues. Many people cannot afford to invest as heavily in the process as necessary, both monetarily and emotionally. Family members unwilling or unable to take their time in exploring family of origin issues may find the approach cumbersome and elect to end counseling before the real work is done. Another challenge is the availability of transgenerational information. In some instances, family members have died or disappeared, leaving others to only guess at often critical information.

too time costly

CASE PRESENTATION: THE CASE OF JASE AND SHUNDRA

In working with couples or families, transgenerational marriage and family counselors are always mindful of the powerful influences of the emotional and behavioral patterns that are passed from generation to generation. Unresolved conflicts can endure for generations and have a profound influence on current family functioning. Transgenerational theory reminds counselors that the relationships and interactions experienced in the family of origin can greatly influence a family member's current level of functioning. This is exemplified in the case of Jase and Shundra.

Presenting Problem

Jase and Shundra reveal to their marriage counselor, Chris, that they are unhappy to the point of considering divorce after 18 years of marriage. They have two children, ages 14 and 12.

Jase:	You are so angry and upset all the time. It is unbearable being around you most days.
Shundra:	If you weren't so quiet all of the time, then perhaps we could work on communication, but you are so emotionally unavailable. That is why I am always angry and upset with you.
Jase:	I just keep to myself because I don't want to say something I regret when I am angry.
Therapist:	What in particular makes you angry Jase?
Jase:	For one, the amount of money she spends on our daughter's dance clothes. It puts a big strain on our financial status.
Therapist:	Can you practice telling her that?
Jase:	It really stresses me out when I see how much you spend on dance clothes.
Shundra:	I wouldn't feel as inclined to spend as much time or money with her dance practices if you did not spend as much time trying to make our son the MVP of the football team. The amount of pressure you put on him has made him want to quit the team.
Jase:	Here we go again. I really want us to be able to resolve these issues for our children.
Shundra:	Me too, but how? It seems like it's too late.
Therapist:	It sounds like you both love your children very much and want them to have the best of everything. I wonder what it would be like if you both equally spent some of the time together, rather than on the football field or at dance practice? How could some time be shaved off of each activity to devote to the marriage?

Role of the Therapist

Bowen believed that therapists must work on their own family of origin issues of differentiation and triangulation before they can be effective working with families. Chris must be sure he has taken those steps before meeting with Jase and Shundra. Otherwise, he may become emotionally reactive to their issues, which would sabotage their work together. Chris must remain calm and differentiated, while encouraging the couple to rationally examine and take responsibility for their behavior patterns in the process leading to change. He will act as a guide or a coach throughout the process, taking an act in directing the conversation.

Assessment

Chris initially focuses on gathering information to better understand the presenting problem within the broader context of the family system. A multigenerational genogram is drawn to provide insight into the nuclear and extended families. The use of process questioning and the genogram reveals that Jase's father moved away when he was 13, leaving his mother to raise him and two younger siblings. Working two jobs, Jase's mom relied on him to take care of his siblings and help out around the house. Shundra's father died when she was young, so she too was counted on by her mother to help with siblings and household chores. Both Jase and Shundra were parentified as children, and, their fusion with their mothers has crippled their ability to differentiate. Both were triangulated by their mothers and now do the same thing with their children. Chris administers the **self-differentiation scale**, which shows both are at very low levels of differentiation.

Treatment Techniques and Outcomes

The ultimate goal of therapy is the differentiation of self. Chris recognizes the family as an emotional unit and continues to use process questioning to prompt further discussion about childhood experiences that are affecting their current relationships. Using the genogram, current patterns of connectedness and reactivity are compared to what was experienced in their family of origins. Jase always promised to be a better father but, when questioned by Chris, admits that he has become as emotionally distant. Jase comes to understand that his isolating behavior in the face of life's stressors is a learned behavior pattern that parallels that of his father and evokes the same emotions in Shundra as those experienced by his mother. Likewise, Shundra comes to understand that her reaction to Jase's emotional detachment mirrors that of her mother's. Chris encourages them to take on more and more responsibility for the reactions and responses by coaching them in the use of I messages. This exercise requires them to own their thoughts and feelings instead of blaming others. Chris also guides them in detriangulating with their children. Jase recognizes his overzealous attention to his son's football activities shields him from spending time and energy on his relationship with Shundra. Likewise, Shundra recognizes her triangulation with her daughter to meet need for intimacy and closeness that she is not getting from Jase. With the goal of differentiation in mind, Chris continues his work with Jase and Shundra in a very calm and neutral manner. Overtime they came to understand the influence of their family of origin issues on their current relationship. Armed with this knowledge and insight, Jase and Shundra were able to increase their levels of differentiation and strengthen their relationship.

SUMMARY

In this chapter, we provided you with an overview of transgenerational family therapy. By introducing you to the major figures responsible for its development and the theoretical frameworks that guided them, we hope that you have a sense of the underpinnings that drive the work of all who practice transgenerational family therapy. Through the Case Presentations, you have been exposed to the process of exploring the unhealthy and generationally entrenched thought and behavioral patterns that surface when families face challenging or stressful circumstances. And we hope you have seen how a recognition and illumination of those unhealthy patterns provide an avenue for family healing. Transgenerational family therapy is not easy work. As a therapist, you must be prepared to examine your own family of origin issues before attempting to practice it with others. However, the opportunity to help families break generational cycles of dysfunction and emerge with new behaviors and attitudes is rewarding work indeed. In the next chapter you will continue to learn about the complexity of family systems by examining strategic family therapy and Milan systemic family therapy. These theories will require you to think more critically about the meaning and influence of behavior in defining the family system. And, just as you have witnessed in this chapter, you will learn the important role that that you as therapist play in creating a constructive environment the supports and encourages change.

KEYSTONES

Among the key points addressed in this chapter are:

- Transgenerational family therapies examine the interactions of family members across three or more generations.
- Current and future problems in a family are rooted in unhealthy behavior patterns that are passed from generation to generation.
- Understanding and breaking the cycle of dysfunctional ways of communicating in a family is paramount to resolving the presenting problem.
- The transgenerational therapist focuses less on the presenting problems and more on unlocking the family of origin issues that are creating them.
- The transgenerational therapist may work with the entire family or some subset of the family (e.g., couples and individuals).
- The pioneering work of Murray Bowen, Ivan Boszormenyi-Nagy, and James Framo provides the foundation for transgenerational family therapy.

[handwritten margin notes: "nuc family / family of origin / ext. family. / have to know / to change / grow"]

REFLECTIONS FROM THE CONTRIBUTOR'S CHAIR
Mary Ballard

When utilizing transgenerational family therapy in my work with families, I determine to view presenting problems as unhealthy ways of relating that have developed over at least three generations. I proceed with the understanding that most dysfunctional behavior patterns have been passed along from generation to generation. I also believe that my client(s) have most likely lost the ability to balance needs for individuality and family togetherness. It is this instability that is producing a disruption in the family system. As members become more and more overwhelmed with emotional reactivity to troublesome problems and situations, the more likely they are to seek my counseling services.

A major goal I have for my client(s) is to learn to respond rationally to problems versus irrationally. I take a nondirective approach, one that almost resembles a coach or a guide, and have them examine past relationships and ways of interacting. I am much less concerned with the presenting problem, because I believe that the past holds the key for resolving whatever the current troubles happen to be in the family. I work at all times to stay peaceful and focused, and I attempt to provide a safe and calm environment by practicing unconditional positive regard and showing empathy for their current situation.

I may incorporate a variety of assessment techniques, but none more vital than process questioning to gather historical data, along with the creation of a genogram. I may ask a lot of questions to get the needed family facts. This information helps me and the client(s) to identify unhealthy triangles and low levels of differentiation, which are paramount to working from a transgenerational perspective. Because an examination of the historical roots of the presenting problem is a means for alleviating current family stress, I will often invite families to "go home again" to better understand their family of origin. With a clearer picture of how past relationships have influenced current ones, I can begin to guide client(s) as they unlearn old behavioral ways of reacting in times of stress to new and improved ways of responding rationally and reasonably.

As a professional counselor, I am often met with resistance when using this approach. Unearthing or shedding a spotlight on past family relationships can be very difficult, due to the often painful reminders that a look at the past can bring. However, because relational conflict is passed on from one generation to the next, I believe this journey to be critical and necessary if family members truly hope to resolve the current crisis and continue to grow.

ADDITIONAL RESOURCES
The following resources provide additional information relating to the chapter topics.

Useful Websites
- American Association for Marriage and Family Therapy
  http://www.aamft.org

This is the website for the American Association for Marriage and Family Therapy.

- Bowen Center for the Study of the Family
  http://www.thebowencenter.org/

This Bowen Center provides training programs, conferences, research, clinical services, audiovisual materials, and publications to further the development of Bowen therapy.

- Family Systems Institute
  http://www.thefsi.com.au

The institute provides information and postgraduate training to further the development of Bowen theory.

- Family Systems Theory
  http://www.familysystemstheory.com

This website provides information about transgenerational theory. It also serves as a locator service for marriage and family therapists.

- Family Therapy Resources
  www.familytherapyresources.net

Family Therapy Resources is a service of the AAMFT. Designed for both therapists and consumers, Family Therapy Resources is a comprehensive source for information about family therapy and other family-related issues.

- Genograms.org
  http://genograms.org/

This site contains information about family interaction patterns of communication and how those patterns are manifested across three or more generations.

- GenoPro
  http://www.genopro.com/

GenoPro is a genealogy software for drawing family trees, or genograms. Genograms can include basic information about the number of marriages, number of children in each marriage, birth order, age, and death. They can also include relationships between individuals and information on disorders running in a family, such as alcoholism, depression, and diseases.

- International Association of Marriage and Family Counselors
  http://www.iamfconline.org

This is the website for the International Association of Marriage and Family Counselors, a division of the American Counseling Association.

- Zur Institute
  www.zurinstitute.com

The Zur Institute offers innovative resources and online continuing education in family therapy. The institute includes resources for transgenerational family therapy.

Readings

AAMFT Clinical Updates

http://www.aamft.org/iMIS15/AAMFT/Content/Resources/Clinical_Updates.aspx?hkey=c9ae0056-4d8e-441b-974b-69c8a51d2528

Advocacy News and Events

http://www.aamft.org/iMIS15/AAMFT/Content/Advocacy/News_Events.aspx?hkey=1844adb8-c18e-40c0-a02d-48417a5832d4

Videos

Assessment and Engagement in Family Therapy: by Monica McGoldrick

Family Therapy With the Experts: 10-video series

Family Secrets: Implications for Theory and Therapy: by Evan Imber-Black

REFERENCES

Boszormenyi-Nagy, I. (1987). *Foundations of contextual therapy: Collected papers of Ivan Boszormenyi-Nagy.* New York: Brunner/Mazel.

Boszormenyi-Nagy, I., & Framo, J. (Eds.). (1965). *Intensive family therapy.* New York: Harper & Row Medical Department.

Boszormenyi-Nagy, I., & Krasner, B. (1986). *Between give and take: A clinical guide to contextual therapy.* New York: Brunner/Mazel.

Boszormenyi-Nagy, I., & Spark, G. M. (1973). *Invisible loyalties: Reciprocity in intergenerational family therapy.* New York: Harper & Row.

Boszormenyi-Nagy, I., & Ulrich, D. N. (1981). Contextual family therapy. In A. Gurman & D. P. Knicskern (Eds.), *Handbook of family therapy* (pp. 159–186). New York: Brunner/Mazel.

Bowen, M. (1978). *Family therapy in clinical practice.* New York: Aronson.

Fairbairn, W. R. D. (1954). *An object-relations theory of the personality.* New York: Basic Books.

Framo, J. L. (1972). On the differentiation of self. *Family interaction: A dialogue between family researchers on family therapists.* New York: Springer.

Framo, J. L. (1976). Family of origin as a therapeutic resource for adults in marital and family therapy: You can and should go home again. *Family Process, 15*, 193–210.

Framo, J. L. (1982). *Explorations in marital and family therapy.* New York: Springer.

Framo, J. L. (1992). *Family-of-origin therapy: An intergenerational approach.* New York: Brunner/Mazel.

Friedman, E. H. (1991). Bowen theory and therapy. In A. S. Gurman & D. P. Kniskern (Eds.), *Handbook of family therapy* (Vol. II, pp. 134–170). New York: Brunner/Mazel.

Gehart, D. R., & Tuttle, A. R. (2003). *Theory-based treatment planning for marriage and family therapists.* Belmont, CA: Brooks/Cole.

Gladding, S. T. (2014). *Family therapy: History, theory, and practice* (6th ed.). Upper Saddle River, NJ: Prentice Hall.

Gladding, S. T. (2015). *Family therapy: History, theory, and practice* (7th ed.). Upper Saddle River, NJ: Prentice Hall.

Kerr, M. E. (1981). Family systems theory and therapy. In A. S. Gurman & D. P. Kniskern (Eds.), *Handbook of family therapy* (Vol. II, pp. 226–266). New York: Brunner/Mazel.

Kerr, M. E. (2003, June 7–10). *Process of differentiation.* Paper presented at the 111th Annual Convention of the American Psychological Association, Toronto, Canada.

Kerr, M. E., & Bowen, M. (1988). *Family evaluation: An approach based on Bowen theory.* New York: Norton.

Kolbert, J. B., Crothers, L. M., & Field, J. (2013). Clinical interventions with adolescents using a family systems approach. *Family Journal: Counseling and Therapy for Couples and Families, 21*(1), 87–94.

Learner, S. (1983). *Constructing the multigenerational family genogram: Exploring a problem in context* (Videotape). Topeka, KS: Menninger Video Productions.

Nelson, T. S. (2003). Transgenerational family therapies. In L. L. Hecker & J. L. Wetchler (Eds.), *An introduction to marriage and family therapy* (pp. 255–293). New York: Routledge Mental Health.

Nichols, M. P., & Schwartz, R. C. (2012). *Family therapy: Concepts and methods* (10th ed.). Boston: Pearson.

Shah, D. P., & Jadav, M. (2016). To what extend does birth order affect our personality? *International Journal of Social Impact, 1*(3), 85–95.

Smith, R. L. (1991). Marriage and family therapy: Directions, theory, and practice. In J. Carlson & J. Lewis (Eds.), *Family counseling* (pp. 13–34). Denver: Love.

Toman, W. (1976). *Family constellation: Its effects on personality and social behavior.* New York: Springer.

Wylie, M. S. (1991). Family therapy's neglected prophet. *Family Therapy Networker, 15*, 24–37.

CHAPTER 10

Strategic and Milan Systemic Family Therapy

Rebecca L. Pender Baum, Torey Portrie-Bethke, and Samir H. Patel

"Psychotherapy is the art of finding the angel of hope
in the midst of terror, despair and madness."

—Cloé Madanes

Families often come into our offices thinking they know what the issue is and blaming one or more family members for the trouble that is being experienced at a collective level. However, as family therapists, we must maintain an awareness that the problems experienced are not singular in nature; rather, the "problem" is the manifestation and maintenance of feedback loops. Our role as family therapists is to disrupt these feedback loops, without placing blame, and help the family discover communicative strategies that promote and sustain functional homeostasis.

In Chapter 9 you learned about the transgenerational family therapies. Now we will focus on strategic family therapy and the Milan communication approach, which are two common family theories. The strategic therapy approach was developed from the original workings of Don Jackson, John Weakland, Cloé Madanes, Paul Watzlawick, and Jay Haley; while the Milan communication approach grew out of strategic family theory under the guidance of leading figures Mara Selvini-Palazzoli, Luigi Boscolo, Gianfranco Cecchin, and Giuliana Prata. The focus in both strategic and Milan communications theories is to determine how families maintain problems due to their interactional patterns and processes. In this chapter, we highlight the similarities and differences of these two theories and provide practical activities to help you conceptualize and integrate the material. Let's get started!

LEARNING OBJECTIVES

After reading this chapter, you will be able to do the following:

- Understand that strategic family therapy is directive and characterized by efficiency, brief in nature, and a nonpathological stance toward client concerns.

- Determine the major techniques utilized in strategic and Milan communications theories.

- Identify the major contributors to these theoretical approaches.

- Examine the therapeutic assumptions inherent in strategic and Milan communication theories.

- Understand the history/development from early strategic models that focused on helping families change their behaviors, to the Milan approach that highlighted the need for families to examine their belief systems and the meaning they attach to behavior.

STRATEGIC FAMILY THERAPY

Strategic family therapy gained attention due to its unorthodox therapeutic techniques (Capuzzi & Stauffer, 2015). Gardner, Burr, and Wiedowere (2006) noted that strategic family theory is directive and often intuitive in nature. Strategic family theory can be complex in nature and requires therapists to gain expertise and an advanced skill level to adequately apply the techniques. This approach is a relatively brief form of therapy that is technique oriented and was developed out of the work of Milton Erickson. The theory itself is less concerned with client insight but rather focuses on pragmatic behavioral change within the family unit.

PROFILE OF MAIN FIGURES

Milton Erickson believed that people possessed the ability to solve their own problems when provided opportunities to implement new behaviors. Instead of creating therapeutic relationships that consisted of hours of arduous interpretation and insight making, he developed specific task-related therapy sessions leading his work to be brief, active, and directive. He thoroughly planned each session and interaction with his clients. Erickson used hypnotic techniques with a focus on removing the symptom (Goldenberg & Goldenberg, 2013). Erickson believed that through indirect suggestions, he could encourage families to change their behavioral patterns, thus eliminating their presenting problem. Erickson was known for use of unconventional techniques inducing hypnosis, metaphor, and paradoxical directives (Haley, 1973).

Jay Haley coined the term *strategic therapy* from the work of Milton Erickson, Don Jackson, and Gregory Bateson at the Mental Research Institute (MRI). Again, the emphasis was on the interactional patterns and how they were connected to the family's behavioral problems. He adapted the work of Milton Erickson so that he could apply it to working with families. Haley worked with Gregory Bateson researching schizophrenia in the 1950s and helped to develop the concept of double bind. During his work with Erickson, Haley noticed symptoms appeared to be based on client interactional patterns. Haley (1973) chose to focus on intergenerational relationships. In 1975, he and Cloé Madanes, his then wife, formed the Family Therapy Institute of Washington, D.C., and he wrote two of his most influential seminal works, *Problem Solving Therapy* in 1976, and *Leaving Home* in 1980.

Cloé Madanes viewed family therapy as a brief problem-solving approach and placed an emphasis on the caring and emotional aspects of family systems. She was a pioneer in using holistic and systemic alternatives to paradoxical interventions. For example, she utilized a technique known as the pretend technique (Madanes, 1981). This was a unique technique that integrated the use of play and play therapy within strategic family therapy (Madanes, 1981), wherein she would encourage the parents to ask a child to pretend he or she has the symptoms and the parents pretend to solve the problem.

Paul Watzlawick was an Austrian American family therapist, psychologist, and communications theorist. Watzlawick was a pioneer of strategic family therapy and one of the original founders of the MRI model. He believed that problems within families were simply the result of faulty solutions. At the MRI, he followed the work of Gregory Bateson and the rest of the research team that included Don Jackson, John Weakland, and Jay Haley (who eventually broke off from the MRI). Watzlawick was also one of the founding members of the Brief Therapy Center.

KEY CONCEPTS

The view of human nature in strategic family therapy parallels that of structural family therapy in that the family is the core unit in which we develop and that behavior is viewed within a social context. Strategic family therapists believe that change happens through action oriented therapy that utilizes directives and paradoxes. Common assumptions in strategic family therapy include people operate within an interactional context, are influenced by others, and problems are created by family members. Therefore, families have the power to change what they do not like. Key concepts within this theory include therapist responsibility, symptoms as an attempt to communicate, redefining symptoms, and units and circularity.

Strategic family therapists tend to conceptualize repetitive patterns as preventing more complex evolving behaviors, adaptive sequences, preventing change in the participants' ability to deal differently with each other and thus tending to confirm belief systems and perpetuate dysfunction. Strategic interventions are geared to support or propel family members toward interrupting repetitive sequences, allowing a wider range of alternatives and instilling a higher level of complexity into the system. For example, a couple who presents for therapy may tend to redirect all present fights so they address past issues and problems. Let's turn to Table 10.1 to review the key concepts, conceptualization, and family and couple actions.

Table 10.1 Family therapist's conceptualization of families and couples actions

Key concepts	Therapist's conceptualization	Families and couples actions
Symptoms: Couple reports interpersonal communication challenges: "When we fight our pattern is to blame the other for the issues from the past in the present."	The therapist interprets this reported problem to be a manifestation of the couple's limited or nonexistent intimacy, managing differences, and taking personal responsibility for action. The symptomatic actions are maintained by the dysfunctional organization.	The therapist engages the couple in gaining motivation through therapeutic strategies for enhancing the relationship through setting goals that lead the individuals to take initiative for improving their relationship.
Triangles: Consciously or unconsciously, triangles occur when a couple draws in a third party to attempt to elevate emotional distress.	The therapist conceptualizes the couples attempt to fill the void of loneliness and dissatisfaction in the relationship to seek out another member to elevate the relationship duress. The most emotionally stressed individual is most likely to seek out a more vulnerable family member for support, such as a child.	The more stressed and lonely member in the relationship may seek an emotional connection and safety with a child, leading to a temporary decrease in the marital dissatisfaction, but the initial presenting problem remains the same and will resurface.
Therapeutic strategies	The therapist conceptualizes the couple's faulty cycles of interaction that maintain the problems as an attempt to solve the problems. The pattern is broken by the therapist reshaping dysfunctional behavioral interactions through the emphasis of positive feedback loops. The strategic family therapist is an active problem solver in the counseling relationship working to identify the problem and solve it.	The couple meets with the therapist and the entire family involved in the couple's relationship so that the therapist may replicate family interactions. The therapists actively engages with the family to define the solvable problem, sets goals to be achieved and measured, and designs and implements interventions for the family to practice in the therapy setting and in the home environment. The response is examined not for the purpose of family members' insight but to measure the attainment of reaching a goal of moving the family beyond the pattern of dysfunctional interactions.

Strategic family therapy: First contact

Social stage
Family interacts with the counselor

Problems stage
Each member's perception of the problem is identified.

Interaction stage
Therapist observes the family members' discussion of the problem to assess communication patterns, organization, and power.

Goal-setting stage
Clarifying the problem and creating measurable therapeutic goals. The solution is obtainable and measurable.

Task-setting stage
Counselor provides the family with a directive to do at home.

The strategic family therapist places a large emphasis on the family's first counseling session. The session is not used to complete paperwork, as that may be setting the expectations for the family to be dismissive of the process. The therapist actively moves the clients toward change by immediately directing the family's involvement in the therapeutic process by way of identifying how each member operates in relation to the defined problem.

Observe how they interact ... in office

The strategic family therapist implements many contact attempt skills in the first session to enhance the family's connection with the problem and gain experiences using effective communication strategies. The benefit is for the family to communicate differently and address the problem in descriptive ways that may promote changed behaviors.

1st appt.

The family identifies the problems and creates agreeable goals in measurable terms. The therapist reflects the family's reality and creates metaphors to move from problematic language to strength-based actions.

Directives: Instructions or actions that address communication in the present.

Paradoxical

The strategic family therapist proposes directives to address two purposes:

To intensify treatment while encouraging family members to engage in more effective communication interactions and behaviors.

To generate family interactions that produce information about (a) the family's systemic structure and (b) the rules that govern the family's behaviors.

The family engages in *directives* in and out of the therapy sessions. The purpose of the *directive* offers the family an in-the-moment example of the reality of the dysfunctional relationship patterns.

The *paradoxical interventions* are to prescribe an action/behavior that is inconsistent with the purpose of therapy. The goal is to prescribe the symptom so it changes from a spontaneous to a conscious act.

argue in *hub.*

Compliance-based paradox: instruct the partner to worry for set period each day, which often reduces worry throughout day.

Defiance-based paradox: the parents are required to ask the triangulated children for permission to set the rules.

Exposure-based paradox: the father gives his son a dollar each time he defies his mother in situations where father and son have a coalition against the mother.

Control-based paradox: the therapist instructs the couple to argue for 10 minutes each morning to gain more awareness of how they start and stop an argument.

Metaphoric task: the therapist instructs the family to discuss a conversation that is assumed not to be problematic, and the outcome is used as a metaphor for behavior change.

PREMISES OF THE THEORY

Set goals

Strategic family therapists are responsible for planning and carrying out therapeutic sessions and homework for in-home sessions occurring in-between therapy. Madanes (1981) noted that the therapist identifies measurable goals based on the interpretation of the problem defined by the individual family members. After goal identification, therapists prescribe directives for solving the presenting problems. The therapist actively engages with the family to generate solutions for the identified problem by maintaining the role of director or intervener.

First- and Second-Order Change

When strategic family theorists think about change, they often speak in terms of first-order and second-order change (Watzlawick, Weakland, & Fisch, 1974). First-order change is experienced when a problematic behavior changes within the family system. An example of first-order change would be a woman changing the way she communicates with her spouse as an attempt to better listen and respond to her spouse's concerns. Second-order change occurs when the rules or rituals of a family begin to change, thus impacting the family homeostasis. A good example of second-order change can be seen in parenting. For example, if you see a family whereby parents are not united concerning child discipline and often display this difference, the child may believe he/she can get away with additional dysfunctional behaviors. However, as a second-order change begins to occur and the parents become united in how they discipline children, a new, more functional approach to family homeostasis begins to take shape.

Symptoms as an Attempt to Communicate and Redefining Problems

Strategic family therapists conceptualize symptoms experienced by the family to be most pronounced when the family is attempting to communicate expectations, needs, and roles. The family's communication attempts are witnessed to prolong the problem or symptoms. One thought that offers strength and a sense of pride for the family is to reframe the communication attempts and ongoing efforts. While reframing a family problem is not unique to this theory, strategic family theory did bring new and innovative ideas regarding how to accomplish this task. As you look at a Case Presentation 10.1, determine what you would want to know, what you might address first, and how you would conceptualize the symptoms that the family is presenting.

CASE PRESENTATION 10.1: REFRAMING

The strategic therapist uses communication to give new meaning to an interpreted problem.

Situation: The 17-year-old son expects his parents to allow him to spend his earned money any way he wishes even if it is against the home rules. The teen is angry and is punishing his parents by returning home hours late after curfew. His father decided to take away the truck keys (truck owned by the parents but driven by the son) and removed one tire from the truck in case the son made a spare key.

The strategic family therapist's role: The therapist engages with the family to conceptualize the problem by reframing the motives the parents have to the son. The goal is to help the son gain a new perspective regarding his parents' actions and thus opening the possibility of communication rather than defiance.

Practice reframing:

1. As the strategic family therapist, practice *reframing* the son's issue with not being able to spend money on large items not approved by the parents.

2. As the strategic family therapist, practice *reframing* the parents' concerns with limiting the son's options to spend money.

3. How would you reframe the presenting problem to gain a greater perspective of the underlying issues creating fear from each family member?

4. Reframing family members' emotions or experiences may offer behavior and emotional changes. Given that not all reframes need to necessarily be true or reflect the therapist's full interpretation of the situation, what concerns might you have generating statements that may not reflect the presenting truth but may lead to a reaction promoting change?

Brief Therapy

Strategic family therapy is brief and spends time focusing on the present life situation. Theorists from this approach do not believe that it is important to find the cause of the problem(s), but rather focus on problem resolution; thus, it is not imperative to gain insight into the cause of the problem to generate change. While this therapy is inherently a brief approach, the therapist does often have to take the family through several stages, which may last months, before the problem is resolved; however, the aim of structural family therapy is to reach second-order change within 12 sessions (Szapocznik, Zarate, Duff, & Muir, 2013). To accomplish this, the strategic family therapist prepares structured sessions offering family members opportunities for equal engagement with the identification of the problem, in the moment behavior change tasks, and homework that is practiced in-between sessions. The therapist strongly believes that lasting change for the presenting problem takes practice and time requiring monthly sessions and regular between session homework.

Units and Circularity

Problems are not viewed in isolation. This stance required a departure from treating the individual to addressing the entire system. For example, acting-out behaviors exhibited by a teenage daughter may be viewed as a problem related to communication between the parents and the daughter.

Strategic family theory denounced the view of linear causality in which one event directly causes another and embraced the idea of circular causality. This means that the cause of an event, for example a son skipping school, is not singular in nature; rather, the problem behavior is a culmination of many events. Viewing problems in terms of circular causality provides the therapist with different ways to view the nature of the presenting problem.

$A \rightarrow B \rightarrow C$

Triangles, Sequences, and Hierarchies

In Chapter 3, we introduced you to the concept of triangles. Haley and Madanes believed that problems involved the interaction of at least three parties typically playing out in a coalition of two against one. Keim (1999) stated that the triangle is the preferred way to describe family interactions related to systemic problems. For example, a strategic family therapist would look at a couple conflict through the lens of how others in the family system impact the couple. *how are the affed*

Strategic family therapists also look at family problem behaviors as occurring in sequences. Therefore, the therapist would look at a child acting out in school as more than just that behavior and would also investigate the actions/events that led up to and followed the behavior. Strategic family therapists would focus on treating the interactional patterns rather than changing the one behavior. *patterns are the result of patterns.*

Lastly, strategic family therapists look at hierarchies within the family system, a concept that originated with Salvador Minuchin. The goal of strategic family therapists regarding hierarchies is not to know or understand whether the family's hierarchical patterns are functional or dysfunctional, but rather to understand what role each family member plays in the problem behavior/situation. In addition, strategic family theorists assess if family members are happy in their roles and, if not, whether this facet contributes to familial problems.

ROLE OF THE THERAPIST

Strategic family therapy is a brief approach directly focused on changing a family's behavior related to the identified problem (Gardner et al., 2006). The therapist plays the role of an expert within this theoretical viewpoint and joins with the family (Sheehan & Friedlander, 2015). Haley (1973) stated, "Strategic therapy is not a particular approach or therapy, but a name for the types of therapy where the therapist takes direct responsibility for directly influencing people" (p. 17). Haley believed it was far more powerful to get the family doing something about their problems than it was to spend time analyzing why the problems were occurring. The therapist acts as a change agent by utilizing straightforward or paradoxical techniques.

The therapist serves as a catalyst to challenge the family's interactional patterns and illustrates the impact on the presenting problem. The therapist must be creative, flexible and engaging when working with the family system. The therapist works with the family to identify the problem, recognize familial patterns related to the problem, and encourage the family to follow through with prescribed directives (Griffin & Greene, 1999). Strategic family therapists are concerned with how to promote change in family structure, power, and control (Gardner et al., 2006).

The therapist is not concerned with the family's past but works to assess and focus on the identified and agreed-upon problem. These therapists encourage the family to engage in conversation regarding the identified problem to assess the family's interactional patterns (Capuzzi & Stauffer, 2015; Gardner et al., 2006; Szapocznik et al., 2013). The therapist may also ask the family to act out the problem in session to gain additional information regarding the family's preferred style of interaction (Haley, 1963).

Strategic family therapists also provide the family with specific directions intended to help eliminate the family problem. Prior to these directives, however, the therapist must establish a trusting relationship with the family system. This trust builds rapport so the family is more willing to explore and actively engage in the directives being prescribed (Haley, 1963). The therapist treats the identified problem rather than the family itself and may utilize techniques that are not fully understood by the family. Finally, the therapist provides opportunities for growth by encouraging, allowing for discussion, examining the motives and providing an environment that is supportive of family expression (Gardner et al., 2006). Let's turn to Guided Practice Exercise 10.1, in which we look at success of treatment.

GUIDED PRACTICE EXERCISE 10.1

A strategic family therapist would take responsibility for the success of the treatment process just like a physician would. How does this concept fit your personal style as a therapist?

ASSESSMENT AND TREATMENT

Jay Haley (1976) believed that for counseling to be successful, it had to start off well. He spent time focusing on the assessment process and developed a four-stage model for assessment. The first stage is the social stage. During this stage, the focus is on helping the family to feel comfortable and begin interacting with each other. While this social interaction is occurring, the therapist is beginning to take note regarding how the family interacts. The second stage is the problem stage. During this stage, the therapist begins to gain perspective from each family member regarding what the problem is. It is important to hear from every family member. The third stage is the interaction stage. During this time, the family members are encouraged to dialogue with each other. The family focuses on discussing the identified problem. This allows the therapist to see the member-to-member interaction and to begin to determine which techniques might be useful for the family. The fourth stage is the goal setting stage. Now, the therapist discusses what was gained from the assessment process and works with the family to develop a unified goal for counseling and the process for achieving the goal.

Treatment within strategic family therapy could utilize many different techniques. Some of the most common techniques include using directives, paradoxical interventions, ordeals, positive connotations, pretending, and rituals; each of these are discussed below. The use of directives involves instructing the family to focus on some task in a specific time frame, usually between sessions. By doing this, the therapist is putting the family in the position of interacting with each other to complete the goal. Therapists collaborate with the family when determining the task. Another common technique is the use of paradoxical interventions, which are often used in the form of directives (Mandanes, 1981). Forms of paradoxical interventions include restraining, prescribing the symptom and redefining the problem. The use of ordeals involves giving the family an unpleasant task to complete when the identified problem arises. The theory behind this intervention is that the family will try to avoid the identified behavior or problem. Positive connotations were derived from the Milan approach. With this technique, the therapist helps the family identify the purpose behind a behavior and how the behavior may be protecting the family homeostasis (Boscolo, Cecchin, Hoffman, & Penn, 1987). Pretending involves having a family member act out an identified behavior and the other members reacting to the behavior in their usual way (Madanes, 1981). This technique has two purposes: it allows the family members to have a sense of control over the behaviors and by engaging in the pretending, they will no longer need to do so outside of session. Rituals involve the whole family in engaging in specific actions to highlight interactions of the family members to preserve the presenting problem (Boscolo et al., 1987). By encouraging family members to alter their behaviors, they learn to interact with each other in a different way and create new patterns of interaction. Let's turn our attention to Guided Practice Exercise 10.2, which explores paradoxical interventions.

GUIDED PRACTICE EXERCISE 10.2

Using paradoxical interventions can be dangerous or damaging to families. Imagine you are a beginning family therapist and determine a family is stuck in their behavioral patterns. You believe using a paradoxical intervention could be beneficial to the family. How would you become ethically prepared to utilize this intervention? What safeguards would you take to ensure you do not harm the family? What do you believe would be your reaction if a therapist was to use a paradoxical intervention with you?

Now that you have had some practice with strategic family therapy, let's turn to a case presentation. The illustration demonstrates how a strategic family therapist utilizes the theory to intentionally guide the work with a multicultural family. As you move through the theory, reflect on the interventions being utilized.

CASE PRESENTATION: THE CASE OF LEENA AND SHANN

Leena is a 36-year-old, Asian Indian (born in the United States) woman with two children (Sia, female age 17; and Shann, male age 13, also born in the United States). Leena divorced the children's biological father, who has since moved back to India and severed all contact with them. Two years ago, Leena married George (Caucasian American), age 37, after two years of dating. George has custody of his two sons (Paul and Greg; 10 and 7 years of age respectively). At the start and throughout the blending process of the two families, Sia has felt isolated and alone, and she has grown distant from both Leena and Shann; however, Shann has bonded with George, Paul, and Greg.

Leena was prompted to seek out family therapy as she has observed Sia not assimilating to the new family during the past three years. She is afraid that Sia will be leaving the family for college after high school with "little to no love for the family." In fact, arguments have been escalating in frequency and intensity between Sia and all the family members.

Introduction to Treatment

Therapist:	So glad you all could make it today. How was the drive? (As part of the social stage, the therapist engages in small talk to note the social interactions, content and relationship messages, and **metacommunication** between family members).
Leena:	It was a bit hard to find, but we managed.
Therapist:	Yes, finding the office can be a bit tricky, but you all found your way!
Paul:	We were lost, but Dad knew how to get here!
Greg:	Yeah, Dad was awesome! And Shann helped too!
Therapist:	Sounds like you guys were working together … like being on a treasure hunt. I hope this is what therapy will be like, a treasure hunt where we all work together. But instead of treasure, we will be hunting for good communication. Now it's critical for all to be heard and understood, as everyone plays a vital role in the overall functioning of the family … good and bad. I specialize in working with families, and the one thing that I am certain of is that for families to function at an optimal level, we do not have to identify how the problem started; rather we will need to focus on remedying the pattern of being with each other.
Leena:	What do you mean?
Therapist:	Well, what I've come to find out is that oftentimes it is unknowable how problems start in the first place, but that all families develop their own way of dealing with problems. And that sometimes a family's response to a problem is not successful, but despite the lack of success associated with that strategy, the family continues be with each other in the same way. This is normal for most, if not all families. However, this way of being can result in stress and frustration, and if there is a problem, then this cycle exacerbates the problem further. (Therapist is discussing the use of **positive feedback loops** and **circular causality**) You see, families have rules and norms that dictate patterns of behavior and ways to communicate, and that this mechanism provides family members with structure, but it is also this mechanism that makes familial change challenging. (Therapist explains role of **homeostasis**). But when all family members are actively hunting for new ways to communicate with each other and changing the rules of how they interact with each other, family functioning will improve. (Therapist is explaining **first- and second-order change**).

Inquiry and Definition of the Problem

Therapist: Because we are all part of this system, if you all could share your thoughts about why you are here. (As part of the problem stage, the therapist invites all members of the family to share their understanding of the issue)

George: It seems that Sia does not like me or my kids. She never wants to go along with the family. I think she is mad at her dad for leaving, but takes it out on us.

Leena: It's as though she is angry at me for moving on with my life. (Leena turns to Sia and speaks.) You can't expect me to be single forever.

Shann: (Looking at Sia.) Why can't you just get along with us? (Paul and Greg sit silently, but both are nodding their heads in agreement with Shann.)

Therapist: Sia, I notice that you are sitting lower in your seat and that your eyes are beginning to tear. Remember, we are not looking to find how the problem started, but we are searching for communication, and each person in the family is responsible for how the system operates today. Sia, tell me your perception of what is happening.

Sia: No one listens to me or does what I want to do. I always have to do what Shann, Paul, and Greg want to do. And when I want to be alone, they say that I am 'distant.' It's not fair that I always have to play second fiddle in this family.

Therapist: That does sound difficult. You feel disconnected from the family. (The therapist begins to conceptualize **possible feedback loops** that maintain the **circular causality.** Does blaming Sia for the stress in the family impede Sia from connecting with the family? Does the lack of connection affect Sia's ability to effectively communicate her needs, further isolating her from the family?)

Estimation of Behavior Maintaining the Problem

Therapist: It seems to me that all members of the family have agreed that Sia has had a difficult go of things since the two families joined to make one family. And then when there is tension, or stress, the family members ban together. But I am wondering that when this banning occurs, if Sia experiences this as 'being left behind;' and perhaps when this happens Sia expresses her hurt and isolation through anger, which in turns causes further feelings of separation from one another, causing more arguments to ensue, causing further separation, and so on and so forth. (Therapist is exploring the potential **circular causality** that could be maintaining **homeostasis.**) This is my interpretation of what is happening, but I would like for you all to discuss this picture as a family. I am wondering if you all think that my understanding of what might be happening is valid. (As part of the interaction stage, the therapist encourages the family members to explore a feedback loop together.)

Goal-Setting Stage

Therapist: Okay, what are some things that you all have tried in the past to make and maintain connections between you all and Sia? (Therapist explores previous first-order change attempts.)

George: We sometimes go to museums because Sia enjoys them, but the boys really aren't into it. (After some further discussion, George speaks to explain.) We have three boys, we typically do what they want to do.

Leena: Sia and I have begun talking about college and planning for the things that we will need to buy so that she is ready for college come August.

Sia: Yeah, we've talked about it, but we haven't gone shopping yet. When will you make time for me?

Therapist: Let me interject for a moment. Sia, your feeling of being disconnected is very real. Let's see if we can look for a connection someplace else. How might your mom describe her worries of sending off her first born to college? (The therapist is moving toward second-order changes by helping family members to become aware of the role that metacommunication plays in maintaining **homeostasis**.)

Sia: Well, I think she might be feeling scared and sad.

Therapist: Mom, is Sia's interpretation accurate?

Leena: It is.

Therapist: How often have you shared those feelings, scared and sad, with Sia?

Leena: I don't think I have.

Therapist: Sia, are there times when you want to be with your brother and stepbrothers but feel like an outsider?

Sia: A lot of times. I want to spend time with them, especially with Shann. I really miss him.

Therapist: And how often have you shared these thoughts and feelings with Shann, Paul, and Greg?

Sia: I haven't.

Therapist: Shann, what do you think Sia experiences when she is not invited to join in on the fun when you, Paul, and Greg are playing?

Shann: Like she does not belong.

Task-Setting Stage

Therapist: I think we're in some uncharted territory with regards to this search for new communication, but I think we are on to something. Each person plays a role in disrupting old ways of being to promote better family functioning. Change does not come overnight; rather, we work toward change; and it seems like you guys are wanting to work toward it. Leena and George, set aside time, at least once a week, to communicate with Sia about her needs and well-being. Second, the family will engage in a family meeting once a month in which the goal will be to identify an activity that all family members will participate in during the subsequent month; doing so will keep the family connected and moving forward with new ways to communicate. (The therapist provides the family with *directives* to minimize the potential for reintegration of the **feedback loop**.)

MILAN SYSTEMIC FAMILY THERAPY

Milan systemic family therapy was developed from the work of Jay Haley. A group of Milan family therapists was intrigued by the work of Haley and adapted the approach to working with families. This group of Milan therapists included Mara Selvini-Palazzoli, Luigi Boscolo, Gianfranco Cecchin, and Giuliana Prata; their approach became known as Milan systemic family therapy.

The theory is based on the notion that families wanted to see change in their system or within an identified person, yet they were also struggling to keep things static. The unique component within the Milan approach is that it utilized a team approach to treating families. The team consisted of four therapists and utilized such techniques as circular questions and hypothesizing (Boscolo et al., 1987). The founders of the Milan approach chose to move away from helping families change problem behaviors, and helped them become aware of the meanings they attach to the behaviors instead. This portion of the chapter will highlight the major contributors to the Milan approach, key concepts, and theoretical tenets of the theory.

PROFILE OF MAIN FIGURES

Mara Selvini-Palazzoli, originally trained as a psychoanalyst and in the 1960s, organized eight psychiatrists, including the other founders of the Milan approach, Luigi Boscolo, Gianfranco Cecchin, and Giuliana Prata. Her goal was to treat families who had severely disturbed children (Goldenberg & Goldenberg, 2013). Together with Boscolo, Cecchin, and Prata, Selvini-Palazzoli developed a group to further investigate the dynamics of strategic family theory. They eventually formed the Milan Center for the Study of the Family. In 1974, they introduced the team approach that promoted positive connotations and innovative techniques (Selvini-Palazzoli, Boscolo, Cecchin, & Prata, 1974). The goal of these techniques was to challenge current family impasses and interactional patterns and promote change in the system.

Eventually the group separated into two pairs (Selvini-Palazzoli and Prata; Cecchin and Boscolo). Each pair pursued different ways of thinking yet remained similar in their views of systems work. The pair of Selvini-Palazzoli and Prata developed techniques for challenging and stopping the destructive interactions among the family systems and returned to earlier work related to strategic and structural theories. This pair utilized a directive known as invariant prescription that aimed to strengthen the parental unit and break down the parent–child coalitions viewed as contributing to family problems. They also aimed to create more open communication within the family system. Eventually, Selvini-Palazzoli began to use more insight oriented/long term therapy approaches.

The second pair, Cecchin and Boscolo, grew in popularity in the United States, England, and Canada. Cecchin and Boscolo wanted to focus more on collaboration, circular questions, and goal setting within the family system. Cecchin and Boscolo took a not-knowing stance and reduced the hierarchy that could be present in family therapy. The Milan approach has much in common with social constructionists. For example, the reflecting team process was developed out of the Milan approach (Andersen, 1991).

The Milan systemic family therapy paradigm contains both the early use of the theory as well as changes in theoretical practice that were made in later years. Key concepts include the format of therapy and structure of the sessions. Also key to this theory, are the interventions which will be discussed in detail later in the chapter.

LONG, BUT BRIEF THERAPY

The Milan Systemic approach to family therapy encompasses two distinguishing factors. First, these therapists utilized a team approach in helping the family. The cotherapist dynamic consisted of two therapists preferably a male and female dyad collaboratively working together with the family system, while the team watched from behind a one-way mirror. The purpose for having the team behind the mirror was to attain differing perspectives. Occasionally, the observers would ask the therapist(s) to speak with them so that they could share their perspectives. After the conference with the team, the therapists would return to the sessions and share the experience with the family.

Another unique method specific to this approach utilized a long, brief therapy format meaning the therapy sessions were spaced out. There were typically around 10 sessions, as indicated by the "brief"; however, the sessions were spaced out over several months, addressing the "long." The intentional purpose of spacing the session was to enhance the meaningful interactions into generalized behaviors rather than changes that are limited in time and often to appease immediate learning. The extended time frame offered the family members time to address the therapy lessons within the environment where the behaviors occurred.

STRUCTURED FAMILY SESSIONS

A typical Milan systemic therapy format was divided into five segments. These will be discussed in depth later in the chapter. The session segments included: presession, the session, the intersession, the intervention, and the postdiscussion. Team conferences would occur prior to each session and were used to plan strategies to carry out during that session. A break would occur during the session (intersession), and, at this time, the family therapists conversed with the observing therapy team. Following this experience, the team would meet and plan for the next session.

PREMISE OF THE THEORY

Theoretical Assumptions

Milan family therapy is the exploration of family members' organization of relationship processes through examining nonverbal and verbal communication patterns, circular interactions, boundaries of behaviors, and maintenance of the family's defined homeostasis/rules (Goldenberg & Goldenberg, 2008). The intent of Milan family therapy is to disturb the meaning and beliefs the family members unconsciously ascribe as the family rules. The therapist aims to create change in the family system that promotes insight into rituals of interactions, behaviors, and prescriptions that capture different meanings within the family process (Selvini-Palazzoli, Boscolo, Cecchin, & Pratta, 1978). The therapist observes the family process to exploit the dysfunctional patterns described as family members' repetitive sequence of communication interactions. These interactions are used solely for maintaining the system in the present moment. Engaging in the family's process involves the implementation of creative therapeutic techniques intended to change behaviors (Selvini-Palazzoli et al., 1978). Look at Table 10.2 in which the key concepts, terms, and techniques of Milan systemic family therapy are summarized.

Table 10.2 Milan systemic family therapy: Key concepts, terms, and techniques

Key concepts, terms, and techniques	Definition	Milan systemic family therapy
Epistemology	Epistemology is the study and investigation of knowledge and knowing. The Milan team describes this as viewing families from an epistemological perspective, described as examining how we think, know, and understand (Liddle, Breunlin, & Schwartz, 1988).	– To examine the origin and roots of the family process is to observe the relationships and differences in the family. – The Milan team promotes the term *epistemology* rather than empirical studies in science and clinical research (Liddle et al., 1988). – In the family therapy process, the Milan team investigates the family and members' interactions to examine how clients perceive their behaviors, actions, and attitudes toward one another, their relationship to another, and their existence in the family and world (Liddle et al., 1988).

Key concepts, terms, and techniques	Definition	Milan systemic family therapy
Epistemological error	An error of knowing what is known may be considered or thought of as an erroneous set of sentiments or distinctions that an individual or family uses to make sense of the world (Selvini-Palazzoli, Cirillo, Selvini, & Sorrentino, 1989). Systemic distress is based on an erroneous set of beliefs and family rules that impede the family interaction, resulting in individuals being isolated and stuck in a pattern of power struggles to maintain homeostasis in the family relationships.	The Milan team observes epistemological error to be the idea that one individual's behavior can be the cause of another's behavior—inferring that as human beings, we are powerless and controlled by others' actions. – Epistemological errors are said to be the origin of family symptomatology. For example: A husband returns from work grumpy and heads to his bed to sleep until dinner. The wife reports that his disregard for her and the children and his curt, grumpy attitude when he returns home from work *makes* her angry and resentful. The husband reports that if the wife was not so unappreciative of his long hours and if she would stop nagging him to engage with her and the children, he would not be *forced* to withdraw. – In summary, one family member's actions are not the direct reason for another person's behaviors or actions.
Meaning vs. action	Two levels of interaction (meaning and action) are when family members are stuck in homeostatic balance. The family functions in a set of beliefs that do not fit the family's current reality.	The Milan systemic family therapist aims to distinguish between the family members' actions and meaning to modify or correct epistemological errors. For example: The family therapist will interpret a child's attempt at defiance from the act itself—the child is not following the overt or covert rules. The new understanding creates an in-the-moment reality to support the new meaning and belief patterns for both the person identifying the rules for the child and the child.

Key concepts, terms, and techniques	Definition	Milan systemic family therapy
Circular and linear	Milan systemic family therapists believe that circular causality or systemic causality relates to the problem. A linear perspective is that behavior holds a direct cause and effect. Given that language and reality is in motion, Milan systemic family therapists generate circular questions to explore family dynamics, the history of the problem, and the emotional issues still impacting the family (Hanna, 2007).	The role of the therapist begins with circular questions addressing present concerns then transitioning to explore past factors that are relevant to the evolving problem. The circular questions address four phases of therapy to explore perceived family dynamics: • Problem definition • Sequence of interaction • Comparison/classification • Intervention The therapist's intent of the questions may be exploratory to connect points in time, identify the defined terms of the problem, and create connections between family members (Hanna, 2007). The intent may extend to provocative questions that lend opportunities to indirectly verbally expose hidden family dynamics (Hanna, 2007). To move the family forward, the therapist uses positive connotations to support the family's progression to work through the problem in small, manageable, and often paradoxical ways.
Reframing and positive connotation	Reframing may be used to denote both positive and negative behaviors/circumstances. Reframing is generally directed to credit meaning to a behavior of one family member. Positive connotation offers a circular causality by ascribing a positive value or purpose to each family member's action/behavior that maintains the family problems (Liddle et al., 1988).	The therapist will ascribe meaning to the problem by positively commenting on the problem's existence to maintain homoeostasis in the family (Metcalf, 2011). For instance: A family is experiencing a transition where the oldest child has left for college and the 9-year-old child has begun to misbehave. The therapist shares with the child, "Having all the responsibilities of your older brother now that he has left for college is challenging. You must be angry that you are left with such big responsibilities in the family. Make sure you continue to express your dissatisfaction in the family so that you are not given more tasks and responsibilities to cover your brother's absence. You want your brother to return and you wonder if you act out, he might need to come back to resume his role." By helping the family begin to realize the homeostatic need for the behaviors, the family may respond to the son's acting out in more empathic ways.

Key concepts, terms, and techniques	Definition	Milan systemic family therapy
Hypothesizing	The therapist generates a working hypothesis of the family's interactions by describing the family interactional relationships among all the family members rather than a defined problem, blaming, or identifying one family member.	The therapist carefully questions the family's actions surrounding the problem to shift the problem from the person to the problem is the context. For instance, the youngest child does not like to sit at the dinner table and is described as tantruming and disrupting the entire evening. When the oldest child is questioned regarding the problem, the therapist may ask, "Who first noticed when the problem began?" Questions are used to generate an understanding of the family relationships.
Neutral hypothesizing	The therapist demonstrates curiosity about each member's point of view through circular questions.	The therapist accepts each member's unique perception and accepts that each member's point of view is not better than another. Therapeutic neutrality supports the therapist's stance on maintaining a professional positive regard for all perspectives of the family member's thoughts and actions. This gives the therapist time to develop hypotheses of the family dynamics. This perspective supports the therapist from being drawn into disputes and coalitions.
First-order change	Action change occurs when a specific behavior within a system changes.	The therapist observes the family arguing over planning and that in many situations the children rule all decisions. The therapist asks the parent to refrain from asking the children's opinion for dinner plans; instead, the parents are to decide the meal. The behavior is the parents oversee major decisions in the family.
Second-order change	A second-order change occurs when new rules are established in family interactions and patterns, and the homeostasis alters to integrate new family dynamics.	The family in the example above integrates the family rule that the parents lead the decision-making process. When the parents model sound decisions that result in benefits for the family, the family unit is relieved of the pressure of functioning under unclear guidelines and rules.
Second-order cybernetics	The therapist becomes part of the system being observed rather than detached and disconnected from the family interactions.	The therapist joins the family in creating new behaviors and roles by engaging the family in rituals and positive connotations.

Key concepts, terms, and techniques	Definition	Milan systemic family therapy
Games	Problem-saturated routines or actions are known as games.	A covert family game is the unacknowledged destructive patterns and strategies of the family dynamics and processes that maintain the symptomatic behavior of family members' attempts to control each other.
	The game's rules hold the power in the family process, not the individuals' involved in the interactions.	The behaviors and attitudes of family members are regarded as *moves* with the purpose of continuing the family game. All family interactions are geared toward the continuation of the game and to increase involvement among its players.
	Games hold power to unacknowledged coalitions and alliances.	The Milan systemic family therapist does not attempt to change the players in the game but engages the family to change the rules of the game.
		In this process, the therapist may develop an understanding of the family's pattern of a *double bind*. This may be described as a person's ability to communicate conflicting and different messages simultaneously.
Paradox	A paradox prescribed by the therapist assists the family by assigning specific tactics and maneuvers that are in direct opposition to the goals of therapy—the paradox is that the prescribed technique is designed to achieve the goals.	When the therapist prescribes a paradox, the family may not understand the request and how it is going to help them.
		The therapist may state that every Monday and Wednesday night, I want the children to begin a fight. After the fight begins, I want the parents to get up and eat in the kitchen away from the fighting children. The family is asked to continue this behavior until the family meets with the therapist again.
		The paradox works to reinforce the behavior the family expects to change. The paradox communicating to the family to stay the same by remaining unchanged and as a result the family begins to generate new actions.

Key concepts, terms, and techniques	Definition	Milan systemic family therapy
Linguistics	Language shapes our reality. Family communication is the creation of multiple realties leading to impossible measures to fully capture the observed reality (Selvini-Palazzoli et al., 1989). Language is a linear construct that is used to define circular constructs such as reality.	The therapist observes the family members' language/communication and works to create an approximate understanding of the reality being observed (Liddle et al., 1988). The Milan systemic family therapist works to describe the behavior in circular terms by replacing the verb *is* with *seems, appears, to show, to act, to act as if, has the effect of* in order to put the behavior in context. For example: The linear description is "He is depressed." Circular language is "He appears/seems depressed" or "he acts as if he is depressed." The Milan systemic family therapist models for the family circular observations rather than making causal implications in describing the observations of the phenomena (Liddle et al. 1988).

Let us now look at Guided Practice Exercise 10.3, in which we evaluate our beliefs on using paradox.

GUIDED PRACTICE EXERCISE 10.3

The use of paradox is a cornerstone of systems theory. Currently, the technique is not used as frequently by strategic or systems theorists. One argument is that the technique is not considered honest. What are your thoughts about using this technique for the benefit of the family system?

Goals of Strategic Family Counseling and Milan Family Therapy

The Milan systemic family therapist works to create a therapeutic environment that supports the family's intrinsic self-corrective nature to alleviate symptomatic patterns. The Milan systemic family therapist focuses on three goals to maintain healthy systemic functioning. In the first goal, the therapeutic process provides the family an environment to accommodate and adjust to new information and beliefs to encourage new family interactions. This process involves the therapist's neutrality, hypotheses, positive connotations, and prescribed rituals. Let's turn to Guided Practice Exercise 10.4, in which we look at one intervention in the Milan systemic family therapy approach.

The second goal for the family is to embrace newly generated meaning created by the family game and build the positive connotations to support the family members' new patterns and rules within the family. The third and following goals are left to the family to decide and achieve. The goals' aim is to provide meaning and understanding as to how the family's problem(s) may be serving a purpose. Improvement is noted when the family recognizes problems as being systemic and a family member no longer serves as a scapegoat.

Role of the Therapist

The role of the therapist in this approach departs somewhat from the traditional counselor as expert model and director role recognized in traditional strategic family therapy. Rather, the Milan systemic family therapist works as a collaborative investigator during a family session. The therapist is more concerned with empowering the family system and works to promote optimism and persistence in the family system. The therapist aids in providing an environment that is participatory and the therapist and family work together to determine the goals, rather than the therapist determining for the family what needs to change. Thus, these therapists create an environment that empowers the family to determine their own improved future system.

Assessment and Treatment

Milan systemic family therapists meta-reflect on the context and relationship present between the therapist and family. This interactional therapy assessment yields the following outcomes and allows these experiences to occur in therapy. The family perceives some risk for change as they engage in the therapeutic process. The family members feel confident that their point of view is being validated and considered by the therapist. The validation and acceptance of family members' thoughts and actions offers family members safety to explore their meaning system. The therapist utilizes a neutral position in the family, tentatively hypothesizes the family rules, and engages the family in circular questions to connect family members in creating meaning of the family's experiences. Let's look at Table 10.3, which outlines the format of a Milan systemic family therapy session.

Table 10.3 Time frame and format of the Milan therapy process

Time frame of Milan therapy	Typically, the 10 months are divided into 10 sessions spaced into monthly therapy sessions.
Initial interview: Presession contact	The Milan therapist begins working with the family from the first phone call. The short initial phone call offers the therapist a tentative hypothesis regarding the reasons the family is seeking therapy.
Therapy sessions—five components	The sessions offer the therapist(s) time to interact, face-to-face, with the family to determine the covert rules of the family system. The therapist uses the session time to validate, modify, and change previous hypotheses and to elicit more information regarding the family's perceived dynamics.
Intersessions	The therapist leaves the family therapy session to consult with the team of Milan systemic family therapists. The therapists who are not directly interacting with the family are observing the family behind a one-way mirror and discussing the tentative hypotheses and interventions.
Intervention	After the intersession, the therapist returns to the family prepared to engage the family in the predefined intervention. The therapist typically leaves the room immediately following the shared intervention so the family members cannot express resistance and disqualify the intervention.
Postsession discussion	The Milan systemic family therapists will discuss and collaborate on the therapy session by exploring how the family responded/reacted to the interventions to derive a working hypothesis for the future therapy sessions.
Termination	Termination occurs when the therapy team perceives themselves to no longer being useful to the family and the family no longer describes themselves as pathological—stuck in the rules of the game.

Now that you have had some practice with Milan systemic family therapy, let's turn to a case presentation. The illustration demonstrates how a Milan systemic family therapist and her team utilize the theory to intentionally guide their work with a divorced family. Reflect on the process as you read.

MILAN CASE PRESENTATION: THE CASE OF NATALIE

Natalie, a 38-year-old Caucasian female, is the mother of two female children (Alecia, 16 years old; Lizzy, 12 years old). Natalie currently has custody of Alecia and Lizzy. Billy is a 37-year-old Caucasian male and is the biological father of Alecia and Lizzy.

Natalie and Billy divorced 11 years ago after Natalie discovered that Billy was having an affair. Since that time, Billy has been in a long-term relationship with the woman with whom he was having an affair. Natalie, on the other hand, has had multiple relationships, with one relationship evolving into a marriage but ending in divorce after only one year.

After the birth of Lizzy, Natalie struggled off and on with abuse of prescription drugs. About a year ago, during one of his weekends with the girls, Natalie showed up at Billy's house intoxicated and began a verbal and physical altercation with Billy. The police were called, and Natalie was arrested. Soon after, Natalie admitted herself into rehab.

Natalie has been sober for the past six months and regularly attends 12-step groups; however, her anger and disdain for Billy has not diminished. In fact, Natalie regularly speaks badly about Billy to the children and tells them that he is to blame for the divorce. Currently, Alecia and Lizzy seem to have a closer relationship with Natalie and have become more distant and angry with Billy. Recently, Billy has become extremely concerned about his relationship with the girls; thus, he initiated contact with a Milan family therapist.

Pre-session

During the intake phone call with Billy, the therapist gathers some basic information about the family (e.g., demographics of the family members, the stated problem, strengths of family members, etc.). The therapist describes to Billy the team format of Milan family therapy. After answering questions regarding therapy, a session is scheduled.

Prior to the session, the Milan team members examine the available information and **hypothesize** about the problem. They discuss the potential of a **dirty game** taking place (i.e., Alecia and Lizzy are angry with Billy on behalf of Natalie). The session begins by explaining the process and drawing attention to the team members observing behind the mirror.

Session

Therapist: Welcome everyone, and thank you for coming in today. Before we get started I want to take some time and talk to you all about our room and the process of today's meeting. You will notice that this room has a one-way mirror, and the rest of the team is on the other side of that mirror. They will be observing our session, and after some time, we'll take a break and I'll have a conversation with them. Basically, we'll chat about what they've observed in the session up that point. I suspect that this might feel unusual, but I want to assure you that though unusual, growth and appreciation of the family dynamics will result. I hope you will trust the process, and if there are any questions, please do not hesitate to ask.

Alecia: So those people that we just met are just watching us on the other side of that mirror? It feels like a science experiment.

Therapist: That's a great analogy. This will be an experiment of sorts as we want to discover perhaps some new and unique things about your family. And I also want to say, Alecia, that I appreciate your skepticism about things that are unfamiliar to you, yet my understanding is that you usually do not hesitate when it comes to trying new things.

Lizzy: How did you know that?

Therapist: Well, Lizzy, when your dad called last week, he shared with me some very cool things about you all. For instance, he told me that you were a great softball player, and that your sister wants to be a doctor, and that your mother loves you all very much.

Therapist:	Alecia, my understanding is that you are part of a medical team in your high school where you all look at case studies and try to come up with diagnoses and treatments. Well the people behind that mirror are also a team where they brainstorm about possible solutions to help families get past their problems.
Alecia:	So they are here to help us.
Therapist:	Exactly. It might take some getting used to, but I suspect that in no time we will forget about the mirror. So, to get started to today, I was hoping that we all could go around the room and share why you all think you are here today. You see I'm a big believer in the metaphor 'it takes a village.' Natalie, have you heard of this metaphor before?
Natalie:	I've heard it in the context of using lots of people to raise kids. Is that what you mean?
Therapist:	That is definitely one way people use that metaphor. So, the variable in that saying is people, or better yet, people's perception of what is best for the children, for the family, for the system, and so forth. Therefore, I ask for all perceptions at the onset of our work together, as we all have our unique outlook on things, and all outlooks are valid. So, who would like to start and share with us why you have come today?
Natalie:	Fine, I'll talk. The only reason I'm here is because Billy threatened me by saying that he would go to the courts and file for permeant custody of the kids if I didn't show up.
Therapist:	Keeping your children nearby like a lioness mother protecting her cubs is very important to you. (Therapist reframes Natalie's statement as a **positive connotation**.) Alecia, Lizzy, what are your thoughts on why family counseling could be a good thing?
Alecia:	Well, I know Mom can't stand Dad, and my friends say that them always fighting can't be a good thing for me and Lizzy.
Therapist:	Oh, I see. Billy, which child is most effected by your arguments with Natalie? (Therapist uses **circular questioning** strategy.)
Billy:	Umm … I am not really sure. I have never really thought about it. But I if I had to pick, I think Alecia takes it more to heart because she probably can remember aspects of life prior to the divorce. Whereas for Lizzy, this is all she knows—a life postdivorce. If that makes sense?
Therapist:	Well let's see. Natalie, what are your thoughts on Billy's response?
Natalie:	The reason it's hard on Alecia is because he cheated on me and he is still with that slut. And Alecia has to see that slut every other weekend.
Alecia:	Yeah, and she is so mean to me.
Billy:	She is not a slut. I love her, and I am sorry that things did not work out between you and me, but you cheated on me with your drugs. We might still be together if it wasn't for your addiction.
Therapist:	Lizzy, it sounds like your parents are in one of those arguments right now. Does it matter to you who wins this fight? (Therapist engages the last family member in the conversation to ensure that **neutrality** is not violated.)
Lizzy:	No. I wish they would just get along.
Therapist:	If they didn't fight as much about their past, then your life in the present, and perhaps in the future, would be much better. I wonder if this an accurate reflection?

Lizzy:	It would be so much better.
Therapist:	Okay, it seems like we are making some good progress here. I am going to take this time to meet with the team and inquire about their thoughts. Feel free to use the restrooms, have some snacks, and relax while I'm gone. I'll be back soon.

Intersession

The therapist meets with the team and asks them to share their understanding of the family to this point. The team confirms that they believe their initial **hypothesis** about the **dirty game** was accurate; however, they indicated that due to age differences, the team believed that Alecia plays the game more so than Lizzy.

They also saw Billy as being the victim in this scenario and quickly viewed Natalie as the aggressor. However, the therapist indicated to the team that this view was in violation of **neutrality** and encouraged them to think about the **purposefulness** of all the behaviors and complaints. In doing so, the team **hypothesized** that the Natalie's interactions were her way of keeping her girls close to her because she was afraid that they would leave her for Billy's girlfriend, just as Billy did many years ago. They also hypothesized that Billy's lack of willingness to see Natalie's addiction as a disease enables him to not take any responsibility in the dissolving of their relationship. The team then discusses possible strategies that the therapist could employ during the second half of the session.

Intervention

Therapist:	Thank you for your patience. In this part of the session, my goal is to help you all develop strategies to move beyond the current hurdle. But first, I want to quickly check in and explore how each of you is experiencing me. I do not want to take sides; my primary objective is to increase the health of the family. (Therapist is confirming her experience as being a **neutral figure** in the process.)
Natalie:	I don't feel like you have taken anyone's side. You seem to be all about us.
Billy:	Yeah, you've stayed pretty neutral. I can appreciate that. (The two girls are shaking their heads in agreement with their parents' observations.)
Therapist:	Excellent. So, you've all felt supported. Let me try something here then…. Billy, Natalie, I want you both to argue more about your all's history in front of the children, specifically about the infidelity and the drug use. (Once acknowledgment of **neutrality** and **trust** is confirmed, the therapist employs the strategy of **paradoxes**.)
Natalie:	Excuse me, you want us to do what?
Therapist:	You know, I want you to act as if I was not in the room. Imagine this was a regular day, and you two are going at it as you typically would.
Natalie:	That's ridiculous … I am not doing that. I can't believe you would even suggest such a thing. Nope, I am not doing that.
Billy:	Yeah, I agree, I am not sure how that would be useful. I thought we were here to fix the issue, not to exacerbate it.

Therapist: Okay, okay. So, I am picking up on the fact that you are both upset with me and my directive in this moment. I wonder if the origin of this anger is not so much the directive but at the understanding that such an argument would adversely impact the well-being of the children. (Therapist processed from where the outrage for this directive was coming.) And I agree, this type of argument could have a negative effect on the children. So, let's try something different. Lizzy sit next to your dad. Alecia, sit next to your mom. Okay, Mom, okay, Dad, I want you both to have side conversations with Alecia and Lizzy where the focus of the conversation will be on ridiculing and criticizing the other parent. (Therapist employs another attempt at a paradoxical strategy.)

Billy: I see what you're getting at. We do this all the time at home, even though we know it is not good for the kids.

Therapist: So you guys won't bite on that directive either. Okay, let's try one more. This one is more of a homework assignment. Billy and Natalie, I want you come together once a month, either at Natalie's home or at Billy's home and have a discussion with the children present where you blame each other for the divorce and current state of the relationship.

Natalie: Okay, okay, I get your point. I think we all get your point.

Therapist: Dang, all my strategies are getting blocked. You know, Natalie, the team hypothesized that despite how you and Billy felt about each other, they sensed that you both experienced the importance of raising happy, healthy, and well-functioning girls. So, when I came back from our meeting, I tested their hypothesis. And it seems, as evidenced by you guys not taking the bait, that arguing and placing blame is understood as unhealthy behavior, while having healthy conversations about the girls' well-being is critical for the children's overall functioning. What do you think about this? (Therapist is moving parents toward **new belief patterns** and **new behavior patterns**, resulting in **second-order change**.)

Natalie: Wow, yes. I know we both love our kids. But sometimes I get so wrapped up in my own thoughts and feelings, that I forget my main goal … to raise happy and healthy and strong girls.

Therapist: And that goal is crystal clear right now, in this moment. Billy, what about you, what are you taking away from this experience?

Billy: You know, I have to agree with Natalie. Getting swept away in the emotion of the moment leaves little room for what really matters, and then I just get stuck there. Lizzy, Alecia, I am so sorry.

Natalie: I am sorry too girls. Mommy will try to do so much better in the future.

Therapist: You guys have made some pretty big steps today. You have learned a lot about yourselves and about your family dynamics. I got one more directive for you, and this time I know that you can and will follow through on it. Natalie and Billy, and I want you to go to dinner once every other week, without the children, and have parenting conversations. Both should listen and be open to suggestions, and be open to disagreements. But instead of becoming defensive, talk them through. If the desire to blame or criticize arises, then recall the work that was done in this session and realign your perspective with the overall goal—to raise happy, healthy, and well-functioning girls. (Therapist suggested a **new ritual** to promote **second-order change**.)

Discussion

After the session, the therapist met with the team to assess the work that was done in the session. The team indicated that that they felt optimistic about the *new ritual*, as it seemed that the parents heard and learned new things about each other, specifically as it related to the problem at hand. They also started the presession planning for the second session (to be scheduled in four weeks), and stated that the focus should be on the children's perception of how the parents are intentionally moving toward the new goal of raising happy, healthy, and well-functioning children.

STRENGTHS AND LIMITATIONS

Strategic family therapy and Milan communications have had a lasting impression on the systems approach to counseling. For instance, fundamental constructs such as meta-communication, homeostasis, and circular causality are typical nomenclature for family therapists despite the theoretical approach that one espouses. Additionally, the strengths of these approaches provide the essence for the longevity and continued implementation with diverse families, presenting concerns, substance use and mental health issues, and so forth.

When considering the efficacy of strategic and Milan family therapy, it seems that the strengths of the approaches are directly tangled with the limitations. For example, strategic family therapy is time sensitive, oriented in the present, and distances the counselor from focusing on the history or the etiology of the problem; however, the therapist is considered the expert and may evoke little input from the family when developing directives. As such, if the therapist lacks training, is unskilled, or is without supervision from a skilled strategic family therapist, then there is a potential for the therapist to harm the family, as opposed to changing the system. In terms of Milan communications, the theory utilizes a team-based approach, whereby the therapist maintains a neutral position to help family members see the problem in a positive light. Though, again, problem evolution is not analyzed; thus, families who are looking for answers to their past issues will be unlikely to find them with a Milan family therapist.

SUMMARY

While brief in nature, strategic and Milan approaches are sophisticated and complex. The approaches are not concerned about the origins of familial issues; rather, those who utilize these approaches are more concerned with enhancing communication patterns within the family so that the unit operates with more functionality. Therefore, at the time of their conception, maintaining a focus on the present and future were considered innovative and novel.

The lasting effects of strategic and Milan approaches are far reaching. Concepts such as first- and second-order change, circularity, and feedback loops are now considered common language within family therapy. Other critical concepts drawn from these approaches include that of neutrality and engaging all family members to work on mutually agreed-upon goals. In fact, tenets from these approaches can be viewed in more postmodern approaches to family work.

In the next chapter, you will learn about another theory equally instrumental to the development of family therapy as that of strategic and Milan approaches. Chapter 11 will address the impact of hierarchical balance and boundaries on homeostasis. You will find there are some similarities with regard to strategic and structural family therapy.

KEYSTONES

Among the key points addressed in this chapter are:

- Strategic family therapy and systemic family therapy (Milan) are relatively brief, technique-oriented approaches that were influenced by the work of Milton Erickson.

- Strategic family theory is based on basic dimensions and principles of family life, including family rules, homeostasis, quid pro quo, and circular causality.

- Strategic family theory focuses on action. The therapists get clients to change by identifying creative actions tailored to the family's situation, otherwise known as directives.

- The role of the therapist in strategic family theory is to identify a solvable problem and then present strategies to change the family dynamics so that the problem can be solved. Each treatment plan is unique to the family.

- The goal in strategic family theory is to help the family resolve problems. The therapists define the problem, investigate previous solutions, define the concrete changes to be made, and formulate a strategy for the change.

- Systemic (Milan) family therapy is based on the notion that symptoms are maintained by the family because they serve a purpose.

- A main component of systemic family therapy is circular causality. One member's distress reflects the disturbance within the family system.

- Systemic family therapy uses techniques such as paradox, hypothesizing, positive connotation, circular questioning, the invariant prescription, and rituals.

- Systemic family therapy is flexible and unique in that the therapists work as a team using a one-way mirror.

REFLECTIONS FROM THE CONTRIBUTOR'S CHAIR
Rebecca Pender Baum

I was originally drawn to the Milan approach when introduced to the reflecting team. The reflecting team process grew out of the Milan approach. I incorporated many of the techniques from this theory in my work with couples and families; specifically, the utilization of circular questioning and positive connotations. I found that many families/couples are stuck because they can only see what is wrong with their family. The use of positive connotations has helped my clients see there are things going well for them as well as given them a new lens from which to view their perceived problems. I once had a client tell me that the team approach helped her see that "they were not some screwed up family and it was helpful to see these are normal problems."

ADDITIONAL RESOURCES
The following resources provide additional information relating to the chapter topics.

Useful Websites
- Family Therapy Institute
  http://www.familytherapyinstitute.net

The Family Therapy Institute of Washington D.C. provides training in systemic methods.

- Mental Research Institute
  http://www.mri.org

The Mental Research Institute is a leading source of ideas in system therapy.

Readings
Fisch, R., Weakland, J. H., & Segal, L. (1982). *The tactics of change: Doing therapy briefly*. San Francisco: Jossey-Bass.

This text explores the principles of brief therapy and discusses the basic elements of treatment from a brief approach.

Haley, J. (1973). *Uncommon therapy: The psychiatric techniques of Milton H. Erickson, M.D.* New York: Norton.

The reading provides a look at Dr. Erickson's strategic therapy and how he utilized hypnotic techniques to allow him to get to the core problem of the client and present a course of action.

Haley, J. (1976). *Problem-solving therapy*. San Francisco: Jossey-Bass.

This resource guides the therapist in thinking in a contextually sensitive, directive, and goal-focused way within the context of the entire social unit.

Haley, J. (1980). *Ordeal therapy: Unusual ways to change behavior.* San Francisco: Jossey-Bass.

Jay Haley reveals how ordeals work in therapy and offers numerous case histories to illustrate how ordeals can help systems solve a wide range of problems.

Madanes, C. (1981). *Strategic family therapy.* San Francisco: Jossey-Bass.

In this text, Madanes highlights the imaginative techniques she uses to help achieve balance within the family and explores specific problems such as violence, drug use, and depression.

Selvini-Palazzoli, M., Boscolo, L., Cecchin, G., & Prata, G. (1978). *Paradox and counter-paradox.* Northvale, NJ: Aronson.

The book reports the therapeutic work carried out at the Milan Center for the Study of the Family by the authors with families and children presenting serious psychotic disturbances, as well as young adults diagnosed with schizophrenia.

Watzlawick, P., Beavin, J., & Jackson, D. (1967). *Pragmatics of human communication: A study of interactional patterns, pathologies and paradoxes.* New York: Norton.

The authors present the idea that problems in life often arise from issues of communication rather than from deep psychological disorders.

Watzlawick, P., Weakland, J., & Fisch, R. (1974). *Change: Principles of problem formation and problem resolution.* New York: Norton.

This resource highlights the idea that the solutions to problems are embedded in the problems themselves.

Videos

Jay Haley Training Fields Series

http://www.jay-haley-on-therapy.com/html/books_in_english.html.

This training series was produced by Jay Haley.

REFERENCES

Andersen, T. (1991). *The reflecting team: Dialogues and dialogues about the dialogues.* New York: Norton.

Boscolo, L., Cecchin, G., Hoffman, L., & Penn, P. (1987). *Milan systemic family therapy.* New York: Basic Books.

Capuzzi, D., & Stauffer, M. D. (2015). Strategic and Milan systemic theories: Approaches and applications. In D. Capuzzi & M. D. Stauffer (Eds.), *Foundations of couples, marriage, and family counseling* (pp. 239–260). Hoboken, NJ: Wiley.

Gardner, B. C., Burr, B. K., & Wiedowere, S. E. (2006). Reconceptualizing strategic family therapy: Insights from a dynamic systems perspective. *Contemporary Family Therapy: An International Journal, 28*(3), 339–352. doi:10:1007/s10591-006-9007-x

Goldenberg, H., & Goldenberg, I. (2008). *Family therapy: An overview* (7th ed.). Belmont, CA: Brooks/ Cole.

Goldenberg, I., & Goldenberg, H. (2013). *Family therapy: An overview* (8th ed.). Belmont, CA: Brooks/ Cole.

Griffin, W. A., & Greene, S. M. (1999). *Models of family therapy: The essential guide.* Philadelphia: Taylor & Francis.

Haley, J. (1963). *Strategies of psychotherapy.* New York: Grune & Stratton.

Haley, J. (1973). *Uncommon therapy: The psychiatric techniques of Milton H. Erickson, M. D.* New York: Norton.

Haley, J. (1976). *Problem-solving therapy.* San Francisco: Jossey-Bass.

Haley, J. (1980). *Leaving home.* New York: McGraw-Hill.

Hanna, S. M. (2007). *The practice of family therapy: Key elements across models* (4th ed.). Belmont, CA: Brooks/Cole.

Keim, J. (1999). Strategic therapy. In D. M. Lawson & F. F. Prevatt (Eds.), *Casebook in family therapy* (pp. 210–231). Pacific Grove, CA: Brooks/Cole.

Liddle, H. A., Breunlin, D. C., & Schwartz, R. C. (1988). *Handbook of family therapy training and supervision.* New York: Guilford Press.

Madanes, C. (1981). *Strategic family therapy.* San Francisco: Jossey-Bass.

Metcalf, L. (2011). *Marriage and family therapy: A practice-oriented approach.* New York: Springer.

Selvini-Palazzoli, M., Boscolo, L., Cecchin, G., & Prata, G. (1974). The treatment of children through brief therapy of their parents. *Family Process, 13,* 429–442.

Selvini-Palazzoli, M., Boscolo, L., Cecchin, G., & Prata, G. (1978). *Paradox and counterparadox.* Northvale, NJ: Aronson.

Selvini-Palazzoli, M., Cirillo, S., Selvini, M., & Sorrentino, A. M. (1989). *Family games: General models of psychotic process in the family.* New York: Norton.

Sheehan, A. H., & Friedlander, M. L. (2015). Therapeutic alliance and retention in brief strategic family therapy: A mixed-methods study. *Journal of Marital and Family Therapy, 41*(4), 415–427. doi:10.111/ jmft.12113

Szapocznik, J., Zarate, M., Duff, J., & Muir, J. (2013). Brief strategic family therapy: Engaging drug using/ problem behaviors adolescents and their families in treatment. *Social Work in Public Health, 28,* 206–223. doi:10.1080.19371918.2013.774666

Watzlawick, P., Weakland, J., & Fisch, R. (1974). *Change: Principles of problem formation and problem resolution.* New York: Norton.

CHAPTER 11

Getting Into the Mix: Structural Family Therapy

Michael Walsh, Angela Catena, Hannah Bowers, and Mark B. Scholl

"The individual influences his context and is influenced by it."

—Salvador Minuchin

My own experience with structural family therapy (SFT) came because of my dad studying SFT as a graduate student in the late 1970s. I recall him reading Minuchin's Families and Family Therapy for his grad school course work. As a kid, I was a voracious reader and would often pick up any book lying about and give it a read. I remember reading about families in context and asking my dad about the unique context of our family. This led to an interesting discussion about varying perspectives of family members, and I clearly remember coming out of that discussion with enhanced empathy for many family members.
As a result, SFT will always be near and dear to me as an approach.

—Michael Walsh

A s you learned in Chapter 2, structural family therapy (SFT) was developed by Salvador Minuchin in the 1960s and 1970s and continues to be a prominent family therapy approach used today. SFT is a strengths-based approach to helping families to redesign the way they relate to each other to make a more functional family system.

According to the Minuchin Center for Family Studies (2012), SFT is based on five basic principles:

- Context is what gives our lives and our interactions meaning. All our behavior is organized around the ways in which we relate to other people. The structural therapist, for that reason, focuses on what is going on between people, as opposed to individual family members.

- The family is the primary context for human beings. Minuchin called the family the "matrix of identity" (Minuchin, 1974, p. 42) and asserted that the family system is always in flux, attempting to adapt to new and changing circumstances.

- The family's structure is found in the recurring pattern of interrelationships that family members develop over time.

- Well-functioning family structures respond to family members' needs and adapt to changing conditions.

- The job of the structural family therapist is to help the family identify and utilize strengths and change nonadaptive patterns of relating to patterns that are more adaptive.

Structural family therapy was one of the first family therapies to be used among people of diverse socioeconomic backgrounds, having been developed by Minuchin and his colleagues while working with families in urban and impoverished areas of New York and Philadelphia. These families were often very different from the idealized and theorized families of the contemporary professional literature of the time. This led to Minuchin and his colleagues placing a great deal of emphasis on the cultural, social, political, and economic context of each family (e.g., Minuchin & Montalvo, 1967). In this way, SFT became one of the most culturally sensitive approaches of its time, and remains so today. In this chapter, we'll explore the ways in which the systems and structures within the family influence its function. You learned in Chapter 10 that family therapists may use unconventional techniques to help families to function better. Minuchin believed that a therapist must go one step further and join the family to see and experience the system at work. Let's take a closer look!

LEARNING OBJECTIVES

After reading this chapter, you will be able to do the following:

- Describe the theoretical tenets of structural family therapy.

- Understand the history and development of structural family therapy.

- Understand the use of context in family therapy and how to help the family adopt solutions within their own context.

- Understand the role and function of boundaries within the family system.

- Understand the role and function of the therapist in structural family therapy.

- Learn to develop key skills central to work as a structural family therapist.

PROFILE OF MAIN FIGURES

Salvador Minuchin

Early background. Salvador Minuchin was the firstborn son of a closely knit Jewish family in Argentina. Minuchin's father was a prominent businessman until the Great Depression took its toll on the family's fortunes. This fostered in Minuchin a sensitivity to the experiences and societal contexts that very much influence our lives and the lives of those around us. In high school, Minchin studied the work of philosopher Jean-Jacques Rousseau, who postulated that so-called delinquents were victims of society and of societal context, rather than criminals. The idea that the context in which an individual lives helps to dictate his or her development was to be central to the development of his structural family therapy approach.

Israeli army service. Minuchin went on to study medicine and began a residency in pediatric medicine in 1946, with a specialty in psychiatry. The Israeli war of 1948 interrupted his residency, and he moved to Israel to join the Israeli army and to work with young Jewish soldiers who had survived the Holocaust. In doing this work, Minuchin noticed the influence that family structures (or lack thereof) had on mental health and emotional development. This was an idea he would go on to develop in the coming years.

Theory Development

Wiltwyck School for Boys. In 1954 Minuchin began psychoanalyst training at the William Allison White Institute in New York. Originally trained as a psychoanalyst, Minuchin quickly concluded that the psychoanalytic approach was not as helpful as he would have hoped in working with kids at the Wiltwyck School for Boys. In fact, Minuchin noticed that unstable family structures seemed to be a problem among poor African American and Puerto Rican families in inner-city New York. This unstable family structure, he reasoned, likely had more to do with the challenges these children faced than individual psychodynamic forces. Further, he reasoned, if he could intervene with the family, he may have a more efficient way of fostering positive change for a full family unit as opposed to working strictly with individuals. Minuchin suggested to his colleagues that they begin to develop interventions designed to reorganize and strengthen these family structures.

Social context as critical. Minuchin also noticed that many of the children with whom he worked had difficulty introspecting and communicating feelings. Minuchin was influenced by the idea proposed by Gregory Bateson (1979) that families were composed of numerous interdependent and interrelated systems. He was also inspired by Nathan Ackerman (1954), who proposed that the individual's behavior within family units is naturally influenced by the interpersonal aspects of the family unit. These interdependent and interpersonal factors were, in Minuchin's view, the most in need of intervention. Consequently, Minuchin and his colleagues began to experiment with directive, intentional approaches designed to facilitate a change in communication and transactional patterns within the family in lieu of the more passive psychoanalytic approach.

Therapist accommodation and adaptation to context. To facilitate change, Minuchin reasoned, the therapist needed to be able to "join" with the family and actively foster a change in patterns and family structure. Thus, "structural family therapy" was born.

The turbulent social and societal upheaval of the 1960s and 1970s began to influence Minuchin's thinking in terms of the ways in which families develop in relation to the social world around them. Perhaps because of his childhood and high school experiences with the impact of social context, Minuchin began to hone his theory while working with people from disadvantaged backgrounds. This led Minuchin to investigate and write on the effect of poverty and social oppression on family dynamics.

In 1967 Minuchin published *Families of the Slums* (Minuchin & Montalvo, 1967), which is based on the work of the authors at Wiltwyck over the course of 8 years. This work established Minuchin as a leader in systemic family therapy and gave birth to the idea that therapeutic intervention could be accomplished from within the family with the therapist as an integral part of the family structure.

Concurrently, in 1965 Minuchin was asked to head the Philadelphia Child Guidance Clinic. Joining Minuchin in Philadelphia were Jay Haley and Braulio Montalvo. This program grew to be the largest facility in the country devoted to family therapy. By the early 1970s structural family therapy was quickly becoming one of the most widely practiced forms of family therapy. In 1974 Minuchin published *Families and Family Therapy*, which detailed his concepts of family therapy and the ways in which families may benefit from the process.

Minuchin on Minuchin: In His Own Words

Minuchin was endlessly fascinated with society and roles that families play within that society. He firmly believed that a family's context led directly to its identity development. He also believed that individual family members took their identity development cues from the primary family unit. Here are a few of his own words on society, family, and identity.

Society and family. "*Although the family is the matrix of its members' psychosocial development, it must also accommodate to society and ensure some continuity to its culture. This societal function is the source of attacks on the family in modern America. American society is changing, and many groups within that society want to hurry the change*" *(Minuchin, 1974, p. 48).*

"*The family will change as society changes*" *(Minuchin, 1974, p. 49).*

Identity. "*In all cultures, the family imprints its members with selfhood. Human experience of identity has two elements: a sense of belonging and a sense of being separate. The laboratory in which these ingredients are mixed and dispensed is the family, the matrix of identity*" *(Minuchin, 1974, p. 47).*

"*I am always concerned with preserving the boundaries that define individual identity*" *(Minuchin, 1974, p. 120).*

KEY CONCEPTS OF STRUCTURAL FAMILY THERAPY

A contemporary analysis of Minuchin's theory contained within *The Craft of Family Therapy: Challenging Certainties* (Minuchin, Reiter & Borda, 2013) reveals and enumerates **11** major principles of structural family therapy categorized as basics, techniques, or subsystems:

Basics. The basic steps are as follows :

1. Joining is the essential element. This process of joining with a family is a process borne of mutual respect and compassion and a commitment to healing. It is essential to the process of SFT.

2. Families are often operating on "wrong" assumptions. Families often assume that their perception of the reality of their situation is the only one, and that there are no alternatives. Good therapists know this is a fallacy. Good therapists also challenge other faulty assumptions that the family may hold dear. The therapist's job is to help the family explore other options.

3. The family's certainty is the enemy of change. Families are often certain of the singularity of their perceptions and their focus. This certainty becomes an obstacle to change. A good therapist knows situations can be viewed from multiple angles and approached in a variety of ways. Helping the family to see this diversity of perspective is important. Let's look at Case presentation 11.1. In this illustration, the therapist sniffs out and challenges the family's certainty on a particular issue

CASE PRESENTATION 11.1: IDENTIFYING AND CHALLENGING FAMILY CERTAINTY

Families often come in certain that a particular family member is the "problem." This is known, as you remember, as **scapegoating.** In the following case presentation, the therapist identifies that certainty, then challenges it.

Mom: This is our son, Erick. Erick was born in an orphanage in Russia. I suspect that he has reactive attachment disorder. I have read about it, and it seems like he might have it.

Dad: We have three kids: Kate, our oldest daughter, who is 15, and John, our middle boy, who is 10, and Erick, who is 8. I can tell you that we have strong family values about lying. Each of our kids knows very clearly that we value honesty in our home.

Mom: Yes. They know they can tell us anything if they don't lie. Erick has been lying about stealing things from his brother's room! I just feel that he has a coldness … and that he has no conscience. I just don't think he can form healthy attachments to his siblings or to us.

John: He does steal my stuff. If he'd just stop doing that, things would be so much better at home.

Kate: He steals my stuff too. You brat. (Smiles at Erick.)

Erick: (Beams at his sister. Nudges his brother, who nudges back. The two begin to push each other.)

Mom: See? This violence! Kate and John never did this. I just think he … (whispering) has brought a foreign element into our home.

Kate: (Rolls her eyes.)

Therapist: Would you mind if I share what I'm seeing? (Nods all around.) In my experience, kids that have a hard time attaching, really have a hard time forming relationships. I see a kid, in Erick that has a rivalry going with his brother and seems to adore his sister. Kate, what do you think?

Kate: He does follow me everywhere. It's annoying. (Makes a face at Erick, who thinks that's funny. She laughs.)

Therapist: Sometimes … and this is human nature, so it happens to all of us at one point or another, I am no exception … it is easier to point to one person's behavior as the problem than it is to change the way the whole family system works. I wonder … do you think that might be happening here?

(Furrowed brows all around.)

Therapist: What if Erick was following Kate around because he is very attached to her? What if he steals their stuff because he wants to be more like them? What if he is trying to express his affection in a unique way? How might that change things for the family? What might need to change to accommodate that point of view?

The therapist identifies the faulty assumption, allows it to play out experientially in the here and now, challenges the family with a new way of looking at the situation, and seeks to involve the family in the accommodation process.

Techniques/how it works. Steps discussing techniques follow:

1. Challenging the family is critical. A good therapist challenges this certainty and these assumptions. He or she does this by introducing doubt to the certainty, encouraging curiosity and exploration of options and offering hope for change.

2. Exploring alternative pathways. The therapist helps the family explore different ways of thinking about the situation and, especially, different ways of interacting with each other. This is often done by "enactment," a process by which the therapist directs the family in acting out alternative ways of interaction designed to change the family dynamics. The therapist also observes this process and shares his or her observations of process with the family to diversify perspective.

3. Using "content" of family interactions to reveal the "process" of family dynamics. A good therapist will go beyond the "content" of a family interaction (the specifics of a given complaint) to help the family to see the interaction in terms of the "process" of the family's dynamics. For example, a mother might complain about her child not tidying up his or her room. The SFT therapist sees this as an opportunity to go beyond the messy room to get at the true nature of what Mom may be expressing. Perhaps she is feeling overwhelmed and unappreciated by her family or perhaps she is feeling "unheard" within the family. This "content" (the messy room) may simply be her way of expressing dissatisfaction with a structural family dynamic (process). An effective SFT therapist uses content as a way to get to process.

4. Using humor and metaphor as therapeutic tools. Minuchin's own personality and talents often led him to utilize humor and metaphor as useful therapeutic tools within sessions. Humor, metaphor, and imagery tend to be less threatening and sometimes pleasantly surprising tools for helping a family perceive alternative ways of looking at or approaching one another and the family.

5. Using knowledge, potential future directions, and ethical responsibilities as therapeutic tools. The SFT therapist uses his or her knowledge of how families interact (and can interact differently) and how families can be organized to initiate dialogue with the family about positive change. This allows the SFT therapist to discuss potential future directions for interactions and conveys hope that positive change is possible. The SFT also can occasionally point to ethical principles such as mutual responsibility and mutual caring within families to illustrate the need and potential for changes within the family's dynamics.

Subsystems and SFT work. Subsystems follow:

1. Individuals as subsystems. A key tenet here is that everyone within a family has multiple identities and multiple roles within and outside of the family. The SFT practitioner helps people begin to understand and reflect on these multiple identities and in so doing helps individuals explore alternative ways of existing within the family structure and alternative ways of relating to other family members.

2. Subsystems as potentials for change. The SFT practitioner helps families to understand the complex nature of how subsystems function within the family. In doing so, he helps the family understand which dynamics are at play and are central for making potential improvements.

3. Unbalancing subsystems. The process for beginning change is to challenge those unhealthy subsystems, which can lead to discomfort within the family system. This discomfort can be a therapeutic tool in that it can force family members to consider alternative ways of relating or interacting. This tool is always used with compassion and with intention to facilitate alternative structural patterns that may be beneficial. In Case Presentation 11.2, we'll examine the process of alliance formation, triangulation, and the subsystem unbalancing process in SFT.

CASE PRESENTATION 11.2: ALLIANCES, TRIANGULATIONS, AND SUBSYSTEMS

We are going to utilize the same case scenario as above to examine three more concepts: alliances, triangulations, and subsystems.

First, alliances and triangulations. In this case, the family has formed an alliance with each other and has triangulated Erick. This meets the family's need to keep the interactional patterns the same and use Erick as a scapegoat. This was likely not done to consciously exclude or alienate Erick. Rather, the family was used to interacting a certain way (among the biological kids, Mom, and Dad). Erick's adoption was a stimulus that required an accommodation. Instead of accommodating in an adaptive way, the family sought to continue to interact together in the same, comfortable ways, leaving Erick on the outside of that alliance. The family could tell themselves that any upheaval was a result of Erick's experience at the orphanage, and this allowed them to stick to old, familiar patterns.

Second, subsystems. The old interactional patterns represent a subsystem of this family. Mom, Dad, Kate, and John are used to interacting a certain way. That structure (subsystem) worked just fine for years. When Erick arrived, he challenged that subsystem and, true to human nature, the family sought a way to stick to the old and familiar. They did this by making Erick the "problem." The therapist sought to identify this pattern and this less functional subsystem and replace that structure with one that is more adaptive. The therapist, in identifying this subsystem and proposing an alternative, **unbalanced** that subsystem. Once unbalanced, a subsystem is harder to maintain. In short, it is difficult to "un-know" something.

PREMISES OF THE THEORY

Structural family therapy conceptualizes the family unit as a structure fundamental to the social, mental, and emotional development of its members. Therefore, structural family therapy seeks to help the family refine its structure so that it suits the best interests of the family as well as each of its members. Because families are made up of interpersonal and interdependent subsystems, the family is a complex machine capable of being fine-tuned for optimal performance.

Subsystems are groupings of family members that unite in a common purpose. For example, there may be a parental subsystem consisting of a mother and father, or a sibling subsystem consisting of the children. Subsystems can either be healthy and adaptive or unhealthy and unproductive. The SFT practitioner helps the family see which is which.

Family structures are made up of recurring interactions between these subsystems that contribute to or detract from the healthy functioning of the system and its members. Structural family therapy seeks to help families interact in ways that maximize family success and individual mental, emotional, and social development.

The structures and subsystems are made of boundaries, which are defined as unspoken or unwritten "rules" that help define the ways in which different family members interact. These boundaries can be rigid, meaning they rarely flex with circumstance, or diffuse, meaning they lack formal definition and direction. Depending on the circumstance, boundaries may be helpful or unproductive in assisting with family functioning. SFT practitioners help families determine what might be most productive within their own unique context.

The SFT practitioner's primary function is to help families embrace, explore, and move toward changes in structure that are helpful; and to recognize, analyze, and change those structures that are less than helpful. This is accomplished by first helping families recognize over- and underutilized strengths. Let's look at this process in Guided Practice Exercise 11.1.

GUIDED PRACTICE EXERCISE 11.1: BUILDING STRENGTH-RECOGNITION SKILLS

As SFT is a strength-based approach, building skills in strength recognition is essential. This Guided Practice Exercise is designed to help you build those skills.

Reflect on your own family. Reflect on Minuchin's thought that families often express their strengths at the expense of their own best interests and that families often have strengths of which they are unaware. Thinking of your own family, record your answers to the following question: What happens when your family underutilizes its strengths? What happens when your family overutilizes its strengths? Now, looking at what you wrote down, ponder this: What did you discover about your own family's strengths in this exercise? How might you extend those same "investigatory skills" to the families with which you interact?

ROLE OF THE THERAPIST

Minuchin et al. (2013) points to the therapist as a central component within the structural family therapy process. More specifically, they assert that the therapist plays a key role in the successful implementation of SFT in three key areas:

1. Being intentional about professional distance. A thorough understanding and ability to judge professional distance is critical to the successful functioning of a structural family therapist. This allows the SFT therapist to be intentional about how close he or she wants to be in the family's structural process. Choosing how close to get to a family's interactions is important and close, medium, and distant options each have advantages and disadvantages. A thorough knowledge and ability to analyze that distance is a critical tool that helps SFT therapists make appropriate choices in these areas.

2. Role of the therapist as expert. The SFT therapist has considerable expertise in the dynamics of human relationships and in the dynamics of families. This expertise is a critical tool in his or her professional toolbox and should be utilized.

3. Self as a central tool. In joining the family, the therapist places him- or herself into the family system. A thorough and complete understanding of what he or she brings to that interaction is a critical tool for the SFT practitioner. Self-awareness and self-knowledge are fundamental to the development of a structural family therapist. The therapist's own self is his or her single best tool.

ASSESSMENT AND TREATMENT PROCESS IN STRUCTURAL FAMILY THERAPY

Assessment and Accommodation to the Family

As you may have noted in Chapter 7, families come into family therapy with well-established patterns of communication and ways of relating to one another. The assessment process gives us the chance to get a firsthand look at those structures and patterns. Central to structural family therapy is the idea that all behavior is an effort to adapt and relate to another person. This process is called *accommodation*. Assessment in SFT work is a matter of evaluating this accommodation process.

Family systems are an ever-evolving entity; constantly adapting to changes within the system, such as the addition of a new child, children becoming adolescents followed by adults, parents becoming grandparents, experiencing the death of a family member, etc. For a family to maintain an effective level of relative strength and productivity, it is necessary for the system to undergo continual accommodation (Minuchin, 1974).

Mutual accommodation among spouses can be used to facilitate a sense of support that actualizes positive characteristics between members of the subsystem that may have otherwise remained inactive; therefore, fostering a supportive and safe environment for all members within a family system. Mutual accommodation can be used as a tool for positive reinforcement among spouses, but one also runs the risk of using it as an opportunity to focus on negative characteristics. Emphasizing a spouse's negative attributes can lead to further dysfunctional transactional patterns and processes within the subsystem.

In the process of mutual accommodation, the couple develops a set of patterned transactions—ways in which each spouse triggers and monitors the behavior of the other and is, in turn, influenced by the previous behavioral sequence. These transactional patterns form an invisible web of complementary demands that regulate many family situations (Minuchin, 1974).

For complementary accommodation among spouses to occur successfully, they cannot be influenced by or interfered with by members from other subsystems, such as children, in-laws, and those outside of the family system. The parental subsystem can be a source of support but also serves as a model for children. Additionally, a child's development of skills required for interacting with peers and learning from siblings requires parents to not interfere (Minuchin, 1974).

Joining the Family Structure

The family's presence is an acknowledgement they want help and are inviting the therapist, as an expert, into their family structure to alleviate the dysfunction they are experiencing (Minuchin & Fishman, 1981). As you may recall from Chapter 7, the therapist's joining the family structure and conceptualizing the challenge as a structural one that can be solved sends a message of hope. The therapist assumes a leadership position by communicating this hope for the future.

A family's structure is not something that is immediately available to an outside observer (Minuchin, 1974). Instead, a therapist joins the family, or becomes a participant within the system they are trying to transform (Minuchin & Fishman, 1981). As the therapist experiences the family, they begin to formulate a diagnosis based on the information and observations of the family structure and dynamics.

It is worth noting that families will often engage in a process by which the family identifies a "problem member" and devotes much of the family's dysfunction to that member. This is a process called *scapegoating*, and is quite normal. Instead of focusing on that family member, however, the structural family therapist aims to change the family's dysfunctional transactions; the identified individual is only the symptom bearer and not the cause of the problem(s) (Minuchin & Fishman, 1981).

Families will either seek to change themselves and their systems (which can be hard and takes lots of work), the environment, or the context, whichever is easiest. Most human systems seek what is most efficient and families are no different. This *scapegoating* tendency is one of the *structural interaction patterns* that the good family therapist begins to challenge as the process moves forward. The good SFT practitioner knows that, if the family dynamics and systems change, the family can become a much more functional and efficient unit, which is good for all family members as well as the family as a whole. Helping families begin to recognize faulty assumption, systems, and patterns and then begin to explore alternative approaches is the role of the structural family therapist. This recognition process can be facilitated by the intentional use of gentle humor and metaphor. Let's turn to Guided Practice Exercise 11.2 where you will practice developing helpful metaphors.

GUIDED PRACTICE EXERCISE 11.2: BUILDING SKILLS IN DEVELOPING HELPFUL METAPHORS

Minuchin often used both humor and metaphor as less threatening ways to help the family accommodate new ideas (Minuchin, 1974). Metaphors can be powerful tools that help symbolize key ideas for families. Metaphors can be used as symbols to represent ideas, ways of interacting, family dynamics or even situations or patterns. Metaphors come easily to some of us and, if that's you, great! For others of us, developing a good metaphor is more of a challenge. That's OK. Developing helpful metaphors is a skill that you can improve. The following exercise is designed to help you to build those skills.

Let's say a family of two parents and a daughter is deeply enmeshed and overinvolved with one another. You, being a strong SFT therapist, recognize that there is a strength being expressed here: a deep caring for each other. That will be helpful. Let's say, however, you'd like to create a metaphor that helps the family recognize that pattern. You might explore the metaphor of a rope binding family members together. You might say, with a smile: "It sounds like you may feel as if your parents are tied to you. Mom and Dad, do you sometimes feel like you are tied to your daughter? Being tied together and moving in two different directions makes for rough going!" It is important that this exploration be lighthearted and filled with humor. This helps the family recognize the pattern in a less threatening way. If both the parents and the daughter can get on board with this metaphor, it can become an ongoing reference symbol for the family. A smile and a gentle inquiry such as "Is the rope back?" can help the family recognize, with some humor, this enmeshment pattern. Metaphors can take functional forms (like the rope), or they can take animal forms using stereotypical animal patterns. For example, "Sounds like you guys really like to sniff out what's going on in each other's lives. Does it sometimes feel like you are being hounded?" It is important that the metaphor developed is explored with the family, can be seen with some humor, and is helpful to the family in building their own relational and adaptive skills.

Let's work on your metaphor-building skills. Think of your own family. Start with a single-family dynamic and develop a metaphor. You can use animal patterns, examples from nature, cartoons, or whatever you like. See if you can develop a metaphor that your family members would find funny and not threatening but that would still help them recognize that dynamic on which you are focusing. Reflect on the following questions: What metaphor did you find? Did is come easily to you, or was it a difficult exercise? How might your family use this metaphor in a constructive way? How did you "tailor" the metaphor to fit for your family? How might you take this process into a clinical setting with a family?

While changing a family's dysfunctional transactions are aimed at alleviating symptoms, members of the family may be hesitant to accommodate, or cooperate. The ways in which family members have learned to approach conflict and stressful situations have become habitual and for some are effective coping mechanisms. The structural family therapist should understand there is always potential for resistance and should be able to navigate those situations effectively.

During the process of altering the dynamics of a family, the therapist's input may disrupt structure within a once homeostatic family system (Minuchin & Fishman, 1981). The therapist's input challenges historically defined rules that defined the relationships among the members of the family. Therefore, the therapist's input is likely to be met with opposition. Oftentimes a family seeks therapy after failed attempts at resolving the problem (Minuchin, 1974). The increased stress placed on the family structure, compounded with their attempts to cope, can lead to an overreliance and use of more familiar responses, thus narrowing their experiences and ability to effectively navigate the situation. The therapist has different options for managing the resistance that the family is likely to display, from the use of humor and metaphor as less threatening tools of change to the variability of the therapist's own position in relation to the family.

The therapist can join the family from different positions of proximity. The levels of proximity provide the therapist with the freedom and flexibility to join, disjoin, and rejoin at different various places within the family structure. The levels of proximity are a close position, median position, and a disengaged position (Minuchin & Fishman, 1981).

POSITIONING OF THE THERAPIST

Close Position

In a close position of proximity, the therapist gains the ability to affiliate with family members, possibly aligning with some members against others. Confirmation is probably the most useful tool of affiliation (Minuchin & Fishman, 1981). The therapist uses confirmation to identify an individual's positive attributes, recognize, and reward them. Through the act of confirmation, the other family members begin to see the confirmed member in a new light. This is a powerful tool when the family views one member as the source of the problem and fails to identify the positive characteristics that person possesses.

Confirmation can also be a sympathetic response to an individual's affective presentation of their self (Minuchin & Fishman, 1981). For example, a therapist might say, "You seem to be … frustrated … angry … sad." Confirmation may also be used as a nonjudgmental description of transactions between family members. A therapist may say, "When you say something your wife … seems to distance herself … disagrees with you … withdraws from the conversation." This method is not an interpretation of the behavior, but rather an observation that the family members are already aware of (Minuchin, 1974; Minuchin & Fishman, 1981). This is the therapist's way of acknowledging the dynamics and demonstrates she or he is willing to work with the family on this problem.

Another method of confirmation is to identify a blatantly negative characteristic of a family member and relinquish them of their responsibility for that behavior. For example, a therapist may say, "You seem to be very defiant toward your parents. How long have you gone without adequate structure?" By using this approach, the family member feels recognized in what would be a rather difficult area, without experiencing guilt or criticism. The family member may feel a sense of confirmation from the approach the therapist has taken (Minuchin & Fishman, 1981).

Median Position

The therapist joins the family as an active and neutral listener in the median position, while assisting others in telling their story. This method of joining is known as tracking and is a useful means for gathering information (Minuchin & Fishman, 1981). Therapists use tracking, a joining technique, to follow the content and information of what members within a family are saying, as well as their process and interactions with one another.

Joining the family structure, even from a distance, can restrict the therapist's ability to move about the family system freely (Minuchin & Fishman, 1981). Therapists should be aware of their actions and interactions when tracking family members. For example, a therapist may not actively track a shy and timid family member as often, or as well, as she or he would track a more verbal and outgoing member of the family; this may even occur without the therapist recognizing what is taking place. The ways in which the therapist tracks the family process can provide a plethora of invaluable information about a family. Joining from the median position allows the therapist the opportunity to observe the family process.

When working with small children within a family, there are two important approaches a therapist can use (Minuchin & Fishman, 1981). One is related to size and the other to the appropriate language level. For tracking to be effective, a therapist must communicate in ways the child understands, both verbally and nonverbally (Minuchin & Fishman, 1981). In addition, a therapist may choose to sit on the floor with a child and engage with the child at an appropriate level developmentally. The therapist can mimic the child's expressions and gestures or repeat words to develop a connection and create a more comfortable and relaxed atmosphere for the entire family.

Disengaged Position

A therapist can also join the family system from a disengaged position. In the disengaged position, the therapist uses his or her position as an expert, facilitating a therapeutic relationship and instilling the family with a sense of hope and competence (Minuchin & Fishman, 1981). Unlike joining the family from a close or median position, the therapist acts as the director of, rather than an actor within, the family system. This detached position of joining allows the therapist to monitor the family's perspectives and determine their transactional patterns. He can understand how members within the family understand and conceptualize experiences. The therapist can achieve this level of understanding by examining communication styles and patterns explicating the experiences of the family and isolating those phrases that are of importance to the family. The therapist may use these communication patterns as a source of support, or a mechanism for changing outlooks within the family system.

Cautions on Joining

Although joining a family may provide the therapist with invaluable information about the structure, patterns, and transactions of a system, there are also cautions. Aligning with family members can prove to be rather challenging for many reasons. A therapist may find him- or herself in a situation in which an alliance with one member may be therapeutically beneficial to the system, but that member may have a different belief or value system, such as political or religious. Additionally, a therapist may be hesitant to join a family in which child abuse is present. There are times when a therapist may be reluctant to support individuals within a family even though creating a therapeutic alliance may facilitate change within the system (Minuchin & Fishman, 1981).

On a related note, as can sometimes happen, once the therapist is able to help an individual family member, he or she may begin to develop affection for that family member. This has the danger of damaging the therapist's objectivity, and the entire family's well-being must be considered. Therefore, the challenge becomes finding the motivation and willingness to continue to find ways in which the therapist can be helpful to the family members. Once the therapist finds a way of being helpful, joining can then be possible. To do this, the therapist utilizes the content (what is happening in the here and now) to look deeper for themes and process patterns (what the person might really be reacting to). In Guided Practice Exercise 11.3, we'll look at an example and you will start to build your own skills in using content to access process.

GUIDED PRACTICE EXERCISE 11.3: USING CONTENT TO ACCESS THEMES AND PROCESS

A key skill in structural family therapy is the use of content (what is happening and being expressed in the here and now) to look deeper for themes and process (what the person might really be reacting to). Earlier, we noted that the mother expressing frustration over her child's messy room may well be expressing a feeling of being underappreciated, or unheard. The "content" is the messy room, but the "process" is Mom feeling undervalued. A good structural family therapist carefully attends to the context of the family to find these underlying "structural process" elements, and then works with the family to explore these processes. It is important to note that these deeper process observations are just guesses and must be carefully and gently explored with the family to be sure that they are on target. The following exercise is designed to help you to build your own skills in this area.

Observe the interactions of a family. It could be your own family or another family that you know well. Carefully take note of the "content" of the family's interactions. Make a list of this content. Now, spend time making a list of the possible "structural process" dynamics; the things that might be driving the behavior of individual family members. For example, let's say the family is talking, and Johnny, the young son, constantly interrupts to ask questions of his dad. Take note of the content of the questions, and then think about the possible why's behind the interruptions. Is Johnny feeling insecure and needs his dad's attention? If so, why? In short, you are looking for the deeper meaning behind behaviors of family members that give you clues as to the structure of the family. As you make this list, reflect on the following questions: If you were working with this family, how might you check out these ideas? What strategies might be helpful in doing this? Was this process easy or hard for you? What did you learn?

Joining and Accommodation to the Family

The therapist must have a strong sense of him- or herself and know the ways in which that "self" may be used a key role in accommodation. First, he or she needs to accommodate the most useful parts of that self into the family's existing structure. For example, if the therapist brings a high level of skill with the use of metaphor or humor, he or she may choose to utilize these aspects of self to be most helpful. Likewise, a family therapist needs to be aware of his or her own patterns. For example, if a therapist has a need to be liked, this is likely to enter the transactional patterns of the family. The good therapist is aware of his or her own patterns and the ways in which those patterns may be helpful or not within the family's unique structure and transactional patterns.

In addition to the therapist accommodating to the family, the family must accommodate to changing conditions. A key feature of assessment in structural family therapy is to have an idea of the ways in which a family may adapt to changing conditions. The therapist's very presence can and does create accommodation needs as the therapist begins to note patterns and challenge the status quo. In this section, we will look at some of the most common ways the accommodation process may play out.

A family may be required to restructure and adapt at various periods of time; such as the addition of a new child, children becoming adolescents and then adults, parents becoming grandparents, etc. Continual accommodation is necessary for a family, and its members, to maintain its productivity and relative strength (Minuchin, 1974). Mutual accommodation among spouses can provide a sense of support that reifies positive characteristics within one another that may have lain dormant, thus fostering a supportive and safe environment for each other. It is also possible for individuals to focus on negative aspects of their spouse rather than the positive. This has the potential to activate dysfunctional transactional processes and patterns within the system.

In the process of mutual accommodation, the couple develops a set of patterned transactions—ways in which each spouse triggers and monitors the behavior of the other and is in turn influenced by the previous behavioral sequence. These transactional patterns form an invisible web of complementary demands that regulate many family situations (Minuchin, 1974).

Complementary accommodation among spouses requires freedom from interference by others, such as children, in-laws, and even those outside of the family system. Additionally, a child's development of skills required for interacting with peers and learning from siblings requires parents to not interfere (Minuchin, 1974).

Observation of Family Structure, Interactions, and Boundaries

The therapist makes many observations about the family structure; through stories the family members share, the ways in which they experience reality, and how the family members relate to him or her and to each other. Other observations include identifying who the family spokesperson is, what that means, how that spokesperson was selected, and the actions of the family while that person speaks (Minuchin, 1974).

Nonverbal communication regarding the content of the verbal communication can serve as an important source of information. Are the other family members agreeing or contradicting what is being said? Are these moments typical of the family's dynamics and interactions? The therapist observes transactions, patterns, and boundaries, and forms hypotheses about the nature of these patterns, whether functional or dysfunctional, through observations and by asking questions. You may recall the concept of family mapping from Chapter 7. SFT utilizes mapping in a very specific way. The observational process we've just examined serves as the basis of a family map (Minuchin, 1974).

Boundaries

The therapist can also gather critical information regarding **boundaries** in the observation process. Minuchin thought of boundaries as fundamental elements in defining a family's structure and responsibilities. Boundaries that are **diffuse**, unclear, and difficult to determine often lead to confusion as to family rules, roles, responsibilities, and functions. These very diffuse and unhelpful boundaries are referred to as **enmeshed**. This enmeshed condition can lead to overinvolvement between family members and a lack of independence. Boundaries that are clear, easy to understand, and help define roles, responsibilities, and family functions are thought of as **clear** boundaries. The establishment of clear boundaries is a goal of structural family therapy. Boundaries that are too **rigid** and do not respond to changing conditions are thought to be **disengaged**. These rigid boundaries can lead to feelings of isolation within family members and do not lend themselves to healthy expression or development. Look at Figure 11.1, which describes Minuchin's various boundaries.

Figure 11.1 Symbols Used in Structural Family Mapping

Subsystems/Transactional Symbols	Boundary Symbols	Subsystems/Transactional Symbols
Symbol Used for *Affiliations*:	Symbol Used for Diffuse (Confusing) Boundary: ⋯⋯⋯⋯⋯	Symbol Used for *Detouring*:
_____	Symbol Used for Clear (Normal) Boundary: _ _ _	=>
	Symbol Used for Rigid (Distancing) Boundary: _____	
	You might combine all of the symbols in this section as a figure. Refer to the Figure in place of the symbols here.	
Subsystems/Transactional Symbols	Subsystems/Transactional Symbols	Subsystems/Transactional Symbols
Symbol Used for *Triangulation* △	Symbol Used for *Conflict Between Members*, represented by an interrupted line _____╎╎_____	Symbol Used for *overinvolvement*, four solid lines connecting individuals: _____ _____ _____ _____

Adapted from: Salvador Minuchin, Families and Family Therapy, pp. 53-54. Copyright © 1974 by Harvard University Press.

It is important for you to remember, however, the importance Minuchin placed on social context. Each boundary observation is a snapshot in time and is fully dependent on the context of the moment. For example, let's suppose a young adult family member experiences a major trauma, accident, or acquires a disability. Shortly after that happens, the family comes in for family therapy. The therapist observes that the relationship between the mother and the young adult child seems enmeshed, with the mother being overly involved with the everyday decisions and roles that might be expected of a young adult. Rather than evidence of "pathology" within the family, this may be evidence of a family accommodating to support the temporary needs of one member. It is only by understanding the full social and familial context that the therapist can make accurate assessments.

CASE CONCEPTUALIZATION IN STRUCTURAL FAMILY THERAPY

Enactment of Dysfunctional Patterns

> *"The only family structure immediately available to a therapist is the dysfunctional structure"*
>
> *(Minuchin, 1974, p. 91).*

Enactment is a therapeutic tool used to observe and modify problematic family functioning and can occur intentionally or spontaneously (Minuchin, 1974; Minuchin & Fishman, 1981). The therapist invites the family to bring an outside conflict into session, thereby allowing the members to demonstrate how they navigate conflict. The therapist can observe how members control their behaviors and identify the source of the problematic behavior(s) based on the family transactions (Schultz, 1984).

A therapist uses enactment as an avenue to interrupt the already established transactions and patterns, examining the system's flexibility and capacity for accommodation of new and more efficient rules. Change comes not from talking about problems, but rather as a direct result of addressing them (Minuchin & Fishman, 1981).

There are three movements of enactment a therapist can use with a family: spontaneous transactions, eliciting transactions, and alternative transactions.

Spontaneous Transactions

This is based on the concept that most deeply transactional patterns will manifest themselves in some way in the here and now. For this reason, the wise therapist stays vigilant and watches for these transactional patterns to appear. When she does notice the pattern, she points it out.

Eliciting Transactions

The therapist creates situations in which family subsystems and dynamics are highlighted. These transactions are done with the full family present, and the therapist shares his observations with the family as it happens. This begins the process of helping families recognize long-held patterns and transactions. Often, these patterns are *nonsupportive* transactions that do nothing to help the family unit function or adapt. Recognizing these patterns is a critical first step to SFT.

Alternative Transactions

Most importantly, the therapist begins to help the family to explore alternative approaches to situations and/or alternative ways of relating to one another that help the family to adapt and accommodate more efficiently and/or that help support the overall functioning of the family unit. Development, exploration and deployment of these *supportive alternatives* are at the heart of good SFT.

Mapping the Family System

In Chapter 7 we examined family mapping and genograms. SFT utilizes this family mapping to visually conceptualize communication and engagement patterns within the family. The SFT family map is a working hypothesis that is continuously tested, refined, and redrawn according to new information gathered by the therapist. Mapping the family system allows the therapist to visually organize information about a family that has been gathered to create hypotheses and inform therapeutic goals.

According to Minuchin (1974),

> *the family map is a powerful simplification device, which allows the therapist to organize the diverse material that*

he is getting. The map allows him to formulate hypotheses about areas within the family that function well and about other areas that may be dysfunctional. It also helps him to determine the therapeutic goals (p. 90).

Minuchin and Fishman (1981) describe the utility of the family map:

This family map indicates the position of family members vis-à-vis one another. It reveals coalitions, affiliations, explicit and implicit conflicts, and the ways family members group themselves in conflict resolution. It identifies family members who operate as "detourers" of conflict and family members who function as switchboards. The map charts the nurturers, healers, and scapegoaters. Its delineation of the boundaries between subsystems indicates what movement there is and suggests possible areas of strength or dysfunction (p. 69).

A family map to an instrumental tool used in identifying the family's problem and goals for therapy.

Diagramming relationship structures. As noted above, a key tool used in conceptualizing the family structure is the use of diagrams to represent relationships. Minuchin characterized several types of transactions and transactional styles and used different symbols to represent them in the family map. Symbols are used to describe different types of boundaries (dotted lines for diffuse boundaries, a dashed line for clear boundaries, and a solid line for rigid, distance-creating boundaries; see Figure 11.1, boundary symbols).

Symbols are also used to describe the types of transactional relationships, or subsystems, among family members. Family members can group themselves in **affiliations** and **alliances/coalitions**. Families can also **triangulate** and **detour.** Ways to diagram these different situations are detailed below (see Figure 11.1, triangulation and detouring symbols).

Minuchin used two lines connecting different people as a representation of an affiliation between those people. **Affiliations** are structural concepts and relate to an individual's position in the family relative to the other members. Affiliations can be either healthy (supporting the good functioning of the family) or unhealthy (nonsupporting of the healthy function of the family (see Figure 11.1, affiliations symbol).

Alliances or **coalitions** are used when family members band together to get certain needs met. Again, this can be supportive of healthy family functioning (siblings banding together to support each other in reaching goals) or nonsupportive (Dad and son banding together to subvert Mom's planning or structure). Minchin used a bracketing symbol to connect coalitions in the family map.

Coalition/alliance. Another example of a **nonsupportive coalition** is called **triangulation**. Triangulation is an example of family members banding together to get their needs met at the expense of another family member. For example, Dad has a goal of saving money to buy a new car, which the family needs. Siblings 1 and 2 want to take a trip to snorkel in the Florida Keys. Siblings 1 and 2 approach Mom and convince her that it is in her best interest and theirs that they take the snorkel trip. Mom gives them the money. In this case, the kids have successfully triangulated the relationships within the family to get their needs met. Triangulation is normal and happens in families quite a bit. The challenge with triangulation is that certain members get needs met at the expense of the overall family unit, and decisions are made without the full input of all family members (see Figure 11.1, triangulation symbol).

Coalition/alliance that is triangulated. Families may also develop strategies to avoid conflict. These strategies or structures are called "detours" and can take the form of a person (the family who always jokes and distracts to lessen tension) or a habit (instead of talking through the conflict, the family retreats to familiar activities that are nonthreatening, such as watching TV or going to a movie). This serves to detour away from conflict but also ensures that no healthy communication or conflict resolution takes place.

Minuchin spoke of a habit some families use to **detour** away from conflict. **Detouring** helps avoid conflict and saves family members from uncomfortable conversations. However, the lack of honest communication leaves underlying issues unaddressed and can lead to long term challenges (see Figure 11.1, detouring symbol).

Families can arrange themselves into subsystems in which family members are **overinvolved** with each other or **enmeshed**. For example, a young adult who is in community college is having trouble in his classes. His mother calls the course instructor to discuss how her son may be more successful in the class. While this may sound like a nice thing for Mom to do, Mom is essentially stepping into a role that, developmentally, her son would be best playing. This is an example of enmeshment and overinvolvement. The challenge with this sort of enmeshment is that it can rob the child of a sense of independence and self-efficacy, leading to an overdependence on the family unit and lack of autonomy. This overdependence can also result in an unwillingness on the part of the developing person to seek involvement outside of the family. As depicted earlier in this chapter, Figure 11.1 illustrates this overdependence using the overinvolvement symbol.

Finally, families can occasionally arrange themselves into structures in which there is conflict between members. This is represented by an interrupted line. Figure 11.1 illustrates this conflict using the conflict between members symbol. Now, let's look at Guided Practice Exercise 11.4, in which you will work on both your observational and family mapping skills.

GUIDED PRACTICE EXERCISE 11.4: DIAGRAMMING THE FAMILY

Minuchin (1974) used *family mapping* to graphically represent the relationship dynamics and underlying structure within the family. This exercise is designed to help you build skills in family mapping.

Arrange to observe a family. Maybe you join them for dinner or are simply able to observe the family's interactions over a period of time. Next, make a family map using the symbols described above. Be sure to use these symbols to represent, as accurately as possible, the underlying family dynamics you observed. Remember to utilize your new skills in using content to investigate process. You may not have a chance to check these assumptions out with family members, but make your best guesses. Reflect on the following questions: What does this family map reveal to you? How might it help you or the family to better understand the underlying family and relationship structures? How might you use these skills in a clinical setting with a family?

STRENGTHS AND LIMITATIONS OF STRUCTURAL FAMILY THERAPY

Limitations and Criticisms of Structural Family Therapy

Structural family therapy's evidentiary base lies in research done in the 1970s, 1980s, and 1990s. Evans, Turner, & Trotter (2012) point out that this early evidence often lacked scientific rigor and that much of the more recent research done with SFT is case study in nature. Other conceptual concerns lie in the notion that some constructs of SFT lack a clear operational definition suitable to future research (Jones, 1980), perhaps suggesting a reason for the paucity of replicative research.

SFT's strong reliance on the evaluation of the therapist has led some to question the multicultural applicability of SFT. More specifically, Gladding (2010) noted that SFT may be disempowering to clients due to its reliance on the assessment and opinions of the therapist. On a related note, Hammond and Nichols (2008) argued that the confrontational nature of the therapist pointing out structural deficiencies could have a negative impact on the working alliance between the therapist and the client family.

Others have criticized SFT on cultural grounds, arguing that the therapist's defining of *enmeshed* or *triangulated* is by definition bound in the cultural norms of the therapist, as opposed to the family (Napoliello & Sweet, 1992). Further, Minuchin's definitions of male and female roles in relationships—specifically, males expected to take executive roles and females expected to take expressive roles—has been criticized on the grounds of cultural relevance (Gladding, 1998).

McGoldrick (1989) advanced a feminist criticism of the structural family therapy model, noting that the assumption of an optimal family unit consisting of a male holding a position of power fails to account for the powerful dynamic of gender and gender roles as a structural variable. McGoldrick (1989) goes on to note that SFT does not consider the impact of cultural and societal stereotypes and norms on women and mothers.

Strengths of Structural Family Therapy

Proponents of structural family therapy cite SFT's involvement of the full family in decision making, as well as SFT's call of consideration of the social and cultural context of the family as evidence of its multicultural utility and appeal. Minuchin (1974) himself noted the need to "look at man within his social context" (p. 4). It is this insistence on context that lends credence to the argument that good SFT is always done within the social and cultural context of the family.

Figley and Nelson (1990) noted that structural family therapy's "simplicity, concreteness and directness" (p. 226) is one of its greatest strengths. On a related note, many researchers found that SFT was a highly teachable form of family therapy and that trainees showed high levels of conceptual and executive skills when compared to control groups (Zaken-Greenberg & Neimeyer (1986). You may note that the Guided Practice Exercises for this chapter focus heavily on the counselor's development of key skills. It is these same skills that are referenced above.

Structural family therapy is based on the tenet that families have options and solutions within themselves and that each family, without exception, has strengths that it may leverage in difficult situations. In this way, SFT is a fundamentally strength-based approach. Additionally, by involving the full family in decision making, a good SFT practitioner bases interventions on what is most important to the family, within its own unique value system. This strength-based and value-based approach is consistent with many modern approaches such as motivational interviewing (Miller & Rollnick, 2013), which base case conceptualization in the positive arena (the positive impact of change), as opposed to the negative arena (what happens if things don't change). That being said, a core tenet of SFT is family choice and the honoring of those choices. Family autonomy is a priority.

Perhaps due in part to its consistency and ease of use, SFT's influence on the world of family therapy is clear. McFarlane, Dixon, Lukens, & Lucksted (2003) noted that SFT's influence in the world of family therapy has been broad, noting that many of its central tenets have been incorporated into later family therapy models.

PUTTING IT ALL TOGETHER: WORKING WITH A FAMILY USING STRUCTURAL FAMILY THERAPY

Regulating Intensity and Meeting the Contextual Needs of the Family

A key tool in the practice of successful structural family therapy is intentionality regarding session intensity and exploration. It is critical to remember that, in structural work, context shapes the structure of the family, and all work should be done within that context and at the intensity level called for by the context. For example, if a family is deeply enmeshed and that enmeshment has evolved over time as an accommodation and an adaptation to the environment around the family, it is important to remember that a family is likely to be very resistant to challenges to that structure. It is incumbent on the structural family therapist to adjust the intensity with which he or she challenges these existing structures to allow the family to entertain the possibility of change.

For example, let's say that a family has evolved a structure that is deeply enmeshed due to the presence of threatening forces outside of the family such as gang, religious or political violence, social struggle, etc. The interventions and intensity utilized by the structural family therapists must take these outside forces into account. In this example, interventions framed around the concept of staying safe from violent forces or even framed around escaping those forces all together stand a much better chance of being entertained by the family than interventions not based within that context. Further, the choice and intensity of intervention makes a huge difference. It may not be beneficial to choose an intervention designed around assertiveness in the face of political violence. Rather, interventions designed to help the family function while staying safe or even escaping that context may be better choices. Practicality and strict attention to context is a critical point of successful SFT.

Shaping competence. In structural family therapy work, the family serves as the primary context for the development of each individual family member. Interventions should be designed to best support that family as whole to maximize the nurturing potential of the family unit. For this reason, interventions in SFT are almost never done without the full family present. This fosters a level of communication and sharing of problem-solving responsibilities that helps to establish clear and healthy boundaries and roles.

Families will always face conflict. The key to shaping competence within the family is to help the family build skill in analyzing situations for alternative pathways, building confidence that families can explore and put into practice alternate approaches to problem solving, and encourage the development of healthy transactional patterns that foster this exploration and discovery.

At its very heart, structural family therapy is a strength-based approach in which the therapist helps the family locate, develop, and employ underutilized and/or underdeveloped strengths.

As a developing structural family therapist, you can help yourself shape your own competence by beginning to "tune your eyes and ears" to look for those underutilized, underdeveloped, or sometimes hidden strengths. Understanding, for example, that "problems" are often characterized by over- or underutilizing strengths may help you begin to refine your skills at spotting these strengths. For example, suppose that you are working with a family that seems deeply enmeshed and overinvolved in each other's lives. This could be a problem, sure. You, however, as a developing structural family therapist, recognize the strength being expressed in this pattern: a deep caring and love within the family. That is a strength that the family can use. Minuchin (1974) held that, in all cases, each family has strengths it can leverage to improve its functioning.

Unbalancing and challenging assumptions. Challenging assumptions provides the family with alternative views of reality by altering the ways in which they relate to each other. When assumptions are challenged through education and new experiences, members within the family can then choose more appropriate and effective responses. This is often the case with the setting and resetting of boundaries.

> *"Change is seen as occurring through the process of the therapist's affiliation with the family and his restructuring of the family in a carefully planned way, so as to transform dysfunctional transactional patterns"* *(Minuchin, 1974, p. 91).*

The term **unbalancing** refers to the process of upsetting the time-honored status quo of the way the family relates to one another. The SFT typically does this by either pointing out old dynamics, suggesting new ways of relating, or putting families into situations in which the old ways of relating are not possible. For example, if there is a rigid boundary between siblings and neither is cooperating with the other, the SFT may suggest that the parents create a collaborative opportunity for the siblings in which they only way they each get their individual needs met is to collaborate with each other. This is done with the full involvement and knowledge of the entire family and with the understanding that the goal of the intervention is to develop new ways of relating. This **unbalances** the status quo by ensuring that existing transactional patterns of conflict and noncooperation won't work. It also challenges the assumption that the previous way of interacting was the only way. Finally, it provides all family members the opportunity for input and models a new and more adaptive way of group problem solving that may previously not have existed within the family structure. The therapist offers process-based feedback throughout and thereby helps the family to "troubleshoot" this new behavior pattern and work out any wrinkles. This helps to ensure that the new pattern is viable and that the family has an increased comfort level with its use.

The effective SFT also helps the family to begin to recognize and define healthy and unhealthy boundaries to build the adaptation and accommodation skills of the family. Recognizing that no family will ever be completely free of conflict, the SFT seeks to build the family's autonomy by equipping the family with these skills. Once the family is beginning to use these skills, the family begins to reset its own boundaries, and the need for the SFT's intervention is lessened. This helps the therapist begin to know when the time is near to begin to terminate the therapeutic relationship.

Case Presentation: Using SFT

Background information:

Dad (41 years old, light skinned and muscular, has been a cop for 18 years)

Mom (40 years old, big boned, happy and healthy, a receptionist in a nursing home)

Denitra (15 years old, freshman at Saluda High School)

Mark (11 years old, in sixth grade at Saluda Middle School)

Therapist:	Welcome back! You know, I've noticed over the past few sessions that Mom and Dad often sit together over there on the couch and that Mark and Denitra take separate chairs in the room. What do you think that's about?
Denitra:	(Shrugs, does not respond.)
Mark:	(Shrugs.)
Mom:	It's like that at home too. She never wants to be anywhere near us.
Dad:	She's a teenager. That's what they do.
Therapist:	(Smiles gently.) Sometimes, when you're 15 and thinking about the big things going on your life, being with family feels like a hassle. And I suspect that sometimes, your family has a hunch that it's hard for you to figure all this stuff out. Maybe what we can try is to see things from the other's perspective. You guys willing to try that?
	(Nods all around.)
Therapist:	OK. Mom, why might it be hard for Denitra to hang around with the family? Let's see how close you get to. Denitra, tell us whether Mom is on track here.
Mom:	I know that you've been having a tough time at school and that kids sometimes approach you and give you grief for your dad being a cop.
Denitra:	(Scowling and hunching her shoulders.) It sucks. Black lives matter. All lives matter. What about my life?
Dad:	You can't let that get to you. It has nothing to do with you…
Denitra:	(Whirling to face Dad.) How would you know what has to do with me?! You don't know what it's like to be me at school…
Dad:	(Shakes his head, frustrated … looks like he wants to speak, doesn't.)
Therapist:	Looks like there is something that you want to say, Dad?
Dad:	No, forget it. She wouldn't listen anyway.
Therapist:	I don't think we know that for sure. What was it that was said? We miss 100% of the shots we don't take…?
Mom:	Go ahead. It will be good for her to hear it.
Dad:	(Quietly.) Maybe I do.
Denitra:	What?
Dad:	Maybe I do know what it's like. I … was (looks at Mom, who nods) I was bullied a ton when I was in school.
Denitra and Mark:	(Stare open mouthed and dumbfounded.)
Mark:	You were…
Dad:	Yep. I was the only Black kid in my neighborhood that was light skinned enough to make people think I had a white parent. I didn't but it didn't stop people from assuming. Somehow, I wasn't 'Black enough' for some of the bigger kids. I got thumped pretty regularly at the bus stop all through fifth and sixth grade.

Denitra:	But you're, like ripped…
Dad:	(Smiles.) I wasn't always. I started lifting that summer after sixth grade. Got tired of being beat up. Decided I was gonna help make sure that didn't happen to other people.
Therapist:	(Turns to family.) How does knowing that change things?
Denitra:	I guess I just figured you always could take care of yourself.
Therapist:	Does it give you hope that maybe your dad understands more about your experience than you thought?
Denitra:	I guess, but … (Turns to face Dad.) Why didn't you ever tell us this? Why don't you ever ask how I am? (Voice cracks.)
Dad:	I just thought … I mean … I guess I was afraid to ask because I was afraid I wouldn't be able to fix it for you …
Therapist:	(Speaks gently.) So, to be effective as a dad, you have to be able to fix it?
Dad:	Yeah. That's kind of how it's supposed to be, right?
Mom:	Maybe she just wants to talk … vent a little. Maybe it would be good if she could do it with you … with us.
Therapist:	That's an interesting idea. Let's get Mark's take on all of this. Mark?
Mark:	(Has been watching all of this like a tennis match. Suddenly, he blurts.) This is some bullsh…
Mom and Dad:	Hey! Watch your language!
Therapist:	Maybe what Mark is trying to say … and it sometimes happens that the youngest member of the family can feel this way … is that he's hoping that somebody notices him. One thing that I've noticed is that Mark has been on the sidelines for this discussion. I've seen that pattern in previous sessions. I'm wondering whether Mark feels excluded or unappreciated. Mark, did I get that right?
Mark:	(Shrugs.) I guess so, yeah.
Therapist:	So let me recap what I have noticed. Denitra, and to some extent, Mark have had a hard time seeing the perspective of Dad. Dad and Mom have had a hard time recognizing the perspective of Mark and Denitra. I also noticed that we have not yet heard from Mom. Is that a dynamic that also plays out at home?
	(The family looks sheepishly around the room, tears well in Mom's eyes. She nods.)
Therapist:	What sometimes happens with families is that we're just spending time trying to survive … and we start not to notice the people and relationships around us. What I have also found is that if we can come together and recognize each other's perspectives, we can change the ways in which we relate. I think we saw that happen earlier with Dad and Denitra. (Looks around the room.)
Therapist:	What would you all think if we worked on ways to build empathy between ourselves over the next sessions? What are some ways that we might do that, do you think?

Reflecting on the case above, what skills and key concepts did you see play out in the session? What techniques did the therapist employ? What did you notice about the dynamics of things as the session moved along?

In Guided Practice Exercise 11.5, you have an opportunity to explore a technique of Minuchin's called family mealtime, in which you will practice noting things like interactional patterns, use of space, family rules and rituals and other key indicators of family subsystems. You will also have the opportunity to describe at least two structural interventions that you would employ as a family therapist to enhance that family's functioning as well as your rationale for those choices.

GUIDED PRACTICE EXERCISE 11.5: FAMILY MEALTIME ACTIVITY

Salvador Minuchin was known for a counseling approach sometimes referred to as the family mealtime session (Rosman, Minuchin, & Liebman, 1975; Grossman, Pozanski, & Banegan, 1983). This session would involve his joining a family for a meal—usually lunch. During the meal with the family, Minuchin would observe and note key family characteristics including the family structure, use of space, rituals, patterns of communication, patterns of behavior, unwritten rules, and salient family subsystems. He would commonly intervene by reframing the **identified patient** (depressed, anorexic) as a problem related to family structure or family interaction patterns. This approach was utilized to take the burden off the identified patient and to facilitate change in entrenched family patterns and rigid family rules to enhance family and individual functioning.

This activity has two options. The first option employs a video of a family at mealtime. The second employs naturalistic observation of an actual family at mealtime.

Option 1: Watch a video of a family having a meal from YouTube titled *Everybody Loves Raymond Thanksgiving* at https://www.youtube.com/watch?v=VmARwxlMJV0

Describe as many of the characteristics of the family as you can identify or describe: use of space, patterns of communication, patterns of behavior, rituals, family rules, roles of family members, and salient family subsystems. Next, describe at least two structural interventions you would employ as a family therapist to enhance family functioning, and provide your rationale for employing each of these.

Option 2 : Arrange to join the family of a friend for either breakfast, lunch, or dinner. Another option might be coffee and dessert if a meal is not possible. After the conclusion of the meal, write descriptions of the following characteristics for the family you observed: use of space, patterns of communication, patterns of behavior, rituals, family rules, roles of family members, and salient family subsystems. Next, describe at least two structural interventions you would employ to enhance the family's functioning, and provide your rationale for employing each of these.

SUMMARY

In this chapter, we looked at Minuchin's structural family therapy, a strengths-based approach that helps families recognize patterns within family relationships and alter those patterns in order to become a more efficient family unit. In SFT, we learned the power of context and role that relational patterns have in determining family outcomes. We also learned that, according to SFT, family is the primary context for human beings and that families are in a constant state of either adaptation or rigidity. According to SFT, families that are best able to adapt that are the ones best able to function. The therapist's role in SFT is to help the family identify and maximize existing strengths, identify existing relational patterns, and modify those patterns to adapt to change.

Therapists accomplish these goals by actively joining with the family and making themselves a part of the family structure. The therapist is then able to recreate (**enactment**) examples of existing family patterns and structure. The therapist can then use family mapping and diagrams to graphically illustrate to family members how these patterns function. This provides the family the opportunity to "see" the family structure as well as the relational connection inherent within that structure. This enables SFT therapists to better illustrate relational patterns (family structure) and to impact those patterns by providing alternative patterns (alternative transactions), while providing support for the family in incorporating these new patterns (supportive alternatives). Fundamentally, Minuchin believed that each and every family has strengths they can use to solve problems. The SF therapist joins the family to help them discover and utilize these strengths. At its core, SFT is an approach that honors the autonomy of the family and its ability to make choices. In this way, structural family therapy is one of the more humanistic approaches in family work.

In our next chapter, we'll take a look at another group of humanistic family approaches, the experiential family therapies. These approaches, like SFT, center on a conviction that families retain their own best healing forces within themselves. The experiential therapist's goal is to create the sort of experiences that help the family identify and utilize these healing forces.

KEYSTONES

Among the key points addressed in this chapter are:

- All families have strengths.
- Families are the primary source of identity and personal and emotional development for members.
- Families are made up of subsystems consisting of relationships among people.
- These subsystems can be supportive of the family as a unit or nonsupportive.
- The family will have a way of operating that it has gotten used to and may resist having that challenged.

- An effective structural family systems therapist will challenge the assumptions and systems present, unbalancing the system or systems before helping the family explore new, more adaptive ways of relating.

REFLECTIONS FROM THE CONTRIBUTOR'S CHAIR

As I reflect on structural family therapy work, and as I use it with families in my practice, I am always struck by the ways in which families benefit from learning of their own dynamics and structure.

It calls to mind an experience with my own family, in which we had occasion to look at some of the structural dynamics within our relationships. I still remember the feeling of satisfaction and deeper empathy that came with a better understanding of my family's motivations and behavior. Suddenly, the ways in which my own family behaved toward each other had context beyond "content" and we could get a deeper look at the "process" of our relationships. This allowed us to have new choices in the ways in which we related to each other. It also developed within us deeper understanding of the emotional and social positions of each family member. We could look beyond "content" and make better choices of response that allowed us to develop better relationships. It was very liberating and enlightening to finally be able to say, "Aha! Maybe THAT's why this happened!"

When working with families, I often find myself looking forward to helping them toward that "aha!" moment. It is that transformative opportunity that then gives the family new choices as to how they understand one another and how they relate with one another. I have also come to understand that these new choices are just that: choices. Some families choose to take these new ideas and run with them, using them to relate differently and improve the family's structure and function. Some do not. That choice is as much about context and family autonomy as anything else. Either way, as I see it, and as my grandfather used to say: "The Buffet is open. Folks can choose as much or as little as they want."

Good luck as you build your skills. May your buffet always be as full as you want it to be.

—Michael Walsh, PhD, CRC

ADDITIONAL RESOURCES

The following resources provide additional information relating to the chapter topic.

Useful Website

- Minuchin Center for the Family
  http://www.minuchincenter.org

This site has excellent resources on SFT and descriptions of training opportunities.

Video

- Video of Minuchin Discussing Structural Family Therapy
  http://www.psychotherapy.net/video/minuchin-family-therapy

An excellent opportunity to see Salvador Minuchin describe SFT in his own words.

Reading

Minuchin, S., Reiter, M., & Borda, C. (2013). *The craft of family therapy: Challenging certainties.* New York: Taylor and Francis.

This is a comprehensive and contemporary look at Minuchin's approach.

REFERENCES

Ackerman, N. (1954). Interpersonal disturbances in the family. *Psychiatry: Interpersonal and Behavioral Processes, 17*(4), 359–364.

Bateson, G. (1979). *Mind and nature: A necessary unity.* New York: Dutton.

Evans, P., Turner, S., & Trotter, C. (2012). *The effectiveness of family and relationship therapy: A review of the literature.* Melbourne: Psychotherapy and Counselling Federation of Australia.

Figley, C. R., & Nelson, T. S. (1990). Basic family therapy skills, II: Structural family therapy. *Journal of Marital and Family Therapy, 16*(3), 225–239. doi:10.1111/j.1752-0606.1990.tb00845.x

Gladding, S. T. (1998). Structural family therapy. In *Family therapy: History, theory and practice* (pp. 209–228). New York: Prentice Hall.

Gladding, S. T. (2010). *Family therapy: History, theory, and practice* (5th ed.). Upper Saddle River, NJ: Pearson Education.

Grossman, J. A., Poznanski, E. O., & Banegas, M. E. (1983). Lunch: Time to study family interactions. *Journal of Psychosocial Nursing and Mental Health Services, 21*, 19–22.

Hammond, R. T., & Nichols, M. P. (2008). How collaborative is structural family therapy? Counseling and therapy for couples and families. *Family Journal, 16*(2), 118–124.

Jones S. L. (1980). *Family therapy.* Bowie, MD: Brady.

McFarlane, W., Dixon, L., Lukens, E., & Lucksted, A. (2003). Family psychoeducation and schizophrenia: A review of the literature. *Journal of Marital & Family Therapy, 29*, 223–245.

McGoldrick, M. (1989). Women through the family life cycle. In M. McGoldrick, C. M. Anderson, & F. Walsh (Eds.), *Women in families: A framework for family therapy* (pp. 200–226). New York: Norton.

Miller, W. R., & Rollnick, S. (2013). *Motivational interviewing: Helping people change.* New York: Guilford Press.

Minuchin, S. (1974). *Families and family therapy.* Cambridge, MA: Harvard University Press.

Minuchin, S., & Fishman, H. C. (1981). *Family therapy techniques.* Cambridge, MA: Harvard University Press.

Minuchin, S., & Montalvo, B. (1967). *Families of the slums: An exploration of their structure and treatment*. New York: Basic Books.

Minuchin, S., Reiter, M., & Borda, C. (2013). *The craft of family therapy: Challenging certainties*. New York: Taylor and Francis.

Minuchin Center for Family Studies. (2012). About structural family therapy. Minuchin Center for the Family. Retrieved from http://www.minuchincenter.org/about_sft

Napoliello, A. L., & Sweet, E. S. (1992). Salvador Minuchin's structural family therapy and its application to Native Americans. *Family Therapy, 19*, 155–165.

Nichols, M. P. (2013). *Family therapy: Concepts and methods* (10th ed.). Upper Saddle River, NJ: Pearson Education.

Rosman, B. L., Minuchin, S., & Liebman, R. (1975). Family lunch session: An introduction to family therapy in anorexia nervosa. *American Journal of Orthopsychiatry, 45*(5), 846–853.

Schultz, S. J. (1984). *Family systems therapy: An integration*. New York: Aronson.

Zaken-Greenberg, F., & Neimeyer, G. J. (1986). The impact of structural family therapy training on conceptual and executive therapy skills. *Family Process, 25*, 599–608.

CHAPTER 12

Becoming, Genuineness, and Open Communication: The Experiential Family Therapies

Michael Walsh, Mark B. Scholl, Angela Catena, and Hannah Bowers

"Being the "best you can be" is really only possible when you are deeply connected to another. Splendid isolation is for planets, not people. "

—Susan Johnson

I gazed up into the planetarium, amazed at the complex nature of the universe and the breathtaking beauty of the planetary structures. I was at once dazzled and suddenly wistful. I sighed and looked down at the empty seat next to me. I had often come to this place with my best friend. We would sit and gaze at the planets or wander the museum, rarely talking and quite comfortable with the silence. There was no need to talk or to have a plan of any sort. We'd know when it was time to leave and go on to do something else. We were connected. Deeply, comfortably connected. We often knew each other's thoughts with a glance and would make decisions without speaking. This place was better with him ... and somehow diminished without him. You see, he had just moved away, and I was back at this museum for the first time since. Despite

its beauty and mystery, the experience just was not the same without that
deep connection. That's why Johnson's quote above really resonated with me.

—Michael Walsh

This chapter deals with approaches that honor both experience and deep connection. Let's get started!

In Chapter 11 you learned about Minuchin's structural family therapy. You learned about the ways in which families accommodate to new circumstances and the ways in which families can find themselves stuck. Minuchin often spoke of the therapist's joining the family as a transformational experience. Indeed, you learned in both Chapters 2 and 9 that this very joining can be therapeutic. At the center of each of these approaches is a meaningful experience that provides a transformative opportunity. In this chapter, we'll examine therapies that consider the experience a primary therapeutic tool. This group of family therapies have, at their very core, a belief that a genuine experience is at the heart of therapeutic change. According to these approaches, the best way to truly grow is to engage fully with other human beings and to fully experience the physical, emotional and cognitive shifts that come with that experience. In this way, participants gain a personal touchstone on which they may base further growth and change.

In Chapter 2 you learned about Virginia Satir. This chapter will go into a great deal more depth on Satir's human validation model and other experiential family approaches. Whether it is Carl Whitaker's use of playful thinking and metaphor to help the family accept themselves and to frame desired change, Satir's family sculpture and reconstruction, or Greenberg and Johnson's emotionally focused family therapy, each contains an experience that aims to allow for the family to connect with genuine emotional resonance, to make new meaning of that experience, and to explore meaningful alternatives. In this way, the experiential family therapies base their interventions in the humanistic belief that human beings and families are inclined toward positive change, are best able to make that change when they can genuinely experience the world around them, and when they have the opportunity to become their best selves.

LEARNING OBJECTIVES

After reading this chapter, you will be able to do the following:

- Understand, describe and apply Carl Whitaker's symbolic-experiential family therapy to conceptualize cases and to design effective marriage and family therapy interventions.

- Understand, describe and apply Virginia Satir's human validation model to conceptualize cases and to design effective marriage and family therapy interventions.

- Understand, describe, and apply Greenberg and Johnson's emotionally focused family therapy model to conceptualize cases and to design effective marriage and family therapy interventions.

PROFILE OF MAIN FIGURES

Carl Whitaker

Early background. In Chapter 2 you briefly learned about Carl Whitaker (1912–1995) and some of his significant accomplishments. Here we will focus on his journey in more detail. He grew up on a dairy farm in upstate New York near the town of Raymondville. Biographer John Neill observed that his family, typical of families who farm for a living, was characterized as being emotionally reserved, and as a result, Whitaker was socially introverted and made a concerted effort to form close friendships with the two of the most popular boys in his high school. An additional positive influence on his social development was his outgoing mother who at one time aspired to becoming a nurse. Further, Whitaker's Calvinist religious upbringing exerted a powerful influence on his personality, including his steadfast belief that "work could provide a sort of salvation, [and] he could "make something" of himself" (Neill & Kniskern, 1982, p. 2).

Medical school training. Whitaker attended the Syracuse University medical school from 1993 to 1936. After a 2-year residency at New York's City Hospital specializing in obstetrics and gynecology, he developed an intense desire to know more about the psychiatric specialization. As a result, he made the unconventional decision to spend the final year of his residency at the Syracuse Psychopathic Hospital (Neill & Kniskern, 1982).

Also highly relevant to his later career, in 1940, he moved with his wife, Muriel to a nearby private hospital in Canandaigua, New York, where he served in the role of assistant physician (Neill & Kniskern, 1982). Brigham Hall was typical of inpatient Mental Hospitals of the day, as the conditions were harsh. However, Neill observed that Whitaker had a rare capacity for spending long periods of time with the psychotic patients as well as viewing them as individuals struggling with the challenges of life that all of us face.

During the period from 1936 to 1940, Whitaker participated in his own psychoanalysis. In 1941 he completed his master's thesis in psychology, titled *Without Psychosis: Chronic Alcoholism: A Follow-Up Study*. At the time, many clinical practitioners believed that organic abnormalities such as tumors were the root cause of psychoses. In his thesis, Whitaker expressed his belief that psychoses were caused by immaturity or disintegration and as a result were treatable through psychotherapy (Neill & Kniskern, 1982).

Oak Ridge, Tennessee—counseling employees working on the atomic bomb. At the beginning of World War II, Whitaker was assigned to a position counseling employees assigned to Eric Clarke's group at the top secret atom bomb project. The psychiatric staff was responsible for supporting the mental health of the workers who were under considerable stress. Whitaker had a heavy case load and employed a nondirective approach that included long silences. These silences were viewed as productive for promoting the accumulation of therapy material (Neill & Kniskern, 1982).

Indicative of Whitaker's psychodynamic orientation, he responded in a permissive manner when an employee in treatment seized a full baby bottle left from a child therapy session and began nursing from the bottle. Whitaker believed that the bottle was a symbol of the worker's need to regress as well as to experience nurturance and acceptance. In effect, the individual needed to regress before he had the ability to "grow up." Whitaker also observed that this case coincided with an internal struggle over whether he could accept his own "craziness" regarding the unorthodox approach to treatment (Neill & Kniskern, 1982).

Finally, Oak Ridge marked the time when the therapist became acutely aware of the need for close professional relationships in his life. At Oak Ridge he met John Warkentin, who was to serve as his cotherapist for the next 20 years. Another colleague Whitaker met there was Thomas Malone, who shared a keen interest in psychoanalytic therapy. Whitaker, Warkentin, and Malone were close friends who formed a creative team and produced many collaborative professional publications (Neill, 1982, p. 9).

Theory development and key concepts: Symbolic-experiential family therapy. Whitaker's unique approach, known as symbolic-experiential family therapy (SEFT), is a synthesis of the psychoanalytic emphasis on symbolism with the existential perspective's emphasis on the potential therapeutic influence of experiences. Whitaker (1989) believed that a wide variety of daily experiences including conversations, playing sports, joining groups, and dating, to name a few, can be therapeutic. In SEFT, the therapist is responsible for bringing about these therapeutic experiences (Smith, 1998). Once the family has had a therapeutic experience, the symbolic meaning they attach to their experience indicates that therapeutic change has occurred (Smith, 1998).

In addition, families commonly present with their own symbols or symbolic language and the therapist operating from an SEFT orientation will seek to understand the family's symbols. As needed, the therapist will introduce one or more symbols intentionally selected for their power to promote therapeutic changes. To comprehend SEFT, it is important to understand the **therapeutic relationship, major constructs**, and **goals** inherent to this approach.

The Therapeutic Relationship and Premises of the Theory

In her book *Mastering Competence in Family Therapy*, Diane Gehart (2013) discussed the nature of the therapeutic relationship in SEFT. Emphasis is placed on the therapist's authentic use of self as well as encouraging (or even pushing) the client to be authentic. Consistent with existential perspective, Whitaker insisted that clients should accept full responsibility for their choices and behaviors. He believed that the therapeutic relationship should be mutually growth producing for the counselor and the clients. Regarding interpersonal style, he recommended a balance between challenging and supporting clients. For this reason, he commonly worked with a supportive cotherapist who could provide the balance for his confrontational style. Finally, he was an advocate for both family unity and the development of each family member's development of individuality.

KEY CONCEPTS

Because of his early experiences with psychoanalysis, Whitaker held a belief that thoughts, feelings, and actions were often symbolic manifestations of the unconscious. Whitaker also applied existential principles to family therapy. Key concepts in SEFT include **symbolism and metaphor, battle for structure, battle for initiative, craziness,** and **flight into health. Symbolism** refers to the unconscious or latent meaning of manifest behaviors or figurative language used by the clients and counselor. **Battle for structure** refers to conflict between the counselor and client regarding the parameters or rules that the counselor establishes for counseling practice. **Battle for initiative** refers to conflict between the counselor and client regarding the direction therapy will take (Whitaker & Keith, 1981). **Craziness** is Whitaker's term for the divergent, creative, and playful thinking that is used to solve problems in therapy (Wetchler & Piercy, 1996). **Flight into health** is Whitaker's term for a family's tendency to prematurely terminate therapy once their anxiety has been reduced (Whitaker & Ryan, 1989). Whitaker did not discourage such flights into health because he believed this was a positive sign the family had become more cohesive, and they would return if they needed additional therapy. Let's turn our attention to Guided Practice Exercise 12.1, in which we'll work on building skills in the development of effective metaphors. As you may recall, we did some work on this in Chapter 11. We'll take a deeper dive here with a focus on using your own life a guide.

GUIDED PRACTICE EXERCISE 12.1: CONCEPTUALIZING: BUILDING SKILLS IN METAPHOR DEVELOPMENT

Central to the development of skill in symbolic-experiential family therapy, as well as the human validation model is the use of metaphor with clients. For some, this skill comes naturally. For others, it takes some practice. This Guided Practice Exercise is designed to help you to sharpen your skills in the development of metaphor by asking you to think about your own life and see if you can find a central metaphor of your own.

1. Think back on your own life. Think of a story from your very early past that stands out to you. We usually remember those stories from way back because they speak to us about who we are and they capture a central theme or belief that we hold about ourselves. What are the themes that you see? Jot down some words that pop to mind.

2. Look at this list of words. Is there one (or a phrase) that "feels" like a good fit? Does that word tell a story or suggest that it captures a theme in your life? If so, this may be a good central metaphor for you.

    (For example, I remember a long walk I took—by myself—at about 6 years old. I wandered off from my grandparents' house in Philadelphia and had a blast of a time wandering around the neighborhood. My family was not amused, but I had a grand adventure that day! For me, that would be a fitting central metaphor for my life: the grand adventure.)

3. What metaphor can you think of that captures a theme in your life? Think about this central metaphor for a moment. How does it influence and/or inform you? How might it influence and/or inform your work with families?

Major Goals and Role of the Therapist

Whitaker and Keith (1981) described some of the goals of SEFT. They stated that SEFT entails goals at both the individual and systems levels. They sought to cultivate an increased sense of belonging and cohesion among the family unit, and to also promote an increased sense of individuality and self-actualization for each family member. They sought to increase the creativity of the family system as well as the creativity of individual members.

Additional goals relate to the terms **battle for structure** and **battle for initiative**. Whitaker believed it was important for the counselor to win the battle for structure to provide the necessary facilitative conditions and supporting ground rules for therapy to succeed. At the same time, he believed it was important for the clients to win the battle for initiative and determine the course of therapy (Gerhart, 2013). If the clients won the battle for initiative, it was more likely they would be invested and do most of the work required for therapy to succeed. Let's turn our attention to Case Presentation 12.1

CASE PRESENTATION 12.1: USING BASKETBALL IN THERAPY

Whitaker used the term *craziness* to describe the type of interaction in which the therapist can use humor, metaphor and/or the language of the client to enhance outcomes.

In this illustration, a therapist notes that his clients seem to be basketball fans. In fact, two are wearing a basketball jersey. This family has been reticent and very reluctant to embrace creative problem solving. This gives the therapist an idea.

Therapist: What say we take this session outside today? In fact, let's take it to the basketball courts. I have an idea.

(Confused looks around the room.)

Mom: Uh, OK, I guess.

(The family packs up and meets at the local public courts. The therapist retrieves a basketball from his trunk.)

Therapist: OK. I think this may work. You ready to play?

Dad: I guess so … but what is this all about?

Therapist: You'll see. Let's just have some fun. Mom and Dad, you're on team A, kids, you're on team B. Here's the trick. Each time you shoot, you've burned your possession. It's the other team's ball whether it goes in or not. Here's the other trick: You can only hold the ball for 10 seconds each, so keep passing. Ready? Go!

(Both teams quickly figure out, after many blown whistles and penalties called, that the key to success is sharing the ball, passing, and using teamwork to set up the best possible shot. Soon, what started as a mundane activity has family members laughing and collaborating. That game ends, and the therapist processes the experience with the family. Once the processing is done, the therapist moves to reinforce coping fluency.)

Therapist: OK. So, here's the question: How are you guys going to share the ball and collaborate at home? I'm going to randomly pass the ball to someone and you've gotta come up with an idea quick. Ready? Go!

(The therapist uses the metaphor of basketball, an experiential activity and a time pressured activity to help the family to build fluency in problem solving ... all with an unconventional, experiential, and fun-based approach.)

Carl Whitaker: In His Own Words

Whitaker believed that the very best therapists showed adaptability and flexibility when they could collaborate with each other. He also felt that flexibility and adaptability were key components to healthy functioning. Here are his words on those subjects:

> ***Whitaker on the cotherapist role.*** *"For a practitioner, the use of a co-therapist not only dramatically extends the range of therapeutic technique, but it fosters growth in both co-therapists as well"* (Whitaker, 1971, p.293) .

> ***Whitaker on flexibility and healthy functioning.*** *"It is not necessary to be immature in order to have irrelevant, free-associative fantasy components ... as Rioch (1944) said many years ago, 'Maturity is the capacity to be immature'"* (Whitaker & Keith, 1981, p. 222).

Virginia Satir

Personal background and family history. Much of Satir's theoretical orientation was based in her own background and experience. Virginia Satir was born on June 26, 1916, to Oscar and Minnie Pagenkopf in Neillsville, Wisconsin. Virginia's parents, as well as her

German immigrant grandparents, would become central figures in the development of her theory in years to come.

At 5 years old, Virginia developed appendicitis. Her mother, a devoutly religious Christian Scientist, initially refused to take Virginia to a hospital. After some time, at her father's insistence, Virginia was taken to the hospital and admitted. In the meantime, however, Virginia's appendix had ruptured, and she was forced to spend several months in the hospital.

Interestingly, Satir never blamed her mother for her extended illness. Rather, she sought to understand her mother's actions in the context of her mother's frame of reference. More specifically, she sought to understand her mother's actions in light of the seeming contradiction between her mother's clear love for her and the decision driven by her mother's religious faith. This led to an intense curiosity on Virginia's part to better understand the motivations of others. In relating the story, which she did often, she spoke of a decision that she made at age 5 to be "a children's detective of parents." In her words: "I didn't quite know what I would look for, but I realized a lot went on in families that didn't meet the eye" (Satir, 1988, p. 17).

This search for context and understanding was to become a hallmark of both her theoretical approach and her work with families. Satir would time and again return to her own family experiences to guide her theoretical development. Satir often told the story of her grandmothers, both from privileged backgrounds, marrying working-class men. Satir initially postulated that this breach of social norms likely led her grandparents to emigrate to the United States. Satir's own mother also made a choice to marry a working-class man. She later came to believe that this choice on the part of her mother may have been the root of a feeling of inadequacy on the part of her father, who often had difficulty expressing emotions. He would often clearly be upset, yet he would claim that everything was just fine. Satir believed her father's reluctance to express emotion was the result of his feelings of inadequacy based on his past generational shame. She would often use this story to illustrate how individual understanding and context impact human decisions (King, 1989).

Satir believed firmly in the power of metaphor and would often include stories from her own background as metaphorical "playgrounds" for use in sessions with families. One story is particularly illustrative of her ability to draw from her past to help a family in the present. Having grown up on a farm, Virginia's family often used what was at hand for its most practical purpose at that very moment. One such item was a large black iron pot in which her family stored various things. In some parts of the year, it was used to store soap, and in other parts of the year, store manure. Said Satir: "We came to call it the '3-S pot.' Anyone who wanted to use the pot faced two questions: What is the pot now full of, and how full is it?" (Satir, 1983, p.285). This story became a metaphor that was occasionally used in sessions with families. One family, in particular, adopted the metaphor of the pot to express the feelings each carried. Satir would continue the use of metaphor as a therapeutic tool throughout her career.

Premise of the Theory

Virginia Satir's (1916–1988) human validation process model is based primarily on the ideal that human beings fully develop to their potential. To develop fully, individuals must fully and genuinely experience life. This means being able to genuinely feel the full range of our emotions and be honest with ourselves and our loved ones about what we feel. The freer we are to feel and express those feelings, the better our relationships will function.

Satir also believed that the foundation for these emotional skill sets, as well as the "unwritten rules" around which we feel and express emotion are established by families. At times, these established, unwritten rules regarding emotion and emotional expression are healthy and help us adapt to our changing circumstances and environments. There are other times when these rules do not serve people as well as they could and other ways of coping and adapting are called for. This situation leads to lower self-esteem and lower confidence in our ability to adapt to challenging situations.

Fundamental to Satir's approach is the idea that the overall coping style can be most influenced by the relationship between the key parental figures. Families, she found, come to adopt and/or are heavily influenced by the complex series of perceptions, social expectations, and anticipated behavior patterns modeled by parental figures. This complex chain forms the basis for the family's overall coping style.

According to Satir, we are often unaware of the ways in which these unwritten rules impact us, our coping styles, and our coping strategies. The role of the therapist is to shed light on these complex patterns, the ways in which they may influence our coping styles and strategies, and to help the family begin to explore alternative patterns of feeling, expression, communication, and ways of being. Because these complex patterns are each interdependent, Satir believed it was critical that any intervention utilized be directed at the full family, as opposed to individual members. This was a very different approach from the more accepted approaches of Satir's time. In this way, the human validation model approach became one of the first true family therapies.

Satir also believed the most important aspect of life was not "what happens" but rather how one copes with what happens. For that reason, perhaps the most fundamental concept in the human validation model is the connection between learning new and more adaptive ways of being within the world and the maximization of human potential.

Satir believed that the development of new and adaptive skills begins with the family unit. More specifically, it begins with the ability of family members to genuinely feel and express the full range of their emotions and thereby build better relationships, leading to better self-esteem and enhanced coping skills for family members.

Key Concepts

Triad as the primary learning vehicle. Satir often expressed the idea that the **triad** was the primary learning vehicle in human development. By triad, she meant the relationships between the primary couple within the family (parents) and the children. According to Satir, it is the complex series of assumptions and interdependent communication and relational styles among these people in the family that form the basis of learned coping strategies employed by family members (Satir, 1983, p.117). If a family is struggling, it is the coping style that has become disordered, as opposed to the individuals within the family. As such, any intervention should be directed at the entire family unit rather than to individual members alone.

Satir went on to note that families can often be unaware of the effects that these coping styles may have on their everyday lives precisely because they have grown so accustomed to utilizing them and because individuals often can only see the world subjectively through their own experiential lens. Often, it takes an "outsider" to help us to see these things. As with many things, Satir describes this concept with a metaphor: "Everyone has a back, yes? But how many of us have ever seen our back? Plenty of other people see our backs, yet we do not.… It points out the absurdity of thinking that the only things that there are in the world are the things that we can see in it" (Satir, 1988).

The role of the therapist, then, becomes pointing those patterns and strategies out as they arise and helping the family to explore alternatives. In this way, the therapist becomes a guide and facilitator and allows the family to retain its own expertise. This focus on family autonomy, compassion, and the development of adaptive decision-making skills within the family is central to the human validation model.

Self-esteem. Self-esteem, Satir believed, was "value neutral" and could either be positive or negative. Self-esteem could be a clue, Satir, reasoned to a person's overall coping strategy. Positive self-esteem tends to be a sign of good, adaptive coping strategies and confidence in handling life's challenges. Low self-esteem tends to be a sign of less effective coping strategies. It is important to note that Satir saw self-esteem as an individually defined and socially learned construct within each person's own social and emotional context. The person's own estimation of their level of self-esteem, Satir (1972) believed, was a good indicator of that person's inner thought processes as well as their interactions with others. Self-esteem is gathered, according to Satir, from social and family-learned norms, family behaviors and parental comments. Because so much of self-esteem is socially constructed, Satir held that self-esteem is malleable, even well into adulthood. Helping people build self-esteem by building confidence in new and more adaptive ways of coping becomes a key role for the therapist.

Communication and maturation. Satir placed a premium on communication. So much so, in fact, that she called communication "a huge umbrella that covers and affects all that goes on between human beings" (Satir, 1988, p. 30). On an individual level, Satir went on to suggest that an individual's communication style could be a clue to the person's level of maturity.

Examples of immature communication styles include the use of sweeping generalizations, using terms such as *always* and *never*, or a strict adherence to dichotomous and absolutist terms such as *right* and *wrong*. These represent a divisive and divergent pattern of thinking that does not lend itself to interpersonal effectiveness.

Examples of mature individual communication styles, according to Satir, are found among people who seek to first learn from others before delivering judgements, and in people who seek dialogue as opposed to conflict. This allows the individual the freedom to realize his own potential by maximizing his interactions with others. Satir believed this to be especially important within the family. Let's turn to Guided Practice Exercise 12.2, in which you will have the opportunity to practice assessing your own communication style. This can be especially critical when working with Satir's human validation model, in which the goal is congruent and consistent communication patterns. Let's jump in!

GUIDED PRACTICE EXERCISE 12.2: ASSESSING YOUR OWN COMMUNICATION STYLE

Central to the development of skills in any experiential family therapy is the ability to assess and recognize different communication styles. For example, if you encounter a client who uses broad, sweeping terms to describe herself and world (the most, the best, etc.), and many "absolute" terms (I always do this … I never do that, etc.), you are likely working with someone whose communication style is based largely in her own judgment. This exercise will help you build skills in recognizing different communication styles, starting with your own.

1. Grab a recording device. Grab a friend or two. Tell them you are doing a project and you just want to record yourself having a conversation. Note: it is important to tell folks that you are doing this. Depending on your state and state law, you may legally need to gain permission from someone before recording a conversation with them! Either way, letting people know is a nice thing to do. Try to have as natural a conversation as you can. If you can, record long enough that you forget the recorder is on.

2. Listen to the recording. Pay attention to phrases that you say repeatedly. For example, when I have done this experiment, I hear myself say, "We'll see" a good bit. I also hear myself say, "Let's see what happens" an awful lot. These repeated phrases are indicators of my communication pattern. I am a wait-and-see guy! I subscribe to the theory that I have two ears and only one mouth … which is a gentle hint: Listen more and talk less! As you listen to your recording, see what phrases and patterns that you notice. What do they tell you about your communication style?

3. Listen to your family's communications. Try to notice if they have open communication styles or closed communication styles. Note: There is no perfect family out there! Some of the best therapists and counselors have come from families who had challenges. There is no wrong way to get to be a good counselor. Everyone and every family has growing edges, so no penalty for any answer here. This is just for your own development in recognizing styles!

Genuine caring and role of the therapist. A critical aspect of the human validation model and the search for a family's full potential, according to Satir, was the relationship between the therapist and the family (Satir & Bitter, 2000). Satir's approach calls for genuine caring on the part of the therapist and open communication between the therapist and the family. This caring and the resulting caring, congruent relationship makes possible the spontaneity, risk taking, and emotional experiencing within the counseling relationship. Satir believed that to develop a human being's full potential, that individual had to be free to genuinely experience and express the full range of his or her emotions.

This, according to Satir (1988), applied to the family unite. The freer each human being is to experience and express emotion in each relationship, the better the relationship will function. Fundamental to the human validation model was the human capacity to realize full potential by learning new and more adaptive ways of being.

Virginia Satir: In Her Own Words

Satir placed a strong emphasis on the role that coping strategies play in the success of a family. Satir also saw the parental unit as a primary driver in the development of healthy and adaptive children. She felt that the best way to achieve that is with true and genuine experience, honesty and communication that is congruent with the actual lived experience. Here are her own words on the subjects:

> ***Satir on coping.*** *"Problems are not the problem; coping is the problem. Coping is the outcome of self-worth, rules of the family systems, and links to the outside world"* (as cited in Andreas, 1991, p. 40).

> ***Satir on parenting.*** *"In the nurturing family ... parents see themselves as empowering leaders not as authoritative bosses. They see their job primarily as one of teaching their children how to be truly human in all situations. They readily acknowledge to the child their poor judgment as well as their good judgment; their hurt, anger, or disappointment as well as their joy. The behavior of these parents matches what they say"* (Satir, 1988, p. 15).

SUSAN JOHNSON AND LES GREENBERG

Early background. Susan Johnson grew up in Kent, England. Johnson reports having grown up in a pub and having been fascinated by the dynamics of couples courting, dating, and interacting. Later, while in her doctoral program, she gravitated to working with couples and reported being immediately enthralled by the delicate nature of the balance between two people. "It's not just about one person's issues. It's a dance that happens between people, these relationships" (Johnson, 2009, p.412). Susan went on to study drama in her undergraduate work, continuing her fascination with human beings and the expression of emotion. After earning her doctorate, she became increasingly interested in working with families. Johnson went on to connect Bowlby's attachment theory to her work with families, eventually formulating emotionally focused therapy (EFT).

Leslie S. Greenberg was born in Johannesburg, South Africa, in 1945. A strong-willed child, he also reported being quite anxious as his family worked through many financial crises. This inherent duality would surface in years to come as he continued to explore what was possible while questioning the status quo. This came to a head at the age of 22.

The army days. Having been drafted into the South African army but being philosophically opposed to apartheid, Greenberg and his wife, Brenda, left South Africa to further their educations and to escape the South African secret police, who reportedly maintained a file on his protest activities. This sense of what was possible versus what existed continued to inform Greenberg as he questioned the status quo. Having studied engineering in college, he made the switch to psychology to formally study his interest, the contrast between "rational" thinking and intuition.

Person-centered mentoring. His mentor during his doctoral studies was Laura Rice, who studied with Carl Rogers at the University of Chicago. Greenberg grew fascinated with the complex ways in which people worked through problems and sought a deeper understanding of emotional processing. It was at this intersection of person-centered emotional processing and problem solving that his career would evolve (APA, 2012).

Greenberg would meet Susan Johnson in 1986 at York University in Toronto, and the two would go on to develop EFT, an innovative intervention for couples that was based in part on Bowlby's theory of attachment (1969, 1982, 1988) and Rogers's person-centered approach.

Theory Development and Key Concepts: Attachment and Emotion

Bowlby's attachment theory (1969, 1982, 1988) is particularly significant in EFT. Bowlby's research dealt with the idea that a human being's most fundamental, basic need is meaningful attachment and relationship with another human being. Johnson postulated that these themes of attachment express themselves best in relationships in the form of emotion. Thus, the primacy of emotion in EFT is a direct reflection of the quality of the attachment between the family and the therapist.

Bowlby (1969, 1982) stressed that if we are better able to understand the environment in which an individual or family forms relationships, we can better understand the emotional reaction of the person, as well as their behavior. In this way, Johnson (2009) asserts, we can have a pathology-free and judgement-free understanding of a family's behavior. In other words, if the therapist can understand a family's context, we are free to accept the family's behavior as a reasonable adaptation to that reality. This allows for a more genuine attachment and emotional connection on the part of the therapist and family, thereby facilitating a good working alliance.

Johnson goes on to point out that research into attachment (Mikulincer, 1995) predicts that securely attached adults would have a more positive sense of self. Translating this same idea to families, Johnson postulates that securely attached families will be healthier, more productive and better able to adapt to life changes and stressors (Johnson, 2009). Thus, the development of relationship and attachment are at the core of EFT.

Humanistic Roots and Premises of EFT

In addition to Greenberg's influence, Johnson also believed in the Rogerian (Rogers, 1961) concept of human tendency toward growth and development. As mentioned at the top of our chapter's exploration, this humanistic idea that human beings are inclined toward growth is central to the experiential therapies. EFT is no exception. Johnson (2009) asserts that strong attachment and a good therapeutic relationship helps to facilitate and enhance this natural growth process. Dysfunction (being unhealthy) is seen in these circles as being a "disconnect" between experienced emotion and the ability to process that emotion and merge with meaningful alternatives. EFT is designed to highlight the importance and experience of genuine emotion and emotional exploration.

Transformative Emotional Experiences

Like Satir's concept of transformative moments, Johnson (2009) asserts that there are key moments within family counseling that allow families and couples to take new risks with expressing emotion and thus discover new attachment themes that allow for different ways of relating. Johnson, like Satir, believes that these Transformative experiences are at the heart of therapeutic growth. Greenberg (2012) agrees, indicating the best way to change emotions is by providing clients and families opportunities to first feel those emotions, and then to process them.

Role of the Therapist

The role of the therapist in EFT is to identify and amplify the role that emotion and attachment play within the primary relationship. As noted above, the goal is to allow couples and families opportunities to genuinely experience the emotional and attachment patterns that are present. The therapist seeks to help the couple or family to identify the ways in which emotion is expressed (or not expressed) and the ways in which that emotion impacts the relationship(s). In this way, the couple or family can make better decisions about altering the ways in which they interact, emote, and communicate.

Susan Johnson: In Her Own Words

Johnson and Greenberg hold that attachment is the best way to conceptualize human relationships, that curiosity leads to flexible and adaptive thinking, and that the best way to a successful relationship is to embrace a genuine experience of emotion. Here are their words on those subjects:

> ***Johnson on attachment.*** *"The first and foremost instinct of humans is neither sex nor aggression. It is to seek contact and comforting connection" (Johnson, 2013, p. 18).*

Johnson on curiosity. *"Curiosity comes out of a sense of safety; rigidity out of being vigilant to threats" (Johnson, 2008, p. 12).*

Les Greenberg: In His Own Words

Greenberg on emotion. *"Emotions are seen as crucial in motivating behavior...To help people change what they think, therapists must help them change what they feel" (Greenberg, 2011 p. 6).*

Greenberg on genuineness. *"We need to live in mindful harmony with our feelings, not attempt to control them" (Greenberg & Paivio 1997, p. 25).*

ASSESSMENT AND CASE CONCEPTUALIZATION PROCESSES IN EXPERIENTIAL THERAPIES

Whitaker's Symbolic-Experiential Family Therapy Example

The Family Crucible **(Napier & Whitaker, 1978).** While working as a professor of psychiatry at the University of Wisconsin, Carl Whitaker mentored August Napier, an intern enrolled in the PhD psychology program at the University of North Carolina. Napier and Whitaker coauthored *The Family Crucible* in 1978. The book, based on their cotherapy with a family, provides a memorable illustration of Whitaker's unique approach to family therapy known as symbolic-experiential family therapy (Scholl, Perepiczka, & Walsh, 2015). In this section, we provide examples from *The Family Crucible* to illustrate four principles that are integral to Whitaker's SEFT.

Battle for structure. Whitaker believed it was important for the family therapist to win the **battle for structure** by establishing authoritative control early in the process (Wetchler & Piercy, 1996). In *The Family Crucible*, cotherapist Napier observed that one of the ways Whitaker attempted to win this battle was by insisting that the first family therapy session not begin until all the family members were present. The Brice family members consist of the parents, David and Carolyn, and their three children: Claudia, Don, and Laura. Claudia is at high risk of committing suicide and is the identified patient in the family.

Symbolism and metaphors. Carl Whitaker's background in psychoanalysis had significant implications for his approach to family therapy. For example, he believed that a statement or behavior made by a family member had both a literal meaning and a latent or symbolic meaning (Whitaker & Ryan, 1989). He sought to uncover the unconscious or latent meaning underlying observable behaviors. Similarly, he believed that metaphor reflected unconscious symbolic content that were useful for understanding the unstated assumptions and rules of family members (Davies, 2011).

A powerful example of the significance of metaphor in SEFT can be found in a session in *The Family Crucible* in which the husband (David) criticizes the wife (Carolyn), and she begins crying. Whitaker told the family that at one point in the argument, David was transformed into a symbol representing Carolyn's critical mother. At this point, the argument reached an impasse because Carolyn was unable to contend with her critical mother. For the couple to arrive at a constructive resolution to the argument, they would have to encounter each other on a here-and-now authentic level as husband and wife.

Symbolic language or verbal play. Whitaker believed that most close families developed symbolic language that reflected their rules and assumptions. To bring about change, he would introduce metaphors that could potentially promote healthier family functioning (Connell, 1996). For example, in working with the Brice family, Whitaker and Napier recognize a characteristic pattern of arguing between the mother, Carolyn, and the identified patient, Claudia. Each of the two viewed the other as the source of the problem and the instigator. To counter the unhealthy tendency of the members of the Brice family to label one another as the problem, the cotherapists used the metaphor of the family dance to describe the argument and the roles played by the entire family in patterns the argument took. In this way they encouraged the family to view the problem as family-wide and one that would require teamwork to resolve (Napier & Whitaker, 1978).

Later in therapy with the family, Whitaker and Napier used metaphor to encourage the family to become more flexible in their roles. They introduced the notion that David and Carolyn lacked intimacy because David was "having an affair" with his work and Carolyn was "having an affair" with her mother. In other words, rather than asking for more closeness directly, David and Carolyn attempted to make one another jealous as an indirect way of getting their needs met. At this point in the therapeutic relationship, this approach did not effectively lead to David and Carolyn using more direct communication to have their needs met. Instead, reflecting the rigidity of the family members' roles, David and Carolyn engaged in a heated argument, loudly accusing each other of being selfish.

Capacity for Engaging in Playful or Metaphorical Thinking

Whitaker used divergent, playful, creative thinking he termed **craziness** to help families solve problems (Wetchler & Piercy, 1996; Whitaker & Keith, 1981). He employed this approach to model flexible creative thinking, to assess the family's capacity for this type of thinking, and to nudge the family into using this approach to solve their problems. For example, the cotherapists refer to the **influence** that Carolyn's mother has on Carolyn's relationship with her daughter as "grandmother's ghost." They tell her that her critical mother has a powerful impact on her parenting style and her relationship with her family members. Carolyn, they assert, derived a vicarious satisfaction from her daughter's rebellious behavior because she did not have the courage to rebel against her own mother.

They believed that understanding this influence exerted by "grandmother's ghost" made it possible for Carolyn to break the behavior pattern she previously did not understand.

Another example of this sort of playful thinking was a suggestion that the family "democratize their fighting." To function as a better team, the fights should be more evenly distributed among the family members. Why weren't Carolyn and David fighting? Why weren't family members criticizing Don or Laura? Although, Whitaker explained that conflict does not have to be expressed through yelling, and he did not condone children degrading their parents, he did believe that more flexible rules for the expression of conflict among family members would make for a healthier family system.

Satir's Human Validation Model Example

Looking for blockage of communication and/or expression. Fundamental to Satir's assessment style was a focus on evaluating the existing communication patterns within the family. As you may recall from Chapter 7, this is a primary function of family therapy assessment; evaluation and consideration of presenting issues as potential therapeutic factors.

Families with functional communication styles, according to Satir (1988) are families with clear, easy-to-understand communication rules. These **open communication patterns** are characterized by genuine exchanges of ideas and emotion, encouragement of the exploration of new and different ideas, and experiences outside of the family. Those rules, although clear, are flexible enough to shift with circumstances and allow the family to adapt to changing circumstances. Each family member is encouraged to explore and fully experience the world and family members communicate openly and fully all that is felt and experienced.

Families with dysfunctional communication patterns operate on distorted or dishonest communications that can be less than complete representations of what is truly being felt. These systems are characterized by **closed communication patterns, family secrets** and/or **family myths**.

Family secrets tend to lead to distrust and less willingness for members to be honest with each other. This pattern of less than complete communication can ripple across families, leading to less information exchange. According to Satir and Baldwin (1983), these secrets are often used to protect the image of the parents or family and are justified with statements such as "The kids are too young to understand" or "What you don't know won't hurt you." Family secrets are often used to perpetuate:

Family myths often exist, such as "Your father is not an alcoholic, he just likes to hang out with his friends at bars" or "Your mother did not spend time in prison, she was staying with her sister in Utah." The thinking is that the less that kids know about "skeletons" in the family closet, the better. The challenge is that these real events tend to shine through and lead to doubt as to other messages received within the family, breeding distrust and resentments. These secrets and myths can, at times, span generations, and so can be even more complex.

These closed communication patterns do not lend themselves to full and honest expression and leave families less equipped to adapt to changing and/or challenging conditions.

A key part of assessment in human validation work is a thorough examination of communication patterns within the unique context of the family with which the clinician is working.

Family sculpture as an assessment and conceptualization tool. As you may remember from Chapter 7, the assessment process in family therapy can be both therapeutic and informative. Satir believed that visceral experience was an excellent teacher and that a demonstration of family dynamics would help people to better understand them. Satir developed **family sculpture activity** to accomplish this end.

Each family member is encouraged to "**sculpt**" their understanding of the family and the ways in which they relate to each other using the actual family members themselves. Members are encouraged to use physical proximity, stances, facial expressions, even pops such as ropes to demonstrate the ways in which they perceived different family members inter-relating. In this way, the activity becomes an experiential activity for each member. For the "**sculptees**" each gets a real, physical sense of the ways in which each member perceives them and the way that they relate with other members. For the "**sculptor**," he or she has an opportunity to fully express the ways in which he or she sees the family. For the family as a unit, it is an opportunity to explore and understand. For the therapist, it is a golden opportunity to assess family dynamics and perceptions.

Family reconstruction as an assessment and conceptualization tool. Family reconstruction is a technique by which a family has an opportunity to actively search for the lived context of three generations of family (Satir & Baldwin, 1983). Born of Satir's conviction that every action has context and is motivated by a complex set of factors, this exercise was designed to shed new light on family members' actions from years past. It was also designed to help people to see new possibilities for the context behind people's actions, let go of old resentments and perhaps begin to see family members as more fully human actors.

The family is encouraged to learn as much as is possible about three generations of family actions, particularly those of real emotional note. The "**recaller**" is then asked to find out as much as is possible about the possible motivations and context of the people involved in that incident. Then, the family reenacts the drama of those key moments, each contributing perspective as to motivation and context. In this way, Satir believed, family members had a chance to reconnect with one another as human beings with reasons and complex emotions, instead of the ways in which they may have traditionally perceived each other. Satir believed this experiential approach to be one of power and potential for insight.

Parts Parties as an Assessment and Conceptualization Tool. This technique, related to psychodrama, is designed to help to highlight specific characteristics to which a client is either attracted or from which he or she is repelled. This "**Parts Party**" can be based on the individual or the family levels. A family member (or individual client) is asked to identify a person (maybe a famous person or just someone the client knows) that exemplifies a trait. For example, a family member might say: "My friend Matt exemplifies courage and honor. He may make mistakes, but he is going to own those mistakes and make amends, whatever the cost." The family continues to identify people and characteristics. The family is asked to concentrate on those "parts" that are most representative of him or herself or another member of the family. This helps the therapist to identify the specific characteristics that seem of most import to the family.

The family is then asked to invite each of these people to a fictional party. As this party develops, conflict develops between the personalities. According to Satir, these conflicts are likely to represent the ways in which the different aspects of one's personhood interact. The client and therapist work together to resolve these conflicts as they arise. The development and eventual resolution of that conflict was thought to be both instructive from an assessment standpoint and therapeutic from a clinical standpoint.

Greenberg and Johnson's EFT Case Presentation

Central to the assessment process of EFT is the identification of negative interactional attachment cycles inherent in the relationship. To identify these cycles, the therapist tracks and reflects to the couple or family the cycles she hears (Johnson, & Greenberg, 1994).

For example:

Therapist: (Turning to the husband.) When your wife made the comment, upon arriving home, that he was disappointed that you hadn't gotten more done, you just shut her out because it hurt too much to hear that kind of disappointment from someone whose opinion is really important to you. (Turning to the wife.) When John shut you out, it felt like a rejection of you, personally, and it also felt like he wasn't listening, so you continued to comment on what he hadn't gotten done. You were angry and hurt and you just wanted him to listen to you.

In this way, the therapist tracks and reflects the interactive patterns that are leading to negative attachment patterns. The therapist identifies the actual emotions experienced, as opposed to the ones that may have been expressed, allowing each member insight into the other's (and their own) actual experience. This allows the client/couple/family to hear those patterns and associate the emotional experience of those negative patterns. The goal of therapy is, once identified and honestly dealt with from an emotional standpoint, the client/couple/family can redesign these interactions, being more honest and genuine in the emotions expressed, and in doing so, develop deeper, more meaningful attachments to each other.

PUTTING IT ALL TOGETHER: WORKING WITH A FAMILY USING EXPERIENTIAL THERAPIES

Carl Whitaker Case Presentation: Symbolic-Experiential Family Therapy

The examples of terms provided below come from a session titled *Therapeutic Three Generation Family Reunion*, in which Whitaker (1990) served as the family therapist.

The quotes were taken directly from the videotape of the family therapy session. The multigenerational Latino family includes the maternal grandmother (Juanita), mother (Elaina), father (Rubin), and their 9-year-old daughter (Rubilita) and 3-year-old son (Ryan). A primary focus of the session is helping the grandmother, with the input and support of Elaina and Ryan, become more flexible regarding her rigid views of her role as a mother and grandmother.

Unorthodox freewheeling interpersonal style. Whitaker's freewheeling interpersonal style reflected his belief in being creative and playful as a means of modeling divergent thinking that was neither rigid nor bound by social convention. Neill (1982) observed that Whitaker affirmed Otto Rank's (1996) notion of the therapist as "creative artist." Such a creative artist creates his own standards from within. As such he distinguishes himself from the neurotic whose will he differs from the approval-seeking neurotic as well as the delinquent whose behavior is indirectly shaped by his need to be defiant. At the beginning of the session, he begins by lying on his side at the feet of the family holding a microphone with his free hand. This posture is consistent with many unconventional suggestions he makes to the family throughout the session.

Modeling fantasy alternatives to real-life stress. Early in the session, Juanita, the grandmother, complained that she was not taken seriously by the other family members. She added that the other family members do not listen to her opinions. Whitaker listened respectfully and paraphrased her concern. A minute later, he suggested that she might go to a public dance with her son-in-law. The grandmother responded that she could never go to a dance because of what people would think. Whitaker (1990) replied, "That is what makes it so much fun." The son-in-law, Rubin, opines that it would be helpful for the grandmother to model playful behavior for their "parental" 9-year-old daughter. This section of the family session illustrates how Whitaker used fantasy to help families expand their emotional life and roles and how he used humor to reduce family members' feelings of anxiety.

Distinguishing Between Interpersonal and Intrapersonal Fantasy Stress

Later in the same session, Whitaker discovered an example of what he might term "fantasy stress." He asked the grandmother, Juanita, whose husband was deceased, if she believed she would ever remarry. She responded that she was too old to consider remarrying. Whitaker asked her how long she thought she had to live, and she ventured that she might have 20 years left before her death. Playfully challenging Juanita's view regarding what constitutes appropriate behavior, Whitaker suggested that 20 years gave her enough time for at least two more marriages. He also suggested that she should have more fun and behave like a teenager rather than a protective mother.

In this example, the open discussion of Juanita's potential for remarrying and having more fun illuminated her intrapersonal stress as based in fantasy rather than the actual views of other family members. She also found out that she could discuss remarrying and having fun without other family members responding critically, and this was a freeing experience.

Adding ambiguous or tongue-in-cheek suggestions. Later in this same family session, the mother, Elaina, complained that the family members relied on her too much. Whitaker suggested that she might go on a vacation by herself and force the family members to fend for themselves. Consistent with his belief that it is healthy to challenge rigid social norms and family roles, he made tongue-in-cheek statements such as this, and usually left it up to the family members to decide whether to adopt his suggestions or ignore them. He believed that family members have autonomy and can decide for themselves. Using tongue-in-cheek suggestions, he challenged rigid roles and norms without taking himself too seriously.

Symbolic-experiential family therapy: Limitations and recommendations. Salvador Minuchin wrote:

> *Whitaker has developed a language of discontinuity as an answer to the absurdity of living. When people insist that the reality they have learned is the only one possible, Carl's response is an impossible question, an absurd answer, a dirty joke, a dream (as cited in Neill & Kniskern, 1982, p. viii).*

When using this playful tongue-in-cheek approach, Whitaker appeared to assume that his clients were capable of processing, understanding, and selectively incorporating his responses into their lives. Whitaker and Keith (1981) acknowledged that this may not be true of some families. When working with diverse populations, family therapists are advised to take more care in processing what occurred during a family session, and to more clearly communicate their recommendations for family change (Scholl et al., 2015). This recommendation also likely holds for individuals who are less philosophical or abstract in their thinking.

On the other hand, a decided strength of symbolic-experiential family therapy is that it emphasizes the priority of establishing rapport with the family who holds the most influence or power in the family. This stance entails being responsive to cultural differences. Whether the most influential family member is mother, father, grandparent, the SEFT therapist begins by forming a quality working relationship with this family member.

Another strength of this approach is Whitaker's encouraging family members to get in touch with their *craziness* meaning to use divergent thinking and have the courage to behave in ways that deviate from societal norms for conventional behavior. Whitaker models craziness by wrestling children and conducting family interview lying on the floor in a casual relaxed manner. He is authentic in that he practices what he preaches and his persona is freeing for families who may have entrenched rigid patterns of behavior and communication. *Craziness* potentially encompasses metaphors and role plays which are engaging and energizing for families. Metaphors and role plays are accessible to a wide age range, and to people from diverse cultural backgrounds. However, a final caution is that SEFT therapists need to be sensitive to cultural norms which might cause family members to become highly uncomfortable or even offended by lighthearted suggestions to change or negotiate traditional roles.

Treatment Process in Human Validation Model: Putting It All Together

Goals of human validation model. As her career moved along, Satir's goals shifted from her original focus on the elimination of pathology toward the optimization of human potential and functioning (Satir & Baldwin, 1983). In this way, Satir's approach was very humanistic in nature.

At the center of Satir's later work was the development of the awareness of growth potential, self-esteem development, and the resulting ability to adapt to changing environments and circumstances. This, according to Satir, was the goal of family therapy.

Satir's (1988) three main goals for family therapy were as follows:

1. Each family member should be able to report openly and honestly about what he or she sees, hears, feels, and thinks.
2. Decisions in a family are best made by exploring individual needs and negotiating to get those needs met in the group context, as opposed to using "power plays" to get wants met.
3. Differences should be used as growth opportunities within the family.

Treatment Process: Relationship Development and Facilitation

The first task of the therapist in human validation work, according to Satir (Satir & Bitter, 2000), is the development of a genuine and congruent relationship with the family while encouraging growth and change. Being outside of the family, the therapist is better positioned to observe and point out the communication styles and patterns that most influence events. These patterns are often not as apparent to the family themselves (recall Satir's "seeing one's own back" analogy). In this way the therapist pinpoints opportunities for growth and change in real time.

COMMUNICATION PATTERNS IN HUMAN VALIDATION MODEL WORK

Communication and Roles within the Family

Satir (1972) found that people tend to fall into one of several categories or communication "roles" within the family:

The placator: Agrees with whatever the speaker says and often defers to others' judgement and often seeks others' help. These individuals may feel inadequate and so do only what others expect of them and do not take initiative.

The blamer: Often disagrees and/or accuses the speaker of being at fault. This person is often feeling unsuccessful and lonely.

The computer: Incredibly reasonable and uses logic instead of true emotion when experiencing a situation. Often uses logic to emotionally distance him or herself. This person often feels vulnerable and uses this position to protect him- or herself or to assert control over a situation.

The distractor: Often uses language to move the conversation away from the actual topic. This person may feel unable to relate effectively to a given situation and may question whether anyone cares. He or she often appears to be in constant motion and lives in fear of stress and confrontation.

The congruent communicator: This person balances fully experiencing a situation with his or her way of communicating. He or she is honest in expressing his or her feelings and is congruent with language, body language and actions.

In Guided Practice Exercise 12.3, we'll look at Satir's method for assessing these types of communication patterns. Satir conceptualized family members as playing various communication-based "roles." We'll work to build our own skill in identifying the various roles in our own families.

GUIDED PRACTICE EXERCISE 12.3: IDENTIFY THE ROLE PLAYERS

Central to assessment of communication in the human validation model is the ability to spot the different "roles" represented in Satir's family model.

1. Head off to a family gathering.
2. Listen for the roles in your own family. Who plays what role? Why might they play that role? Note: No judgments here! Recognize that everyone develops these roles as an adaptive response to something. See if you can objectively note which roles are being played by whom and what they may be getting out of playing that role.

The Satir Change Model

Satir (1988) found that the process of facilitating family change had common elements that flow from one another:

Status quo. The established, agreed-upon (by use, if not explicitly) behavior, interaction, and communication patterns existing within the family are part of the family status quo. This status quo tends to continue to exist "as is" until challenged and disrupted by some person or event.

Foreign element. Satir called the event that challenges the status quo the *foreign element.* Families often only change when the status quo is challenged by this foreign element and traditionally employed coping strategies fail.

Chaos. When these coping strategies fail, there is often a period of chaos as the family resists any potential change. The family will often seek to find new ways to employ old strategies, and only reluctantly will families seek new solutions.

Transformative idea. This is the "big idea" that helps the family shift from one coping strategy to a new and more adaptive one. It is likely this idea will come from the family itself, once it has gotten through the chaos phase and is ready and willing to consider new options. The therapist may act as a facilitator of the idea development, or in some cases, may even provide the idea him or herself. Turn to Case Presentation 12.2 to see how these concepts are applied.

CASE PRESENTATION 12.2: THE CASE OF JENNY AND HER PARENTS

Satir believed that the best positive change flowed from the interruption of a family's **status quo**, or ingrained patterns. The **foreign element** disrupts the status quo and this leads to *chaos*. Then, the transformative idea comes along and helps to resolve things.

Mom and Dad are having trouble in their relationship. Jenny (16), Debbie (12), and Kimmie (9) are having some trouble with behavior in school and seem depressed. Dad has been drinking heavily for years. The marriage has gotten stale, and both partners seem bored with the lack of stimulation within the marriage. The kids have accepted that Dad drinks a bit too much but are worried about him, as is Mom. Dad isn't worried about it (**status quo**). One day Dad is coming home from the bar when he gets pulled over. Dad is arrested for a DUI, and his car, one of the primary cars used for family transportation, is impounded and his driver's license suspended (**foreign element**). The family is left one car short, with kids to get to practice and no way to get them there (**chaos**).

The family shows up at the family therapist's office and begins to process different ways of coping with challenges. The therapist helps the family to explore alternative ways of communicating. It seems that Jenny, the oldest daughter, has been feeling disconnected and uninvolved in family decisions and family life. She didn't mention it because, she says, "This family doesn't talk about things like that."

The therapist suggests that perhaps each week Jenny, with her new driver's license, may be helpful in getting folks to practice and to school. He also suggests a regular Saturday family meeting, in which family members talk about their week and share one feeling, one genuine appreciation of another family member, and one concern (**transformative idea**). Soon, the family is actively communicating about their feelings, Dad is in recovery, and the family is functioning at a much higher level.

Case Presentation: Human Validation Model

A family comes into family therapy to cope with recent life stressors. Dad, a 42-year-old engineer, has recently lost his job at a local building company. Mom, a 38-year-old physician, is financially supporting this family of five. Mom does well but has expressed frustration at being the only one in the house who is working. Paula, 19, lives at home while attending community college. Lisa, 17, is finishing her senior year of high school and will graduate magna cum laude in just a few months. Chad, 15, is finishing his freshman year of high school and plays on a traveling AAU baseball team.

Therapist: Welcome, everyone! Thanks for coming back today! How was everyone's week?

Lisa: It was fine. I have a few finals to finish, but if I buckle down, I should be ok.

Mom:	It was a rough one this week. I was on call through the weekend in the ER and it was a doozy. I'm exhausted.
Dad:	You've had a tough week.
Chad:	Cruisin' along in my 64…
Mom:	Stop.
Chad:	(Grins and leans back in his chair.)
Dad:	He didn't mean any harm. It's just music.
Paula:	He's an idiot. Did he tell you what he did in school today?
Mom:	What?
Paula:	Go ahead. Tell them.
Chad:	I got an in-school suspension.
Mom:	What?! Why? What did you do?
Chad:	(Unable to suppress a grin.) I may or may not have mooned the opposing team.
Mom:	Chad! How many times do we have to talk about this? See? This is what I'm talking about. I work my butt off and for you guys, it's all fun and games…
Therapist:	Mom, you sound frustrated. It would be normal to feel frustrated at a time like this. Let me ask: How does the family typically deal with a stressful situation?
Dad:	I wouldn't say that this is stressful … boys will be boys…
Paula:	Don't stick up for him, Dad! I can't believe the crap he gets away with.
Mom:	Paula is right. Chad, what you did was stupid and selfish. They're not going to let you pitch this weekend, are they? You're going to have to be at ISS this weekend and I must work. You were supposed to wait for the plumber. (Tearing up.) Don't you people understand?! I need help here. This is unbelievable. Paula, I'm going to need you to stay home and wait for the plumber.
Paula:	(Fumes and looks daggers at Chad, who smiles sweetly at her.)
Lisa:	(Emotionless.) He won't pitch this weekend. That's for sure.
Chad:	(Sobering.) Nope.
Therapist:	It seems like when a problem comes up, Paula points it out, Dad plays it down, Mom gets frustrated, Lisa just spits out the facts and Chad tells a joke. Is that about right?
	(Looks and nods around the room. Mom shakes her head.)
Paula:	If Chad would just get his stuff together…
Dad:	Now Paula, let's just calm down and think about this.
	(Therapist notes that body language has shifted so that folks are angled away from one another.)

Therapist: It sounds like the family's coping style results in a frustrated Mom, little resolution and folks feeling isolated. Maybe we can work on some ways to tackle problems that are more adaptive? How would folks feel about changing the playbook? (Smile.) Maybe without the mooning...

Therapist: I have an idea. Often, we can be creative when we must be. If each of you could reshape or "sculpt" this family, what choices would you make? What would you shape differently and why?

Paula: (Glaring at Chad.) I'd give scarecrow over there a brain...

In this example, the therapist has identified some key communication and interactional roles and a coping style that is not adapting to family needs. She will go on to identify these roles and suggest alternative patterns, but she first invites the full family into the change process. This focus on family "buy-in" to changing coping styles is critical in the human validation model. The therapist is focused on optimizing function, and is enlisting the family in the growth process.

Food for thought: What roles did you notice in this case example? What coping style did you notice? If you were the therapist, how might you move forward here?

Human Validation Model: Limitations and Recommendations

The humanistic approaches to experiential family therapy encourage genuineness and tremendous creativity on the part of the therapist/counselor. Therapists should be sure that the model is a good fit for their own interpersonal styles. While other approaches lend themselves to a series of techniques, the experiential approaches require the therapist/counselor to be creative, spontaneous and very much in tune with the needs of the entire group. Much cognitive and personal flexibility is required to maximize the effectiveness of these interventions. Counselors should ensure the approach matches both the family's personality and skill set.

Like many of the humanistic approaches, Satir's human validation model places tremendous value on individualism, the human capacity for growth, and the drive toward growth. Critics assert that such approaches fail to account for systemic factors such as discrimination, oppression and racism. The encouragement toward authenticity and genuineness, some argue, may be dangerous in a scenario in which societal or systemic oppression discourages such expression. Therapists should be intentional and cautious in settings in which systemic oppression may be a danger to the client/family.

Finally, due to the less structured nature of experiential therapies, clients need a level of cognitive sophistication and cultural congruence to maximize the benefit that they receive. Counselors should use caution with these less structured approaches with clients who have limited cognitive functioning or with clients who struggle with a lack of structure. In addition, counselors should be sure that the less structured experiential approach is a good fit from a cultural standpoint. While some cultural positions and backgrounds would gravitate to such an approach, it may be less effective for others. The counselor's cultural competence is a key factor.

Treatment Process in Greenberg and Johnson's Emotion-Focused Family Therapy: Putting It All Together

Attachment, EFT, and the role of the therapist. Attachment (Bowlby, 1988) is considered a fundamental human drive and is at the heart of EFT interventions. Secure attachment grows from individual autonomy, partner accessibility, and responsiveness. Relationship distress grows from fear, uncertainty, anxiety, and/or avoidance. The EFT professional acts as a consultant for the client/family on interactional process. In this way, she can be helpful in recognizing reflecting and helping to reorganize emotional interactions and responses. The client/family can then apply these new emotional interactional styles to current and past problems, building new interactional patterns of trust and positive attachment.

Assumptions and emotions in EFT. According to Johnson (2009), there is a critical need to understand each person's reality as a subjective experience and each person's behavior as a largely reasonable response to that reality. This enables the therapist and family members to stay free of judgement and creates safe and more accepting space within the family for change.

In addition to this major tenet, there are three main goals in EFT:

1. Access, reorganize, and expand key emotional responses, as emotion is the strongest change agent available to enhance attachment.

2. Create a change in the interactional patterns between partners/family members. It is these patterns that are the most accessible signs of change. The responsiveness of each partner is key to the possibility of change.

3. Development and enhancement of a more secure and functional attachment between partners/family members by developing more attachment-friendly and genuine emotional exchanges.

Greenberg and Johnson (1998) indicate that emotions can fall into two levels:

1. Primary emotions: Deeper and more vulnerable. These include sadness, hurt, fear, shame, and loneliness. These primary emotions are the ones more likely to bring people closer together.

2. Secondary emotions: Reactive and defensive. These include anger, jealousy, resentment, and frustration. These secondary emotions tend to push people further away.

Effective EFT aims to increase and amplify the experience and expression of primary emotions and identify when these may be being masked by secondary emotions.

Distressed couples often are caught in patterns in which secondary emotions cover up primary emotions. This both exacerbates and leads to (circular pattern) less secure attachments. Successful change involves shifting emotional relationship dynamics and opening family members up to new emotional exchange experiences. Being able to assess primary and secondary emotions is central to EFT work. In Guided Practice Exercise 12.4, we'll practice doing just that. Let's get started!

GUIDED PRACTICE EXERCISE 12.4: ASSESSING PRIMARY AND SECONDARY EMOTIONS

Central to being able to work in EFT is being able to recognize primary and secondary emotions. Review those definitions. Now, haul out those tapes that you made of yourself or head off to a family gathering. Listen for primary and secondary emotions.

1. What do you hear more of? How do you think that ratio impacts people's relationships?
2. How might you develop more primary emotional interaction? What might need to change?

Rheem, Woolley, and Johnson (2011) identified nine steps in EFT:

1. Create a good working alliance and identify the issues present from an attachment perspective (negative attachment/positive attachment, etc.).
2. Identify the interactional style contributing to attachment insecurity or relationship distress.
3. Identify unexpressed emotions within these patterns.
4. Reframe the problem in terms of unexpressed emotions, the pattern observed, and attachment needs.
5. Encourage identification with unmet/previously unidentified needs and aspects of self.
6. Promote acceptance of each partner/family member's new conceptualization of needs and self as well as new relationship behaviors.
7. Promote new interactional patterns and new experience of the relationship dynamics.
8. Facilitate the development and utilization of new solutions to old problems using the new interactional patterns.
9. Reinforce new relationship positions and connect with new patterns of attachment.

Let's look at Case Presentation 12.3, in which the family therapist applies what we just learned.

CASE PRESENTATION 12.3: THE COUPLE WITHOUT SPONTANEITY

A couple comes to couple's therapy complaining of a lack of spontaneity in their lives. The therapist notes that each seems disconnected from the other, often checking their phones in session and frequently interrupting each other. The therapist also notes dismissive behaviors from the partner when one or the other speaks. The therapist conceptualizes this as a lack of attachment. The therapist decides to design an intervention designed at facilitating a genuine emotional exchange and fostering attachment.

Therapist:	I have a hunch that you two are feeling disconnected from each other. Would you be open to an activity designed to help change that?
	(Nods from the couple.)
Therapist:	Today, I want each of you to make a list of the things that made you fall in love with the other. Starting tonight, you'll light some candles, put on soft music, and sit together on the floor. For at least 10 minutes, I'd like you to stare into each other's eyes. Then, only after ten minutes, one at a time, share one thing on your list with the other. Do this each night for a week. Let's reconvene after the week and process.

GREENBERG AND JOHNSON'S EFT: LIMITATIONS AND RECOMMENDATIONS

Safety and emotional space is of paramount importance in EFT work. EFT is contraindicated if any condition exists that precludes emotional safety. Ongoing violence, abuse or affairs, and serious addiction or substance use issues are all factors which preclude effective EFT work.

Culture is also a factor in considering EFT intervention. Although EFT has shown success with traditional male/female couples across demographic groups, there is limited evidence of EFT's effectiveness in cultural milieus in which emotional expression is less valued or actively frowned on. The counselor must involve the client/family in the choice of interventions.

SUMMARY

In this chapter, we examined several family therapy approaches that utilize an experiential platform. We looked at Carl Whitaker's use of emotional logic as a primary processing tool, as well as his use of symbolism, humor, and play as experiential tools for fostering family growth and development. We also looked at Virginia Satir's human validation model, with its focus on emotional congruence and genuine experience as a primary teaching tool. Finally, we examined Greenberg and Johnson's emotion focused therapy, which holds at its core that genuine emotional experience is the best way for couples and families to understand the role that attachment plays within relationships. The hope is that after reading this chapter, you will be able to intentionally conceptualize and plan the ways in which experience may be used as a therapeutic factor in helping families grow. In our next chapter, we'll look at behavioral and cognitive behavioral therapy with couples and families.

KEYSTONES

Among the key points addressed in this chapter are:

- At the heart of the experiential family therapies lies the assumption that families do best when they are able to genuinely experience the relationships, emotions, and attachment to the world around them.
- Families are also at their very best functionally when they can achieve congruence with their emotional reality and the ways in which they communicate those emotions.
- Families function best when they can demystify long-standing patterns of family myths and misunderstandings and develop new and more adaptive patterns of communicating, relating, and experiencing one another.

REFLECTIONS FROM THE CONTRIBUTOR'S CHAIR

As I reflect on the experiential family therapies, I am reminded of things that stand out in my own emotional life. Without exception, memories that flow to me now are experiences, as opposed to simple cognitive insights.

As the child of a counselor myself, I was exposed very early in my life to groups of people who spoke of emotion and experience. In fact, I attended (as a child of a single dad) many meetings of the Philadelphia Humanistic Psychology Association, even attending the national conference in 1977. I less than half listened as adults sat around dusty tables at the local university and spoke of the potential of human learning, the enhanced value of experience, and the human tendency to optimize growth and learning. I was fortunate to have these experiences and others.

As I moved through school, I found that I learned well through traditional methods. However, when I got into a less traditional educational setting, I learned the value of experiential learning. In this less structured but more experiential learning environment, my curiosity soared and my drive to learn grew! What I learned in this time was that my most meaningful learning was done via experience. Suddenly, the things I understood on an intellectual level I also understood at a visceral level. Best of all, I got to add my own interpretation and meaning to these experiences. I quickly realized that this experiential learning was at the heart of much of what was being discussed at those dusty, sepia-toned tables in the 1970s.

I am also attracted by the less structured and more experimental nature of the experiential models, as I am engaged by their humanistic philosophy. Specifically, I am attracted to the inherent idea within these experiential models that genuine experience is primary human learning source. In my experience, experience itself has often proven to be the best teacher. This approach also allows for each individual and family to make their own meaning of experience. I find that meaning making is one of the most fundamental humanistic tenets, and I am drawn to those approaches that place emphasis on that process.

Best of all, I think experiential family therapies appeal to the part of me that suspects human beings simply are better able to access experience as a learning tool. I have seen evidence of this as a counselor educator over the years. I have often explained concepts; drawn maps, tables, and diagrams; and developed assignments designed to enhance learning. I have found with few exceptions that many of the most valuable lessons for learners come at the hands of experience, as opposed to traditional didactic pedagogy.

Likewise, many of my clients have had huge "aha!" moments during an exploration of family sculpting or in experiencing a reframe of an emotional interaction. It seems human beings excel when they have opportunities to experience insight through engagement rather than through discussion alone.

I hope you can utilize the experiential family therapies discussed above for the benefit of your clients. If, however, you find they are not a good fit for your temperament or skill set, my hope is that you find something within these pages you can apply to your understanding of human relationships and processes. Best of luck on your journey to be the best counselor you can be! May your experience exceed your dreams!

—Michael Walsh, PhD, LPC, CRC

ADDITIONAL RESOURCES

The following resources provide additional information relating to the chapter topics.

Useful Websites

Carl Whitaker Project

- http://www.carlwhitaker.org/

This site maintains a list of articles, books, videos, and a bibliography devoted to Whitaker's work.

- Satir Global Network
  https://satirglobal.org/

This site was developed by Satir and contains links to resources, training materials, and publications related to Satir's work.

- Emotion-Focused Therapy Clinic
  http://www.emotionfocusedclinic.org/

This site is maintained by Leslie Greenberg and is devoted to resources and training opportunities for clinicians in EFT.

Readings

Whitaker, C. A., & Keith, D. V. (1981). Symbolic-experiential family therapy. In A. S. Gurman & D. P. Kniskern (Eds.), *Handbook of family therapy* (Vol. 1, pp. 187–225). New York: Guilford Press.

Excellent primer on Whitaker's approach to therapy.

Satir, V. (1988). *The new people making*. Mountain View, CA: Science and Behavior Books.

An essential piece of Satir's later work that explores her ideas on families and family therapy.

Johnson, S. M. (2009). Attachment and emotionally focused therapy: Perfect partners. In J. Obegi & E. Berant (Eds.), *Attachment theory and research in clinical work with adults* (pp. 410–433). New York: Guilford Press.

Wonderful piece that explores the link between emotional experience and attachment theory in relationships

Video

Mishlove, J. (Producer). (1995). *Virginia Satir: Communication and congruence* (Thinking Allowed Series) [Video]. Oakland, CA: Thinking Allowed Productions.

Wonderful video interview with Virginia Satir on her approach to therapy and to life.

REFERENCES

American Psychological Association. (2012). Leslie S. Greenberg: Award for Distinguished Professional Contributions to Applied Research: Biography. *American Psychologist, 67*(8), 695–697.

Andreas, S. (1991). *Virginia Satir, the patterns of her magic*. Palo Alto, CA: Science and Behavior Books.

Bowlby, J. (1969). *Attachment and loss* (Vol. 1). New York: Basic Books.

Bowlby, J. (1982). *Attachment and loss* (Vol. 1: *Attachment*). (2nd ed.). New York: Basic Books.

Bowlby, J. (1988). *A secure base*. New York: Basic Books.

Connell, G. M. (1996), Carl whitaker in memoriam. *Journal of Marital and Family Therapy, 22*: 3–8. doi:10.1111/j.1752-0606.1996.tb00182.

Gerhart, D. (2013). *Mastering competence in family therapy: A practical approach to theory and clinical case documentation*. Belmont, CA: Brooks/Cole.

Greenberg, Leslie S. (2011). Emotion-focused therapy. Theories of psychotherapy series. Washington, DC: American Psychological Association.

Greenberg, L. S. (2012). Emotions, the great captains of our lives: Their role in the process of change in psychotherapy. *American Psychologist, 67*(8), 697-707.

Greenberg, L. S., & Paivio, S. (1997). *Working with emotions in psychotherapy.* New York: Guilford Press.

Johnson, S. M. (2009). Attachment and emotionally focused therapy: Perfect partners. In J. Obegi & E. Berant (Eds.), *Attachment theory and research in clinical work with adults* (pp. 410–433). New York: Guilford Press.

Johnson, S. M. (2013). *Love sense: The revolutionary new science of romantic relationships.* New York: Little, Brown.

Johnson, S., & Greenberg, L.S. (1994). Emotion in intimate interactions: A synthesis. In S. M. Johnson & L. S. Greenberg (Eds.), *The heart of the matter: Perspectives on emotion in marital therapy* (pp. 297–323). New York: Brunner/Mazel.

King, L. (1989). *Women of power.* Berkeley, CA: Celestial Arts.

Mikulincer, M. (1995). Attachment style and the mental representation of the self. *Journal of Personality and Social Psychology, 69,* 1203–1215.

Napier, A. Y., & Whitaker, C. A. (1978). *The family crucible.* New York: Harper & Row.

Neill, J. R., & Kniskern, D. P. (1982). *From psyche to system: The evolving therapy of Carl Whitaker.* New York: Guilford Press.

Rank, O. (1996). A psychology of difference: The American lectures. Selected, Edited, and Introduced by Robert Kramer, with a foreword by Rollo May. Princeton, NJ: Princeton University Press.

Rheem, K.D., Woolley, S.R., & Johnson, S.M. Emotionally focused couple therapy: A military case study. In D. Carson & M. Casado-Kehoe (Eds.), *Case Studies in Couple Therapy: Theory-Based Approaches,* New York: Taylor and Francis.

Rogers, C. R. (1961). *On Becoming a person: A psychotherapists view of psychotherapy.* New York, NY: Houghton Mifflin.

Satir, V. (1972). *People making.* Mountain View, CA: Science and Behavior Books.

Satir, V. (1988). *The new people making.* Mountain View, CA: Science and Behavior Books.

Satir, V., & Baldwin, M. (1983). *Satir step by step: A guide to creating change in families.* Palo Alto, CA: Science and Behavior Books.

Satir, V. M., & Bitter, J. R. (2000). The therapist and family therapy: Satir's human validation process model. In A. M. Horne (Ed.), *Family therapy and counseling* (3rd ed.) (pp. 62-101). Itasca, IL: F. E. Peacock.

Scholl, M. B., Perpiczka, M., & Walsh, M. (2015). Experiential and humanistic theories: Approaches and applications. In D. Capuzzi & M. D. Stauffer (Eds.), *Foundations of couples, marriage, and family counseling* (pp. 159–183). Hoboken, NJ: Wiley.

Smith, G. L. (1998). The present state and future of symbolic-experiential family therapy: A post-modern analysis. *Contemporary Family Therapy, 20*(2), 147–161.

Wetchler, J. L., & Piercy, F. P. (1996). Experiential family therapies. In F. P. Piercy, D. H. Sprenkle, & J. L. Wetchler (Eds.), *Family therapy sourcebook* (2nd ed., pp. 79–105). New York: Guilford Press.

Whitaker, C. (1971). Multiple therapy and its variations. In G. D. Goldman & D. S. Milman (Eds.), *Innovations in Psychotherapy* (pp. xxii, 293. New York: Thomas.

Whitaker, C. A. (1989). A panoramic view of psychotherapy. In M. O. Ryan (Ed.), *Midnight musings of a family therapist* (pp. 151–156). New York: Norton.

Whitaker, C. A. (1990). *Therapeutic three generation family reunion* [Videotape]. Phoenix, AZ: Milton H. Erickson Foundation.

Whitaker, C. A., & Keith, D. V. (1981). Symbolic-experiential family therapy. In A. S. Gurman & D. P. Kniskern (Eds.), *Handbook of family therapy* (Vol. 1, pp. 187-225). New York, NY: Guilford Press.

Whitaker, C. A., & Ryan, M. O. (1989). *Midnight musings of a family therapist.* New York: Norton.

CHAPTER 13

Behavioral and Cognitive Behavioral Therapy with Couples and Families

Rochelle Cade, Esther Benoit, Katherine Hermann-Turner, and Robika Mylroie

"You feel as you think."

—Albert Ellis

The birth of behavioral and cognitive behavioral couples and family therapy can be tracked to the beginning of the 20th century and the pioneering work of Ivan Pavlov, B. F. Skinner, and John B. Watson. The influence of learning theory and linear, cause-and-effect understanding of behavior underlies the four therapeutic approaches (behavioral, cognitive behavioral, functional family therapy, and integrative) to couples and families discussed in this chapter. While the four share common theoretical origins of learning theory and behaviorism, other elements such as emphasis on cognitions, systemic thinking, or relational interactions shape the approaches to make them distinct. The general purpose of the chapter is for readers to learn about behavioral and cognitive behavioral approaches in couple and family counseling. In this chapter, we examine the four approaches of behavioral and cognitive behavioral therapy: cognitive therapy, behavioral therapy, functional family therapy, and integrative behavioral therapy.

LEARNING OBJECTIVES

After reading this chapter, you will be able to do the following:

- Discuss the theoretical assumptions of behavioral and cognitive behavioral therapy.

- Describe four behavioral and cognitive behavioral approaches to therapy with couples and families.

- Identify the major figures associated with these approaches.

- Examine the role(s) of therapists operating from these approaches in couples and family therapy.

- Explore the theoretically consistent techniques, interventions, and assessment in behavioral and cognitive behavioral therapy.

Cognitive Couple and Family Therapy

Profile of Main Figures

Several behavioral and cognitive behavioral theorists formed the landscape of cognitive couple and family therapy. Behaviorism was shaped by the work of Ivan Pavlov and John B. Watson. Pavlov, perhaps best known for his work identifying classical conditioning, helped pioneer the field of behavioral science. Watson's work focused heavily on the external behavioral reactions people exhibit, rather than on the internal processes that might underlie these reactions. Behavioral theory was further enhanced by the work of Joseph Wolpe, a South African psychiatrist who is credited with developing several reciprocal disinhibition techniques, including systematic desensitization. Another key figure in the field of behaviorism is Burrhus Frederic (B. F.) Skinner, who championed the principle of reinforcement. His work centered on the concept of operant conditioning and learned responses. Skinner's work led to the school of thought known as radical behaviorism.

Behaviorism laid the foundation for the emergence of cognitive sciences. Cognitive scientists built on many of the tenets of behaviorism, incorporating learning and development as they relate to our cognitions, perceptions, and emotions. Cognitive couple and family therapy is heavily influenced by both cognitive and behavioral approaches.

KEY CONCEPTS

Classical conditioning was developed from experiments completed by Ivan Pavlov. He observed that dogs would reliably salivate (unconditional response) when given food (unconditional stimulus) but did not salivate to the ringing of a bell (neutral stimulus). Pavlov then started ringing a bell just before he would present the dogs with food. The dogs began to associate the sound of the bell with food. The repeated pairing of the bell (neutral stimulus) with the food (unconditional stimulus) resulted in the bell becoming a conditional stimulus. As a result, the dogs would salivate to the sound of the bell (conditioned response) even if it was **not** immediately followed by food. Pavlov could elicit a conditioned response (salivation) to a previously neutral stimulus (bell).

Operant conditioning is the concept that learning is shaped through the consequential rewards and punishments associated with specific behaviors. Where classical conditioning is focused on stimulus and response, operant conditioning involves response reinforcement. Unlike classical conditioning, in operant conditioning individuals have some agency or control over the events in their environment. In operant conditioning, behavior is shaped by the individual's desire to maximize reward and minimize punishment.

PREMISE OF THE THEORY

Cognitive approaches examine both behavioral and emotional elements that contribute to dysfunctional relational responses. The cognitive couple and family therapist addresses how family members think about themselves both individually and relationally. Schemas or core beliefs about relationships influence behaviors and emotions within dyadic and familial family structures. Cognitive couple and family therapy theory addresses those thought patterns by examining expectations, assumptions, and roles.

Theoretical Assumptions

Cognitive family therapy theory examines the role of cognitions in shaping our patterns of interaction within relationships. These cognitions influence the overall functioning of relationships by shaping how individuals behave in relational systems. With its roots firmly planted in learning theory, change is often focused on individual family members or smaller subunits/subsystems of the larger family system. While the theory addresses systemic components, it is less systemically focused than other family therapy theories.

Goals of Cognitive Family Therapy

The cognitive family therapist works with couples and families to enhance family communication, dispute irrational beliefs, increase parenting skills, and encourage positive patterns of family interaction. While this section focuses specifically on cognitive family therapy approaches, in practice, cognitive and behavioral approaches are often combined.

Therapeutic Structure

Cognitive couple and family therapy centers on the modification of behaviors by examining thought and relational patterns between and among family members. The therapist works to build skills with members of the family system to help them adapt to current and future challenges. Thoughts and thought patterns are examined in the context of one's primary relationships. While cognitive family therapy addresses the family unit, individuals and dyads are often the focus of clinical work, and parent training is often a key component of therapeutic work.

Couple/Family Assessment

Couple and family assessment helps to identify presenting problems and examine individual, couple, and family schemas. A therapist may also wish to assess relationship satisfaction, communication patterns, normative and non-normative family life events, potential abusive behavior, relationship beliefs, and other pertinent elements of family life. Examples of assessments that you read about in Chapter 8 include the *Dyadic Adjustment Scale (DAS)* and the *Marital Satisfaction Inventory-Revised (MSI-R)*.

Working Stage

Cognitive restructuring is the goal of the working stage. This restructuring addresses unrealistic beliefs that partners may have about each other, replacing them with more helpful and productive beliefs. Education is also an important component of the working stage of counseling. The therapist helps clients understand developmentally appropriate behaviors and expectations as they pertain to specific family relationships.

Several cognitive interventions or techniques can be used during the working stage of counseling. **Guided behavior change** includes both identifying and then modifying core beliefs and couple/family schemas. The therapist works to challenge the beliefs held by clients around patterns of interaction and then supports clients in making incremental behavior changes. Cognitive restructuring underlies this guided behavior change process. **Socratic questioning** is a type of questioning that helps clients identify unrealistic ideas and thought patterns about their relationships, including unproductive attitudes and assumptions. Rather than have the therapist point out counterproductive beliefs and family schemas, Socratic questioning aims for the client to discover these beliefs themselves (Dattilio, 2010). **Role rehearsal** and **modeling** are observational learning techniques grounded in social learning theory. As family members become aware of their thought patterns around relationships within the family, role rehearsal is used to try new ways of interacting. Modeling new behaviors and shaping new patterns of interaction in the counseling session helps couples and families practice new skills. The therapist can then observe what the clients have understood and then provide support in continuing to shape those new patterns of thought and behavior.

Termination

Goals in cognitive family therapy are dynamic and shift as the clients' needs grow and change. Once the stage is set for change, the therapist works to support the couple or family in trying on new roles, practicing skills, addressing persistent thought and belief patterns, and working toward self-sufficiency and termination.

Role of the Therapist

The cognitive couple and family therapist is flexible in shifting between roles as an educator, coach, expert, and collaborator. Skills-based interventions are often used to help provide couples and families with didactic instruction at the onset of counseling. As skills are learned, therapists facilitate opportunities for clients to practice new behaviors and patterns of interacting relationally. Therapists seek to facilitate systemic change through education, cognitive restructuring, modeling, shaping, and other cognitive and behavioral interventions.

Strengths and Limitations

Cognitive couple and family therapy is well supported in the research literature as an effective therapeutic intervention approach (Baucom, Epstein, & Gordon, 2000; Northey, Wells, Silverman, & Bailey, 2003). As with any theoretical approach, certain limitations exist. Cognitive approaches tend to focus on specific relational cognitions and their related behaviors rather than on larger patterns; thus, this therapy is less systemically focused than other theories of family therapy. Action is emphasized over insight, which can result in a failure to explain why or how partners maintain maladaptive patterns of relating (Fischer, Baucom, & Cohen, 2016).

BEHAVIORAL COUPLE AND FAMILY THERAPY

Profile of Main Figures

Albert Bandura

Albert Bandura is well known for discovering observational learning through his Bobo doll studies in the 1950s and 1960s. In other research, Bandura explored self-efficacy and discovered that a positive cognitive self-perception is a strong predictor of positive behavioral outcomes. Throughout his life, he advanced the understanding of behavioral influences on human functioning.

Albert Ellis

Albert Ellis is one of the most famous and recognizable psychologists. After focusing his clinical practice on psychoanalysis early in his career, Ellis changed to a behavioral perspective and created rational emotive behavior therapy (REBT), originally rational emotive therapy. As a therapist and theorist, Ellis was known for his straightforward communication style, challenging the thinking of individuals and the counseling profession through direct confrontation, dry humor, charisma, and logical problem solving.

Aaron Beck

Aaron Beck began his career in medicine with a specialization in neurology. He later changed his emphasis to psychiatry and began treating clients using his psychoanalytic training. He later rejected Freudian beliefs during his groundbreaking research on depression and development of the Beck Depression Inventory. Beck is described as gentle, supportive, practical, and cooperative, all characteristics that have influenced his clinical practice and the development of cognitive behavior therapy.

PREMISE OF BEHAVIOR THEORY

Behavioral therapy originated in the 1950s as part of the second force in psychotherapy, challenging the established psychoanalytical therapeutic perspective. The approached originated from classical and operant conditioning, which emphasized behavioral changes as a path to improved wellness and functioning. In the 1970s the theory emerged from primarily residential treatment to outpatient populations (Patterson, 2005).

Theoretical Assumptions

Behavioral therapists believe individuals are influenced by their experiences and learning (social learning). In response to these experiences, an individual learns adaptive or maladaptive behaviors, both of which can be modified to improve well-being. Therapeutic growth occurs through behavioral interventions that require action, not insight.

Global Goals

The overarching goal of behavioral therapy is to facilitate client well-being by changing, reducing, or eliminating unwanted behaviors. These goals are accomplished by teaching skills, which can be implemented, monitored, and maintained by clients.

Behavioral Parent Training

In behavioral parent training (BPT), parents learn strategies to help improve their children's behavior using behavioral modification techniques. Parents learn approaches to identify and revise behaviors based on social learning and operant conditioning strategies, such as establishing a reward system and implementing disciplinary practices such as a time-out. Throughout the therapeutic process, parents learn and practice skills inside of therapy to be applied outside of sessions.

Key Concepts

Shaping is a behavioral technique used to progressively move a client to a larger goal through the reinforcement of small, manageable changes. This allows clients to make gradual changes from a previous behavior to a new behavior.

Token economy is the most frequent and commonly used operant conditioning technique. Children receive a "token" to reinforce positive behaviors, and these tokens can then be exchanged for a reward or privilege.

Contingency contracting or management is based on the belief that the environment affects the probability of behavior. As such, some contexts enable or reinforce the behavior and other contexts reduce or punish the occurrence of the behavior. Therefore, in a contingency contract either a behavior is rewarded or a specified reward is not received when a desired behavior does not occur.

When constructing a token economy or a contingency contract, it is important for parents and therapists to define the positive behavior, setting, timeline, exchange rate or reward, punishment, and methods for monitoring progress.

Role of the Therapist

When implementing BPT, a therapist must employ a multisystemic focus to achieve two simultaneous goals: teaching parents skills and improving a child's behavior. To accomplish these goals, the therapist may function as a teacher when introducing behavior-training strategies to parents. As parents implement these strategies, the therapist may function as a coach that supports parents in their efforts.

Prior to implementing techniques and behavioral modifications, a therapist must observe and assess the parent and child's level of functioning and adjust interventions accordingly. Once a therapeutic relationship and accurate understanding of a client has been established, a therapist can begin training parents in the specific techniques described above.

The overarching goal of BPT is a reduction in the negative behavior of the child. Nevertheless, secondary goals include parent education and training and improved overall functioning of both the child and parent. With skillful attentive implementation, BPT can result in positive systemic change.

Behavioral Couple Therapy
Behavioral couple therapy (BCT) is a goal-oriented, present-focused form of therapy aimed at improving the quality of a couple's relationship. Therapists operating from this approach believe problems result from the absence of positive reinforcement of positive actions. Therefore, negative behaviors are believed to have been learned and maintained. To improve the couple relationship, communication, problem solving, and behavior exchange are used to positively reinforce the desired behaviors.

Key Concepts

Behavior exchange is an intervention in which the therapist and couple collaborate to uncover, plan, and agree on changes that will help both the individual and couple relationship. Each person commits to positive, specific, attainable behaviors (e.g., emptying the dishwasher, calling during the work day) to be performed for 1 day with the explicit goal of making their partner happier. Unlike **quid pro quo** discussed below, each individual is responsible for making changes independent of their partner's efforts.

Quid pro quo is a form of contingency contracting among couples. In these agreements, one partner agrees to do something depending on the other partner performing a task. For example, if one partner takes the car to get washed, the other partner will then pick up the dry cleaning.

Role of the Therapist
Behavioral couple therapists assume an active and directive stance as they educate and support behavioral skill development. They model positive behaviors and provide interventions aimed at improving behavioral exchanges and each individual's actions.

At the start of therapy, a behavioral couple therapist describes the therapeutic process and explains additional problems may arise as awareness increases. Second, the therapist observes the couple and identifies behaviors and communication patterns that would benefit from reshaping. Third, the therapist determines a target behavior and develops a plan for removing current problematic behavior or adding a new behavior. Fourth, the therapist models the desired behavior and reshapes the couple's behavior to match the intended goal. Finally, the couple and therapist assess the progress and replan, if necessary.

The goal of BCT is to reduce distress among a couple by improving behavioral interactions. Through the process of shaping and rehearsing behaviors, rather than simply education, a couple not only changes their actions but also modifies their reactions to their partner's behaviors. Using the operant conditioning techniques and the therapy process discussed above, many find long-term relational satisfaction. Let's turn our attention to a Case Presentation 13.1, in which a therapist uses these techniques with a family.

CASE PRESENTATION 13.1: THE CASE OF MADDISON AND MICHAEL

Maddison and Michael are a dual-income, biracial couple who entered family counseling at the recommendation of their son's school therapist. Peter, their son, had begun to into trouble at school for disrupting class and fighting, new behavior for him. When Peter was asked by the family therapist why the family was in counseling, he responded, "I don't know. I guess because I am always in trouble. No matter what I do, it's wrong. It's just not fair!" The therapist understood some of Peter's irrational beliefs and lack of accountability for his actions. Once this relationship with the family was established, the therapist taught the entire family about irrational beliefs and how to evaluate activating events, beliefs, and consequences and develop playful ways to dispute one another's beliefs. The therapist had the family create a "to be avoided" word list for the family's refrigerator that included the words *should*, *must*, and *always*. The family counted every time someone used one of these words, and each day there was a winner. Peter was very competitive, and he loved beating his parents at this game. Finally, the therapist made a contract with the family outlining new behaviors to use in their home and a plan to report the results in their weekly therapy sessions.

RATIONAL EMOTIVE BEHAVIOR THERAPY

REBT was developed by Albert Ellis in 1955 as an active form of therapy to address cognitions, emotions, and behaviors. This theory believes people are goal directed and that their distorted thoughts lead to emotional problems. While this short-term form of therapy (1–10 sessions) is primarily behavioral, it also incorporates the existential–humanistic perspective of other therapeutic approaches to alter a client's way of thinking and reacting to problems.

Key Concepts

Irrational beliefs are the foundation of most individual's emotional difficulties. These beliefs are characterized by rigidity, extremism, inconsistency, intolerance, and illogical reasoning. REBT therapists challenge and restructure beliefs so a client is more rational. This restructuring process includes confronting irrational problem solving as well as eliminating specific absolutist verbiage such as *should* and *must*.

Negative cognitions are believed to be the source of maladaptive reasoning. These thoughts may revolve around past experiences, present treatment, or a current outlook. Often clients are unaware they process and view things through a lens of negativity; thus, a therapist first identifies and then presents these negative cognitive patterns to the client.

Cognitive restructuring is based on the belief that individuals can change their thoughts. With practice, an individual can learn to think and respond differently.

Role of the Therapist

REBT therapists believe a therapist should be a collaborator and educator, teaching skills, assigning homework, and challenging unproductive thoughts. Thus, a warm relationship between the client and therapist is unnecessary or sufficient for therapeutic change in this approach, a distinct difference from humanistic approaches to therapy.

An REBT therapist uses the ABC(DE) model to assess and teach clients. In this model, A is defined as the activating event (identification of the cause of the problem). B is the belief about that event (clarification of the belief and reaction to the event). C isolates the consequences and resulting feelings about the event. D disputes the irrational thoughts related to the reaction to the event. E assesses the effects of a new way of thinking about a solution to the activating event. This model is used as both a baseline for understanding a client's behavior as well as a topic for educating clients to dispute their own irrational thoughts.

REBT therapy aims to help a client become more realistic and rational through "deep-seated emotional and behavioral change" (Ellis, 1980, p. 327). Because of the therapeutic process, a client revises their outlook and responds more functionally and positively to stimulus that previously produced maladaptive responses.

Strengths and Limitations

One of the primary strengths of behavioral interventions is their applicability to a variety of presenting problems and body of research supporting their use. In addition, the open communication, psychoeducational component, established goals, and ongoing assessment helps demystify the therapeutic process for clients.

Specific criticisms of this therapy include a lack of attention to cultural factors, the therapist's high level of influence, a lack of development of client insight and understanding as to the origin of the problem, and restricted relational development (Christensen, Dimidjian & Martell, 2015; Patterson, 2005). While many of these limitations are thought to be unnecessary areas of development by behaviorists, other theories may emphasize their importance.

Functional Family Therapy

Profile of Main Figures

Functional family therapy (FFT) was developed in the 1970s by James F. Alexander in collaboration with Bruce Parsons to work with adolescents with delinquent behavior and their families. Alexander and Tom Sexton cofounded training groups that helped disseminate FFT nationally and internationally. Alexander currently serves as a faculty member in the Psychology Department at the University of Utah and as clinical and research director of Functional Family Therapy, LLC. Sexton is a professor in the Counseling Psychology Program at Indiana University–Bloomington and director of the Center for Adolescent and Family Studies. The two continue to contribute to the growing body of literature and research on FFT.

Key Concepts

In FFT a key concept and part of the name of the approach, is the focus on the **function** of behavior within a system. An FFT therapist views all behavior as adaptive and serves a function in the family system. Because of the focus on the **function** of the behavior, FFT therapists do not view behavior as good or bad nor right or wrong. Therapists work with families to find more adaptive or functional expressions of the problem behavior. For example, a family may enter therapy to address their adolescent daughter's skipping part of the school day and repeatedly receiving disciplinary referrals at school. The FFT therapist would assess the function of her behavior within the family. This would be different than other forms of therapy that would focus on the individual or intrapsychic nature of the daughter's issues or the elements of her conduct that would warrant a mental health diagnosis. Instead, the FFT therapist would consider the function of the adolescent's behavior and might discover it is her means to gain attention from her parents who are regularly inattentive. The therapist would work with the family to have the adolescent female get her needs meet in ways other than skipping school. Additionally, the therapist would aid the parents in connecting to their daughter in ways other than attending parent conferences at the school to address her absences and problematic conduct. In Guided Practice Exercise 13.1, you will practice framing behaviors according to their function, rather than assigning a value to them.

GUIDED PRACTICE EXERCISE 13.1

In the paragraphs above, you read that the FFT therapist takes a neutral position and does not view behavior as good or bad but instead focuses on the function of the behavior. Given that FFT is a therapeutic approach to work with adolescents with conduct issues and their families, it might be challenging for a therapist to remain neutral on adolescent behavior like truancy, drug abuse, theft, or profanity. Find a partner in class and discuss how this can be a challenge for you as a therapist and how you might overcome these challenges and remain focused on the function of the behavior.

Premise of the Theory

Theoretical Assumptions

The integration of systems theory and behaviorism are the theoretical origins that inform FFT. The integration of these two theories is rooted in the idea that to understand behavior, therapists need to consider the relationships in which the behavior occurs. FFT therapists widen their conceptual lens from the individual to the system and the interpersonal or relational landscape in which behavior is situated. The FFT model considers the **function** of behavior within relationships or systems. The most critical feature or function of behavior is the relationship outcome that it produces: intimacy or distance. It should be noted that family members can achieve these outcomes without understanding of how or why they produce them.

Goals of FFT

The goals of FFT are for the family to establish new patterns of behavior to replace problematic or dysfunctional ones. The FFT therapist does not diagnose or define "bad" behavior, nor does the therapist prescribe a right way for the family to feel, think, behave, or function.

Therapeutic Structure

The goals of FFT are accomplished in a three-phrase process. In the first phase, **engagement and motivation**, the therapist focuses on developing a relationship with all members of the family. Additionally, the therapist attempts to foster hope and optimistic expectations within the family. The therapist takes a respectful, nonblaming position and interrupts negativity and blame in session as these are considered behavior that "dismotivates" (Onedera, 2006, p. 308). While sessions occur, the therapist is assessing the **function** of the problem behavior(s).

Behavior change, the second phase, focuses on changing behavior by establishing new patterns of interaction within the family to replace old patterns or behaviors. The therapist works with the family to gain the tools needed to establish the new patterns and behaviors. Tools the family may need include but are not limited to modification of cognitions, communication, or time-management skills. The therapist may utilize techniques from other evidence based cognitive behavior or behavioral models that are not specific to the FFT model to aid the family in this phase.

The third phase, **generalization**, aims to support the maintenance of change through broadening the families external support within their environment or community. This includes creating and strengthening the family's connection to positive resources and social systems like schools, 12-step programs, extended family, and faith-based services. The therapist may help the families identify, access, or reaccess these resources. In addition, the therapist helps the family anticipate challenges and obstacles to maintaining change. The family then makes plans for how they will address these. Through three phases of the FFT, therapists work with families to develop the motivation, tools, and resources or supports to establish and maintain new family patterns of behavior. In Guided Practice Exercise 13.2, you will examine the concept of generalization by helping the client access community resources and identify challenges associated with those resources.

GUIDED PRACTICE EXERCISE 13.2

In the above section, you read about third phase of FFT, *generalization*, in which the therapist works to aid families in identifying, accessing, or reaccessing positive community resources or support systems. Consider that you are a therapist working to with family in this phase of FFT. Make a list of challenges families could face as they attempt to identify and access community resources. Once you have made the list, identify skills a therapist would need to help the family address these challenges.

Role of the Therapist

The primary tasks of the FFT therapist are to identify the function of the problem or dysfunctional behaviors and help the families become more functional. These tasks are accomplished by first building a relationship with each family member and helping the family build or rebuild relationships with each other. Therapists can aid in the relationship building by expecting all family members to participate in session. This can help to engage all family members in the counseling process and avoid any perception of a single person as the problem. The therapist also understands that motivation and engendering hope are important, as many families will enter therapy feeling overwhelmed, reluctant, uncertain, or frustrated. Because many families are mandated by another system to attend counseling, it is important that the therapist consider how this may influence their perception of the therapist. It can be helpful for the therapist to clearly indicate his or her role as a helping professional and how this is different from other roles and functions (i.e., case managers, probation officers) with whom the family may interact.

Strengths and Limitations

FFT has several strengths for therapists and researchers to consider. First, FFT can be considered a preventative approach. Though families will typically enter therapy because of an adolescent with conduct issues, it is preventative in nature because by changing the family system in a positive direction, FFT prevents the appearance of those same conduct issues in younger siblings or family members (Onedera, 2006). Another strength of FFT is that it considers the culture of the family and local or larger social systems of the family and how these can be respected, appreciated, and included as support. FFT's inclusion of extended family and significant community members or elders can be consistent with the values of the family. A final strength of FFT is its empirical support. FFT has been listed in the Substance Abuse and Mental Health Services Administration's National Registry of Evidence-Based Programs and Practices. FFT therapists may also appreciate the measurable treatment outcomes in their own clinical practice that can prove useful when reporting therapeutic outcomes for grants or insurance companies

Although FFT has noteworthy strengths, there are some limitations to consider. FFT aims for all members of the family to engage and participate in therapy. Getting all members of the family to attend a session together can be thwarted by many challenges including conflicting schedules and transportation issues. A second limitation is that FFT may not align with the mission, philosophy of treatment, or organizational culture of the agency or organization in which it is implemented (Duncan, Davey, & Davey, 2011). Larger systems, like the criminal justice system or community mental health system, may operate from a problem or deficit-focused model of treatment, which does not align with FFT's emphasis on reframing problems into functions within relational systems. Finally, this relational focus may preclude opportunities for therapists to seek reimbursement for their services from insurance companies.

INTEGRATIVE BEHAVIORAL COUPLES THERAPY

Profile of Main Figures

Neil Jacobson and Andrew Christensen developed integrative behavioral couple therapy (IBCT). In their clinical practice, they observed short-term, immediate improvement for couples that was not long lasting. Their dissatisfaction with traditional BCT led them to collaborate and develop IBCT. Jacobson and Christensen published a manual of delivery for IBCT, engaged in research, and began offering training in this approach to therapy.

Key Concepts

Healthy versus Distressed Couples

In IBCT, differences and incompatibilities between partners are to be expected, and the subsequence discord that follows is cocreated by the couple. Their problematic interactions and behaviors are conceptualized as the couples' attempts to resolve these differences. Distressed couples are those whose reactions to problem behavior are as problematic as the behavior itself.

Context of Change

In couple's therapy, it is common for one partner to want the other partner to change, and traditional behavioral therapy can focus on facilitating these desired changes. However, in IBCT, change occurs alongside the twin goal of acceptance. Instead of focusing energy and efforts on changing partners or their behaviors, IBCT therapists work with the couple to first accept each other, and this acceptance becomes a catalyst for natural change to occur.

Premise of the Theory

Jacobson and Christensen observed most traditional behavior couples therapy produced results but that the results were not long lasting. A key element the two observed to be missing was the idea of acceptance as a facilitator of change. These two concepts, acceptance and change, were incorporated into their approach, IBCT. The theory is also integrative in that in utilizes a variety of behavioral treatment strategies or techniques. In Case Presentation 13.2, you will observe how a therapist might use IBCT to help a couple use acceptance as part of their change process.

CASE PRESENTATION 13.2: THE CASE OF KAYLA AND MALCOLM

Kayla and Malcolm enter couples therapy and describe a deep love for each other and commitment to their 8-year relationship. However, they feel discouraged that after this many years, they tend to get stuck in the same arguments. A typical argument starts with Malcolm coming home and questioning or criticizing something Kayla has done. Kayla feels judged and hurt and tends to shut down and withdraw. Malcolm feels misunderstood and then tries to rephrase his comments. Kayla retreats further, and Malcolm then responds with criticism of her inability to engage in the conversation. A therapist operating from an IBCT approach would facilitate discussion for the couple to uncover that Malcolm feels overwhelmed at work and then comes home and takes it out on Kayla. Malcolm would learn that constant criticism leads Kayla to feel unappreciated and worthless. Kayla would reveal that her retreating helps her move away from these feelings but in doing so leads to Malcolm feeling alone in solving the issues. The couple would not be prescribed rules as in traditional therapy but instead would be moving toward emotional acceptance. This acceptance can generate minor changes in the couple. Malcolm would learn to be mindful in his questions and how to move toward Kayla's emotional experience when he does. With this in mind, Malcolm would learn to connect to her hurt and make an attempt at repair. Kayla also would learn that when Malcolm questions and criticizes, this is an indicator that he is feeling overwhelmed at work and that she can move toward him with support.

Theoretical Assumptions

IBCT is informed by elements of behaviorism including functional analytic behavior views and contingency shaped behavior. IBCT focuses on problematic patterns of interactions and emotional acceptance. This focus is based on the following assumptions: All couples have some incompatibilities; their reactions to these incompatibilities can be as problematic as the incompatibilities; and efforts at direct change of these incompatibilities can exacerbate rather than ameliorate them. Thus, IBCT therapists do not focus their efforts on direct change efforts; instead, they focus more on the emotional reactions of couples to the problems or incompatibilities.

Goals of IBCT

The main goal of IBCT is to promote acceptance and change in the couple. Though these may seem like opposing concepts, Christensen, Doss, and Jacobson (2014) contend the combination is needed for the couple to proceed with change.

Structure of Counseling

In this form of therapy, assessment and feedback occur in the first four sessions. Initial assessment occurs as a conjoint interview. To understand the couple's situation, the therapist explores conditions that control behavior, or what is known as a functional analysis of behavior. The therapist will rely on informal assessment and observations of couple behavior but can also incorporate more formal assessment measures. Next, the therapist will complete individual interviews with each partner separately. The therapist then brings the partners back together for a clinical formulation and feedback session. In this session, the therapist uses his or her case formulation to establish treatment goals. The active phase of treatment is next and includes 8 to 20 joint sessions. As the couples makes progress and moves toward termination, the time between joint sessions will increase until termination of counseling.

Role of Therapist

Assessment and treatment. In addition to formal assessments you read about in Chapter 8, the following are six informal assessment questions that may aid therapists in the formulation of a treatment plan (Jacobson & Christensen, 1996):

1. How distressed is the couple?
2. How committed is the couple to this relationship?
3. What are the issues that divide them?
4. Why are these issues such a problem for them?

5. What are the strengths holding them together?

6. What can treatment do to help them?

Process and techniques. Techniques include those aimed at acceptance, tolerance, and change. To move the couple toward acceptance, the therapist may use **empathic joining or unified detachment**. In **empathic joining**, the therapist shifts the couple away from problem focused, blaming approaches to hearing the experience of their partner. The therapist asks couples to use soft disclosures rather than hard disclosures to allow for this to occur. Hard disclosures are described as those statements that show dominant power or stronger position. For example, a wife may say, "I won't let myself be taken for granted." Soft disclosures show vulnerability. Switching from a hard disclosure to soft, the wife may say, "I do not feel cared for." Though soft disclosures do not always soften the listener, they can help partners listen and move toward acceptance. **Unified detachment** is a technique that asks the couple to detach from the problem so that it becomes a common enemy for them to combat together. Rather than accusing one another of problems and behaviors, the couple can now blame the problem itself and talk about it in a detached way.

Techniques may also be used to move the couple toward tolerance. The idea of **tolerance building** is like exposure therapy where the couple is slowly exposed to the problem without reinforcing it. Exposing the partners in a safe environment with the therapist present can lead to acceptance through tolerance.

Jacobson and Christensen (1996) discuss four strategies for building tolerance. First, *pointing out the positive* features of negative behavior. The therapist can point out that positive place of origination or the purpose the problem behavior serves. The second strategy is **practicing negative behavior** in therapy sessions. The safety of the therapy sessions allows for couples to play out their negative behavior and observe the results of the behavior. A third strategy is **faking negative behavior**. It allows partners to realize the influence or impact of their behavior when they are calm and can view the experience without the emotional filters. This also allows the person receiving the faked behavior to build a tolerance for that experience. A fourth strategy is to **build tolerance through self-care**. This includes partners learning to become less dependent and more self-reliant. Too often, partners can expect or depend on each other to meet every need. This expectation is unrealistic and too great a responsibility for any one partner to bear. Thus, self-care aids couples in learning to get their needs met both independently and dependently. Additional techniques from traditional BCT, such as **behavior exchange** or communication skills, may also be utilized.

Strengths and Limitations

A strength of IBCT is that its introduction of specific acceptance strategies to be used with couples: empathic joining, unified detachment, and building tolerance. Although researchers have shown that IBCT is indeed able to help couples sustain long term change (Mairal, 2015), at present the body of research promising but limited. Future research could add support to Jacobsen and Christenson's assertion that acceptance was a missing link in traditional behavior couples therapy that facilitates and sustains change.

Case Presentation: The Case of Jennifer and Barry

Now that you have gained knowledge about behavioral and cognitive behavioral therapy, let's late a look at a case.

Jennifer and Barry entered therapy after many months of heated conflict in their marriage. Jennifer manages a day care center and is enrolled in evening classes at the local community college to become a nurse. Barry is a mechanic and has recently had his hours cut at work. This has exacerbated the couple's existing conflicts, as their financial situation has become much more difficult to manage. The couple is in their mid-30s, has been married for 15 years, and has two teenage sons together.

The couple has come to marriage and family therapy after realizing they were unable to solve their conflicts on their own. The couple has entered their first counseling session with a cognitive behavioral therapist. In the first session, the therapist will focus on a specific complaint or issue the couple is facing, listen for their cognitions related to the issue and each other, and then collaborate with them to devise a plan and treatment goals.

Therapist: Tell me what brings you in to couple's therapy.

Jennifer: Well, we have never been in therapy before and some friends of ours went and said it was helpful to their marriage. So, here we are ready to work on our own marriage.

Therapist: Barry, what brings you to couples therapy?

Barry: Fighting. We fight about the same things every week and nothing changes. I am tired of nothing getting solved. So, we are hoping that counseling will help us solve some things in our marriage.

Therapist: So, you have tried to solve things on your own and are now ready to try therapy.

Jennifer: Well, I do not know if I am ready for therapy, but I am ready to stop so much fighting.

Therapist: You are unsure about therapy.

Jennifer: Yeah. I always thoughts couples therapy was for people on the verge of divorce. That is not where we are, but I do not want us to get their either. So here we are.

Barry: Yeah, we aren't near divorce at all. We just need some help in making changes.

Therapist. You are committed to your marriage and coming to therapy before divorce conversations is another way in which you are showing your commitment to your marriage. So, tell me about what you would issue or issues you would like to focus on in our time together.

As the therapist listens to the couple identify their issues, she will be careful not to align with either partner and will keep the couple focused on the present and not the past. The therapist is engaging in the assessment process and listening for cognitions, antecedents, and consequences of the issue identified by the couple.

Therapist: While there are several areas you identified, both of you agreed that the intensity and frequency of the fights are what you would like to focus on.

Barry: Yeah, I don't even know why we fight or what we fight about.

Jennifer: I know what we fight about, seems like the same things, but I don't know why we keep fighting or what starts it all off. Seems like one minute we are eating dinner and then the next minute we are yelling at each other.

Therapist: You would like to slow it down and understand what is happening.

Jennifer: Exactly. I just don't know how it goes from fine to yelling.

Barry: Yeah, what happens at dinner to set her off or me off.

Therapist: So far, we know that you guys want to work on reducing the amount of fighting that is happening and the yelling that occurs in the fights. What you do not know and are curious to find out what happens with each of you that starts down the path toward a fight.

Jennifer: Yes, the path to a fight. I want to know when and how I step on that path. I want to see when I get on it and then how to get off the path.

Therapist: This week between sessions, let's find out more about the path for each of you by doing some record keeping.

Barry: So, we are going to do some homework this week?

Therapist: Yes, keeping a record or homework can give us more information about these fights.

The therapist then describes the homework assignment to the couple. She instructs the couple to each keep a log of the fighting that happens in the upcoming week. She asks them to record the situation, what happened before the situation, their thoughts associated with the situation, their emotions associated with the situations, and what happened afterward. When the couple returns for their next session, the therapist will review their homework, discuss any challenges they had in completing their homework, and introduce them to cognitive distortions and how to challenge them. The therapist will continue to have the couple identify their cognitive distortions as part of the path to a fight and have them challenge these and generate alternates. The couple is early in their therapy process and will need to practice these thoughts and behaviors over time. The therapist will engage in ongoing assessment to see what is working and adjust treatments so they are specific to the couple and their progress.

SUMMARY

In this chapter, we examined the influence of learning theory and linear, cause-and-effect understanding of behavior and how that underlies the four therapeutic approaches (behavioral, cognitive behavioral, functional family therapy, and integrative) to couples and families. While the four share a common theoretical origin of learning theory and behaviorism, other elements such as emphasis on cognitions, systemic thinking, or relational interactions shape the approaches to make them distinct approaches. In the next chapter, we will turn our attention to solution-focused brief therapy.

KEYSTONES

Among the key points addressed in this chapter are:

- Behavioral and cognitive behavioral couples and family therapies are based on learning theory, a theory originating from the work of Albert Bandura.

- Cognitive couple and family therapy addresses how family members think about themselves both individually and relationally and how this informs problem behaviors.

- The major premise of behavioral couple or family therapy is that behavior is continued or discontinued by reinforcements or consequence. Because behavior is learned, adaptive behaviors can be learned and maladaptive behavior unlearned to bring about change in couples or families.

- Functional family therapy focuses on the function of behavior within a system. FFT views all behavior as adaptive and serves a function in the family system.

- Integrative behavioral couple therapy gets its name from the integration of acceptance and change. The theory is also integrative in that in utilizes a variety of behavioral treatment strategies or techniques.

REFLECTIONS FROM THE CONTRIBUTORS CHAIR
Esther Benoit

Cognitive and behavioral approaches to therapy influence most of us who are in clinical practice. Even though we may not operate from purely or primarily cognitive or behavioral approaches to therapy, we cannot avoid the concept that behaviors and thoughts are inextricably linked. Couples and families can learn to see this link and use it to make lasting change. The dynamic nature of relationships calls for examination—and what better way to examine one's life than to uncover assumptions, family schemas, and ingrained patterns of behavior. As I (Esther) completed my training in marriage, couples, and family counseling, I found myself drawn to cognitive behavioral approaches both for their simplicity and for their ability to help me help my clients make movement toward change.

ADDITIONAL RESOURCES

The following resources provide additional information relating to the chapter topics.

Useful Websites

Association for Behavioral and Cognitive Therapies

- http://www.abct.org/Home/

This website provides information for those interested in an association of professionals that operate from behavioral and cognitive therapies.

- Beck Institute for Cognitive Behavior Therapy
  https://www.beckinstitute.org/

This website provides information about cognitive behavioral therapy for clinicians as well as clients.

- Functional Family Therapy
  http://fftllc.com/

This website provides a wealth of information research that supports FFT and training opportunities for clinicians.

- Integrative Behavioral Couple Therapy
  http://ibct.psych.ucla.edu/about.html

This website provides information and resources for those interested in learning more about IBCT or locating a therapist that practices from this model.

Readings

Alexander, J. F., Waldron, H. B., Robbins, M. S., & Neeb, A. A. (2013). *Functional family therapy for adolescent behavior problems.* Washington, DC: American Psychological Association.

This text is a comprehensive resource for clinicians interested in learning about FFT and how to implement it with adolescents and their families.

Dattilio, F. M. (2001). Cognitive-behavioral family therapy: Contemporary myths and misconceptions. *Contemporary Family Therapy, 23,* 3–18.

This article helps readers have an accurate understanding of cognitive behavioral family therapy.

Dattilio, F. M., & Beck, A. T. (2010). *Cognitive–behavioral therapy with couples and families: A comprehensive guide for clinicians.* New York: Guilford Press.

This text provides readers with research and case presentations to demonstrate how cognitive behavioral therapy can be utilized with couples and families.

Fischer, D., & Fink, B. (2014). Clinical processes in behavioral couple's therapy. *Psychotherapy, 51*(1), 11–14.

This article provides case presentations to demonstrate how behavioral techniques are used with couples.

Gurman, A. S. (2013). Behavioral couple therapy: Building a secure base for therapeutic integration. *Family Process, 52,* 115–138.

This article provides a description of the theoretical origins of integrative behavioral couple therapy.

Jacobson, N. S., Christensen, A., Prince, S. E., Cordova, J., & Eldridge, K. (2000). Integrative behavioral couple therapy: An acceptance-based, promising new treatment for couple discord. *Journal of Consulting and Clinical Psychology, 68*(2), 351–355.

This article provides a description of integrative behavioral couple therapy.

Sexton, T. L., & Alexander, J. F. (2002). FBEST: Family-based empirically supported treatment interventions. *Counseling Psychologist, 30*(2), 238–261.

This article provides an overview of family-based treatments, along with research that supports their use.

Sexton, T. L. (2010). Functional family therapy in clinical practice: *An evidenced-based treatment model for working with troubled adolescents.* New York: Routledge.

This text is another comprehensive resource for clinicians interested in learning about functional family therapy.

Wolpe, J. (1969). *The practice of behavior therapy.* New York: Pergamon Press.

This text is a comprehensive resource that includes a review of the theory, its implementation in clinical practice, and research that supports it use.

REFERENCES

Baucom, D. H., Epstein, N., & Gordon, K. C. (2000). Marital therapy: Theory, practice, and empirical status. In C. R. Synder & R. E. Ingram (Eds.), *Handbook of psychological change: Psychotherapy processes and practices for the 21st century* (pp. 65–90). New York: Guilford Press.

Christensen, A., Dimidjian, S., & Martell, C. R. (2015). Integrative behavioral couple therapy. In A. S. Gurman J. Lebow & D. K. Snyder (Eds.), *Clinical handbook of couple therapy* (pp. 61–96). New York: Guilford Press.

Christensen, A., Doss, B. D., & Jacobson, N. S. (2014). *Reconcilable differences: Rebuild your relationship by rediscovering your partner you love–without losing yourself* (2nd ed.). New York: Guilford Press.

Dattilio, F. M. (2010). *Cognitive-behavioral therapy with couples and families: A comprehensive guide for clinicians.* New York: Guilford Press.

Duncan, T. M., Davey, M., & Davey, A. (2011). Transporting functional family therapy to community-based programs. *Family Journal, 19*(1), 41–46. doi:10.1177/1066480710387269

Ellis, A. (1980). Rational-emotive therapy and cognitive behavior therapy: Similarities and differences. *Cognitive Therapy and Research, 4*(4), 325–340.

Fischer, M. S., Baucom, D. H., & Cohen, M. J. (2016). Cognitive-behavioral couple therapies: Review of the evidence for the treatment of relationship distress, psychopathology, and chronic health conditions. *Family Process, 55*(3), 423–442.

Jacobson N. S., & Christensen, A. (1996). *Acceptance and change in couple therapy: A therapist's guide to transforming relationships.* New York: Norton.

Mairal, J. B. (2015). Integrative behavioral couple therapy (IBCT) as a third wave therapy. *Psicothema, 27,* 13–18.

Northey, W. F. Jr., Wells, K. C., Silverman, W. K., & Bailey, C. E. (2003). Childhood behavioral and emotional disorders. *Journal of Marital and Family Therapy, 29,* 523–545.

Onedera, J. D. (2006). Functional family therapy: An interview with Dr. James Alexander. *Family Journal: Counseling and Therapy for Couples and Families, 14*(3), 306–311.

Patterson, T. (2005). Cognitive behavioral couples therapy. In M. Harway (Ed.), *Handbook of couples therapy* (pp. 119–140). Hoboken, NJ: Wiley.

CHAPTER 14

Solution-Focused Brief Therapy: A Constructivist Couples and Family Approach

Janet Froeschle Hicks, Stephan Berry, Brandé Flamez, and Tom Knowles-Bagwell

"Problem talk creates problems. Solution talk creates solutions."

—Steve De Shazer

When I first heard this quote, I was not sure what was meant by "solutions." I was instantly skeptical, and my first thought was, "If the family knew the solution, they wouldn't be in therapy." Now I laugh because I realize that solutions, while always present, are often hidden. With solution-focused brief therapy (SFBT), therapists empower families to recognize what works based on what worked previously. Because families describe their own solutions, results are often rapid, and pressures therapists face to demonstrate results are lessened. For this reason, SFBT, which seeks solutions rather than problems, has become an important treatment approach in recent years.

Treatment is often conducted in a short amount of time or in a limited number of sessions, although progress is measured by results, not by the number of sessions. SFBT values planning, focusing on wants and goals, building on successes, deemphasizing the past, and emphasizing behavior changed as the most effective and efficient way to help people improve their lives (DeJong & Berg, 2002; O'Hanlon & Weiner-Davis, 2003). One of solution-focused therapists' basic assumptions is that individuals and their families have the resources to build their own solutions (de Shazer & Miller, 1992).

SFBT is a social constructionist theory that focuses on finding solutions rather than dissecting problems. Social constructionism is based on the premise that reality is finite and subjective. Further, this reality is based on a person's knowledge, beliefs, experience, and communication with and perception of others (Bannink, 2007). As such, social constructionism believes a person can construct a unique success or defeat reality. To encourage a focus on the former (success and solutions), SFBT supporters do not tout spending inordinate amounts of time discussing problems. Rather, they suggest therapists focus on times when problems are not occurring or are less intense. In other words, past accomplishments are believed to be keys to future successes or solutions (de Shazer, 1988).

To fully understand the application of SFBT in family therapy, one must first understand the foundations of the theory. As a result, the first section of this chapter explores the history of SFBT, followed by a theoretical description and premises including goals, techniques, and multicultural and ethical considerations. Special issues and topics that lend themselves to the use of SFBT are discussed as part of case studies and key points family therapists should consider when using the theory.

LEARNING OBJECTIVES

After reading this chapter, you will be able to do the following:

- Explore the history of SFBT and the major theorists.
- Describe the goals, techniques and multicultural and ethical considerations evident when using SFBT.
- Identify techniques and interventions associated with SFBT to special issues and topics.
- Integrate SFBT when working within marriage and family therapy.

HISTORY AND BACKGROUND OF SFBT

Profile of Main Figures

Steve de Shazer and Insoo Kim Berg are a husband-and-wife team credited with the development of SFBT (MacDonald, 2011; Trepper, Dolan, McCollum, & Nelson, 2006). De Shazer and Berg were introduced to one another by John Weakland, their mentor, at the Mental Research Institute (MRI) in 1977. Prior to this introduction, de Shazer worked as a professional saxophonist, and Berg, a Korean native, moved to the United States to study pharmacy. After moving to the United States, Berg developed an interest in social work and psychotherapy (Visser, 2013). Following their introduction, de Shazer and Berg became a couple, married, and decided to move to Milwaukee, Wisconsin, where they founded the Brief Family Therapy Center (BFTC) in 1978. Over the course of their careers, the two worked alongside their team at the BFTC to create and refine the tenets of SFBT. After presenting a workshop on SFBT in London in 2005, de Shazer contracted pneumonia while traveling to Austria and died 2 days later. Berg died in 2007 at age 72. However, their legacy will always be linked to the introduction and establishment of SFBT as a viable and effective therapy.

Evolution of the Theory

De Shazer and Berg were influenced by several theorists. Milton Erickson (O'Connell, 2012), Gregory Bateson (Visser, 2013), peers at the MRI (Ratner, George, & Iveson, 2012), and the BFTC (Visser, 2013) each provided foundational pieces and constructs that de Shazer and Berg incorporated into the principles of SFBT as we know it today.

Milton Erickson. Erickson was a psychiatrist and hypnotherapist who used unconventional techniques to effect change in his clients. Erikson, who practiced from the 1920s to the 1970s, believed that individuals possess the strengths and resources needed to resolve their problems. He also proposed that people were more likely to benefit from treatment if therapists accepted and used whatever material clients presented and focused on current behavior (Weakland,Watzalwick, & Fisch, 1974). Erickson did not believe in the philosophy that therapy needed to be a long, drawn out process or that diagnostic labels were necessary (O'Connell, 2012). Reflecting a stance foundational within current SFBT perspectives, Erickson also believed a small change could set in motion a series of bigger changes and that people have the power to solve their own problems.

Gregory Bateson. Bateson was an anthropologist who began studying the communication patterns of families. Bateson understood the importance of systems as they related to the development of solutions that effect change. Also reminiscent of SFBT, Bateson stated, "The social system in which people function is of great importance to the development and solution of problems" (as cited in Visser, 2013, p. 11). This statement reflects two of the key ideas in SFBT, that of taking a systems approach and of seeking solutions. In addition, Bateson's work was foundational in the development of the "do something different" principle in SFBT.

Mental Research Institute. The Brief Therapy Center was founded in 1966 under the umbrella of the MRI. The Brief Therapy Center developed a succinct, goal-oriented, practical method of therapy. As a forerunner to SFBT, this approach to therapy included the concepts of viewing the person seeking therapy as a client or customer rather than a patient, a here-and-now focus to therapy, and the replacement of ineffective behaviors with more effective ones (Visser, 2013).

Brief Family Therapy Center. Both de Shazer and Berg were social workers who were dissatisfied with traditional methods of therapy and wanted to find more effective approaches. When de Shazer met Berg, he had been using a one-way mirror to observe therapists in action to determine the mechanisms of effective therapy. The clinic's resistance to using the one-way mirror or other innovative approaches to therapy caused de Shazer and Berg to open the BFTC in 1978 (de Shazer et al., 2007). Originally, the BFTC was in de Shazer and Berg's living room, until they could set up an office. It was at the BFTC that de Shazer, Berg, and their colleagues began to investigate what worked in therapy. Rather than start with a theoretical perspective, they worked to discover what inductively led to change in therapy (Visser, 2013). Guided Practice Exercise 14.1 asks you to analyze pros and cons of this method.

GUIDED PRACTICE EXERCISE 14.1: NON–THEORETICALLY BASED RESEARCH

As you learned in Chapter 6, the ACA Code of Ethics (ACA, 2014) states, "Therapists have a responsibility to the public to engage in counseling practices that are based on rigorous research methodologies" (p. 8). What risks did de Shazer and Berg's first clients face? Would some therapists see these research practices as unethical today? Discuss your thoughts with a partner.

The research done via observation of live sessions and videotape at the BFTC yielded surprising results. De Shazer and Berg found that the absence of problem analysis and diagnosis in the therapeutic process did not affect client outcomes. Further, techniques and approaches began to emerge that helped clients articulate desires and attain goals. It became evident that what worked for one client did not necessarily work for another. This fact led the group to theorize that what mattered most in therapy was not the specific intervention implemented by the therapist but "interventions that helped the client formulate more clearly what they wanted to achieve, that helped the client become more confident in their possibilities, and that helped identify ideas for steps forward" (Visser, 2013, p. 12).

The couple continued to work on the principles and core concepts that would become SFBT, and in 1982 de Shazer published his first book on SFBT, called *Patterns of Brief Family Therapy: An Ecosystemic Approach* (1982). Although the book was not well received, it did introduce the world to de Shazer's theory of brief therapy. De Shazer then followed up his book with an article he and Alex Molnar cowrote, entitled "Four Useful Interventions in Brief Therapy" (1984), which introduced the SFBT concepts of doing something different, overcoming the urge, and redefining of stability as change. In de Shazer's (1985) second book, *Keys to Solution in Brief Therapy*, his concepts of creating an expectation of change, the lack of detailed problem analysis, and past successes as keys to future solutions were described and articulated for the first time in print. After the publication of this book, *solution focused* became the term most associated with de Shazer's brand of therapy. Over the next few years, other SFBT concepts and techniques, such as scaling, the miracle question, and exceptions, were introduced and became accepted practices. In the 1990s Berg began to write extensively about the application of SFBT in both therapeutic and nontherapeutic contexts (Visser, 2013). Today de Shazer and Berg's work serves as the foundation for the widespread acceptance and use of SFBT in couples and family settings.

O'Hanlon and Weiner-Davis. In addition to de Shazer and Berg, others have played prominent roles in the development of solution-focused therapy throughout the past 30 years. Two such figures are Bill O'Hanlon and Michele Weiner-Davis. O'Hanlon, a former graduate student of Milton Erikson's who exchanged gardening services for academic mentorship, and Wiener-Davis, a marriage and family therapist specializing in divorce prevention, codeveloped solution-oriented therapy following their work with the BFTC. Solution-oriented therapy is a form of therapy based on the premise that clients should be directed to identify and use their own personal strengths to overcome challenges and reach their goals. Like de Shazer and Berg, O'Hanlon and Weiner-Davis believed that the root cause of a problem was irrelevant, and only a discussion of the steps needed to solve the problem was warranted. The works of these individuals also provided the foundation for the development of the solution-focused approach practiced today.

KEY CONCEPTS

Solution-focused therapy is based on several unique premises. Each of the concepts that form a framework for the theory follows in the next sections.

Definition of Constructivism, Constructionism, Social Constructionism, and Humanism

It is important to note that unlike other theories you have learned about thus far, an underlying conceptualization of human nature is not included in the solution-focused response (Flamez & Watson, 2014). What do we mean by this? SFBT is a theory of practice rather than, say, a theory of human nature. This theory is based on the philosophical principles of social constructionism and humanism. Let's talk about the first underlying principle, social constructionism, and then we will discuss the second underlying principle, humanism.

Social construction. An understanding of the distinction between the terms *constructivism*, *constructionism*, and *social constructionism* is crucial if one is to understand the theoretical premises and evolution of SFBT. Constructivism, constructionism, and social constructionism all evolved from Vygotsky's (1962) social development theory (Learning Theories, 2015). In his theory, Vygotsky (1962) focused on the connection between people and the sociocultural context in which they interact. Bruner (1966) expanded these connections by further defining constructivism as a philosophical concept, placing emphasis on an individual's ability to learn from the past. Thus, with constructivism, everyone creates their own reality based on previous events, interactions, experiences, and trainings. For example, a person who has been bitten by or exposed to vicious dogs may have learned to fear certain animals and has constructed a personal reality that animals are not trustworthy.

Papert and Idit (1991) reinforced the educational perspective of constructivism by defining constructions as educational products created based on constructivist learning. Thus, the constructionist paradigm views reality as being constructed through interactions or even language. The cognitive processes themselves are a "reality" constructed through interaction. When referring to constructionism, a person whose constructivist reality believes dogs are not trustworthy shares these notions with others who cognitively adopt the ideas and educate others on this shared reality. Thus, the cognitions become collective rather than individual ideas.

Social constructionism incorporated both aspects by considering the understanding between a person, society, language, and subjective reality (Berger & Luckmann, 1966). Thus, with social constructionism, persons within society consider teachings but also incorporate their own reality. For example, several persons in society may question that all animals are vicious based on their own experiences and collectively revisit teachings as they understand the systemic contributions to the cognitions. Society then constructs its own reality based on all aspects. De Shazer and Berg applied the concepts of social constructionism within SFBT by intentionally focusing on solutions rather than problems, using specific wording as a component within session techniques, and discussing previous times when problems were reduced or nonexistent.

Humanism. Humanism views the human condition holistically and therefore gives little credence to genes, the unconscious mind, or observable behaviors alone. The stance resulted in humanistic theory which grew out of the existential premise of free will and continued with Rogers (1959) and Maslow's (1968) contentions that all persons inherently move toward growth and fulfillment. Considered the third force in the realm of counseling, humanism focuses on the unique qualities of human beings and consequently rejects behavioral and psychodynamic approaches as being inadequate and discards animal studies used to make human comparisons (Maslow, 1968). Although SFBT is not traditionally classified as a humanistic theory, many contend it is based first upon constructivism and second on humanism. Humanism is evident in SFBT through use of empathy, a belief in innate personal growth, and the stance that all humans have unique needs and must have focused treatment.

PREMISES OF THE THEORY

Theoretical Description

SFBT asks a unique question: "How do we construct meaningful solutions for couples and families?" Solution-focused brief therapists believe the answer to this question lies in the ability to determine what the couple or family wants, utilize what is already working for them, and have them do something different. Many of the premises and tasks given SFBT aim to help clients find out desired goals and instill positive futuristic thinking in lieu of a problematic focus (DeJong & Berg, 2002; Walter & Peller, 1992). Much insight about the theory can be gleaned through an understanding of the theoretical worldview, time orientation, role of the therapist, and assumptions and goals of the theory as described below.

Worldview. An integral paradigm within SFBT is looking at clients through a positive, hopeful lens. The solution-focused brief therapist views human beings as the experts on their own problems. Due to a belief in the competency of their clients, the SFBT therapist focuses on helping couples and families formulate problems in concrete terms and in a manner that can be solved. Solution-focused therapists believe that families are not only strong and resilient but also possess the self-efficacy to implement the strategies they created to solve their own problems (De Jong & Berg, 2002; Trepper et al., 2006).

Time orientation. SFBT is different than most traditional therapies in that it does not focus on the past but instead has couples and families look to the future. History is not relevant, in the sense that a detailed history of the problem is not needed or desired. The past is only examined when it provides examples of when the problem was not as severe or did not exist.

Role of the Therapist

In SFBT the therapist exhibits a positive, respectful, and hopeful approach to therapy. The therapeutic relationship is built on the premise of the client as the expert on the problem and its solution and the therapist as a facilitator of change. Cooperation is the primary ingredient in the client–therapist relationship (Davis & Osborn, 2000; DeJong & Berg, 2013); thus, the therapist's function is that of collaborator and consultant. To accomplish these tasks, therapists need to set a positive tone, engage in active listening, ask open questions, give reassurance, communicate acceptance, and clearly communicate the purpose and objectives of counseling (Davis & Osborn, 2000; De Jong & Berg, 2013). Engaging in an empathetic, genuine, and respectful manner with the client is also important.

To establish a positive, cooperative therapeutic alliance with the client, Osborn (1999) suggests several guidelines for the therapist to consider:

> *Listen, do not label; investigate, do not interrogate; level, do not lecture; cooperate, do not convince; clarify, do not confront; solicit solutions, do not prescribe them; consult, do not cure; commend, do not condemn; explore, do not explain; be directive, not dictatorial. (p. 176)*

Every couple or family demonstrates "a unique way of attempting to cooperate, and the therapist's job becomes, first, to describe that manner to himself that the family shows and, then, to cooperate with the family's way and, thus, to promote change" (de Shazer, 1982, pp. 9–10). The therapist conveys to the family that "the therapist expects changing and that he is confident that changing will occur" (de Shazer, 1984, p. 15). The therapist functions as a gatherer of information and a sounding board for the client's consideration of their solution creating abilities. The focus of the relationship is always predicated on the therapist helping the couple or family discover their own strengths.

ASSESSMENT AND TREATMENT

Assessment

Assessment is an ongoing process in SFBT. From the moment the first session begins, the assessment process also begins. However, the type of assessment done in SFBT is not the formal, standardized testing that is generally thought of when the term assessment is mentioned. When it comes to assessment, the SFBT therapist assumes a different role compared with the other approaches you have read about thus far. SFBT therapists do not seek to establish formal diagnoses using assessment; rather, the assessment is the process of continually addressing the client's movement toward their goals. Questions are the primary assessment tool used by SFBT (e.g., miracle, scaling, coping, exceptions, fast-forward questions, and relationship questions), as they allow us to see where clients currently stand and where they hope to be in the future, monitor progress, and discover which approaches were beneficial or not (Flamez & Watson, 2014).

This assessment of goal attainment begins with the client's description of the presenting problem. The SFBT therapist works with the couple or family to clarify and operationalize the problem. Questions such as "What is being said or done?," "What happens next?," "How long has this been going on?," "Where are you on the scale?," and "How often is this happening?" are examples of questions used to formulate a statement that is measurable and solvable (Institute for Solution-Focused Therapy, 2017; MacDonald, 2011). This initial assessment also involves discerning whether presession changes have occurred. The therapist asks questions to detect small changes occurring between the time of the initial appointment and the first session.

Scaling questions are another technique utilized to determine goal attainment. Scaling questions allow the client to describe the severity of the problem or the progress they have made in resolving the problem. Ongoing scaling and assessment continues until the client resolves the problem and therapy is no longer needed or desired. To more fully understand this process, let us examine the assumptions, goals, and techniques involved in SFBT.

Assumptions

Walter and Peller (1992) describe 12 working assumptions used when counseling couples and families with SFBT. First, the therapist must adhere to the belief that a focus on the positive is therapeutic. Second, it must be assumed that exceptions or past successes can lead to future accomplishment. Third, the therapist must believe that change is constant, and fourth, that small changes lead to larger changes. The fifth and sixth assumptions state that clients are doing the best they can and are cooperating to the greatest extent possible. The last six assumptions include the premise that people have a need to solve their problems; meaning and experience are constructed; descriptions of actions affect the action itself; the meaning of the message should be the focus; the client has the expertise needed to fix him- or herself; and a description of a solution affects interactions within the family or couple. Once the therapist buys into these assumptions, a few additional ground rules help set a positive outlook for sessions.

Rules of thumb. De Shazer (1985) outlines a few rules of thumb that set the stage for positive outcomes and guide actions and techniques in SFBT. The first rule states, "If it works, don't fix it." So often therapists try to change something that the family does not need fixed. Unfortunately, well-intended therapists can inflict additional stress and harm. The second rule says, "If everything you are doing is not working, do something different." It is important that the couple or family continue to try new things to correct problematic issues. The third rule states, "Keep it simple." Helpful interventions do not have to be sophisticated or complicated to work. Often, interventions viewed as simple are the most effective. The last rule states, "Approach each session as if it were the last and only time you will see that client." Therapists focus on what can be done to help the couple or family immediately and within the current session.

Berg and Miller (1992) and de Shazer (1988) identify additional philosophies relevant to understanding the theory. Berg and Miller state that if something works, do more of it. They also tout that if something doesn't work, it should be eliminated. De Shazer makes it clear that the client, in this case the couple or family, is the expert. Often, therapists forget to ask couples and families what has or has not been successful and give little credence to the client's unique understanding of self.

GOALS

Once assumptions and ground rules have been established philosophically, the therapist can focus on the direction clients must take to achieve positive life changes. The first goal is to help couples and families construct solutions by identifying and utilizing exceptions to problems and avoid dissecting the problem. The second goal is to identify and reinforce strengths and competencies within each family or couple. The third goal is to help establish specific goals and use client resources in helping the couple or family change self-defeating behaviors (Davis & Osborn, 2000). Guided Practice Exercise 14.2 asks you to consider the goals of SFBT in relationship to your personal values and beliefs.

GUIDED PRACTICE EXERCISE 14.2: A SOLUTION FOCUS

SFBT surmises that a focus on solutions and the positive is more therapeutic than spending time dissecting problems. It further states that people are the experts on themselves and have the innate ability to "fix" themselves. Do you agree or disagree with this stance? How much time should a therapist spend discussing a couple or family's problems in your opinion? Have you ever been in a situation in which a negative conversation made you feel down? Do you think a relationship exists between negative conversations and mood? Why or why not? How might your opinions relate to your ability to use SFBT within the couples and family setting?

TECHNIQUES

Several techniques are unique to SFBT and lend themselves to the final goal, an agreement as to which problem families would like solved. These techniques include complimenting, the miracle question, exception questions, scaling, coping questions, relationship questions, identifying relationship types, and feedback (De Jong & Berg, 2013). Each technique is described as follows.

Complimenting. Complimenting is a technique utilized throughout sessions and serves several purposes in SFBT. First, complimenting reveals family strengths and successes that are important to the client and therefore assists in meeting goals. Some of these strengths may not have been previously considered by the couple or family. In this way, complimenting not only empowers families but also reframes issues.

Compliments can be given as either direct spoken compliments or indirect compliments. You can think of direct compliments as positive evaluations and reactions in response to what your client stated (De Jong & Berg, 2013). For example, "You are quite persistent" is a direct and spoken compliment. Indirect compliments are questions implying strengths within the family. For example, "How have you managed to stay connected as a family despite excessive homework and work demands?" This statement implies the family is persistent, hardworking, and dedicated to the system. As you can see from this example and unlike compliments given in individual therapy, marriage and family therapists often offer direct and indirect systemic compliments. For example, the family may receive a direct compliment such as, "As a family, you seem to show great perseverance and unity when one family member is persecuted."

Miracle question. The miracle question is used to elicit unlimited possibilities regarding a nonproblematic future (DeJong & Berg, 2002). In this technique, couples and families are asked to imagine how life will be different once the problem disappears. For example, the therapist might say, "Pretend that tonight while you are asleep a miracle occurs. While you are sleeping your family or relationship problems disappear. When you wake up you notice things are different in your relationship. What will be different that lets you know this miracle occurred?" This future vision requires much thought from the couple or family and patience on the part of the therapist. Many couples and families are unprepared for the miracle question and need time and follow-up questions to process the information. For example, questions such as "How would your relationship be different if this occurred?" and "Who would notice if this miracle occurred?" offer the ability to process and reframe miracles that may be outside the couple's locus of control.

Exception questions. A major tenet of SFBT involves exploring times when problems were less severe or nonexistent. Therapists can ask specific questions to elicit these descriptions of exceptions. For example, the therapist asks, "Have there been times when the problem did not exist or was not as severe? Tell me about those times." Next, the therapist can listen for differences between times of exception and those deemed problematic. Therapists can help in this process by asking follow-up questions such as "What was different during those times?" Exception questions help couples and families understand their own inherent power in creating solutions. Unlike exceptions used in individual therapy, family therapists explore exceptions occurring within and affecting the family system.

Scaling. Scaling questions are used to determine progress over time, to define the severity of the problem, and to describe motivation levels (DeJong & Berg, 2002). Scaling helps clients formulate a concrete explanation for abstract feelings. When used to determine progress and problem severity, the therapist might say, "On a scale from 0 to 10 with 0 being as bad as the problem gets and 10 meaning an absence of the problem, where are you as a family?" Regardless of the answer given, a positive focus is given to the response. For example, if the family says, "We are at a 0," the therapist might respond with a compliment and coping question, such as, "You have great tenacity because even though you are at a 0 you came to counseling today. How did you do that?" Should the family say, "We are at a 2 today," the therapist might say, "Wow! You are already up to a 2. What have you done to get yourselves up to a 2? What would it take to move up to a 3?"

Scaling is also used to determine motivation levels. By measuring motivation, the therapist can determine how likely families will be to follow through with tasks and goals. Once again, scaling is used to measure this motivation level and might be stated, "On a scale from 0 to 10 with 0 meaning you are willing to do nothing to solve this problem and 10 meaning you will do anything, where are you?" Responses to this question help the therapist elicit end-of-session feedback and determine accuracy of goals.

Coping questions. Coping questions offer a method whereby couples and families transition from a problem to solution focus. For example, a family who states their life is "unmanageable and awful" would be asked, "How have you managed to keep everyone healthy and maintain job and school productivity?" or "How have you handled this for so long?" These questions elicit strengths such that clients become aware of strengths and successes they minimized or did not previously recognize. Recognition of these strengths offers hope that things can improve.

Relationship questions. Relationship questions were derived from the family systems intervention of circular questioning. Often people get stuck in a problem, and they are unable to think of other alternatives or clients respond to solution talk with statements such as, "I don't know." Relationship Questions allow families to view themselves from the perspective of one another and therapists can use these questions to point out exceptions or encourage clients to avoid self-defeating behaviors (De Jong & Berg, 2013). By weaving those for whom the family cares deeply into the conversation, all persons may be more apt to make positive changes or think more globally. For example, when asked if there are times the problem was not occurring, the family might say, "I am not sure." The therapist might then turn to the grandparents and say, "How would you answer this question?" Another example might be if a family member states, "My drinking is never a problem for the family." The therapist might turn to the children and say, "Describe the impact of Dad's drinking."

Relationship types. While SFBT does not advocate labeling clients, it does describe three different types of relationships therapists establish with couples and families. These relationship types serve as a guide when determining feedback, tasks, and session goals.

The first and often most difficult of the relationship types is the "visitor relationship." The visitor relationship is one in which the therapist and client do not mutually agree on a problem, let alone a goal. When working in this type of relationship, solution-focused therapists take the stance that client perceptions make sense. Asking questions that elicit "proof" of perceptions in a calm stance of pretended ignorance helps clients in a visitor relationship own behaviors (DeJong & Berg, 2002). For example, the parents who say "Arguing in front of our children is not hurting anyone" might be asked, "What happens that indicates no harm exists? How does arguing in front of the children help your family?"

The second type of relationship described in SFBT is the "complainant-type relationship." With this type of relationship, therapists and couples or families mutually agree on a problem but cannot agree on the client's role in the process. Couples or families in this type of relationship may say things that blame others, such as, "If the kids would stop screaming all the time, we would be fine" or "If he would just stop, get up and do chores, I would not need to be here." The client does not recognize their role in the problem and therefore, does not see a role in the solution. Therapists can respond by listening and asking questions that place personal ownership on the client. For example, the therapist might ask, "How would your family relationship be different if your husband did chores?" The therapist can capitalize on responses that elicit problem ownership and may often transform the relationship to that of a customer-type relationship.

As mentioned above, the third type of relationship is entitled the "customer-type relationship." These ideal couples and families both recognize the problem and see their part in the solution. These clients are ready to utilize exceptions and establish goals right away (DeJong & Berg, 2002). Families establishing customer-type relationships are often given behavioral tasks as part of session feedback.

Feedback. Feedback consists of three connected parts: compliment, bridge, and task. First, the therapist offers a sincere compliment to the couple or family followed by a bridge, or rationale for a task. The bridge offers the therapist an opportunity to agree with the problem discussed while leading into an appropriate client task. The task consists of either an observation or behavioral homework assignment. For example, the family might be asked to observe a situation or perform a task involving a behavior. When the three parts of feedback are linked, it might appear as follows. "I respect that your family is working very hard to improve the climate in your home and I agree that you all deserve to be treated with respect. As a result, I suggest you observe times when you do not feel disrespect in a conversation and write down what is happening that is different at that time." Levels of motivation, confidence, relationship type, and progress, as determined when scaling earlier in the session, should be considered when assigning a task (DeJong & Berg, 2002). Case Presentation 14.1 asks you to apply the techniques with a specific couple.

CASE PRESENTATION 14.1: USING TECHNIQUES

Betty and Jane are in a committed relationship. Betty says that Jane is irresponsible, can't hold a job, and does nothing to help at home. Jane responds by stating that Betty is a slob who "strings her clothes all over the house." Betty and Jane come to you saying, "We seem to be drifting apart and would like to rekindle our relationship." Betty and Jane also state that their parents have "disowned" them because of their "lesbian lifestyle." Which techniques might you immediately use with Betty and Jane? What type of relationship are Betty and Jane probably exhibiting? What would you do for Betty and Jane? Using the three steps mentioned as part of feedback, how might you phrase this feedback?

Multicultural Considerations

SFBT has been shown to be an effective intervention in terms of implementing culturally sensitive therapy (De Jong & Berg, 2013). In SFBT, the relationship between the therapist and client is one of cooperation and collaboration. "By understanding and incorporating a minority client's ethnic or cultural values and experiences, a solution-focused clinician can help further build a collaborative relationship by lessening the burden on minority clients who must retell and explain their stories" (Kim, 2014, p. 10). The SFBT adopts a position of "not knowing" and "leading from one step behind" (De Jong & Berg, 2013, p. 20), all the while remaining "curious about and intrigued by the client's idiosyncratic perspectives" (Lewis & Osborn, 2004, p. 42). The techniques in SFBT can be adapted as a way of bridging the culture gaps between clients and therapists. One example is using coping questions. The strengths elicited from coping questions can include such cultural supports as spiritual beliefs, community resources, and family supports that enable the client to mitigate the effects of the problem.

SFBT has been successfully used with various cultural groups such as Asian immigrants, African Americans, LGBTQ, and the economically disadvantaged (Kim, 2014). SFBT has also been adapted for use with Native Americans (Meyer & Cottone, 2013), children and adolescents (Corcoran, 2002), and persons with disabilities (Estrada & Beyebach, 2007). Given the social constructivist underpinnings of SFBT and the therapist's stance of "not knowing," the client's cultural viewpoint is always being acknowledged and informs the process.

Ethical Considerations

Ethical practice should be a primary consideration no matter what theoretical orientation is used. This is no less true when using SFBT. Issues such as the imposition of personal values, definition of who the client is, and the misuse of techniques of SFBT are all issues for which the ethical therapist must be aware of, and address, in therapy.

The personal values of a therapist can affect the counseling relationship. This is especially true should the therapist utilize gender stereotyping. The proper use of SFBT eliminates this imposition of values by a therapist, because it is the client who defines the problem, creates the solution, and evaluates the amount of success achieved. The opportunity for the therapist to impose personal values is therefore minimized provided the therapist adheres to the theoretical principles.

When working with couples or families it can be difficult to explain that the client being served is the intact couple or family unit. This definition can be difficult since the presence of two or more people often results in conflicting individual issues. An important question in these instances is: Whose issue gets served? Guman (2013) suggested resolving this issue by advocating for the family system rather than individuals within the system. This way, one member of the couple or family system does not have needs placed above another member's needs.

Strengths and Limitations

As with any theory, SFBT has both strengths and weaknesses. Many of SFBT's strengths are based on its brief nature. For example, consumers and insurance companies experience reduced costs due to fewer sessions. While many might associate fewer sessions with poor outcomes, several studies suggest that SFBT has the potential to improve client outcomes as early as the first or second session (Adams, Piercy, & Jurich, 1991; de Shazer, 1985; Jordan & Quinn, 1994). It is not surprising, therefore, that strong evidence supports the notion that SFBT is an effective treatment method (Gingerich & Peterson, 2013).

Critics state that SFBT spends too little time delving into problems and uncomfortably elevates clients into the role of expert (Lightfoot, 2014). These critics argue this deemphasis on problems results in a shallow, insufficient, and ineffective result (Hermann & McWhirter, 1996; Lightfoot, 2014). Supporters of SFBT respond to this criticism by stating that other theories go too in-depth and solve problems that do not exist, thereby wasting client time and resources. When interviewed, de Shazer stated that many theorists become too involved with the science of mental illness such that they forget to look at what works for mental health (Hoyt, 2001). He also believed these practitioners discounted the client's ability and knowledge to determine both the problem and the solution (Hoyt, 2001). Guided Practice Exercise 14.3 asks you to consider your own perceptions of the theory's strengths and weaknesses.

GUIDED PRACTICE EXERCISE 14.3: STRENGTHS AND WEAKNESSES

Thus far, you have read about the assumptions, goals, and techniques imbedded within SFBT. You have also read the strengths and weaknesses related to the theory. As you read through the techniques, did any appeal or not appeal to you? In addition to the strengths and weaknesses listed in the chapter, what criticisms or compliments do you have of this theory? When working with couples and families, what issue(s) might be best handled with the techniques learned as part of this theory? Do you agree that SFBT does not delve far enough into a client's problems? Why or why not?

Special Issues in the Couples and Family Setting
Substance Use

The National Institute on Drug Abuse (2013) reported that 17.3 million Americans either abused or were dependent on alcohol, and 9.4% of those aged 12 or older used illicit drugs within the past month. It comes as no surprise, therefore, that substance use issues are prevalent in counseling. Many clients require inpatient treatment programs that typically involve a 28-day residential stay. In these inpatient facilities, clients receive a combination of medical detoxification, therapy (individual, group, and family), and immersion in 12-step programs (Marion & Oliver, 2014). SFBT serves as an alternative to this inpatient model and offers several advantages.

Unlike many inpatient models, SFBT can be used by itself or in conjunction with other substance abuse treatment modalities, can involve the entire family system, and does not assume abstinence from all chemicals is the only solution (Berg & Miller, 1992; Linton, 2005). The client decides if they want to seek abstinence, reduce the amount they use, or reduce the problems associated with their use (Berg & Miller, 1992). Case Presentation 14.2 asks you to consider how SFBT might help a couple suffering because of alcohol use.

CASE PRESENTATION 14.2: SUBSTANCE USE TREATMENT AND SFBT

Danny is a 54-year-old man who presented to counseling along with his wife, Lydia, for help dealing with the marital strife and discord they are currently experiencing. Lydia states Danny's use of alcohol has created multiple stressors for the couple, including increased fighting between Danny and Lydia, financial stress due to Danny's frequent absenteeism from work, and pending legal issues due to Danny's recent arrest for DWI. Danny says things are not as bad as his wife is making them out to be, but he is afraid that if things don't get better between them, she will end up divorcing him after 29 years of marriage. Danny states his job as an accountant is very stressful and that his drinking helps him "blow off steam". Danny states if he could just learn how to cope with stress better, everything would be okay. Lydia says things were fine in the marriage until 2 years ago, when Danny began drinking a half to a full bottle of wine every night. Lydia says Danny falls asleep on the couch each night by nine o'clock and that they never do anything together anymore. She wants Danny to stop drinking altogether. How do you go about resolving Danny and Lydia's conflicting goals for treatment? Is Danny's use of alcohol an issue that needs to be addressed from the beginning of therapy, and if so, how do you as a therapist bring it up when Danny does not see it as an issue? What aspects of this case might you need help with from other professionals?

Counseling Parents and Children in the School Setting

The literature touts the importance of involving families in the school setting as stakeholders in their child's academic experiences (Gerrard, 2008, 2015). This emphasis changes school counseling from the traditional therapist-student only sessions approach to one where parents are included in some sessions. This new school based family counseling approach requires training and an integration of both school and family counseling.

When involving these families in the school setting, SFBT is mentioned as an effective and preferred counseling modality (Bond, Woods, Humphrey, Smyes, & Green, 2013; Brasher, 2009; Kim & Franklin, 2008). Issues such as negative student behaviors, emotional problems, lowered self-esteem, poor peer relationships, and academic failure have been discussed in the literature as being effectively reduced through school-based solution-focused brief family therapy (Kim & Franklin, 2008; Taathadi, 2014). Case Presentation 14.3 discusses a case wherein a school therapist helps a student improve her grades and self-esteem using SFBT.

CASE PRESENTATION 14.3: SOLUTION-FOCUSED BRIEF FAMILY THERAPY IN THE SCHOOL

Rosa is a 14-year-old eighth-grade student who has been referred to the therapist for help improving her grades. After visiting with Rosa for a short time, the therapist learns that Rosa was recently removed from her biological parents' home due to abuse inflicted upon Rosa by her older brother. Because Rosa's biological parents could not remove her brother from the home and therefore ensure her safety, Child Protective Services moved Rosa to a foster home. Rosa states that she does not like her foster mother because she is "so bossy." Rosa also says she doesn't care about her grades because she "just wants to go home." Rosa can see her biological parents under supervision, provided her older brother is not present. As a result, Rosa's biological parents meet with her regularly at the school. Because Rosa's foster mother is required to be present for meetings between Rosa and her biological parents, they have met and want what is best for Rosa. Should the therapist work with Rosa alone or involve her parents? If you worked with Rosa and her biological parents, would you also involve the foster mother? As a therapist, what would you do to help Rosa?

Case Presentations: The Cases of Danny, Lydia, and Rosa

Several sidebars in this chapter discuss case studies with unanswered counseling-related questions. Following is a discussion offering potential responses to these case studies based on counseling standards of practice. These responses are suggestions and should not be regarded as the only possibility for working with these fictional couples or families.

The case of Danny and Lydia. The case of Danny and Lydia poses several challenges for any therapist who works with them. One pressing issue that needs to be given immediate attention is the possibility of Danny experiencing withdrawal symptoms should he significantly decrease his alcohol use. Danny will need to be evaluated by a physician who is familiar with the effects and treatment of alcohol withdrawal to determine if monitoring or treatment of withdrawal symptoms is indicated.

Since Danny feels his main issue is stress and not drinking, the SFBT therapist should be "apprehensive about prescribing abstinence from AOD [alcohol or other drugs] as the goal of treatment, at least at the onset of therapy, if the client did not consider abstinence as a desired goal" (Linton, 2005, p. 303). Danny should be allowed to develop his own goals and solutions and then test them out to see if they work.

Following is a portion of a counseling session that might occur with Danny and Lydia using SFBT. The session begins after Danny and Lydia state the presenting problem.

Therapist: Danny and Lydia, I hear that you are having relationship problems. Lydia, you feel the problem started 2 years ago when Danny starting drinking. Danny, you think stressors at work are the issue and drinking helps you unwind. First, I want to commend both of you for seeking help. It takes courage and a strong belief this relationship can work for you to be here. (**Complimenting.**) Tell me about a time when things were better between you. (**Exception question.**)

Lydia: Five years ago, Danny would come home and hug me. We would cuddle on the couch and watch a movie at night. Danny would not come home, ignore me, and drink all night.

Danny: Yeah, well, 5 years ago I had a different job and my commute was shorter. Now my boss yells at me all the time and I can't keep up at work. I come home and Lydia instantly starts fussing at me not to drink.

Therapist: So, things were better 5 years ago (paraphrase). Describe what each of you said or did 5 years ago that was different. What was working then? (**Exception question.**)

Lydia: Danny was happy to see me when he came home. He kissed me, hugged me, and acted glad to have me around.

Danny: Lydia was not yelling about drinking when I came home.

Therapist: So now I know how you view the other person's behavior differently but how did YOU act differently? (**Creating personal responsibility for the exception.**)

Danny: I guess I did come home and kiss Lydia. We would spend more time together. I was drinking less.

Lydia: I would cook Danny's favorite foods and make sure he was included in family decisions. Now I feel I am forced to do everything alone.

Therapist: So, I hear there are several things you used to do that you no longer do such as kissing, cooking, less drinking, and including each other. (**Paraphrasing; establishing future tasks.**) If you woke up tomorrow and your relationship was perfect, what would be different? (**Miracle question.**)

Lydia: We would go back in time to when we were happy.

Danny: My job would be less stressful and Lydia would be nicer.

Therapist: That would be nice but these may be things beyond your control. How would YOU be different if this occurred. How would you behave differently? (**Processing the miracle question.**)

Danny: I would come home and hug Lydia. We might even go out for dinner. I would have only a few drinks at the end of the day.

Lydia: I would think about Danny during the day and not dread his arrival. I would never have to discuss his drinking.

Therapist: On a scale from 0-10 with one meaning the problem is in control and 10 meaning you have complete control, where are you? (**Scaling.**)

Lydia: About a 5.

Danny: About a 6.

Therapist: Wow! You are already around a 5 or 6. What did you do to get up that high?

Danny and Lydia discuss specific reasons they stated a 5 or 6. The therapist notes what is working so these things can be continued and enhanced in the future. Using the exceptions from above (i.e., kissing, cooking, less drinking, and inclusion), along with those from the scaling above, Lydia and Danny create a list of tasks to incorporate before the next session.

At this point and when possible, the therapist consults with other SFBT therapists who view sessions through a one-way mirror and offer input.

Therapist: First, I want to say how impressed I am at your tenacity in dealing with your problems. I also respect the patience you show one another while dealing with so much. I agree with you that things need to improve. Over the next week, which tasks would you be willing to work on? (**Feedback.**)

Danny and Lydia develop goals for the following week and attend follow-up sessions. In the subsequent follow-up sessions, Danny can report on the effectiveness of the solutions he has developed. However, given Lydia's feelings about the problem, Danny faces a difficult task in reducing his stress if Lydia's concerns are not addressed. The therapist must avoid the perception of taking sides while also addressing Lydia's concerns.

The use of SFBT can be an effective intervention strategy in cases where alcohol or drug is a concern. Using SFBT, Danny and Lydia will be able to address the issues they face as a couple. Danny will be able to determine if he is able to lessen the stress in his life with or without addressing his alcohol use. Working together as a couple and with the help of the SFBT therapist, the solution to Danny and Lydia's issues can be achieved.

The case of Rosa. The case of Rosa involves many facets. For example, Rosa has been abused by a loved one, removed from her home, and placed in foster care with a stranger. So what is the therapist to do for Rosa?

First, therapists must recognize that being removed from home, although offering safety, causes enormous emotional pain (Sanders, 2016). Rosa probably feels abandoned, anxious about her new home environment and uncertain future, and even guilty for causing disruption in her biological family. Further, she is grieving many recent losses (family, home, neighborhood friends). Because Rosa needs help bonding with her foster mother and will probably return home to her biological parents once her brother is of age, it is probably best to involve foster and biological parents in the counseling sessions. Having all adults present shows Rosa that her biological parents respect and value her foster mother as a parent and decision maker. It also allows a connection between Rosa and her biological parents to continue despite her absence in the home. The positive future-oriented nature of SFBT is helpful because it empowers Rosa to determine her own solutions while focusing on a better future. The school therapist can work with Rosa individually and with the family unit through two separate weekly sessions.

When applying techniques, the therapist must remember that Rosa will most likely demonstrate wishes instead of goals. For example, if asked the miracle question, Rosa will probably respond, "Everything in my life would be perfect if I could go home." Because this is not a possibility and certainly not in the safety interests of Rosa, the therapist can place emphasis on things Rosa does control by responding, "If you were home, how would you be different?" This questioning strategy illustrates to Rosa that while she doesn't control her circumstance, she does control her reactions. Over time, Rosa will bond with her foster mother, worry less about her future, and begin to focus on her academic work again.

SUMMARY

SFBT originated in the work of Steve de Shazer and Insoo Kim Berg at the BFTC in Milwaukee, Wisconsin. It is rooted in the social learning theory of L. S. Vygotsky (1962), the human systems theory of Gregory Bateson (Visser, 2013), and the unique therapeutic approach of Milton Erickson (O'Connell, 2012). The central distinguishing feature of SFBT is its reliance on the ability of human systems to resolve their problems by focusing on system resilience and the formulation of paths to solution. Rather than an expert treating patients, the SFBT therapist functions as a collaborator with clients, utilizing techniques such as complimenting, miracle question, scaling, exception questions, or relationship questions to facilitate change in the system. Its approach and techniques are readily adaptable to culturally diverse contexts and conform to ethical practice guidelines.

KEYSTONES

Several techniques are mentioned in the chapter and discussed in the cases. Proper use of these techniques is critical, therefore; the following list summarizes important techniques and point discussed in the chapter while also leaving you with a few last minute tips.

- When exposed to complimenting, therapists often state, "Don't clients feel complimenting is fake?" or "What if they don't accept your compliment?" One thing to remember is that compliments are not intended to make the client feel good. Rather, they point out strengths that can be used to fulfill goals set later in the session. If clients do not easily accept compliments, the therapist can say, "You may not believe this but I think you are organized (or insert whatever compliment is genuine)" (De Jong & Berg, 2013).

- Another question often asked is, "What if the client wants something dangerous when you ask the miracle question?" The therapist can use relationship questions to focus on significant others or data that would not endorse the dangerous behavior. For example, state, "What would your wife say about your drinking?" or "What evidence exists to support that your drinking is not affecting your family?" This tactic forces the client to accept that the family is systemic and their actions affect others.

- Often clients will state they want things that are not within their control. For example, should a child respond to the miracle question by saying, "I would be fine if my mother was not dying from cancer," the therapist can respond with a question that places control in the child's hands. For example, the therapist might say, "How would you be different if your mother was well?" These responses reframe the conversation to one that is empowering.

REFLECTIONS FROM THE CONTRIBUTOR'S CHAIR
Janet Hicks

When I was a middle school therapist working with families, it was common to see issues escalate when parents focused only on problems faced by their child. I remember one child who was unable to make friends at school, demonstrated lowered academic achievement, and was extremely argumentative. The parents visited the school regularly and requested help with the child's problems. The child was the scapegoat for all family issues and things seemed to go from bad to worse. Finally, after asking this family to focus on what was different when things were better, they began to focus on how they interacted differently during nonstressful times. Once the child was no longer considered the problem and the entire family concentrated on making systemic changes, the family began to heal.

This left me with three major premises. First, family therapy is crucial in most settings because it helps both the unit and individuals within that unit. Second, creating solutions based on what worked previously has power to reveal issues for which the family was previously blind. Finally, my experience taught that often big problems require only small interventions. As touted by de Shazer (1985), do not make things more complicated out of a desire to be helpful or sophisticated. For example, simply asking the family "What is better this week?" can immediately frame the session in a positive manner and facilitate systemic change. Couples and families find this positive stance offers hope, empowerment, and encouragement. For this reason, SFBT is a tool a therapist can use in schools, with managed care, and even when few sessions are possible. I wish you well in your future and as you empower families in a variety of settings through techniques such as the miracle question, exception questions, relationship questions, coping questions, complimenting, and feedback.

ADDITIONAL RESOURCES

The following resources provide additional information relating to the chapter topics.

Useful Website

Solution-Focused Brief Therapy Association

- http://www.sfbta.org/

This organization's website offers the latest news, resources, and training for therapists.

Readings

De Jong, P., & Berg, I. K. (2013). *Interviewing for solutions* (4th ed.). Pacific Grove, CA: Wadsworth.

This book takes the reader step-by-step through SFBT and explains the theory in detail.

De Shazer, S., & Dolan, Y. (with Korman, H., Trepper, T., McCollum, E., & Berg, I. K.). (2007). *More than miracles: The state of the art of solution-focused brief therapy*. Binghamton, NY: Haworth Press.

This book is the final work of de Shazer. The reader can find new advances to this approach and real-life case examples.

Associations

- Brief Therapy Institute of Sydney
  http://www.brieftherapysydney.com.au/btis/links/html
- Solution-Focused Brief Therapy Association
  http://www/sfbta.org/

REFERENCES

Adams, J. F., Piercy, F. P., & Jurich, J. A. (1991). Effects of solution-focused therapy's formula first session task on compliance and outcomes in family therapy. *Journal of Marital and Family Therapy, 17*, 277–290.

American Counseling Association. (2014). *ACA code of ethics*. Alexandria, VA: Author.

Bannink, F. P. (2007). Solution focused brief therapy. *Journal of Contemporary Psychotherapy, 37*(2), 87–94. doi:10.1007/s10879-006-9040-y

Berg, I. K., & Miller, S. (1992). *Working with the problem drinker: A solution-focused approach*. New York: Norton.

Berger, P. L., & Luckmann, T. (1966). *The social construction of reality: A treatise in the sociology of knowledge*. Garden City, NY: Anchor Books.

Bond, C., Woods, K., Humphrey, N., Smyes, W., & Green, L. (2013). Effective counseling interventions with youth and families. Retrieved from https://www.umass.edu/schoolcounseling/uploads/Research%20Brief%2010.2.pdf

Brasher, K. L. (2009). Solution-focused brief therapy: Overview and implications for school therapists. *Alabama Counseling Association Journal, 34*, 20–30.

Bruner, J. (1966). *Toward a theory of instruction*. Cambridge, MA: Harvard University Press.

Corcoran, J. (2002). Developmental adaptations of solution-focused family therapy. *Brief Treatment and Crisis Intervention, 2*, 301–313.

Davis, T. E., & Osborn, C. J. (2000). *The solution focused counselor: Shaping professional practice.* New York: Brunner-Routledge.

De Jong, P., & Berg, I. K. (2002). *Interviewing for solutions.* Pacific Grove, CA: Brooks/Cole.

De Jong, P., & Berg, I. K. (2013). *Interviewing for solutions* (4th ed.) Pacific Grove, CA: Brooks/Cole.

de Shazer, S. (1982). *Patterns of brief family therapy.* New York: Guilford Press.

de Shazer, S. (1984). The death of resistance. *Family Process, 23*, 11–17.

de Shazer. S. (1985). *Keys to solution in brief therapy.* New York: Norton.

de Shazer, S. (1988). *Clues: Investigating solutions in brief therapy.* New York: Norton.

de Shazer, S., Dolan, Y., Korman, H., Tepper, T., McCollum, E.E., & Berg, I.K. (2007). *More than miracles: The state of the art of solution-focused brief therapy.* Binghamton, NY: Hawthorn Press.

de Shazer, S., & Molnar, A. (1984). Four useful interventions in brief family therapy. *Journal of Marital and Family Therapy, 10*, 297–304.

Estrada, B., & Beyeback, M. (2007). Solution-focused therapy with depressed deaf persons. *Journal of Family Psychotherapy, 18*(3), 45–63. doi:10.1300/J085v18n03_04

Flamez, B., & Watson, J. C. (2014). Solution-focused brief therapy. In R. Parsons & N. Zhang (Eds.), *Counseling theory: Guiding reflective process* (pp. 311–344). Thousand Oaks, CA: Sage.

Gerrard, B. (2008). School-based family counseling: Overview, trends, and recommendations for future research. *International Journal for School-Based Family Counseling, I.* Retrieved from http://www.school-basedfamilycounseling.com/docs/IJSBFC%20-%20Volume%20I(1)%20-%20Gerrard.pdf

Gerrard, B. (2015). School based family counseling. Retrieved from http://webcache.google-usercontent.com/search?q=cache:Jeq0-SILz9IJ:www.usfca.edu/soe/ctrs_institutes/ccfd/school_based_counseling/+&cd=20&hl=en&ct=clnk&gl=us

Gingerich, W. J., & Peterson, L. T. (2013). Effectiveness of solution focused brief therapy: A systematic qualitative review of controlled outcome studies. *Research on Social Work Practice, 23*, 266–283.

Guman, A. S. (2013). *Handbook of family therapy.* New York: Brunner/Mazel.

Hermann, D. S., & McWhirter, J. (1996). A review of better, deeper, and more enduring brief therapy: The rational emotive behavior therapy approach. *Contemporary Psychology, 41*, 1146–1147.

Hoyt, M. (2001). *Interview with brief therapy experts.* Ann Arbor, MI: Edwards.

Institute for Solution-Focused Therapy. (2017). What is solution focused therapy? Retrieved from https://solutionfocused.net/what-is-solution-focused-therapy

Jordan, K. B., & Quinn, W. H. (1994). Session two outcome of the formula first session task in problem-and solution-focused approaches. *American Journal of Family Therapy, 22*, 3–16.

Kim, J. S., & Franklin, C. (2008). Solution-focused brief therapy in schools: A review of the outcome literature. *Children and Youth Services Review, 31*, 464–470.

Kim, J. S. (2014). *Solution-focused brief therapy: A multicultural approach.* Thousand Oaks, CA: Sage.

Learning Theories. (2015). Constructivism. Retrieved from https://www.learning-theories.com/constructivism.html

Lewis, T. F., & Osborn, C. J. (2004). Solution-focused counseling and motivational interviewing: A consideration of confluence. *Journal of Counseling & Development, 82*, 39–49.

Lightfoot, J. M. (2014). Solution focused therapy. *International Journal of Scientific & Engineering Research, 5*, 238–240.

Linton, J. (2005). Mental health counselors and substance abuse treatment: Advantages, difficulties, and practical issues to solution-focused interventions. *Journal of Mental Health Counseling, 27*, 297–310.

MacDonald, A. (2011). *Solution-focused therapy: Theory, research & practice.* London: Sage.

Marion, N. E., & Oliver, W. M. (2014). *Drugs in American society: An encyclopedia of history, politics.* Denver: ABC-CLIO.

Maslow, A. H. (1968). A dynamic theory of human motivation. In C. L. Stacey & M. DeMartino (Eds.), *Understanding human motivation* (pp. 26–47). Cleveland, OH: Allen.

Meyer, D. D., & Cottone, R. R. (2013). Solution-focused therapy as a culturally acknowledging approach with American Indians. *Journal of Multicultural Counseling and Development, 41,* 47–55.

National Institute on Drug Abuse. (2013). DrugFacts: Nationwide trends. Retrieved from

http://www.drugabuse.gov/publications/drugfacts/nationwide-trends

O'Connell, B. (2012). *Solution focused therapy.* Thousand Oaks, CA: Sage.

O'Hanlon, W., Weiner-Davis, M. (2003). *In Search of Solutions—a new direction in psychotherapy.* New York: W. W. Norton & Company

Osborn, C. J. (1999). Solution focused strategies with involuntary clients: Practical applications for the school and clinical setting. *Journal of Humanistic Counseling, 37,* 169-181. doi 10.1002/j.2164-4683.1999. tb00418.x

Papert, S., & Idit, H. I. (1991). *Constructionism.* New York: Ablex.

Ratner, H., George, E., & Iveson, C. (2012). *Solution focused brief therapy: 100 key points and techniques.* New York: Routledge.

Rogers, C. R. (1959). A theory of therapy, personality, and interpersonal relations as developed in the Soclient-centered framework. In S. Koch (Ed.), *Psychology: A study of a science* (Vol. 3, pp. 184–256). New York: McGraw-Hill.

Sanders, D. (2016). *Within our reach: A national strategy to eliminate child abuse and neglect.* Washington, DC: Government Printing Office.

Taathadi, M. S. (2014). Application of solution focused brief therapy to enhance high school students' self-esteem. *International Journal of Psychological Studies, 6*(3), 96–105.

Trepper, T., Dolan, Y., McCollum, E., & Nelson, T. (2006). Steve de Shazer and the future of solution-focused therapy. *Journal of Marital and Family Therapy, 32,* 133–139.

Visser, C. (2013). The origin of the solution-focused approach. *International Journal of Solution-Focused Practices, 1,* 10–17.

Vygotsky, L. S. (1962). *Thought and language.* Cambridge, MA: MIT Press.

Walter, J. L., & Peller, J. E. (1992). *Becoming solution focused in brief therapy.* Levittown, PA: Brunner/Mazel.

Weakland, J., Watzalawick, P., & Fisch, R. (1974). *Change: Principles of Problem Formation and Problem Resolution.* New York: WW. Norton.

CHAPTER 15

Narrative Therapy: Principles and Practices

Marvarene Oliver and Adriana Dyurich

"The most powerful therapeutic process I know is to
contribute to rich story development."

—Michael White

N arrative therapy as discussed in this chapter primarily refers to the approach developed by Michael White and David Epston. While there are ways in which other theorists have adopted some of the hallmark narrative therapy strategies, a foundation in some of the basics of narrative therapy as defined herein will assist aspiring counselors in determining whether their own beliefs about how people change are a good fit with this theoretical orientation. In addition, the material may help in assessing how narrative therapy practices, as opposed to narrative therapy, may fit within other orientations.

To understand narrative therapy, it is important to have some grounding in the conceptualizations that underlie the theory. These conceptualizations provide the contexts in which the approach is founded, and as readers will find, context is critical from a narrative therapy perspective. Understanding the basic worldview held by narrative therapists is particularly important because it is a view that is in opposition to much of the current dominant view in counseling, psychology, and marriage and family therapy. In this chapter, we provide an overview of philosophical and theoretical ideas that were intriguing to White and Epston as well as to others who are key figures in narrative therapy. In addition, we highlight specific strategies that are considered hallmarks of narrative therapy practice by most narrative therapists.

After reading this chapter, you will be able to do the following:

- Describe philosophical foundations of narrative therapy.
- Describe strategies frequently used in narrative therapy.
- Identify major contributors to narrative therapy.
- Describe the therapist's role in narrative therapy.
- Describe current research in efficacy of narrative therapy.

PROFILE OF MAIN FIGURES

Michael White and David Epston are considered the originators of narrative therapy. Although they had been working on this approach together since the 1980s, it wasn't until they published *Narrative Means to Therapeutic Ends* in 1990 that they introduced narrative therapy to the world. Other key figures include Stephen Madigan, Jill Freedman, and Gene Combs. Except for White, who died in 2008, these individuals are still actively involved with the development of narrative therapy.

Michael White

White, with David Epston, is considered the cocreator of this innovative approach to therapy. White was born on December 29, 1948, in Adelaide, Australia, where he lived his entire life. He worked as a probation officer while obtaining an undergraduate degree in social work. After graduating in 1979, he became a psychiatric social worker for the Adelaide Children's Hospital. In 1983 he founded the Dulwich Centre and began his private family therapy practice. Up until his death, he was the codirector of the Dulwich Centre. He also set up the Adelaide Narrative Centre, a facility for counseling and training. White was awarded the honorary doctorate of humane letters from John F. Kennedy University in 1996 and the Distinguished Contribution to Family Therapy Theory and Practice Award from the American Family Therapy Academy in 1999. To the shock of his friends, family, and all those who followed his work, Michael White died of a heart attack in San Diego, California, where he had just completed the first day of a workshop. He passed away on April 4, 2008, at the age of 59 (Epston, 2008; Gallant, 2008; Pearce, 2008; White, 2009).

White was a prolific writer. He coauthored, with David Epston, the book that would mark the emergence of the narrative movement, *Literate Means to Therapeutic Ends* (1989), followed soon after by the version that would take narrative therapy to the rest of the world, *Narrative Means to Therapeutic Ends* (1990). He wrote numerous other books and articles that have been translated into several languages. He and Epston developed and adapted innovative therapeutic ideas and strategies fundamental to narrative therapy, including externalizing the problem, reauthoring life stories, scaffolding conversations, mapping the problem, and utilizing rites and ceremonies as a therapeutic tool.

David Epston

Epston, the cocreator of narrative therapy, was born in Ontario, Canada, in 1944. At age 19, he moved to New Zealand, where he obtained a BA in sociology and anthropology. A few years later, he started studies in the United Kingdom, earning a diploma in community development, an MA in applied social studies, and a certificate of qualification in social work. At the time of this writing, he offers workshops, lectures, and trainings on narrative therapy in diverse parts of the world. He is currently the codirector of the Family Therapy Centre in Auckland, New Zealand. He is also an active faculty member in different narrative therapy centers around the world. He has published many books and articles that have shaped the development of the narrative movement, several of which were written with Michael White. Epston has been recognized as an important contributor to family therapy and was presented with the Distinguished Contribution to Family Therapy Theory and Practice award in 2007 by the American Family Therapy Academy (Dulwich Centre, n.d.a) and an honorary doctorate of humane letters by John F. Kennedy University in 1996. White recognized Epston as the encourager in incorporating the story and text analogies into the practice of narrative therapy (Denbourough, 2014; White, 2009; White & Epston, 1990).

Stephen Madigan

Madigan holds two master's degrees (MSW and MSc) and a PhD in marriage and couples therapy. He apprenticed with White and Epston early in his professional life. In 1992, encouraged by his mentors and in partnership with Yaletown Family Therapy, he founded the Vancouver School for Narrative Therapy (VSNT). It became the first narrative therapy training site located in the Northern Hemisphere. Subsequently, he was instrumental in founding the first training center in Toronto, Canada, and in bringing VSNT trainings to Norway (Stephenmadigan.ca, n.d.). Epston has referred to him as one of narrative practice's first scholars and practitioners. He has been a prolific writer of books and articles on the topic. The APA featured him in a live-session video series demonstrating the work of narrative therapy with children (Psychotherapy.net, 2002). The APA also published Madigan's *Narrative Therapy* (2011) as part of its Theories of Psychotherapy Series. He currently practices as a family therapist and regularly offers workshops and lectures. He also hosts the annual Therapeutic Conversations narrative conferences as part of his work for VSNT.

Jill Freedman and Gene Combs

Freedman and Combs are the codirectors of the Evanston Family Therapy Center, located in Chicago. The center offers narrative training and workshops as well as therapy and consulting. Freedman and Combs also provide international trainings and presentations and work closely with the Dulwich Centre in Australia. Together and individually, as well as with others, they have written numerous articles and books—including *Narrative Therapy: The Social Construction of Preferred Realities* (Freedman & Combs, 1996); *Symbol, Story, and Ceremony: Using Metaphor in Individual and Family Therapy* (Combs & Freedman, 1990); and *Narrative Therapy with Couples* (Freedman & Combs, 2000)—that address the theory and practice of this approach. In 2009 Freedman and Combs were honored with the Award for Innovative Contribution to Family Therapy by the American Family Therapy Academy (Evanston Family Therapy Center, n.d; Dulwich Centre, n.d.a).

KEY CONCEPTS

White was and Epston is a social worker. Their histories and how they came to family therapy are different; however, social movements, including community development, were part of their early professional lives. Feminist and social justice theories and practices also had a significant impact on their thinking. The first model of therapy learned by White was Rogers' person-centered therapy, and the profound respect Rogers demonstrated for individuals remains evident in narrative therapy. Both believed that anthropology, with its emphasis on social and kinship structures, provides a critical perspective to family therapy. Epston was trained as an anthropologist and White once stated that anthropology should be a fundamental part of training for family therapists (Beels, 2001). In addition, philosophical writings about social constructionism and poststructuralist ideas were important in the development of White and Epston's thoughts about how to work with individuals and families. While it is beyond the scope of this chapter to fully discuss postmodernist philosophies, some understanding of basic concepts as viewed by narrative therapy scholars is critical to making sense of both theory and practice of narrative therapy.

Social constructionism emerged in the 1900s as a theoretical orientation that offered radical alternatives to psychology, sociology, and other disciplines (Burr, 1995), in large part by challenging the meaning-giving process in people's lives. In classical theories, the therapist is viewed an expert who can diagnose, offer meanings, and suggest solutions to client problems. This way of viewing individuals and their problems shifted somewhat to the view that clients give meaning to events that occur in their lives and can change via a process of insight and trust in an inherent tendency toward growth and development. This perspective still promotes the idea that problems are located within the individual and reflect realities engrained in the individual's identity or nature as well as in the identity of others around them. Both perspectives provide an internalizing understanding of problems with which people struggle.

Social constructionism is a postmodernist way of thinking that posits that what people view as reality is socially constructed, primarily through language. Social constructionist ideas challenge the separation of the individual knower from the world they know. Human identity is described as relational, contextual, and even anti-individualistic (Burr, 1995; Geertz as cited in Madigan, 2011). From this perspective, the relational and social aspects of the individual's life are critical in the construction of that person's reality. Identity and reality are viewed as being formed through stories that are cocreated with others and informed by their relationships and culture. Further, ideas about disorder, disease, and health are part of these stories, and are social constructs formed by those with story-naming rights (in other words, by those with power) and accepted by society and the individual as truth. As an example, Madigan (2011) pointed out that the accepted ideas about disorder and health change overnight for millions of people whenever a new edition of the *Diagnostic and Statistical Manual of Mental Disorders* is published.

Poststructuralism includes theories put forward by a range of philosophers. Some of the best known include Derrida, Foucault, and Deleuze (Khoja-Moolji, 2014). Poststructuralism was a response to structuralism, which remains the dominant worldview in counseling and psychology today. Structuralist theorists view individuals as occupying specific positions that can be understood as structures. From this perspective, human culture follows specific patterns of structure that reflect a preexisting reality. Poststructuralists, on the other hand, are concerned about how the patterns establish and maintain hierarchies and power structures. Specifically, poststructuralist theorists maintain that meanings in language are not fixed; rather, they are really tied to specific historical and social contexts and reflect a shared practice rather than reality (Combs & Freedman, 2012). Foucault, whose work is difficult to categorize within a specific philosophical stance, studied the relationship between knowledge and power and defended the idea that knowledge is a construction of those with intellectual power (Gutting, 2005; Rabinow, 1984). The impact of Foucault's thinking on narrative therapy is clear, perhaps most identifiably in the concept of story-telling rights and recognition of client as the expert.

PREMISES OF THE THEORY

Narrative therapy may be considered more a philosophical perspective than a theoretical one. Consistent with the ideas discussed above, narrative therapy is arguably concerned first and foremost with the counselor's philosophical stance and worldview, including how the counselor understands individuals and families as well as the problems they experience. White and Epston indicated that social constructionist and poststructuralist ideas offer a rich understanding of the ways that stories and narratives, which provide a sense of meaning, identity, and understanding good and evil, come to be accepted as reality (White, 2007; White & Epston, 1990).

Narrative therapists concentrate on the stories individuals and families have constructed about their lives, and include consideration of the dominant social and cultural ideas that ascribe meaning and identity to experiences. These narratives are not objective; rather, they are constructed around events that have become dominant and express the concepts others and we have about ourselves. If the narratives, which have been informed by common beliefs, societal rules, and accepted conceptions, are problematic or *single-storied*, narrative therapists collaborate with clients to explore their often-unrecognized complexity and to discover subordinate plots (Morgan, 2002). Guided Practice Exercise 15.1 illustrates how single-storied ideas can impact how we view others.

GUIDED PRACTICE EXERCISE 15.1

Go to https://www.youtube.com/watch?v=D9lhs241zeg&index=1&list=PLhLpcBrSiNgkZ. Once you have watched it, think about the following questions and make notes about your responses. In what areas of my life do I have a single story about myself? In what areas of my life do I have a single story about another person or group of people? How do these single stories serve as identities I believe to be true about myself and others? Make notes of your answers to give yourself a point of reference as the chapter continues. *If you are tempted to think there are no people or groups about which you have single-storied ideas, you should look further. Those single stories need not be about deficit; indeed, they could be about exceptional virtue or heroism.*

A fundamental concept in narrative therapy theory is the narrative metaphor. The narratives people have about their lives provide a sense of meaning and continuity. These narratives are shaped and changed as people adapt the telling of their stories and make meaning of events in their lives to more closely fit with the narratives they, others, and the dominant culture tell about them and their identity. These stories are important and defining in that they provide the meaning given to particular experiences and shape people's sense of identity. While people may have little control over the events that occur in their lives, they can make choices about how to talk about them. Narrative conversations enable the client to talk about the meaning they are giving to their experiences (White & Epston, 1990). Once able to recognize and describe these stories and narratives, clients can decide if the story reflects a meaning in their lives that is of real importance to them (McQueen & Hobbs, 2014).

ROLE OF THE THERAPIST

The role of the narrative therapist is as a collaborator or consultant who engages in therapeutic conversations. The therapist is not the expert; from a narrative therapy perspective, only clients can provide expert knowledge about their lives. The therapist does not dispense advice or solutions nor make judgments. Neither is the role of the therapist to exercise authority. The therapist does not even seek to correct or eliminate problem-centered stories (White, 2007). However, the therapist is active in helping clients construct a preferred alternative story by joining with them in consultation to look for ways of opening up new, neglected, and preferred stories about their own lives (Combs & Freeman, 2012; Walther & Carey, 2009). The position of the therapist is a decentered yet influential one; thus, the therapist must be aware of and reflective about his or her own influence (White, 1997; Morgan, 2002; White, 2007). In fact, the therapist should be mindful that therapeutic conversations are two-way, and thus have an impact on the clinician as well as the client (White, 1997). The narrative therapist is not seen as a provider of treatment; rather, the therapist is a coauthor of sorts in creating a coherent narrative of the client's life that provides the opportunity for the client to develop a richer, preferred identity. The therapist asks questions with honest curiosity with the intention of exploring or stimulating a fuller narrative of experiences, filled with details about specific events in their lives (Gallant, 2008). As Denborough (2011) indicated, the therapist's role is to

> *rescue what was said, and the meaning of what was said, and to document this in ways that the person can examine in the future and put to continuing use in his or her life in a way that the person can examine and use in the future ... honoring and extending the life of words that otherwise may pass unnoticed. (p. xv)*

Practitioners of narrative therapy are concerned with deconstructing problematic stories and coauthoring these new and preferred narratives, and not with diagnosing, problem solving, and advice giving. The therapist works from a nonpathologizing stance and joins with clients to develop thick descriptions that include overlooked details and marginalized accounts of events so that richer stories and preferred identities may be developed (Combs & Freedman, 2012). The position of narrative therapists is that telling and retelling one's story, finding neglected and nondominant elements of the story, and developing multistoried lives allow people to reshape their identities and life stories (Morgan, 2000).

KEY CONCEPTS AND STRATEGIES

Externalizing the Problem

The practice of externalizing the problem is one of the interventions that most closely resonates with its theoretical foundation. The phrase "The person is not the problem, the problem is the problem," commonly attributed to Michael White, helps summarize the idea behind externalizing the problem. According to narrative therapy thought, most people recognize the problem as part of their own identities. They internalize it. If the problem is part of one's identity, then changing it significantly or getting rid of it might be experienced as an act of self-destruction (White, 2007). Because language is the tool through which a person understands and expresses meaning, the way one talks about problems is critical. Therefore, narrative therapists use language that situates the problem away from the person and that is conducive to more accurate and in-depth explorations of the effects of the concern, and how the concern is affecting the client's life. This is a more favorable avenue to the discovery of resources and abilities that could be used in responding to a problem's influence in one's life (McQueen & Hobbs, 2014; for an in-depth description of externalizing grammar see Freeman, Epston & Lobovits, 1997).

Externalizing conversations happen in two phases. In the first phase, externalizing conversations are an exploratory tool. White (2007) compared the role of the therapist in the early phase of therapy as being akin to that of the investigative reporter. The client and therapist approach the issue with curiosity and a sense of inquiry, trying to locate, describe, and characterize the problem to build up their case for an exposé. After the problem has been exposed and objectified, the process of externalizing conversations enters an action phase during which the client starts to weaken the problem and give place to a preferred narrative of their live and identity. Narrative therapists do not engineer conversations in such a way as to portray a problem as completely negative. It is essential to include the benefits a person might be obtaining from the problem both during externalizing conversations that characterize and those that weaken problems. Externalizing conversations are held in such a way that the problem is recognized as a construct outside the identity of the person that is exacerbated, sustained, or perhaps created by shared beliefs rather than by innate personal flaws (White, 2007).

Some authors have expressed concern that externalizing conversations could exonerate clients from taking responsibility for their problems (White, 2007). Externalization of problems does not separate people from their responsibilities regarding their behavior in continuing the problem. Rather, it provides clients with an enhanced sense of personal agency that allows them to assume responsibility for the problem. Narrative theorists believe the separation between the client and the problem allows clients to recognize and further explore exceptions to the problem and understand the real consequences the problem has had. Further, externalizing conversations can provide the opportunity for concepts such as responsibility to take on meaning that was previously unclear (White & Epston, 1990; White, 2007, 2011). See Case Presentation 15.1 for a brief illustration of how externalizing conversations may have an impact.

CASE PRESENTATION 15.1: EXTERNALIZING CONVERSATIONS

Irene and Joe came in for consultation with their 11-year-old son, Dario. The parents said that Dario used to be witty and sweet but that in recent months he had lost his "joie de vivre." They said that, even though he is a straight-A student, he has begun having intense anxiety related to school and has a hard time finishing tasks on time, resulting in missing recess and bringing home extra work. At the recommendation of the school, Dario's parents had him assessed by the school psychologist. Results indicated sub-clinical results on assessment for attention-deficit/hyperactivity disorder, an above-average IQ, and heightened worry on anxiety measures. Their pediatrician indicated that the problem wasn't physical. The narrative consultant asked carefully worded questions designed to help the family characterize and understand the problem and how it was affecting all of them. Dario said that when he was doing school work, he would "get worried about not finishing and kind of blank out." The "blank-outs," as they named the problem, made him forget what he was doing and have to start over, which just increased his worry. The family began to see the blank-outs as something that could be derailed, giving Dario the opportunity to limit their effects.

Thin and Thick Stories

As noted previously, social constructionism proposes that what we accept as truth is merely a post-facto description of events. This description has been constructed in conjunction with others and has been agreed upon. Nevertheless, these descriptions or stories leave out many important details that could provide a different perspective on the events in question. This process is mimicked within an individual as well. When constructing their stories, people generally choose and highlight a limited number of experiences from which they draw meaning. The description of experiences and narratives about meaning are generally ones that resonate with other people or broader systems in individuals' lives. These narratives and descriptions play a significant role in how people understand themselves and their lives. Omitted details and ignored or minimized ideas about the experiences could provide a very different sense of meaning and identity (Morgan, 2000; White, 2007). In addition, there are many other events in individuals' lives that are not included at all in the stories that make up their identities (Denborough, 2014). Thin stories are limited and restricted. During the process of narrative therapy, the therapist collaborates with the client to reveal subordinate stories, including overlooked details and unmentioned events, that include possibilities for change and development of the client's preferred identity. Thickening and supporting the new stories and identities is a critical part of narrative therapy (Denborough, 2014; Freedman & Combs, 1996; McQueen & Hobbs, 2014). Guided Practice Exercise 15.2 includes questions to ask yourself that can help you identify ways in which you may unknowingly support thin stories about yourself or others.

GUIDED PRACTICE EXERCISE 15.2

Read back through your answers to the single-story exercise. How would those ideas affect your work with someone who is like the person or group you identified? What assumptions might you make about them? What might you miss from your single-story perceptions? Make notes of your answers. Now think about how any single stories you may have about yourself? How might those stories limit you in aspirations, self-expression, or other important areas of life? Make notes about your thoughts.

Storytelling Rights and Reauthoring Conversations

Epston once asked, "Who has the storytelling rights to the story being told?" (personal communication as cited by Madigan, 2007, p. 138). This critical question has to do with ideas about issues of power, social structures, the nonneutrality of stories we tell, and the interconnectedness of how we form ideas about identity (Madigan, 2007). Madigan (2011) pointed out that the one (or group) who tells the story has the power to define significant parts of identity of individuals or groups and that storytelling rights of personhood belong to the person. In fact, he held that storytelling by dominant groups (whether larger society, cultural groups, or uninvited family storytellers) can influence perpetuation of problems. Thus, narrative therapists discuss storytelling rights with clients and have reauthoring conversations that facilitate clients' repossession of the right to tell their own stories. Unique outcomes that arise out of externalizing conversations provide an entry point that allows clients to consider alternative storylines of their lives and provide space for people to reauthor their own stories (Freedman & Combs, 1996; Madigan, 2011; White, 2007).

Once clients have uncovered events, experiences, and subordinate stories that have been neglected or obscured by the problem story, they have additional or broader understanding of what is happening in their lives. The natural next step to follow the empowerment that results from discovering themselves as the authors of their own stories is to engage in their lives and relationships and begin thickening their stories as they develop preferred narratives of their lives (Madigan, 2011). Guided Practice Exercise 15.3 will encourage you to think not only about your stories, but where they came from.

GUIDED PRACTICE EXERCISE 15.3

Look at your notes from Guided Practice Exercise 15.1. Where did your single-story ideas come from? What parts of your experiences and what people may have played a part in your single story, including religious, ethnic, political, and other important influences? In what ways? Make notes of your ideas. Then add notes about what you care about and value and about your hopes and dreams. Are there ways in which your ideas about yourself or your dreams may have been limited by dominant narratives in your world?

Landscape of Action and Landscape of Identity

White (2007) was intrigued by literary theory ideas about story structure and incorporated ideas about dual landscapes into the practice of narrative therapy. The landscape of action refers the plot and underlying themes (what happens, when it happens, and who was involved), and the landscape of identity has to do with the intentions, hopes, meanings, values, and reflections of the client about the events described in the landscape of action. White noted out that the role of the therapist is not the same as the role of an author. As he pointed out, therapists are not the originators of the story and remain decentered. However, he indicated that thinking in terms of these two landscapes helped him shape therapeutic conversations in a way that contribute to rich development of varied aspects of people's lives and the multiple stories within them. Questions asked by narrative therapists that thicken and enrich stories provide information about both landscape of action and landscape of identity.

Therapeutic Letters and Documents

Narrative therapy makes use of letter writing as an important tool in the therapeutic process. The use of letters and documents is arguably one of the best-known practices of this approach. Letters can serve several purposes and provide evidence of the constructed reality of therapy (White & Epston, 1990). They act as a way of referring to the narrative conversation, to sustain preferred stories and serve as witnesses' proof or evidence, and even to invite clients to begin therapy (White & Epston, 1990; Morgan, 2000; McQueen & Hobbs, 2014). Epston (2009) expressed his hope for the legacy of these therapeutic documents to be adapted to new technologies and current ways of communication, such as emails, in accordance with Bruner's (1991) idea that the principal function of cultural endeavors is to produce works that could take on a life of their own. Letters assist with externalizing ideas and creation of community by facilitating thinking as a group (Epston, 2009). Some of the types of letters common in narrative therapy are discussed below.

Letters of invitation. As the name indicates, letters of invitation are used to invite someone to join therapy. It is not uncommon for a client to be referred for therapy and then be reluctant to follow through. Letters of invitation might be used when additional participants are believed to be important in the therapeutic process or when family members are concerned about a family member who will not attend sessions. Invitation letters may be written by the clinician or by a participant in therapy with the collaboration of the therapist (White & Epston, 1990).

Redundancy letters. Letters of redundancy are often written by clients who benefitted in some way from the service of others who assumed roles they were not prepared or supposed to have or roles that are no longer needed. Clients in this case express their readiness and willingness to take on their responsibility. When appropriate, the person receiving the letter may write back accepting that they are being released from extra roles and responsibilities (White & Epston, 1990).

Letters of prediction. Epston (White & Epston, 1990) described the practice of writing a letter at the end of therapy. The letter provides a prediction for a client's or family's future and includes the instruction to open on a specific date six months in the future. The letter serves to propose a six-month follow-up. In addition, because Epston thinks most people won't wait six months to read it, his expectation is that the letter will serve as a prophesy that may fulfill itself.

Therapeutic letter-writing campaigns. While not a particular form of letter, therapeutic letter-writing campaigns are designed to address difficulties of problem identities growing stronger within structures and systems that seem to support problems. Letter-writing campaigns are a way to counterbalance the problem-saturated story and its memory and help people to re-remember lost aspects of themselves. Communities of concern are enlisted to hold the preferred story of the client and to write letters about these preferred stories (Madigan, 2011).

Other letters. There are many other types of letters used by narrative therapists (Majchrzak, 2003; White & Epston, 1990). Letters for special occasions, letters of reference that reinforce strengths of the client, and counter-referral letters that underscore for referral sources new identities clients are creating can all be used to document the story of therapy and to sustain new narratives. Letters can easily be adapted to the needs of clients and can be brief. Epston and White (1990) explained that many of their brief letters were expressions of their thoughts at the conclusion of a session and were intended to communicate those thoughts to the clients in the near future. Research suggests that the most effective approach when using letter writing as a therapeutic device is to follow a narrative plot (a story with a beginning, middle and end) instead of listing disjointed fragments that do not offer a story (Goldberg, 2000; Smyth, True & Souto, 2001). Use what you have read about letters to complete Guided Practice Exercise 5.4.

GUIDED PRACTICE EXERCISE 15.4: WRITE YOURSELF A LETTER

Read back through all the notes you made during the exercises in this chapter. Then write yourself a letter about the observations you have made about yourself and what you have learned in the process. Include any ideas you have about ways that you may have opened possibilities for expanding your own stories and ideas about your identity. If you are willing to do so, share your observations with a witness of your choosing.

Documents. Narrative therapists may use a variety of documents that are counter to the problem-saturated story and identity of clients. It is particularly common to see such documents used with children, who may be presented with certificates that celebrate a new story or declarations that document a new identity that a client is announcing. While some of these documents may be developed by the therapist, others may be coauthored by clients, who are thus consciously participating in defining their own identity. Having an audience to witness these documents (definitional ceremonies) helps to solidify the consolidation of new meanings in clients' lives and revises preexisting meanings in a venue important to the client (White & Epston, 1990).

Definitional Ceremonies and Outsider Witness Practice

Definitional ceremonies allow clients to tell their stories before an audience of outsider witnesses. Narrative therapists acknowledge their clients' preferred narratives of identity and help them make their preferred accounts visible to others if clients choose to do so. The term definitional ceremony was taken from the work of Myerhoff, a cultural anthropologist who wrote about the act of being as a social and psychological construct (Freedman, 2014; Madigan, 2011; Walther & Fox, 2012; White, 2007; White & Epston, 1990). White (2007) considered the definitional ceremony metaphor as potentially the most powerful of his practices. White outlined the importance of choosing *outsider witnesses* for definitional ceremonies carefully. He noted that outsider witnesses were originally drawn primarily from family, friends, and school and work environments, and included acquaintances and even people unknown to the clients. However, as he and Epston continued to work, they began to include communities of people who had previously consulted them.

Definitional ceremonies that include audiences to bear witness to a person's retelling of a story consist of three defined stages (White, 2007). First the therapist interviews the person for whom the definitional ceremony is being held while the audience is listening.

These observers are instructed to listen for phrases that seem interesting to them and be aware of the images these phrases generate as they listen—things that resonate with them as witnesses and what they take away from the experience of listening. Next, the person listens while the therapist interviews the outside witnesses. Then the person at the center of the ceremony is interviewed again about what he or she heard in the retelling. White (2007) and Freedman (2014) provided extensive detail about preparation of outsider witnesses and the structure of this type of definitional ceremony.

Scaffolding Conversations

While Vygotsky was not an influence in Epston and White's conceptualization of narrative practice, White (2007) indicated that Vygotsky's conclusions about learning lent clarity to important facets of narrative conversations and reinforced various narrative practices. Two specific ideas were of interest to White. One was the notion that learning is a result of social collaboration. The second was Vygotsky's description of the zone of proximal development. From a narrative therapy perspective, conversational partnerships and collaboration are required to support people as they proceed in manageable steps away from what is known to a distance that allows them to have greater ability to influence their own lives. Scaffolding conversations in narrative therapy involve areas of inquiry that move from low-level distancing from what is familiar and immediate to very high in distancing from the immediate and familiar. White pointed out that therapists have a responsibility to provide the conditions that support personal agency, and that scaffolding is an important part of that responsibility (White, 2007).

ASSESSMENT AND TREATMENT

Assessment

Although assessment was discussed in detail in Chapter 8, it is important to note that assessment in narrative therapy is different from approaches that locate problems within individuals or families. Narrative therapists are more concerned with discovering what a problem means to a client, how it impacts the client and the world in which the client lives, and how the problem behaves. A narrative therapist might map the influence of the problem and have conversations with a client to clarify the landscape of action and the landscape of identity. The therapist is genuinely curious and asks questions designed not to arrive at a diagnosis, but to collaborate with the client in understanding the client's relationship with a problem.

Assumptions underlying traditional formal assessments are inconsistent with the philosophy of narrative therapy; thus, many narrative therapists are unlikely to use traditional assessments because of the assumption of a single reality implicit in such assessments, a pathology orientation, and lack of attention to cultural and other contextual factors. Instead, assessment is a process wherein the therapist pays attention to clients' perspectives on their lives as well as to cultural and other contexts of clients' lives. Local knowledge provided by clients and others they wish to include is privileged rather than expert knowledge provided by assessment results and clinicians.

Process of Treatment

White and Epston prefer the word consultation to treatment, which is consistent with the perspective of the client holding the position of authority on his or her culture and experience (Beels, 2001). White (2007) noted that he did not always spend time in externalization and the idea that a clinician should always work through a series of steps is not characteristic of White's later work. However, it can be helpful to think about the process in a series of stages. Beels (2001) described treatment as occurring in essentially three phases: recasting of the problem narrative, or externalization; identifying exceptions, or unique outcomes; and recruiting support.

Externalizing involves encouraging individuals to objectify and even personify problems that are experienced as oppressive. Externalizing is a coconstructive process involving the therapist and clients in which they create mutually acceptable descriptions that encourage or allow separation of the person or family and the problem (Gallant, 2013). The problem becomes separate and external to the individual or relationship that was formerly considered the problem, and the client begins to think of the problem as the problem. When problems are externalized, clients can move away from identification with problem-saturated stories and descriptions of themselves and open possibilities of new, alternative, preferred stories (White and Epston, 1990). Identifying exceptions and unique outcomes allows the client to identify times when the problem does not have the same ability to dominate or impact the client's life (Beels, 2001). Not only is the influence of the problem over clients addressed, but the influence of clients over problems is explored (Gallant, 2012). When clients recruit support, they identify and enlist allies in reducing the impact and influence of the problem on clients' lives (Beels, 2001; White & Epston, 1990). It is important to note that removal of problems is not the goal; rather, the goal is to reduce influence of problems in client's lives so that they are free to identify and live their preferred stories.

Another important part of the process of narrative therapy is the making and using of notes. Narrative therapists will often use extensive note-taking during sessions, using the words of their clients rather than the therapists' own ideas. These notes may then be used to create case files that provide a narrative of client experiences over time and which can be used to craft letters or create documents that reflect the preferred stories of individuals and families (Freedman & Combs, 1996).

Strengths and Limitations

One strength of narrative therapy is the recognition of and explicit conversations about the impact of dominant cultural stories on clients' lives and the explicit conversation concerning dominant familial and cultural narratives. The contexts in which clients exist are a critical part of the process. A focus on understanding of how culture and external forces play a significant role in identified problems and in the ways clients view their identities is a hallmark of narrative therapy practice. These ways of thinking are consistent with the aims of multicultural competence (Semmler & Williams, 2000). Clients are encouraged to examine the impact of their cultural milieu so that they can consider the impact of dominant cultural and societal storylines on their own stories about themselves. In addition, narrative therapists are sensitive to issues of power and its impact in clients' lives and recognize that the therapeutic process itself can reinforce, rather than challenge, dominant cultural stories that are not preferred by clients.

A second strength of narrative therapy is its flexibility. In addition to having room for adaptation of the process of therapy, narrative scholars and practitioners continue to add to and adapt the work for use with individuals and families as well as communities. In fact, the importance of the contributions of others to the body of work about narrative therapy was an important consideration in why White and Epston did not intend to establish a "school" of therapy (Epston & White, 1992).

Another strength is the common forms of research conducted by narrative practitioners. Combs and Freedman (2012) discussed the most common and noted that insider knowledge (e.g., regarding experiences of problems such as eating disorders or depression) that comes from such research can provide a wealth of information for individuals who are impacted by those problems as well as for the clinicians who work with them. Coresearch, involving clients and therapists working together to clarify how problems work, results in careful notes using clients' language. Documents are created from these notes and can become archives of insider knowledge that may be passed on to others. Collecting and circulating insider knowledge is more like research methods of anthropologists than it is to traditional methods in counseling and psychology.

One thing that may be considered a limitation of narrative therapy is that it utilizes language that is different from most other approaches and that may be difficult for novices to understand. Additional training is generally required for a clinician to become skilled in this approach, which can be expensive or logistically difficult. In addition, clinicians may use narrative strategies without understanding how, when, and why to use them or how they fit (or not) with the clinician's primary orientation, resulting in confusion for both client and clinician. The latter is not unique to narrative therapy, however, and as with all approaches, counselors should take care to be intentional about what they do.

Another limitation is in research. There is a lack of large-scale studies that point to the effectiveness of narrative therapy with certain populations of individuals or with specific problems. Etchison and Kleist (2000) noted that qualitative approaches are particularly suited to researching the effectiveness of narrative therapy and noted several potential reasons for the limited research base in narrative therapy. They acknowledged that, while narrative therapy could not be said to be the preferred treatment for particular problems, narrative therapy has been demonstrated to be useful in working with a variety of family problems. Combs and Freedman (2012) disagreed with some of Etchison and Kleist's conclusions, and pointed to the breadth of research on the use of narrative therapy with specific problems that is currently available. There are many qualitative studies and small quantitative studies as well as case study presentations that narrative therapists indicate demonstrate the effectiveness of narrative therapy. Depression, childhood stealing, soiling, autism, attention deficit/hyperactivity symptoms, body image, cutting, and eating disorders are all problems that have been addressed successfully with individual or group narrative therapy (see Dulwich Centre, n.d.b).

CASE PRESENTATION: 15.2: GEORGE AND RAMONA

George and Ramona

George and Ramona came in for consultation about their relationship and the arguments they were having. They indicated concern that, while they had always had what they called normal arguments, in the past year their arguments had become more frequent. They agreed that they were becoming more distant and generally angry with each other. Ramona said that the arguments really started escalating about a year ago. Both stated that they were frustrated and seemed to be at an impasse about making anything better.

George and Ramona have a 7-year-old daughter, Sarah, who had just begun second grade, and a 4-year-old son, Mathias. Both George and Ramona work full time, and Ramona's mother takes care of Mathias during the day as well as Sarah in the afternoon after school until her parents get home. George and Ramona said that a lot of their arguments are about problems Sarah is having at school and how to respond to them.

Consultation Process

The consultant, or therapist, would listen carefully to what George and Ramona said about themselves and their relationship, understanding that the stories they told individually and together had many possible meanings. The therapist would listen for gaps and ambiguities in their narrative and ask them to fill in details. A narrative therapist might ask questions designed to check whether the therapist's understanding of the meaning is the same as what Ramona and George intend. The therapist would also be listening for new meanings and subordinate story lines as they emerge. The therapist might have externalizing conversations to first explore the problem story and then to separate the problem from Ramona and George and from their relationship. In other words, the problem would not be viewed as resident within Ramona and George or within their relationship.

The influence of the problem would be explored, including the impact that problem might be having on others. The therapist would explore unique outcomes—times when the arguments were not happening or times when the couple did not feel distant and angry. Depending on the stories and views of the couple, Sarah, Mathias, Ramona's mother, or others the couple believed would provide expertise or understanding might be invited to meet with them. New, alternative stories that offered a preferred identity for Ramona, George, and their relationship would be developed and strengthened. If Ramona and George agreed, outsider witnesses might be invited to participate in a definitional ceremony that supports the enriched and multistoried sense of identity that Ramona and George were declaring.

Throughout the process of consultation, questions would be used extensively, though the questions would have purposes different than fact-finding. Questions might be designed to deconstruct, to open space for new stories or unique outcomes, to find out client preferences about the stories that are arising, to aid in rich story development, or to invite clients to reflect on meaning. The consultation process described here is deliberately vague, because George and Ramona's responses to questions would determine what questions were asked next and how the process would proceed. A narrative therapist, while having thoughts about what could be contributing to the increasing arguments, would not direct clients in a way that presupposed that Sarah's problems were causing the arguments or that Ramona's mother was an influence in the arguments. The therapist would consult with the couple about whether and when to invite the children or Ramona's mother into the consultation process, honoring the expertise of the clients about their own lives. These ideas might well be explored during conversations throughout the process, but the therapist would remain decentered and out of an expert position.

ETHICAL AND CULTURAL CONSIDERATIONS

Freedman and Combs (1996) discussed relationships and ethics at length and included ideas about assumptions made about people and therapy and the role of community in defining ethical practice. They indicated that modernist ideas about ethics that are generally based on "sweeping meta-narratives" (p. 265) that can be set out in rules and then enforced are viewed with some skepticism from a post-modernist perspective. They noted the importance of making room for "marginalized voices and marginalized cultures" (p. 265) as well as the importance of therapists and counselors being clear about where they stand, recognizing that where one stands has local, interpersonal effects. They stressed the importance of recognizing the effects of our practices on individuals and cultures, especially those who are not part of the dominant storyline of current culture. How therapists situate themselves in relationships with others is itself an ethical practice from a narrative therapy point of view.

Combs and Freedman (2012) pointed out that narrative therapists work to separate people from problems, thus creating space for people to make choices in line with their preferences for their lives. Narrative therapists support people's preferred choices even when those choices are different from those identified as preferred by the dominant culture. From a narrative perspective, this is an ethical imperative. Narrative therapists are aware of and attend to the use of power in their therapeutic relationships to avoid being complicit in marginalizing clients.

Recognition that the client is the expert rather than the therapist is one way that power in the therapist–client relationship is addressed. The therapist admittedly knows nothing about what an experience means to the client. Acknowledgement of that lack of understanding is an acknowledgement of a fundamental truth that may be particularly important to members of nondominant cultures. In addition, narrative therapists believe that the client is the best consultant in his or her own case. Thus, the client has the freedom to identify anyone he or she believes might help the therapist understand and who may serve as supporters and perhaps coauthors of the client's preferred story.

Narrative scholars have also addressed ethical and cultural considerations in research. One such consideration has to do with identifying the participants and the audience for research. Being transparent about to whom researchers intend to aim research efforts is important if the impact of power and dominant discourses is to be understood. Academic researchers, for example, may be more concerned about contributing to conversations with previous researchers, thinking about what editors and peer reviewers might want to see, and generally participating in the production of scholarly knowledge. Some researchers may be more concerned with clients and clinicians who are part of the conversation about a specific topic. In either event, clarity and transparency about the purpose of the conversation (i.e., the research) is "always either implicitly or explicitly relevant" (Crocket, Drewery, McKenzie, Smith, & Winslade, 2004, p. 65). The intended purposes often fall along a continuum, with the intention of adding to knowledge in both academic and more local settings; however, lack of transparency inadvertently privileges a kind of knowledge that in and of itself may serve to maintain dominant ways of thinking about reality.

SUMMARY

This chapter provided an overview of philosophical perspectives critical to narrative therapy, as well as many strategies commonly used by therapists and counselors who work from a narrative stance. Understanding the context and philosophical underpinnings of narrative therapy allows counselors to determine not only whether this orientation is a good fit with how they think about the counseling process but also whether and how narrative strategies may be effectively incorporated into other approaches that may be compatible with narrative work.

Now that several main schools and models of family therapy have been covered, we will turn our attention to psychoeducational and enrichment programs.

KEYSTONES

Among the key points addressed in this chapter are:

- Narrative therapy, with its strong core philosophical perspective, is concerned first and foremost with the counselor's philosophical stance.

- White and Epston posited that social constructionist and poststructuralist ideas offer critical understanding of the ways that particular narratives come to be accepted as reality. One philosopher, Foucault, argued that there is a relationship between knowledge and power and that knowledge is a social construction of those with intellectual power. Some basic understanding of philosophical ideas of individuals such as Foucault, Derrida, Deleuze, and others is important to understanding White and Epston's conceptualization of narrative therapy.

- Narratives that people hold to be true about themselves, including sense of identity and meaning of their experiences, are impacted in often unrecognized ways by dominant familial, community, and societal ideas. Practically, this can mean that the right to name and define one's own experience and identity is superseded by so-called expert knowledge of the larger society.

- However, narrative clinicians insist that clients are the ones who can competently tell their stories and are the ultimate authorities on the meaning of their experiences.

- Narrative metaphor is a fundamental concept in narrative therapy and provides a sense of meaning and continuity. Narratives people hold about themselves change as they tell them, initially often to better fit with the stories of dominant familial and community ideas.

- Contrary to much current thinking in counseling and psychotherapy, the therapist does not seek to correct or eliminate problems, diagnose, problem solve, or change problem-centered stories; instead, the clinician joins with clients to look for new and preferred stories about their own lives. These stories may challenge in significant ways the stories supported by local and larger communities.

- Common ideas important to understanding narrative practice include narrative conversations, thick and thin stories, storytelling rights and reauthoring conversations, and the landscape of action and landscape of identity.

REFLECTIONS FROM THE CONTRIBUTOR'S CHAIR
Marvarene Oliver and Adriana Dyurich

We are not narrative therapists. With that said, we have each been influenced by narrative thought and practices. The first author was a clinician for many years and at the time of this writing is a faculty member and supervisor. The second author worked with organizations and communities in various countries as a political scientist prior to becoming a counselor. Both of us have worked extensively with those who have been marginalized or underrepresented and with those who have experienced significant trauma in their lives. We are also both aware that the contexts in which we have lived our lives have played a role in how we each define ourselves and that, as those contexts have changed over time, our own perspectives about power, the use of language, and who gets to own stories has continually evolved.

While we are not narrative therapists per se, in concert with the philosophies inherent in narrative therapy, how we practice is at least as much about our theoretical stances as about particular strategies. For both of us, profound respect for the people *with whom* we work forms the bedrock for *how* we work regardless of the setting. Like Michael White, Carl Rogers's way of being with people is something we were individually taught early in our counseling training and impacts our attitudes when we are "in the room." We believe that we are privileged to be invited into people's lives. In addition, we both have an unwavering curiosity about people, their lives, and especially how they experience and make sense of them. We share the conviction that we need to hear directly from clients and supervisees. While knowledge that comes from research and theory is necessary and useful, we believe it alone is not sufficient to understand how particular clients and supervisees experience themselves and their lives.

In our respective work, we found that having a space in which clients and communities can not only talk about their experiences but define and expand the meaning of those experiences is critical for empowerment. We share the belief that clients' stories matter and that clients have the right to tell them. The nuanced ways in which narrative therapists and scholars phrase questions and use language to recognize clients as the experts and remain themselves decentered are important to both of us in our own work.

ADDITIONAL RESOURCES

The following resources provide additional information relating to the chapter topics.

- David Epston website
  http://www.narrativeapproaches.com

This link will take you to David Epston's website from Auckland, New Zealand. Epston is considered the cofounder of narrative therapy. This web page provides a summary by S. Roth and D. Epston of a framework for a White–Epston type interview that details critical aspects of the interview as well as providing rationales for each aspect.

- Dulwich Centre
  http://www.dulwichcentre.com.au/

Founded in 1983 by Michael White, the Dulwich Centre is now an international main hub for narrative therapy, resources, training, and publishing related to narrative approaches. It is in Adelaide, Australia. There are many free articles and presentations available, as well as extensive bibliographies of narrative therapy materials.

- Evanston Family Therapy Center
  https://www.narrativetherapychicago.com/

The center offers narrative training and workshops, as well as therapy and consulting. It is situated in Chicago and codirected by Jill Freedman and Gene Combs.

- Evanston Family Therapy Center- Narrative World View
  https://www.narrativetherapychicago.com/narrative-worldview/

Part of the Evanston Family Therapy Center, this page includes information regarding basic assumptions of a narrative approach and characteristics of a narrative worldview. It also includes a list of questions pertaining to ethics from a narrative perspective

- *Explorations: An E-Journal of Narrative Practice*
  http://www.dulwichcentre.com/au/e-journal.html

Published by the Dulwich Centre, this journal is an international peer-reviewed journal.

- Narrative Therapy Library
  http://www.narrativetherapylibrary.com/

This website provides information concerning books, articles, DVDs, and journals related to narrative therapy.

- Yale Town Family Therapy
  http://www.yaletownfamilytherapy.com

This center was founded by Stephen Madigan and is a major training center in North America, providing narrative training, consultation, and workshops in Vancouver, Canada.

REFERENCES

Beels, C. C. (2001). *"A different story . . ." The rise of narrative in psychotherapy*. Phoenix, AZ: Zeig, Tucker, & Theisen.

Bruner, J. (1991). The narrative construction of reality. *Critical Inquiry, 18*(1), 1–21. Retrieved from http://dx.doi.org/10.1086/448619

Burr, V. (1995). *An introduction to social constructionism*. New York: Routledge.

Combs, G., & Freedman, J. (1990). *Symbol, story, and ceremony: Using metaphor in individual and family therapy*. WW Norton & Co.

Combs, G., & Freedman, J. (2012). Narrative, poststructuralism, and social justice: Current practices in narrative therapy. *Counseling Psychologist, 40*(7), 1033–1060. doi:10.1177/0011000012460662

Crocket, K., Drewery, W., McKenzie, W., Smith, L., & Winslade, J. (2004). Working for ethical research in practice. *International Journal of Narrative Therapy and Community Work, 3*, 61–66.

Denborough, D. (Ed.). (2011). Editor's note. In M. White, *Narrative practice: Continuing the conversation.* New York: Norton.

Denborough, D. (2014). *Retelling the stories of our lives: Everyday narrative therapy to draw inspiration and transform experience* [Kindle edition]. New York: Norton.

Dulwich Centre. (n.d.a). Our people. Retrieved from http://dulwichcentre.com.au/about/our-people

Dulwich Centre. (n.d.b). Research, evidence and narrative practices. Retrieved from http://dulwichcentre.com.au/narrative-therapy-research

Epston, D. (2008). Saying hullo again: Remembering Michael White. *Journal of Systemic Therapies, 27,* 2008, 1–15.

Epston, D. (2009). The legacy of letter writing as a clinical practice. Introduction to the special issue on therapeutic letters. *Journal of Family Nursing, 15,* 3–5.

Epston, D., & White, M. (1990). Consulting your consultants: The documentation of alternative knowledges. *Dulwich Centre Newsletter, 4,* 25–35.

Epston, D., & White, M. (1992). *Experience, contradiction, narrative and imagination: Selected papers of David Epston & Michael White, 1989-1991.* Adelaide, South Australia: Dulwich Centre Publications.

Etchison, M., & Kleist, D. M. (2000). Review of narrative therapy: Research and utility. *Family Journal: Counseling and Therapy for Couples and Families, 8*(1), 61–66. doi:10.1177/1066480700081009

Evanston Family Therapy Center. (n.d.). About us: Jill Freedman and Gene Combs. Retrieved from http://www.narrativetherapychicago.com

Freedman, J. (2014). Witnessing and positioning: Structuring narrative therapy with families and couples. *Australian & New Zealand Journal of Family Therapy, 35*(1), 20–30. doi:10.1002/anzf.1043

Freedman, J., & Combs, G. (1996). *Narrative therapy: The social construction of preferred realities.* New York: Norton.

Freedman, J., & Combs, G. (2000). Narrative therapy with couples. In F. M. Datillo & L. J. Bevilacqua (Eds.), *Comparative Treatments for Relationship Dysfunction.* 342–361. New York, NY: Springer Publishing Company.

Freeman, J., Epston, D., & Lobovits, D. (1997). *Playful approaches to serious problems: Narrative therapy with children and their families.* New York: Norton.

Gallant, P. (2008). Michael White: In memoriam: Therapist, teacher, innovator. *Journal of Marital and Family Therapy, 34,* 427–428.

Gallant, P. (2013). No worry allowed. Get out! A case study tribute to the life and work of Michael White. *Contemporary Family Therapy: An International Journal, 35,* 29–40. Retrieved from http://dx.doi.org/10.1007/s10591-012-0225-3

Goldberg, D. (2000). "Emplotment": Letter writing with troubled adolescents and their families. *Clinical Child Psychology and Psychiatry, 5*(1), 63–76. doi:10.1177/1359104500005001007

Gutting, G. (2005). *Foucault: A very short introduction.* New York: Oxford University Press.

Khoja-Moolji, S. (2014). Constructionist and poststructuralist theories. In L. Ganon, M. Coleman, & G. Golson (Eds.), *The social history of the American family: An encyclopedia.* Thousand Oaks, CA: Sage.

Madigan, S. (2007). Watching the other watch. In C. Brown & T. Augusta-Scott (Eds.), *Narrative therapy: Making meaning, making lives* (pp. 133–150). Thousand Oaks, CA: Sage.

Madigan, S. (2011). *Narrative therapy.* Washington, DC: American Psychological Association.

Majchrzak, M. A. (2003). An invitation to therapeutic letter writing. *Journal of Systemic Therapies, 22*(1), 15–32. doi:10.1521/jsyt.22.1.15.24097

McQueen, C., & Hobbs, C. (2014). Working with parents: Using narrative therapy to work towards genuine partnership. *Educational & Child Psychology, 31*(4), 9–17.

Morgan, A. (2000). *What is narrative therapy? An easy to read introduction.* Adelaide, Australia: Dulwich Centre.

Morgan, A. (2002). Beginning to use a narrative approach in therapy. *International Journal of Narrative Therapy and Community Work, 1*, 85–90.

Pearce, J. (2008, April 28). Michael White, 59, dies; used stories as therapy. *New York Times*. Retrieved from http://www.nytimes.com/2008/04/28/us/28white.html

Psychotherapy.net (Producer). (2002). *Narrative therapy with children with Stephen Madigan, PhD*. [DVD]. Mill Valley, CA: Author.

Rabinow, P. (1984). *The Foucault reader*. New York: Random House.

Semmler, P. L., & Williams, C. B. (2000). Narrative therapy: A storied context for multicultural counseling. *Journal of Multicultural Counseling & Development, 28*, 51–60.

Smyth, J., True, N. & Souto, J. (2001). Effects of writing about traumatic experiences: The necessity for narrative structuring. *Journal of Social and Clinical Psychology, 20*(2), 161–172. doi:10.1521/jscp.20.2.161.22266

Stephenmadigan.ca. (n.d.). About Dr. Madigan. Retrieved from http://www.stephenmadigan.ca/about-dr-madigan

Walther, S., & Carey, M. (2009, October). Narrative therapy, difference and possibility: Inviting new becomings. *Context*, 5–10.

Walther, S., & Fox, H. (2012). Narrative therapy and outsider witness practice: Teachers as a community of acknowledgement. *Educational & Child Psychology, 29*, 8–17.

White, C. (2009, October). Where did it all begin? Reflecting on the collaborative work of Michael White and David Epston. *Context*, 59–60.

White, M. (1990). Consultation interviews and accountability. *Dulwich Centre Newsletter, 4*, 36-40.

White, M. (1995). Reflecting teamwork as definitional ceremony. In M. White (Ed.), *Re-authoring lives: Interviews and essays* (n.p). Adelaide, Australia: Dulwich Centre. Retrieved from https://www.dulwich-centre.com.au/reflecting-teamwork-as-definitional-ceremony-michael-white.pdf

White, M. (1997). The mouse stories. In C. White & J. Hales (Eds.), *The personal is the professional: Therapists reflect on their families, lives and work* (pp. 105-113). Adelaide, Australia: Dulwich Centre.

White, M. (2007). *Maps of narrative practice*. New York: Norton.

White, M. (2011). *Narrative practice: Continuing the conversation* (D. Denborough, Ed.). New York: Norton.

White, M., & Epston, D. (1989). *Literate means to therapeutic ends*. Adelaide, South Australia: Dulwich Centre Publications.

White, M., & Epston, D. (1990). *Narrative means to therapeutic ends*. New York, NY: Norton.

CHAPTER 16

Family Psychoeducation and Enrichment

Bret Hendricks, Loretta J. Bradley, Melissa Gaa,
Derek Robertson, and Brandé Flamez

*"The stored experience of relationship becomes the
template on which future experience is modeled."*

—Donald Bloch

The term *psychoeducation* was first used in 1911 by John E. Donley in his article, "Psychotherapy and Re-education," which appeared in the *Journal of Abnormal Psychology*. In 1941 Brian E. Tomlinson published a book, *The Psychoeducational Clinic*, in which he referred to psychoeducation in a clinical mental health setting. Tomlinson (1941) further discussed the need to use psychoeducation with staff and clients in a mental health clinic to begin the process of therapy. Thus, psychoeducation was identified as a necessary component of family counseling for mental health issues. In Section III of the book, you have learned about various models and therapeutic approaches to working with families. In this chapter, we will focus on family psychoeducation and enrichment. We will discuss psychoeducation programs for persons with family members hospitalized for mental illness, childhood disorders, as well as programs for families experiencing mental disorders. We will then turn our attention to various enrichment programs. Throughout the chapter we will include case presentations to help you apply the information. Let's get started!

After reading this chapter, you will be able to do the following:

- Define the term *psychoeducation* and be able to describe *psychoeducation* and its use in family counseling.
- Identify historical persons who developed family psychoeducation.
- Understand the historical context of psychoeducation and double bind theory.
- Identify key persons who developed marriage and relationship enhancement.
- List major components of marriage enrichment programs.
- Identify psychoeducational programs for families dealing with adult and childhood illness.
- Be familiar with marriage and family enrichment programs.
- Identify key constructs of psychoeducation with stepfamilies.

OVERVIEW AND HISTORY OF PSYCHOEDUCATION

While psychoeducation was discussed as a component of family therapy, it wasn't until the 1950s that psychoeducation was more formally studied. The true origins of psycho-education originated as a response to the 1950s models of treatment related to medical conditions and psychopathology. In 1956 Bateson, Jackson, Haley, and Weakley proposed the double bind theory of schizophrenia. According to the double bind theory, families' faulty and contradictory interaction patterns predispose their own family members to schizophrenia (Bateson et al., 1956). Thus, according to this theory, families "create" systems that lead to the development of schizophrenia. The medical community quickly embraced this theory because it accounted for the high relapse rates which were 72% to 74% for patients who returned to living with their families 6 months or less (Schooler, Solomon, Golberg, Booth, & Cole, 1966). In essence, the clients and their families were "blamed" for the pathology and ensuing relapses.

Early researchers in family therapy did not agree that families should be "blamed" for their mental health diagnoses. Donald Bloch and Nathan Ackerman began closely examining the interactions of clients and clinicians in mental health hospitals. During this time, researchers were discovering that mental health clients routinely received inhu-mane treatment (Paul, 1969; Paul & Lentz, 1977). In direct reaction to these realizations, the concept of the therapeutic community was born. The primary aim of therapeutic communities was and is to respect clients and their innate abilities to cope with and recover from mental illnesses through the creation of a democratic user-led form of therapeutic environment. Therapeutic communities use psychoeducation as means of empowering clients through knowledge. Therapeutic communities avoid authoritarian practices, enabling clients and clinicians to work together to provide a therapeutic envi-ronment. Through the utilization of social interactions, clinicians leveraged positive peer pressure to develop clients' coping skills. Thus, as clients worked on their own goals, they participated in and facilitated positive outcomes for their peers.

RELATIONSHIP ENHANCEMENT: HISTORICAL BACKGROUND

Concurrently, as researchers were beginning to recognize the importance of positive family interventions for persons with severe mental illness, another movement was being developed in Spain. Father Gabriel Calvo began leading retreats in 1961 for married couples in which the husband and wife would learn from other couples as they modeled communication and intimacy techniques. Likewise, in the 1960s in the United States, David and Vera Mace began exploring couple enrichment and enhancement. The Maces, who later wrote their groundbreaking book, *How to Have a Happy Marriage: A Step by Step Guide* (Mace & Mace, 1977), were seeking to remediate the high divorce rates of the time. They began conducting marriage enhancement retreats in 1962. They worked under the premise that if couples would strengthen their marriages when they were not in a crisis stage, they could deal with future crisis and conflict in positive ways.

During the 1980s and 1990s, programs for the chronically mentally ill became more community-based, thereby directly involving family members in the therapeutic process. Carol Anderson (1988) developed programs designed to provide information to family members about the patients' illness, life skills, ways to improve family functioning, ways to access community supports, ways to access social service, and methods for the families and patients to cope after the patients' hospital release. In 1998 the World Schizophrenia Fellowship adopted a strategy for family training, education, and support that was to be integrated into each client's treatment plan, with the primary focus being the health and support of the patient with schizophrenia while also integrating family enrichment strategies. Thus, with this inclusion psychoeducation was legitimately viewed as integral to the patient's recovery process, if the patient was returning to her or his parental family.

THE 2000S: THE GROWTH OF PSYCHOEDUCATION AND ENRICHMENT PROGRAMS

The years since 2000 have been filled with immense growth and internationalization of psychoeducation, family enrichment, and marriage enrichment. In particular, marriage enrichment programs are reaching almost all parts of the globe. By 2003 it was estimated that between one quarter and one third of all marrying couples in Australia, the United Kingdom, and the United States had attended some form of marriage enrichment seminar (Halford, Markman, Kline & Stanely, 2003). Communication skills, financial management, conflict resolution skills, and parenting are focal points of most family psychoeducation programs.

Role of the Therapist

The role of the therapist in marriage and family enrichment is varied and unique. As illustrated in this chapter, marriage and family enrichment theorists were from varied backgrounds. For example, Donald Bloch (1973) was a psychoanalytic psychiatrist. Father Calvo was a Catholic priest (White, 1999). Carol Anderson is a professor of psychiatry and social work at the University of Pittsburgh (Singer, 2007). These theorists, examples of the diverse backgrounds of researchers in marriage and family enrichment, provided a foundation in which eclectic practice is valued and encouraged. Many of the actual practitioners of marriage and family enrichment are paraprofessionals or volunteers, particularly in religious settings. The roles of therapists are highlighted in the following discussions related to the researchers.

Psychoeducation and Mental Illness

In the preceding paragraphs, we recounted milestones in the history of family psycho-education. We also discussed the psychiatric community's early views of the double bind theory, which essentially blamed families for their own illnesses. Soon after its inception, early family researchers reacted strongly to the blaming stance, believing instead that the family system was part of the solution, not the problem. Thus, treatment of mental health clients foundationally changed because of their research. Moreover, through implementation of their strategies, clients who had been considered "hopeless cases" transformed as they learned to cope with their illnesses. Thus, family members became active coparticipants in treatment, rather than the perceived cause of dysfunction. In the following paragraphs, we will discuss these pioneering researchers more in depth, examining the context and the background of their work. Later in the chapter, we will also discuss the evolution of psychoeducation for families with mental health issues and how psychoeducation has now become an integral part of treatment today.

Profile of Main Figures

Donald Bloch's Systemic Family Therapy in Medicine

Donald Bloch was a pioneer advocate in systemic thought regarding treatment of clients with mental illness. Bloch, a psychoanalytic psychiatrist, completed medical school in 1943. At that time, few medications existed to effectively treat clients as they had aggressive episodes or "psychotic excitements," as they were known then. During these episodes, clients were self-harming, disoriented, and aggressive to staff and peers.

To study treatment options, Bloch turned to other disciplines outside medicine. Thus, Bloch's research combined cultural anthropology, sociology, general systems theory, cybernetics, and semiotics; that is, the study of "meaning-making." He used research from Frank Parsons, Margaret Mead, Gregory Bateson, Ludwig von Bertalanffy, and Harry Stack Sullivan as the foundations of his work. Because of his studies, Bloch became a vocal proponent of holistic methods of psychiatric treatment, demanding that clients receive treatment for their physical and emotional struggles. Let's take a moment and turn out attention to Guided Practice Exercise 16.1 in which consider our own wellness plan.

GUIDED PRACTICE EXERCISE 16.1

Donald Bloch (1973) insisted that clients receive holistic treatment addressing physical and emotional struggles. For you to better understand holistic treatment, design a wellness plan for yourself that includes physical and emotional supports. Create specific and time limited goals that are relevant to your own emotional and physical development. For example, you may be feeling anxious about meeting new friends. Thus, you might want to create a plan to increase positive self-talk and go to a gym regularly where you might exercise and meet others; thereby increasing socialization and decreasing anxiety through self-talk and exercise. Assess your progress after two or three weeks and at defined times in the future.

Foundationally, Bloch believed effective treatment of mental disorders included physical and mental intervention as they incorporated family treatment, education, resource information, and life-skills. During the 1960s and 1970s, Bloch began to present his ideas to the family therapy community, calling his collective concepts family systemic medicine. In 1965 he began working with Nathan Ackerman, a pioneer in Family Therapy known for, among other things, integrating individual psychotherapy constructs with family systems. After Ackerman's sudden death in 1971, Bloch served as director of the Ackerman Institute from 1972 until 1991. In 1973 he wrote *Techniques of Family Psychotherapy: A Primer*, considered a seminal work in family therapy (Bloch, 1973). His tenure at the Ackerman Institute enabled him to further study and disseminate information about his work, now called family systemic medicine, or FSM. In 1983 Bloch began a journal, *Family Systems Medicine*, now known as *Family, Systems, and Health*, focusing on medicine and systemic treatment. This quarterly journal, now edited by Colleen Fogerty of the University of Rochester Medical Center and Larry Mauksch of the University of Washington School of Medicine, is a major journal in family therapy. Today therapists use FSM with families dealing with a wide range of illnesses, including but not limited to intellectual developmental difficulties, autism, diabetes, HIV, Parkinson's disease, and multiple sclerosis.

Carol Anderson's Psychoeducation Model Development

Carol Anderson, a professor at the University of Pittsburg, began developing a program, later known as Family Psychoeducation, in 1978. The recipient of a grant focused on working with clients with schizophrenia, Anderson, observed that stressors facing family members of these clients were almost insurmountable. She noted that families did not understand what schizophrenia was; therefore, their lack of understanding led them to treat the person with schizophrenia in ways that intensified or exacerbated their symptoms. Thus, from its inception, Anderson's behavioral therapeutic program consisted of four distinct elements designed to assist families cope while also learning about schizophrenia.

As she worked with her clients and saw firsthand the mistreatment of persons with mental illness, Anderson became an outspoken advocate for persons with schizophrenia and their families. In a 2007 interview, Anderson said the following:

We have blamed each other, the patients themselves, their parents and grandparents, public authorities, and society for the cause and for the terrible course of these mental disorders. When hope and money become exhausted, we frequently tear schizophrenic patients from their families consigning them to the existential terror of human warehouses, single occupancy hotels and more recently to the streets and alleys of American cities. (as cited in Singer, 2007, p. 1)

Carol Anderson: Psychoeducation Program Components and Key Concepts

Carol Anderson focused significant portions of her psychoeducational program on information about the illness and symptom management. She noted early in her program that patient's families had little or no correct information about schizophrenia, thereby limiting their ability to care for the identified patient. Further, Anderson believed that assessment of preexisting family stressors must occur to deliver information in ways the family could understand. Moreover, she found that families were unintentionally causing stress for themselves and the person diagnosed with schizophrenia simply because they were uninformed. The components of her program are listed below:

Phase 1: Connecting phase. In this phase, therapists build rapport with family members by listening to their experiences, obtaining information about strategies they use to cope with illness. The person with the illness does not attend sessions during this phase.

Phase 2: Survival Skills Workshop. The second phase of treatment is the Survival Skills Workshop, which helps families prioritize their attention so the illness is not the center of family concern. They are also given instructions regarding stimulation minimization and ways to set clear limits and boundaries with the family member who has schizophrenia. The person with schizophrenia does not attend this phase.

Phase 3: Reentry phase. Phase 3 assists clients and their families to implement knowledge application from the Survival Skills Workshop. Reentry is done very gradually, as the first 3 months after a psychotic episode are the highest risk time for episode recurrence. Phase 3 is considered mastered when the client with schizophrenia has 6 months of stability; that is, no evidence of psychotic episodes. Thus, this phase might last anywhere from 6 months to 2 years.

Phase 4: Applying skills in social context. During this phase, clients apply social skills they have learned earlier in the program. The client might attend vocational rehabilitation, community support groups, and peer groups. Examples of applied social skills include training in meeting and greeting others in social and work contexts and communicating with peers at a mental health center or group.

Phase 5: Family therapy. The client and family attend family therapy sessions with the duration being determined by the family therapist. Frequently, therapists focus on stressors the family encounters during the illness, such as marriage stress and financial stress. During Phase 5, the Family Enrichment Scale, fourth edition, could be used to assess the social environment of the family. The scale provides information that will enable the therapist to develop treatment plans and assist families as they interact with their environments (Moos & Moos, 2009).

Anderson's program challenged the prevailing psychiatric community, which maintained that clients relapsed after hospital release because their families did not maintain enough structure for the client to be medication compliant. Anderson's program results further challenged the psychiatric community by its high success rate. Specifically, Anderson had almost 100% success in relapse prevention, compared to high relapse rates of other prevailing programs.

Carol Anderson: Role of the Therapist

Carol Anderson's program requires the therapist to do psychoeducation, guidance, and assessment. During Phase 1 of the program, the Connecting Phase, therapists simultaneously assess the family coping skills while building rapport. During Phase 2, the Survival Skills Workshop, therapists provide psychoeducation regarding schizophrenia and provide instruction to the family regarding stimulation minimization and boundary setting. During Phase 3, the reentry phase, the therapist provides feedback to the family regarding implementation of knowledge they have gained in the previous phases. Phases 4 and 5 of the program are focused on providing family support as the family applies skills in the social context and deals with stressors related to their situation. Thus, the therapist may use any theory that is relevant to the family as the therapist and family coconstruct goals for counseling.

TREATMENT OF DISORDERS OF CHILDHOOD

Psychoeducation for families with a child with mental illness is vital. Parents and siblings of a child experiencing mental illness will benefit from psychoeducation at multiple levels. As discussed above, Carol Anderson (1988) found that family members obtained benefits from gaining information about the etiology, diagnosis, and prognosis of the illness impacting their family. Second, parents who have a child who has been diagnosed with a mental health condition may have only rudimentary or wrong information about the condition. Through psychoeducation, family members gain information about the illnesses they face in ways they understand, without using overly complicated jargon and clinical terminology. Further, psychoeducation helps family members feel less isolated and increases the chances of interventions being successfully implemented outside the counseling sessions.

CASE PRESENTATION: PARENT MANAGEMENT TRAINING

In this fictional case, Dr. Boroughs, a family therapist, is working with Wanda, the mother of a 15-year-old named Jackie. Originally, Wanda came to Dr. Boroughs seeking help after she was reprimanded by the school for Jackie's excessive absences. To assist Wanda, Dr.

Boroughs is using parent management training techniques; namely, data collection and reinforcers. Note the use of these techniques in the following case presentation.

Family therapist: Hello, Wanda. Tell me how things are this week with Jackie.

Client: Well, Dr. Boroughs, we are still working on her going to school. I swear I got called again this week by the principal who said that she did not go to her first period class twice this week. I was so frustrated that I am glad we talked about anger management last week! I kept my self-talk positive. I just kept telling myself that we are seeing progress, though it's slow.

Family therapist: Sounds as if you practiced what we talked about regarding staying cognitive and not letting your emotions take over. I'm glad to hear that you are practicing positive self-talk and even more glad to hear that you find it beneficial. Now, let's talk about Jackie's behavior. You said that you are seeing progress? What progress are you seeing?

Client: She missed two classes last week. That made me really mad until I looked at the chart that we made and I saw that she missed four classes the week before last. She missed classes after lunch and in the morning. Last week, she missed two morning classes. Now, I am not happy she missed those classes, but it's better than the week before. So, I told her I see room for improvement, but I am happy that she came back from lunch on time and went to class every day last week. In fact, I told her I am so happy with her that I will get her a gift card for the coffee shop so she can go and take a friend to get something to drink. Any 16-year-old would like that. I think she will be excited about this.

Family therapist: So, you plan to talk to her and review her attendance as well as reward her positive behavior.

Client: Yes, and I am really glad to see improvement. Thank goodness it is getting better. We were going to be referred to court if she didn't start going to class more often.

Family therapist: Now, it's important for you to set a goal with her for next week.

Client: I know. Of course, I want her to be in every class. I think that if she goes to every class, I will give her movie passes. Oh my, she would like that. I will even volunteer to drive her and a friend to the movie theater.

Family therapist: Whatever you do has to mean something to her. It sounds as if she would look forward to going to a move with a friend. 'Be sure that she understands that she has to abide by the rules and go to every class to get the reinforcer; that is, the movie tickets. Also, make sure she knows that you will check her attendance with the assistant principal just to be sure that she is going to every class and keep writing her attendance on the chart so she can see that you are tracking the attendance.

CHILDREN'S MENTAL HEALTH: STATISTICAL INFORMATION

Children's mental health disorders cover a wide range of dysfunction and may include developmental difficulties, depression, conduct disorder, attentional difficulties, and social isolation related to the autism spectrum. The Centers for Disease Control and

Prevention (2013) reported the following about mental health disorders among children and adolescents ages 3 to 17 during 2011:

- Millions of American children live with depression, anxiety, attention deficit/hyperactivity disorder (ADHD), autism spectrum disorders, Tourette syndrome. or a host of other mental health issues.

- ADHD was the most prevalent current diagnosis among children aged 3–17 years; it affects some 5.9 million children ages 3 to 17 in the United States.

- The number of children with a mental disorder increased with age, except for autism spectrum disorders, which was highest among 6- to 11-year-old children.

- Boys were more likely than girls to have ADHD (the diagnostic rate in the United States for girls is less than half that of boys), behavioral or conduct problems, autism spectrum disorders, anxiety, Tourette syndrome, and cigarette dependence.

- Adolescent boys aged 12–17 years were more likely than girls to die by suicide.

- Adolescent girls were more likely than boys to have depression or an alcohol use disorder.

PREMISES OF PARENT MANAGEMENT TRAINING

Parent management training (PMT) developed in the early 1960s as people came to realize that treatments for children with disruptive behaviors were largely ineffective (Forgatch & Patterson, 2010; Kazdin, 2005). During PMT, parents are taught Bandura's social learning theory principles (Bandura, 1969). PMT takes several months for parents to complete and focuses on the application of positive reinforcements as foundations for prosocial behaviors

PMT focuses on parent training and children do not attend the training sessions. Over the course of PMT, parents are trained to record data describing their children's positive and negative behaviors. When their children exhibit appropriate or positive behaviors, they are rewarded with social reinforcements that are both social and concrete in nature. Positive social reinforcements are hugs, smiles, and verbal praise. Examples of concrete reinforcements are stickers or check marks on a chart. Additionally, parents may sometimes develop a point system to provide further motivation for the child to achieve larger rewards. Point systems are devised cooperatively with children to ensure that their participation is meaningful.

Effects of PMT. PMT has been extensively studied and researched. The use of PMT has been positively correlated with increasing positive parental behavior and confidence while decreasing parental depression, anxiety, overall stress, irritability, and anxiety

(Bjørnebekk, Kjøbli, & Ogden, 2015;Lali, Malekpour, Molavi, Abedi, & Asgari, 2012; Levy-Frank, 2012). PMT is also viewed as a cost-effective way to treat under-controlled behaviors (Skotarczak & Lee, 2015). Effectiveness of family interactions is integral to PMT. Too assess familial interaction effectiveness, therapists may use the Family Task Interview, or FTI (Kinston & Loader, 1988). See Chapter 8 for a thorough discussion of the FTI and its use in family assessment. Guided Practice Exercise 16.2 illustrates one assessment that might be used to uncover family interactions through personality traits.

GUIDED PRACTICE EXERCISE 16.2

Mercedes is a single mother of an adopted 16-year-old son, Shane. Mercedes constantly complains that Shane doesn't talk to her. Further, she declares that he is constantly late and very disorganized. On the other hand, Shane reports that his mother won't give him any peace because she wants him to immediately tell her about everything at school at the moment he arrives home from school. "I just want to be quiet for a while when I get home, but you bug me to tell you everything," Shane says. Sensing that there are major personality preference differences between Shane and Mercedes, you ask Shane and Mercedes to each complete the Myers–Briggs Type Indicator (MBTI) (Myers, McCaulley, Quenk, & Hammer, 1998). The MBTI, discussed at length in Chapter 8, indicates that Mercedes has strong extroversion and judging traits, whereas Shane has strong introversion and perceiving traits. How would you discuss these results with Shane and Mercedes so they see these traits as personality preferences rather than personality deficits? How would you use their MBTI results in treatment planning for them?

ADHD and PMT. PMT has been used to assist parents in working with children diagnosed with ADHD. Children with ADHD tend to be disorganized, overactive, and unable to sit still; they also have difficulty with waiting and have impulse behaviors, such as blurting out or poking others because they are unable to control it (Flamez & Sheperis, 2015). Additionally, they may be obstinate and bossy (Bell, 2011). They miss social cues and misinterpret the actions of others. These symptoms obviously interfere with their ability to function in at least two normal environments, home and school. ADHD is viewed as a long-term chronic condition that one manages over time and, like other long-term disorders, is treated with medication alone or a combination of medication and psychotherapy (Flamez & Sheperis, 2015). Stimulant medication is frequently used to control symptoms. Further, parents of children diagnosed with ADHD tend to feel high levels of stress and low parental efficacy (Lali et al., 2012). Furthermore, ADHD is more common in single-parent families (12%) compared to two-parent families (7%; Flamez & Sheperis, 2015).

PMT shows significant effectiveness in reduction of aggressiveness and behavioral problems associated with ADHD (Vazari, Kashani, & Sorati, 2014). While it should be noted that PMT addresses the behavioral components of ADHD, PMT also addresses the organic components of ADHD, such as innate impulsivity, distractibility, and excessive activity. Management of these behaviors, while possible, will be inconsistent at best

(Nichols & Schwartz, 1998). However, researchers do find that PMT combined with parent and teacher participation may be effective in managing a variety of behaviors related to ADHD (Östberg, 2012).

PMT: Role of the Therapist

Therapists are very active as they work with families in PMT. Specifically, during PMT, therapists educate the family regarding Bandura's (1969) social learning theory. Further, during PMT, therapists instruct parents' use of reinforcers to encourage their children's targeted prosocial behaviors. To record progress of the therapy, therapists teach parents ways to record data. Therapists also work with parents to devise point systems and charts with stickers or check marks to indicate the frequency of prosocial behaviors.

Psychoeducation and treatment of autism spectrum disorder. Autism spectrum disorder (ASD) is a neurodevelopmental disorder that is characterized by social communication and social interaction impairments along with repetitive patterns of behavior, interests, or activities (American Psychiatric Association, 2013). The range of difficulties and social communication first appear in infancy and early childhood (Flamez & Sheperis, 2015). In 2014, 1 in 45 children in the United States was diagnosed with ASD (Zablotsky, Black, Maener, Schieve, & Blumberg, 2015). Children with ASD have problems relating to others or have little or no social interest. Further, children with autism avoid eye contact with others and want to be alone. If children with autism are interested in people, they struggle to relate to others and often miss social cues (Baio, 2014).

Ivar Lovaas (1987) instituted an early intervention treatment program like PMT for use with children with autism who were less than 4 years old. In his program, parents were trained extensively for treatment to occur during almost all the child's waking hours. In the program, parents rewarded children for being less aggressive, more compliant, and prosocial. The goal of the program was to mainstream children. As behaviors became more frequently positive, they would have more activity with "normal" peers. The treatment program lasted more than forty hours per week for more than 2 years. Nineteen children were in the treatment group, which was compared to a control group of 55 children who received 10 hours or less of training per week. Lovaas (1987) reported that the results of the study indicated 47% of the children with autism who received 40 hours of Lovaas's treatment protocol were mainstreamed into regular classrooms and classified as "indistinguishable" from their peers in follow-up studies.

In 2010 researchers investigated a psychoeducational and support program for parents and children with autism (Lock, Hendricks, Bradley, & Layton, 2010) In this program, families participated in weekly activities designed to simultaneously provide social support and psychoeducation. In each session of the program, families with a member who had autism participated in a short psychoeducational program followed by a structured game time designed for the families' enjoyment. The research indicated that families were much more likely to participate in psychoeducation when the psychoeducation was paired with activities the family considered "fun." Further, families reported strong bonding and support because of the program. This bonding and support led to increased participation and attendance.

Psychoeducation and treatment of childhood mood disorders. Psychoeducation can also be quite helpful for clients with mood disorders and their families. Mary Fristad has published many articles regarding the use of psychoeducation in the treatment of children with mood disorders (Fristad, 2010; Fristad, Davidson, & Leffler, 2007; Fristad, Verducci, Walters, & Young, 2009; Fristad & Goldberg-Arnold, 2011; Fristad, Goldberg-Arnold, & Leffler, 2011). Similarly, David Miklowitz, professor of psychiatry in the Division of Child and Adolescent Psychiatry at the UCLA Semel Institute, has published articles supporting the use of psychoeducation in treatment of families who have a child with bipolar disorder.

Miklowitz (2004) developed a program for children with mood disorders. Miklowitz's program consists of 21 sessions with three components. The program is designed for parents, siblings, and clients. Miklowitz's family-focused treatment approaches therapy on a single-family basis and generally focuses on older children and teens with bipolar spectrum disorders. Parents, siblings, and patients are invited to sessions. After an initial introduction and a thorough diagnostic evaluation, the program proceeds with 3 major components: (a) psychoeducation of families and children (usually 7–8 sessions), (b) communication enhancement training (7–8 sessions), and (c) problem solving (3–4 sessions).

CASE PRESENTATION 16.1: JOSE AND IMELDA

Jose and Imelda are a married couple with two grown children and three grandchildren. Jose has been through chemotherapy treatments the past 3 months for his cancer diagnosis. Jose attended chemotherapy twice a week and increasingly felt nauseated and fatigued after each appointment. This has been very difficult for both Jose and Imelda. Jose's boss recently told him he only has 4 more days of sick leave, and if he needs more time off after that, he will need to take an unpaid leave of absence. However, his boss assured Jose he could come back to work after that time. Jose and Imelda were called into the doctor's office to discuss Jose's progress. Imelda told the doctor she is worried because Jose is taking longer each time to recover from the chemotherapy treatment and he only takes his medicine when she reminds him. She also states she is confused about when he needs to take his medications, as each bottle states something different. She is worried she is not giving him the correct medicine and dosage. She feels the medicine and treatments are making him sicker rather than better. The doctor discussed putting Jose on a new medication and speaks very quickly with them. Both Jose and Imelda are confused but nod and agree to the new medication.

The day before the doctor's appointment, Imelda spoke to their oldest daughter, Irene. Irene stated a social worker just left her house telling Irene she would need to move out with the kids because her husband had been hitting them. Irene denies that her husband is mistreating the children, but the social worker stated they would remove the children from the home if she did not move them out herself. Irene has asked Imelda if they could move back home with her and Jose. Imelda said of course, but she has not discussed this with Jose yet because of his illness. She is worried what this added stress will do to him. Imelda is worried, as they live in a three-bedroom one-bath home. She is not sure how Irene and the three children will all fit comfortably in their home.

PSYCHOEDUCATION: FAMILIES AND MEDICAL ILLNESS

Families who are dealing with physical illness of a family member face a myriad of problems and stressors. Please refer to Case Presentation 16.1, illustrating an example of a family dealing with the effects of chronic illness. Stressors related to medical illness are experienced singularly and collectively. Singularly, a person who is diagnosed with a major chronic or acute illness experiences denial, anticipatory anxiety and grief and confusion. Collectively, a family experiences similar emotions along with other stressors related to physical and emotional exhaustion. In the following paragraphs, we will discuss psychoeducational interventions that have been used to work with families who are facing physical illnesses. We will discuss how researchers and clinicians covered earlier in the chapter adapted their models to use with physical illnesses, followed by a discussion of other researchers who focused their work specifically on psychoeducational interventions with physical illness.

Psychoeducation: Role of the Therapist

Therapists are trainers and educators in psychoeducation. Ivar Lovaas (1987) emphasizes training parents to implement a program that rewards children for aggression reduction and rule compliance. Lock et al. (2010) created a program in which therapists combine social support and psychoeducation. In this program, the therapist educates families regarding parenting and autism and assists families in creating effective wellness strategies. David Miklowitz (2004) emphasized parent education and diagnostic evaluation by the therapist to effectively treat mood disorders. In each of these examples, therapists are active participants in therapy as they teach and encourage families to become more educated and independent.

DONALD BLOCH AND NATHAN ACKERMAN: TRAUMA AND FAMILIES WITH MEDICAL ILLNESS

Donald Bloch and Nathan Ackerman, both psychiatrists, were pioneers in working with families with medical illnesses. Ackerman was a prolific writer; one of his most widely read books, the *Psychodynamics of Family Life* (1958), outlined his groundbreaking concepts regarding systemic family therapy and psychodynamic family therapy. In the mid-1960s Bloch and Ackerman worked with orthopedic and obstetric patients at New York hospital (Weiner, 1996). During their work, both Bloch and Ackerman were surprised at the high levels of trauma that patients and their families experienced. Notably, most of the patient trauma they treated was unrelated to the illnesses for which the patients were being treated. Bloch and Ackerman also noted the prevalence of divorce among families who experienced physical illness. The work that Bloch and Ackerman pursued involved systemic family intervention with medical issues and formed the basis of Bloch's future establishment of FSM.

JOHN ROLLAND: PREMISES OF FAMILY SYSTEMS ILLNESS MODEL

John Rolland, clinical professor of psychiatry at the University of Chicago, Pritzker School of Medicine, developed strategies to help families cope effectively with the multidimensional levels of illness and corresponding family characteristics. Rolland studied more than 500 families who were experiencing illness. In his research, he found that families deal with illness in different ways, depending on the type and course of illness. Other factors influencing how families deal with illness, according to Rolland (1994), include illness onset, illness course, and the degree of incapacitation the disease causes. Further, treatment outcomes are dependent on the family life cycle stage and the role of the family member who is ill. Rolland (1994) also found that culture and ethnicity of family and the family member's beliefs about the illness impact the ways that families cope with illness.

Rolland (1994) based his model on four core beliefs. These core beliefs form the foundation of his psychoeducational treatment. The core beliefs are described below:

1. Diseases exert an inward pull and require increased family cohesion. This inward pull creates dissonance with families as they are in transition between individual autonomy and less cohesion as they cope with the stressors of the disease.

2. Chronic conditions create a time of transition. The intensity and length of transitions related to chronic conditions depend on the family's life phase and the type of illness. If the family is at a stable or stabilizing phase, the transition created by illness is particularly debilitating and impactful on the family.

3. If the condition or illness is relapsing, increasingly debilitating, and/or life threatening, distinct phases of the disease are marked by transitions. Depending on the progression illness, the family alters its life structure to accommodate the illness.

4. Families dealing with chronic illness have a marked transition as the illness progresses from crisis to chronic stages and vice versa. These transitions are key points for the family to make decisions about future socialization. As the family deals with the crisis nature of the disease, their interactions are centered on the disease and its effects. At this stage, the family has the opportunity to define its' living style as they transition to the realization that the disease will be a present factor in the future of the family. As they transition to crisis stage, family members realize that the disease is becoming increasingly pervasive in their interactions.

Premises of Rolland's psychoeducation model: Phases. John Rolland (1994) wrote that family therapists must work with families who are experiencing medical illness contextually as they experience phases related to illness. Further, he wrote that therapists usually focus their work with families in the terminal phase of illness and do not concentrate their interventions on earlier stages of illness; namely, the initial phase and the chronic phase. Rolland's phases of illness are described below:

Initial phase. In this phase, the therapist assists the family in framing the illness. Therapists help families define their contextual beliefs about disability and death. Contextual beliefs include the family's beliefs about culture, religion, and normalcy in family life.

Chronic phase of illness. The chronic phase of illness is the stage in which the symptoms of the illness remain relatively stable. Rolland maintains that the chronic phase of illness has its own distinct stressors, which therapists frequently ignore. During the chronic stage of illness, families become hyper-vigilant and worried about symptoms, which may be very vague. Thus, the family is constantly seeking information regarding whether the chronic stage is progressing to the terminal stage of illness.

Terminal phase of illness. Rolland (1994) stated that family therapists must help family members complete the process of anticipatory grief and finish any unfinished business. Further, family therapists should assist family members as they begin the reorganization process; that is, they must help the family begin to function as they anticipate the death of the family member who is ill.

Today many programs incorporate John Rolland's concepts. Through his establishment of Chicago Center for Family Health, Rolland and his staff provide programs for low-income and minority families providing psychoeducation for those dealing with physical illness. Rolland and his staff, including Mona Fishbane, Mary Jo Barrett, and others, write about these topics and present Rolland's constructs nationally and internationally.

PRESENT TRENDS: MEDICAL FAMILY THERAPY

Medical family therapy is an emerging area of family therapy. Medical family therapy is an extension of relational systemic understanding, which blends family therapy and medicine. In medical family therapy, the therapist connects patient and provider conceptualizations of issues and goals and client understanding of issues and goals while providing consultation psychoeducation with families dealing with physical illness (Marlowe, 2013). Researchers are now pointing to medical family therapy as the "new frontier of family therapy;" stating that this new subspecialty must be more specifically defined and researched (Tyndall, Hodgson, Lamson, White, & Knight, 2012) write that not only does this new subspecialty need empirical definition, it also needs medical family researchers to identify core curriculum standards, core competencies for training, and research regarding this subspecialty's efficacy. Now that you understand psychoeducation, let's turn our focus to family and marriage and enrichment.

Family Enrichment and Marriage Enrichment

History of Psychoeducational Marriage and Family Enrichment

The goal of relationship education or enrichment programs is to help participants learn, practice, and maintain healthy relationship skills. Nonprofessionals often facilitate these classes and retreats. The first programs of this kind were created in the 1950s by the Catholic Church to strengthen Catholic marriages and families. The programs became more widespread in the 1960s and 1970s as they integrated emerging psychological theories and interpersonal models. Foundationally, marriage and family enrichment models assert that healthy relationships require learned skills that must be practiced and maintained. Thus, some people may have observed healthy couple skills in their families of origin; others may never have observed these skills being practiced. Whether observed or not, family enrichment researchers maintain that everyone needs to build her/his skills to enhance their family relationships. Furthermore, family researchers believe that healthy relationship skills can be taught, practiced, and learned just as one can learn to ride a bike or speak a foreign language (Wetzler, Frame, & Litzinger, 2011).

Marriage and Family Enrichment: Role of the Therapist

Nonprofessionals often facilitate marriage and family enrichment activities.

Family Enrichment

Profile of main figures and key concepts. In the 1970s Bernard Guerney Jr., PhD, developed relationship enhancement (RE); a model of brief therapy and a psychoeducational program used to help families and couples develop relational skills. As a psychoeducational program, RE is used in non-clinical settings, facilitated or taught by laypersons. As a therapeutic adjunct, clinicians use RE to enhance couples counseling.

Bernard Guerney greatly respected the work of Carl Rogers and Salvador Minuchin, with whom he coauthored the family therapy book *Families of the Slums* (Montalvo, Guerney, Rosman, Schumer, & Minuchin, 1967). While Guerney advocates the use of person-centered constructs, RE integrates concepts from psychodynamic, behavioral, humanistic, and interpersonal theories (Guerney, 1994). In his work as a marital/family therapist Guerney noted the importance of emotions and their influence on familial relationships. Although most are unaware of all the ways in which emotions impact our interactions with others, Guerney contended that emotions influence individuals' thoughts, actions, and interpretations of others' behaviors. Thus, as emotions affect interpersonal interactions in ways that are often outside of one's awareness, Guerney believed that it was crucial for clients to examine their emotions and share their feelings to develop more satisfying relationships. Therefore, RE's primary goal is to facilitate family members' awareness of and expression of their deepest emotions. Guerney was opposed to the medical model of counseling which he felt was and is based on problem solving. Indeed, Guerney believes that the medical approach to counseling creates client defensiveness. Contrary to the medical model, RE focuses on the therapeutic process while deemphasizing "problems." RE clinicians do not identify a client per se, instead, RE practitioners believe the relationship is the client.

Premises of family enrichment. Bernard Guerney maintains that meaningful change and growth only occur when individuals fundamentally change the way they interact in their most intimate relationships. Therefore, it is crucial to involve those closest to the client in the therapeutic process. With this in mind, RE therapists and educators emphasize teaching relationship skills to clients, while deemphasizing behavioral change. As couples and families learn relationship skills, RE therapists and educators facilitate integration of these skills. Ultimately, the therapeutic goal is for the family to resolve relationship problems using their newly acquired skills.

RE focuses on skills acquisition. Bernard Guerney, as stated above, believes relationship skills must be learned and practiced. Namely, the relationship skills Guerney identifies as crucial to relationship development are **empathy, expression, discussion/negotiation, problem/conflict resolution, facilitation, conflict management, self-change, generalization, and maintenance** (http://www.skillswork.org). RE programs promote participants' learning, practice, and maintenance of these skills. The RE program, according to Guerney, is appropriate for use with families who are experiencing highly stressful situations, such as infidelity. He also promotes the use of RE for premarital counseling to prevent future problems (Scuka, 2012).

The National Institute of Relationship Enhancement (http://www.nire.org) offers RE training and RE certification for mental health professionals. Further, RE has been adapted to use with clients as they learn parenting skills, and to assist stepfamilies. RE has also been used to address refugee and immigrant family issues (http://www.skillswork.org). Additionally, RE programs are used to improve communication in work and corporate settings (http://www.nire.org).

Marital Enrichment

History of Marital Enrichment: Calvo and Marriage Encounter

Profile of main figures. Religious institutions, invested in the health of their memberships' marriages and families, began developing experiential and educational programs designed to teach couples the skills they need to maintain fulfilling relationships. One of the earliest models is the **Marriage Encounter** Program, developed by a Spanish priest, Gabriel Calvo. Father Calvo was ordained as a Catholic priest in 1952. In 1961 Calvo met with 28 couples for a weekend. This weekend program, called the *Encuentro Conyugal*, or Marriage Encounter, was the first program of its kind, and it became extremely popular. In fact, couples who participated in ensuing Marriage Encounter weekends were so enthusiastic that the program became popular throughout the larger Catholic Church (White, 1999).

Key concepts and theoretical premises. The format of the Marriage Encounter has remained the same since its inception. The programs or retreats are held for 2 to 3 days as a weekend group experience. Priests or married couples facilitate the program. Since the mid-1970s, the Marriage Encounters have expanded their focus to include unmarried couples, couples who do not identify as Catholic, and couples with no religious affiliation whatsoever (Sayers, Kohn, & Heavey, 1998). Please refer to Case Presentation 16.2, which describes the hesitancies of a same-sex couple as they contemplate a marriage enrichment workshop led by a church. The couple wrestle with the dilemma of whether they will be accepted in the church environment. To address these questions, Marriage Encounters are increasingly inviting diversity related to gender identity, racial and ethnic identity, and language. Since 2000 Father Calvo's manuals have been translated into many different languages, with programs conducted in over 100 countries (http://wwme.org). The "Additional Resources" section in this chapter provides information on several other marital and relationship enrichment programs.

CASE PRESENTATION 16.2: ABDUL AND GREG

Abdul and Greg are a couple in their late 30s and have been together 11 years. Until recently, marriage was not a legal option, and now Abdul and Greg are struggling with the decision of whether to get married. They feel pressure from friends and family continuously asking when they are going to marry. They both agree marriage would provide legal and financial advantages they currently do not have; they also see their relationship has been and continues to be satisfying in its present state. That is, they have agreed on the meaning and the commitment of their relationship in its present context and are reluctant to change the relationship from its present status.

Greg and Abdul had known each other since adolescence; however, their relationship did not evolve into a couple relationship until they were both in college. In high school Greg and Abdul had painful experiences as they came out to themselves and friends and family. They both struggled deeply as they sought further understanding of their sexual orientation and increasingly became confused as they witnessed peers openly dating. They did not feel "normal."

Greg spent many years trying to be "straight"; thus, his experience of coming out to friends and family was a long and painful process. Although many of Greg's friends and family were supportive, others made it clear they disapproved of him. As he struggled with others' disapproval, he felt emotionally depleted and reluctant to allow people to get close to him. Further, Abdul's family loves Greg and accepts Greg completely into their family. However, Greg's family does not accept Abdul's role in Greg's life. Abdul is aware of how Greg's family feels about their relationship and that those attitudes are unlikely to change. Abdul has obtained a level of peace about his relationship with them.

Although Greg and Abdul have had hardships in the past, they now enjoy a comfortable and fulfilling relationship. While there are stressors typical to all couples, their arguments are infrequent; often diffused quickly with humor. They are now faced with the decision of whether to marry and realize they need help dealing with this. Greg also wonders if marriage would appease his family as their relationship becomes more "legitimate." As Greg reads a local online newspaper, he reads about a couple enrichment workshop. Intrigued, he reaches toward his keyboard to register for the workshop. Then, suddenly, he stops and laughs quietly to himself. The workshop is offered at a community center in conjunction with a local church. Quietly, he says to himself, "I wonder what they will think of THIS couple coming to enrich their relationship?"

PSYCHOEDUCATION: STEPFAMILY PREPARATION

According to the Pew Research Center (2011), 40% of new marriages in the United States are remarriages for one or both partners. In response to the prevalence of stepfamilies and their unique needs, step-couple education classes have been offered since the late 1970s (Lucier-Greer, Adler-Baeder, Harcourt & Gregson, 2014). Between 1978 and 2007, many stepfamily programs were developed. Participants in these programs learned communication skills, characteristics and unique needs of stepfamilies, and ways to facilitate blending family systems. The programs were offered in a variety of formats including group discussions, family group therapy, and self-directed education (Skogrand, Dansie, Higginbotham, Davis, & Barrios-Bell, 2011). Since the inception, stepfamily education has been expanded to offer stepfamilies assistance particularly with discipline techniques, finances, and parenting (Skogrand, Reck, Higginbotham, Adler-Baeder, & Danise, 2010).

Profile of Main Figures

John and Emily Visher: Pioneers in stepfamily research. John and Emily Visher are considered pioneers in stepfamily psychoeducation. Married in 1959, the Vishers each had four children, ranging in age from 5 to 13. The Vishers, both psychologists, entered the marriage believing they could easily face the challenges of their newly blended family. However, they very quickly realized they were ill equipped to deal with the ensuing complications of combining their families. The Vishers' stepparenting experiences provided rich resources as they wrote and researched stepfamilies. Realizing the need for stepfamily support, they established the Stepfamily Association of America in 1979 to help families with adopted and stepchildren. The Vishers wrote *How to Win as a Stepfamily* in 1982 (Visher & Visher, 1982), which provided stepfamilies new information about how to be successful as a stepfamily. Focusing on family therapy interventions, The Vishers wrote *Therapy with Stepfamilies* in 1996 (Visher & Visher, 1996), providing therapists with strategies for counseling stepfamilies.

Key concepts. Throughout their writing, John and Emily Visher referred to 15 constructs designed to help stepfamilies as they create new family systems (Visher & Visher, 1982; Visher & Visher 1996). According to the Vishers, stepfamilies should follow the 15 constructs or "tips" to achieve maximum positive stepfamily communication and general functioning (Coalition for Marriage, Family, and Couples Education 2015). The Vishers' 15 tips are listed below:

1. Families should begin their "new lives" in their home if possible. This will decrease "turf" arguments, hurt feelings, and give the family more ability to rid itself of unpleasant memories of the past.

2. Stepfamilies should not expect the new family system to be the same as their first marriage families. Stepfamilies have characteristics that make them different and these characteristics have their own challenges and rewards. For example, stepfamilies are formed after relationship

changes and losses, thereby the adults and children in the family have preconceived ideas about how family life "should" be. Thus, the adults and the children in the "new" system are establishing parent–child relationships that never existed before the couple relationship was formed. Conversely, children and parents in stepfamilies must integrate new relationships into their existing family system, creating confusion and conflict. While these stepfamily characteristics can add richness and diversity to the family, they also result in formidable challenges for the family.

3. Stepfamilies should let relationships and systems develop gradually. Relationships do not develop on demand. Trust takes time. Integration of families and family systems may take 4 to 6 years, according to Visher & Visher (1996).

4. Stepfamilies should develop new traditions. New traditions hasten the sense of belonging and connectedness as they develop familiar "rituals" and special celebrations.

5. Stepfamilies should negotiate differences. For example, whether the dog sleeps at the foot of the bed or in the garage should not be considered an argument related to "right or wrong;" but rather a difference of opinion and expectations.

6. Stepfamilies should share past family histories. As family members share past experiences, they gain knowledge and understanding of each other.

7. Stepparents should assume parenting roles very slowly. Stepparents must build relationships with stepchildren before attempting to set limits with the stepfamilies.

8. Couples with stepfamilies must form a solid bond. When couples have a good relationship, they can work together to meet the needs of the children.

9. Stepfamilies must develop and maintain relationships on a one-on-one basis. Parents should plan to spend individual time with their biological and stepchildren.

10. Stepparents must provide access to both biological parents. If stepparents provide access to both biological parents, they are less likely to be "caught in the middle" of conflicting emotions and confusion.

11. Stepfamilies need to develop family schedules with input from the children.

12. Children in stepfamilies need a "special spot" in the household. Providing a drawer or desk facilitates a sense of belonging.

13. Stepparents must understand that children's anger may be due to changes and losses. Further, they may feel they have no control over the losses and changes they have experienced.

14. Stepfamilies must learn to communicate.

15. Stepfamilies should contact the Stepfamily Association of America. This association provides many resources.

Source: http://www.smartmarriages.com/stepfamily.tips.html

Now that you understand these key concepts, let's turn to Guided Practice Exercise 16.3

GUIDED PRACTICE EXERCISE 16.3

Stepfamilies should, as discussed in this chapter, develop new traditions to hasten the sense of belongingness. What are your family traditions? What are the family traditions of your spouse or partner? How do these traditions differ from your family? How have you developed new traditions with your spouse or partner? If you are not in a committed relationship, think about your family traditions. Which of these traditions would you have difficulty giving up or changing? Are there family traditions you have which you would not change?

The "Additional Resources" section provides information on several resources for stepfamilies.

In summary, psychoeducation programs use education to empower clients and families while enabling them to support, learn from, and connect with others who share common goals for happiness and wellbeing. Psychoeducation and enrichment programs are available to clients and families who are struggling with long-term illness or mental disorders. Programs are also available to improve parenting, strengthen marriages, or provide support for stepfamilies. Within a supportive community families are empowered through knowledge that is specific to their needs. Thus, it is crucial that therapists are aware of these important resources, so that they can insure families receive the help and support they need beyond the counseling session.

SUMMARY

In this chapter, we discussed marriage and family enrichment, which has a long and rich history that now provides insights and knowledge to current family counselors. The pioneers of marriage and family enrichment paved the way for today's couple and family counselors to address such diverse areas as holistic treatment, wellness, and communication. The continued work of those now focused on marriage and family enrichment brings together theorists, researchers, and multidisciplinary mental health practitioners with a common goal: making life better for couples and families. In Chapter 17 the theme of systemic mental health is further discussed as the authors explore integrative family therapy approaches. In an era of increasing diversity awareness and emphases on systemic treatment, integrative approaches to couples and family counseling are increasingly utilized. Accordingly, the following chapter focuses on integrative theories of couples and family counseling.

KEYSTONES

Among the key points addressed in this chapter are:

- 1911: John Donley used the term *psychoeducation* for the first time (Donley, 1911).
- 1941: Brian E. Tomlinson wrote *The Psychoeducational Clinic* (Tomlinson, 1941).
- 1943: Donald Bloch began his observations related to systemic medicine.
- 1956: Bateson, Jackson, Haley, and Weakley proposed the double bind theory of schizophrenia.
- 1961: John Calvo had his first marriage encounter weekend in Barcelona, Spain.
- 1965: Donald Bloch began his work with Nathan Ackerman, further enhancing his work with families with medical needs.
- 1973: Donald Bloch wrote *Techniques of Family Psychotherapy: A Primer* in which he outlined his concepts of medical illness and systemic family treatment (Bloch, 1973).
- 1977: David and Vera Mace wrote *How to Have a Happy Marriage: A Step by Step Guide* (1977).
- 1977: Bernard Guerney wrote *Relationship Enhancement* (Guerney, 1977).
- 1978: Carol Anderson developed her program for family psychoeducation with families dealing with schizophrenia.
- 1982: John and Emily Visher wrote *How to Win as a Step-Family* (Visher & Visher, 1982).
- 1994: John Rolland wrote *Families, Illness, and Disability* (Rolland, 1994).
- 1998: The World Schizophrenia Fellowship adopted a strategy for family training, education, and support that was to be integrated into each client's treatment, thus integrating psychoeducation into treatment planning for clients with schizophrenia.

REFLECTIONS FROM THE CONTRIBUTORS' CHAIR
Derek Robertson

In the late 1990s and early 2000s, I worked at a community agency that served clients living with HIV/AIDS and their families. One of the services that seemed to be the most beneficial in helping clients find peace and emotional healing was the psychoeducation groups. Many clients, upon receiving their diagnosis of HIV or AIDS, assumed that the diagnosis was a death sentence. Due to the stigma of HIV at the time, they often suffered in isolation. These groups provided clients and their families the opportunity to learn facts about the disease and how to best manage it. But, most importantly, the groups provided access to people who had been living successfully with HIV. Some of the long-term survivors, having found a new lease on life, were fully engaged in healthy living. They worked or volunteered, they dated, and they raised families. Some would even say they had the best years of their lives *after* their HIV diagnosis. Attendance at these groups helped my clients move beyond the worst-case scenarios in their heads and begin to paint a picture of how they may have meaningful and happy lives despite HIV.

ADDITIONAL RESOURCES
The following resources provide additional information relating to the chapter topics.

Useful Websites

- PAIRS Practical Application of Intimate Relationship Skills
  http://www.pairs.com

The goal of the PAIRS program is to help couples build an enjoyable intimate relationship. The nonprofit PAIRS Foundation also offers relationship skills training for same-sex couples, military families, adoptive families, unmarried couples, singles, and disadvantaged youth.

- PREP Prevention and Relationship Enhancement Program (Markman, Floyd, Stanley, & Storaasli, 1988)
  http://Prepinc.com

An evidenced-based psychoeducation model for building healthy relationships and reducing incidence of divorce.

Videos
Better Marriages

- http://www.bettermarriages.org/for-couples/marriage-enrichment-groups/replay-of-marriage-enrichment-groups-megs/

This video offers clips of marriage enrichment groups.

- John Gottman and the Gottman Institute
  http://www.gottman.com

The Gottman Institute, established in 1996 in Seattle, Washington, offers programs for clients seeking relationship skills as well as training for mental health professionals. The Gottman Institute also offers programs for same-gender couples.

Readings

PREPARE: PREPARE/ENRICH Program: Customized Version. Minneapolis, Minnesota, Life Innovations, Inc. https://wwwprepare-enrich.com.

A relationship skills and education model that assesses a couple's relationship strengths and vulnerabilities. Online assessments are customized to each couple (Olson, Larson, & Olson, 2009).

Dr. Pat Love has written many well-regarded books about marriage and family enrichment. These books can be accessed at http://www.patlove.com.

REFERENCES

Ackerman, N. (1958). *Psychodynamics of family life*. New York: Basic Books.

Anderson, C. M. (1988). Psychoeducational model different than paradigm. *Family Therapy News, 19*, 10–12.

American Psychiatric Association. (2013). *Diagnostic and statistical manual of mental disorders* (5th ed.). Arlington, VA: Author.

Baio, J. (2014). The prevalence of autism spectrum disorder among children aged 8 years. *Surveillance Summaries, United States Centers for Disease Control and Prevention, 63*(2), 1–21.

Bandura, A. (1969). *Principles of behavioral modification*. New York: Holt, Rinehart, & Winston.

Bateson, G., Jackson, D. D., Haley, J., & Weakland, J. (1956). Toward a theory of schizophrenia. *Behavioral Science, 1*, 251–264.

Bell, A. S. (2011). A critical review of ADHD diagnostic criteria: What to address in the "DSM V." *Journal of Attention Disorders, 15*(1), 3–10.

Bjørnebekk, G., Kjøbli, J., & Ogden, T. (2015). Children with conduct problems and co-occurring ADHD: The caregiver's burden, coping, and psycho-education in Indian household with single- and multiple affected members with schizophrenia. *International Journal of Mental Health, 43*(1), 30–49.

Bloch, D. (1973). *Techniques of family psychotherapy: A primer*. New York: Grune and Stratton. Centers for Disease Control and Prevention. (2013). Mental health surveillance among children-United States, 2005-2011. (2013, May, 16). Report retrieved April 18, 2015 from www.cdc.gov/Features/ChildrensMentalHealth.

Coalition for Marriage, Family, and Couples Education. (2015). Tips for stepfamilies by Emily & John Visher founders of stepfamily association of America. Retrieved from http://www.smartmarriages.com/stepfamily.tips.html

Donley, J. E. (1911). Psychotherapy and re-education. *Journal of Abnormal Psychology, 6*(1), 1–10.

Flamez, B., & Sheperis, C. (Eds.). (2016). *Diagnosing and treating children and adolescents: A guide for mental health professionals*. Hoboken, NJ: Wiley.

Forgatch, M. S., & Patterson, G. R. (2010). Parent management training—Oregon model: An intervention for antisocial behavior in children and adolescents. In J. R. Weisz & A. E. Kazdin (Eds.), *Evidence-based psychotherapies for children and adolescents* (2nd ed., pp. 159–178). New York: Guilford Press.

Fristad, M. A. (2010). Development of emotion regulation in children of bipolar parents: Treatment implications. *Clinical Psychology: Science and Practice, 17*(3), 187–190.

Fristad, M.A., Davidson, K.H., & Leffler, J. (2007). Thinking-Feeling-Doing: A therapeutic technique for children with bi-polar disorder and their parents. *Journal of Family Psychotherapy, 18(4)* 81–104.

Fristad, M.A., Goldberg Arnold, J.S. (2011). *Multifamily Psychoeducation Psychotherapy (MF-PEP): Parent workbook.* Columbus OH: CFPSI Press.

Fristad, M.A., Goldberg Arnold, J.S., & Leffner, J. (2011). *Multifamily Psychoeducation (MF-PEP): Child workbook.* Columbus, OH: CFPSI Press.

Fristad, M. A., Verducci, J. S., Walters, K., & Young, M. E. (2009). The impact of multi-family psychoeducational psychotherapy in treating children aged 8–12 with mood disorders. *Archives of General Psychiatry, 66*(9), 1013–1021.

Guerney, B. G., Jr. (1977). *Relationship enhancement: Skill training programs for therapy, problem prevention and enrichment.* San Francisco: Jossey-Bass.

Guerney, B. G., Jr. (1994). The role of emotion in relationship Enhancement marital/family therapy. In S. M. Johnson & L. S. Greenberg (Eds.), *The heart of the matter: Perspectives on   emotion in marital therapy* (pp. 124–147). New York: Brunner/Mazel.

Halford, W. K., Markman, H. J., Kline, G. H., & Stanley, S. M. (2003). Best practice in couple relationship education. *Journal of Marital and Family Therapy, 29*, 385–406.

Kazdin, A. E. (2005). *Parent management training: Treatment for oppositional, aggressive, and antisocial behavior in children and adolescents.* New York: Oxford University Press.

Kinston, W., & Loader, P. (1988). The Family Task Interview: A tool for clinical research in family interaction. *Journal of Marital and Family Therapy, 43*, 67–87.

Lali, M., Malekpour, M., Molavi, H., Abedi, A., & Asgari, K. (2012). The effects of parent management training, problem-solving skills training and eclectic training on conduct disorder in Iranian elementary school students. *International Journal of Psychological Studies, 4*(2), 154–161.

Levy-Frank, I. D. (2012). A narrative evaluation of a psychoeducation and therapeutic alliance intervention for parents of persons with a severe mental illness. *Family Process, 51*(2), 265–280.

Lock, R., Hendricks, C. B., Bradley, L. J., & Layton, C. (2010). Using family leisure activities to support families living with autism spectrum disorders. *Journal of Humanistic Counseling, 49*(2), 163–180.

Lovaas, O. I. (1987). Behavioral treatment and normal educational and intellectual functioning in young autistic children. *Journal of Consulting and Clinical Psychology, 55*, 3–9.

Lucier-Greer, M., Adler-Baeder, F., Taylor Harcourt, K., Gregson, K.D. (2014). Relationship education for step-couples reporting relationship instability- Evaluation of the Smart Steps Embrace the Journey Curriculum. *Journal of Marital and Family Therapy, 40*(4), 454–469.

Mace, D., & Mace, V., (1977). *How to have a happy marriage: A step by step guide.* Nashville: Abingdon Press.

Markman, H. J., Floyd, F. J., Stanley, S. M., & Storaasli, R. D. (1988). Prevention of marital distress: A longitudinal investigation. *Journal of Consulting and Clinical Psychology, 56*(2), 210–217. doi:10.1037//0022-006X.56.2.210

Marlowe, D. (2013). Bridging conversations: Discussing the intra-professional relationship between medical family therapy and family therapy. *Journal of Family Therapy, 35*(2), 119–138.

Miklowitz, D.J. (2004). The role of family systems in severe and recurrent psychiatric disorders: a developmental psychopathology view. *Developmental Psychopathology, 16*(3), 677-688. Montalvo, B., Guerney, B. G., Rosman, B. L., Schumer, F., & Minuchin, S. (1967). *Families of the slums: An exploration of their structure and treatment.* New York: Basic Books.

Montalvo, B., Guerney, B. G., Rosman, B. L., Schumer, F., & Minuchin, S. (1967). *Families of the slums; an exploration of their structure and treatment.* New York: Basic Books.

Moos, R. H., & Moos, B. S. (2009). *Family Environmental Scale manual and sample set: Development, applications, and research* (4th ed.). Menlo Park, CA: Mind Garden.

Myers, I. B., McCaulley, M. H., Quenk, N. L., & Hammer, A. L. (1998). *The MBTI® Manual: A Guide to the Development and Use of the Myers-Briggs Type Indicator*. Palo Alto: Consulting Psychologists Press.

Nichols, M. P., & Schwartz, R. C. (1998). *Family therapy: Concepts and methods*. Boston: Allyn and Bacon.

Olson, D. H., Larson, P. J., Olson, A. K. (2009). *PREPARE/ENRICH Program: Customized version*. Minneapolis: Life Innovations.

Östberg, M. A. (2012). An efficacy study of a combined parent and teacher management training programme for children with ADHD. *Nordic Journal of Psychiatry, 66*(2), 123–130.

Paul, G. L. (1969). Chronic mental health patient: Current status-future directions. *Psychological Bulletin, 71*, 89–94.

Paul, G. L., & Lentz, R. J. (1977). *Psychosocial treatment of chronic mental patients: Milieu versus social-learning programs*. Cambridge, MA: Harvard University Press.

Pew Research Center. (2011). A portrait of stepfamilies. Retrieved from http://www.pewsocialtrends.org/2011/01/13/a-portrait-of-stepfamilies

Rolland, J. S. (1994). *Families, illness, and disability*. New York: Harper.

Sayers, S. L., Kohn, C. S., & Heavey, C. (1998). Prevention of marital dysfunction: Behavioral approaches and beyond. *Clinical Psychology Review, 18*(6), 713–744. doi:10.1016/S02727358(98)00026-9

Schooler, N.R., Solomon, C., Goldberg, Booth, H., Cole, J.R. (1967). One year after discharge: Community adjustment of schizophrenic patients. *American Journal of Psychiatry, 123* (8), 986–995.

Scuka, R. F. (2012). Repairing a relationship imperiled by infidelity: Combining individual work, Relationship Enhancement® couple therapy and guided visualization to break through an emotional impasse. *Sexual and Relationship Therapy, 27*(4), 335–343. doi:10.1080/14681994.2012.735768

Singer, J. B. (Host). (2007, October 24). Family psychoeducation: Interview with Carol Anderson, Ph.D. [Episode 27]. *Social Work* [Podcast]. Retrieved from http://socialworkpodcast.com/2007/10/family-psychoeducation- interviewwith.html

Skogrand, L., Dansie, L., Higginbotham, B. J., Davis, P., & Barrios-Bell, A. (2011). Benefits of stepfamily education: One-year post-program. *Marriage & Family, 47*(3), 149–163.

Skogrand, L., Reck, K. H., Higginbotham, B., Adler-Baeder, F., & Dansie, L. (2010). Recruitment and retention for stepfamily education. *Journal of Couple & Relationship Therapy, 9*(1), 48–65.

Skotarczak, L., & Lee, G. K. (2015). Effects of parent management training programs on disruptive behavior for children with a developmental disability: A meta-analysis. *Research in Developmental Disabilities, 38*, 272–287.

Tomlinson, B. E. (1941). *The psychoeducational clinic*. New York: Macmillan.

Tyndall, L. J., Hodgson, J., Lamson, A., White, M., & Knight, S. (2012). Medical family therapy: A theoretical and empirical review. *Contemporary Family Therapy, 34*(2), 156–170.

Vazari, S., Kashani, F. L., & Sorati, M. (2014). Effectiveness of family training in reduced symptoms of the children with attention deficit hyperactivity disorder. *Procedia- Social and Behavioral Sciences, 128*, 337–342.

Visher, E. B., & Visher, J. S. (1982). *How to win as a stepfamily*. New York: Routledge.

Visher, E. B., & Visher, J. S. (1996). *Therapy with stepfamilies*. New York: Brunner-Mazel.

Weiner, E. (1996). An interview with Dr. Donald Bloch. *Family, Systems, and Health, 14*(1), 95–105.

Wetzler, S., Frame, L., & Litzinger, S. (2011). Marriage education for clinicians. *American Journal of Psychotherapy, 65*(4), 311–336.

White, R. (1999). *The origin and vision of marriage encounter*. Washington, DC: FIRES.

Zablotsky, B., Black, L. I., Maenner, M. J., Schieve, L. A., & Blumberg, S. J. (2015). Estimated prevalence of autism and other developmental disabilities following questionnaire changes in the 2014 National Health Interview Survey. *US Department of Health and Human Services National Health Statistics Report, 87*, 1–20.

CHAPTER 17

Integrative Models

Michael Moyer, Stephen Jennings, Lynn Jennings,
Jarryn Robinson, and Janet Froeschle Hicks

"Every time we ask a question, we're generating a possible version of a life."

—David Epston

Integrative models of counseling are a combination of effective and appealing theories for working with clients (Prochaska & Norcross, 2009). Upon graduation, new counselors commonly strive to integrate learned theories into an effective model. Some therapists choose to combine only a few theories and others are more flexible, picking and choosing techniques at random to meet the needs of clients (Kottler & Montgomery, 2011). In contrast to the 1950s and 1960s, when therapists generally worked within one theoretical orientation, most counselors and family therapists today report using an integrative approach to counseling (Prochaska & Norcross, 2009).

Integrative approaches are becoming more common, with over 34% of counseling psychologists and 23% of counselors describing themselves as integrative (Norcross & Goldfried, 2005; Prochaska & Norcross, 2009). Even counselors who claim to practice using only one theory likely integrate several theories when working with clients. We believe that holding to only one theory is extremely difficult especially when working with a diverse population. People are complex, come from a variety of backgrounds, and seek out mental healthcare for an assortment of concerns. The most effective family counseling theoretical orientation is not necessarily a specific theory, but more so a blending of theories that best fit the personality of the therapist and the needs of the family.

Miller, Duncan, and Hubble (2002) found new therapists were more likely to follow a select few theories whereas more experienced therapists were more flexible, integrating a wider range of theories into their practice. However, before family therapists can integrate theories into practice, they must have a firm understanding of not only general counseling theories, but also common integrative approaches. Therefore, in the remaining parts of this chapter, we will focus on providing an in-depth understanding of internal family systems, the metaframeworks model, integrative problem-centered therapy, the narrative solutions approach, and integrative couples therapy. A case presentation is provided to help you apply the concepts.

LEARNING OBJECTIVES

After reading this chapter, you will be able to do the following:

- Describe the goals, techniques, therapists' roles, and ethical considerations evident when using various integrative models.
- Describe the metaframeworks model and associated techniques.
- Understand similarities and differences between traditional behavioral couple therapy and integrative behavioral couple therapy.
- Understand integrated problem-centered therapy, narrative solutions approach, and integrative couples therapy models (including history, techniques, and key figures associated with each model).
- Explore the historical background, key theorists, and theoretical foundations of narrative solutions.
- Describe commonalities among five integrative models of couples' therapy.

INTERNAL FAMILY SYSTEMS

History, Background, and Profile of Main Figures

The internal family systems (IFS) model is an integrative approach to individual psychotherapy developed by Richard Schwartz in the early 1990s. IFS is based on the general concept of **systems theory**, which is a generic term with several concepts that, taken together, enable therapists to address problems by working with the contexts in which they occur. These concepts began to influence the field of psychotherapy in the 1950s and were instrumental in challenging the prevailing notion of mental illness as a disease caused by defects within the individual (Breunlin, Schwartz, & Kune-Karrer, 2001). Following is a specific description of the **internal family systems model** of Richard Schwartz (1995).

KEY CONCEPTS: DEFINITIONS OF PARTS

Some of the basic assumptions within IFS, as they were recently articulated by Schwartz (2014) at the Cape Cod Institute Conference, are as follows. First, Schwartz stated that all humans have multiple personalities, and second, he says it is the nature of the mind to be subdivided

(Schwartz, 2014). Schwartz goes on to point out that these **parts** are not seen as pathology as in dissociative identity disorder in the DSM-5 (American Psychiatric Association, 2013), but are valuable resources for the survival of our *self.* Schwartz (2014) points out that IFS therapists see dissociative identity disorder as one end of a spectrum of personalities.

The next basic assumption of IFS, according to Schwartz, is that **parts** carry **burdens.** These *burdens* a person's various *parts* carry, find their origin in past hurts that are not yet resolved. These unresolved issues cause a person's various **parts** to take on roles that force them out of their natural and valuable states resulting in undesirable feelings of being stuck. Unfortunately, taking on these undesirable charades are necessary for survival. Fortunately, these identified **parts** can **unburden** themselves and return to their naturally valuable states (Schwartz, 2014).

Premises of the Theory

IFS is described by Schwartz as a model of transformation. The therapy process begins with identifying a person's **parts** within a client's personality. The therapist then goes to these **parts** in a loving way, and witnesses their stories. The therapist then helps the **parts** out of the past in which they were stuck and can unload the emotions and beliefs that are called "the burdens they carry." These **burdens they carry**, which tend to drive extreme behaviors, can transform back to their natural and valuable state, once they are unloaded (Schwartz, 1995).

ROLE OF THE THERAPIST

In IFS, the therapist's role is to invite the client to open up, welcome in the client's various aspects of personality, and help the client identify the various **parts**. Congruence is brought to the various parts found within a client's personality without labeling any as good or bad (Schwartz, 2014). It's about getting into this place of huge compassion and from that place, relating to these **parts** which become stuck (referred to as **exiled parts**), and helping them heal (Schwartz, 2014).

IFS therapists will also seek to identify what are referred to as **protective parts**. These **protective parts** are called **manager parts** and **firefighter parts**. These **managers** and **firefighters** are designed to stop antecedent triggers and consequential anxiety, thus, keeping our lives managed. When **managers** and **firefighters** are in conflict or **polarized**, the controlling **managers** can conflict with the overcompensating **firefighters** leading to loss of control. Polarizing behavior tends to be bothersome to a client's friends and associates and will typically be why the client is seeking therapy. Therapists assist in resolving these conflicts (Schwartz, 2014).

Theoretical Strengths and Limitations

As with any theory, IFS has both strengths and weaknesses. One strength described by both therapists as well as clients, is that IFS develops a deep sense of self-awareness, and can be useful when working with supervisees as they become more aware of their own issues. On the other hand, it can be challenging and take time and patience to convince clients to accept and talk to their various parts. In Case Presentation 17.1, Angela is a therapist working with her client, Jill, who suffers from anxiety. Look to see how Angela might apply the IFS model to help her client.

CASE PRESENTATION 17.1: THE CASE OF JILL

Angela is a therapist who is comfortable working with clients who present with anxiety and she has had success using *cognitive behavioral therapy*. Angela recently received her level 2 certification as an *internal family systems* therapist and has a new client, Jill, who is practically immobilized by anxiety attacks. This anxiety is affecting Jill's family life, since she cannot help with family tasks such as transporting her children to school or contributing to the family finances. Angela and Jill, along with the Jill's partner, have identified this anxiety as a *part*, and during a recent session Jill had an anxiety attack. Previously, Angela would have attempted to calm Jill using deep breathing exercises and talking through the issue; however, this time she welcomed in the *anxiety part* and asked it to explain what it feared. The goal of this technique is for Jill's *anxiety part* to become familiar and comfortable with *manager parts* so she will stop having anxiety attacks. Jill could express fear that her partner would leave if they did not "fix" this problem. A basic assumption of IFS therapists is that all *parts* are welcome. The process of addressing a *part's* hurt is referred to by the IFS therapist as a *transformation* (Schwartz, 2014). Angela can begin to work with the couple to address these issues by continuing to identify various *parts* within the couple.

Now that you understand how the IFS model can be applied, take a moment to consider and discuss some ethical concerns that might arise when using this strategy. Guided Practice 17.1 asks you to evaluate and discover limitations of use.

GUIDED PRACTICE EXERCISE 17.1

The ACA Code of Ethics (ACA, 2014) states, "Counselors discuss the required limitations to confidentiality when working with clients who have been mandated for counseling services. Counselors also explain what type of information and with whom that information is shared prior to the beginning of counseling" (p. 4). What concerns might a parent have with IFS therapy, knowing that his employer or a judge might view his therapy records? Would IFS be a good fit for working with a divorced couple mandated to parenting classes? Discuss these potential issues with the class.

MULTICULTURAL ISSUES INVOLVED IN IFS

Research in the field of psychotherapy is clear that one of the most important predictors of positive therapeutic outcomes is the alliance between the client and the therapist (Lambert, 1992). Therapists using the IFS model, by design, will be assessing the needs of their clients throughout the process. When therapists are unfamiliar with a client's cultural beliefs, they may make biased assumptions leading to misunderstandings and potentially harm the client. According to the ACA Code of Ethics (ACA, 2014), counselors are to recognize the effects of age, color, culture, disability, ethnic group, gender, race language preference, religion, spirituality, sexual orientation, and socioeconomic status when assessing the needs of a client. Similarly, the American Association for Marriage and Family Therapy (2015) ethical standards require members to provide services without discrimination based on race, age, ethnicity, disability, gender, religion, sexual orientation, gender identification, or relationship status. IFS can aid in this regard because it provides a simplified process for identifying and working with internal processes (e.g., thoughts, emotions, physiological responses) and can consequently aid novice therapists in their ability to form a nonbiased therapeutic alliance (Mojta, Falconier, & Huebner, 2014).

METAFRAMEWORKS MODEL

History, Background, and Profile of Major Figures

The metaframeworks approach was developed by Douglas Breunlin, Richard Schwartz, and Betty Mac Kune-Karrer. The framework is a compilation of works such as strategic, structural, Milan, and Bowenian models in combination with six additional categories: organization, sequences, mind, development, gender, and culture.

Key Concepts: Terminology and Techniques

The metaframeworks approach focuses on **constraints** as a key to identifying areas for exploration in therapy. **Constraints** are typically the complaints the individual or family members bring to therapy. Breunlin identified the problem with constraints by pointing out, that as therapists, "the client system we treat cannot, themselves, solve the problems they present in therapy because they are often caught in a web of constraints that keep them from doing so (Breunlin, 1999). Breunlin posited that using the six metaframeworks described below and consisting of organization, sequence, mind, development, gender, and culture, creates an adequate model to assist in identifying and working within the constraints.

Organization. The organization metaframework examines two core constructs; boundaries and leadership (Breunlin et al., 2001; Wood, 1985). Organizational constraints appear when the leadership within a system or across system levels becomes unbalanced or when the boundaries of the system are inappropriate for the needs of the system.

Sequences. The sequences metaframework uses four classes of sequences: brief face-to-face sequences, sequences of daily routine, sequences that ebb and flow over a period of time from a week to a year, and transgenerational sequences (Breunlin, 1999).

Development. The development metaframework examines the competencies required for each level of a system, and the system as a whole, to function effectively and develop appropriately (Breunlin, 1999).

Gender. Gender is a biological reality and a major construct of personhood. The politics of gender deeply affect relationships, and gender-prescribed roles can severely impact how a family functions (Breunlin, 1999).

Culture. Building on the work of Karrer (1989), therapists construct a multicultural metaframework that adopts a broad definition of culture. The definition reflects sensitivity to the multiple contexts in which people are embedded and learn a variety of ways to be human. These contexts are classified by economics, education, ethnicity, religion, gender, generation, race, minority or majority status, and regional background (Breunlin et al., 2001).

Mind. The metaframework of mind captures the domain of ideas about mental processes in human systems (Breunlin, 1999).

The previously mentioned metaframeworks are a recursive set of ideas that interact with and complement one another. To understand a human system, we often draw on more than one metaframework, and our hypotheses are often hybrids, constructed from the ideas contained in several metaframeworks (Breunlin et al., 2001).

Premises of the Theory

Breunlin posits that metaframeworks prescribe a blueprint that consists of four interrelated processes of therapy: hypothesizing, planning, conversing, and reading feedback (Breunlin et al., 2001). The blueprint is the overview that ties together the six individual metaframework subsections and identifies the direction for therapy. The metaframeworks and the presuppositions form the basis for hypothesizing, and the collaborative approach forms the basis for planning.

Role of the Therapist

The process of therapy itself is a conversation in which the therapist draws distinctions by asking questions, making statements, and giving directives while constantly attempting to make sense of and use the family's feedback. The final goal of therapy is to address such constraints as hierarchy, power, and control and replace it with leadership, balance, and harmony (Breunlin et al., 2001).

Theoretical Strengths and Limitations

Metaframeworks, like all theories, has strengths and weaknesses. The most common weakness is the lack of research on the approach. Other than research conducted by the framework's creators, little research can be found to validate the process. One strength, on the other hand, is the integrative approach's inherent ability to structure large amounts of theoretical complexity into manageable, nonconfusing techniques (Breunlin et al., 2001).

Let's turn our attention to Case Presentation 17.2, in which Jon, Mary, and their son Jace seek out counseling to address Jace's recent behavior change.

CASE PRESENTATION 17.2: THE CASE OF JON, MARY, AND JACE

Jon and Mary brought their 14-year-old son, Jace, to see Samuel, a therapist in their suburban town, to which the family has just moved from a rural town in another state. Jon and Mary visited with Samuel about their son's recent behaviors and lack of motivation to finish his chores. After listening to sufficient examples of Jace's poor behavior, Samuel worked with Jace using a behavior chart whereby Jon and Mary offered Jace behavioral rewards and consequences at the end of each week. After several weeks, Jace was not having much success, so Samuel asked the parents to come back in. With consent, Samuel asked another therapist to sit in on the session. The consulting therapist, Bill, an experienced counselor in using the metaframeworks model, asked the parents several more questions. Bill addressed other metaworks, such as culture, and Bill discovered that Jon grew up on a farm and expected his son to perform chores such as yard work before breakfast and before school. Mary disagreed with this requirement and would cover for Jace despite indicating she was in sync with Jon's wishes. Bill placed this information in the organization metawork, since there was an imbalance between the parent's boundaries and leadership. After talking further with Jace, Bill discovered that Jace had become apathetic about the rules of the home, since he would overhear his parents argue and they were sending mixed signals. Bill placed this information in the metawork of sequence since this involved face to face sequences and daily routines. Bill developed a blueprint to address each of these metaworks and address such constraints as hierarchy, power, and control and replace it with leadership, balance, and harmony.

Now that we have discussed Case Presentation 17.2, reflect on and discuss your responses to Guided Practice Exercise 17.2.

GUIDED PRACTICE EXERCISE 17.2

Using the case presentation of Jon and Mary, who brought their son Jace to a therapist, discuss how you might address each of the six domains to assist this family.

Multicultural Issues Involved in Metaframeworks

Client culture is a major consideration when using metaframeworks. A therapist must be aware of the client's culture as well as the extended culture in which the client lives. The multiculturally sensitive therapist strives to understand both these issues and attains awareness, knowledge, and skills to assist.

Ethical Considerations

Metaframeworks theory is based on multiple systems within the family. When counseling an entire family system, the therapist must continually balance confidential needs of each family member with therapeutic needs of the client, or entire family system. According to Gladding (2015), "Just as the family is a system, so the field of family therapy is systemic. For family clinicians to stay healthy, they and their colleagues must abide by ethical codes and legal statutes and practice according to the highest standards possible" (p. 141).

INTEGRATIVE PROBLEM-CENTERED THERAPY

History, Background, and Profile of Main Figures
Profile of Main Figures

William M. Pinsof, licensed clinical psychologist and a licensed marriage and family therapist, founded Pinsof Family Systems, an organization dedicated to healing and strengthening complex family systems (Pinsof, 2016). He created integrated problem-centered therapy (IPCT) after experiences working in the Family Institute of Chicago (later reorganized into the Family Institute at Northwestern University) and the Department of Psychiatry at the Northwestern Medical School.

Evolution of the Theory

Since the late 1970s, the field of psychotherapy has slowly shifted from utilizing pure form therapy models (e.g., cognitive therapy, behavioral therapy, etc.) to integrative or eclectic models of therapy, which incorporate more than one model of therapy (Pinsof, 1994). The driving force behind this shift is the inability of the pure form models to independently work in all situations, with all clients, thus at some point in time, the pure form models fail to effectively treat a given family system. IPCT is the framework that integrates individual, family, and biological therapies in a coherent, comprehensive manner (Pinsof, 1995). Pinsof (1983) based this theory on dual assumptions: Each pure form model has an area of expertise, and these models can be interrelated as they build upon strengths and decrease deficiencies.

Though they are similar, integrative approaches differ from eclectic approaches. Pinsof (1995) identified three primary criteria to distinguish between integrative and eclectic approaches. First, integrative approaches have an "underlying and unifying theoretical framework" (Pinsof, 1995, p. 104). Second, the integrative approach "addresses and integrates core theoretical and pragmatic tenets of the major pure form approaches it draws" from (Pinsof, 1995, p. 104). Third, the integrative approach "must have explicit principles of application" which specifies the appropriate application of the theories and practices for each client and their presenting problem (Pinsof, 1994, p. 105). In addition, Pinsof asserted the use of an integrative approach to be more practical, cohesive, predictable, and organized than an eclectic approach, specifically on a theoretical level.

Key Concepts of IPCT Therapy as Human Problem Solving

According to Pinsof (1995), "therapy is human problem solving" (p. 1). The premise of this being that clients seek therapy when their psychological, psychosocial, or biopsychosocial problems interfere with their ability to function in their everyday life (Pinsof, 1994). Though a client may first attempt to decipher their own problems, they will often seek therapy once their attempts to correct the problem have been unsuccessful.

A client's presumption of the issues in their life is referred to as their presenting problem. Presenting problems can range from what seems to be a minor issue, to a much more complex issue, and may include multiple issues that will likely change over the course of the therapeutic intervention due to resolution or significant improvement of the issue. Ultimately, the assumption is there is always a presenting problem with which a client needs assistance. In problem-centered therapy, it is the presenting problem that drives therapy throughout the therapeutic process; however, it does not mean that the therapist cannot address other issues that arise (Pinsof, 1995). When utilizing problem-centered therapy, the therapist can address other issues as they arise, if the new issue is linked to the presenting problem. If the new issue is not linked, nor potentially linked to the presenting problem, the therapist would breach the integrity of the problem-centered framework if he attempted to manage the new, unrelated issue and therefore could not address it until it was either found to be linked or the current presenting problem was resolved (Pinsof, 1995).

Since IPCT treats the patient system, it is important to identify client human system(s). This identification can act as an aide to determine which elements may be potentially maintaining the presenting problem, or could potentially help resolve the presenting problem (Pinsof, 1995). These systems are typically composed of social, psychological, biological elements, or a combination of these. Utilizing the patient system allows the therapist to confront relevant biopsychosocial information present without breaking the system down into individual parts. Pinsof (1995) postulated that "every problem has its own unique patient system" (p. 4). Thus, whether the biological, social, or psychological system affects the maintenance of a problem, or the resolution thereof, it needs to be included in the patient system.

Pinsof (1994, 1995) asserted that in addition to every problem having its own patient system, every presenting problem has its own problem maintenance structure. The therapeutic process of "IPCT is designed to progressively and pragmatically reveal the nature of the problem structure in the form of a process diagnosis" (Pinsof, 1994, p. 115). If the structure is simple, then behaviorally oriented interventions should be successful. However, if this mode of intervention is not successful, the assumption is the structure is deeper than initially assessed, and will need a higher level intervention.

Premises of the Theory

Dimensions of IPCT. Pinsof (1994) delineated two dimensions that IPCT integrates: modality/context and orientation. The *modality/context dimension* involves who is directly involved in therapy and the focus of the intervention. IPCT integrates three therapeutic modality/contexts, which consist of family/community, couple/dyadic, and individual. Let's turn to Table 17.1 for a visual description of the problem-centered orientation/modality matrix.

Table 17.1 The Problem-Centered Orientation/Modality Matrix

Orientations	Family/community	Couple/dyadic	Individual

Behavioral/interactional
-Social learning
-Strategic
-Functional
-Structural

Experiential
-Cognitive
-Affective
-Communication
-Interpersonal

Historical
-Family of origin
-Psychodynamic
-Psychoanalytic

When addressing family/community, the therapist looks at therapeutic approaches that focus on two or more people within a family unit, typically from different generations, such as parents and children. The focus can also be on larger systems, which could include extended, divorced,and blended families, as well as community or social systems that affect the family system (Pinsof, 1994). When looking at the couple/dyadic modality/context, the therapist looks at therapeutic approaches, which focus primarily on the interaction of the couple. This modality/context would include two people from the same generation in a family, such as two parents, or two people coparenting within the same family system. Finally, when looking at the individual modality/context, the therapist looks at any therapeutic approach that addresses the individual child or adult. Their presenting problem is viewed as the major treatment focus. (Pinsof, 1994).

The **orientation dimension** frames the aspects of a therapeutic approach that identify theories of formation and resolution of problems, or basically how clients get themselves into difficult situations and how therapy helps them resolve the situation. Pinsof (1995) identified three orientations within this dimension: behavioral, experiential, and historical. Behavioral orientation refers to theoretical approaches that primarily focus on behavior or action. Behavioral approaches argue that people get into trouble due to the way they behave, and when appropriate, changes made to behavior lead to problem resolution. When looking at Table 17.1, behavioral/family, the pure form behavioral theorists include Patterson, Haley, the MRI, Minuchin, and Alexander (Pinsof, 1994). When looking at behavioral/couple, behavioral marriage theorists include Baucom, Stuart, Jacobsen, and Milton Erickson (Pinsof, 1994). When looking at behavioral/individual, this would include classic behavioral terrorists such as Wolpe, Lovass, and Kazdin, as well as Milton Erickson and Speigel (Pinsof, 1994).

Experiential orientation is composed of theories focused on the family's experience and their internal experiences with themselves and within interactions, whereas behavioral orientation focuses primarily on external aspects, experiential orientation focuses on internal, cognitive, and affective aspects. In this perspective, clients are experiencing trouble due to negative cognitions or affective patterns of functioning. Modification of the cognitive and affective patterns is the primary intervention in experiential theory. Experiential approaches focus on communicating the meaning and the development of empathy between the therapist, the client, and the patient system (Pinsof, 1994; 1995). When looking at Table 17.1, the experiential/family refers to gestalt therapists such as Satir, Kempler, and Reiss (Pinsof, 1994). The experiential/couple refers to couple theorists such as Greenberg and Johnson, Guerney and Gordon, and Beck (Pinsof, 1994). The experiential/individual refers to cognitive theorists such as Beck and Meichenbaum; client-centered theorists such as Rogers, Gendlin, and Rice; and gestalt theorist such as Perls (Pinsof, 1994).

In contrast to behavioral and experiential orientations that emphasize the here and now, the historical orientation centers on what has happened in the past that is causing trouble currently. The historical orientation has two subcategories: family of origin and psychodynamic/psychoanalytic. These subcategories deal with family history and the impact family history has on current functioning, as well as clients' personal experiences within their families. Again, referring to Table 17.1, theorists who would be included in historical/family are family and analytical theorists such as Bowen, Framo, McGoldrick, Carter, Stierlin, and Boszormenyi-Nagy (Pinsof, 1994). In Table 17.1, the historical/couple section, object relations theorists and analytical theorists like Scharfs, Paul, and Bowen are listed (Pinsof, 1994). In the final section, historical/individual, psychoanalytical, and object relations theorists would include Gruntrip, Fairbairn, Winnicott, Kernberg, Greenberg, and Mitchell (Pinsof, 1994). In addition, Pinsof (1994) includes self-psychologists such as Kohut, Wolf, and Goldberg.

Theoretical Framework

The theoretical framework of IPCT is composed of three components: interactive constructivism, systems theory, and mutual causality. Utilizing these components, the underlying theoretical framework can unify the various pure form approaches drawn on by IPCT. **Interactive constructivism** suggests that an independent reality exists, but the human knowledge of this reality is partial yet progressive (the more we learn the more we understand what are trying to learn). There is also an implication that diagnosing is an ongoing endeavor (Pinsof, 1994). The basic assumption is that the longer we work with a system (e.g., individual, family, couple), the more we learn about that system, and thus we have knowledge about what is valuable within that system.

Systems theory contends that the world operates as a set of interactive and organized systems (e.g., smaller systems are within larger systems). No system is ever completely knowable, and boundaries between systems are often undefined. For example, human systems are open, dynamic, interdependent, and mainly self-regulating, though they may experience periods of change and instability followed by periods of equilibrium (Pinsof, 1994). Therapy is considered the ongoing interaction between the patient system, and the therapist system (Pinsof, 1989). The therapist system is very much the same, and the interaction between the two systems, the patient system and the therapist system, are what establish the therapy system.

Mutual causality contends that causality is mutual (Pinsof, 1994). A system is a fluid group of subsystems that influence one another in an ongoing basis, both independently and collectively. For example, parents influence children, and children influence parents. However, even though this is the case, as interactive processes escalate, not everyone in the process can be held equally responsible for the result. For example, parents and children cannot be held accountable for negative actions on the same level.

These components can be easily applied as a base theory in Table 17.1. Theories can be formulated about behavioral systems in individuals, couples and families. Cohesiveness within the family or the self can be discussed. The self can fragment parts of itself, and the family can cut off members. Family interaction and influence on the cognitive and affective processes within the system can be discussed, as well as influence the family's interactions. Questions can be posed, such as, to what extent does "marital homeostasis" jeopardize each individual's efforts to maintain their personal balance? The "underlying and unifying framework" (Pinsoff, 1994, p. 111) equips the therapist with a base theory for the whole system, or "matrix as well as each cell within it" (Pinsof, 1994, p. 111).

Principles of Application

When utilizing IPCT in therapy, the initial focus is on the behavioral issues that prevent the system from problem resolution. If therapeutic intervention at the behavioral level is unsuccessful, then a shift is made to focus more on the cognitive and affective (experiential) level of the maladaptive behavior patterns (Pinsof, 1994). If intervention on that level is unsuccessful, then the therapeutic focus will be on family of origin patterns linked to the maladaptive behavior. When the focus shifts to the family of origin, this may involve direct work with the family to gain a more comprehensive understanding of multi-generational patterns within the family (Pinsof, 1994). To further explore the family of origin issues, especially if the basic family of origin intervention fails, the therapist will need to explore historical sources of the maladaptive patterns that began with key members in the family of origin (Pinsof, 1994). In doing this transference, patterns are identified within the patient system, and clarity improves while moving through the matrix toward the Historical/Individual section (see Table 17.1). This movement ultimately focuses on the therapist/patient dyad (Pinsof.1994). In IPCT, the therapeutic progression is in the here and now, and the interpersonal (Pinsof, 1994, 1995). Though this may not be ideal, it is necessary if the prior level of intervention was unsuccessful.

Role of the Therapist

In IPCT the primary goal of the therapist is to create a therapeutic alliance with the client. According to Pinsof (1995), therapy without this alliance will not be productive. The creation and maintenance of the therapeutic alliance "takes priority over the problem-centered principles of application, and resolving deeper and more complex problem-maintenance structures" (Pinsof, 1995, p. 87). The effort and experience (e.g., tearing and repair, etc.) that comes with the deepening of this alliance creates a critical, and potentially positive move within the alliance. This alliance is seen by IPCT therapists as ever changing from case to case and phase to phase—an evolving event that establishes relational context in therapy.

Now that you have a solid understanding of IPCT, take time to reflect on and discuss the question(s) posed in Guided Practice Exercise 17.3.

GUIDED PRACTICE EXERCISE 17.3

The role of the therapist in IPCT is to create a therapeutic alliance with the family. In what ways can this be accomplished utilizing what you have learned about IPCT? Are there any ethical or multicultural concerns you might face when using IPCT with a client? Discuss your thoughts with a partner.

INTEGRATIVE BEHAVIORAL COUPLE THERAPY

History, Background, and Profile of Main Figures

Integrative behavioral couple therapy (IBCT) is a modification of traditional behavioral couple therapy (TBCT) and promotes acceptance to the more traditional focus of behavioral couple therapy. It was created by Neil Jacobsen and Andrew Christiansen and was first published in 1995 (Dimidjian, Martell, & Christensen, 2008). TBCT was the most commonly practiced treatment for couples' therapy for over 20 years and was a skill-based treatment; relying on behavioral exchange and communication. Its success with couples was widely documented and TBCT is still the only couple therapy to stand up to the strictest empirical research standards (Dimidjian et al., 2008). However, Jacobsen and Christensen were not happy with the success rates of TBCT, which were about 50% of couples who would improve and maintain their improvement long term. The two renowned family therapists found that by adding components to promote acceptance within the couple, couples could not only improve their relationships, but maintain that improvement long term (Nichols & Schwartz, 1998).

Key Concepts, Terminology, and Techniques

IBCT begins with the formulation stage which consists of three parts: the **theme, polarization**, and the **mutual trap**. The formulation stage's focus is to encourage couples to stop blaming one another and to promote acceptance and change (Nichols & Schwartz, 1998). During the formulation stage, **themes** typically emerge and may include (but are not limited to) conflicts that trigger maladaptive behaviors from one or both partners and/or tendencies toward handling conflict. Once **themes** have emerged, the therapist works with the couple during the **polarization process** to describe maladaptive communication patterns. Finally, the IBCT therapist uses metaphors and other experiential activities to highlight the *mutual trap* or circular process preventing the couple from breaking the cycle (Dimidjian et al., 2008; Gladding, 2015).

Premises of the theory. No formal techniques are used with IBCT. To foster acceptance, couples are encouraged to see differences as inevitable rather than as a means for concern. Couples are further encouraged to talk about their own experiences and emotions using I statements (Nichols & Schwartz, 2015). After understanding their partner's experiences, they are further guided to use traditional behavioral change techniques such as behavior contracts. For example, partners might be encouraged to list behaviors they can exhibit which would be appreciated by their counterpart. In contrast to TBCT which encourages rules to oversee behavior, IBCT focuses on adjusting the tendencies of each partner and how each reacts to their counterparts' behaviors. Instead of setting up rules to govern the couple's interactions IBCT therapists create experiences whereby couples use active listening skills and communicate nondefensively to shift behavior patterns (Dimidjian et al., 2008; Nichols & Schwartz, 2015).

IBCT is typically used in outpatient settings. It consists of only the therapist and couple with no other family members involved. The length and frequency of sessions may vary but typically consist of 50-minute sessions administered in weekly or biweekly sessions over the course of a year. At the onset, an agenda is codeveloped by the couple and therapist. The agenda may be adjusted at any time, but sessions usually focus on one of four areas: discussions about differences in partners, upcoming events that may cause conflict, recent negative interactions, or recent positive events (Dimidjian et al., 2008).

Role of the Therapist

The role of the therapist in IBCT is flexible, depending on the nature of the session. Interventions may vary, and the therapist is active and directive while working with clients (Dimidjian et al., 2008). In addition to taking on the therapist role, IBCT therapists play the role of coach and teacher. They guide couples on effective methods of communication and provide feedback to the couple. Still, the therapist's core function is to be a compassionate listener, show empathy, and develop a genuine understanding of the couple's concerns no matter which role he/she assumes.

As an active member of the session, the IBCT therapist acts as a mediator and points out themes in communication patterns contributing to the couple's unhappiness. Once attention has been given to specific behaviors, the therapist's role is to identify themes within behaviors and the function of the behaviors (Nichols & Schwartz, 2008). IBCT therapists are skilled at choosing words that have meaning to the couple and frequently use metaphors to describe communication patterns. Throughout the session, IBCT therapists fluctuate between teacher and mediator roles to highlight ineffective themes and patterns of communication and then reteach more effective methods (Dimidjian et al., 2008). Consider Case Presentation 17.3 and how Marcus and Sharon work on their communication concerns by using IBCT.

CASE PRESENTATION 17.3: THE CASE OF MARCUS AND SHARON

Marcus and Sharon came to therapy and reported "constant arguing since their son was born 2 years ago." Marcus is a law enforcement officer and Sharon is a grade school teacher. The two claim to be constantly "at each other's throats" and frequently argue over work schedules and ways to care for their son. When the two met, Marcus fell in love with Sharon's kind nature and nurturing soul. He says she brought peace to his life. Similarly, Sharon, reported that among other things, she loved Marcus for his protective spirit and always felt safe being around him. What the couple once saw as attractive personality traits, became triggers to their conflict. Marcus claims Sharon does not live in the "real" world and has the benefit of living in a protected world. Conversely, Sharon claims she feels as though Marcus does not respect her career and she withdraws from him when she feels conflict arising. Marcus, on the other hand, is more assertive and tries to pursue Sharon even more when she withdraws.

During the first sessions, their therapist, Kevin, learns that Sharon's parents were both educators and that this played a major role in her and her family's life. Conversely, both Marcus's parents dropped out of high school due to financial constraints. His father was employed as a manual laborer and his mother stayed home to take care of him and his brothers. Marcus describes the male as primary caregiver and resource for physical and financial needs as all he has ever known. Kevin highlights theme's in the couple's communication patterns and provides an environment in which they can practice more acceptance based behaviors. Kevin also works with the couple to understand the triggers to their conflict. He explains the mutual trap the couple has fallen into, in which Sharon's withdrawal causes Marcus to pursue even more. The more Marcus pursues Sharon, the more she continues to withdraw. The two are encouraged to use I statements rather than blaming language (i.e., he always, she always) to share their experiences during conflict. The couple is also encouraged to list behaviors they can exhibit to satisfy their partner's needs.

Theoretical Strengths and Limitations

IBCT has shown to be useful with both heterosexual and same-sex married and co-habitating couples. Couples who have with a history of abuse may be inappropriate for treatment. Couples in which one or both partners have a psychological disorder may also be inappropriate for treatment. The effectiveness of treatment may be inhibited unless the diagnosed disorder is treated simultaneously (Dimidjian et al., 2008).

At the time this text was written, only three empirical studies had been conducted on the effects of IBCT. In all three instances, couples demonstrated significantly improved communication and overall relationship satisfaction (Dimidjian et al., 2008). Christensen, Atkens, Burns, Wheeler, Baucom, and Simpson (2004 stated that while too early to determine the overall effectiveness of the treatment, couples exposed to ICBT showed "steady improvement over the course of therapy" (p. 188).

NARRATIVE SOLUTIONS APPROACH

Historical Background and Profile of Main Theorists

Joseph Eron is a licensed clinical psychologist and founder of the Catskill Family Institute. Eron has a distinguished background in clinical work with couples and families Catskill Family Institute, 2016). Upon establishing the Catskill Family Institute in Kingston, New York, in 1981, he actively utilized and trained professionals in MRI brief therapy (Eron & Lund, 1996). It was this journey of education that introduced him to Thomas Lund in 1985. Lund is a licensed psychologist and certified school psychologist, whose clinical works focused on addressing the needs of adolescents and their families (Catskill Family Institute, 2017). Together Eron and Lund codirected the Catskill Family Institute, established the narrative solutions approach, and actively developed, published, and practiced from this systemic psychotherapy model (Eron & Lund, 1996).

Evolution of the Theory

One cannot discuss the creation of the narrative solutions approach to family therapy without critically exploring its remarkable roots in many of the originating psychotherapy ideologies. As previously mentioned, the narrative solutions approach to family therapy is heavily influenced by the MRI's conceptualization of clients and client problems (Eron & Lund, 1996). Specifically, rearticulating Milton Erickson's **utilization approach** and establishing *reframing* as instrumental components to the model. **Reframing** and the **utilization approach** are praised for their ability to engage clients and reduce resistance; however, Eron and Lund identified gaps in their ability to holistically understand people with these interventions (Dagirmanjian, Eron, & Lund, 2007). The MRI's constructivist perspective of truth and reality is then introduced to the clinical works of Carl Rogers. Carl Rogers offered **unconditional positive regard** as a means of closing the gap that existed between therapist and client, as well as, the ideal versus perceived self of the client. Integrating these ideologies required the incorporation of one final concept, R.D. Laing's "interpersonal perceptions" (Dagirmanjian et al., 2007, p. 77). The integration of these very distinct perspectives birthed the narrative solutions (NS) approach.

NARRATIVE SOLUTIONS THEORETICAL PREMISES AND INTERVENTIONS

Key Concepts

The Narrative Solutions (NS) integrative approach is based on the exploration of client perceptions and stories. The following information discusses how therapists use this theory to reframe life issues into manageable experiences.

Assumptions of the Problem

It is impossible to discuss the NS integrative approach without examining how problems are conceptualized from this perspective. The three general assumptions NS makes about problem evolution is a product of MRI brief therapy. The first assumption infers that problems are simply a mismanagement of life experiences. Often people are faced with ordinary life struggles that require immediate action and occur at pivotal times in our development (e.g., marriage, retirement, relocation, starting a graduate program). Sometimes these actions are unintentionally the beginning of "problem cycles" (Eron & Lund, 1996). Like many systemic family therapy models, pathology is never the goal in identifying the origin of these problems or resolving them.

The second assumption of problem evolution is that the behaviors chosen to resolve a problem often inadvertently prolong its existence. This means that many times well-intended solutions become an active component of the "problem cycle" (Eron & Lund, 1996) or the solution "itself is the problem" (Watzlawick, Weakland, & Fisch, 1974, p. 55).

The third and final assumption of problem evolution is that decreasing the prevalence of an intended solution creates the space for change. In other words, severing the connection between clients and their attempted solutions can be enough to promote growth and alleviate the problem (Lund, Eron, & Dagirmanjian, 2016). Collectively, these assumptions act as the foundational understanding of client problems, behaviors that maintain these problems, and potential interruption of these patterns.

Premises of the Theory

Preferred view. The assumptions of problem evolution speak explicitly to the behavioral component of maintaining a "problem cycle" (Eron & Lund, 1996). While this information is pertinent to resolving any issue in family therapy, the narrative solutions approach successfully integrates the cognitive and emotional hindrances to problem resolution. The **preferred view**, according to NS, is derived from Carl Rogers's stance on how "intrapersonal perceptions" (Dagirmanjian et al., 2007, p. 77) impact behavior. In other words, when people perceive themselves as acting in a way that is not congruent with their ideal, cognitive and emotional dissonance occurs (Dagirmanjian, et al., 2007; Lund, et al., 2016).

This is key to establishing a holistic conceptualization of your client, their problem, and the thoughts and behaviors that maintain that problem. People set personal standards of character, and according to NS, when these standards are not met, problems may be maintained (Dagirmanjian et al., 2007; Lund et al., 2016). It is important to remember that these standards may fall anywhere along the continuum of viability. As previously stated, the preferred view is one of the most influential concepts within the narrative solutions approach. Collaborating with a client to identify qualities of the preferred self can be a facilitator of change in the therapeutic process (Lund et al., 2016).

Gaps. Throughout the clinical and literary works of Eron and Lund, the concept of **gaps** has remained pertinent to the theoretical development of the narrative solutions approach. **Gaps** are indicative of disconnects between the preferred view of a client and reality as it is experienced internally and relationally (Lund et al., 2016). Identifying these discrepancies and honestly dialoguing, within the context of therapy, helps eliminate that gap.

Role of the Therapist

Until now, we have discussed the eclectic history of NS theorists and the philosophical foundation that it is built on. Now, what is your role? How do you engage clients in a way that motivates and facilitates space for the changes that they want to see? Understanding your role is essential to answering these questions.

When approaching treatment with narrative solutions the goal is to create a therapeutic environment that fosters discussion. The narrative component of this integrative theory highlights the benefit of exploring stories as they enable the clinician to identify connections amongst every dimension of an existing problem (e.g., emotions, cognitions, behaviors, relationships). As the clinician, your goal is to establish a relationship with every client that is void of judgment and overflowing with support. To accomplish this, it is essential that the therapist facilitates discussions in which the client is viewed as independent from the problem. This narrative philosophy is known as **externalizing conversations**. **Externalizing conversations** promote a balanced relationship with the client, while sustaining active awareness of their goals (White & Epston, 1990).

The ambitious goals of therapy are achieved when the space for change is not only collaborative and supportive, but also intentional. This means that outside of establishing the relationship, building rapport, and creating a safe space, the NS approach requires that you be intentional with your line of questioning and purposeful with interventions (Lund et al., 2016).

Interventions

Now that we have explored the historical context of the narrative solutions approach key concepts, and the role of the therapist, this section will highlight clinical interventions specific to this model and offer practical examples.

Utilization principle. The MRI approach to family therapy is strongly influenced by the early works of Milton Erickson. Erickson demonstrated an undisputable ability to meet clients where they were. His early clinical and literary works regarded this distinctive method as the utilization principle (Dagirmanjian et al., 2007).

This clinical intervention ensures that all aspects of the problems presented in therapy (e.g., client/problem conceptualization, language) are regarded as instrumental in facilitating change (Dagirmanjian et al., 2007). The utilization principle also reduces the amount of resistance experienced within the context of therapy and creates the space for a collaborative therapeutic atmosphere.

Reframing. Reframing is the act of applying contextual information about the presenting problem and translating that information into a new and often more constructive ideal (Watzlawick et al., 1974). This shift, ideally, will challenge the clients existing perspective and corresponding behaviors that feed into the "problem cycle" (Dagirmanjian et al., 2007).

Unconditional Positive Regard. With this Rogerian counseling intervention, therapists are challenged to offer support regardless of the content of therapeutic discussions or client behaviors. Unconditional positive regard ensures that clients can experience life in its entirety without fear of judgement or dismissal (Wilkins, 2000). As previously mentioned, one of the primary goals of NS based therapy is to stimulate change inducing conversations. Often, clients experience internal dissonance when the reality of their behaviors does not match their **preferred self** (Dagirmanjian et al., 2007). Utilizing unconditional positive regard within client interactions assists in creating an environment conducive to change.

Externalizing the problem. If you recall from Chapter 15, you are already somewhat familiar with the final intervention we will explore that originated with narrative therapy (White & Epston, 1990). According to Gehart and Tuttle (2003), "Externalization involves linguistically separating the problem from the person and often entails personifying the problem" (p. 218).

When this intervention is integrated into therapeutic conversations the client may begin to release negative feelings associated with the problem that stagnate personal growth and feed the problem cycle. It is imperative to understand that externalization is not intended to relinquish the client of responsibility for behaviors. The goal of externalization is to increase the dialogue of events, interactions, thoughts, or behaviors that feed the problem (White & Epston, 1990).

Strengths and Limitations of Narrative Solutions

As with any theoretical model, strengths and limitations are evident in the narrative solutions approach. The conversational and collaborative nature of the approach allows for diverse populations to benefit from this model. As diversity and multiculturalism continue to permeate daily interactions, the establishment of relationships, and the context of problem formation it is essential that systemic models, utilized by professionals, effectively address cultural variation. The narrative solutions approach integrates systemic philosophical concepts with psychotherapy interventions that promote the restoration of relationships (inter- and intrapersonal) and reconciliation of gaps in identity (Lund et al., 2016).

Lund et al. (2016) discussed theoretical limitations in their most recent article publication. According to the literature, the primary theoretical limitation is the lack of empirical support (Lund et al., 2016). While the integrative theory has roots in prominent systems theories, there is not significant evidence of its practicality independent of research supporting MRI brief therapy, narrative therapy, person-centered therapy, and so on. Future empirical research utilizing this model and demonstrating effectiveness is essential.

Assessment and Treatment with Integrative Theories

When using integrative theories, assessment and intervention are inseparable dual purposes, and span the "entire course of therapy" (Pinsof, 1995, p. 89). Every action or behavior can be seen dually as assessment and intervention. Pinsof (1995) used the example of the genogram (see Chapters 3 and 7). He pointed out that genograms typically serve the purpose of assessment but can also serve as an intervention, as well. As you learned in Chapter 7, from the assessment perspective, genograms can be used to tell about family rules, roles, structure, and so on. As an intervention, genograms can also be used to identify triangulation, and subsequently used to detriangulate an "11-year-old precocious daughter who continually interrupts her parents' efforts to communicate with each other" (Pinsof 1995, p. 89).

Pinsof (1995) explained that this action allows the therapist to state certain observations and assumptions to the parents, thus unveiling the parents' response to the intervention and the family's underlying problem-maintenance structure. These family system structures are only exposed when they are probed and worked with through intervention and assessment.

CASE PRESENTATION: THE CASE OF AMANDA, BOBBY, AND SARA

Now that you have learned about various integrative models, let's look at the following case and see how IPCT may look when applied to the case of Sara.

Therapist:	Let's start by discussing the ways the two of you attempted to deal with Sara's school problems and her relational problems at home.
Amanda:	Well, we have increased the amount of time we have spent with her on about 3 days a week. I work 4 nights a week, so that is the most we can do consistently. We work with her on school nights to help her with her homework. It seems to be helping some, but we are still having issues with her interactions with us, though school seems to be going better.
Therapist:	Let's talk about what you have done to help the situation improve.
Bobby:	Well, we eat together at least 3 nights a week. I try to help her with her homework. I try to remain positive, and not get frustrated even though she has a teenage attitude that drives me crazy most days. At least 3 days a week, Sara gets upset with me, and then it usually leads to an argument between us. My wife comes in and tries to save the day and makes me feel like I don't know what I am doing. I feel like it undermines my authority with Sara.

Amanda: Well, Bobby, if you would do as I tell you, and interact with her like I do, then things would go more smoothly.

Therapist: Amanda, one of the challenges with your statement is you cannot be there all the time. Your work schedule prevents you from being in the home, in the evenings, 4 nights a week, so more often than not, your husband has to deal with Sara alone.

Amanda: I understand that, but Sara doesn't give me as much push back as she does her dad. She knows I'm serious when I make threats to take her phone away, etc. if she doesn't do what I have asked, especially with her homework.

Sara: My relationship with my mom is different than my dad. My mom has always been the strict parent and my dad has always been more playful, even when they both seemed kind of lost after Janet left for college. Since we have been making changes in our family, and Mom has been working different hours that I am used to, things have been harder in some ways and better in others. I have enjoyed the time with my dad, but having to do homework and stuff with him is weird since that is something I have done previously with my mom. It does make me and Dad argue at times, but I feel bad when Mom comes in and yells at Dad and tells him that he isn't doing it right.

Therapist: So, Amanda what do you hear your husband and your daughter telling you about your efforts in trying to intervene to make the situation better?

Amanda: I guess that when I interrupt in the arguments, I make him feel unsupported and like I don't trust him. I guess it's not really helping him, and is making him feel bad. And my daughter feels like I am attacking him. Even though I am trying to help, I am making it them feel bad.

This interaction defines Amanda's problem-solving strategy as ineffective. As much as she tries to help, it is not working in the manner she intends it to; in fact, it makes matters worse. A critical piece to this interaction is Amanda's awareness that though the approach made sense to her, it does not work for the family. An essential component to this is helping Amanda see that what they have been doing to solve the presenting problem is ineffective and unlikely to work in the future. This awareness will help augment the search for more adaptive solutions.

SUMMARY

In this chapter, we highlighted the benefits of integrating theoretical approaches to family therapy. Diverse client populations with varying presenting concerns require clinicians to tailor treatment to best benefit the needs and cultural demands of the client. For family therapists, one foundational ideology that permeates integrative theories is the systems epistemology. Therapists utilizing integrated family therapy models are sensitive to the contextual and systemic influences on the client and problem maintenance. IFS focuses on identifying **parts** of a client's personality and addressing the **burdens** associated with those parts. From this perspective, we learned that burdens create immovable and unvalued responses that prevent clients from being healed from their presenting concerns. The IPCT approach assumes that patients seek counseling for help with a presenting problem; however, that does dictate the direction of therapy. We learned that therapists operating from this framework address not only the problem but also the biological, psychological, and social elements that maintain it. IPCT requires that therapists are aware how effective treatment is on a cognitive, emotive, and behavioral level. On the other hand, the NS integrative approach emphasizes problem formation and development, while also critically examining the clients preferred view of reality versus the reality they experience.

Utilizing integrative approaches to family therapy requires that clinicians are immersed in each of the theoretical components of the approach chosen, to ensure effective services are delivered. This concludes our exploration of integrative family therapy approaches. Next, we will explore nonnuclear families in Chapter 18.

KEYSTONES

Among the key points addressed in this chapter are:

- Integrative approaches to couples and family counseling is becoming more prevalent and even the norm.
- IFS is based on the general concept of *systems theory* and enables therapists to address problems by working with the contexts in which they occur.
- Integrated behavioral couple therapy is a modification of traditional behavioral couple therapy and promotes acceptance of the more traditional focus of behavioral couple therapy.
- The metaframeworks approach was based on earlier theories of family therapy, such as strategic, structural, the Milan model, and Bowenian models from the 1970s through the 1990s.
- Integrative problem-centered therapy is the framework that integrates individual, family, and biological therapies in a coherent, comprehensive manner.
- The narrative solutions approach to family therapy is heavily influenced by the MRI's conceptualization of clients and client problems.
- Integrative behavioral couple therapy begins with the formulation stage, which consists of three parts: the *theme*, *polarization*, and the *mutual trap*.
- In problem-centered therapy, assessment and intervention are dual purposes, are inseparable, and span the entire course of therapy.
- Research in the field of psychotherapy is clear that one of the most important predictors of positive therapeutic outcomes is the alliance between the client and the therapist, regardless of theory incorporated.

REFLECTIONS FROM THE CONTRIBUTOR'S CHAIR
Michael Moyer

All the contributors to this chapter share a background in both teaching and clinical practice. In our private practices, we see clients on an individual basis as well as in couples' therapy and family therapy. While we tend to utilize an integrative family systems approach, narrative solutions and IBCT, and find metaframeworks appealing, we find its application is directly correlated to the level of client desire to participate in the therapy. Simply stated, when a family wants solution focused therapy, we will not have success laying out the complicated overview and terminology required to implement metaframeworks.

On the other hand, when families show a desire to understand underlying dynamics of their issues and are patient with a process of change, metaframeworks or other more time intensive therapies can be very productive therapeutic approaches. In the initial interview with families, our experiences have been that it is best to have the family members articulate how they would like therapy to look. A key question we often ask is "Have you been in therapy before, and if so, what seemed to work or not work?" We find family members will typically let the therapist know if they want more insight based therapy or don't particularly like an overly complicated process.

In conclusion, we believe all theoretical approaches can be useful when working with clients, since none have proven superior effectiveness when used individually. We believe it is important for therapists to have knowledge of various theories and be able to integrate multiple theories into practice. We believe using integrative models or integrating multiple theoretical approaches strategically may best target family needs.

ADDITIONAL RESOURCES
The following resources provide additional information relating to the chapter topics.

Useful Websites

- Catskill Family Institute
http://www.catskillfamilyinstitute.com/home

The Catskill Family Institute of Kingston, New York, opened in 1981 with the goal of providing quality psychotherapy for individuals, couples, and families using a practical, solution-focused approach.

- Center for Self Leadership
https://selfleadership.org

This website is dedicated to the internal family systems model. It provides information about training/certification and provides valuable resources.

- IFS Growth Programs
  http://personal-growth-programs.com

This website is dedicated to helping IFS become known throughout the United States and the world, both in the professional psychotherapy community and among personal growth enthusiasts.

- Mental Research Institute
  http://mri.org/

This website provides information about the Mental Research Institute, which is the leading source of ideas in interactional/systemic studies, psychotherapy, and family therapy.

- Personality Pathways
  http://www.personalitypathways.com/type_inventory2.html

This website gives additional information in understanding your Myers–Briggs Type Indicator and 16PF results. It also provides additional reading and resources related to personality assessment.

Readings

Neustadt, P. (2017). From reactive to self-led parenting: IFS therapy for parents. In M. Sweezy & E. L. Ziskind (Eds.), *Innovations and elaborations in internal family systems therapy* (pp. 70–89). New York: Routledge.

This chapter describes the difference between reflective and self-led parenting based on the IFS model.

Russell, W. P., Pinsof, W., Breunlin, D. C., & Lebow, J. (2016). Integrated problem centered metaframeworks (IPCM) therapy. In T. L. Sexton & J. Lebow (Eds.), *Handbook of family therapy* (pp. 530–544). New York: Routledge.

This chapter describes integrated metaframeworks therapy. It integrates theory and research in a practitioner-friendly modality.

Tennant, M. (2012). The narrative solutions approach. In A. Rambo, C. West, A. Schooley, & T. V. Boyd (Eds.), *Family therapy review: Contrasting contemporary models* (pp. 191–195). New York: Routledge.

This book provides a detailed history of and describes the narrative solutions approach.

REFERENCES

American Association for Marriage and Family Therapy. (2015). *AAMFT code of ethics*. Alexandria, VA: Author.

American Counseling Association. (2014). *ACA code of ethics*. Alexandria, VA: Author.

American Psychiatric Association. (2013). *Diagnostic and statistical manual of mental disorders* (5th ed.). Arlington, VA: Author.

Breunlin, D. C. (1999). Toward a theory of constraints. *Journal of Marital and Family Therapy, 25*(3), 365–382. doi:10.1111/j.1752-0606.1999.tb00254.x

Breunlin, D., Pinsof, W., Russell, W., & Lebow, J. (2011). Integrative problem centered meta framework therapy 1: Core concepts and hypothesizing. *Family Process Journal, 50*, 293–313.

Breunlin, D. C., Schwartz, R. C., & Kune-Karrer, B. M. (2001). *Metaframeworks: Transcending the models of family therapy, revised and updated.* San Francisco: Jossey-Bass.

Catskill Family Institute. (2017). Our psychologists. Retrieved from http://www.catskillfamilyinstitute.com

Christensen, A., Atkens, D. C., Burns, S., Wheeler, J., Baucom, D. H., & Simpson, L. E. (2004). Traditional versus Integrative Behavioral Couples Therapy for significantly and chronically distressed married couples. *Journal of Counseling & Clinical Psychology, 72*, 176–191.

Dagirmanjian, S., Eron, J., & Lund, T. (2007). Narrative solutions: An integration of self and systems perspectives in motivating change. *Journal of Psychotherapy Integration, 17*(1), 70–92. doi:10.1037/1053-0479.17.1.70

Dimidjian, S., Martell, C. R., & Christensen, A. (2008). Integrative behavioral couple therapy. In A. S. Gurman (Ed.), *Clinical handbook of couple therapy* (4th ed., pp. 73–106). New York: Guilford Press.

Eron, J. B., & Lund, T. W. (1996). *Narrative solutions in brief therapy.* New York: Guilford Press.

Gehart, D. R., & Tuttle, A. R. (2003). *Theory-based treatment planning for marriage and family therapists.* Pacific Grove, CA: Brooks/Cole.

Gladding, S. T. (2015). *Family therapy: History, theory, and practice* (6th ed.). Upper Saddle River, NJ: Pearson.

Karrer, B. M. (1989). The sound of two hands clapping: Cultural interactions of the minority family and the therapist. In G. W. Saba, B. M. Karrer, & K. V. Hardy (Eds.), *Minorities and family therapy* (pp. 209–237. New York: Hawthorn Press.

Kottler, J. A., & Montgomery, M. J. (2011). *Theories of counseling and therapy: An experiential approach* (2nd ed.). Thousand Oaks, CA: Sage.

Lambert, M. (1992). Psychotherapy outcome research: Implications for integrative and eclectic therapists. In J. C. Norcross & M. R. Goldfried (Eds.), *Handbook of psychotherapy integration* (pp. 94–129). New York: Basic Books.

Lund, T., Eron, J., & Dagirmanjian, S. (2016). Narrative solutions: Using preferred view of self to motivate individual and family change. *Family Process, 55*(4), 724–741. doi:10.1111/famp.12207

Miller, S. D., Duncan, B. L., & Hubble, M. A. (2002). Client-directed, outcome-informed clinical work. In F. W. Kaslow & J. Lebow (Eds.), *Comprehensive handbook of psychotherapy: Vol. 4: Integrative/eclectic* (pp. 185–212). New York: Wiley.

Mojta, C., Falconier, M. K., & Huebner, A. J. (2014). Fostering Self-Awareness in novice therapists using internal family systems therapy. *American Journal of Family Therapy, 42*(1), 67–78. doi:10.1080/01926187.2013.772870

Nichols, M. P., & Schwartz, R. C. (1998). *Family therapy: concepts and methods* (4th ed.). Boston: Allyn & Bacon.

Nichols, M. P., & Schwartz, R. C. (2008). *My helping kit: The essentials of family therapy.* Boston, MA: Allyn & Bacon.

Norcross, J. C., & Goldfried, M. R. (Eds.). (2005). *Handbook of psychotherapy integration.* Oxford: Oxford University Press.

Pinsof, W. M. (1983). Integrative problem centered therapy: Toward the synthesis of family and individual psychotherapies. *Journal of Marital and Family Therapy, 9*, 19–35.

Pinsof, W. M. (1989). A conceptual framework and methodological criteria for family therapy process research. *Journal of Consulting and Clinical Psychology, 57*, 53–60.

Pinsof, W. M. (1994). An overview of integrative problem-centered therapy: A synthesis of family and individual psychotherapies. *Journal Family Therapy, 16*, 103–120.

Pinsof, W. M. (1995). *Integrative problem centered therapy: A synthesis of biological, individual and family therapies*. New York: Basic Books.

Pinsof, W. (2016). Pinsof Family Systems. Retrieved from https://www.pinsof-familysystems.com/home

Prochaska, J. O., & Norcross, J. C. (2009). *Systems of psychotherapy: A transtheoretical analysis* (7th ed.). Pacific Grove, CA: Brooks/Cole.

Schwartz, R. C. (1995). *Internal family systems therapy*. New York: Guilford Press.

Schwartz, R. C. (2014). The 2014 IFS Conference at the Cape Cod Institute. Retrieved from http://www.selfleadership.org/dick-at-cap-cod.html

Watzlawick, P., Weakland, J., & Fisch, R. (1974). *Change: Principles of problem formation and problem resolution*. New York: Norton.

White, M., & Epston, D. (1990). *Narrative means to therapeutic ends*. New York: Norton.

Wilkins, P. (2000). Unconditional positive regard reconsidered. *British Journal of Guidance & Counselling, 28*(1), 23–36. doi:10.1080/030698800109592

Wood, B. (1985). Proximity and hierarchy: Orthogonal dimensions of family interconnectedness. *Family Process*, 1985, *24*(4), 487–507.

PART IV

Special Issues

CHAPTER 18

Nonnuclear Family Constellations

Laura Haddock, Abby Dougherty, and Tracy Calley

"Feelings of worth can flourish only in an atmosphere where individual differences are appreciated, mistakes are tolerated, communication is open, and rules are flexible—the kind of atmosphere that is found in a nurturing family."

—Virginia Satir

In the previous chapters, you focused on the various schools and models of family therapy. Now we will shift our focus to discussing special issues throughout the remaining chapters. Families of adopted children, single-parent families, blended families, families with gay parents, children living with relatives other than, or in addition to, their birth parents—these family structures are frequently represented in school classrooms and family therapy sessions. Culturally competent therapists are charged to work with families from these and other backgrounds. Children can get the implicit message from society that nontraditional families are less than normal, and marriage and family therapists have a powerful opportunity to provide an affirming and nurturing environment that promotes self-acceptance and healthy self-concept.

The information in this chapter will acquaint therapists with many nonnuclear family constellations. Intended to promote sensitivity to the needs of family systems that do not meet the traditional model of a biological parental unit and biological children, this chapter includes information that may assist marriage and family therapists in individualizing work with a variety of family systems. For each family constellation, an overview of common characteristics, cultural considerations and intervention strategies are provided, as well as information and activities to promote contextual application and understanding.

LEARNING OBJECTIVES

After reading this chapter, you will be able to do the following:

- Identify characteristics common to unified families, single-parent families, adoptive families, same-sex parent families, multigenerational family systems, and immigrant families.
- Describe ethical considerations for each of these family systems.
- Understand cultural considerations for each of these family systems.
- Designate common intervention strategies for each of these family systems.

SINGLE-PARENT FAMILIES

Single-parent families are a common theme throughout the United States and account for over 20% of households (Deal, 2014a). This population has steadily increased over the past decade and continues to warrant the attention of mental health professionals. A single-parent home is defined as one parent taking on most or all child-rearing responsibilities, including but not limited to financial obligations, emotional and mental health concerns, academic and developmental progress, as well as the overall well-being of the child. These responsibilities can be overwhelming, and the transformations that single parents endure can be quite complex.

CHARACTERISTICS AND TYPES OF SINGLE-PARENT FAMILIES

Single-parent families are characterized in several different ways that include divorce, death, individual choice (unwed pregnancy, adoption), or types of temporary work-related situations, such as military deployment (Gladding, 2015). Regardless of what leads to the family being restructured, the hardships and stressors that the family faces during this time are quite similar. Every aspect of the family system tends to change, which includes but is not limited to income, housing, parenting styles, and relationships with family members and friends.

Single-parent families formed because of divorce are the most common type of family unit. Up until the mid-20th century, most single-parent families formed because of the death of a parent or the abandonment of a spouse (Gladding, 2015). According to the U.S. Census Bureau (2016), 31% of the children living in the United States reside in a home that does not include two parents. Markowitz (2015) reported that two-parent homes have declined and single-parent homes are steadily increasing. More than half of U.S. children today will spend at least part of their childhoods not living with two biological parents (Fremstad & Boteach, 2015). Currently, one fourth of all U.S. children are residing in a single-parent family and spend roughly one third, or 5 years, of their childhood in this type of nontraditional family setting (Deal, 2014a). These are alarming statistics when considering how many families are impacted daily; clearly, the issues surrounding single-parent families can be complex. In many instances, the family structure was fractured prior to the finality of the relationship and often the family was in distress throughout the separation and divorce process.

Divorce and the creation of a single-parent home can lead to a multitude of issues including poverty, stress, depression, lowered household income and creating new social relationships (Gladding, 2015). Also, the new family structure initiates new roles for all family members. These new roles can include a decline in parental involvement, changes in parenting styles, and increased responsibilities of children in the home. These changes can add another layer of psychological and emotional distress within the family.

Single-parenting because of the death of a partner poses unique challenges to the family and to practitioners. The family unit and dynamics change drastically regardless of whether the family was prepared for the loss or it was a sudden death. The surviving partner and children face many emotions during this time that range from disbelief, anger, depression, and feelings of hope for a loved one to return. Coping strategies and resiliency can be related to the attachment and relationship to the deceased spouse/parent, familial support, and religiosity. A family who loses a spouse/parent is treated much differently by family, friends, and the community, when compared to a couple who have chosen to divorce. There tends to be a greater outpouring of support from loved ones when a spouse/parent dies, and the loss can unite the family and create a stronger bond (Milstead & Perkins, 2010). Working with families who have lost a parent or spouse requires practitioners to not only focus on change within the family structure but also focus on grief and bereavement. Let's pause to consider how a therapist might work with a family dealing with the sudden death of a parent. Work through Guided Practice Exercise 18.1 and the issues faced by Ed and his children after the sudden death of his wife, Kay. Challenge yourself to answer all the questions.

GUIDED PRACTICE EXERCISE 18.1

Ed and Kay have been married for 12 years and have two children, Tim (12 years old) and Jenny (6 years old). Ed and Kay have been arguing frequently over finances and the children's grades. The children have begun to realize that Ed and Kay are not getting along and the arguing has intensified. One Saturday afternoon, Kay begins to feel sick and disoriented. Ed checks in on her and decides to call 911 due to her frequent alcohol abuse. On the way to the hospital, Kay passes away of a seizure. Although terminating the relationship had been discussed by means of separation, her sudden passing has turned the family upside down. Ed is depressed and not able to cope due to all the arguing they have had and recent discussions of separation and the overwhelming process of figuring out what it means to be a single father. Tim is angry and Jenny thinks Mommy will be coming home soon. Based on what you have read in this chapter, how would you work with Ed and the children? What resources would be beneficial to them at this time? What approaches would you take to best assist them in their loss and grief?

Single-parent-families-by-choice are a growing trend within our society. Since the 1980s women have been putting off marriage and having children to pursue educational endeavors or careers. More and more women (predominately educated individuals with a strong sense of job security) in their late 30s and 40s are staying single by choice and are intentionally having children later in life (Gladding, 2015). An individual's choice to have a child out of wedlock or to pursue other means of having children (such as adoption) has become much more socially acceptable as negative connotations have declined.

Temporary, single-parent families have also emerged in recent decades and gained the attention of mental health practitioners. Temporary, single-parent families can include military personnel, oil field workers, individuals who change careers and move before the family can join as well as those working in global occupations (Gladding, 2015). Preparing for these temporary changes, open communication, and reintegration are vital components in the success of families who are separated for an extended amount of time.

Parents impacted by divorce are only a fraction of the family therapist's concerns. According to Gladding (2015), children of divorce can be challenged when attempting to form intimate relationships, have higher rates of cohabitation and divorce than children who come from traditional families. Children of divorced parents tend to struggle academically, have higher rates of sexual promiscuity, lowered self-esteem, and increased behavioral problems when compared to peers with intact families (Haskins, 2015; Deal, 2014b). Child temperament, continued dual parental involvement, and parental avoidance of child conflict inclusion can result in increased adjustment and fewer long-term challenges (Deal, 2014b). It is vital for both parents to assist the children throughout this transition and promote positive coping mechanisms as each child has unique needs during such a critical time in development.

Cultural Considerations

Being that single-parent families are continuing to grow, mental health professionals must consider how culture plays a role within family systems and therapeutic modalities. As discussed in Chapter 5, therapists must display sensitivity, acceptance, ingenuity, and experience when working with culturally diverse, single-parent families (Gladding, 2015). Also, therapists must remain cognizant of their individual cultural differences and biases while remaining client centered and focusing on the family dynamics the clients are facing. Minorities are more likely to be a part of a single-family system and face issues of poverty, depression, and stress (Sawhill, 2015). Research continues to grow within this domain to ensure clients are receiving the best treatment and interventions available.

Intervention Strategies

Role of Therapist

Families are unique structures, and no two are the same. Therapists should approach this population with careful consideration and assess family needs regarding diversity. This means considering the type of single-family unit with whom you are working. As mentioned earlier in the section, a family becomes a nonnuclear family constellation through a variety of issues. The therapist must avoid exhibiting bias or prejudice and work to build a positive rapport with the existing family unit. Many emotions can emerge from families while going through this transition and the therapist must be prepared to work with the associated challenges. Emotions can range from anger to despair, feelings of relief to regret, and feelings of volatility (Gladding, 2015). In addition, mental health professionals must be prepared and have resources readily available for clients. Familial support, social support, and local support can significantly assist clients' overall well-being throughout these life changes.

Treatment

Families who are going through significant life changes such as divorce, loss of a loved one, or having children in a nontraditional setting require skilled therapists and varied resources. Literature reveals that psycho-educational and behavioral interventions can be beneficial during this challenging time (Gladding, 2015). Also, therapists may consider utilizing various creative forms of interventions such as sand tray therapy, play therapy, family sculpting and music therapy. Counseling single-parent families requires unique and innovative approaches. As single-parent families become an increasingly diverse landscape within the counseling profession, mental health practitioners must consider innovative techniques and interventions to best meet the needs of this population.

UNIFIED FAMILIES

The blended family, or stepfamily, is a prevalent family system in the American family landscape. According to Deal (2014a), about 40% of new marriages in the United States are remarriages for one or both partners. In addition, close to 42 million adults are in a second or subsequent marriage, and 40% of married couples with children in the United States are stepfamilies (Manning, 2015). When adults with children unite, a unified family is born. The new commitment merges the child or children of both members of the new couple. While unified families often form through remarriage, blended families are also born when two parents with children from a previous relationship live together, resulting in a combined family household though the parents have not married. The distinguishing feature of unified families from the countless variations of other family types lies in the fusion of one or more members of a previous family with one or more new members.

What Do We Call This Nonnuclear Family Constellation?

A review of current literature reveals that many terms are used synonymously when referring to two or more systems that come together to form a new one. *Stepparent* originated in the marriage and family literature as a term that referred to new people in the household who substituted for the "real" parent who had died (Berman, 1980). Let's face it, Cinderella stacked the deck against stepmothers everywhere. *Blended family* is commonly used to describe a system in which a new spousal relationship has formed and includes children from previous relationships (Zeleznikow & Zeleznikow, 2015). However, it is somewhat difficult to escape the picture that surfaces from the word "blended." The term paints a mental picture of tossing items in the kitchen aide, throwing the switch, and potentially creating a mess! *Merged family* sounds more like a business transaction than a loving family system. *Unified* does offer a positive connotation for integrated systems and offers great potential for a new term to symbolize united systems.

If merely finding terms to describe a unified family is complicated, what must the experience of landing in middle of this situation be like? It is critical for marriage and family therapists not to underestimate the impact this unification will have. One key to successful treatment is for therapists to take the time to get to know each system and subsystem and establish a plan for interventions to meet the needs of every member of the system. Research is clear that the increase in divorce throughout the second half of the 20th century generates risk for negative consequences for women and children's well-being (Jappens & Van Bavel, 2016). Children are often forced to move into a new house or are expected to welcome a new and strange person or persons into their own home. After all, unified families are "instant" families and children are part of the remarriage package. Adjusting to a stepparent may prove to be the lesser of the evils in the eyes of a child who faces the much more complicated event of getting to know or at least learn how to live with new siblings on top of a new stepparent. Keep in mind, this only describes the difficulties of transitioning to new family dynamics and forming new relationships. It does not consider other significant matters such as dealing with birth parents' divorce, the death of a parent, or the choice one parent made to remarry. Unmistakably, the mixing of families is a complex and disconcerting experience. With the incidence of divorce and subsequent development of new families, the blended family is today less the exception and more the rule (Purswell & Taylor, 2013). It is critical for marriage and family therapist to maintain awareness that unified families are different from nuclear families. The structure, roles, and functions of unified families are multifaceted and can be indistinct leaving these new systems in need of assistance with working through issues. For decades, researchers have illuminated that blended families face a lack of available resources and absence of cultural rules and guidelines (Hurwitz, 1997). Unfortunately, this means that unified families are often left with little idea of what to expect or how to deal with problems when they emerge.

Characteristics of Unified Families

As discussed earlier, unified families come in many shapes and sizes. The key difference is that within unified families at least one biological parent is elsewhere. Every member of the new family system feels the absent parent, whether living or dead. Dealing with the loss of the family structure or a biological parent through death or divorce are two of the most difficult stressors any individual can live through (Luecken & Roubinov, 2013). There are also wide variations in both custody and visitation arrangements. Shared parenting is common today (DiFonzo, 2014). This means children may move back and forth between family homes with multiple household arrangements. When children are members of more than one household, they can struggle with ever changing patterns of interaction and lack of stability in household expectations. The rules in the households may be very different leading to confusion, frustration and loyalty conflicts.

Further complicating family dynamics in unified families is lack of clarity about roles. The role definition of a stepparent is not static. While a stepparent is not biologically related to the children, there is typically an expectation that they will participate in financial, educational, and parenting responsibilities. So, while stepparents are often expected to provide nurturing roles in the family, the authority or power remains with the biological parent. In addition, stepfamily functioning and couple functioning appear to be intimately linked (Martin-Uzzi & Duval-Tsioles, 2013). For example, in a remarried family system there are often intrapersonal dynamics that can cause conflict among or between the couple, the stepparent, and the children. For example, power struggles may emerge between the biological parent–child dyad and the new marital dyad, with the biological dyad often winning (Deal, 2014b). The biological parent and child share a history and patterns of interaction that typically have more history than the remarried dyad. There is no doubt that many stepparents enter into a unified marriage with solid commitments to care for the children, yet there is often fear of rejection lurking beneath the surface (Martin-Uzzi & Duval-Tsioles, 2013). Simultaneously, the parent who is trying to maintain ties to his or her children may feel guilty about the new marriage or time spent with the new spouse (Martin-Uzzi & Duval-Tsioles, 2013). Overall, confusion over the rights, roles, and duties of the unified family members can lead to family dysfunction.

While societal norms are more inclusive of unified family systems than ever before, there can still be challenges that create discomfort even with everyday tasks like filling out forms. Preschool or elementary age children often create cards in celebration of holidays potentially leaving a child to choose which parent will receive the card and potentially leaving one parent feeling rejected. Researchers have asserted for years that for some children who may carry feelings of guilt over the divorce or death of a biological parent, these sorts of daily challenges may manifest in an even greater load of guilt and worry that their choices will result in a second divorce. "Guilt breeds resentment and anger" (Prosen & Farmer, 1982, p. 394). Finally, the nuances of the family unit may result in a shortage of social support. For example, you could have two divorced same-sex adults with a child from a previous opposite-sex relationship who become involved in a same-sex relationship. This is not to suggest that all gay or lesbian families are unified families but to illustrate that when working with families, it is incredibly important to understand the dynamics and needs of every member of the system and consider the cultural implications of each system.

Intervention Strategies

Role of the Therapist

Building a therapeutic alliance with a unified family is the foundation for therapeutic success. Validating the unique experience of each family member, including the emotional response to the presenting problem, can be quite powerful in promoting a secure therapeutic relationship. The therapist's attention and responsiveness to each member of the system honors the integrity and identity of the family.

Treatment

More than 30 years ago, Prosen and Farmer (1982) established assumptions that interventions for stepfamilies rest upon which hold true today. First, children demonstrating emotional and/or behavioral dysfunction while coping with family unification are more likely responding to the stress of the situation rather than demonstrating psychopathology. Second, the therapist is well served by focusing treatment on problem solving, feelings, communication, and interpersonal processes.

During the assessment phase of the process, learning what each member of the system perceives to be the presenting problem is critical to understand the family dynamics on both a macro and a micro level. In addition, a family discussion on the perceived problems may allow you to observe intra-relational responses and begin to identify problematic interactional behaviors. You should respond to the personal reactions of the family members with reflection and validation of feelings. Your ability and willingness as the therapist to listen empathically is an important component of the therapeutic process. It also falls on you to determine which issues are best resolved through system work versus those that could benefit from one on one intervention.

Once you, as the therapist have established an understanding of the systemic issues, you should be prepared to investigate the concerns of each of the subsystems. For example, the children may benefit from having their feelings affirmed as "normal" in relation to their peers as well as being given permission to experience their own feelings. Using support and encouragement, you can assist the children with addressing stressful issues with parents and stepparents.

In Chapters 1, 3, and 5, you learned how important it is for therapists to recognize that the foundation of a unified family is a pair of adults who sought a relationship as a couple. If you can assist the couple in strengthening the relationship, the stress levels of the child(ren) may naturally subside. See Case Presentation 18.1 to practice determining next steps after the parental unit in a unified family shares their presenting problem.

CASE PRESENTATION 18.1: THE CASE OF ELIZABETH AND MICHAEL

Marriage and family counselors must orient themselves to the unique circumstances of each family. However, there are some general counseling goals that are likely to apply to most unified families:

1. Understanding the effects, both positive and negative, of the integration of the family for each member of the system.
2. Clarifying the roles of each member of the system and facilitating positive attitudes and acceptance of the new family structure.
3. Increasing the adult couples understanding of the importance of bonding within their relationship apart from the relationship with the children and stepchildren.
4. Improving the quality of the communication among and between all members of the systems and subsystems.

Consider the following case presentation:

Elizabeth and Michael arrive at their counseling appointment requesting an intake to initiate family therapy. Between the two of them, Elizabeth and Michael have four children. McKenna is the 4-year-old biological daughter of Elizabeth and Michael. Kenzy is 15, and Connor is 16; both were adopted by Elizabeth prior to her marriage to Michael. Everly is 10 years old and was adopted by Michael prior to his marriage to Elizabeth.

Michael:	I think it is important that we start some counseling because we are really having a hard time.
Elizabeth:	It was recently discovered that my son, Connor has bullied Everly. After Michael discovered that he had hurt Everly, there have been a lot of changes in the house.
Michael:	After all this came to light, I called the police so they would talk to Connor. I took what happened seriously. But after the police got involved, Everly went to live with my ex-wife and Connor went to live with his grandparents until we figure out whether he is a risk to the other children.
Michael:	Now Kenzy is angry all the time because she can't be with her brother. She is rude, sullen, and basically won't come out of her room. Elizabeth cries all day, every day. I haven't noticed much with McKenna, but she does say she misses Everly living with us.
Elizabeth:	I am just so angry! I can't believe this has happened! For so many years Kenzy and Connor were all I had and now it feels like I have lost both of them!

If you were their therapist, how would you proceed from here?

ADOPTIVE FAMILIES

Adoptive families are not a new familial trend within our society. Children being placed in a home that does not include a biological parent grew in the early 20th century because of the high number of homeless children in urban areas (Palacios & Brodzinsky, 2010). Currently, adoption rates are increasing due to innovations in reproductive technology that identify genetic disorders, age as the result of delaying the start of a family, infertility, as well as same-sex couples and single individuals wishing to adopt (Berk, 2014). Adoption procedures can be an emotional roller coaster, extremely stressful and overwhelming for all parties involved. Counseling families throughout the adoption process and well into the integration of a new family member is of special interest to mental health practitioners.

Characteristics and Types of Adoptive Families

Every adoptive family exhibits very diverse characteristics and come in many complex family constellations. For instance, there are heterosexual couples without children seeking to adopt, heterosexual couples with children, single individuals and same-sex couples selecting to expand their family. The reasons for a family to consider adoption are quite extensive. Some examples include: the inability to conceive naturally, the risk of genetic disorders, desiring more children and individuals that have full custody of a biological child and chose to allow their significant other adoption options (Berk, 2014). Interestingly, adoptive families take on many of the characteristics noted in other sections of this chapter. Adoptive families can be embedded in a blended family, single-parent family, same-sex-parent family, and within a multigenerational family constellation.

Adoption has long served to connect families and children. Adoptive families can encounter substantial amounts of stress and complications; however, most families overcome this and experience a very fulfilled life. Adoption has the potential to offer children and adults "the prospect of stability, loving care, security, and lifetime family connections for boys and girls whose biological parents are unable to raise them" (Brodzinsky, 2011, p. 200).

Adoptive family systems face complicated boundaries and roles when compared to biological family systems (Kalus, 2014). Complexities can also arise with respect to the adoptee's ethnicity and age at which adoption occurs. Adoptive children show higher rates of emotional disturbances and learning difficulties than nonadoptive children (Berk, 2014). These emotional and learning challenges increase with the child's age prior to adoption. Essentially, children adopted as an infant have lower levels of emotional distress and learning disabilities than children adopted at a later age (Berk, 2014). Adoptive families also have differences in personality and intelligence due to genetic predispositions that biological families do not experience (Berk, 2014). These differences can lead to familial conflict if not addressed particularly in the adoptees adolescent development. During this time, adolescents are not only experiencing puberty but trying to find their identity. Familial relationships are influential on one's identity development therefore the adoptee may become increasingly inquisitive about their biological family (Berk, 2014; Brodzinsky, 2011). Despite the myriad of challenges adoptive families face, most adoptees become secure, well-balanced adults (Berk, 2014; Brodzinsky, 2011). Pause for a moment and complete Guided Practice Exercise 18.2. You will have the opportunity to strengthen your case conceptualization skills as you consider how to help David and Karen, a married couple struggling to cope with the emotional and behavioral strife of their adopted son, Patrick, and the implications this has for their family.

GUIDED PRACTICE EXERCISE 18.2

David and Karen are a happily married couple with two biological children, Chloe (20) and Emily (18). They adopted David's nephew, Patrick (16), shortly after he was born. Patrick knows that he is adopted and that his biological mom is his aunt. They do not have a strong relationship, due to her drug and alcohol use. The family has started counseling services, due to Patrick having episodes of anger, showing resentment to David and Karen, and poor academic performance. Patrick feels close to Chloe, but his relationship with Emily has become strained. Emily is angry with Patrick for what he is doing to the family but also sad that they are not as close as they once were. David and Karen's marriage remain intact, but Karen's relationship with Patrick is fragmented. She is struggling with his outbursts and feels that his rage is directed toward her.

As the therapist, how would you best work with the family? Please identify the presenting problems within the family. What interventions strategies would you employ? Would you recommend any other types of therapy (individual, couple, group)?

Cultural Considerations

Cultural factors are vital to working with this population. Adoptive families may have various ethnicities rooted within the family. As mentioned in Chapter 5, differences in ethnicity and culture can impact the family dynamics and if not considered by the therapist, could impede the entire counseling process. Exploring the culture of the adoptee can enhance the relationship of the family and assist in creating a positive identity for the child. Considering cultural considerations when working with adoptive families can be a powerful tool within the counseling process.

Intervention Strategies

Role of Therapist

Working with adoptive families can be an intricate and complex process. The role of the therapist must be centered around family needs and dynamics. Therapists must consider where the family is in the adoption and integration process. The therapist would work quite differently with a family that is beginning the adoption process versus a family that has decided to reveal to an adolescent that they were adopted. Practitioners should exhibit high levels of unconditional positive regard, genuineness, empathy and respect to adoptive family clients. The role of the therapist should be adaptable in order best meet the needs of the family.

Treatment

A variety of approaches should be employed when working with adoptive families. As earlier explored, adoptive families present themselves in many ways. Therapists must first identify the type of family they will be working with and where they are in the adoption process. Once this is defined, therapists can work from a systems based perspective while considering the multidimensionality of the family. Approaches must remain client centered and be dependent upon what the family is seeking to adapt.

In addition, Brodzenski (2011) offers guidelines for mental health professionals when working with adoptive families, which are found in Guided Practice Exercise 18.3 Take a few moments to challenge yourself to develop strategies for approaching working with adoptive families.

GUIDED PRACTICE EXERCISE 18.3

The following list provides an overview of clinical considerations for marriage and family therapists working with adoptive families. Consider your role as the therapist and identify strategies or techniques you might employ to facilitate these issues:

1. Discussing adoption with children is a process, not an event.
2. Adoption revelation is a dialogue, not a process of talking to children.
3. Early telling has advantages over late telling.
4. Be emotionally available for the child and listen.
5. Begin the adoption story with birth and family diversity, not adoption.

6. Keep in mind the child's developmental level and readiness to process specific information.
7. Validate and normalize children's curiosity, questions, and feelings about their adoptions, birth parents, and heritage.
8. Be aware of your own feelings and values related to birth parents and the children's history.

- Avoid negative judgments about birth parents or the child's heritage.
- Discussing "difficult" background information.
- Be prepared to help children cope with adoption related loss and grief.
- Foster open, honest, and respectful parent–child communication about adoption.

Same-Sex-Parent Family Constellation

The family as an institution seems to be in a constant state of change. As traditional male and female roles are redefined, various alternative family constellations have become an integral part of the social structure. It is estimated that there are more than two million gay and lesbian parents raising from 6 million to 14 million children in the United States (U.S. Census Bureau, 2011). From 2000 to 2010, the number of people reporting to be living in a household with a same-sex partner rose by 80.4% (Nhan, n.d.). Six million American children and adults have at least one gay or lesbian parent. Lesbian and gay families are diverse, and each family is unique. These families share many of the same concerns as households headed by heterosexual parents and, in addition, deal with issues specific to being members of an oppressed group. Studies that have directly compared gay and lesbian parents with heterosexual parents have consistently shown that the former are as fit and capable as the latter, and that their children are as psychologically healthy and well adjusted. Empirical research shows that parental sexual orientation has no quantifiable conclusion on the quality of parent–child interactions or on children's mental health or social adjustment (Webb & Chonody, 2014). Another study noted the pervasive findings inferring no differences when comparing families of heterosexual couples with those of lesbian or gay couples (Massey, Merriweather, & Garcia, 2013)

Characteristics of Same-Sex-Parent Families

Same-sex couples often become parents following one partner's heterosexual relation-ship history, through adoption, or through donor insemination or surrogate parenting (Rosenfeld, 2010). Parenthood is often more difficult to achieve for same-sex couples than for heterosexual couples which could lead to the question of whether these systems, which may have had to work harder to become parents, are even more dedicated to the hard work of parenting. Perhaps these challenges are ultimately beneficial for their children.

> *Myths and misperceptions about lesbian and gay parents*
> *continue to present the greatest obstacle to adoption for*
> *LGBT adults. In recent years, however, a growing body of*

research on LGBT parents and their children is clear and affirming about the ability of LGBT individuals and same-sex couples to parent, and it alleviates concerns about the outcomes of children raised by LGBT parents [Massey et al., 2013]. It is essential that professionals have access to and can draw from evidence-based information about LGBT adoptive families in making decisions in the best interests of children. Without this body of knowledge, professionals will continue to overlook the great potential of LGBT individuals and couples to be a resource for children.... [Counseling] research [Frias-Navarro, Monterde-i-Bort, Pascual-Soler, & Badenes-Ribera, 2015; Massey et al., Garcia, 2013; Webb & Chonody, 2014] shows the following:

Children raised by LGBT parents do not differ in any key areas of adjustment or functioning (Goldberg, 2009).

Quality of parenting and level of family functioning are not related to the sexual orientation of the parents (Erich, Leung, Kindle, & Carter, 2005).

Adults who have been raised by LGBT parents report feeling more tolerant of all types of human diversity (Biblarz & Stacey, 2010).

These are just a few findings among dozens of studies conducted with children of LGBT parents over more than three decades. In short, the research shows that children raised by LGBT parents do not experience negative effects or outcomes because of their parents' sexual orientation, and, in fact, there are positive outcomes for children raised by LGBT parents. (Child Welfare Information Gateway, 2011)

Persons identifying as lesbian, gay, bisexual, and transsexual (LGBT) come from all walks of life and from within a variety of cultures (LaSala & Frierson, 2012). Families of origin for this population also vary greatly. Some families embrace and accept sexual minority status and relationships whereas others ostracize these family members, thus, leading to secrecy and distance. For this reason, many sexual minorities choose to hide their sexuality from families as well as others within society. This ostracism can even extend to levels of verbal and physical abuse that bring about devastating consequences. Marriage and family therapists must educate themselves so they are prepared to work with diverse LGBT couples and families. This often means learning as much as possible about same-sex families and countering personal biases that impede the relationship.

Cultural Considerations

> Not all LGBT people identify as lesbian, gay, bisexual, or transgender. Other terms might include "same-gender loving," having a "fluid" sexuality, or being "two-spirited." Many younger LGBT Americans reclaimed the term "queer" and may choose that term to self-identify. The terms, expressions, and ways of defining oneself are often tied to cultural understandings of sexuality and gender and can also be influenced by popular culture, generational experience, and region of the country. Additionally, like most groups, the language, and terminology used within and about the LGBT community evolve over time. (Child Welfare Information Gateway, 2011)

Therapists should consider that their therapeutic decisions are rarely fully neutral. Awareness of these ethical and political considerations plays a key role when counseling LGBT clients and their family's therapist. This also includes adopting a position against counseling clients based on their sexual orientation. Therapists should consider their ethical stance on counseling with LGBT couples and families. Examples include:

ACA Code of Ethics (ACA, 2014) C.5. instructs, "Counselors do not condone or engage in discrimination against prospective or current clients, students, employees, supervisees, or research participants based on age, culture, disability, ethnicity, race, religion/spirituality, gender, gender identity, sexual orientation, marital/ partnership status, language preference, socioeconomic status, immigration status, or any basis proscribed by law" (p. 9).

AAMFT Code of Ethics (AAMFT, 2015) 1.10 requires: "Marriage and family therapists respectfully assist persons in obtaining appropriate therapeutic services if the therapist is unable or unwilling to provide professional help" (p. 3).

The International Association of Marriage and Family Counselors (2017) mandates: "Couple and family counselors do not abandon clients and do not withhold treatment to clients for discriminatory reasons such as race, disability, religion, age, sexual orientation or identification, cultural background, national origin, marital status, affiliation or socioeconomic status" (p. 2).

Given that clinical competence in family counseling and proficiency in individual counseling with LGBT clients is a prerequisite for working with LGBT clients and families, therapists need to explore how these ethical and cultural obligations are met in training, practice, and supervision. Being able to make culturally and ethically appropriate referrals for LGBT clients also requires close examination. Other critical issues include the need to address heterosexist bias particularly in family counseling. The shifting landscape of American family life, institutional bias, internalized homophobia and heterosexism, conflicting views on the etiology of same-sex attraction, and the very nature of human sexuality all create the need for ongoing research, training, supervision, and consultation. Despite this complex range of cultural and ethical challenges when counseling with or considering the referral of LGBT clients and couples and their families, marriage and family therapists are in a unique position to validate, affirm, and advocate for LGBT clients and their families. Given the cultural stigma of homosexuality borne by LGBT persons, their history of oppression and marginalization, and the ethical complexities of family counseling with this population, working with LGBT clients will often generate more questions than answers, and perhaps the most aspirational guidance can be found by promoting client safety, security, and place of belonging.

Marriage and family therapists are called to become proficient in working with LGBT clients and families. Ethical professionals carefully consider referrals and use them only when they do not have adequate training to assist with a client's presenting concerns. Inappropriate and heterosexist referrals have the power to damage sexual minorities as they may invalidate them as human beings. In contrast, culturally competent marriage and family therapists have the power to affirm sexual minority clients and families and should utilize ongoing supervision, consultation, and training opportunities to become even more culturally competent when working with this population (Janson & Steigerwald, 2002).

Intervention Strategies

The Role of the Therapist

The stigma gay and lesbian families face, a hostile social and political climate, and myths and misconceptions are obstacles that can be overcome. Self-awareness of personal beliefs and biases is essential and must be examined and when necessary, amended. Family therapists should promote affirming language and be willing to speak out when antigay language is encountered. It is important to be cautious and use inclusive language and materials with clients and avoid reflecting heterosexism. Formal policies, forms, and brochures will ideally reflect this same acceptance and inclusivity. The inclusion of books and posters within the counseling environment that affirm gay and lesbian families can facilitate a welcoming setting. Awareness of specific issues that may affect gay and lesbian families and knowledge of resources and support groups is the therapist's responsibility. Therapists have an ethical responsibility to obtain the training, education, and experience necessary to understand the lived experience of the same-sex family. Each family is unique. Families come into counseling seeking cohesion. Yet therapists must not overlook the potential for the family to face opposition, discrimination or prejudice at any given time, and be prepared to help hold this pain throughout any intervention. Families may enter the counseling process for guidance or support that has not been available from their support system or the community. It is exquisitely important for therapists not to display an uninformed or judgmental attitude.

Treatment

The techniques of enactment and reframing can be particularly useful for this family constellation (LaSala, 2013). Enactment is a technique shared with multiple empirically supported models of family therapy, which allows therapists to facilitate having family members communicate with each other during the sessions, and interaction patterns are targeted for assessment and modification (Nichols, 2013). Family members are encouraged to talk to each other, and the therapist observes and evaluates their interactions, and then assists family members with exchanging destructive communication patterns with more positive and productive ones. When family interaction consists of complaints, blaming, or silence, the technique of reframing is a way of reorganizing communication to make it more agreeable to therapeutic adjustment (Nichols, 2013). For example, parents struggling with a child's behavior may raise their concerns in an angry, anxious way that can provoke defensiveness. Thus, reframing the interactions to communicate less combatively and more authentically can be particularly useful for these families. See Case Presentation 18.2 and consider how reframing and enactment could be used to access parents' underlying worries about their children along with the child's wishes for unconditional love and acceptance.

CASE PRESENTATION 18.2: THE CASE OF DAN AND MICHELLE

Dan and Michelle were married for 11 years and had three children together. Dan knew he could no longer hide his sexuality, and he came out as gay to his wife. Michelle was very upset with Dan. She had given up her career to care for their children and was devastated by Dan's admission. Dan soon moved out of their family home, and the couple agreed they would divorce.

He has come to see you for help.

Dan: Over this last year, I met and fell in love with Mike. He is my soul mate and we have started discussing the possibility of marriage. I am totally baffled by how to introduce Mike to my children. My ex-wife thinks that it is un-natural for kids to have "two dads" and I am not sure how to handle that. I know from my own research that LGBT parents have had their sexual orientation used against them in custody cases. I'm scared people will think I am a freak! I can't sleep, I feel nervous all the time and I have lost 20 pounds!

MULTIGENERATIONAL AND IMMIGRANT FAMILIES

The nuclear family, which is typically composed of two married parents and their biological or adopted children, has become just one of many different types of family systems in the United States today. One type of family system that is becoming the norm, rather than the exception, is multigenerational family households. Multigenerational families can be described as a family system that typically resides in the same residence and exchanges support and resources (Bailey, Johnson, & Wilson, 2014). Fry and Passel (2014) (2012 noted three common types of multigenerational households:

(1) Two generations: parents (or in-laws) and adult children ages 25 and older (or children-in-law); either

*generation can "head" the household, (2) Three genera-
tions: parents (or in-laws), adult children (and spouse or
children-in- law), grandchildren, (3) "Skipped" generation:
grandparents and grandchildren, without parents (including step-generation). (p. 2)*

The Pew Foundation (2014) further reported that as of 2012, there were 57 million
Americans living in multigenerational family households, double the number from 1980
(Pew Foundation, 2014). There are several contributing factors that have influenced the
rise of multigenerational households. Divorce, longer life span, economic instability, mi-
nor-parents, disability, poverty, and delayed marriage have all contributed to the increase
in multigenerational families.

Single-parent households, which are also on the rise, are at much greater risk for
experiencing poverty (Coontz, 2016). It is no surprise why many families are increasingly seeking family structures that place a premium on shared expenses and resources.
Additionally, many older adults are seeking to live independently longer. This led to more
adult children caretaking for two generations; their parents, and their children. Older
adults who need care benefit from living with extended family. Another contributing
factor to the surge in multigenerational households is the 2008 economic recession (Pew
Foundation, 2014). This led to an increase in the number of adult children moving back
in with their parents after graduating from college. Many Americans experienced long-
term unemployment. It is easy to forget that the nuclear family of the 1950s was possible
due to a thriving middle class and a newly established social safety net. African American,
Hispanic, and Asian families, who disproportionately experience poverty and have a
higher rate of single parents, have traditionally lived in multigenerational households in
the United States (Lofquist, 2013). In cultures that place a high value on interdependent
family relationships, multigenerational family households are the norm rather than the
exception.

Parenting in Extended Families

Multigenerational family structures can be both a source of comfort and a source of pain
for parents. New parents, particularly single parents and their children, greatly benefit
from the additional child-care and financial support. However, several generations in
one household can cause relational difficulties. Grandparents may have different values
and norms for child rearing than their children. Sometimes this can lead to anger and
resentment for parents who may feel their parents have overstepped parental boundaries
regarding roles and responsibilities. While there can be difficult emotional experiences for
caregivers in multigenerational households, there is also the possibility that the children
have more opportunities to receive positive parenting. Researchers have demonstrated
some influence on intergenerational transmission of parenting practices (Conger, Neppl,
& Schofield, 2014). Warm, supportive parenting involves plenty of encouragement,
praise, support, and active involvement in children's activities (Conger et al., 2014). These
parenting behaviors have been shown to positively support healthy child and adolescent

development across cultures and family structures (Conger et al., 2014). Thus, there can be more opportunities for positive caretaking in multigenerational households.

Cultural Considerations

In Western cultures, an expectation has existed that once children reach adulthood it is developmentally appropriate for them to individuate from their families of origin and develop their own families. This is a very different worldview and expectation than that seen in families from collectivist cultures. American Indian, African American, Hispanic, and Middle Eastern cultures have traditionally defined family from a worldview that places a heavy value on the extended family network. Socio-political forces have also influenced the family structure in the United States. Low income and housing discrimination have made it more difficult for minority children to live without their extended family (Darrah & DeLuca, 2014). Increased hurdles must be overcome when the family care provider is not the biological relative of the children under their care. A rise in immigration has also increased the number of multigenerational households in the United States (Pew Foundation, 2014). The level of acculturation across generations can be a source of conflict for multigenerational families. Immigrant families have the complex task of figuring out how to maintain and honor their culture of origin, while navigating assimilation, integration, and possible marginalization within their communities (Han, Berry, & Zheng, 2016). Children from immigrant families often acculturate at a faster pace than their parents (Lazarevic, 2017). Lazarevic noted that immigrant children often serve as cultural brokers in immigrant families, helping their parents and extended family with translation and understanding cultural nuances. The author further discussed the psychological impact of cultural brokering on immigrant youth. For some immigrant youth, engaging in cultural broking leads to increased maturity and a greater sense of self-efficacy. Yet for many immigrant youths there can be feelings of discomfort, stress, embarrassment, and guilt. Eastern European immigrants are often expected to live with their parents until marriage (Gungor & Perdu, 2017). Yet in the United States young adults are expected to move out of their parents' homes and live independently. This cultural conflict can have a profound impact on young adult development and immigrant family dynamics.

Another cultural dimension for therapists who are working with multigenerational families is that many older adults want to stay living independently longer than past generations. This has contributed to an increase in older adults moving in with their adult children. Additionally, many grandparents step in to provide parenting when their adult children cannot care for their children (Dancy, Julion, Sumo, & Wilbur, 2015). Multigenerational family systems can be beneficial for the aging family member, as many older adults and elderly suffer from isolation and higher rates of depression (Sun, 2016). Multigenerational family homes can provide more opportunities for companionship and emotional support.

Intervention Strategies

One of the essential roles of therapists working with multigenerational family households is to support the development of multigenerational interdependence. Interdependence within a multigenerational family context reflects a valuing of relational functioning and collective reliance (Johnston et al., 2014). Healthy systems within an interdependent family system have a healthy balance between collaboration and autonomy (Bailey et al., 2014). In the process of wanting to support multigenerational families, therapists must develop awareness of family structural concerns. Therapists working with parents in multigenerational households need to explore how chores are negotiated. Who is responsible for the day-to day care of any children? To what extent do family members exchange support? What is the quality of child care available from both parents and grandparents? Is the current housing situation temporary or permanent? Who will be responsible for which bill?

Poor communication can lead to family members wanting to isolate from one another. Further, family members may expect other members within the family system to know what they want without expressing their desire (this often referred to as "mind reading"). Another concern when working with multigenerational and immigrant families regarding communication is whether family members have discussed their spoken and unspoken norms for the family system. For example, what are the expectations for privacy and personal space? When adult children are returning home, leaving at a time when they were adolescents, and now reentering the family system, family members may revert to the family norms that were present when their child left home at age eighteen. This can cause suffering for family members as they figure out what their new family norms will be. Through the process of exploring roles and responsibilities, therapists have an opportunity to identify positive behaviors and interactions that support the multigenerational family's resilience. Take a moment to practice your clinical skills with Case Presentation 18.3.

CASE PRESENTATION 18.3: THE CASE OF ASAMI

Asami is a 21-year-old Japanese American. Asami is feeling quite apprehensive about graduating from college. While she has worked very hard at getting her bachelor's degree, she chose to follow her passion and received a degree in education which has not gone over well with her family.

Asami: I really need your help. I am freaking out.

Counselor: Help me understand what is going on.

Asami: My parents think I am a failure. I got my degree but I can't find a job.

Counselor: So, you are feeling anxious because you haven't found a job since graduating?

Asami: Yes. I am the first one in my family to go to college. My parents and grandparents immigrated to the United States before I was born. And now, I've taken out all these loans to go to school, but can't find a job!

Counselor: I am sure that has you worried. Tell me a little bit about how that is affecting you.

Asami: I have no appetite and it seems like I wake up every hour all night long! I don't want to move back in with my parents because I am scared they will expect me to take care of my grandparents, which is only going to make it harder to look for a job! I love my grandparents, but my parents are really strict and that would probably mean no phone, no internet, and no going out. I will be so lonely!! They just don't understand me!

Asami has come to see you about her worries and would like to invite her parents and grandparents to counseling. Asami knows her parents and grandparents will be apprehensive about coming to counseling, but she knows they love her very much and will be willing to attend with her invitation. She would like you, her therapist, to help tell her parents that she would like to move to another community with more job opportunities. How would you begin working with Asami and her family? How can you address Asami's concerns from an approach that honors her cultural heritage?

Ethical Considerations When Working with Nonnuclear Family Constellations

Therapists working with nonnuclear families need to be attentive to their own ethical duty to remain nonjudgmental. The ACA Code of Ethics (2014) and the IAMFC (2017) stated that therapists who practice ethically need to be educated in multicultural models and multiple cultural frameworks that acknowledge the cultural complexities of the clients they are counseling. For example, same-sex couples may present to counseling with issues concerning gender identities and subsequent role responsibilities that are very different from couples who embrace traditional gender norms. Therapist who are working with nonnuclear families require unique competencies and continual self-reflection into ones' biases, and how their biases may impact the counseling process and outcomes.

Therapists working with multigenerational and immigrant families from eastern countries such as India or Japan should develop cultural competencies when working with clients who have a collectivist worldview. Additionally, when working with nonnuclear families, therapists need to take great care in developing a therapeutic alliance with all members of that family system. When therapists are working with blended families, therapist they need to be cognizant of the status of legal guardianship of any children in the marriage (APA, 2017). If guardianship is shared, the therapist will want to obtain permission from all legal caretakers before engaging in counseling (APA, 2017). Nonnuclear families may experience barriers in accessing mental health treatment. Families may struggle with access to counseling providers who have the expertise to address nonnuclear family concerns. Single-parent families and multigenerational immigrant families are at a higher risk for experiencing poverty (Bratter, Damaske, & Frech, 2017). These families may struggle with an inability to pay for services or transportation problems.

It is important for therapists to be aware of available community resources such as support groups for single, blended, adoptive, same-sex, or multigenerational families. It is also advantageous for therapists working with nonnuclear families to address any concerns they may have about receiving counseling. In some cultures, receiving mental health counseling is a quite stigmatized and a shame-filled experience which can lead the clients to experience a lack of trust in the counseling process. Therapists need to take the time to explore their clients' perceptions of receiving counseling. Along with understanding culture specific competencies for nonnuclear families, therapists need to be aware of using theoretical approaches and treatment interventions that have demonstrated-effectiveness for use with the cultural background of the client (ACA, 2014; IAMFC, 2017).

When working with families, just like counseling groups, the therapist cannot guarantee that members of the family will not disclose what has been discussed in session. Special attention to the limits of confidentiality need to be discussed and reviewed with all family members involved in the counseling process.

FUTURE DIRECTIONS

The family structure in the United States today is in continual flux. Thus, there is a need for therapists to develop research exploring the impact of the needs and experiences of nonnuclear family households. There is not only a need for more research exploring nonnuclear family experiences, but also for therapists to further develop their skills in working with families. Single-parent, blended family and multigenerational family households are continuing to increase (Pew Foundation, 2014). While many single-parent households are a result of divorce or death of a spouse, many more individuals are making a conscious decision to raise children within single-parent households. Therapists will also need to develop comfort in exploring their own sexual and gender identity, and how this may impact their work with same-sex couples. Further, therapists will need to pay special attention to any heterosexual bias in their diagnostic instruments (Moleiro & Pinto, 2015).

Fifty percent of families will experience divorce during their lifetime, and more interventions are needed to support parents and children adjusting to blended family life (Baugh, 2014). There is also a need to explore the concerns of adoptive parents and their adopted children. Parents who are adopting children from a differing birth country than their own need support and education to help their children work with any discrimination they may encounter (Juffer, Reinoso, & Tieman, 2013). While much of the research exploring the mental health of adoptive children has focused on developmental processes, there is still a gap in the research literature exploring the needs of pre-and postadoptive families (Brabender & Fallon, 2015).

Finally, therapists need to continue to develop their advocacy competencies. As "nonnuclear families" become "traditional," therapist will need expertise in multiculturally relevant family counseling frameworks. Therapist need to have enough flexibility in their clinical approach to incorporate the worldview of nonnuclear families. Finally, therapists can provide an invaluable service to nonnuclear families by developing the competencies to provide competent care, and by documenting and publishing their outcomes to further the counseling profession knowledge of best practices.

SUMMARY

An endless number of nonnuclear family constellations are in existence. The dynamics that make each family distinctive can also contribute to the need for support from counseling professionals. Through the course of this chapter, we have covered numerous family compositions that demonstrated the need for marriage and family therapists to be fully dedicated to meeting each family where they are and taking the time to understand the characteristics of every system that walks through the door. In addition, we highlighted the need for ethical practice that fully integrates a commitment to self-awareness of personal beliefs and cultural competence.

Ideally, marriage and family therapists will offer nonpathologizing and empowering methods of understanding with thoughtful consideration for every family constellation. We encourage you to seek innovative and enriching interventions that invite both therapist and families to enter into a transformational relationship in which healing can occur. In Chapter 19 you will have the opportunity to consider another important issue; the role of parental functioning on the family system.

KEYSTONES

Among the key points addressed in this chapter are:

- It is critical for therapists to remember that unified families are different from nuclear families. The structure, roles, and functions will need to be intentionally negotiated. Children can struggle living in multiple households where expectations and household rules vary.

- Therapists working with nonnuclear families often support family members clarifying and redefining their roles and responsibilities.

- There is a growing need to explore and support the well-being of temporary single-parent families. Temporary single-parents include military families in which one member is deployed, oil field workers, or family members with new employment and move before their family.

- Adoptive families may need support from therapists due to differences in parent–child ethnicity, if the child has developmental disabilities, or the age of the child when the adoption took place.

- LGBT families face prejudicial views and societal misperceptions, despite a large body of evidence demonstrating the health and well-being of children raised in LGBT households. Therapists working with LGBT families need to promote affirming language and speak out when antigay language is used.

- There are now 57 million families living in multigenerational households in the United States.

- Poor communication can lead to family members wanting to isolate from one another. Further, family members may expect other members within the family system to know what they want without expressing their desire.

- Psychoeducation, behavioral interventions, and creative therapies can be beneficial for nonnuclear families going through difficult times.
- Therapists need knowledge in multicultural frameworks that are flexible enough to incorporate the world view of nonnuclear families.

REFLECTIONS FROM THE CONTRIBUTOR'S CHAIR
Laura Haddock

If there is one takeaway from this chapter, it should be a reminder that there is no "one way" to effectively treat any family. Because every family is unique, competent therapeutic practice requires an individualized approach to treatment with attention to the specific needs of the full system on a macro level and the subsystems on a micro level. You may find yourself asking how in the world you can accomplish that. How can you keep up? How do you honor the identity of everyone involved when there are so many moving parts? Families are not static and they are not linear. So how do you know what to do? From a practical perspective, you are challenged to stay current with evidence based literature, maintain ongoing education and training, and invest in quality supervision. While there are an endless array of techniques, interventions, and theories to serve as tools in service delivery, you cannot overemphasize the importance of the human factor. Know yourself and get to know your clients. Staying keenly self-aware of your own thoughts, feelings, values, and bias that inform your decision making and perceptions is not only a necessity, but an ethical responsibility. And take the time to know your clients. Learn what they bring to the table and how their life experiences have impacted their approach to the world, to interpersonal communication, and to the familial relationships that they are part of.

Though the years, hundreds of families have come through the office doors for treatment. The variety of shapes and sizes of those families are vast. In fact, that informed the title of this chapter. Because when you are a therapist working with couples and families, there are as many different constellations as stars in the sky! While it may be challenging sometimes, the flip side is that it is work that can offer an endless variety of opportunities for creative and fulfilling work!

ADDITIONAL RESOURCES
The following resources provide additional information relating to the chapter topics.

- Adoptive Family Resources
  http://www.adoptingfamilyresources.com

The Adoptive Family Resources website contains a substantial amount of information. It includes resources on adoption choices, financial help, and adoption laws and rights.

- Coalition for Marriage, Family and Couples Education
  http://www.afccnet.org/

An interdisciplinary and international association of professionals dedicated to improving the lives of children and families through the resolution of family conflict.

- Family Equality Council
  http://www.familyequality.org/

The Family Equality Council connects, supports, and represents parents who are lesbian, gay, bisexual, transgender, and queer in the United States.

- *Family Journal*
  https://www.iamfconline.org/members/login.cfm?hpage=The-Family-Journal.cfm

The *Family Journal* features current research articles in relation to marriage, couples, and families.

- Generations United: Because We Are Strong Together
  http://www.gu.org/OURWORK/Multigenerational/
  MultigenerationalHouseholdInformation.aspx

The mission of Generations United is to improve the lives of children youth and older people through intergenerational collaboration, public policies, and programs for the enduring benefit of all.

- International Association of Marriage and Family Counselors
  http://www.iamfconline.org/public/main.cfm

This website provides various links with information on counseling families. It provides ethical codes of conduct, credentialing, publications, and CEU opportunities.

- National Council on Aging
  http://www.ncoa.org/

The National Council on Aging is a nonprofit service and advocacy organization that improves the lives of all older adults and community organizations.

- National Parenting Education Network
  http://npen.org/

This site offers therapists resources, continuing education, and certifications in parenting education.

- Parents Without Partners
  http://www.parentswithoutpartners.org

Parents Without Partners is website for single parents that has various membership chapters across the United States and Canada. The website provides information on single parenting, articles, books, and conference information. The mission of Parents Without Partners is to assist in the welfare of all single parents and children.

- Single Parents Network
  http://www.singleparentsnetwork.com

The Single Parents Network website provides resources for single parents and blended families. Some examples include employment links, articles, support forums, hot topic discussions, and other information.

- SmartStepfamilies
  http://www.smartstepfamilies.com

This website offers videos, articles, statistics, and training information for stepfamilies and therapists working with families.

REFERENCES

American Association for Marriage and Family Therapy. (2015). *AAMFT code of ethics*. Retrieved from http://dx5br1z4f6n0k.cloudfront.net/imis15/Documents/Legal%20Ethics/AAMFT-code-of-ethics.pdf

American Counseling Association. (2014). *ACA code of ethics*. Retrieved from http://www.counseling.org/resources/aca-code-of-ethics.pdf

American Psychological Association. (2017). *Guidelines for child custody evaluations in family law proceedings*. Retrieved from http://www.apa.org/practice/guidelines/child-custody.aspx

Bailey, W., Johnston, J., & Wilson, G. (2014). Mechanisms for fostering multigenerational resilience. *Contemporary Family Therapy, 36*, 148-161.

Baugh, E. (2014). *Encouraging effective coparenting in blended families*. National Resource Center for Healthy Marriage and Families. Retrieved from http://cchrwy.org/index_htm_files/cchr%20web%20Effective%20Coparenting

Berk, L. E. (2014). *Development through the lifespan* (6th ed.). Boston: Pearson.

Berman, C. (1980). *Making it as a step parent: New roles new rules*. Garden City, NY: Doubleday.

Biblarz, T. & Stacey, J. (2010). How does the gender of parents matter? *Journal of Marriage and Family, 72*(1), 3–22. doi 10.1111/j/1741-3737.2009.00678.x

Brabender, V. M., & Fallon, A. E. (Eds.). (2015). *Working with adoptive parents: Research, theory, and therapeutic interventions*. Hoboken, NJ: Wiley.

Bratter, J. L., Damaske, S., & Frech, A. (2017). Single mother families and employment, race, and poverty in changing economic times. *Social Science Research, 62*, 120–133.

Brodzinsky, D. (2011). Children's understanding of adoption: Developmental and clinical implications. *Professional Psychology: Research and Practice, 42*(2), 200–207. doi:10.1037 a0022415

Child Welfare Information Gateway. (2011). Working with lesbian, gay, bisexual, and transgender (LGBT) families in adoption. Retrieved from http://www.centerforchildwelfare.org/kb/AdoptPub/HelpingLGBTAdoptCWIG2011.pdf

Conger, R., Neppl, T., & Schofield, T. (2014). Positive parenting, beliefs about parental efficacy and active coping: Three sources of intergenerational resilience. *Journal of Family Psychology, 28*(6), 973–978.

Coontz, S. (2016). *The way we never were: American families and the nostalgia trap.* Philadelphia: Basic Books.

Dancy, B., Julion, W., Sumo, J., & Wilbur, J. (2015). Rationales for support that African American grandmothers provide to their children who are parenting adolescents. *Journal of School Nursing, 31*(6), 441–449.

Darrah, J., & DeLuca, S. (2014). "Living here has changed my whole perspective": How escaping inner-city poverty shapes neighborhood and housing choice. *Journal of Policy Analysis and Management, 33*(2), 350–384.

Deal, R. (2014a). Marriage, family, and stepfamily statistics. Retrieved from http://www .smartstepfamilies.com/view/statistics

Deal, R. L. (2014b). *The smart stepfamily: Seven steps to a healthy family.* Bloomington, MN: Bethany House.

DiFonzo, H. (2014). From the rule of one to shared parenting: Custody presumptions in law and policy. *Family Court Review, 52*(2), 213–239.

Erich, S., Leung, P., Kindle, P. & Carter, S. (2005). Gay and lesbian adoptive families: An exploratory study of family functioning, adoptive child's behavior, and familial support networks. *Journal of Family Social Work, 9*(1), 17–32.

Fremstad, S., & Boteach, M. (2015). *Valuing all our families: Progressive policies that strengthen family commitments and reduce family disparities.* Washington, DC: Center for American Progress Retrieved from https://cdn.americanprogress.org/wp-content/uploads/2015/01/FamilyStructure-report.pdf

Frias-Navarro, D., Monterde-i-Bort, H., Pascual-Soler, M., & Badenes-Ribera, L. (2015). Etiology of sexuality and attitudes towards same sex parenting: A randomized study. *Journal of Sex Research, 52*(2), 151–161. doi:10.1080/00224499.2013.802757

Fry, R. & Passel, J. (2014). In post recession era, young adults drive continuing rise in multigenerational living. Retrieved from http://www.pewsocialtrends.org/files/2014/07/ST-2014-07-17-multigen-households-report.pdf.

Gladding, S. (2015*). Family Therapy: History, Theory and Practice* (6th Ed.). Upper Saddle River, New Jersey: Pearson.

Goldberg, A. E. (2009). *Lesbian and gay parents and their children: Research on the family life cycle.* Washington, DC: American Psychological Association.

Gungor, D., & Perdu, N. (2017). Resilience and acculturative pathways underlying psychological well-being of immigrant youth. *International Journal of Intercultural Relations, 56*, 1–12.

Han, L., Berry, J. W., Zheng, Y. (2016). The relationship of acculturation strategies to resilience: The moderating impact of social support among Qiang ethnicity following the 2008 Chinese earthquake. *PLoS ONE, 11*(10), e0164484. Retrieved from https://doi.org/10.1371/journal.pone.0164484

Haskins, R. (2015). The family is here to stay—or not. *Future of Children, 25*(2), 129–153.

Hurwitz, J. (1997). *Coping in a blended family.* New York: Rosen.

International Association of Marriage and Family Counselors. (2017). *IAMFC code of ethics.* Alexandria, VA: Author.

Jappens, M., & Van Bavel, J. (2016). Parental divorce, residence arrangements, and conflict between grandchildren and grandparents. *Journal of Marriage and Family, 78*(2), 451–467. doi:10.1111/jomf.12275

Juffer, F., Reinoso, M., & Tieman, W. (2013). Children's and parents' thoughts and feelings about adoption, birth culture identity and discrimination in families with internationally adopted children. *Child and Family Social Work, 18*, 264–274.

Kalus, A. (2014). Methodological findings on adoptive families. *Archives of Psychiatry and Psychotherapy(3).* 19–23.

LaSala, M. C. (2013). Out of the darkness: Three waves of family research and the emergence of family therapy for lesbian and gay people. *Clinical Social Work Journal, 41*, 267–276. doi:10.1007/s10615-012-0434-x

LaSala, M. C., & Frierson, D. (2012). African American gay youth and their families: Redefining masculinity, coping with racism and homophobia. *Journal of GLBT Family Studies, 8*, 428–445.

Lazarevic, V. (2017). Effects of cultural brokering on individual wellbeing and family dynamics among immigrant youth. *Journal of Adolescence, 55*, 77–87.

Lofquist, D. (2013). Multigenerational households. Paper based on roundtable presentation at the annual meeting of the American Sociological Association, New York.

Luecken, L., & Roubinov, D. (2013). Pathways to lifespan health following childhood parental death. *Social and Personality Psychology Compass, 6*(3), 243–257. doi:10.1111/j.1751-9004.2011.00422.x

Manning, W. (2015, June 2). Remarriage in the United States: If at first they don't succeed, do most Americans "try, try again?" Briefing paper prepared for the Council on Contemporary Families, Austin, TX. Retrieved from https://contemporaryfamilies.org/remarriage-brief-report

Martin-Uzzi, M., & Duval-Tsioles, D. (2013). The experience of remarried couples in blended families. *Journal of Divorce and Remarriage, 54*(1), 43–57. doi:10.1080/10502556.2012.743828

Massey, S., Merriweather, A., & Garcia, J. (2013). Modern prejudice and same sex parenting: Shifting judgements in positive and negative parenting situations. *Journal of GLBT Family Studies, 9*(2), 129–151. doi:10.1080/1550428X.2013.765257

Milstead, K., Perkins, Gerra. (2010). Family Structure Characteristics and academic success: Supporting the work of school counselors. *Academic Leadership Online Journal 8*(4).

Moleiro, C., & Pinto, N. (2015). Sexual orientation and gender identity: Review of concepts, controversies and their relation to psychopathology classification systems. *Frontiers in Psychology, 6*, 1511. Retrieved from https://www.ncbi.nlm.nih.gov/pmc/articles/PMC4589638

Nhan, D. (n.d.). Same-sex parents: U.S. demographic snapshot. Retrieved from http://www.nationaljournal.com/thenextamerica/statistics/same-sex-parents-u-s-demographic-snapshot-20120618

Nichols, M. P. (2013). *Family therapy: Concepts and methods* (10th ed.). New York: Pearson.

Palacios, J., & Brodzinsky, D. (2010). Adoption trends, topics, outcomes. *International Journal of Behavioral Development, 34*(3), 270–284.

Prosen, S., & Farmer, J. (1982). Understanding step-families: Issues and implications for therapists. *Personnel and Guidance Journal, 60*(7), 393–397.

Purswell, K., & Taylor, D. (2013). Creative use of sibling play therapy: An example of a blended family. *Journal of Creativity in Mental Health, 8*, 162–174.

Rosenfield, M. (2010). Nontraditional families and childhood progress through school. *Demography, 47*(3), 755–775.

Sawhill, I. (2015). Purposeful parenthood: Better planning benefits new parents and their children. *Education Next, 15*(2), 51–55.

Steigerwald, F., & Janson, G. R. (2003). Family counseling and ethical challenges with gay, lesbian, bisexual, and trangendered clients: More questions than answers. *The Family Journal, 10*, 415–418. doi 10.1177/106648002236761

Sun, R. (2016). Intergenerational age gaps and a family member's well-being: A family systems approach. *Journal of Intergenerational Relationships, 14*(4), 320–337.

US Census Bureau. (2011). American Community Survey briefs: Same-sex couple households. Retrieved from http://www.census.gov/prod/2011pubs/acsbr10-03.pdf

US Census Bureau. (2016). Current population survey annual social and economic supplement. Retrieved from https://www.census.gov/newsroom/press-releases/2016/cb16-192.html

Webb, S., & Chonody, J. (2014). Heterosexual attitudes towards same sex marriage: The influence of attitudes towards same sex parenting. *Journal of GLBT Family Studies, 10*(4), 404–421. doi:10.1080/1550428X.2013.832644

Zeleznikow, L., & Zeleznikow, J. (2015). Supporting blended families to remain intact: A case study. *Journal of Divorce and Remarriage, 56*(4), 317–335. doi:10.1080/10502556.2015.1025845

CHAPTER 19

Influences of Parental Functioning on the Family

Mary G. Mayorga, Elizabeth Ann Wardle, Cassandra Riedy, Kathryn Helmers, and Janet Froeschle Hicks

> *"The path of development is a journey of discovery that is clear only in retrospect, and it's rarely a straight line."*
>
> —Ellen Kennedy Moore

The family can be the greatest source of strength or the weakest. This is determined by the unity of the family and its members. Will they band together during a crisis or disintegrate during troubled times? Children and adolescents are aware when there is a crisis occurring within a family system. Parents and relatives who rally together and support each other during crises need to be aware that children and adolescents are observing everything. Adolescents may see themselves as having the ability to understand what is going on yet will feel left out when parents choose to not include them in conversations about the family crisis or conflict. This can easily lead to feelings of anger and frustration for children and adolescents, and it may even impact their social and school life. Embracing them into the fold during these times and allowing them to be part of the process will make a positive impact on their developmental process.

As family therapists, it is important to help families who are in crisis or conflict embrace this idea of child/adolescent "inclusion" when attending therapy sessions, making decisions, and resolving crises and conflicts (WebMD, 2015). This is true regardless of family structure, as we discussed in detail in Chapter 18, or when confronted with a variety of issues, such as parental physical or mental illness, addictions, divorce, and even managing the aftermath of abuse. Most parents' or parental figures' first thought is to "protect the children" from problems, yet shutting out children and adolescents may do the opposite and enhance youths' levels of anxiety. As we will discuss in this chapter, family therapists can teach families how to communicate with their children and/or adolescents in a gentle, realistic manner and can help family functioning improve during times of crises.

LEARNING OBJECTIVES

After reading this chapter, you will be able to do the following:

- Understand the nature of parental health within the family structure.
- Explain the impact of parental health on children and adolescents and their developmental process.
- Describe perspectives of parental health from a child's or adolescent's perspective.
- Understand the models of addiction and its impact on family dynamics.
- Explain the impact of family violence on the family structure.

PARENTAL HEALTH

Mental Health

Mental health and mental illness have increasingly been used as if they mean the same thing, but they do not (Earley, 2014). All people have mental health, but not all people have mental illness. During a person's lifetime, not everyone experiences mental illness, but everyone struggles or has challenges with their mental well-being. Mental health has been defined as the absence of psychopathologies, such as depression and anxiety (Trompetter et al., 2016).

Parental health includes mental health, and parents who are experiencing mental health wellness have ability to understand how they feel about themselves, how they feel about their work, and are better able to manage their own personal life (Prinz, 2013). They also have ability to solve problems, overcome challenges, build relationships with others, contribute to their community, and can achieve their own goals (National Alliance on Mental Illness [NAMI], 2015). These abilities are a positive influence on the family (Kaneez, 2015).

On the other hand, mental health illness interferes with a parent's cognitive, emotional, or social abilities (Komarek & Schroer, 2014; Van Loon, Van Ven, Van Doesum, Witteman, & Hosman, 2013). These inabilities interfere with the parent's ability to relate to each member of the family, including children and adolescents. The parent's ability to function daily becomes a difficult occurrence and can be an emotionally charged experienced for everyone (George, 2013; Wiener, Battles, & Heilman, 1998). Considerable evidence exists supporting that children in families with mental health issues are at heightened risk for many adverse outcomes, including multiple psychosocial problems (Beardslee, Keller, Seifer, & Lavori, 1996; Chen, 2014; George, 2013).

The term *mental illness* has been used as a broad term to refer to difficulties that interfere with a person's daily functioning (NAMI, 2017). These issues range from mental health problems to more severe mental disorders. When the person with the mental health issue is a parental figure, consequences may occur for all members in the family system. These consequences may include lack of bonding between the parent and other family members, increased levels of anxiety and depression for all family members, and psychosocial and behavioral problems, such as delinquency for the child and/or adolescent (Chen, 2014; Pedersen, 1994). A parent's untreated mental illness, such as depression, will result in the child suffering. A study conducted by the Drexel University School of Public Health looked at more than 1 million Swedish students from 1984 to 1994 and compared their grades with the state of their parents' mental health (Schlozman, 2016). The findings inferred that children whose parents were depressed received lowered academic grades during the period of their parent's illness.

Influence on Development

Parental health influences the well-being of children and adolescents (George, 2013). Parents who have mental health issues may maintain a poor relationship with their children resulting in the development of psychosocial problems (Chen, 2014; George, 2013; Pedersen, 1994). It is noted that adolescence is a critical stage that is marked by significant mental, physical, and psychological changes (Kaneez, 2015). Family dynamics and interaction patterns serve in important contexts as children try to discover their own personal self and establish themselves as individuals. Parental health can positively or negatively affect an adolescent's sense of psychological well-being, especially self-esteem, self-evaluation, and peer relationships (Cripps & Zyromski, 2009; George, 2013). A family's healthy functioning patterns enhance the mental health of family members, including children and adolescents. Adolescents and children determine their personal self-worth, self-efficacy, and self-esteem based on the level of parental involvement. When a parent is experiencing mental health issues, levels of parental involvement may drop, putting the children at risk for poor psychological development resulting in psychological health symptoms (George, 2013; Seiffge-Krenke, 1995).

Family environment acts as a protective or risk factor for children's cognitive, social, and psychological development (Centers for Disease Control and Prevention [CDC], 2016). Adolescents and children who come from homes characterized by warmth, caring, communication, understanding, and support develop less psychological health symptoms. Children and adolescents thrive in stable and nurturing environments where they have a routine and know what to expect (Sandstrom & Huerta, 2013). Parental mental illness creates a disruption in the family domain, which triggers disruption among other domains. For example, behaviors in the school environment or social environment may result in a stressors leading to deviant behaviors (Ojukwu, & Chigozirim, 2015). Guided

Practice Exercise 19.1 asks you to consider how therapists might help parents achieve a balanced home environment.

GUIDED PRACTICE EXERCISE 19.1

Warm, structured, nurturing, and organized home environments tend to foster better mental health and adjustment for children. The word *organized* is often misinterpreted. What is meant by this term? How much organization is good and how much is too much? How does a therapist help parents find the optimal amount of organization?

Child and Adolescent Perspective

Mental illness of a parent can have a significant impact on children and adolescents (Chen, 2014; Flamez & Sheperis, 2015). For example, the role the child or adolescent takes on in the family structure is affected by the parent's illness, which often poses great challenges and monumental tasks for children (Chen, 2014; Ross, 1990). This unbalanced role formation may even increase the risk of the child or adolescent developing their own mental illness. Many challenges face the children or adolescents during this stressful time, including taking on inappropriate levels of responsibility in caring for themselves and managing the household. The child or adolescent may also experience embarrassment or shame because of the stigma associated with mental illness (APA, 2017a). This may lead to social isolation from peer and community support systems, along with the risk of not getting emotional and physical needs met.

Alongside these issues, the child or adolescent will also develop a point of view or perspective regarding handling the parent's mental illness. Although some parents with mental illness may try to protect their children, inadvertently the child or adolescent may end up unable to manage the stress and have difficulty focusing on academic achievement (Royal College of Psychiatrists, 2017). In these situations, many children may perceive that somehow, they are responsible for what is occurring to their parent. This thought pattern may influence their behavior at home and at school and lead to the child or adolescent experiencing feelings of depression or anxiety (Royal College of Psychiatrists, 2014).

Environmental and Hereditary Influences

The effect of having a mentally ill parental figure impacts the family in several ways (Doidge, Higgins, Delfabbro, & Segal, 2017; Murphy, Peters, Wilkes, & Jackson, 2017). It is recognized that mental disorders affect not only the individual but those around him or her. If there is a history of mental illness in the family of either parent, the possibility of experiencing a mental health illness episode increases within that family structure (American Academy of Child & Adolescent Psychiatry, 2015). This is due to both heredity and family environment.

How does the family environment influence parental mental health? Families faced with social and economic hardships and instability may have a hard time establishing a family environment that positively impacts family members, including children and adolescents. These hardships can increase family conflict and create a hostile environment for family members (Doidge et al., 2017). Factors such as unemployment, lack of extended family support, and financial issues related to costly medical treatments may make it difficult to maintain physical, psychological and emotional wellness (Chen, 2014). Children and adolescents may be at risk for child abuse or mistreatment (Higgins, Delfabro, & Segal, 2017). Families who grapple with an unhealthy environmental experience may find themselves dealing with physical disease, poor personal satisfaction of life, less social involvement, and lack of purpose (Work Group for Community Health and Development, 2016).

Families whose environmental experience includes physical, psychological and emotional wellness may have a lower incidence of experiencing mental issues and have better outcomes (Chen, 2014; Westerhof & Keyes, 2010). These consequences include a more positive level of self-acceptance; establishing goals, beliefs, and a sense of direction and purpose in life; improved academic achievement; and the ability to be autonomous (Chen, 2014; Ryff & Keyes, 1995). Case Presentation 19.1 demonstrates a family session in which stress is impacting the family environment.

CASE PRESENTATION 19.1: THE CASE OF SHEILA AND GRAYSON

Sheila and her son Grayson are in their second session with you in family therapy. It becomes clear they are experiencing stress that is negatively impacting their family environment. Grayson, a 13-year-old adolescent, states that his mother is "trying to run his life" and "won't let him even think." It seems that Sheila comes home after a stressful day at work and vents her frustrations as soon as she enters the home. She says she doesn't want to do this but doesn't know how else to cope with the stress. What can a family therapist do to improve the environment and reduce stress levels?

As discussed in Chapter 6, the therapist first conducted several assessments, including a specific assessment for anxiety. Finding Sheila to be absent major anxiety, the therapist decided to evaluate family environmental severity using the observational assessments as discussed in Chapter 8. After assessments were completed, the therapist decided Sheila's stress was impacting the family environment. The therapist offered the family stress management and muscle relaxation techniques as part of family therapy during the following session. Following is a synopsis of this session.

Sheila and Grayson brought pillows and blankets to the session and lay on the floor in a comfortable position. The therapist dimmed the lights and made calming statements, such as "Take a deep breath in through your nose and as you exhale mentally state, I am relaxed. Your head is feeling very heavy and warm. You can visualize all the tension in your head flowing down out of your body. You are becoming just as relaxed as you wish to be." The therapist mentioned each body part one at a time from head to toe until all parts of the body were relaxed. Sheila and Grayson continued to breathe deeply and mentally stated, "I am relaxed," as coached throughout the process. Once a full state of relaxation was achieved, the therapist brought the family back to an alert state by counting backward from 10 to 1. Sheila and Grayson slowly opened their eyes and sat up. At this point the therapist asked the family to process current feelings, their state of relaxation, and feeling toward one another. Tips were then given to the family to practice these techniques at home. After several weeks of practicing these techniques as family homework, Sheila and Grayson reported an improved home environment and lowered stress levels.

Medical Diagnosis, Disease, and Disability

When a parent receives a medical diagnosis, the effect is felt among all family members. The medical diagnosis can be one that leads to either a temporary or permanent disability or it may be chronic, sudden, or life-threatening. Any life-threatening illness can instill a fear of being a burden on family. This burden can have an emotional, physical, social and financial impact (Chen, 2014).

Children whose parent is coping with a medical diagnosis, chronic disease, or disability may find themselves struggling to manage. They must maintain a sense of balance in continuing their normal daily routine while also acknowledging the possibility of losing a parent forever (Chen, 2014). There may be a radical change in a child's or adolescent's behavior after a parent's disclosure of his or her diagnosis. The behavior may involve sleeping problems, wetting the bed, or acting younger than their chronological age (Schoenfeld, 2015).

Parents with chronic illness can detrimentally affect that parent's ability to adequately respond to a child or adolescent's needs due to fatigue, pain management issues, or the progression of the condition. It is important to remember that children and adolescents of parents with either a chronic, sudden or life-threatening disease may experience any of the following emotional reactions during this trying time, such as annoyance, confusion, fear, distress, and fear of losing the parent, resentment, anger, and depression (Schoenfeld, 2015). One way of managing the emotional roller coaster the family is experiencing is to engage in a family meeting (Dinkmeyer, 2017). Family meetings are invaluable in that they offer family members the opportunity to enhance communication, enhance family inclusion, share information, and help negotiate decisions.

Unfortunately, illness often results in death and can have a lifelong psychological effect on youth (Akerman & Statham, 2014). There can be a wide range of emotional and behavioral responses to grief, which may include anxiety, depressive symptoms, fears, angry outbursts, and regression regarding developmental milestones (Akerman & Statham, 2014). Although many children and adolescents have a good support system after the loss of a parent, others that may lack the needed support and may make them more vulnerable for psychological issues. Case Presentation 19.2 demonstrates a case involving a parent's medical illness and its impact on a child.

CASE PRESENTATION 19.2: THE CASE OF TREVOR, LINDA, FRAN, AND TRUDY

Trevor, Linda, and their daughter Trudy arrive at your office in tears. Linda has been diagnosed with terminal cancer and the family is unsure how to handle the emotions. Trudy, their 8-year-old daughter, says she is afraid her mom will die, so she has started having problems in school and refuses to talk to her mother for fear she will "get sick." Trevor says he now feels like he is parenting alone, wants Trudy to have a close relationship with Linda, and is completely overwhelmed trying to keep up at work and be a care giver and parent. How can the therapist help this family?

As discussed in Chapter 8, the therapist decided to conduct family mapping activities to not only determine family issues but to discover supportive family connections. After conducting these assessments and discussing possibilities with the family, it was decided that Sheila's mother, Trudy's grandmother, be invited to take a more active role in helping the family cope.

Trudy's grandmother, Fran, was invited to attend the next session. Fran was delighted to assist the family and moved into the spare room in the family's home. Because this transition was difficult and Trudy was still avoiding Linda, the therapist decided to train the family in filial play therapy, a family-based play therapy model. Following is a synopsis of the sessions.

First, the therapist conducted a play therapy session with Trudy as Fran, Linda, and Trevor observed. All adults were then taught specific techniques, such as tracking, reflecting, and limit setting, and asked to practice them over the next couple of weeks. On the third session, Linda conducted play therapy with Trudy as the therapist and other family members watched. After the session, the therapists offered feedback to Linda. Linda was proficient in her techniques so by the fourth session, she was conducting sessions at home and reporting to the therapist for weekly family feedback. A partial transcript of one of the family's post filial play therapy training sessions follows.

Therapist:	Linda, tell me how things are going at home.
Linda:	Trudy is now talking to me and things are better but I do have one problem.
Therapist:	Tell me about the problem.
Linda:	When I am doing the filial play therapy with Trudy, she often gets upset and throws her doll at me.
Therapist (to Trudy):	Tell me about throwing the doll.
Trudy:	I just wanted to throw the doll because it felt good.
Therapist:	I bet the doll wants to say something about being afraid your mom is sick but she doesn't know how.
Linda:	Oh! I get it. She is using the doll to express how she is feeling.
Trudy (starts to cry):	I don't like you being sick.
Therapist (to Trudy):	The doll loves her mom.
	(Trudy hugs her mom as though she has finally been understood.)
Trevor:	Wow! I just thought Trudy was misbehaving but I think things are clear now.
Fran:	I am so happy right now. It just broke my heart to see Trudy and Linda so distant. They need each other.

At the end of the session, the therapist also reviewed setting limits with Linda so she knew how to respond should Trudy later throw something that might be harmful. The family continued filial sessions for several weeks. Fortunately, Linda found her cancer was in remission and was soon on the mend.

PARENTAL ADDICTION

Overall Impact

In the United States, an estimated 12% of children live with a least one parent that is dependent on alcohol or drugs and not receiving the appropriate treatment (Brooks & McHenry, 2015; Van Wormer & Davis, 2017. Families witness more preventable deaths, illnesses and disabilities due to substance abuse than any other cause (Gladding, 2015). Substance use invites physical illness and disabilities through biological effects on the abuser, direct effects on the abuser's family members, and the indirect toll of a life habituated to stress and dysfunction. Substance use is also responsible for approximately half of the federal incarcerations that lead to the physical separation of parents from their children (Sentencing Project, 2017).

Along with the physical impact of addiction, parental alcohol or drug dependency presents severe challenges to families' mental health. As an addiction forms, the most intimate relationship in an addict's life becomes the one shared with a substance, and all other relationships become secondary. The children of addicted parents are four times more likely to be physically abused and suffer neglect, which can lead to persistent, deep-seated struggles for mental health (Brooks & McHenry, 2015). Without effective parental bonding, children miss out on one of the most protective factors against developing their own addictive behaviors (Kalaitzaki & Birtchnell, 2014; Lake et al., 2015). The lack of a primary relationship with an addicted parent exposes children to greater risk for emotional, psychological, and social problems, such as difficulty forming intimate relationships, depression and anxiety, and antisocial behavior such as aggressiveness (Brooks & McHenry, 2015; Gladding, 2015).

Parental addiction's effects run deeper and are more complicated than perceived physical and mental health problems. Addiction restructures the family, its members' identities, and all members' interactions (Van Wormer & Davis, 2016). Often, addiction is not the presenting problem because a family has found homeostasis, having self-regulated to maintain balance despite the dysfunction an addiction causes (Brooks & McHenry, 2015). The family expends its energy maintaining as much stability and predictability as possible, rendering itself rigid and blind to the novel changes that could more aptly address the addiction (Reiter, 2014). An addict's recovery is undermined if his or her family does not receive treatment due to the family's contributions to the development and maintenance of addiction. (Gladding, 2015; Miller, 2014).

Models of Addiction

Models of addiction define addiction and serve as a lens through which to conceptualize the cause, development, maintenance, and treatment of addiction. In doing so, they provide a foundation from which a therapist bases his or her assessment, techniques, and treatment. Models range in their attribution of responsibility for an addiction and apply a wide array of labels to the nature of addiction, such as biological, psychological, social, and spiritual, or an integration of many factors. For example, 12-step programs function based on a spiritual disease model, where biological determinants lead powerless individuals to the need for a spiritual awakening (Thombs & Osborn, 2013).

Disease model. The biological etiology of the disease model attributes a chronic, progressive condition of addiction to a taxonomy of clinically identifiable symptoms to physiological aberrations (Szott, 2015). Medical research focuses on susceptibility, the role of genes, and exposure, the role of chemical alterations of the brain, to shed further light on biological causal mechanisms leading to the contraction of addiction (National Council on Alcoholism and Drug Dependence [NCADD], 2015; Thombs & Osborn, 2013). The disease model removes the onus for addiction from the individual, conceptualizing him or her as "sick" rather than "willfully deviant" (Miller, 2014).

Often in family therapy, the presenting problem is not the addiction, and it takes a nonjudgmental, empathetic environment to invite disclosure of an addiction. Framing addiction as a disease serves to reduce stigma and, therefore, increase help-seeking behavior (Szott, 2015). The concept of disease is relatively simple and familiar, readily lending itself to family education (Thombs & Osborn, 2013). Extending the disease model to the metaphor of a "family disease" has proved extremely fruitful in therapy sessions, research and scholarly publications addressing parental addiction (Thombs & Osborn, 2013). The concept of "family disease" highlights important aspects of addiction, such as all family members displaying symptoms, in a nonblaming manner (Klostermann & O'Farrell, 2013).

Cognitive–social learning model. According to the cognitive–social learning model, addiction is a learned, maladaptive behavior that arises from reciprocal relationships between an actions, thoughts, and environment (West & Brown, 2014). The individual is neither wholly responsible nor completely at the mercy of mechanisms beyond their control in the forming and maintenance of addiction (NCADD, 2015; Thombs & Osborn, 2013). The nature of addiction is psychosocial in that the internal forces of thinking and learning interact with external forces such as family, society, and culture to produce behavior (Miller, 2014).

Addiction is developed and maintained by an individual's beliefs and perceived reinforcements. Advocates of the cognitive–social learning model typically use cognitive-behavioral therapy to promote self-awareness and self-control regarding the thoughts and adaptive learning regulating behavior (Thombs & Osborn, 2013). Some cognitive behavioral methods treat addiction as a maladaptive coping mechanism, a form of self-medication for emotional, psychological, or social problems, by directly challenging the addiction's efficacy in promoting adaptive, productive coping skills (West & Brown, 2014).

The cognitive–social learning model sheds light onto the significant, formative impact of the lessons an individual learns from his or her family, whether directly or indirectly through modeling and vicarious learning. It provides a lens through which family members can identify and attempt to correct their beliefs and behaviors that serve as reinforcements for another's addiction and could inhibit recovery (Lamb, Maguire, Ginsburg, Pinkston, & France, 2016). As well, it can emphasize to each family member the importance of social modeling and its influence on learned addiction. Studies have demonstrated that modeling can instigate substance use and greatly impacts the amount of a substance consumed (Thombs & Osborn, 2013). The most successful application of this model has been in relapse prevention. Studies have shown that self-efficacy expectancies, an individual's beliefs about his or her ability to succeed, are a crucial component to avoiding relapse (Nikmanesh, Baluchi, & Motlagh, 2016). Both positive family rhetoric around an individual's ability to succeed as well as vowed familial support can be huge factors in engendering high self-efficacy.

Family systems model. The family systems model views addiction as an adaptation that serves a purpose as the family system confronts the challenges and complexities of life (Thombs & Osborn, 2013). Addiction is a family's coping mechanism, and the addict bears symptoms on the family's behalf to maintain homeostasis (Reiter, 2014). The family system, itself, is, in large part, responsible for the addiction's development and maintenance. Addiction is by nature a social problem, enacted and perpetuated by the reciprocal interactions of social beings, not distinct biological or psychological entities (Miller, 2014).

The family system maintains an addiction as it becomes the fundamental principle dictating family organization and structure (Reiter, 2014). As family members fill roles to ensure the system's homeostasis, the addiction infiltrates individuals' beliefs, interactional patterns, routines and rituals (Walrond-Skinner, 2013). Treatment based on the family systems model uses the family, not the addiction, as its starting point. The organization of interconnected relationship is the primary focus, the addiction secondary (Thombs & Osborn, 2013). Treatment addresses and leverages circular causality, the concept that one family member's change will precipitate changes in the rest of the family's members, inherit in a family system and the self-regulating nature of the family system (Wetchler & Hecker, 2014). Therapy based on family systems focuses on appropriate boundaries to enable individual members the flexibility and the ability to innovate in coping (Thombs & Osborn, 2013).

The family systems model is emphatic about the necessity of family involvement in successful recovery and invites therapists to use the lens of an overarching system of interconnected relationships within a family rather than focus on individuals separately. In doing so, it sheds light on the concept of systemic homeostasis, circular causality, and how family members act and assume roles on behalf of overall balance (Thombs & Obsorn, 2013). It introduces the concepts of role rigidity and inappropriate boundaries enabling addiction and the need for family members to assume new roles and responsibilities for recovery to occur (Walrond-Skinner, 2013).

Family Roles

Addiction threatens the balance of a family, and members respond with various coping mechanisms. With time, their responses can become rigidly ingrained in the fabric of the family's interactions as the whole family seeks to find stability and predictability in the face of chronic stress (Reiter, 2014). Sharon Wegscheider-Cruse, a student and coworker of Virginia Satir, gave names to the roles she observed family members fulfilling based on their habituated coping mechanisms: chief enabler, family hero, scapegoat, lost child, and mascot (Brooks & McHenry, 2015).

Chief enabler. The chief enabler copes by working diligently to mitigate the consequences of the addiction, assuming responsibilities, trying to be in control and establish order, and shielding the addict from the full weight of his or her actions (Van Wormer & Davis, 2016). The chief enabler may take pride in having the most intimate relationship with the addict but also can experience a sense of martyrdom and even develop physical illness from over functioning (Reiter, 2014).

Family hero. The family hero copes by overachieving, believing that he or she is responsible for the family's self-worth and trying to elevate the family with his or her successes (Brooks & McHenry, 2015). The hero tends to be the oldest child who sometimes is "parentified" and plays the role of chief enabler (Reiter, 2014). He or she may eventually develop into a workaholic or have trouble forming relationships due to a need to control others (Reiter, 2014).

Scapegoat. The scapegoat copes by diverting energy and attention from the addiction through negatively perceived actions, often presenting as the family problem and enabling continued familial denial regarding the addiction (Miller, 2014). The scapegoat tends to be the second child and feels unable to live up to the hero's accomplishments (Brooks & McHenry, 2015). Often, the scapegoat has difficulty forming intimate relationships due to an impulse to create conflict or chaos (Reiter, 2014).

Lost child. The lost child copes by evading the family situation, deflecting attention from him- or herself, and retreating inward (Reiter, 2014). Marked by shyness and amenability, the lost child does not assert him- or herself in a relationship and may keep talents hidden so as not to stand out (Reiter, 2014).

Mascot. The mascot copes by making light of serious situations. He or she keeps stress at a distance through humor and distracts the family in efforts to keep everyone happy (Miller, 2014). Other family members may be inclined to protect the mascot as they view him or her as fragile (Reiter, 2014). Mascot's may maintain immaturity beyond when appropriate and lack important problem-solving skills (Reiter, 2014).

Family Rules

As you learned in Chapters 1 and 11, the concepts of family rules and roles has roots in structural family therapy (SFT), pioneered by Salvador Minuchin (Minuchin, Lee, & Simon, 1996). The family system adopts rules that dictate the role and function of each family member, and, in doing so, the system can find balance despite dysfunction (Brooks & McHenry, 2015). Each member can anticipate the behaviors of others, feeling a sense of security in knowing his or her place and continued loyalty to the system by playing his or her role (Brooks & McHenry, 2015).

Steinglass, Bennett, Wolin, and Reiss (1987) described families struggling with alcoholism as systems in which the entire family reconfigures itself according to the addiction of one member, so that addiction is both the major theme as well as the shared condition of the entire family. To maintain the homeostasis of this addictive environment, the family develops ways of functioning in both their internal relationships with each other as well as in their external relationships with the outside world. The term *family rules* describes these repetitive ways in which the alcoholic family functions (Ford & Herrick, 1974).

Such family rules are inferred means of reinforcing the deeply ingrained behaviors of family members as they maintain their coping-induced roles within the system. Because the rules are not codified and communicated overtly except in their application, family members become aware of them only when they break them via the swift and certain—sometimes escalating to violent—consequences meted out by other family members who perceive such transgression as betrayal that cannot be tolerated for the survival of the family system. The covert existence of the rules ensures their repetitive reinforcement. Steinglass et al. (1987) observed that family rules emphasize "the binding rather than the organizing nature of belief systems" (p. 59). Thus, a closed system feels confusing and chaotic when closure is repeatedly reinforced with unhealthy patterns of relationship.

The presence of family rules pervades all aspects of family identity and function, from abstract philosophical concepts such as what "family" means to expectations for routine details of everyday life. Ford and Herrick (1974) identified five key characteristics of family rules: (a) *unwritten law*—which loses its power when written down or made explicit; (b) *inferences* from repeated behavior; (c) having the dimension of *repetition and redundancy over time*; (d) having the *attributes of systems*, which develop complexity such as rules about the rules; and (e) having *autonomy*, or taking on a self-perpetuating life of their own. They distinguish between "large" rules governing a family's distinctive lifestyle and "small rules" that carry out that lifestyle. Recurring "small rules" across the five major family lifestyles they identified include:

- Don't say what you think or feel.
- Don't listen to what anyone says.
- Don't say what you want or even admit that you want anything.
- Do "the right thing" instead of making your own choices.
- Don't get your hopes up.
- Don't make sense of what's going on.
- Don't make somebody else the bad guy (you're probably to blame).
- Don't point out differences or differentness.

A key therapeutic implication for family rules is the reality that simply by making these rules explicit and commenting on them, the therapist breaks them. This breaking of the rules—i.e., the rules can be surfaced and talked about—is called a counter-rule, which opens an interventional wedge of change into the family system. Colapinto (1982) described the therapeutic solution for enmeshed families as the modification of the family structure governing their homeostasis. When a therapist intervenes with a counter-rule, the resulting disturbance can provide a springboard of conflict and ambivalence, a ripe setting for intervention and change. This context is 'the "therapeutic system which offers a unique chance to challenge the rules of the family" (p. 8).

The therapist's role in challenging family rules introduces a paradox:

> *The therapist is asked to support while challenging, to attack while encouraging, to sustain while undermining. A crucial conceptual distinction is necessary here to protect the therapist from confusion or hypocrisy: he [sic] is requested to be for the people in need of help, against the system of transactions that cripple them. (Colapinto, 1982, p. 11)*

Miller and Rollnick (1991) pioneered the treatment modality known as *motivational interviewing* (MI) as a way of being with clients rather than the application of a set of techniques. Here the therapist's role is in part directive, focused on evoking self-motivational statements and enhancing family member's motivation for positive change (Davidson, 1994). The nature of the collaborative partnership between therapist and client is Rogerian in its person-centered roots: the environment best suited to this method requires empathy, unconditional acceptance, an optimistic regard for the client's ability to problem solve and work toward change, and the therapist's respect for the client's autonomy in choosing to move toward growth and actualization. The idea is to create a climate in which clients choose to make healthy changes on their own and without external rewards.

Motivational Interviewing Techniques for Effectuating Change

Steinglass (2009) documented the early success of MI in catching on quickly as a substance abuse treatment with individuals, arguing that although its primary use was initially viewed as applicable for work with individuals, it may be equally effective when used with families. His research documented the effectiveness of *systemic-motivational therapy*—a combination of family systems therapy combined with techniques from MI.

Miller and Rollnick (2002) defined MI as being a directive and person-centered approach used to overcome client ambivalence. Four methods used to instill change are: express empathy, develop discrepancy, roll with resistance, and support self-efficacy. Combining these techniques with the need to overcome ambivalence and motivate change results in family interventions as follows:

1. Increase intrinsic motivation. Clients are assumed to be competent and to have inherent resources needed to create change. The therapist's role is to influence the client such that motivation evolves. Clients are not manipulated, rather, therapists use techniques and skills to help clients overcome ambivalence.

The process of building on personal motivation may require different amounts of time, depending on where clients are in their relationship to change: not having thought about it, or having been forced into counseling under threat of consequences; ambivalent about change, not sure yet whether they are ready to act; or ready to change, desiring guidance and confirmation for their choices.

2. Express empathy. Carl Rogers's (1977) emphasis on "accurate empathy" is the foundation of the therapist's role in MI. Unconditional acceptance is neither agreement nor approval. It is reflective listening to and understanding of clients' feelings and perspectives without judgment or criticism. A therapist may even disagree or challenge clients' thinking without violating this principle of unconditional acceptance.

Miller and Rollnick (2002) described why empathy is so crucial to the change process:

> *Paradoxically, this kind of acceptance of people as they are seems to free them to change, whereas insistent non-acceptance ("You're not OK; you have to be different") tends to immobilize the change process. Family therapists call this sort of phenomenon "ironic process," because as in Greek tragedy, the action causes the very outcome that it was meant to avert. Happily, self-fulfilling prophecies work both ways. The attitude of acceptance and respect builds a working therapeutic alliance and supports the client's self-esteem, which further promotes change. (p. 37)*

3. Develop discrepancy. Discrepancy refers to the gap between where clients are now and where they want to be. Therapists can help make this gap explicit by asking clients to reflect on their own goals and values and how their behavior might conflict with those goals and values. They can ask clients to separate out what they do and how they behave from who they really are. They can highlight any mention that clients make of their concern over potential negative consequences.

A way to ensure that therapists refrain from inadvertently pressuring or coercing clients is to ensure that clients voice their own goals and values, not someone else's goals and values. Once clients recognize the discrepancy between where they are and where they want to be, they—not the therapist, not other family members—can give voice to reasons for and possibilities of change. The client, never the therapist, is the generator and articulator of the desire for change.

The Center for Substance Abuse Treatment (1999) cites on tactic for developing discrepancy as "the 'Columbo approach'" (Kanfer & Schefft, 1988). This approach is particularly useful with a client who prefers to be in control. Essentially, the clinician expresses understanding and continuously seeks clarification of the client's problems but appears unable to perceive any solution. A stance of uncertainty or confusion can motivate the client to take control of the situation by offering a solution to the clinician (Van Bilsen, 1991).

4. Roll with resistance. It is tempting to meet client resistance with persuasion, but Miller and Rollnick (1991) pointed out that it can lead to the opposite effect and increase rather than reduce resistance to change. Telling clients they are **in denial** or **resistant** or

addicted may make clients more likely to increase or maintain behaviors than to change. Instead, Miller and Rollnick (1991) state therapists should change thought patterns, avoid labels, and stay in the client's frame of reference.

Thus, the term "roll" with resistance means that instead of trying to combat it, therapists use it to create momentum toward change by helping to reframe it. Clients exhibit resistance in therapy through behaviors such as arguing, interrupting, denying, or ignoring (Miller & Rollnick, 1991). Therapeutic responses to such behaviors can include such verbal techniques as simple reflection, amplified reflection, double-sided reflection, agreement with a twist, reframing, and siding with the negative (Center for Substance Abuse Treatment, 1999). If therapists find themselves arguing for change in appealing to their clients, it is a clear red flag that they are opposing, not rolling with, their clients' resistance.

5. Support self-efficacy. When clients cannot believe in themselves, therapists carry that belief for them—a hopeful, optimistic posture of "you can do this." Miller and Rollnick (2002) point out that such support can become a self-fulfilling prophecy. Once clients recognize that they want to change, therapists can help them build confidence as they take positive steps in coping with obstacles and experiencing the change that results.

Other ways that therapists can support self-efficacy is through their clients' exposure to others who have faced similar situations and succeeded in overcoming obstacles and experiencing change. This tactic can provide tested ideas as well as a hedge against clients' feeling isolated and hopeless.

Additionally, therapists can identify educational resources that will provide understanding and insight, helping clients feel empowered with information and giving them perspective on how to break down huge challenges into small, manageable steps. Guided Practice Exercise 19.2 asks you to consider how therapists integrate treatment for the individual with concurrent family therapy. Case Presentation 19.3 offers insight into a family session utilizing motivational interviewing.

GUIDED PRACTICE EXERCISE 19.2

Motivational interviewing has been touted as an efficacious method for working with individuals addicted to substances. The integration of this approach with family therapy may be especially advantageous to all members of the family. Having read the previous chapters in this text, which family therapies would best integrate with motivational interviewing? Explain your stance to others in your class.

CASE PRESENTATION 19.3: THE CASE OF MELINDA AND KERA

Melinda and her daughter have been referred to family therapy by a judge to maintain child custody. While discussing family problems, Kera, Melinda's 15-year-old daughter, states that Melinda often stays out all night and when home, Melinda is "gloomy and doesn't want to do anything."

As discussed in Chapter 6, depression and addiction often play a role in family dysfunction. The therapist decided to assess Melinda for these disorders and evaluated the family system using family sculpting as mentioned in Chapter 8. While the depression was not evident, the therapist realized the family system was suffering from role confusion and Melinda was dealing with substance abuse. Following is a partial transcript of one of Kera and Melinda's sessions.

Melinda (to therapist):	I go out with my friends and just have fun. Kera is 15, she is fine.
Therapist:	Kera, what are your thoughts about this?
Kera:	I am not fine. I want to go out with my friends too but I have to clean the house and do my homework. I just wish she would stay home and be a mom. She would rather go out drinking than be my mom though.
Melinda:	I only drink a little.
Kera:	A LITTLE! You come home drunk all the time.
	The therapist incorporates motivational interviewing techniques into the session since Melinda is abusing alcohol.
Melinda:	I don't need either of you to tell me what to do.
Therapist:	Melinda, I am not here to try and preach to you. I am here to help you make the changes you would like to make. How does that sound?
Melinda:	Ok. But I know what is best.
Therapist:	How happy are you with the way you are managing your health?

The therapist explores changes Melinda would like to make in her health as well as in her relationship with Kera. The therapist never pushes but helps Melinda explore pros and cons of her behavior while using reflections. At the end of the session, Melinda summarizes the pros and cons of her behavior. Kera is also asked to discuss her thoughts on these pros and cons. Melinda is referred to a therapist who specializes in working with addictions but continues to see the family therapist to heal her relationship with Kera.

PARENTAL BEHAVIORS

Intimate Partner Violence

In Chapter 4, we discussed intimate partner violence (IPV). Recall that according to the CDC (2015b), the term *intimate partner violence* describes physical, sexual, or psychological harm by a current or former partner or spouse. This type of violence can occur among heterosexual or same-sex couples and does not require sexual intimacy. It occurs among both heterosexual and same-sex couples and is often a repeated offense. Statistical data from the National Intimate Partner and Sexual Violence Survey (2014) showed that 1 in 4 women and 1 in 7 men have experienced some form of intimate partner violence that had a long-term impact on their life.

The definition of an intimate partner is someone in a relationship who is characterized by emotional connectedness, regular contact, ongoing physical contact and/or sexual behavior, identity as a couple or familiarity and knowledge about each other's lives (Breiding, Basile, Smith, Black, & Mahendra, 2015).

Types of Violence

According to the National Institute of Justice (U.S. Department of Justice, 2017), there are four main types of intimate partner violence:

- Physical violence—the intentional use of physical force with the potential of causing death, disability, injury or harm.
- Sexual violence, which is divided into three categories:
  - The use of physical force to compel a person to unwillingly engage in a sexual act
  - A sexual act involving a person who, because of illness, disability, or the influence of alcohol or other drugs, or because of intimidation or pressure is unable to understand, decline participation, or communicate unwillingness in a sexual act.
  - Abusive sexual contact.
- Threats of physical or sexual violence—threat of death, disability, injury, or physical harm with the use of words, gestures, or weapons.
- Psychological/emotional violence—traumatizes the victim by acts, threats, or coercive tactics, such as humiliating the victim, controlling what they can or cannot do, withholding behaviors, isolating the victim from family and friends, or denying access to money or other basic resources.

Stalking is another form of intimate partner violence (CDC, 2016) and includes harassing or threatening behavior engaged in repeatedly. It can include following, lying in wait, spying, damaging property, spreading rumors, and posting personal information on the Internet as a means of control over the victim (U.S. Department of Justice, 2016).

Impact of Exposure in Childhood

A plethora of research exists examining the effects of witnessing incidents of intimate partner violence. When the mother is struggling to survive in an abusive environment, she is may not be able to be present in her children's life. The father may be so consumed with controlling everyone, he not be able to be present for his children, either. The children in this abusive environment feel isolated and vulnerable, having been physically, emotionally and psychologically abandoned (Domestic Violence Roundtable, n.d.).

These children can experience a multitude of feelings, such as self-blame, helplessness, fear, shame, and anger. They might exhibit behavior such as poor concentration, disturbed sleep, nightmares, withdrawal, low self-esteem, and physical symptoms. The extent of the impact on children will depend on multiple factors, such as the length of time the child was exposed to the violence, the age of the child when the exposure began, and whether the child has also experienced child abuse (Domestic Violence Prevention Centre, Gold Coast, n.d.). According to the Domestic Violence Prevention Centre, Gold Coast (n.d.), "Often the behavioral and emotional impacts of domestic and family violence will improve when children and their mothers are safe, the violence is no longer occurring and they receive support and specialist counselling" (p. 2). Guided Practice Exercise 19.3 asks you to consider the therapist's role when family abuse is disclosed.

GUIDED PRACTICE EXERCISE 19.3

Family therapists often find themselves stunned as they hear of the numerous abuses suffered by family members. Using the "State Law" link found in the "Additional Resources" section below, what is the therapist's responsibility in your state for reporting various types of abuse? Discuss this with others in your class.

SEPARATION AND DIVORCE

According to the APA (2017b), between 40% and 50% of couples experience divorce. Remarriage divorce rates are even greater. These high divorce rates resulted in more than one million children suffering consequences of divorce with 6% of children living with a stepparent and 15% living with two parents in a subsequent marriage (Cohen & Weitzman, 2016; Pew Research Center, 2014).

Nature of Conflict

The first 2 or 3 years following a divorce can be a time of strong reactions (Cohen & Weitzman, 2016) but most children adjust well within the 2 years that follow a divorce (APA, n.d.; Herrick, Haight, Palomares, & Bufka, n.d.). Children of parents in a high-conflict relationship fear future relationships, exhibit conduct disorder, attempt suicide more frequently and are diagnosed with posttraumatic stress disorder more often than children who are from homes not experiencing divorce (Cohen & Weitzman, 2016). Female children in abusive homes experience heightened depression (Cohen & Weitzman, 2016). Unfortunately, when parents are in high conflict relationships, the children often feel caught between their parents (Cohen & Weitzman, 2016).

Children may lose important relationships with friends, relatives, and the noncustodial parent, which is usually the father. Problems can be further compounded with restricted visitation times, financial considerations, custody arrangements, geographical distance due to a move, and a new parental father figure if the mother has remarried. This can be especially difficult for boys who need a close relationship with their father for optimal development (Cohen & Weitzman, 2016).

Mothers with custody of their children will most often have to deal with reduced income, (Cohen & Weitzman, 2016; Hopf, 2010; Hetherington & Elmore, 2003. This could mean a move to a less expensive home and neighborhood, a new school that may not provide the same advantages, and new friends and less desirable peers. Financial support from the noncustodial father can be beneficial and protect their children from harmful influences, and lead to better relationships with their children (Cohen & Weitzman, 2016; Hopf, 2010).

Children who have a poor relationship with one or both parents may have a much more difficult time coping with the divorce. Parent education and family counseling have been touted as effective methods for improving child outcomes and enhancing family relationships (APA, n.d.; Cohen & Weitzman, 2016; Velez, Wolchick, Tein, & Sandler, 2011). Most children do adjust and function well after divorce with appropriate intervention (Cohen & Weitzman, 2016).

Child Abuse and Neglect

Child abuse and neglect are defined in both state and federal laws. State laws may be defined in both the civil and criminal statutes. State laws differ depending on the state. It is the responsibility of every licensed provider to know the laws of the state in which you practice, and the reporting requirements for suspected abuse and/or neglect.

According to the APA (2017c), federal laws are defined by the Child Abuse Prevention and Treatment Act as follows:

> *Any recent act or failure to act on the part of a parent or caretaker, which results in death, serious physical or emotional harm, sexual abuse, or exploitation, or an act or failure to act which presents an imminent risk of serious harm. (p. 1)*

Types of Abuse

The following are definitions of the different types of abuse, as provided by Child Welfare Information Gateway (2016).

- Physical abuse is generally defined as purposeful physical injury to the child and can include striking, kicking, burning, or biting the child, or any action that results in a physical impairment of the child.

- Neglect is frequently defined as the failure of a parent or other person with responsibility for the child to provide needed food, clothing, shelter, medical care, or supervision to the degree that the child's health, safety, and well-being are threatened with harm.

- Some states refer in general terms to sexual abuse, while others specify various acts as sexual abuse. Sexual exploitation is an element of the definition of sexual abuse in most jurisdictions. Sexual exploitation includes allowing the child to engage in prostitution or in the production of child pornography.

- Emotional abuse is an injury to the psychological capacity or emotional stability of the child as evidenced by an observable or substantial change in behavior, emotional response, or cognition and injury as evidenced by anxiety, depression, withdrawal, or aggressive behavior.

- Abandonment is when the parent's identity or whereabouts are unknown, the child has been left by the parent in circumstances in which the child suffers serious harm, or the parent has failed to maintain contact with the child or to provide reasonable support for a specified period.

- Parental substance abuse is an element of the definition of child abuse only in some states. Circumstances that are considered abuse or neglect in some states include:

  1. Prenatal exposure of a child to harm due to the mother's use of an illegal drug or other substance (14 states and the District of Columbia)

  2. Manufacture of a controlled substance in the presence of a child or on the premises occupied by a child (12 states)

  3. Allowing a child to be present where the chemicals or equipment for the manufacture of controlled substances are used or stored (3 states)

  4. Selling, distributing, or giving drugs or alcohol to a child (7 states and Guam)

  5. Use of a controlled substance by a caregiver that impairs the caregiver's ability to adequately care for the child (8 states)

Child Protective Services Interventions

Child protective services are a state agency in most states. They are known by different names, such as the Department of Children and Family Services or Child Protective Services (CPS). Therapists who suspect that a child is being abused or neglected must report their concerns to the agency within their state.

When a CPS worker comes to the home, it can be intimidating for the parent. CPS will be looking to see if there is any reason to believe that it is not safe for the child to live there, and that there are no drugs or evidence of abuse or neglect. Since each state has different laws, families may wish to seek legal advice, especially if court proceedings follow the visit. Family therapists are often utilized to help families heal and stay together after these proceedings.

SUMMARY

Parental health plays a major role on child and adolescent development. Parental physical health and mental health are impacted by issues such as addiction, abuse, separation, divorce, and violence, and often affect the entire family system. Children exposed to these issues can also face mental health issues as a result. Chapter 20 focuses more intently on child illness and its effects on the family system. As you have learned in the chapters within this book, the family is a system and all members' crises and behaviors affect the entire family.

KEYSTONES

Among the key points addressed in this chapter are:

- Healthy family functioning is important to enhance the mental health of family members, including children and adolescents.
- Parental physical and mental illness impacts the entire family system resulting in a need for enhanced communication patterns and support.
- Motivational interviewing and family meetings may be effective techniques for assisting families suffering from addictions.
- Children from divorced and abusive homes suffer from a variety of emotional and psychosocial problems but do adapt and function well with intervention.

REFLECTION FROM THE CONTRIBUTOR'S CHAIR
Janet Hicks

When I first started working as a school therapist many years ago, I thought I would work with children individually in the school and make a tremendous difference. It didn't take long to realize that optimal change occurs in children when involving the entire family system. I found that when parents sought help alongside their children, the youth showed the greatest gains. Obviously, parental functioning plays a tremendous role in the success of children and is very important to consider. Personal growth is a passage where children trek, and the parents are the path on which they walk. As therapists, let's smooth the path so society's children are less apt to stumble. Good luck as you help future families blaze their trails.

ADDITIONAL RESOURCES

The following resources provide additional information relating to the chapter topics.

Useful Websites

- Effects of Substance of Abuse on Parenting
  https://www.ncsacw.samhsa.gov/files/TrainingPackage/MOD2/EffectsofSubstanceAbuse.pdf

Here you can find information regarding types of substances and parenting effects of drug use.

- Consequences of Child Abuse
  https://www.cdc.gov/violenceprevention/childmaltreatment/consequences.html

This site provides information on child abuse, neglect, and prevention

- State Laws Regarding Abuse
  https://www.childwelfare.gov

This website provides information regarding types of abuse, standards for reporting, persons responsible for the child, exceptions, and summaries of state laws for each state.

Readings

Akerman, R., & Statham, J. (2014). Bereavement in childhood: The impact on psychological and educational outcomes and the effectiveness of support services. Working Paper No. 25, Childhood Wellbeing Research Centre, Thomas Coram Research Unit, Institute of Education, University of London.

This reading discusses facts on grief and bereavement and ways to assist children.

Blume, J. (2014). *It's not the end of the world*. Scarsdale, NY: Bradbury.

This children's book helps explain the divorce in an understandable manner to youth.

REFERENCES

Akerman, R., & Statham, J. (2014). Bereavement in childhood: The impact on psychological and educational outcomes and the effectiveness of support services. Working Paper No. 25, Childhood Wellbeing Research Centre, Thomas Coram Research Unit, Institute of Education, University of London.

American Academy of Child & Adolescent Psychiatry. (2015). Facts for families. Retrieved from https://www.aacap.org/AACAP/Families_and_Youth/Facts_for_Families/Facts_for_Families_Pages/Children_Of_Parents_With_Mental_Illness_39.aspx

American Psychological Association. (n.d.). Healthy divorce: How make your split as healthy as possible. Retrieved from: http://www.apa.org/helpcenter.healthy-divorce.aspx.

American Psychological Association. (2017a). How to cope when a loved one has a serious mental illness. Retrieved from http://www.apa.org/helpcenter/serious-mental-illness.aspx

American Psychological Association. (2017b). Marriage and divorce. Retrieved from http://www.apa.org/topics/divorce

American Psychological Association. (2017c). Understanding and preventing child abuse and neglect. Retrieved from http://www.apa.org/pi/families/resources/understanding-child-abuse.aspx

Beardslee, W., Keller, M. B., Seifer, R., & Lavori, P. W. (1996). Prediction of adolescent affective disorder: Effects of prior parental affective disorders and child psychopathology. *Journal of the American Academy of Child & Adolescent Psychiatry, 35*(3), 279–288.

Breiding, M. J., Basile, K. C., Smith, S. G., Black, M. C., Mahendra, R. (2015). Intimate partner violence surveillance, uniform definitions, and recommended data elements. Centers for Disease Control. Retrieved from https://www.cdc.gov/violenceprevention/pdf/intimatepartnerviolence.pdf

Brooks, F., & McHenry, B. (2015). *A contemporary approach to substance use disorders and addiction counseling.* Alexandria, VA: American Counseling Association.

Center for Substance Abuse Treatment. (1999). *Enhancing motivation for change in substance abuse treatment.* Rockville, MD: Substance Abuse and Mental Health Services Administration. Retrieved from https://www.ncbi.nlm.nih.gov/books/NBK64964/

Centers for Disease Control and Prevention. (2015b). Intimate partner violence: Violence prevention. Retrieved from http://www.cdc.gov/violenceprevention/intimatepartnerviolence/html

Centers for Disease Control and Prevention. (2016). Intimate partner violence: Definitions. Retrieved from http://www.cdc.gov/violenceprevention/intimatepartnerviolence/definitions.html

Chen, Y. (2014). Exploration of the short-term and long-term effects of parental illness on children's educational and behavioral functioning. *Western Journal of Nursing Research, 36*(5), 664–684. doi:10.1177/0193945913509899

Child Welfare Information Gateway. (2016). *Definitions of child abuse and neglect.* Washington, DC: US Department of Health and Human Services, Children's Bureau. Retrieved from http://www.childwelfare.gov

Cohen, G. J., & Weitzman, C. C. (2016). Helping children and families deal with divorce and separation. *Pediatrics, 138,* 1–9.

Colapinto, J. (1982). Structural family therapy. Retrieved from http://www.colapinto.com/files/SFT.doc

Cripps, K., & Zyromski, B. (2009). Adolescents psychological well-being and perceived parental involvement: Implications for parental involvement in middle schools. *Research in Middle Level Education, 33*(4), 1–13. Retrieved from http://files.eric.ed.gov/fulltest/EJ867143.pdf

Davidson, R. (1994). Can psychology make sense of change? In G. Edwards & M. Lader (Eds.), *Addiction: Processes of change* [Society for the Study of Addiction Monograph No. 3]. New York: Oxford University Press.

Dinkmeyer, D. (2017). Guidelines for family meetings. Retrieved from http://www.steppublishers.com/articles/guidelines-family-meetings

Doidge, J., Higgins, D., Delfabbro, P., & Segal, L. (2017). Risk factors for child maltreatment in an Australian population based cohort. *Child Abuse and Neglect, 64*, 47–60.

Domestic Violence Prevention Centre Gold Coast. (n.d.). Impact of domestic violence on children and young people. Retrieved from http://www.domesticviolence.comau/pages/impact-of-domestic-violence-children-and-young

Domestic Violence Roundtable. (n.d.). The effects of domestic violence on children. Retrieved from http://www.domesticviolenceroundtable.org/effect-on-children.html

Earley, P. (2014). Mental health advocate vs mental illness advocate: You decide. Retrieved from http://www.peteearley.com/2014/11/21/mental-health-advocate-vs-mental-illness-advocate-decide

Flamez, B., & Sheperis, B. (2015). *Diagnosing and treating children and adolescents: A guide for mental health professionals.* Hoboken, NJ: Wiley.

Ford, F., & Herrick, J. (1974). Family rules: Family life styles. *American Journal of Orthopsychiatry, 44*(1), 61–69.

Gladding, S. T. (2015). *Family therapy: History, theory, and practice.* Boston: Pearson.

George, L. (2013). Life course perspectives on mental health. In C. S. Aneshensel, J. C. Phelan, & A. Bierman (Eds.), *Handbook on the sociology of mental health* (pp. 585–602). Dordrecht, Netherlands: Springer International.

Herrick, L., Haight, R. S., Palomares, R., & Bufka, L., (n.d.). Healthy divorce: How to make your split as smooth as possible. Retrieved from http://www.apa.org/helpcenter/healthy-divorce.aspx

Hetherington, E. M., Elmore, A. M. (2003). Resilience and vulnerability: Adaptation in the context of childhood adversities. In S. S. Luthar, (Ed.). *Adaptation in the context of childhood adversities* (pp. 182-212). New York: Cambridge University Press.

Higgins, D. J., Delfabro, D., & Segal, P. L. (2017). Risk factors for child maltreatment in an Australian based population cohort. *Child Abuse & Neglect, 64*, 47–60.

Hopf, S., (2010). Risk and resilience in children coping with parental divorce. Dartmouth Undergraduate Journal of Science. Retrieved from http://dujs.dartmouth.edu/2010/05/risk-and-resilience-in-children-coping-with-parental-divorce

Kalaitzaki, A. E., & Birtchnell, J. (2014). The impact of early parenting bonding on young adults' Internet addiction, through the mediation effects of negative relating to others and sadness. *Addictive Behaviors, 39*(3), 733–736.

Kaneez, S. (2015). Family environment and psychological well-being of adolescents. *Indian Journal of Positive Psychology.* Retrieved from https://www.questia.com/library/journal/1P3-3931412941/family-environment-and-psychological-well-being-among

Kanfer, F. H., Schefft, B. K. 1988. *Guiding the Process of Therapeutic Change.* Champaign, 1L: Research Press.

Komarek, P., & Schroer, A. (2014). *Defying mental illness: Finding recovery with community resources and family support.* Cincinnati, OH: Church Basement Press.

Lake, S., Wood, E., Dong, H., Dobrer, S., Montaner, J., & Kerr, T. (2015). The impact of childhood emotional abuse on violence among people who inject drugs. *Drug Alcohol Review, 34*(1), 4–9.

Lamb, R., Maguire, D. R., Ginsburg, B. C., Pinkston, J. W., & France, C. P. (2016). Determinants of choice, and vulnerability and recovery in addiction. *Behavioural Processes, 127*, 35–42.

Miller, G. A. (2014). *Learning the language of addiction counseling.* Hoboken, NJ: Wiley.

Miller, W. R., & Rollnick, S. (1991). *Motivational interviewing: Preparing people to change addictive behavior.* New York: Guilford Press.

Miller, W. R., & Rollnick, S. (2002). *Motivational interviewing: Preparing people for change.* New York: Guilford Press.

Minuchin, S., Lee, W., & Simon, J. (1996). *Mastering family therapy: Journeys of growth and transformation.* Hoboken, NJ: Wiley.

Murphy, G., Peters, K., Wilkes, L., & Jackson, D. (2017). Adult children of parents with mental illness: Navigating stigma. *Child and Family Social Work, 22,* 330–338.

National Alliance on Mental Illness. (2015). Mental health conditions. Retrieved from https://www.nami.org/Learn-More/Mental-Health-Conditions

National Association on Mental Illness (NAMI). (2017). Understanding your diagnosis. Retrieved from https://www.nami.org/Find-Support/Living-with-a-Mental-Health-Condition/Understanding-Your-Diagnosis

National Council on Alcoholism and Drug Dependence. (2015). Family history and genetics. Retrieved from https://www.ncadd.org/about-addiction/family-history-and-genetics

National Intimate Partner and Sexual Violence Survey. (2014). National data on intimate partner violence, sexual violence, and stalking. Retrieved from https://www.cdc.gov/violenceprevention/pdf/nisvs-fact-sheet-2014.pdf

Nikmanesh, Z., Baluchi, M. H., & Motlagh, A. A. (2016). The role of self-efficacy beliefs and social support on prediction of addiction relapse. *International Journal of High Risk Behaviors and Addiction, 6*(1), 1–6.

Ojukwu, M. O., & Chigozirum, N. A. (2015). Influence of insecurity on school environment on the behavior of secondary student in Isiala-Ngwa north and south local government areas of Abia State, Nigeria. *International Journal of Education and Literacy, 3*(4), 49–55. doi:10.7575/aiac.ijels.v.3n.4p.49

Pedersen, W. (1994). Parental relations, mental health, and delinquency in adolescents. *Adolescence, 29*(116), 1–21.

Pew Research Center. (2014). Fewer than half of kids today live in a traditional family. Retrieved from http://www.pewresearch.org/fact-tank/2014/12/22/less-than-half-of-u-s-kids-today-live-in-a-traditional-family

Prinz, C. (2013). How your mental health may be impacting your career. Retrieved from http://www.pbs.org/newshour/rundown/how-mental-health-impacts-us-workers

Reiter, M. D. (2014). *Substance abuse and the family.* New York: Routledge.

Rogers, C. (1977). *A way of becoming a person.* New York: Little, Brown.

Ross, C. E. (1990). The impact of the family on health: The decade in review. *Journal of Marriage and Family, 52*(4), 1059–1078. Retrieved from http://www.jstor.org/stable/353319

Royal College of Psychiatrists. (2014). Parental mental illness: The impact on children and adolescents: Information for parents, careers and anyone who works with young people. Retrieved from http://www.recpsych.ac.uk/healthadvice/parentsandyyouthinfo/parents

Royal College of Psychiatrists. (2017). Parental mental illness information for parents, caregivers, and anyone who works with young people. Retrieved from http://www.rcpsych.ac.uk/healthadvice/parentsandyouth-info/parentscarers/parentalmentalillness.aspx

Ryff, C. D., & Keyes, C. L. M. (1995). The structure of psychological well-being revisited. *Journal of Personality and Social Psychology, 69*(4), 719–727. doi:10.1037/0022-3514.69.4.719

Sandstrom, H., & Huerta, S. (2013). The negative effects of instability on child development: A research synthesis. Low-Income Working Families Discussion Paper 3, Urban Institute, Washington, DC. Retrieved from https://www.urban.org/sites/default/files/publication/32706/412899-The-Negative-Effects-of-Instability-on-Child-Development-A-Research-Synthesis.pdf

Schlozman, S. (2016). Parents' untreated mental illnesses affect their children. Clay Center for Healthy Young Minds. Retrieved from http://www.mghclaycenter.org/parenting-concerns/families/parents-untreated-mental-illnesses-affect-children

Schoenfeld, P. (2015). Helping children cope when a parent is sick. Everett Clinic. Retrieved from http://everettclinic.com/blog/helping-children-cope-when-a-parent-sick

Seiffge-Krenke, I. (1995). *Stress, coping, and relationships in adolescence.* Mahwah, NJ: Erlbaum.

Sentencing Project. (2017). Drug policy. Retrieved from http://www.sentencingproject.org/issues/drug-policy

Steinglass, P. (2009). Systemic-motivational therapy for substance abuse disorders: An integrative model. *Journal of Family Therapy, 31*, 155–174.

Steinglass, P., Bennett, L. A., Wolin, S. J., & Reiss, D. (1987). *The alcoholic family*. New York: Basic Books.

Substance Abuse and Mental Health Services Administration. (2005). TIP 39: Substance abuse treatment and family therapy (Publication No. SMA 05-4006).

Szott, K. (2015). Contingencies of the will: Uses of harm reduction and the disease model of addiction among health care practitioners. *Health: An Interdisciplinary Journal for the Social Study of Health, Illness and Medicine, 19*(5), 507–522.

Thombs, D. L., & Osborn, C. J. (2013). *Introduction to addictive behaviors*. New York: Guilford Press.

US Department of Justice, Office of Justice Programs, National Institute of Justice. (2017). Intimate partner violence. Retrieved from https://www.jij.gov/topics/crime/intimate-partner-violence/Pages/welcome.aspx

Van Bilsen, H. P. J. G. (1991). Motivational interviewing: Perspectives from The Netherlands, with particular emphasis on heroin-dependent clients. In W. R. Miller & S. Rollnick, *Motivational interviewing: Preparing people to change addictive behavior* (pp. 214–224). New York: Guilford Press

Van Loon, L. M., Van Ven, M. O., Van Doesum, K. T., Witteman, C. L., & Hosman, C. M. (2013). The relation between parental mental illness and adolescent mental health: The role of family factors. *Journal of Child and Family Studies, 23*(7), 1201–1214.

Van Wormer, K., & Davis, D. R. (2017. *Addiction treatment: A strengths perspective*. Boston: Cengage Learning.

Velez, C. E., Wolchik, S. A., Tein, J.-Y., & Sandler, I. (2011). Protecting children from the consequences of divorce: A longitudinal study of the effects of parenting on children's coping processes. *Child Development, 82*, 244–257.

Voydanoff, P., & Donnelly, B. W. (1998). Parents' risk and protective factors as predictors of parental well-being and behavior. *Journal of Marriage and Family, 60*(2), 344–355. DOI: 10.2307/353853

Walrond-Skinner, S. (2013). *Family therapy (psychology revivals): The treatment of natural systems*. London: Routledge.

WebMD. (2015). Family therapy. Retrieved from http://www.webmd.com/balance/family-therapy-6301

West, R., & Brown, J. (2014). *Theory of addiction*. Chichester, UK: Wiley-Blackwell.

Westerhof, G. J., & Keyes, C. L. M. (2010). Mental illness and mental health: The two continua model across the lifespan. *Journal of Adult Development, 17*(2), 110–119. doi:10.1007/s10804-009-9082-y

Wetchler, J. L., & Hecker, L. L. (Eds.). (2014). *An introduction to marriage and family therapy*. New York: Routledge.

Wiener, L., Battles, H., & Heilman, N. E. (1998). Factors associated with parents' decision to disclose their HIV diagnosis to their children. *Child Welfare, 77*(2), 115–135.

Work Group for Community Health and Development. (2016). Addressing social determinants of health and development. University of Kansas. Retrieved from http://ctb.ku.edu/en/table-of-contents/analyze/analyze-community-problems-and-solutions/social-determinants-of-health/main

CHAPTER 20

Child and Adolescent Influences on the Family

Joshua Francis and Leslie Neyland-Brown

> *"One of the luckiest things that can happen to you in life, I think, is to have a happy childhood."*
>
> —Agatha Christie

The child and adolescent years of a person's life are foundational for all areas of future life development. As clinicians working with youth for many years, we both feel passionate about the importance of early life interventions that bring biopsychosocial stability, health, and happiness into the lives of children and adolescents. In both functional and dysfunctional family dynamics, children and adolescents are major players. Throughout the entire evolution and development of the human species, child bearing and child rearing has been an essential element of the human condition. Raising children to an age of independence is vital to the continuation of the any living species.

Family therapists must possess a comprehensive knowledge of the complex issues involving children and adolescents to adequately provide therapeutic interventions to families in need. According to the U.S. Census Bureau (2012), about 40% of U.S. households have children under 18. Vast, broad, and ongoing societal issues continue to burden the family with unprecedented stressors. Rapid changes in technology, communication, and lifestyle make it more imperative than ever for family therapists to be diversely skilled to meet the dynamics needs of family systems. This chapter will provide an overview of the variety of influences both children and adolescents have on the modern family system, with special emphasis placed on treatment interventions, physical and neurological development, physical and emotional health issues, family dysfunction, trauma, peer-related difficulties, technology, and addictions. In the final chapter of this book, we will focus on the children and adolescent influences on the family.

After reading this chapter, you will be able to do the following:

- Increase your understanding of the ways children and adolescent influence the family system.

- Develop competency through a clinical familiarity of the important issues affecting youth and adolescents.

- Recognize the variety of externalized behaviors and internalized emotional symptoms that can contribute negatively to the family system.

- Identify physical health conditions in youth that contribute to the family unit.

- Conceptualize the numerous psychosocial and environmental contributions to the lives of children and adolescents and their impact on the family.

- Develop greater awareness of the importance of biological, neurological, and physiological factors that affect human development, functioning, and behavior in children and adolescents.

History of Child and Adolescent Treatment

Therapeutic interventions involving children and adolescents have long been a component of mental health treatment. Family interventions began being commonly employed since the 1950s (Broderick & Schrader, 2013). As previously mentioned in this textbook, there exist a multitude of theories, orientations, styles, and licensures that therapists can employ to intervene at the family level. Early family interventions were strongly influenced by religious and moral ideologies (Zink, 2008). Old-fashioned biblical ideology such as "spare the rod, spoil the child" accompanied early American, puritanical views of child rearing. Religious texts often contained vague references to child-rearing practices and the hierarchical power structures in the family system. It was not until the second half of the 20th century that conventional psychotherapy and family interventions began to treat the individual components of the family unit, including the treatment of children and adolescents.

Importance of Clinical Interventions

Clinical interventions can be vital to the effective and efficient functioning of family systems. The last decade of mental health treatment and research has consistently emphasized the importance of evidence-based treatment approaches (Goorden et al., 2016). Tremendous variability exists in the type, setting, style, and application of therapeutic interventions. Endless debate has taken place over which of these variables is the most effective in producing a positive change in the lives of those treated. Regardless of the modality employed, expansive research has suggested that type of treatment administered is important and suggested that family-based treatments produce better results than individual or group interventions (Dakof et al., 2015).

The Modern Family

Human families have existed since the beginning of the species, with the anatomically modern human being estimated to have originated around 200,000 to 250,000 years ago (Smithsonian Institute, 2017). Primitive environmental and biological demands have influenced the formation of early family structure. This early family structure heavily emphasized the role of the mother as the primary and often exclusive caregiver in early humans. Paternal investment began only a few thousand years ago as males began balancing the need to spread their gene pool against the need to protect their young. Humans are biologically unique in that we have developed a life history strategy that involves intensive parenting over a long developmental period. The length of this developmental period has not changed and places tremendous importance on early life and familial events and dynamics.

Modern Family Demographics

As you learned in the earlier chapters and chapter 18 (non-nuclear family constellations) the demographic profiles of the family and household structures have changed significantly over the past centuries. Modernity has left a strong impression on the contemporary family, changing the way U.S. families live, relate, and interact. According to the Pew Research Center (2016) several significant changes in the family system and structure have occurred in the past few years. The number of two-parent households continues to decline, while divorce, remarriage, and cohabitation are increasing. Blended families are also more common, with about 1 in 6 American children living in this situation (Pew Research Center, 2016). An additional phenomenon affecting the modern family demographic is the increase in mothers entering the workforce. Almost half of all two-parent households have both parents in the workforce, increasing the domestic roles of father tending to household chores and child care duties.

Need for Competence

Since the family system contributes tremendously to the mental health of society, professional competency is vital to the delivery of mental health interventions. In the classic work on the competency theory, Boyatzis (1982) described competence as the underlying attributes of individuals in relation to the diverse knowledge, skills, or abilities they possess. The roots of competency theory have spurred significant ongoing research and understanding of competence in the human services field.

Professional competency in the clinical world of child and adolescent mental health is imperative for the well-rounded marriage and family therapist. At any given time while working with a family in treatment, a family therapist may be tasked with the needs and demands of a vast array of physical, emotional, and developmental needs of family members. Let's review Case Presentation 20.1 to better understand the diversity of issues presented within a single-family system.

CASE PRESENTATION 20.1: THE CASE OF THE MONROE FAMILY

The Monroe family presents to the family therapist (Dr. Denise) for assistance in helping improve overall family relations and lessen the intensity of argument and disagreement in the household. The family consists of Stephanie (birth mother); Derrick (husband of Stephanie and father of one child with her); Seth (17, biological son of Stephanie); Callie (12, biological daughter of Stephanie); and Shawn (4, biological child of Derrick and Stephanie). Stephanie and Derrick have been together for 5 years. Seth and Callie rarely see their birth father, who abused alcohol and was verbally abusive to them and their mother before their parents went through an ugly and traumatic divorce and custody battle. In the initial family assessment, Derrick and Stephanie reported increased defiance and attitude from Seth and Callie over almost everything—starting arguments and showing complete disrespect for Derrick. Derrick and Stephanie also report going through a rough time in their marriage, and are considering separation or divorce. Seth and Callie report that Derrick often oversteps his boundaries with them, and shows a strong preference for his biological son, Shawn. In addition, they do not like how Derrick treats their mother, their arguing, and his binge use of alcohol. Dr. Denise recognized the importance of establishing trust and rapport with Seth and Callie and had two separate individual sessions prior to the family sessions. Using a variety of "real talk" with the children, she found success in breaking through their resistance with the following dialogue.

Dr. Denise: So, Callie, I heard what your mom thinks the problems is, but I am sure you probably disagree with her point of view. I am really interested in having you describe in your own words what is causing all of the problems with your family?

Callie: It's pretty much Derrick—he thinks he is my dad and tells Seth and I what to do. He also treats Mom bad and I pretty much hate him!

Dr. Denise: It sounds like Derrick can be a real jerk at times—what do you think we can do to help your family get along better?

Callie: I don't know—Derrick is the one who has to change. I wish he would just leave.

Dr. Denise: I am sure Derrick leaving would make you feel a lot more comfortable in your own house; but since we cannot control what Mom and Derrick do, let's identify some things that only you can do to try to make everyone get along better.

These lines of questions empower the children and help engage them in treatment. Dr. Denise initially assessed the children using a semi structured clinical interview and Child Behavioral Checklist/6–18 (Achenbach & Rescorla, 2001). Additionally, Dr. Denise is trained and competent in the administration of projective drawings and used the house-tree-person (Buck, 1948) and kinetic family drawing (Burns & Kaufman, 1970). The projective tests helped reveal the intense resentment and origin of the children's anger with Derrick. Through several sessions of intense therapy, Dr. Denise stabilized the family unit, increased healthy communication, and assisted the Monroe family in greater functionality and happiness.

This case demonstrates the common complexity and broad range of clinical competence that a therapist must possess to adequately meet the needs of the family.

Depending on the clinical issues being addressed, the therapist in this case must have a minimal competence in the following clinical areas: marriage/couples counseling; child developmental issues (teenage autonomy, pre-teen angst, preschool behavior); high conflict divorce, blended family dynamics, drug/alcohol abuse, and posttraumatic stress.

The ACA (2014) and AAMFT (2015) Codes of Ethics demand competence throughout various sections of the code. For example, in Section C of the ACA Code of Ethics (ACA, 2014): Professional Responsibility, directly emphasizes competence by stating, "Counselors practice only within the boundaries of their competence, based on their education, training, supervised experience, state and national professional credentials, and appropriate professional experience" (p. 8).

BEHAVIORAL AND EMOTIONAL ISSUES

There are many issues children and adolescents face that parents may not be prepared for. Even in instances where parents are made aware of potential concerns during pregnancy, the magnitude of how developmental, psychological or medical conditions will impact the family may not be fully understood, creating a myriad of unexpected challenges for the child, the parents and the family as a unit. A thorough understanding of these issues is critical when working with those affected.

Behavioral Contributions

Externalizing disorders are characterized by problematic behaviors that often include impulsivity, hyperactivity, aggression and defiance (American Psychiatric Association, 2013). Signs of externalizing disorders can present in early childhood where parents may notice frequent temper tantrums, a reluctance to follow directions or the inability to play cooperatively with others. If signs are missed or not present in the early years, parents are usually alerted to a problem during the school-age years when self-regulation is required for the educational setting. Children and adolescents with externalizing behaviors may have difficulty concentrating, staying on task or interacting appropriately with peers. Oppositional behaviors such as explosive outbursts, fighting, and verbal aggression towards authority figures, usually warrant disciplinary action by the school. At home, children and adolescents may be confrontational and combative with both parents and siblings. More violent and anti-social behavior such as vandalism, truancy or stealing, consistent with conduct disorder, often results in legal trouble. In addition, children and adolescents with externalizing behaviors may also have emotional problems such as depression, low self-esteem or anxiety, contributing to impairment.

Children and adolescents with externalizing behaviors require a great deal of supervision and attention in comparison to their unaffected counterparts. Due to behavior problems, parents often have difficulty securing child care and appropriate school placements. School aged children may face disciplinary action that requires them to be picked up from school during the school day or kept home during a suspension. Parents may be asked to attend meetings to discuss student issues as well as seek additional mental health services from outside agencies. Adolescents with conduct issues may need to retain legal counsel, attend court dates and fulfill legal obligations that often rely heavily on parent participation. These requirements can be both costly and time consuming, therefore putting a great deal of strain on parents, a marriage and the family unit.

Siblings of children and adolescents with externalizing behaviors may find the affected child difficult to be around resulting in fear or resentment. Likewise, other family members and close friends may not want children with behavior problems around, limiting social interaction and support for the family. As discussed in Chapter 16, psychoeducation for family members is important to help all those impacted gain a better perspective of the externalizing behaviors and how they impact the child and the family. Family therapy can provide an opportunity to process individual feelings and potential threats to familial cohesiveness. More covert antisocial behaviors that impose threats of safety for others, including siblings, may require parents to make difficult decisions regarding temporary placements and request for emergency services. Let's turn our attention to Case Presentation 20.2 about the importance of having the appropriate resources for treatment and the overall well-being of everyone involved.

CASE PRESENTATION 20.2: THE CASE OF MARVIN

Marvin is a 5-year-old boy who lives with his mother (Tammy), stepfather (Dave), older sister Kara, and baby brother Jacob. Marvin was excited throughout his mother's pregnancy but was very standoffish when they brought baby Jacob home from the hospital. Over the next few months, Marvin became very distant from the family. He did not want to do things with the family, and his teacher complained that his behavior was becoming very disruptive in class. Tammy received a call from Marvin's school asking her to come pick Marvin up. His teacher reported that he became physically aggressive, throwing things around the room and forcing her to remove all other students from the room. He ended up curled up in a ball crying. Shortly after many similar incidents, Marvin was not permitted to return to school. Marvin was very angry at home and had told his mother on many occasions that he hated her and would become physically aggressive with her. Tammy could not prove it, but she also had concerns that Marvin may have been trying to harm the baby. Marvin's counselor encouraged Tammy to be patient with Marvin and suggested she allow Marvin to have time to cool down when his behavior becomes disruptive. Tammy has followed all suggestions but has not seen any progress. Marvin's stepfather believes that Marvin is being babied and that Tammy is not disciplining him for his behavior. Both Tammy and Dave love Marvin but are frustrated with how he has been behaving. Marvin's counselor suggests family therapy to be added to Jacob's treatment plan.

Discussion questions: In what ways is Marvin's behavior impacting members of his family? What additional issues must Tammy and Marvin face?

Emotional Contributions

Contrary to the previous section on externalizing disorders, youth struggling with internalizing disorders are more likely to isolate themselves and keep negative emotions inside; yet are equally afflicted. Internalizing disorders may go undetected in the absence of problematic behaviors that often result in conflict with others and authority. Younger children may not be able to verbalize feelings of uneasiness or distress, but instead exhibit physical and emotional symptoms that may seem to appear without an identified stressor. Adolescents may disconnect from others and present as moody or irritable impairing social functioning and motivation in other areas. Using the categorical approach to clinical diagnosis, internalizing disorders are divided into two categories, anxiety disorders and mood disorders (American Psychiatric Association, 2013). Symptoms of anxiety and depression may present similarly or occur together, making it difficult to differentiate the actual diagnosis. In addition, it is not unusual for a child with an internalizing disorder to also have a co-occurring externalizing disorder or at minimum exhibit externalizing behaviors.

Anxiety disorders. Anxiety disorders are characterized by uncontrollable stress, worry or fear that prompts avoidant behaviors and interferes with normal daily function. Feeling nervous, tense or uneasy yields both physiological and behavioral responses that often make it difficult for children and adolescents to attend school, stay with child care providers, interact with peers, and participate in age appropriate activities. Children and adolescents may report feeling physically ill to avoid stressful situations prompting parents to keep them home or pick them up early from school or social events. Like children with externalizing disorders, parents of children with anxiety disorders must allocate time to consult with both school and mental health providers to manage anxiety and help children feel safe. It is also important that parents and caretakers are on one accord as it relates to how anxiety will be addressed. Inconsistency can be counterproductive for the affected child and decrease familial cohesion.

Siblings of children with anxiety disorders may feel the child with the disorder receives more attention or gets special privileges. They may also develop resentment in instances where accommodations must be made for the affected child that limits the activities they would like to do individually or as a family. Parents and other family members will need to have a clear understanding of anxiety disorders to provide a supportive environment for the affected child while ensuring the individual needs of all family members are also addressed.

Mood disorders. Mood disorders are broken into two categories, Depressive disorders and Bipolar Disorders (American Psychiatric Association, 2013). It can be difficult to pinpoint the existence of a mood disorder when the presenting problems may be masked by more problematic behaviors often associated with externalizing disorders (Bilginer & Kandil, 2016; Breton et al., 2012). For this reason, childhood depression often goes undetected. Children and adolescents diagnosed with Bipolar disorders may present with elevated mood, impulsivity and irritability during periods of mania, followed by periods of depressed mood. Periods of mania may include verbal or physical aggression that may seem out of character for the adolescent making them uncooperative and difficult to be around. Like adults struggling with depression, children and adolescents may become distant from friends and family, lose interest in normal activities, exhibit changes in eating and sleeping habits, and appear very emotional or sensitive. Although there may be signs of academic struggle, there may not be behavior problems present that warrant an alert to parents of a more serious issue. Mood disorders left untreated worsen and often cause more serious issues for those affected. More severe symptoms include self-injurious behavior, substance abuse and suicide, which typically warrant more intensive treatment.

Parents of children and adolescents with mood disorders may struggle with understanding the changes in mood and behavior as a symptom of the disorder as opposed to intentionally being distant, overly dramatic or attention seeking. This may make it difficult for parents to know when to seek help, leading to feelings of guilt, helplessness, frustration and resentment when symptoms do not improve. Psychoeducation is necessary to assist parents in recognizing the warning signs of mood disorders and knowing when to seek help. Living with a family member with a mood disorder can be emotionally draining for everyone involved. In Guided Exercise 20.1, consider the scenario presented and the emotions it elicits.

GUIDED PRACTICE EXERCISE 20.1

Many parents struggle with disciplining their children in public due to fears of being judged harshly. This can be even more difficult for parents of children who have a behavior or emotional disorder. Recall a time when you have seen a child behaving inappropriately in a store or at an event. What do you remember about the incident? How did the parent handle it? What was your first reaction and what were the reactions of others who were observing? Now imagine you are the parent in this situation. How might you feel knowing others are judging you without any knowledge of what may be going on with your child?

PHYSICAL HEALTH CONTRIBUTIONS

There are many conditions that impact children and adolescents both physically and psychologically. These disorders create unique challenges for families having to adjust and cope with physical ailments and medical treatment while being supportive of the affected child. This includes disorders found in the following categories of diagnosis in the DSM-5: feeding and eating disorders, elimination disorders and sleep-wake disorders, in addition to chronic health conditions of childhood that interfere with daily function and living.

Feeding and Eating Disturbances

Issues with feeding are not uncommon during infancy, causing a great deal of concern for parents and pediatricians. Mothers of infants who are resistant to breast-feeding or reject breast milk often experience feelings of inadequacy and disappointment. Failed attempts at feeding can be emotionally draining and increase the likelihood of mothers developing depression (Fahlquist, 2015). Inadequate nutrition poses threats to proper growth and development and can be life-threatening if left to persist. Infants and toddlers who have issues with feeding may be fussy and irritable due to discomfort caused by hunger or involuntary regurgitation (Benoit, 2009). Regardless of causation, failure to receive proper nourishment is concerning, and medical attention should be sought.

Eating disorders not limited to infants and early childhood include avoidant/restrictive food intake disorder, anorexia nervosa (AN), and bulimia nervosa (BN). Often confused with AN, children and adolescents struggling with avoidant/restrictive food intake disorder do not meet appropriate nutritional needs due to a restricted diet, not eating enough or not eating at all. Unlike AN, refusal and restriction is not motivated by weight management, but instead is associated with lack of appetite, sensory concerns with food and/or anxiety about eating. Regardless of motivation or method, inadequate consumption of nutrients is physically harmful and causes a great deal of psychosocial issues for children and adolescents (American Psychiatric Association, 2013). Whether at home or in school, meal times are usually accompanied by social interaction with peers or family members. Children and adolescents with eating disorders may avoid meal times due to embarrassment or other consequences of making others aware of the issue. This can be very isolating and contribute to greater emotional disturbance for the affected individual (Choate & Ginter, 2015).

Sleep Disturbances

Children and adolescents affected by sleep disorders often wake feeling irritable and tired. Other symptoms of inadequate sleep include hyperactivity, difficulty concentrating and lack of energy, which can affect both academic performance and behavior (Sheperis, Calley, Jones-Trebatoski, & Wines, 2015). In addition to impairment in functioning, sleep disorders may limit opportunities for age appropriate social activities such as parties and school trips that require overnight stays. Sleep disturbance not only affects the child, but also disrupts the sleep of parents and potentially any siblings that may sleep nearby. For this reason, some parents opt for co-sleeping in hopes of eliminating future sleep interruptions.

Co-sleeping may interfere with partner intimacy and contribute to marital discord when it is not agreed upon or planned by both parents. Parents of children with sleep problems resulting in "reactive co-sleeping" are less likely to experience satisfaction with sleep arrangements and more likely to have marital issues (Germo, Chang, Keller, & Goldberg, 2007). Although pediatricians in the United States discourage co-sleeping, it is a socially accepted practice for many cultural groups (Jain, Romack & Jain, 2011). Psychoeducation for parents should include culturally sensitive strategies for developing consistent bedtime routines, setting appropriate limits and creating a supportive sleep environment for everyone in the household. Now, let's review Case Presentation 20.3 which describes this complex dynamic.

CASE PRESENTATION 20.3: THE CASE OF JAMIE, JANE, MIKE, AND JOANNE

Jamie and Jane are 7-year-old twin girls who were conceived after years of trying and fertility treatments that were worth it but very costly for Mike and Joanne. Joanne really wanted to be a stay-at-home mom until the girls were school age, but due to finances she had to return to work when the girls were 18 months old. Jamie never slept well as a baby, resulting in many sleepless nights for Joanne. This continued throughout Jamie and Jane's toddler years. Joanne would often have to go into Jamie's room and stay with her until she fell asleep. At around 5 years old, Jamie began having night terrors that would cause her to wake up hysterical. The first few times this happened, Mike and Joanne allowed Jamie to get in bed with them, but after the third time, Jane also wanted to get in the bed. Mike and Joanne agreed that this would not be a healthy arrangement, and instead they established a consistent bedtime routine for the girls in which they both participated. Jamie continued to have night terrors, but Joanne stuck to the agreement and recommendation from their pediatrician that Jamie should continue to sleep in her own bed. Joanne would go into Jamie's room at night to help soothe her until she fell asleep. This would happen a couple of nights a week. Mike would often wake up in the middle of the night and go get Joanne, who would fall asleep in Jamie's room, but sometimes he would just let her stay.

Elimination Issues

Toilet training is a major developmental milestone in early childhood and typically begins during the toddler years. This can be a smooth process for children who catch on quickly, or a daunting process for children who may take more time. Child readiness does not always align with parent expectations for when a child should be fully toilet trained, causing anxiety for both the parent and the child when progress is not observed. Child care is often a major concern for parents of children who struggle with elimination management, as daycare or school enrollment may be contingent on the child being fully toilet trained.

Even after toilet training has been achieved, it is not uncommon for younger children to have occasional accidents that involve urinating while sleeping or during the day when a restroom is not reached in enough time. These incidents, even when isolated, can be stressful for the child who may experience feelings of embarrassment or defeat. Even more distress is experienced for children who fear chastisement from a disappointed caretaker. Frequent accidents that continue to persist or that involve soiling clothes by means of defecation typically indicate the presence of an elimination disorder.

Elimination disorders are characterized by the passing of feces (encopresis) or urine (enuresis) into inappropriate places. Enuresis is not diagnosed in children under age 5, distinctively developmental age as opposed to chronological age (American Psychiatric Association, 2013). Prevalence of enuresis declines with age, however social impairment becomes even greater for older children than younger. Likewise, children with daytime, diurnal, enuresis are more likely to have social and self-esteem issues than those who primarily suffer from nighttime, nocturnal, enuresis, which is often easier to conceal from peers (Thibodeau, Metcalfe, Koop, & Moore, 2013). Parents of children with enuresis may fear judgment from others, assuming full responsibility for what may be perceived as failed toilet training.

Treatment of elimination disorders usually includes both medical and behavioral approaches. Both approaches require full buy in from caretakers who will be responsible for implementation. Psychoeducation for parents and close family members is critical for treatment compliance. In instances where encopresis or enuresis is voluntary, family or parent–child therapy may be necessary to get to the root of the issue.

Chronic Illness

There are many changes that take place for a family when a child is diagnosed with a chronic condition. Roles and responsibilities may be disrupted and social interaction may be limited. Parents often experience feelings of grief, guilt and frustration. Other challenges include managing finances and maintaining employment with frequent doctor's appointments and costly medical treatment. Families need to be educated on the chronic condition and work together to maximize treatment compliance. This may be difficult for young siblings who may not fully understand. Family therapy and support groups may be beneficial to help members adjust and support family functioning.

The following section reviews some of the most common chronic conditions for children and adolescents.

Asthma. Asthma is a chronic condition of the respiratory system that causes the airways of the lungs to close making it difficult to breathe. It is estimated that 8.6% of children and adolescents suffer from asthma making it one of the most common chronic conditions of childhood and the number one reason school aged children miss school (CDC, 2014). Asthma affects poor and minority children at the highest rates with Puerto Rican and African American children at the greatest risk. These groups are also at the highest risk for hospital stays and asthma related deaths (minorityhealth.hhs.gov).

Children and adolescents must be educated on the seriousness of their condition to reduce exposure to triggers. Some triggers may be unavoidable making access to medication critical and very stressful for parents when they are away. For this reason, parents of children with severe asthma may have to limit certain activities and places to keep children safe.

Diabetes. Diabetes is one of the most common chronic diseases of childhood with an estimate of about 208,000 individuals under age 20 living in the United States (www.diabetes.org). Diabetes affects the way the body processes sugar in the blood due to the inability to produce insulin (type 1 diabetes) or resistance to insulin (type 2 diabetes). Treatment of diabetes includes regularly testing blood, a modified diet and eating schedule, and insulin injections when necessary. Adherence to treatment is critical for symptom management and to reduce the risk of major complications. When managed, children and adolescents can participate in normal daily activities. Dietary restrictions may be an adjustment for children and adolescents who are unable to consume the same foods as peers. Leaving class or an activity to check blood glucose levels or to have a snack may also bring youngsters unwanted attention. In the early years, parents and caretakers assume most of the responsibility for treatment.

Chronic pain. Chronic pain is not a condition that most people associate with childhood, however, it is estimated that 15% of children may be suffering from chronic pain (Eccleston & Malleson, 2003). Common areas in which children and adolescents experience pain include the abdomen, bones and joints. Many children and adolescents also suffer from chronic headaches. Chronic disorders that involve pain include sickle cell anemia, arthritis, and fibromyalgia. The pain experienced from these chronic conditions can be physically debilitating, preventing individuals from performing normal daily tasks or even leaving the house. In addition to the physical pain, children and adolescents often struggle with the inability to live normal lives and actively engage with peers.

Parents of children with chronic pain are at high risk for developing anxiety and depression (Palermo, 2000). The emotional weight of watching a child suffer in pain while having to make solid judgment calls, as the primary advocate for appropriate pain management, is a heavy burden for parents to bear. Studies on parental and family factors impacting chronic pain in children and adolescents suggest that poor parental and family functioning is linked with poor adjustment and functioning for children with chronic pain (Ross et al., 1993; Palermo & Armstrong, 2007; Logan, 2005). As it is important that the mental health needs of the affected child are evaluated and addressed, the mental health needs of the parents should also be monitored and appropriate referrals should be made as necessary.

Neurological disorders. Neurological disorders are disorders that involve any dysfunction of the brain, spinal cord or nervous system. Children born with Cerebral Palsy have physical impairments stemming from brain damage or malformation. Physical impairments often limit movement and coordination, which impact a child's ability to master fine gross and motor skills. Other impairments include issues with speech, vision, hearing and learning. Up to half of children diagnosed with cerebral palsy are also diagnosed with the seizure disorder, epilepsy (Hundozi-Hysenaj & Boshnjaky-Dallku, 2008). Children with cerebral palsy can benefit from physical and occupational therapy as well as use of a variety of assistance devices. Cerebral palsy is a recognized disability in the Individuals with Disabilities Education Act, granting children and adolescents with special services until age 21. Having a child with a disability is very challenging for parents, as there will be many things the child may not be able to do on his or her own. Parents of children with neurological disorders must advocate for appropriate services and seek support for themselves when needed.

Cancer. Children and adolescents make up 1% of all individuals diagnosed with cancer (www.cancer.gov). Treatment like surgery, chemotherapy and radiation, which often help individuals live longer, are invasive, painful, and come with a list of negative side effects. In the unfortunate circumstance that treatment has failed and death is inevitable, both the child and family will need psychological support throughout the process and after.

COGNITIVE AND DEVELOPMENTAL CONTRIBUTIONS

A variety of cognitive and developmental issues within the lives of adolescents and children can contribute dramatically to the family system and impact clinical treatment. Development, as it occurs throughout the human life span, is complex and powerful. A solid knowledge of these issues can help the marriage and family therapist better assess, conceptualize, and treat the family unit.

Early Life Development

As scientific research on prenatal and early life events expands, greater emphasis continues to be placed on early life development and environmental factors. Compared to all other animal species, even other hominids, humans have a strikingly and significantly longer period of gestation (280 days), delay in appearance of permanent teeth (20.5 years), and completion of general physical growth (20 years; Narvaez, 2014). Additionally, in comparison to other animal species, humans have the longest period of child rearing (human number of years versus animal years) and take the longest time to reach adult physical maturation. Conversely, the human brain volume at birth is only 25% of its adult size, but quickly grows to 90% of its adult size by age 3 (Dettwyler, 1997; Montagu, 1978; Trevathan, 2011), revealing a tremendous amount of importance placed on the human child's early life environment and experience.

Prenatal and Infant Care

Healthy and successful life functioning for the child and adolescent begins in the womb and during infancy. The conception and early development of a human child brings into existence an amazingly complex explosion of physiological processing requiring an adequate level of nutrition and environmental care and stability. Physical development, including skeletal, brain, and sensorimotor growth and maturation, are dynamic during the early years of life. Prominent influences on early life care include heredity and hormones, emotional well-being, and nutrition; as well as avoiding disease and childhood injuries (Jenkins, Fineran, & Lange, 2016). Neglected prenatal care can create irrevocable problems in a child's development. Malnutrition, drug or alcohol use, and infectious disease can all contribute to the unhealthy development of a child. Physical and mental health professionals can often assist in the prevention of these maladies through proactive educational efforts.

Nurturance and Attachment

Developmental and early life research continues to place importance on nurturance and attachment as essential elements of the maturation process (Narvaez, Panksepp, Schore, & Gleason, 2013). Nurturance is generally defined as the emotional and physical nourishment that a parent or caregiver gives to an infant. Similarly, attachment is understood as a deep and enduring emotional bond that comes about through the active and healthy connection between a caregiver and a child. The seminal work on attachment is Bowlby's (1969) attachment theory, which emphasizes the importance of the mother child relationship during the first 5 years of life. The theory believes that maternal separation/deprivation in the child's early life can cause life-long social, relational, and emotional damage. Numerous other research has supported these findings. For example, Dozier, Zeanah, and Bernard (2013) found that a lack of attachment and nurturance in early life can lead to a variety of behavioral, emotional, and physiological dysregulation and challenges. Let's pause now and read Guided Practice Exercise 20.2 to reflect upon your own childhood.

GUIDED PRACTICE EXERCISE 20.2

Many developmental theorists identify a child's infancy and early childhood (0–6 years) physical development, cognitive development, emotional development, and social development as imperative in the overall growth and health of a child. Take a moment to reflect and examine your own infancy and early childhood, and identify the domain (physical, cognitive, emotional or social) that was the most important in contributing to your personal early life development and making you who you are. Contemplate and elaborate on why this domain was the most significant during this this developmental period.

Neurodevelopmental Disorder and Issues

Neurodevelopment and neuroprocesses emerged as important areas of both clinical and research elements in the social sciences (Kindsvatter & Geroski, 2014). According to the Environmental Protection Agency (2013), up to 15% of children in the United States ages 3 to 17 were affected by neurodevelopmental disorders. Once predominantly the work of the fields of neurology and neuropsychology, mental health professionals, including marriage and family therapists, are now finding themselves assessing, diagnosing, and treating an array of neurodevelopmental issues (Flamez, King, & Francis, 2014). The importance of neurodevelopment is most profound in childhood, but its effects persist into adulthood, resulting in impairment or delay in various central nervous system functioning. Mental or emotional disorders because of impairment in neurodevelopment rarely experience remission or relapses, and commonly follow a stable and persistent course over time (World Health Organization, 2014).

Understanding neurodevelopmental disorders is very challenging, as early developmental trajectories are inherently unpredictable, influenced by complex genetic, biological, environmental, and psychosocial factors (Insel, 2014). Recent advances in pediatric neuroscience revealed increasingly complex systems that continue to evolve and modify (Fine & Sung, 2014). A diverse and comprehensive understanding of the concepts and processes associated with neurodevelopment is needed for a deep understanding of child and adolescent issues as they related to the family system.

Intellectual Disabilities

Healthy neurodevelopment is essential for the mental health of all individuals. As the human brain governs most behavioral, social, cognitive, and emotional functioning, abnormal neurodevelopment can result in altered functioning of the brain systems (Perry, 2008). Accordingly, the specific nature of the mental health dysfunction is a result of which areas, networks, and stages are altered (Flamez, King, & Francis, 2015). Intellectual disabilities are one such phenomena that can occur because of disordered neurodevelopment. Intellectual disability is defined as "deficits in general mental disabilities, such as reasoning, problem solving, planning, abstract thinking, judgment, academic learning, and learning from experience" (American Psychiatric Association, 2013, p. 31). In addition, intellectual disability is scaled on four levels of severity: mild, moderate, severe, and profound.

Intellectual disability can impact the family system in multiple ways, and add an additional element of complexity to the family practitioner. Webb-Peploe and Fredman (2015) suggested that family communication which includes a family member with intellectual disability can be a challenge, as the person often feels their voices are frequently subjugated or silenced. Recognizing and empathizing with both the individual with the developmental disability and the family members provides a strong foundation to therapeutic services.

Autistic Spectrum Disorder

The mental health profession's awareness and recognition of autistic spectrum disorder has drastically increased in the past decade. This increase has greatly improved the identification of the disorder and its symptoms as they apply and contribute to the family system. Autistic spectrum disorder (ASD) is characterized by persistent deficits in social communication and social interaction throughout multiple environments, including deficits in social and emotional reciprocity, nonverbal communicative behaviors used for social interaction, and skills in developing, maintaining, and understanding relationships (American Psychiatric Association, 2013). Families play a tremendously important role in aiding the development and well-being of children with autism spectrum conditions.

A significant variable in the assessment and understanding of ASD is the severity of the symptoms and level of impairment in functioning caused by the disorder (Helps, 2016). Severity levels range from level 1 (requiring support), level 2 (requiring substantial support), and level 3 (requiring very substantial report). The severity level for ASD often equates to the level of impact and involvement of family members in the day-to-day management of the disorder. According to the Center for Disease Control and Prevention (2014), 1 in 68 children have ASD. With no sign indicating these numbers will decrease, families, and the therapeutic professionals that serve them, will need to grow in knowledge and competence to meet the demands of this population.

Trauma

In addition to the biologically driven neurodevelopmental disorders, environmental trauma can also profoundly impact the lives of children and adolescents within the family context. Rates of trauma on children vary, with some studies finding that as high as 68% of children and adolescents had experienced a potentially traumatic event by age 16 (Costello, Erkanli, Fairbank, & Angold, 2002). Trauma can take many forms including abuse (physical, emotional, verbal, sexual), violent, crime, accidents, neglect, and witnessing violent acts on others (Finkelhor, Turner, Shattuck, & Hamby, 2013). Institutionalized trauma and generational family trauma also contribute to the scale of trauma on youth and the myriad of emotional dysfunction they lead to. Trauma, in its various forms and iterations, can directly cause symptoms of depression, anxiety, behavioral problems, and interpersonal problems in childhood and adolescents (Eslinger, Sprang, & Otis, 2015).

Marriage and family therapists cannot underestimate the impact of trauma on either the individual or family system participating in treatment.

Healthy Development

The absence of prominent biological or environmental stress or dysfunction leads to the healthy development of our youth. Capuzzi and Stauffer (2016) suggest that development occurs within the physical, cognitive, emotional, and social domains of a person's life. The physical domain occupies the basic nutritional and biological needs of the youth, as well as the genetic and inherited contributions of their biochemistry. The cognitive domain consists of the brain's acquisition of senses, including psychomotor, language, communication, and memory. Additionally, the emotional domain includes the development of a vast array of complex feelings, reactions, and sensations in reaction to the physical environment. Lastly, the social domain includes a child's interactions with other people in their lives, including family, peers, and caregivers. In many ways, healthy development is the totality of the almost infinite number of variables that contribute to the well-being of a person. Early intervention in the form of competent marriage and family therapy has the potential to prevent or mitigate the barriers to healthy development among children and adolescents.

PSYCHOSOCIAL AND ENVIRONMENTAL CONTRIBUTIONS

Chaotic Family Environments

The family environment in which children and adolescents grow and develop have profound effects on the child. Chaotic and unstable family environments can significantly damage the physical and emotional development of a child, leading to lifelong ramifications. As previously discussed in this chapter, disruptions in early healthy development can negatively impact the biological, psychological, and social health of the young child. As children grow beyond infancy, environmental chaos and instability can induce other disturbances in the health development of the youth.

Divorce and Conflicted Parent Relations

Each year, 1.2 million marriages ended in divorce in the United States (U.S. Census Bureau, 2013), with an average length of 8 years for the first marriage (Henry, Fieldstone, Thompson, & Treeharne, 2011). Sixty-five percent of divorces in the United States involve families with minor children (Cohen, 2002), and 10% of divorcing families had disagreements over the custody of dependents (Luftman, Veltkamp, Clark, Lannacone, & Snooks, 2005). Divorce is a significant life stressor to youth and involves a variety of losses and adjustments, including emotional, financial, and physical (Cohen & Levite, 2012).

The effects of conflicted divorce on children and adolescents can be profound. Divorce and conflicted parent relations can cause instability and division in the child's life (Moore, Ordway, & Francis, 2013). Children are built and wired for consistency, stability, and predictability in their immediate environment and family system. The youth brain requires relative homeostasis to function optimally during these years. Conflicted parental divorce and disagreements disrupts this need, leading to a host of potential developmental and emotional problems including depression, anxiety, school and peer issues, behavioral problems, and substance abuse (Chun, Jang, Choi, Shin, & Park, 2016; Gustavsen, Nayga, & Wu, 2016).

Please take a moment now to reflect in a small group as directed in Guided Practice Exercise 20.3.

GUIDED PRACTICE EXERCISE 20.3

Divorce is very prevalent in our current society. The effects of divorce on children and adolescents are also potentially profound and developmentally significant. In dyads or a small group discussion, share your experiences with parental divorce (either your own experience or someone you were close to growing up). Identify the age of the person when the divorce occurred, the level of conflict associated with the divorce, and discuss what (if any) effect this had on the biopsychosocial health of the person as they went through parental divorce.

Changing Educational Environments

The beginning of the 21st century brought profound technological changes to most aspects of human life. One area where advances in technology have rapidly advanced the field is in the world of education. Smartboards, tablets, digital learning, and online schooling are all examples of the technological changes influencing the modern academic environment. With the increase in access and public perception of home-schooling and web-based primary and secondary educational environments, more families are educating children in their own homes.

Educational environments are also experiencing changes with the proliferation of postsecondary educational opportunities, dual enrollment, and college credit plus. These terms are used to imply the ability for high school students to earn college credit during their high school years. This movement is part of the larger societal trend in the United States to introduce more rigorous academic opportunities for students at a younger age. There are both proponents and opponents to the movement, but it is unlikely to change as the pressure for global educational competition continues to heat up.

Peer Pressure and Peer-Related Issues

Human beings are social creatures strongly influenced and affected by the people within their peer and environmental circles. Research continues to confirm the strength of peer relations on the development of children and adolescents (Dishion, 2013). Strong attachments to peer groups can lead to conformity, which is understood as a person changing their behavior to match the responses of others (Cialdini & Goldstein, 2004). Successful peer relationships can drastically enhance the social and emotional development of childhood (Capuzzi & Stauffer, 2016). Conversely, negative peer relationships can adversely impact development in numerous ways. Youth are easily influenced by the group identity associated with a peer group. Examples of an overallegiance to a negative group identity can be found in street gangs and other unhealthy peer environments that promote violence and risk-taking behaviors (Masland & Lease, 2013).

Problems with Technology

Undoubtedly, advances in technology over the past 2 decades drastically changed the way we live our lives. Although technological advances have been occurring throughout human evolution, the recent explosion in technology exposed children and adolescents to innovations never seen in our history. Children growing up today have never known a world without the Internet and electronic media and communication. Improvements and changes in communication, travel, social and intimate relationships, and access to information have had a most profound impact on children and adolescents and how they influence the family system. Technology is changing the way the family unit lives their lives. Not all of these changes have a positive impact on the family system, and an inability to moderate its use can lead to significant levels of dysfunction. Excessive gaming, Internet addictions, and problematic use of social media are common examples of this problem.

Excessive and compulsive use of video gaming has been found to have a host of negative effects on children and adolescents. More than 90% of all U.S. children participate in some type of video gaming activity (APA, 2015). Research has clearly demonstrated numerous concerns for excessive gaming including compulsive use, feelings of distress and loneliness, disregard for school work and other pro-social behaviors, and a variety of mental health issues (Livingston & Hadden, 2009; Rikkers, Lawrence, Hafekost, & Zubrick, 2016). A specific concern found throughout the professional literature is on the link between excessive gaming and violence among children and adolescents. Many popular video games portray violent acts including murder, death, shooting, and other forms of mayhem. Multiple associations can be made between violent video game participation and various acts of aggressiveness and violence (APA, 2015).

Internet addiction is defined as excessive and uncontrollable use of the Internet that leads to various negative results and impairment in functioning (Baysan-Arslan, Cebeci, Kaya, & Canbal, 2016). Internet addiction in adolescents has been correlated with higher risk of aggression, anxiety, and depression, as well as other mental health disorders (Ko, Yen, & Yen, 2012; Kuss, Griffiths, Karila, & Billieux, 2014; Lim et al., 2015). Excessive Internet use has also been found lead to emotional withdrawal, intolerance if desired use is not met, and a variety of negative physical and social consequences (Block, 2008). Familial problems often arise when parents or caregivers attempt to reduce or restrict the use of the Internet. The attempts to limit can create defiance and oppositional responses from the child, leading to yelling and screaming matches, hiding and sneaking use, and struggles for power and control.

Social media has also been found to negatively impact children and adolescents' emotional, physical, and relational health. Of primary concern in the world of social media and children is the phenomenon of cyberbullying. Cyberbullying is the intentional targeting of an individual through some form of electronic medium to intimidate and humiliate a person in an intentionally aggressive and abusive manner that persists over time and deploys an imbalance of power between the perpetrator and victim (Merrill & Hanson, 2016). Cyberbullying is unique from traditional bullying in that the perpetrator can hide behind online anonymity and reach a much greater audience, furthering the humiliation and impact on the victim. The effects of cyberbullying can be tragic and can include depression, anxiety, lowered self-esteem, substance abuse, obesity, and even suicide (Carpenter & Hubbard, 2014; Hinduja & Patchin, 2010; Richards, Caldwell, Go, & Caldwell, 2015).

Although many negative contributions are credited to advances in technology, numerous positive influences on children, adolescents, and the family unit are also noted. Marked improvements in communication, learning/education, access to information, medical science, transportation, and others have created applications and opportunities for the betterment of family health well into the 21st century and beyond. Balancing and moderating the pros and cons of technological advances will be the vital to the future of the human species.

Trends in Addictions in Children and Adolescents

Long before the struggle with addiction to technology, addiction to substances took its toll on individuals and the larger family system. Unfortunately, children and adolescents are not immune to the ravages of substance abuse and chemical dependency. Like changes in technology, addiction trends in youth also fluctuate with time. In monitoring trends in youth substance abuse, the National Institute on Drug Abuse (2016) found a slightly declining use of alcohol, nicotine, cocaine, and inhalants; however, use of marijuana remained unchanged.

Marijuana use among youth is trending in recent times and continues to have high popularity as more states in the United States pass both medical and recreation marijuana use laws. Colorado was the first state in the union to legalize recreation use of marijuana. As a result, solid data continues to compile on the effects of legalization on children and adolescents. According to the Office of National Drug Control Policy (2016), a developing negative impact of the legalization of marijuana is increases in use among youth. Research indicated that past-month use among youth was up 20%, compared to the 2-year average prior to legalization. Marijuana legalization increases the amount of marijuana and ease of access for youth. Medical and recreational legalization of marijuana also sends a strong message of acceptance to adolescents, allowing them to more easily justify and condone personal and group use. Dangers of marijuana youth among children and adolescents include a lack of motivation, changes in perception and mood, lack of coordination, difficulty thinking and problem solving, and impairment in learning and memory (National Institute on Drug Abuse, 2016). If recent marijuana legalization trends continue across the United States, youth use will also increase and will continue to have a powerful effect on the family system.

Other psychoactive and illegal substances are becoming increasingly problematic in children and adolescents. Of all substances being used and abused by children and adolescents, heroin is emerging as the most addicting and dangerous. Predominantly an issue with young adults and adults, the ravages of heroin are creeping into the adolescent and late adolescent demographic. The use of heroin among youth continues to grow as they advance into late adolescence (Johnston, Miech, O'Malley, Bachman, & Schulenberg, 2016). Heroin is a highly addictive drug made from morphine, a powerful derivative of the poppy plant. Heroin use and overdose deaths have significantly increased in the past decade (Substance Abuse and Mental Health Services Administration, 2015). The power behind heroin addiction is found in the potency of its clinical withdrawal syndrome. Individuals addicted to heroin and its opiate relatives must endure horrible withdrawal symptoms that include flu-like symptoms, nausea, aches and pains, and profound cravings. With one use of the substance, the withdrawal symptoms disappear immediately, adding to the cycle of chronic use.

Youth Addiction's Effect on the Family

Substance use, abuse, and dependency (addiction) in children and adolescents also takes its toll on the family system. Generational substance abuse and addiction is common in families where use frequent use is pervasive in the family history. The family patterns often trickle down to multi-generational use. Use among children and adolescents, whether in a family system with generational substance abuse or not, can also have a profound impact on the family. Parents of addicted children can be placed in terrible situations for which they feel incredible unequipped to manage. Family members of substance abusing or addicted youth struggle with many facets of the addiction cycle. It is important for marriage and family therapists to have a sufficient knowledge of the signs and symptoms of addiction, available community and professional resources, and treatment approaches to better assist families through this substantial challenge.

SUMMARY

In Chapter 20 we reviewed the variety of powerful and diverse contributions that children and adolescents have on the family system and the importance of professional competence when working with this population. Important topics included the rapidly evolving changes in the family structure because of modern influences such as technology, changes in education, and transformations in family demographics. Children and adolescents demonstrate both externalized behaviors (disruptive or problematic outward expressions) and internalized behaviors (inward emotional symptoms) that influence the family unit, including a variety of physical health issues. Family therapists need to develop an awareness of the numerous psychosocial and environmental contributions to the lives of children and adolescents and their impact on the family. Lastly, we want to wish you success on your journey in the counseling profession. We hope you have found the information throughout all the chapters helpful and have gained a greater knowledge of family therapy.

KEYSTONES

Among the key points addressed in this chapter are:

- Professional competency of child and adolescent issues is essential for marriage and family therapists.
- The family unit continues to evolve and modify as a product of societal and technological changes.
- Children and adolescents consist of several complex, independent, yet interconnected parts that greatly impact the family structure.
- Physical/environmental, emotional, social/relational, and cognitive life domains all impact the development of youth and significantly influence the family system.

REFLECTIONS FROM THE CONTRIBUTORS' CHAIR

Joshua Francis

The importance of the human developmental period between birth and young adulthood cannot be overestimated. As research continues to demonstrate the power and potency of this time, it also reveals a harsh paradox. As a clinician actively working with youth in a private counseling practice, I struggle with this paradox daily. The paradox is that the human body matures exponentially faster than the human brain. Regrettably, children I treat are exposed to environmental stressors and factors that exceed their emotional or cognitive capacity to manage them, creating early life challenges that can last a lifetime. The advancement of modernity has only expedited this process and created a powerful conundrum for myself and all child and family therapists. Family interventions are vital (and maybe essential) to addressing the issues, as the family can be both the cause of the problem, and the ultimate solution to the problem. As clinicians working with youth and families, we must recognize this and intervene diligently on both ends, attempting to repair the source of the dysfunction, as well as using the family system as the foundation to rebuild the mental health and stability of the unit. If we prioritize this, we CAN make a difference—a hefty challenge indeed!

ADDITIONAL RESOURCES

The following resources provide additional information relating to the chapter topics.

Useful Websites

- American Diabetes Association
  http://www.diabetes.org

This website provides information on diabetes to spread awareness and promote advocacy efforts for prevention and treatment.

- Centers for Disease Control and Prevention
  http://www.cdc.gov

This U.S. government website provides an abundance of information and resources on various diseases and conditions.

- DARE Research on Marijuana Use and Youth
  http://www.dare.org/impact-of-marijuana-upon-colorado-youth/

This website provides up-to-date information about marijuana in early recreational legalization states.

- National Cancer Institute
  https://www.cancer.gov

This U.S. government website provides information on the different types of cancer, treatment options, available resources, and current research.

- National Institute of Mental Health
  http://www.nimh.gov

This U.S. government website provides information on various mental disorders, treatment, and current research.

- National Institute on Drug Abuse
  https://www.drugabuse.gov

This U.S. government site provides an abundance of information on youth drug abuse.

- National Institute on Drug Abuse for Teens
  https://teens.drugabuse.gov

This website provides specific information on drug abuse related to the teenage and adolescent population as well as many pragmatic resources for families and treatment providers.

REFERENCES

Achenbach, T. M., & Rescorla, L. A. (2001). *Manual for the ASEBA school-age forms & profiles*. Burlington, VT: University of Vermont, Research Center for Children, Youth, & Families.

American Association of Marriage and Family Therapy. (2015). *Code of ethics*. Retrieved from http://www.aamft.org/iMIS15/AAMFT/Content/Legal_Ethics/Code_of_Ethics.aspx

American Counseling Association. (2014). *Code of ethics*. Retrieved from http://www.counseling.org/docs/ethics/2014-aca-code-of-ethics.pdf?sfvrsn=4

American Psychiatric Association. (2013). *Diagnostic and statistical manual of mental disorders* (5th ed.). Washington, DC: Author.

American Psychological Association. (2015). Technical report on the review of the violent video game literature. Retrieved from http://www.apa.org/pi/families/review-video-games.pdf

Baysan-Arslan, S., Cebeci, S., Kaya, M., & Canbal, M. (2016). Relationship between Internet addiction and alexithymia among university students. *Clinical & Investigative Medicine, 39*(6), S111–S115.

Benoit, D. (2009) Feeding disorders, failure to thrive and obesity. In C. H. Zeanah Jr. (Ed.), *Handbook of infant mental health* (3rd ed., pp. 377–391). New York: Guilford Press.

Bilginer, C., & Kandil, S. (2016). Emotional and behavioral characteristics of childhood depression. *Journal of Experimental & Clinical Medicine, 33*(2), 85–92.

Block, J. (2008). Issues for DSM-V: Internet addiction. *American Journal of Psychiatry, 165*, 306–307.

Bowlby, J. (1969). *Attachment. Attachment and loss: Vol. 1. Loss*. New York: Basic Books.

Boyatzis, R. E. (1982). *The competent manager: A model for effective performance*. New York: Wiley.

Broderick, C. B., & Schrader, S. S. (2013). The history of professional marriage and family therapy. In A. S. Gurman & D. P. Kniskern (Eds.), *Handbook of family therapy* (Vol. 1, pp. 5–35). London: Rutledge.

Buck, J.N. (1948). The H-T-P test. *Journal of Clinical Psychology, 4*, 151–159.

Burns, R. C., & Kaufman, S. H. (1970). *Kinetic family drawings (K-F-D)*. New York: Brunner/Mazel.

Capuzzi, D., & Stauffer, M. D. (Eds.). (2016). *Human growth and development across the lifespan: Applications for counselors*. Hoboken, NJ: Wiley.

Carpenter, L. M., & Hubbard, G. B. (2014). Cyberbullying: Implications for the psychiatric nurse practitioner. *Journal of Child & Adolescent Psychiatric Nursing, 27*(3), 142–148. doi:10.1111/jcap.12079

Centers for Disease Control and Prevention. (2014). Prevalence of Autism Spectrum Disorder among children aged 8 years. Retrieved from https://www.cdc.gov/mmwr/preview/mmwrhtml/ss6302a1.htm?s_cid=ss6302a1_w

Choate, L. H., & Ginter, G. G. (2015). Feeding and eating disorders. In B. Flamez (Ed.), *Diagnosing and treating children and adolescents: A guide for mental health professionals* (pp. 315–339). Hoboken, NJ: Wiley.

Chun, S., Jang, S., Choi, J., Shin, J., & Park, E. (2016). Long-term effects of parental divorce timing on depression: A population-based longitudinal study. *International Journal of Social Psychiatry, 62*(7), 645–650.

Cialdini, R. B., & Goldstein, N. J. (2004). Social influence: Compliance and conformity. *Annual Review of Psychology, 55*(1), 591–621.

Cohen, G. J. (2002). Helping children and families deal with divorce and separation. *Pediatrics, 110*(5), 1019–1023. doi:10.1542/peds.2006-0676

Cohen, O., & Levite, Z. (2012). High-conflict divorced couples: Combining systemic and psychodynamic perspectives. *Journal of Family Therapy, 34*, 387–402.

Costello, E. J., Erkanli, A., Fairbank, J. A., & Angold, A. (2002). The prevalence of potentially traumatic events in childhood and adolescence. *Journal of Traumatic Stress, 15*(2), 99–112.

Dakof, G. A., Henderson, C. E., Rowe, C. L., Boustani, M., Greenbaum, P. E., Wang, W., … & Liddle, H. A. (2015). A randomized clinical trial of family therapy in juvenile drug court. *Journal of Family Psychology,* *29*(2), 232–241.

Dettwyler, K. A. (1997), On parents and children sleeping together. *American Journal of Orthopsychiatry, 67*: 159–160. doi:10.1037/h0085078

Dishion, T. J. (2013). Stochastic agent-based modeling of influence and selection in adolescence: Current status and future directions in understanding the dynamics of peer contagion. *Journal of Research on Adolescence, 23*(3), 596–603.

Dozier, M., Zeanah, C. H., & Bernard, K. (2013). Infants and toddlers in foster care. *Child Development Perspectives, 7*(3), 166–171. doi:10.1111/cdep.12033

Eccleston, C., & Malleson, P. (2003). Managing chronic pain in children and adolescents. *British Medical Journal, 326*(7404), 1408–1409.

El Sheikh, M., Buckhalt, A., Cummings, M. E., & Keller, P. (2007). Sleep disruptions and emotional security are pathways of risk for children. *Journal of Child Psychology and Psychiatry, 48*, 88–96.

Environmental Protection Agency. (2013). *Neurodevelopmental disorders.* Retrieved from http://www.epa.gov/ace/pdfs/Health-Neurodevelopmental.pdf

Eslinger, J., Sprang, G., & Otis, M. (2015). Children with multi-trauma histories: Special considerations for care and implications for treatment selection. *Journal of Child & Family Studies, 24*(9), 2757–2768.

Fahlquist, J. N. (2015). Experience of non-breastfeeding mothers: Norms and ethically responsible risk communication. *Nursing Ethics, 23*(2), 231–241.

Fine, J. G., & Sung, C. (2014). Neuroscience of child and adolescent health development. *Journal of Counseling Psychology, 61*(4), 521–527. doi:10.1037/cou0000033

Finkelhor, D., Turner, H. A., Shattuck, A., & Hamby, S. L. (2013). Violence, crime, and abuse exposure in a national sample of children and youth. *JAMA Pediatrics, 42*, 1–8.

Flamez, B., King, J. H., & Francis, J. D. (2015). Conceptualizing DSM-5 disorders in children and adolescents. In B. Flamez (Ed.), *Diagnosing and treating children and adolescents: A guide for mental health professionals* (pp. 3–27). Hoboken, NJ: Wiley.

Germo, G. R., Chang, E. S., Keller, M. A., & Goldberg, W. A. (2007). Child sleep arrangements and family life: Perspectives from mothers and fathers. *Infant and Child Development, 16*, 433–456.

Goorden, M., Schawo, S. J., Bouwmans-Frijters, C. M., Van der Schee, E., Hendriks, V. M., & Hakkaart-Van Roijen, L. (2016). The cost-effectiveness of family/family-based therapy for treatment of externalizing disorders, substance use disorders and delinquency: A systematic review. *BMC Psychiatry, 16*(1), 237.

Gustavsen, G. W., Nayga, R. J., & Wu, X. (2016). Effects of parental divorce on teenage children's risk behaviors: Incidence and persistence. *Journal of Family and Economic Issues, 37*(3), 474–487.

Helps, S. (2016). Systemic psychotherapy with families where someone has an autism spectrum condition. *Neurorehabilitation, 38*(3), 223–230.

Henry, W. J., Fieldstone, L., Thompson, M., & Treharne, K. (2011). Parenting coordination as an antidote for high-conflict divorce and court prelitigation. *Journal of Divorce & Remarriage, 52*, 455–471.

Hinduja, S., & Patchin, J. W. (2010). Bullying, cyberbullying, and suicide. *International Academy for Suicide Research, 14*, 206–221.

Hundozi-Hysenaj, H., & Boshnjaku-Dallku, I. (2008). Epilepsy in children with cerebral palsy. *Journal of Pediatric Neurology, 6*, 43–46.

Insel, T. R. (2014). Mental disorders in childhood: Shifting the focus from behavioral symptoms to neurodevelopmental trajectories. *JAMA: Journal of The American Medical Association, 311*(17), 1727-1728. doi:10.1001/jama.2014.1193

Jain, S., Romack, R., & Jain, R. (2011). Bed sharing in school-age children: Clinical and social implications. *Journal of Child and Adolescent Psychiatric Nursing, 2*, 185–189.

Jenkins, C., Fineran, K. R., & Lange, A. (2016). Birth and infancy: Physical and cognitive development. In D. Capuzzi & M. D. Stauffer (Eds.), *Human growth and development across the lifespan: Applications for counselors* (pp. 113–150). Hoboken, NJ: Wiley.

Johnston, L. D., Miech, R. A., O'Malley, P. M., Bachman, J. G., & Schulenberg, J. E. (2016). *Teen use of any illicit drug other than marijuana at new low, same true for alcohol.* Ann Arbor: University of Michigan News Service. Retrieved from http://www.monitoringthefuture.org

Kindsvatter, A., & Geroski, A. (2014). The impact of early life stress on the neurodevelopment of the stress response system. *Journal of Counseling & Development, 92*(4), 472–480.

Ko, C. H., Yen, J. Y., & Yen, C. F. (2012) The association between Internet addiction and psychiatric disorder: A review of the literature. *European Psychiatry, 27*, 1–8.

Kuss, D., Griffiths, M., Karila, L., & Billieux, J. (2014). Internet addiction: A systematic review of epidemiological research for the last decade. *Current Pharmaceutical Design, 20*(25), 4026–4052. doi:10.2174/138 16128113199990617

Lim, J., Gwak, A. R., Park, S. M., Kwon, J., Lee, J., Jung, H. Y., ... & Choi, J. (2015). Are adolescents with Internet addiction prone to aggressive behavior? The mediating effect of clinical comorbidities on the predictability of aggression in adolescents with Internet addiction. *Cyberpsychology, Behavior & Social Networking, 18*(5), 260–267. doi:10.1089/cyber.2014.0568

Logan, D. E., & Scharff, L. (2005). Relationships between family and parent characteristics and functional abilities in children with recurrent pain syndromes: An investigation of moderating effects on the pathway from pain to disability. *Journal of Pediatric Psychology, 30*, 698–707.

Luftman, V. H., Veltkamp, L. J., Clark, J. J., Lannacone, S., & Snooks, H. (2005). Practice guidelines in child custody evaluations for licensed clinical social workers. *Clinical Social Work Journal, 33*(3), 327–357.

Masland, L. C., & Lease, A. M. (2013). Effects of achievement motivation, social identity, and peer group norms on academic conformity. *Social Psychology of Education: An International Journal, 16*(4), 661–681.

Merrill, R. M., & Hanson, C. L. (2016). Risk and protective factors associated with being bullied on school property compared with cyberbullied. *BMC Public Health, 16*(1), 145. doi:10.1186/s12889-016-2833-3

Montagu, A. (1978). Touching: The human significance of the skin. New York: Harper & Row.

Moore, R., Ordway, A., & Francis, J. (2013). The tug-of-war child: Counseling children involved in high conflict divorce. *ACA VISTAS, 43.* Retrieved from http://www.counseling.org/docs/vistas/the-tug-of-war-child-counseling-children-involved.pdf?sfvrsn=2

Narvaez, D. (2014). Neurobiology and the development of human morality. New York: Norton.

Narvaez, D., Panksepp, J., Schore, A., & Gleason, T. (Eds.) (2013). Evolution, early experience and human development: From research to practice and policy. New York: Oxford University Press.

National Institute on Drug Abuse. (2016). Marijuana. Retrieved from https://teens.drugabuse.gov/drug-facts/marijuana

Office of National Drug Control Policy. (2016). The legalization of marijuana in Colorado: The impact. Retrieved from http://www.rmhidta.org/html/FINAL%20NSDUH%20Results-%20Jan%202016%20Release.pdf

Palermo, T. M. (2000). Impact of recurrent and chronic pain on child and family daily functioning: A critical review of the literature. *Journal of Developmental Behavior Pediatrics, 21*, 58–69.

Perry, B. D. (2008). Child maltreatment: A developmental perspective on the role of trauma and neglect in psychopathology. In T. Beauchaine & S. P. Hinshaw (Eds.), *Child and adolescent psychopathology* (pp. 93–129). Hoboken, NJ: Wiley.

Pew Research Center. (2016). 10 demographic trends that are shaping the U.S. and the world. Retrieved from http://www.pewresearch.org/fact-tank/2016/03/31/10-demographic-trends-that-are-shaping-the-u-s-and-the-world

Richards, D., Caldwell, P. H., Go, H., & Caldwell, P. Y. (2015). Impact of social media on the health of children and young people. *Journal of Pediatrics & Child Health, 51*(12), 1152–1157. doi:10.1111/jpc.13023

Rikkers, W., Lawrence, D., Hafekost, J., & Zubrick, S. R. (2016). Internet use and electronic gaming by children and adolescents with emotional and behavioural problems in Australia—results from the second Child and Adolescent Survey of Mental Health and Wellbeing. *BMC Public Health, 16*(1), 399.

Sheperis, C. J., Calley, T. K., Jones-Trebatoski, K., & Wines, L. A. (2015). Sleep-wake disorders. In B. Flamez (Ed.), *Diagnosing and treating children and adolescents: A guide for mental health professionals* (pp. 340–365). Hoboken, NJ: Wiley.

Smithsonian National Museum of Natural History (2017). Retrieved from http://humanorigins.si.edu/evidence/human-fossils/species/homo-sapiens

Substance Abuse and Mental Health Services Administration. (2015). CBHSQ report. Trends in heroin use in the United States: 2002 to 2013. Retrieved from http://www.samhsa.gov/data/sites/default/files/report_1943/ShortReport-1943.html

Thibodeau, B. A., Metcalfe, P., Koop, P., & Moore, K. (2013) Urinary incontinence and quality of life in children. *Journal of Pediatric Urology, 9*(1), 78–83.

Travathan, W.R. (2011). Human birth: An evolutionary perspective, 2nd ed. New York: Aldine de Gruyter

US Census Bureau. (2012). America's families and living arrangements: 2012. Retrieved from https://www.census.gov/prod/2013pubs/p20-570.pdf

US Census Bureau. (2013) Number, timing, and duration of marriages and divorces: 2009. Retrieved from http://www.census.gov/prod/2011pubs/p70-125.pdf

Webb-Peploe, H., & Fredman, G. (2015). Systemic empathy with adults affected by intellectual disabilities and their families. *Journal of Family Therapy, 37*(2), 228–245. doi:10.1111/j.1467-6427.2012.00605.x

World Health Organization. (2014). Mental disorders. Retrieved from http://www.who.int/mediacentre/factsheets/fs396/en

Zink, D. W. (2008) The practice of marriage and family counseling and conservative Christianity. In J. D. Onedera (Ed.), *The role of religion in marriage and family counseling* (pp. 55–72). New York: Routledge.

Code of Ethics

PREAMBLE

The Board of Directors of the American Association for Marriage and Family Therapy (AAMFT) hereby promulgates, pursuant to Article 2, Section 2.01.3 of the Association's Bylaws, the Revised AAMFT Code of Ethics, effective January 1, 2015.

Honoring Public Trust

The AAMFT strives to honor the public trust in marriage and family therapists by setting standards for ethical practice as described in this Code. The ethical standards define professional expectations and are enforced by the AAMFT Ethics Committee.

Commitment to Service, Advocacy and Public Participation

Marriage and family therapists are defined by an enduring dedication to professional and ethical excellence, as well as the commitment to service, advocacy, and public participation. The areas of service, advocacy, and public participation are recognized as responsibilities to the profession equal in importance to all other aspects. Marriage and family therapists embody these aspirations by participating in activities that contribute to a better community and society, including devoting a portion of their professional activity to services for which there is little or no financial return. Additionally, marriage and family therapists are concerned with developing laws and regulations pertaining to marriage and family therapy that serve the public interest, and with altering such laws and regulations that are not in the public interest. Marriage and family therapists also encourage public participation in the design and delivery of professional services and in the regulation of practitioners. Professional competence in these areas is essential to the character of the field, and to the well-being of clients and their communities.

Seeking Consultation

The absence of an explicit reference to a specific behavior or situation in the Code does not mean that the behavior is ethical or unethical. The standards are not exhaustive.

Marriage and family therapists who are uncertain about the ethics of a particular course of action are encouraged to seek counsel from consultants, attorneys, supervisors, colleagues, or other appropriate authorities.

Ethical Decision-Making

Both law and ethics govern the practice of marriage and family therapy. When making decisions regarding professional behavior, marriage and family therapists must consider the AAMFT Code of Ethics and applicable laws and regulations. If the AAMFT Code of Ethics prescribes a standard higher than that required by law, marriage and family therapists must meet the higher standard of the AAMFT Code of Ethics. Marriage and family therapists comply with the mandates of law, but make known their commitment to the AAMFT Code of Ethics and take steps to resolve the conflict in a responsible manner. The AAMFT supports legal mandates for reporting of alleged unethical conduct.

Marriage and family therapists remain accountable to the AAMFT Code of Ethics when acting as members or employees of organizations. If the mandates of an organization with which a marriage and family therapist is affiliated, through employment, contract or otherwise, conflict with the AAMFT Code of Ethics, marriage and family therapists make known to the organization their commitment to the AAMFT Code of Ethics and take reasonable steps to resolve the conflict in a way that allows the fullest adherence to the Code of Ethics.

Binding Expectations

The AAMFT Code of Ethics is binding on members of AAMFT in all membership categories, all AAMFT Approved Supervisors and all applicants for membership or the Approved Supervisor designation. AAMFT members have an obligation to be familiar with the AAMFT Code of Ethics and its application to their professional services. Lack of awareness or misunderstanding of an ethical standard is not a defense to a charge of unethical conduct.

Resolving Complaints

The process for filing, investigating, and resolving complaints of unethical conduct is described in the current AAMFT Procedures for Handling Ethical Matters. Persons accused are considered innocent by the Ethics Committee until proven guilty, except as otherwise provided, and are entitled to due process. If an AAMFT member resigns in anticipation of, or during the course of, an ethics investigation, the Ethics Committee will complete its investigation. Any publication of action taken by the Association will include the fact that the member attempted to resign during the investigation.

Aspirational Core Values

The following core values speak generally to the membership of AAMFT as a professional association, yet they also inform all the varieties of practice and service in which marriage and family therapists engage. These core values are aspirational in nature, and are distinct from ethical standards. These values are intended to provide an aspirational framework within which marriage and family therapists may pursue the highest goals of practice.

The core values of AAMFT embody:

1. Acceptance, appreciation, and inclusion of a diverse membership.

2. Distinctiveness and excellence in training of marriage and family therapists and those desiring to advance their skills, knowledge and expertise in systemic and relational therapies.

3. Responsiveness and excellence in service to members.

4. Diversity, equity and excellence in clinical practice, research, education and administration.

5. Integrity evidenced by a high threshold of ethical and honest behavior within Association governance and by members.

6. Innovation and the advancement of knowledge of systemic and relational therapies.

Ethical Standards

Ethical standards, by contrast, are rules of practice upon which the marriage and family therapist is obliged and judged. The introductory paragraph to each standard in the AAMFT Code of Ethics is an aspirational/explanatory orientation to the enforceable standards that follow.

STANDARD I
Responsibility to Clients

Marriage and family therapists advance the welfare of families and individuals and make reasonable efforts to find the appropriate balance between conflicting goals within the family system.

1.1 Non-Discrimination. Marriage and family therapists provide professional assistance to persons without discrimination on the basis of race, age, ethnicity, socioeconomic status, disability, gender, health status, religion, national origin, sexual orientation, gender identity or relationship status.

1.2 Informed Consent. Marriage and family therapists obtain appropriate informed consent to therapy or related procedures and use language that is reasonably understandable to clients. When persons, due to age or mental status, are legally incapable of giving informed consent, marriage and family therapists obtain informed permission from a legally authorized person, if such substitute consent is legally permissible. The content of informed consent may vary depending upon the client and treatment plan; however, informed consent generally necessitates that the client: (a) has the capacity to consent; (b) has been adequately informed of significant information concerning treatment processes and procedures; (c) has been adequately informed of potential risks and benefits of treatments for which generally recognized standards do not yet exist; (d) has freely and without undue influence expressed consent; and (e) has provided consent that is appropriately documented.

1.3 Multiple Relationships. Marriage and family therapists are aware of their influential positions with respect to clients, and they avoid exploiting the trust and dependency of such persons. Therapists, therefore, make every effort to avoid conditions and multiple relationships with clients that could impair professional judgment or increase the risk of exploitation. Such relationships include, but are not limited to, business or close personal relationships with a client or the client's immediate family. When the risk of impairment or exploitation exists due to conditions or multiple roles, therapists document the appropriate precautions taken.

1.4 Sexual Intimacy with Current Clients and Others. Sexual intimacy with current clients or with known members of the client's family system is prohibited.

1.5 Sexual Intimacy with Former Clients and Others. Sexual intimacy with former clients or with known members of the client's family system is prohibited.

1.6 Reports of Unethical Conduct. Marriage and family therapists comply with applicable laws regarding the reporting of alleged unethical conduct.

1.7 Abuse of the Therapeutic Relationship. Marriage and family therapists do not abuse their power in therapeutic relationships.

1.8 Client Autonomy in Decision Making. Marriage and family therapists respect the rights of clients to make decisions and help them to understand the consequences of these decisions. Therapists clearly advise clients that clients have the responsibility to make decisions regarding relationships such as cohabitation, marriage, divorce, separation, reconciliation, custody, and visitation.

1.9 Relationship Beneficial to Client. Marriage and family therapists continue therapeutic relationships only so long as it is reasonably clear that clients are benefiting from the relationship.

1.10 Referrals. Marriage and family therapists respectfully assist persons in obtaining appropriate therapeutic services if the therapist is unable or unwilling to provide professional help.

1.11 Non-Abandonment. Marriage and family therapists do not abandon or neglect clients in treatment without making reasonable arrangements for the continuation of treatment.

1.12 Written Consent to Record. Marriage and family therapists obtain written informed consent from clients before recording any images or audio or permitting third-party observation.

1.13 Relationships with Third Parties. Marriage and family therapists, upon agreeing to provide services to a person or entity at the request of a third party, clarify, to the extent feasible and at the outset of the service, the nature of the relationship with each party and the limits of confidentiality.

STANDARD II
Confidentiality

Marriage and family therapists have unique confidentiality concerns because the client in a therapeutic relationship may be more than one person. Therapists respect and guard the confidences of each individual client.

2.1 Disclosing Limits of Confidentiality. Marriage and family therapists disclose to clients and other interested parties at the outset of services the nature of confidentiality and possible limitations of the clients' right to confidentiality. Therapists review with clients the circumstances where confidential information may be requested and where disclosure of confidential information may be legally required. Circumstances may necessitate repeated disclosures.

2.2 Written Authorization to Release Client Information. Marriage and family therapists do not disclose client confidences except by written authorization or waiver, or where mandated or permitted by law. Verbal authorization will not be sufficient except in emergency situations, unless prohibited by law. When providing couple, family or group treatment, the therapist does not disclose information outside the treatment context without a written authorization from each individual competent to execute a waiver. In the context of couple, family or group treatment, the therapist may not reveal any individual's confidences to others in the client unit without the prior written permission of that individual.

2.3 Client Access to Records. Marriage and family therapists provide clients with reasonable access to records concerning the clients. When providing couple, family, or group treatment, the therapist does not provide access to records without a written authorization from each individual competent to execute a waiver. Marriage and family therapists limit client's access to their records only in exceptional circumstances when they are concerned, based on compelling evidence, that such access could cause serious harm to the client. The client's request and the rationale for withholding some or all of the record should be documented in the client's file. Marriage and family therapists take steps to protect the confidentiality of other individuals identified in client records.

2.4 Confidentiality in Non-Clinical Activities. Marriage and family therapists use client and/or clinical materials in teaching, writing, consulting, research, and public presentations only if a written waiver has been obtained in accordance with Standard 2.2, or when appropriate steps have been taken to protect client identity and confidentiality.

2.5 Protection of Records. Marriage and family therapists store, safeguard, and dispose of client records in ways that maintain confidentiality and in accord with applicable laws and professional standards.

2.6 Preparation for Practice Changes. In preparation for moving a practice, closing a practice, or death, marriage and family therapists arrange for the storage, transfer, or disposal of client records in conformance with applicable laws and in ways that maintain confidentiality and safeguard the welfare of clients.

2.7 Confidentiality in Consultations. Marriage and family therapists, when consulting with colleagues or referral sources, do not share confidential information that could reasonably lead to the identification of a client, research participant, supervisee, or other person with whom they have a confidential relationship unless they have obtained the prior written consent of the client, research participant, supervisee, or other person with whom they have a confidential relationship. Information may be shared only to the extent necessary to achieve the purposes of the consultation.

STANDARD III
Professional Competence and Integrity
Marriage and family therapists maintain high standards of professional competence and integrity.

3.1 Maintenance of Competency. Marriage and family therapists pursue knowledge of new developments and maintain their competence in marriage and family therapy through education, training, and/or supervised experience.

3.2 Knowledge of Regulatory Standards. Marriage and family therapists pursue appropriate consultation and training to ensure adequate knowledge of and adherence to applicable laws, ethics, and professional standards.

3.3 Seek Assistance. Marriage and family therapists seek appropriate professional assistance for issues that may impair work performance or clinical judgment.

3.4 Conflicts of Interest. Marriage and family therapists do not provide services that create a conflict of interest that may impair work performance or clinical judgment.

3.5 Maintenance of Records. Marriage and family therapists maintain accurate and adequate clinical and financial records in accordance with applicable law.

3.6 Development of New Skills. While developing new skills in specialty areas, marriage and family therapists take steps to ensure the competence of their work and to protect clients from possible harm. Marriage and family therapists practice in specialty areas new to them only after appropriate education, training, and/or supervised experience.

3.7 Harassment. Marriage and family therapists do not engage in sexual or other forms of harassment of clients, students, trainees, supervisees, employees, colleagues, or research subjects.

3.8 Exploitation. Marriage and family therapists do not engage in the exploitation of clients, students, trainees, supervisees, employees, colleagues, or research subjects.

3.9 Gifts. Marriage and family therapists attend to cultural norms when considering whether to accept gifts from or give gifts to clients. Marriage and family therapists consider the potential effects that receiving or giving gifts may have on clients and on the integrity and efficacy of the therapeutic relationship.

3.10 Scope of Competence. Marriage and family therapists do not diagnose, treat, or advise on problems outside the recognized boundaries of their competencies.

3.11 Public Statements. Marriage and family therapists, because of their ability to influence and alter the lives of others, exercise special care when making public their professional recommendations and opinions through testimony or other public statements.

3.12 Professional Misconduct. Marriage and family therapists may be in violation of this Code and subject to termination of membership or other appropriate action if they: (a) are convicted of any felony; (b) are convicted of a misdemeanor related to their qualifications or functions; (c) engage in conduct which could lead to conviction of a felony, or a misdemeanor related to their qualifications or functions; (d) are expelled from or disciplined by other professional organizations; (e) have their licenses or certificates suspended or revoked or are otherwise disciplined by regulatory bodies; (f) continue to practice marriage and family therapy while no longer competent to do so because they are impaired by physical or mental causes or the abuse of alcohol or other substances; or

(g) fail to cooperate with the Association at any point from the inception of an ethical complaint through the completion of all proceedings regarding that complaint.

STANDARD IV
Responsibility to Students and Supervisees
Marriage and family therapists do not exploit the trust and dependency of students and supervisees.

4.1 Exploitation. Marriage and family therapists who are in a supervisory role are aware of their influential positions with respect to students and supervisees, and they avoid exploiting the trust and dependency of such persons. Therapists, therefore, make every effort to avoid conditions and multiple relationships that could impair professional objectivity or increase the risk of exploitation. When the risk of impairment or exploitation exists due to conditions or multiple roles, therapists take appropriate precautions.

4.2 Therapy with Students or Supervisees. Marriage and family therapists do not provide therapy to current students or supervisees.

4.3 Sexual Intimacy with Students or Supervisees. Marriage and family therapists do not engage in sexual intimacy with students or supervisees during the evaluative or training relationship between the therapist and student or supervisee.

4.4 Oversight of Supervisee Competence. Marriage and family therapists do not permit students or supervisees to perform or to hold themselves out as competent to perform professional services beyond their training, level of experience, and competence.

4.5 Oversight of Supervisee Professionalism. Marriage and family therapists take reasonable measures to ensure that services provided by supervisees are professional.

4.6 Existing Relationship with Students or Supervisees. Marriage and family therapists are aware of their influential positions with respect to supervisees, and they avoid exploiting the trust and dependency of such persons. Supervisors, therefore, make every effort to avoid conditions and multiple relationships with supervisees that could impair professional judgment or increase the risk of exploitation. Examples of such relationships include, but are not limited to, business or close personal relationships with supervisees or the supervisee's immediate family. When the risk of impairment or exploitation exists due to conditions or multiple roles, supervisors document the appropriate precautions taken.

4.7 Confidentiality with Supervisees. Marriage and family therapists do not disclose supervisee confidences except by written authorization or waiver, or when mandated or permitted by law. In educational or training settings where there are multiple supervisors, disclosures are permitted only to other professional colleagues, administrators, or employers who share responsibility for training of the supervisee. Verbal authorization will not be sufficient except in emergency situations, unless prohibited by law.

4.8 Payment for Supervision. Marriage and family therapists providing clinical supervision shall not enter into financial arrangements with supervisees through deceptive or exploitative practices, nor shall marriage and family therapists providing clinical supervision exert undue influence over supervisees when establishing supervision fees. Marriage and family therapists shall also not engage in other exploitative practices of supervisees.

STANDARD V
Research and Publication

Marriage and family therapists respect the dignity and protect the welfare of research participants, and are aware of applicable laws, regulations, and professional standards governing the conduct of research.

5.1 Institutional Approval. When institutional approval is required, marriage and family therapists submit accurate information about their research proposals and obtain appropriate approval prior to conducting the research.

5.2 Protection of Research Participants. Marriage and family therapists are responsible for making careful examinations of ethical acceptability in planning research. To the extent that services to research participants may be compromised by participation in research, marriage and family therapists seek the ethical advice of qualified professionals not directly involved in the investigation and observe safeguards to protect the rights of research participants.

5.3 Informed Consent to Research. Marriage and family therapists inform participants about the purpose of the research, expected length, and research procedures. They also inform participants of the aspects of the research that might reasonably be expected to influence willingness to participate such as potential risks, discomforts, or adverse effects. Marriage and family therapists are especially sensitive to the possibility of diminished consent when participants are also receiving clinical services, or have impairments which limit understanding and/or communication, or when participants are children. Marriage and family therapists inform participants about any potential research benefits, the limits of confidentiality, and whom to contact concerning questions about the research and their rights as research participants.

5.4 Right to Decline or Withdraw Participation. Marriage and family therapists respect each participant's freedom to decline participation in or to withdraw from a research study at any time. This obligation requires special thought and consideration when investigators or other members of the research team are in positions of authority or influence over participants. Marriage and family therapists, therefore, make every effort to avoid multiple relationships with research participants that could impair professional judgment or increase the risk of exploitation. When offering inducements for research participation, marriage and family therapists make reasonable efforts to avoid offering inappropriate or excessive inducements when such inducements are likely to coerce participation.

5.5 Confidentiality of Research Data. Information obtained about a research participant during the course of an investigation is confidential unless there is a waiver previously obtained in writing. When the possibility exists that others, including family members, may obtain access to such information, this possibility, together with the plan for protecting confidentiality, is explained as part of the procedure for obtaining informed consent.

5.6 Publication. Marriage and family therapists do not fabricate research results. Marriage and family therapists disclose potential conflicts of interest and take authorship credit only for work they have performed or to which they have contributed. Publication credits accurately reflect the relative contributions of the individual involved.

5.7 Authorship of Student Work. Marriage and family therapists do not accept or require authorship credit for a publication based from student's research, unless the marriage and family therapist made a substantial contribution beyond being a faculty advisor or research committee member. Co-authorship on student research should be determined in accordance with principles of fairness and justice.

5.8 Plagiarism. Marriage and family therapists who are the authors of books or other materials that are published or distributed do not plagiarize or fail to cite persons to whom credit for original ideas or work is due.

5.9 Accuracy in Publication. Marriage and family therapists who are authors of books or other materials published or distributed by an organization take reasonable precautions to ensure that the published materials are accurate and factual.

STANDARD VI
Technology-Assisted Professional Services

Therapy, supervision, and other professional services engaged in by marriage and family therapists take place over an increasing number of technological platforms. There are great benefits and responsibilities inherent in both the traditional therapeutic and supervision contexts, as well as in the utilization of technologically-assisted professional services. This standard addresses basic ethical requirements of offering therapy, supervision, and related professional services using electronic means.

6.1 Technology Assisted Services. Prior to commencing therapy or supervision services through electronic means (including but not limited to phone and Internet), marriage and family therapists ensure that they are compliant with all relevant laws for the delivery of such services. Additionally, marriage and family therapists must: (a) determine that technologically-assisted services or supervision are appropriate for clients or supervisees, considering professional, intellectual, emotional, and physical needs; (b) inform clients or supervisees of the potential risks and benefits associated with technologically-assisted services; (c) ensure the security of their communication medium; and (d) only commence electronic therapy or supervision after appropriate education, training, or supervised experience using the relevant technology.

6.2 Consent to Treat or Supervise. Clients and supervisees, whether contracting for services as individuals, dyads, families, or groups, must be made aware of the risks and responsibilities associated with technology-assisted services. Therapists are to advise clients and supervisees in writing of these risks, and of both the therapist's and clients'/supervisees' responsibilities for minimizing such risks.

6.3 Confidentiality and Professional Responsibilities. It is the therapist's or supervisor's responsibility to choose technological platforms that adhere to standards of best practices related to confidentiality and quality of services, and that meet applicable laws. Clients and supervisees are to be made aware in writing of the limitations and protections offered by the therapist's or supervisor's technology.

6.4 Technology and Documentation. Therapists and supervisors are to ensure that all documentation containing identifying or otherwise sensitive information which is electronically stored and/or transferred is done using technology that adhere to standards of best practices related to confidentiality and quality of services, and that meet applicable laws. Clients and supervisees are to be made aware in writing of the limitations and protections offered by the therapist's or supervisor's technology.

6.5 Location of Services and Practice. Therapists and supervisors follow all applicable laws regarding location of practice and services, and do not use technologically-assisted means for practicing outside of their allowed jurisdictions.

6.6 Training and Use of Current Technology. Marriage and family therapists ensure that they are well trained and competent in the use of all chosen technology-assisted professional services. Careful choices of audio, video, and other options are made in order to optimize quality and security of services, and to adhere to standards of best practices for technology-assisted services. Furthermore, such choices of technology are to be suitably advanced and current so as to best serve the professional needs of clients and supervisees.

STANDARD VII
Professional Evaluations
Marriage and family therapists aspire to the highest of standards in providing testimony in various contexts within the legal system.

7.1 Performance of Forensic Services. Marriage and family therapists may perform forensic services which may include interviews, consultations, evaluations, reports, and assessments both formal and informal, in keeping with applicable laws and competencies.

7.2 Testimony in Legal Proceedings. Marriage and family therapists who provide expert or fact witness testimony in legal proceedings avoid misleading judgments, base conclusions and opinions on appropriate data, and avoid inaccuracies insofar as possible. When offering testimony, as marriage and family therapy experts, they shall strive to be accurate, objective, fair, and independent.

7.3 Competence. Marriage and family therapists demonstrate competence via education and experience in providing testimony in legal systems.

7.4 Informed Consent. Marriage and family therapists provide written notice and make reasonable efforts to obtain written consents of persons who are the subject(s) of evaluations and inform clients about the evaluation process, use of information and recommendations, financial arrangements, and the role of the therapist within the legal system.

7.5 Avoiding Conflicts. Clear distinctions are made between therapy and evaluations. Marriage and family therapists avoid conflict in roles in legal proceedings wherever possible and disclose potential conflicts. As therapy begins, marriage and family therapists clarify roles and the extent of confidentiality when legal systems are involved.

7.6 Avoiding Dual Roles. Marriage and family therapists avoid providing therapy to clients for whom the therapist has provided a forensic evaluation and avoid providing evaluations for those who are clients, unless otherwise mandated by legal systems.

7.7 Separation of Custody Evaluation from Therapy. Marriage and family therapists avoid conflicts of interest in treating minors or adults involved in custody or visitation actions by not performing evaluations for custody, residence, or visitation of the minor. Marriage and family therapists who treat minors may provide the court or mental health professional performing the evaluation with information about the minor from the marriage and family therapist's perspective as a treating marriage and family therapist, so long as the marriage and family therapist obtains appropriate consents to release information.

7.8 Professional Opinions. Marriage and family therapists who provide forensic evaluations avoid offering professional opinions about persons they have not directly interviewed. Marriage and family therapists declare the limits of their competencies and information.

7.9 Changes in Service. Clients are informed if changes in the role of provision of services of marriage and family therapy occur and/or are mandated by a legal system.

7.10 Familiarity with Rules. Marriage and family therapists who provide forensic evaluations are familiar with judicial and/ or administrative rules prescribing their roles.

STANDARD VIII
Financial Arrangements

Marriage and family therapists make financial arrangements with clients, third-party payors, and supervisees that are reasonably understandable and conform to accepted professional practices.

8.1 Financial Integrity. Marriage and family therapists do not offer or accept kickbacks, rebates, bonuses, or other remuneration for referrals. Fee-for-service arrangements are not prohibited.

8.2 Disclosure of Financial Policies. Prior to entering into the therapeutic or supervisory relationship, marriage and family therapists clearly disclose and explain to clients and supervisees: (a) all financial arrangements and fees related to professional services, including charges for canceled or missed appointments; (b) the use of collection agencies or legal measures for nonpayment; and (c) the procedure for obtaining payment from the client, to the extent allowed by law, if payment is denied by the third-party payor. Once services have begun, therapists provide reasonable notice of any changes in fees or other charges.

8.3 Notice of Payment Recovery Procedures. Marriage and family therapists give reasonable notice to clients with unpaid balances of their intent to seek collection by agency or legal recourse. When such action is taken, therapists will not disclose clinical information.

8.4 Truthful Representation of Services. Marriage and family therapists represent facts truthfully to clients, third-party payors, and supervisees regarding services rendered.

8.5 Bartering. Marriage and family therapists ordinarily refrain from accepting goods and services from clients in return for services rendered. Bartering for professional services may be conducted only if: (a) the supervisee or client requests it; (b) the relationship is not exploitative; (c) the professional relationship is not distorted; and (d) a clear written contract is established.

8.6 Withholding Records for Non-Payment. Marriage and family therapists may not withhold records under their immediate control that are requested and needed for a client's treatment solely because payment has not been received for past services, except as otherwise provided by law.

STANDARD IX
Advertising

Marriage and family therapists engage in appropriate informational activities, including those that enable the public, referral sources, or others to choose professional services on an informed basis.

9.1 Accurate Professional Representation. Marriage and family therapists accurately represent their competencies, education, training, and experience relevant to their practice of marriage and family therapy in accordance with applicable law.

9.2 Promotional Materials. Marriage and family therapists ensure that advertisements and publications in any media are true, accurate, and in accordance with applicable law.

9.3 Professional Affiliations. Marriage and family therapists do not hold themselves out as being partners or associates of a firm if they are not.

9.4 Professional Identification. Marriage and family therapists do not use any professional identification (such as a business card, office sign, letterhead, Internet, or telephone or association directory listing) if it includes a statement or claim that is false, fraudulent, misleading, or deceptive.

9.5 Educational Credentials. Marriage and family therapists claim degrees for their clinical services only if those degrees demonstrate training and education in marriage and family therapy or related fields.

9.6 Employee or Supervisee Qualifications. Marriage and family therapists make certain that the qualifications of their employees and supervisees are represented in a manner that is true, accurate, and in accordance with applicable law.

9.7 Specialization. Marriage and family therapists represent themselves as providing specialized services only after taking reasonable steps to ensure the competence of their work and to protect clients, supervisees, and others from harm.

9.8 Correction of Misinformation. Marriage and family therapists correct, wherever possible, false, misleading, or inaccurate information and representations made by others concerning the therapist's qualifications, services, or products.

International Association of Marriage and Family Counselors Code of Ethics

PREAMBLE

The International Association of Marriage and Family Counselors (IAMFC) is a division of the American Counseling Association dedicated to advancing research, training and practice of couple and family counseling. Members of IAMFC are dedicated to the advocacy of the counseling profession, advocacy of clients and the professionalism of counselors. Members of IAMFC commit themselves to enhancing family relationships and advocate for the healthy development of families while also considering the uniqueness of individuals within family systems.

The guidelines presented in the Ethical Code of the International Association of Marriage and Family Counselors (IAMFC) supplement the current ethical standards of the American Counseling Association (ACA).

This code of ethics provides guidelines for counselors who provide couple and family counseling. The code is divided into ten sections:

SECTION A: THE COUNSELING RELATIONSHIP AND CLIENT WELFARE

Couple and family counselors advocate for the family as a whole system while considering the uniqueness of each family member. Couple and family counselors use systems perspectives and theories as they practice counseling. In addition, couple and family counselors understand that each family presents diverse cultural backgrounds and actively attempt to promote their cultural awareness and knowledge. Couple and family counselors promote multicultural inclusion and do not promote bias or stereotyping regarding family status and/or roles within families.

International Association of Marriage and Family Counselors, "IAMFC Code of Ethics," http://www.iamfconline.org/public/IAMFC-Ethical-Code-Final.pdf, pp. 1-10. Copyright © 2017 by International Association of Marriage and Family Counselors. Reprinted with permission.

Couple and family counselors promote client autonomy and facilitate problem solving skills to prevent future problems. They do not make decisions for families or family members when the decision-making rightfully belongs to the family and/or family members. When it is beneficial, couple and family counselors share clinical impressions and recommendations for the purpose of better informing families.

Couple and family counselors do not participate in keeping secrets for or from clients and maintain professional relationships with clients, refraining from multiple relationships with clients involving business and social contacts, whenever possible. Couple and family counselors also generally refrain from nonprofessional relationships with clients and former clients. At all times, couple and family counselors do not harass, exploit, coerce, or manipulate clients for personal gain.

Couple and family counselors adhere to the following:

1. Couple and family counselors do not discriminate or condone discrimination based on age, color, culture, disability, ethnic group, gender, race, language preference, religion, spirituality, sexual orientation, or socio-economic status.

2. Couple and family counselors inform clients of the goals of counseling.

3. Couple and family counselors inform clients in writing of their counseling qualifications, costs of services, goals of counseling and reasonable expectations for outcomes.

4. Couple and family counselors inform clients that they cannot guarantee that counseling will produce positive results for the couple and/or family.

5. Couple and family counselors inform clients if they have any potentially conflictual relationships with the identified client(s) and a third party or institution.

6. Couple and family counselors must monitor their places of employment and make recommendations to promote cultural awareness, inclusivity, and human growth and development.

7. Couple and family counselors do not harass, exploit, coerce, or manipulate clients for personal gain.

8. Couple and family counselors avoid multiple relationships with clients, including but not limited to, business, social, or educational relationships.

9. Couple and family counselors must refrain from sexual relationships with clients, former clients, and family members of clients.

10. Couple and family counselors withdraw from a counseling relationship if the continuation of the relationship is not in the best interests of the client or would result in a violation of ethical standards.

11. Couple and family counselors do not abandon clients and do not withhold treatment to clients for discriminatory reasons such as race, disability, religion, age, sexual orientation or identification, cultural background, national origin, marital status, affiliation or socioeconomic status.

12. Couple and family counselors arrange appropriate termination of counseling relationship.

13. Couple and family counselors maintain accurate and up-to-date records.

14. Couple and family counselors establish fees that are reasonable and customary based upon the scope and location of their practices.

15. Couple and family counselors do not solicit gifts or fees for referrals.

16. Couple and family counselors recognize that gifts as tokens of respect and gratitude are culturally appropriate with certain clients and may receive gifts of small value.

17. All treatment notes must include the date and time of service.

18. All treatment notes must include the names of those present during the counseling session.

19. All treatment notes must include the name of the clinician(s) providing the counseling services.

SECTION B: CONFIDENTIALITY AND PRIVACY

Couple and family counselors recognize that trust is fundamental to the counseling relationship and client(s) information must not be shared without prior written consent of the client(s). Couple and family counselors must know and understand the limits of confidentiality, privacy, and privileged communication, including the fact that family members may disclose counseling-related information outside counseling thereby rendering the counselor no control over information thus shared. Therefore, couple and family counselors inform clients that in these instances, confidentiality, while desired, cannot be guaranteed.

1. Couple and family counselors must disclose to clients the conditions upon which counselors must legally disclose confidential counseling information.

2. Each person who is legally competent and deemed an "adult" must be provided a confidentiality agreement with the couple and family counselor(s). The agreement must be time limited, consistent with legal

statutes. The parameters of confidentiality must be agreed upon by the client and counselor.

3. Clients must be informed of their rights and the limitations of their rights to confidentiality.

4. Clients must be informed of their rights to terminate or rescind any existing authorization to disclose confidential counseling information.

5. Couple and family counselors inform parents and legal guardians about the confidential parameters of the counseling relationship. When working with minor or juvenile clients and/or adults who lack the capacity to authorize release of confidential information, couple and family counselors seek consent of appropriate custodial parent or guardian to disclose information.

6. Couple and family counselors should, prior to counseling of any minor client, obtain all court orders pertinent to that child's custody in order to assure they have obtained appropriate legal consents of treatment of their minor clients. Further, copies of the relevant court orders should be placed into the client's file along with their signed consents for treatment.

7. Couple and family counselors inform clients of exceptions to confidentiality in accordance with state and federal law.

8. Couple and family counselors inform clients that third party payers have access to their counseling records and adhere to state and federal law regarding the release of confidential counseling information related to billing and collections.

9. Couple and family counselors maintain records according to state and federal statutes.

10. Couple and family counselors maintain the same types of record storage and security regardless of client reimbursement type or status. That is, client records are maintained in consistent manner regardless of whether or not the client pays directly for services or receives third party reimbursement.

11. Couple and family counselors must inform clients if sessions are to be recorded via external media and the purpose of the recording must be provided. Each person who is legally competent must provide informed consent in writing for the recording.

12. Couple and family counselors provide their clients access to records within the timeframes mandated by state and federal statutes.

13. In situations involving multiple clients, couple and family counselors provide only the records directly related to a particular individual, protecting confidential information related to any other client.

14. Couple and family counselors have a written plan or professional will to ensure clients' access to records and client confidentiality in the event of a counselor's incapacitation.

15. Couple and family counselors maintain privacy and confidentiality in research, teaching, publication, case consultation, teaching, supervision and other professional activities.

SECTION C: COMPETENCE AND PROFESSIONAL RESPONSIBILITIES

Couple and family counselors actively seek training, ongoing supervision and/or consultation, and continuing education directly related to couples and family counseling, including the ethical standards of couples and family counseling. Couple and family counselors develop and maintain their skills in counseling through ongoing training, supervision and consultation and recognize the need to familiarize themselves with new research in couples and family counseling.

1. Couple and family counselors must maintain basic skills and knowledge in couples and family counseling as outlined by the Council for Accreditation of Counseling and Related Educational Programs (CACREP).

2. Couple and family counselors recognize the need to know current developments and research in couples and family counseling and actively pursue continuing education opportunities related to couples and family counseling.

3. Couple and family counselors accurately represent their education, expertise, training and experience. Membership in professional organizations, including IAMFC, is not used to suggest competency.

4. Couple and family counselors do not advertise or communicate with the public in ways that misrepresent counseling or counseling outcomes. Thus, couple and family counselors neither guarantee nor predict that counseling outcomes will be consistent with clients' views of "success."

5. Couple and family counselors do not attempt to diagnose or treat problems beyond the scope of their training and abilities.

6. Couple and family counselors do not engage in specialized counseling interventions or techniques unless they have received appropriate training and preparation in the methods they are using.

7. Couple and family counselors do not participate in any professional activity; including but not limited to, counseling, supervision, teaching,

research, in which their professional objectivity may be obscured by personal issues.

8. If couple and family counselors have personal issues which impact their professional objectivity, they seek supervision and/or counseling in order to address these issues.

9. Couple and family counselors do not engage in actions that violate the legal standards of their community and do not encourage client or others to engage in unlawful activities.

10. Couple and family counselors provide public information based upon sound, scientific theories, techniques and approaches that enhances couple and family life.

11. Couple and family counselors provide services to those whom they can provide follow-up care and comprehensive assessment; thus, they do not provide specific advice to individuals through public media, although they may provide general information about couples and family counseling to the media.

12. Couple and family counselors promoting media for commercial sale make every effort to ensure that announcements and advertisements are presented in a professional and factual manner.

SECTION D: COLLABORATION AND PROFESSIONAL RELATIONSHIPS

Couple and family counselors maintain professional relationships with other mental health professionals within and outside the field of counseling. Since interdisciplinary relationships may be required to best serve clients, couple and family counselors actively promote these relationships while maintaining their own ethical boundaries. Further, couple and family counselors are knowledgeable of the roles and functions of other mental health disciplines, such as psychiatry, psychology and social work, as well as other specialties of professional counseling. As they work with others, couple and family counselors promote and maintain healthy boundaries and organizational climate. Thus, couple and family counselors avoid splitting, triangulation, gossip and other indirect forms of communication that are harmful to colleagues or organizations.

1. Couple and family counselors shall not charge a fee for offering or accepting referrals.

2. Couple and family counselors do not engage in harmful relationships with individuals over whom they have supervisory, evaluative, or

instructional control. They adhere to their respective state statutes which may prohibit dual relationships with supervisees.

3. Couple and family counselors working as subcontractors of counseling services for a third party have a duty to inform clients in writing of the limitations that the contracting entity may place on the counseling or consulting relationship.

4. Couple and family counselors do not participate in triangulation, splitting, or other indirect forms of communication that could be harmful to colleagues or the organization they share.

In order to prevent duplication of counseling services, couple and family counselors do not offer services to clients who are being served by other couple and family counselors without securing a referral, thereby preventing duplication of counseling services. The couple and family counselor should obtain written authorization from the client(s) authorizing contact with the other couple and family counselor regarding the transfer of care. This ethical standard applies to prospective and current clients.

SECTION E: ASSESSMENT AND EVALUATION

Couple and family counselors use assessment procedures to promote the well-being of the client. Couple and family counselors only use assessments and evaluations that are scientifically sound and relevant to client(s') goals.

1. Couple and family counselors use assessment methods that are reliable, valid and relevant to the goals of the client(s).

2. Couple and family counselors do not use assessments that are based upon outdated items or normative data.

3. Couple and family counselors do not use assessments that are biased or prejudiced.

4. Couple and family counselors do not use assessment methods or instruments that are outside their scope of training and/or qualifications.

5. Couple and family counselors who conduct custody evaluations use information from both parents and do not make custody recommendations based solely upon information from one parent. If a parent refuses to participate in the evaluation process, this refusal should be noted in the evaluation.

6. Couple and family counselors do not make custody recommendations based solely on test and inventory scores.

7. Couple and family counselors insure that their clients are aware of the differences in counseling and forensic examination. If clients are in a

forensic relationship with the couple and family counselor, the couple and family counselor must, in their initial informed consent, inform the clients of the scope and nature of the forensic counseling, including the entity(ies) to whom the couple and family counselor is reporting client information, and obtain written consent from the client to release counseling information. The written release must specify the types of information that will be released, to whom the information will be released, the time span of the release, and the purpose of the release of information.

8. Couple and family counselors follow current guidelines and standards for testing published or disseminated by the American Counseling Association, American Educational Research Association, American Psychological Association, and the Association for Assessment in Counseling and Education, and other groups dedicated to professional expertise in assessment.

SECTION F: COUNSELOR EDUCATION AND SUPERVISION

Couple and family counselors recognize the inherent power differentials when they engage in teaching, supervision, and consultation. They do not use their power in these relationships for personal gain or exploitation. As teachers, supervisors and consultants, couple and family counselors maintain professional boundaries while recognizing and respecting cultural differences.

1. Couple and family counselors actively seek current knowledge related to supervision practice and theory.

2. Couple and family counselors who provide supervision respect the balance of power in the supervisory relationship and do not exploit students, supervisees, or employees for personal gain, including financial gain.

3. Supervisors do not ask supervisees to engage in behaviors not directly related to the counseling relationship.

4. Supervisors clearly separate supervision and evaluation activities in the supervision relationship. Supervisors clearly identify the goals of supervision and the process(es) of supervision.

5. Supervisors avoid multiple relationships that might impair their professional judgement or increase the possibility of exploitation of supervisee(s).

6. Sexual intimacy with students and/or supervisees is prohibited.

7. Supervisors inform supervisees and students of specific expectations regarding skill building, knowledge acquisition, and development of competencies.

8. Supervisors provide ongoing and timely feedback to supervisees.

9. Supervisors are responsible for protecting the rights and well-being of their supervisees' clients and provide ongoing monitoring of their supervisees' counseling to ensure that clients are receiving beneficial and appropriate counseling services.

10. Couple and family counselors who provide supervision maintain the ethical standards for counselor supervision by the Association for Counselor Education and Supervision.

11. Supervisors and counselor educators implement advocacy awareness for students and supervisees and infuse culturally relevant ethical studies throughout supervision and teaching.

12. Supervisors adhere to the American Counseling Association Code of Ethics throughout their training and supervision and inform students and supervisees that this code is being used throughout their training and supervision.

SECTION G: RESEARCH AND PUBLICATION

Couple and family counselors should engage in research and publication that advances the profession of couple and family counseling and proactively prevent harm to research participants. Couple and family counselors solicit input from peers, institutional review boards, and other stakeholders to adhere to and maintain best practices of research. Couple and family counselors are aware of their obligations to be role models for graduate students and future researchers and act in accordance with the highest standards of research and publication.

1. Couple and family counselors must not present research findings that are misleading.

2. Couple and family counselors must allow for the inclusion of alternative hypotheses and limitations of their research.

3. Couple and family counselors safeguard the privacy of research participants and data about individuals is not released unless the individual is informed of the exact nature of the information to be released and gives written permission for the disclosure.

4. Couple and family counselors protect the safety of their research participants, following the guidelines of peer review committees or institutional review boards, where applicable.

5. Research participants are informed in writing about any potential risk associated with a study and are notified before and during any study that they can withdraw at any time.

6. Couple and family counselors only take credit for research in which they have made a substantial contribution and give credit to all contributors. Authors are listed from greatest to least amount of contribution.

7. Couple and family counselors make their original data available to other researchers upon request.

8. Couple and family counselors do not plagiarize. They give due credit for ideas and data that did not originate with the author and are not common knowledge. Data and ideas must be credited to original source.

9. Couple and family counselors respect the rights of those who submit their research for publication and other scholarly purposes and encourage publication efforts of their colleagues to advance research in couples and family counseling.

10. Couple and family counselors refrain from personal biases in review of research by other authors.

11. Couple and family counselors respect confidentiality as they review research materials submitted for research publications, presentations, and other scholarly purposes, respecting the proprietary rights of those who submit their products for review.

12. Couple and family counselors who review research materials use valid and defensible standards, act within their competencies, and refrain from personal biases in the review process.

13. Couple and family counselors respect the present and future confidentiality of partners or family members in publishing or presenting clinical case studies, especially when the case involves minors or other persons who cannot give consent and may be harmed in the future.

14. Couple and family counselors protect the rights and confidentiality of clients presented in case studies by obtaining written consent from the client(s) after their review of the descriptive case material. The counselor must not misuse not exploit clients in publications or presentations.

15. When written consent cannot be obtained, clinical case studies should be disguised by altering several salient characteristics provided the alteration does not invalidate the research or contribute to false conclusions. Clinical case studies may be disguised by offering composite cases, restricting details, or adding extraneous material, as well.

SECTION H: ETHICAL DECISION-MAKING AND RESOLUTION

Couple and family counselors engage in ethical decision-making in all aspects of couple and family counseling. In so doing, couple and family counselors hold other counselors accountable to their respective ethical codes to ensure that best practices of counseling are followed and no harm occurs to clients. Couple and family counselors work proactively with other counselors to resolve ethical dilemmas and issues.

1. Couple and family counselors are responsible for understanding and implementing the American Counseling Association Code of Ethics, the Ethical Code of the International Association of Marriage and Family Counselors, and other applicable codes of professional associations, certification and licensure boards and credentialing organizations who provide regulation pertinent to them.

2. Couple and family counselors confront unethical behavior of other counselors and therapists by discussing matters directly with the counselor or therapist at alleged fault, unless to do so would potentially harm a client.

3. Couple and family counselors have the responsibility to contact the professional organization and/or the licensure board of a counselor or therapist who persists in unethical behavior after the counselor or therapist has been made aware of his/her ethical infraction(s).

4. Couple and family counselors work within organizations to prevent ethical conflicts and do not compromise ethical standards to accommodate organizational policies, procedures, and practices.

5. Couple and family counselors follow reporting requirements specified by laws and regulations in their jurisdictions and do not knowingly engage in invalid ethical complaints against another therapist or counselor.

6. Couple and family counselors cooperate with ethics committees and other organizations having jurisdiction over any professional or professionals who have alleged ethics violations.

7. Counselors assist professional associations in promoting ethical behavior of couple and family counselors.

SECTION I: TECHNOLOGY ASSISTED COUPLES AND FAMILY COUNSELING

Couple and family counselors may use technology in counseling when the use of technology is deemed appropriate. Couple and family counselors must be compliant with all state and federal laws concerning technology assisted counseling. The following section deals with technology in the use of couples and family counseling.

1. Couple and family counselors must inform clients of the limits of confidentiality related to technology and must meet all applicable laws related to insuring that records are kept confidential and stored in a confidential manner.

2. Couple and family counselors must inform clients in writing of the limitations and risks of confidentiality related to technology assisted counseling.

3. Couple and family counselors follow all jurisdictional regulations related to technology assisted counseling and do not practice outside their legal jurisdiction.

4. Couple and family counselors only use technology that they are familiar with and that meets all legal requirements related to protected health information (PHI).

5. Couple and family counselors do appropriate assessment before using technology in counseling to determine that technology will be useful in counseling.

6. Couple and family counselors adhere to the most current American Counseling Association guidelines regarding technology assisted counseling.

SECTION J. DIVERSITY AND ADVOCACY

Couple and family counselors respect the dignity, worth, uniqueness, and potential of couples and families in their cultural contexts. They infuse counseling with advocacy strategies at all levels of counseling and advocate systems which promote positive growth, development and empowerment. They actively seek to eliminate oppression of human rights.

1. Couple and family counselors are aware of and implement the Advocacy Competencies endorsed by the American Counseling Association.

2. Couple and family counselors are aware of and implement the Multicultural Counseling Competencies endorsed by the American Counseling Association.

3. Couple and family counselors respect the rights of individuals and members to define their relationships and family units beyond boundaries imposed by dominant culture or tradition.

4. Couple and family counselors are especially sensitive to the rights of sexual minorities to define and express their identities, preferences, and relationships.

5. Couple and family counselors recognize sexual health is the integration of the physical, emotional, intellectual, and social aspects of sexual well-being, such that sexuality can be enriching and empowering.

Authored by the International Association of Marriage Counselors (IAMFC) Ethics and Bylaws Committee:

Bret Hendricks (Co-chair), Loretta Bradley (Co-Chair), Mary Ballard (Member), Paul Peluso (Member), Stephen Southern (Member)

2014 ACA
Code of Ethics
As approved by the ACA Governing Council

MISSION

The mission of the American Counseling Association is to enhance the quality of life in society by promoting the development of professional counselors, advancing the counseling profession, and using the profession and practice of counseling to promote respect for human dignity and diversity.

CONTENTS

American Counseling Association, "2014 ACA Code of Ethics," https://www.counseling.org/resources/aca-code-of-ethics.pdf, pp. 1-21. Copyright © 2014 by American Counseling Association. Reprinted with permission.

ACA CODE OF ETHICS PREAMBLE

The American Counseling Association (ACA) is an educational, scientific, and professional organization whose members work in a variety of settings and serve in multiple capacities. Counseling is a professional relationship that empowers diverse individuals, families, and groups to accomplish mental health, wellness, education, and career goals.

Professional values are an important way of living out an ethical commitment. The following are core professional values of the counseling profession:

1. enhancing human development throughout the life span;

2. honoring diversity and embracing a multicultural approach in support of the worth, dignity, potential, and uniqueness of people within their social and cultural contexts;

3. promoting social justice;

4. safeguarding the integrity of the counselor–client relationship; and

5. practicing in a competent and ethical manner.

These professional values provide a conceptual basis for the ethical principles enumerated below. These principles are the foundation for ethical behavior and decision making. The fundamental principles of professional ethical behavior are

- *autonomy*, or fostering the right to control the direction of one's life;

- *nonmaleficence*, or avoiding actions that cause harm;

- *beneficence*, or working for the good of the individual and society by promoting mental health and well-being;

- *justice*, or treating individuals equitably and fostering fairness and equality;

- *fidelity*, or honoring commitments and keeping promises, including fulfilling one's responsibilities of trust in professional relationships; and

- *veracity*, or dealing truthfully with individuals with whom counselors come into professional contact.

ACA CODE OF ETHICS PURPOSE

The *ACA Code of Ethics* serves six main purposes:

1. The *Code* sets forth the ethical obligations of ACA members and provides guidance intended to inform the ethical practice of professional counselors.
2. The *Code* identifies ethical considerations relevant to professional counselors and counselors-in-training.
3. The *Code* enables the association to clarify for current and prospective members, and for those served by members, the nature of the ethical responsibilities held in common by its members.
4. The *Code* serves as an ethical guide designed to assist members in constructing a course of action that best serves those utilizing counseling services and establishes expectations of conduct with a primary emphasis on the role of the professional counselor.
5. The *Code* helps to support the mission of ACA.
6. The standards contained in this *Code* serve as the basis for processing inquiries and ethics complaints concerning ACA members.

The *ACA Code of Ethics* contains nine main sections that address the following areas:

Section A:	The Counseling Relationship
Section B:	Confidentiality and Privacy
Section C:	Professional Responsibility
Section D:	Relationships With Other Professionals
Section E:	Evaluation, Assessment, and Interpretation
Section F:	Supervision, Training, and Teaching
Section G:	Research and Publication
Section H:	Distance Counseling, Technology, and Social Media
Section I:	Resolving Ethical Issues

Each section of the *ACA Code of Ethics* begins with an introduction. The introduction to each section describes the ethical behavior and responsibility to which counselors aspire. The introductions help set the tone for each particular section and provide a starting point that invites reflection on the ethical standards contained in each part of the *ACA Code of Ethics*. The standards outline professional responsibilities and provide direction for fulfilling those ethical responsibilities.

When counselors are faced with ethical dilemmas that are difficult to resolve, they are expected to engage in a carefully considered ethical decision-making process, consulting available resources as needed. Counselors acknowledge that resolving ethical issues is a process; ethical reasoning includes consideration of professional values, professional ethical principles, and ethical standards.

Counselors' actions should be consistent with the spirit as well as the letter of these ethical standards. No specific ethical decision-making model is always most effective, so counselors are expected to use a credible model of decision making that can bear public scrutiny of its application. Through a chosen ethical decision-making process and evaluation of the context of the situation, counselors work collaboratively with clients to make decisions that promote clients' growth and development. A breach of the standards and principles provided herein does not necessarily constitute legal liability or violation of the law; such action is established in legal and judicial proceedings.

The glossary at the end of the *Code* provides a concise description of some of the terms used in the *ACA Code of Ethics*.

SECTION A

The Counseling Relationship

Introduction

Counselors facilitate client growth and development in ways that foster the interest and welfare of clients and promote formation of healthy relationships. Trust is the cornerstone of the counseling relationship, and counselors have the responsibility to respect and safeguard the client's right to privacy and confidentiality. Counselors actively attempt to understand the diverse cultural backgrounds of the clients they serve. Counselors also explore their own cultural identities and how these affect their values and beliefs about the counseling process. Additionally, counselors are encouraged to contribute to society by devoting a portion of their professional activities for little or no financial return (*pro bono publico*).

A.1. Client Welfare

A.1.a. Primary Responsibility
The primary responsibility of counselors is to respect the dignity and promote the welfare of clients.

A.1.b. Records and Documentation
Counselors create, safeguard, and maintain documentation necessary for rendering professional services. Regardless of the medium, counselors include sufficient and timely documentation to facilitate the delivery and continuity of services. Counselors take reasonable steps to ensure that documentation accurately reflects client progress and

services provided. If amendments are made to records and documentation, counselors take steps to properly note the amendments according to agency or institutional policies.

A.1.c. Counseling Plans

Counselors and their clients work jointly in devising counseling plans that offer reasonable promise of success and are consistent with the abilities, temperament, developmental level, and circumstances of clients. Counselors and clients regularly review and revise counseling plans to assess their continued viability and effectiveness, respecting clients' freedom of choice.

A.1.d. Support Network Involvement

Counselors recognize that support networks hold various meanings in the lives of clients and consider enlisting the support, understanding, and involvement of others (e.g., religious/spiritual/community leaders, family members, friends) as positive resources, when appropriate, with client consent.

A.2. Informed Consent in the Counseling Relationship

A.2.a. Informed Consent

Clients have the freedom to choose whether to enter into or remain in a counseling relationship and need adequate information about the counseling process and the counselor. Counselors have an obligation to review in writing and verbally with clients the rights and responsibilities of both counselors and clients. Informed consent is an ongoing part of the counseling process, and counselors appropriately document discussions of informed consent throughout the counseling relationship.

A.2.b. Types of Information Needed

Counselors explicitly explain to clients the nature of all services provided. They inform clients about issues such as, but not limited to, the following: the purposes, goals, techniques, procedures, limitations, potential risks, and benefits of services; the counselor's qualifications, credentials, relevant experience, and approach to counseling; continuation of services upon the incapacitation or death of the counselor; the role of technology; and other pertinent information. Counselors take steps to ensure that clients understand the implications of diagnosis and the intended use of tests and reports. Additionally, counselors inform clients about fees and billing arrangements, including procedures for nonpayment of fees. Clients have the right to confidentiality and to be provided with an explanation of its limits (including how supervisors and/or treatment or interdisciplinary team professionals are involved), to obtain clear information about their records, to participate in the ongoing counseling plans, and to refuse any services or modality changes and to be advised of the consequences of such refusal.

A.2.c. Developmental and Cultural Sensitivity

Counselors communicate information in ways that are both developmentally and culturally appropriate. Counselors use clear and understandable language when discussing issues related to informed consent. When clients have difficulty understanding the language that counselors use, counselors provide necessary services (e.g., arranging for a qualified interpreter or translator) to ensure comprehension by clients. In collaboration with clients, counselors consider cultural implications of informed consent procedures and, where possible, counselors adjust their practices accordingly.

A.2.d. Inability to Give Consent

When counseling minors, incapacitated adults, or other persons unable to give voluntary consent, counselors seek the assent of clients to services and include them in decision making as appropriate. Counselors recognize the need to balance the ethical rights of clients to make choices, their capacity to give consent or assent to receive services, and parental or familial legal rights and responsibilities to protect these clients and make decisions on their behalf.

A.2.e. Mandated Clients

Counselors discuss the required limitations to confidentiality when working with clients who have been mandated for counseling services. Counselors also explain what type of information and with whom that information is shared prior to the beginning of counseling. The client may choose to refuse services. In this case, counselors will, to the best of their ability, discuss with the client the potential consequences of refusing counseling services.

A.3. Clients Served by Others

When counselors learn that their clients are in a professional relationship with other mental health professionals, they request release from clients to inform the other professionals and strive to establish positive and collaborative professional relationships.

A.4. Avoiding Harm and Imposing Values

A.4.a. Avoiding Harm

Counselors act to avoid harming their clients, trainees, and research participants and to minimize or to remedy unavoidable or unanticipated harm.

A.4.b. Personal Values

Counselors are aware of—and avoid imposing—their own values, attitudes, beliefs, and behaviors. Counselors respect the diversity of clients, trainees, and research participants and seek training in areas in which they are at risk of imposing their values onto clients, especially when the counselor's values are inconsistent with the client's goals or are discriminatory in nature.

A.5. Prohibited Noncounseling Roles and Relationships

A.5.a. Sexual and/or Romantic Relationships Prohibited

Sexual and/or romantic counselor–client interactions or relationships with current clients, their romantic partners, or their family members are prohibited. This prohibition applies to both in-person and electronic interactions or relationships.

A.5.b. Previous Sexual and/or Romantic Relationships

Counselors are prohibited from engaging in counseling relationships with persons with whom they have had a previous sexual and/or romantic relationship.

A.5.c. Sexual and/or Romantic Relationships With Former Clients

Sexual and/or romantic counselor–client interactions or relationships with former clients, their romantic partners, or their family members are prohibited for a period of 5 years following the last professional contact. This prohibition applies to both in-person and electronic interactions or relationships. Counsel-ors, before engaging in sexual and/or romantic interactions or relationships with former clients, their romantic partners, or their family members, demonstrate forethought and document (in written form) whether the interaction or relationship can be viewed as exploitive in any way and/or whether there is still potential to harm the former client; in cases of potential exploitation and/or harm, the counselor avoids entering into such an interaction or relationship.

A.5.d. Friends or Family Members

Counselors are prohibited from engaging in counseling relationships with friends or family members with whom they have an inability to remain objective.

A.5.e. Personal Virtual Relationships With Current Clients

Counselors are prohibited from engaging in a personal virtual relationship with individuals with whom they have a current counseling relationship (e.g., through social and other media).

A.6. Managing and Maintaining Boundaries and Professional Relationships

A.6.a. Previous Relationships

Counselors consider the risks and benefits of accepting as clients those with whom they have had a previous relationship. These potential clients may include individuals with whom the counselor has had a casual, distant, or past relationship. Examples include mutual or past membership in a professional association, organization, or community. When counselors accept these clients, they take appropriate professional precautions such as informed consent, consultation, supervision, and documentation to ensure that judgment is not impaired and no exploitation occurs.

A.6.b. Extending Counseling Boundaries

Counselors consider the risks and benefits of extending current counseling relationships beyond conventional parameters. Examples include attending a client's formal ceremony (e.g., a wedding/commitment ceremony or graduation), purchasing a service or product provided by a client (excepting unrestricted bartering), and visiting a client's ill family member in the hospital. In extending these boundaries, counselors take appropriate professional precautions such as informed consent, consultation, supervision, and documentation to ensure that judgment is not impaired and no harm occurs.

A.6.c. Documenting Boundary Extensions

If counselors extend boundaries as described in A.6.a. and A.6.b., they must officially document, prior to the interaction (when feasible), the rationale for such an interaction, the potential benefit, and anticipated consequences for the client or former client and other individuals significantly involved with the client or former client. When unintentional harm occurs to the client or former client, or to an individual significantly involved with the client or former client, the counselor must show evidence of an attempt to remedy such harm.

A.6.d. Role Changes in the Professional Relationship

When counselors change a role from the original or most recent contracted relationship, they obtain informed consent from the client and explain the client's right to refuse services related to the change. Examples of role changes include, but are not limited to

1. changing from individual to relationship or family counseling, or vice versa;
2. changing from an evaluative role to a therapeutic role, or vice versa; and
3. changing from a counselor to a mediator role, or vice versa.

Clients must be fully informed of any anticipated consequences (e.g., financial, legal, personal, therapeutic) of counselor role changes.

A.6.e. Nonprofessional Interactions or Relationships (Other Than Sexual or Romantic Interactions or Relationships)

Counselors avoid entering into nonprofessional relationships with former clients, their romantic partners, or their family members when the interaction is potentially harmful to the client. This applies to both in-person and electronic interactions or relationships.

A.7. Roles and Relationships at Individual, Group, Institutional, and Societal Levels

A.7.a. Advocacy

When appropriate, counselors advocate at individual, group, institutional, and societal levels to address potential barriers and obstacles that inhibit access and/or the growth and development of clients.

A.7.b. Confidentiality and Advocacy

Counselors obtain client consent prior to engaging in advocacy efforts on behalf of an identifiable client to improve the provision of services and to work toward removal of systemic barriers or obstacles that inhibit client access, growth, and development.

A.8. Multiple Clients

When a counselor agrees to provide counseling services to two or more persons who have a relationship, the counselor clarifies at the outset which person or persons are clients and the nature of the relationships the counselor will have with each involved person. If it becomes apparent that the counselor may be called upon to perform potentially conflicting roles, the counselor will clarify, adjust, or withdraw from roles appropriately.

A.9. Group Work

A.9.a. Screening

Counselors screen prospective group counseling/therapy participants. To the extent possible, counselors select members whose needs and goals are compatible with the goals of the group, who will not impede the group process, and whose well-being will not be jeopardized by the group experience.

A.9.b. Protecting Clients

In a group setting, counselors take reasonable precautions to protect clients from physical, emotional, or psychological trauma.

A.10. Fees and Business Practices

A.10.a. Self-Referral

Counselors working in an organization (e.g., school, agency, institution) that provides counseling services do not refer clients to their private practice unless the policies of a particular organization make explicit provisions for self-referrals. In such instances, the clients must be informed of other options open to them should they seek private counseling services.

A.10.b. Unacceptable Business Practices

Counselors do not participate in fee splitting, nor do they give or receive commissions, rebates, or any other form of remuneration when referring clients for professional services.

A.10.c. Establishing Fees

In establishing fees for professional counseling services, counselors consider the financial status of clients and locality. If a counselor's usual fees create undue hardship for the client, the counselor may adjust fees, when legally permissible, or assist the client in locating comparable, affordable services.

A.10.d. Nonpayment of Fees

If counselors intend to use collection agencies or take legal measures to collect fees from clients who do not pay for services as agreed upon, they include such information in their informed consent documents and also inform clients in a timely fashion of intended actions and offer clients the opportunity to make payment.

A.10.e. Bartering

Counselors may barter only if the bartering does not result in exploitation or harm, if the client requests it, and if such arrangements are an accepted practice among professionals in the community. Counselors consider the cultural implications of bartering and discuss relevant concerns with clients and document such agreements in a clear written contract.

A.10.f. Receiving Gifts

Counselors understand the challenges of accepting gifts from clients and recognize that in some cultures, small gifts are a token of respect and gratitude. When determining whether to accept a gift from clients, counselors take into account the therapeutic relationship, the monetary value of the gift, the client's motivation for giving the gift, and the counselor's motivation for wanting to accept or decline the gift.

A.11. Termination and Referral

A.11.a. Competence Within Termination and Referral

If counselors lack the competence to be of professional assistance to clients, they avoid entering or continuing counseling relationships. Counselors are knowledgeable about culturally and clinically appropriate referral resources and suggest these alternatives. If clients decline the suggested referrals, counselors discontinue the relationship.

A.11.b. Values Within Termination and Referral

Counselors refrain from referring prospective and current clients based solely on the counselor's personally held values, attitudes, beliefs, and behaviors. Counselors respect the diversity of clients and seek training in areas in which they are at risk of imposing their values onto clients, especially when the counselor's values are inconsistent with the client's goals or are discriminatory in nature.

A.11.c. Appropriate Termination

Counselors terminate a counseling relationship when it becomes reasonably apparent that the client no longer needs assistance, is not likely to benefit, or is being harmed by continued counseling. Counselors may terminate counseling when in jeopardy of harm by the client or by another person with whom the client has a relationship, or when clients do not pay fees as agreed upon. Counselors provide pretermination counseling and recommend other service providers when necessary.

A.11.d. Appropriate Transfer of Services
When counselors transfer or refer clients to other practitioners, they ensure that appropriate clinical and administrative processes are completed and open communication is maintained with both clients and practitioners.

A.12. Abandonment and Client Neglect
Counselors do not abandon or neglect clients in counseling. Counselors assist in making appropriate arrangements for the continuation of treatment, when necessary, during interruptions such as vacations, illness, and following termination.

SECTION B

Confidentiality and Privacy

Introduction
Counselors recognize that trust is a cornerstone of the counseling relationship. Counselors aspire to earn the trust of clients by creating an ongoing partnership, establishing and upholding appropriate boundaries, and maintaining confidentiality. Counselors communicate the parameters of confidentiality in a culturally competent manner.

B.1. Respecting Client Rights
B.1.a. Multicultural/Diversity Considerations
Counselors maintain awareness and sensitivity regarding cultural meanings of confidentiality and privacy. Counselors respect differing views toward disclosure of information. Counselors hold ongoing discussions with clients as to how, when, and with whom information is to be shared.

B.1.b. Respect for Privacy
Counselors respect the privacy of prospective and current clients. Counselors request private information from clients only when it is beneficial to the counseling process.

B.1.c. Respect for Confidentiality
Counselors protect the confidential information of prospective and current clients. Counselors disclose information only with appropriate consent or with sound legal or ethical justification.

B.1.d. Explanation of Limitations

At initiation and throughout the counseling process, counselors inform clients of the limitations of confidentiality and seek to identify situations in which confidentiality must be breached.

B.2. Exceptions

B.2.a. Serious and Foreseeable Harm and Legal Requirements

The general requirement that counsel-ors keep information confidential does not apply when disclosure is required to protect clients or identified others from serious and fore-seeable harm or when legal requirements demand that confidential information must be revealed. Counselors consult with other professionals when in doubt as to the validity of an exception. Additional considerations apply when addressing end-of-life issues.

B.2.b. Confidentiality Regarding End-of-Life Decisions

Counselors who provide services to terminally ill individuals who are considering hastening their own deaths have the option to maintain confidentiality, depending on applicable laws and the specific circumstances of the situation and after seeking consultation or supervision from appropriate professional and legal parties.

B.2.c. Contagious, Life-Threatening Diseases

When clients disclose that they have a disease commonly known to be both communicable and life threatening, counselors may be justified in disclosing information to identifiable third parties, if the parties are known to be at serious and foreseeable risk of contracting the disease. Prior to making a disclosure, counselors assess the intent of clients to inform the third parties about their disease or to engage in any behaviors that may be harmful to an identifiable third party. Counselors adhere to relevant state laws concerning disclosure about disease status.

B.2.d. Court-Ordered Disclosure

When ordered by a court to release confidential or privileged information without a client's permission, counselors seek to obtain written, informed consent from the client or take steps to prohibit the disclosure or have it limited as narrowly as possible because of potential harm to the client or counseling relationship.

B.2.e. Minimal Disclosure

To the extent possible, clients are informed before confidential information is disclosed and are involved in the disclosure decision-making process. When circumstances require the disclosure of confidential information, only essential information is revealed.

B.3. Information Shared With Others

B.3.a. Subordinates

Counselors make every effort to ensure that privacy and confidentiality of clients are maintained by subordinates, including employees, supervisees, students, clerical assistants, and volunteers.

B.3.b. Interdisciplinary Teams

When services provided to the client involve participation by an interdisciplinary or treatment team, the client will be informed of the team's existence and composition, information being shared, and the purposes of sharing such information.

B.3.c. Confidential Settings

Counselors discuss confidential information only in settings in which they can reasonably ensure client privacy.

B.3.d. Third-Party Payers

Counselors disclose information to third-party payers only when clients have authorized such disclosure.

B.3.e. Transmitting Confidential Information

Counselors take precautions to ensure the confidentiality of all information transmitted through the use of any medium.

B.3.f. Deceased Clients

Counselors protect the confidentiality of deceased clients, consistent with legal requirements and the documented preferences of the client.

B.4. Groups and Families

B.4.a. Group Work

In group work, counselors clearly explain the importance and parameters of confidentiality for the specific group.

B.4.b. Couples and Family Counseling

In couples and family counseling, counselors clearly define who is considered "the client" and discuss expectations and limitations of confidentiality. Counselors seek agreement and document in writing such agreement among all involved parties regarding the confidentiality of information. In the absence of an agreement to the contrary, the couple or family is considered to be the client.

B.5. Clients Lacking Capacity to Give Informed Consent

B.5.a. Responsibility to Clients

When counseling minor clients or adult clients who lack the capacity to give voluntary, informed consent, counselors protect the confidentiality of information received—in any medium—in the counseling relationship as specified by federal and state laws, written policies, and applicable ethical standards.

B.5.b. Responsibility to Parents and Legal Guardians

Counselors inform parents and legal guardians about the role of counselors and the confidential nature of the counseling relationship, consistent with current legal and custodial arrangements. Counselors are sensitive to the cultural diversity of families and respect the inherent rights and responsibilities of parents/guardians regarding the welfare of their children/charges according to law. Counselors work to establish, as appropriate, collaborative relationships with parents/guardians to best serve clients.

B.5.c. Release of Confidential Information

When counseling minor clients or adult clients who lack the capacity to give voluntary consent to release confidential information, counselors seek permission from an appropriate third party to disclose information. In such instances, counselors inform clients consistent with their level of understanding and take appropriate measures to safeguard client confidentiality.

B.6. Records and Documentation

B.6.a. Creating and Maintaining Records and Documentation

Counselors create and maintain records and documentation necessary for rendering professional services.

B.6.b. Confidentiality of Records and Documentation

Counselors ensure that records and documentation kept in any medium are secure and that only authorized persons have access to them.

B.6.c. Permission to Record

Counselors obtain permission from clients prior to recording sessions through electronic or other means.

B.6.d. Permission to Observe

Counselors obtain permission from clients prior to allowing any person to observe counseling sessions, review session transcripts, or view recordings of sessions with supervisors, faculty, peers, or others within the training environment.

B.6.e. Client Access

Counselors provide reasonable access to records and copies of records when requested by competent clients. Counselors limit the access of clients to their records, or portions of their records, only when there is compelling evidence that such access would cause harm to the client. Counselors document the request of clients and the rationale for withholding some or all of the records in the files of clients. In situations involving multiple clients, counselors provide individual clients with only those parts of records that relate directly to them and do not include confidential information related to any other client.

B.6.f. Assistance With Records

When clients request access to their records, counselors provide assistance and consultation in interpreting counseling records.

B.6.g. Disclosure or Transfer

Unless exceptions to confidentiality exist, counselors obtain written permission from clients to disclose or transfer records to legitimate third parties. Steps are taken to ensure that receivers of counseling records are sensitive to their confidential nature.

B.6.h. Storage and Disposal After Termination

Counselors store records following termination of services to ensure reasonable future access, maintain records in accordance with federal and state laws and statutes such as licensure laws and policies governing records, and dispose of client records and other sensitive materials in a manner that protects client confidentiality. Counselors apply careful discretion and deliberation before destroying records that may be needed by a court of law, such as notes on child abuse, suicide, sexual harassment, or violence.

B.6.i. Reasonable Precautions

Counselors take reasonable precautions to protect client confidentiality in the event of the counselor's termination of practice, incapacity, or death and appoint a records custodian when identified as appropriate.

B.7. Case Consultation

B.7.a. Respect for Privacy

Information shared in a consulting relationship is discussed for professional purposes only. Written and oral reports present only data germane to the purposes of the consultation, and every effort is made to protect client identity and to avoid undue invasion of privacy.

B.7.b. Disclosure of Confidential Information

When consulting with colleagues, counselors do not disclose confidential information that reasonably could lead to the identification of a client or other person or organization with whom they have a confidential relationship unless they have obtained the prior consent of the person or organization or the disclosure cannot be avoided. They disclose information only to the extent necessary to achieve the purposes of the consultation.

SECTION C

Professional Responsibility

Introduction

Counselors aspire to open, honest, and accurate communication in dealing with the public and other professionals. Counselors facilitate access to counseling services, and they practice in a nondiscriminatory manner within the boundaries of professional and personal competence; they also have a responsibility to abide by the *ACA Code of Ethics*. Counselors actively participate in local, state, and national associations that foster the development and improvement of counseling. Counselors are expected to advocate to promote changes at the individual, group, institutional, and societal levels that improve the quality of life for individuals and groups and remove potential barriers to the provision or access of appropriate services being offered. Counselors have a responsibility to the public to engage in counseling practices that are based on rigorous research methodologies. Counselors are encouraged to contribute to society by devoting a portion of their professional activity to services for which there is little or no financial return (*pro bono publico*). In addition, counselors engage in self-care activities to maintain and promote their own emotional, physical, mental, and spiritual well-being to best meet their professional responsibilities.

C.1. Knowledge of and Compliance With Standards

Counselors have a responsibility to read, understand, and follow the *ACA Code of Ethics* and adhere to applicable laws and regulations.

C.2. Professional Competence

C.2.a. Boundaries of Competence

Counselors practice only within the boundaries of their competence, based on their education, training, supervised experience, state and national professional credentials, and appropriate professional experience. Whereas multicultural counseling competency is required across all counseling specialties, counselors gain knowledge, personal awareness, sensitivity, dispositions, and skills pertinent to being a culturally competent counselor in working with a diverse client population.

C.2.b. New Specialty Areas of Practice

Counselors practice in specialty areas new to them only after appropriate education, training, and supervised experience. While developing skills in new specialty areas, counselors take steps to ensure the competence of their work and protect others from possible harm.

C.2.c. Qualified for Employment

Counselors accept employment only for positions for which they are qualified given their education, training, supervised experience, state and national professional credentials, and appropriate professional experience. Counselors hire for professional counseling positions only individuals who are qualified and competent for those positions.

C.2.d. Monitor Effectiveness

Counselors continually monitor their effectiveness as professionals and take steps to improve when necessary. Counselors take reasonable steps to seek peer supervision to evaluate their efficacy as counselors.

C.2.e. Consultations on Ethical Obligations

Counselors take reasonable steps to consult with other counselors, the ACA Ethics and Professional Standards Department, or related professionals when they have questions regarding their ethical obligations or professional practice.

C.2.f. Continuing Education

Counselors recognize the need for continuing education to acquire and maintain a reasonable level of awareness of current scientific and professional information in their fields of activity. Counselors maintain their competence in the skills they use, are open to new procedures, and remain informed regarding best practices for working with diverse populations.

C.2.g. Impairment

Counselors monitor themselves for signs of impairment from their own physical, mental, or emotional problems and refrain from offering or providing professional services when impaired. They seek assistance for problems that reach the level of professional impairment, and, if necessary, they limit, suspend, or terminate their professional responsibilities until it is determined that they may safely resume their work. Counselors assist colleagues or supervisors in recognizing their own professional impairment and provide consultation and assistance when warranted with colleagues or supervisors showing signs of impairment and intervene as appropriate to prevent imminent harm to clients.

C.2.h. Counselor Incapacitation, Death, Retirement, or Termination of Practice

Counselors prepare a plan for the transfer of clients and the dissemination of records to an identified colleague or records custodian in the case of the counselor's incapacitation, death, retirement, or termination of practice.

C.3. Advertising and Soliciting Clients

C.3.a. Accurate Advertising

When advertising or otherwise representing their services to the public, counselors identify their credentials in an accurate manner that is not false, misleading, deceptive, or fraudulent.

C.3.b. Testimonials

Counselors who use testimonials do not solicit them from current clients, former clients, or any other persons who may be vulnerable to undue influence. Counselors discuss with clients the implications of and obtain permission for the use of any testimonial.

C.3.c. Statements by Others

When feasible, counselors make reasonable efforts to ensure that statements made by others about them or about the counseling profession are accurate.

C.3.d. Recruiting Through Employment

Counselors do not use their places of employment or institutional affiliation to recruit clients, supervisors, or consultees for their private practices.

C.3.e. Products and Training Advertisements

Counselors who develop products related to their profession or conduct workshops or training events ensure that the advertisements concerning these products or events are accurate and disclose adequate information for consumers to make informed choices.

C.3.f. Promoting to Those Served

Counselors do not use counseling, teaching, training, or supervisory relationships to promote their products or training events in a manner that is deceptive or would exert undue influence on individuals who may be vulnerable. However, counselor educators may adopt textbooks they have authored for instructional purposes.

C.4. Professional Qualifications

C.4.a. Accurate Representation

Counselors claim or imply only professional qualifications actually completed and correct any known misrepresentations of their qualifications by others. Counselors truthfully represent the qualifications of their professional colleagues. Counselors clearly distinguish between paid and volunteer work experience and accurately describe their continuing education and specialized training.

C.4.b. Credentials

Counselors claim only licenses or certifications that are current and in good standing.

C.4.c. Educational Degrees

Counselors clearly differentiate between earned and honorary degrees.

C.4.d. Implying Doctoral-Level Competence

Counselors clearly state their highest earned degree in counseling or a closely related field. Counselors do not imply doctoral-level competence when possessing a master's degree in counseling or a related field by referring to themselves as "Dr." in a counseling context when their doctorate is not in counseling or a related field. Counselors do not use "ABD" (all but dissertation) or other such terms to imply competency.

C.4.e. Accreditation Status

Counselors accurately represent the accreditation status of their degree program and college/university.

C.4.f. Professional Membership

Counselors clearly differentiate between current, active memberships and former memberships in associations. Members of ACA must clearly differentiate between professional membership, which implies the possession of at least a master's degree in counseling, and regular membership, which is open to individuals whose interests and activities are consistent with those of ACA but are not qualified for professional membership.

C.5. Nondiscrimination

Counselors do not condone or engage in discrimination against prospective or current clients, students, employees, supervisees, or research participants based on age, culture, disability, ethnicity, race, religion/spirituality, gender, gender identity, sexual orientation, marital/partnership status, language preference, socioeconomic status, immigration status, or any basis proscribed by law.

C.6. Public Responsibility

C.6.a. Sexual Harassment

Counselors do not engage in or condone sexual harassment. Sexual harassment can consist of a single intense or severe act, or multiple persistent or pervasive acts.

C.6.b. Reports to Third Parties

Counselors are accurate, honest, and objective in reporting their professional activities and judgments to appropriate third parties, including courts, health insurance companies, those who are the recipients of evaluation reports, and others.

C.6.c. Media Presentations

When counselors provide advice or comment by means of public lectures, demonstrations, radio or television programs, recordings, technology-based applications, printed articles, mailed material, or other media, they take reasonable precautions to ensure that

1. the statements are based on appropriate professional counseling literature and practice,
2. the statements are otherwise consistent with the *ACA Code of Ethics*, and

3. the recipients of the information are not encouraged to infer that a professional counseling relationship has been established.

C.6.d. Exploitation of Others

Counselors do not exploit others in their professional relationships.

C.6.e. Contributing to the Public Good
(Pro Bono Publico)

Counselors make a reasonable effort to provide services to the public for which there is little or no financial return (e.g., speaking to groups, sharing professional information, offering reduced fees).

C.7. Treatment Modalities

C.7.a. Scientific Basis for Treatment

When providing services, counselors use techniques/procedures/modalities that are grounded in theory and/or have an empirical or scientific foundation.

C.7.b. Development and Innovation

When counselors use developing or innovative techniques/procedures/modalities, they explain the potential risks, benefits, and ethical considerations of using such techniques/procedures/ modalities. Counselors work to minimize any potential risks or harm when using these techniques/procedures/modalities.

C.7.c. Harmful Practices

Counselors do not use techniques/procedures/modalities when substantial evidence suggests harm, even if such services are requested.

C.8. Responsibility to Other Professionals

C.8.a. Personal Public Statements

When making personal statements in a public context, counselors clarify that they are speaking from their personal perspectives and that they are not speaking on behalf of all counselors or the profession.

SECTION D
Relationships With Other Professionals

Introduction

Professional counselors recognize that the quality of their interactions with colleagues can influence the quality of services provided to clients. They work to become knowledgeable about colleagues within and outside the field of counseling. Counselors develop positive working relationships and systems of communication with colleagues to enhance services to clients.

D.1. Relationships With Colleagues, Employers, and Employees

D.1.A. DIFFERENT APPROACHES

Counselors are respectful of approaches that are grounded in theory and/or have an empirical or scientific foundation but may differ from their own. Counselors acknowledge the expertise of other professional groups and are respectful of their practices.

D.1.b. Forming Relationships

Counselors work to develop and strengthen relationships with colleagues from other disciplines to best serve clients.

D.1.c. Interdisciplinary Teamwork

Counselors who are members of interdisciplinary teams delivering multifaceted services to clients remain focused on how to best serve clients. They participate in and contribute to decisions that affect the well-being of clients by drawing on the perspectives, values, and experiences of the counseling profession and those of colleagues from other disciplines.

D.1.d. Establishing Professional and Ethical Obligations

Counselors who are members of interdisciplinary teams work together with team members to clarify professional and ethical obligations of the team as a whole and of its individual members. When a team decision raises ethical concerns, counselors first attempt to resolve the concern within the team. If they cannot reach resolution among team members, counselors pursue other avenues to address their concerns consistent with client well-being.

D.1.e. Confidentiality

When counselors are required by law, institutional policy, or extraordinary circumstances to serve in more than one role in judicial or administrative proceedings, they clarify role expectations and the parameters of confidentiality with their colleagues.

D.1.f. Personnel Selection and Assignment

When counselors are in a position requiring personnel selection and/or assigning of responsibilities to others, they select competent staff and assign responsibilities compatible with their skills and experiences.

D.1.g. Employer Policies

The acceptance of employment in an agency or institution implies that counsel-ors are in agreement with its general policies and principles. Counselors strive to reach agreement with employers regarding acceptable standards of client care and professional conduct that allow for changes in institutional policy conducive to the growth and development of clients.

D.1.h. Negative Conditions

Counselors alert their employers of inappropriate policies and practices. They attempt to effect changes in such policies or procedures through constructive action within the organization. When such policies are potentially disruptive or damaging to clients or may limit the effectiveness of services provided and change cannot be affected, counselors take appropriate further action. Such action may include referral to appropriate certification, accreditation, or state licensure organizations, or voluntary termination of employment.

D.1.i. Protection From Punitive Action

Counselors do not harass a colleague or employee or dismiss an employee who has acted in a responsible and ethical manner to expose inappropriate employer policies or practices.

D.2. Provision of Consultation Services

D.2.a. Consultant Competency

Counselors take reasonable steps to ensure that they have the appropriate resources and competencies when providing consultation services. Counselors provide appropriate referral resources when requested or needed.

D.2.b. Informed Consent in Formal Consultation

When providing formal consultation services, counselors have an obligation to review, in writing and verbally, the rights and responsibilities of both counselors and consultees. Counselors use clear and understandable language to inform all parties involved about the purpose of the services to be provided, relevant costs, potential risks and benefits, and the limits of confidentiality.

SECTION E
Evaluation, Assessment, and Interpretation

Introduction

Counselors use assessment as one component of the counseling process, taking into account the clients' personal and cultural context. Counselors promote the well-being of individual clients or groups of clients by developing and using appropriate educational, mental health, psychological, and career assessments.

E.1. General

E.1.a. Assessment

The primary purpose of educational, mental health, psychological, and career assessment is to gather information regarding the client for a variety of purposes, including, but not limited to, client decision making, treatment planning, and forensic proceedings. Assessment may include both qualitative and quantitative methodologies.

E.1.b. Client Welfare

Counselors do not misuse assessment results and interpretations, and they take reasonable steps to prevent others from misusing the information provided. They respect the client's right to know the results, the interpretations made, and the bases for counselors' conclusions and recommendations.

E.2. Competence to Use and Interpret Assessment Instruments

E.2.a. Limits of Competence

Counselors use only those testing and assessment services for which they have been trained and are competent. Counselors using technology-assisted test interpretations are trained in the construct being measured and the specific instrument being used prior to using its technology-based application. Counselors take reasonable measures to ensure the proper use of assessment techniques by persons under their supervision.

E.2.b. Appropriate Use

Counselors are responsible for the appropriate application, scoring, interpretation, and use of assessment instruments relevant to the needs of the client, whether they score and interpret such assessments themselves or use technology or other services.

E.2.c. Decisions Based on Results

Counselors responsible for decisions involving individuals or policies that are based on assessment results have a thorough understanding of psychometrics.

E.3. Informed Consent in Assessment

E.3.a. Explanation to Clients

Prior to assessment, counselors explain the nature and purposes of assessment and the specific use of results by potential recipients. The explanation will be given in terms and language that the client (or other legally authorized person on behalf of the client) can understand.

E.3.b. Recipients of Results

Counselors consider the client's and/or examinee's welfare, explicit understandings, and prior agreements in determining who receives the assessment results. Counselors include accurate and appropriate interpretations with any release of individual or group assessment results.

E.4. Release of Data to Qualified Personnel

Counselors release assessment data in which the client is identified only with the consent of the client or the client's legal representative. Such data are released only to persons recognized by counselors as qualified to interpret the data.

E.5. Diagnosis of Mental Disorders

E.5.a. Proper Diagnosis

Counselors take special care to provide proper diagnosis of mental disorders. Assessment techniques (including personal interviews) used to determine client care (e.g., locus of treatment, type of treatment, recommended follow-up) are carefully selected and appropriately used.

E.5.b. Cultural Sensitivity

Counselors recognize that culture affects the manner in which clients' problems are defined and experienced. Clients' socioeconomic and cultural experiences are considered when diagnosing mental disorders.

E.5.c. Historical and Social Prejudices in the Diagnosis of Pathology

Counselors recognize historical and social prejudices in the misdiagnosis and pathologizing of certain individuals and groups and strive to become aware of and address such biases in themselves or others.

E.5.d. Refraining From Diagnosis

Counselors may refrain from making and/or reporting a diagnosis if they believe that it would cause harm to the client or others. Counselors carefully consider both the positive and negative implications of a diagnosis.

E.6. Instrument Selection

E.6.a. Appropriateness of Instruments

Counselors carefully consider the validity, reliability, psychometric limitations, and appropriateness of instruments when selecting assessments and, when possible, use multiple forms of assessment, data, and/or instruments in forming conclusions, diagnoses, or recommendations.

E.6.b. Referral Information

If a client is referred to a third party for assessment, the counselor provides specific referral questions and sufficient objective data about the client to ensure that appropriate assessment instruments are utilized.

E.7. Conditions of Assessment Administration

E.7.a. Administration Conditions

Counselors administer assessments under the same conditions that were established in their standardization. When assessments are not administered under standard conditions, as may be necessary to accommodate clients with disabilities, or when unusual behavior or irregularities occur during the administration, those conditions are noted in interpretation, and the results may be designated as invalid or of questionable validity.

E.7.b. Provision of Favorable Conditions

Counselors provide an appropriate environment for the administration of assessments (e.g., privacy, comfort, freedom from distraction).

E.7.c. Technological Administration

Counselors ensure that technologically administered assessments function properly and provide clients with accurate results.

E.7.d. Unsupervised Assessments

Unless the assessment instrument is designed, intended, and validated for self-administration and/or scoring, counselors do not permit unsupervised use.

E.8. Multicultural Issues/Diversity in Assessment

Counselors select and use with caution assessment techniques normed on populations other than that of the client. Counselors recognize the effects of age, color, culture, disability, ethnic group, gender, race, language preference, religion, spirituality, sexual orientation, and socioeconomic status on test administration and interpretation, and they place test results in proper perspective with other relevant factors.

E.9. Scoring and Interpretation of Assessments

E.9.a. Reporting

When counselors report assessment results, they consider the client's personal and cultural background, the level of the client's understanding of the results, and the impact of the results on the client. In reporting assessment results, counselors indicate reservations that exist regarding validity or reliability due to circumstances of the assessment or inappropriateness of the norms for the person tested.

E.9.b. Instruments With Insufficient Empirical Data

Counselors exercise caution when interpreting the results of instruments not having sufficient empirical data to support respondent results. The specific purposes for the use of such instruments are stated explicitly to the examinee. Counselors qualify any conclusions, diagnoses, or recommendations made that are based on assessments or instruments with questionable validity or reliability.

E.9.c. Assessment Services

Counselors who provide assessment, scoring, and interpretation services to support the assessment process confirm the validity of such interpretations. They accurately describe the purpose, norms, validity, reliability, and applications of the procedures and any special qualifications applicable to their use. At all times, counselors maintain their ethical responsibility to those being assessed.

E.10. Assessment Security

Counselors maintain the integrity and security of tests and assessments consistent with legal and contractual obligations. Counselors do not appropriate, reproduce, or modify published assessments or parts thereof without acknowledgment and permission from the publisher.

E.11. Obsolete Assessment and Outdated Results

Counselors do not use data or results from assessments that are obsolete or outdated for the current purpose (e.g., noncurrent versions of assessments/ instruments). Counselors make every effort to prevent the misuse of obsolete measures and assessment data by others.

E.12. Assessment Construction

Counselors use established scientific procedures, relevant standards, and current professional knowledge for assessment design in the development, publication, and utilization of assessment techniques.

E.13. Forensic Evaluation: Evaluation for Legal Proceedings

E.13.a. Primary Obligations

When providing forensic evaluations, the primary obligation of counselors is to produce objective findings that can be substantiated based on information and techniques appropriate to the evaluation, which may include examination of the individual and/or review of records. Counselors form professional opinions based on their professional knowledge and expertise that can be supported by the data gathered in evaluations. Counselors define the limits of their reports or testimony, especially when an examination of the individual has not been conducted.

E.13.b. Consent for Evaluation

Individuals being evaluated are informed in writing that the relationship is for the purposes of an evaluation and is not therapeutic in nature, and entities or individuals who will receive the evaluation report are identified. Counselors who perform forensic evaluations obtain written consent from those being evaluated or from their legal representative unless a court orders evaluations to be conducted without the written consent of the individuals being evaluated. When children or adults who lack the capacity to give voluntary consent are being evaluated, informed written consent is obtained from a parent or guardian.

E.13.c. Client Evaluation Prohibited

Counselors do not evaluate current or former clients, clients' romantic partners, or clients' family members for forensic purposes. Counselors do not counsel individuals they are evaluating.

E.13.d. Avoid Potentially Harmful Relationships

Counselors who provide forensic evaluations avoid potentially harmful professional or personal relationships with family members, romantic partners, and close friends of individuals they are evaluating or have evaluated in the past.

SECTION F
Supervision, Training, and Teaching

Introduction

Counselor supervisors, trainers, and educators aspire to foster meaningful and respectful professional relationships and to maintain appropriate boundaries with supervisees and students in both face-to-face and electronic formats. They have theoretical and pedagogical foundations for their work; have knowledge of supervision models; and aim to be fair, accurate, and honest in their assessments of counselors, students, and supervisees.

F.1. Counselor Supervision and Client Welfare

F.1.a. Client Welfare

A primary obligation of counseling supervisors is to monitor the services provided by supervisees. Counseling supervisors monitor client welfare and supervisee performance and professional development. To fulfill these obligations, supervisors meet regularly with supervisees to review the supervisees' work and help them become prepared to serve a range of diverse clients. Supervisees have a responsibility to understand and follow the *ACA Code of Ethics*.

F.1.b. Counselor Credentials

Counseling supervisors work to ensure that supervisees communicate their qualifications to render services to their clients.

F.1.c. Informed Consent and Client Rights

Supervisors make supervisees aware of client rights, including the protection of client privacy and confidentiality in the counseling relationship. Supervisees provide clients with professional disclosure information and inform them of how the supervision process influences the limits of confidentiality. Supervisees make clients aware of who will have access to records of the counseling relationship and how these records will be stored, transmitted, or otherwise reviewed.

F.2. Counselor Supervision Competence

F.2.a. Supervisor Preparation

Prior to offering supervision services, counselors are trained in supervision methods and techniques. Counselors who offer supervision services regularly pursue continuing education activities, including both counseling and supervision topics and skills.

F.2.b. Multicultural Issues/Diversity in Supervision

Counseling supervisors are aware of and address the role of multiculturalism/ diversity in the supervisory relationship.

F.2.c. Online Supervision

When using technology in supervision, counselor supervisors are competent in the use of those technologies. Supervisors take the necessary precautions to protect the confidentiality of all information transmitted through any electronic means.

F.3. Supervisory Relationship

F.3.a. Extending Conventional Supervisory Relationships

Counseling supervisors clearly define and maintain ethical professional, personal, and social relationships with their supervisees. Supervisors consider the risks and benefits of extending current supervisory relationships in any form beyond conventional parameters. In extending these boundaries, supervisors take appropriate professional precautions to ensure that judgment is not impaired and that no harm occurs.

F.3.b. Sexual Relationships

Sexual or romantic interactions or relationships with current supervisees are prohibited. This prohibition applies to both in-person and electronic interactions or relationships.

F.3.c. Sexual Harassment

Counseling supervisors do not condone or subject supervisees to sexual harassment.

F.3.d. Friends or Family Members

Supervisors are prohibited from engaging in supervisory relationships with individuals with whom they have an inability to remain objective.

F.4. Supervisor Responsibilities

F.4.a. Informed Consent for Supervision

Supervisors are responsible for incorporating into their supervision the principles of informed consent and participation. Supervisors inform supervisees of the policies and procedures to which supervisors are to adhere and the mechanisms for due process appeal of individual supervisor actions. The issues unique to the use of distance supervision are to be included in the documentation as necessary.

F.4.b. Emergencies and Absences

Supervisors establish and communicate to supervisees procedures for contacting supervisors or, in their absence, alternative on-call supervisors to assist in handling crises.

F.4.c. Standards for Supervisees

Supervisors make their supervisees aware of professional and ethical standards and legal responsibilities.

F.4.d. Termination of the Supervisory Relationship

Supervisors or supervisees have the right to terminate the supervisory relationship with adequate notice. Reasons for considering termination are discussed, and both parties work to resolve differences. When termination is warranted, supervisors make appropriate referrals to possible alternative supervisors.

F.5. Student and Supervisee Responsibilities

F.5.a. Ethical Responsibilities

Students and supervisees have a responsibility to understand and follow the *ACA Code of Ethics*. Students and supervisees have the same obligation to clients as those required of professional counselors.

F.5.b. Impairment

Students and supervisees monitor themselves for signs of impairment from their own physical, mental, or emotional problems and refrain from offering or providing professional services when such impairment is likely to harm a client or others. They notify their faculty and/or supervisors and seek assistance for problems that reach the level of professional impairment, and, if necessary, they limit, suspend, or terminate their professional responsibilities until it is determined that they may safely resume their work.

F.5.c. Professional Disclosure

Before providing counseling services, students and supervisees disclose their status as supervisees and explain how this status affects the limits of confidentiality. Supervisors ensure that clients are aware of the services rendered and the qualifications of the students and supervisees rendering those services. Students and supervisees obtain client permission before they use any information concerning the counseling relationship in the training process.

F.6. Counseling Supervision Evaluation, Remediation, and Endorsement

F.6.a. Evaluation

Supervisors document and provide supervisees with ongoing feedback regarding their performance and schedule periodic formal evaluative sessions throughout the supervisory relationship.

F.6.b. Gatekeeping and Remediation

Through initial and ongoing evaluation, supervisors are aware of supervisee limitations that might impede performance. Supervisors assist supervisees in securing remedial assistance when needed. They recommend dismissal from training programs, applied counseling settings, and state or voluntary professional credentialing processes when those supervisees are unable to demonstrate that they can provide competent professional services to a range of diverse clients. Supervisors seek consultation and document their decisions to dismiss or refer supervisees for assistance. They ensure that supervisees are aware of options available to them to address such decisions.

F.6.c. Counseling for Supervisees

If supervisees request counseling, the supervisor assists the supervisee in identifying appropriate services. Supervisors do not provide counseling services to supervisees. Supervisors address interpersonal competencies in terms of the impact of these issues on clients, the supervisory relationship, and professional functioning.

F.6.d. Endorsements

Supervisors endorse supervisees for certification, licensure, employment, or completion of an academic or training program only when they believe that supervisees are qualified for the endorsement. Regardless of qualifications, supervisors do not endorse supervisees whom they believe to be impaired in any way that would interfere with the performance of the duties associated with the endorsement.

F.7. Responsibilities of Counselor Educators

F.7.a. Counselor Educators

Counselor educators who are responsible for developing, implementing, and supervising educational programs are skilled as teachers and practitioners. They are knowledgeable regarding the ethical, legal, and regulatory aspects of the profession; are skilled in applying that knowledge; and make students and supervisees aware of their responsibilities. Whether in traditional, hybrid, and/or online formats, counselor educators conduct counselor education and training programs in an ethical manner and serve as role models for professional behavior.

F.7.b. Counselor Educator Competence

Counselors who function as counselor educators or supervisors provide instruction within their areas of knowledge and competence and provide instruction based on current information and knowledge available in the profession. When using technology to deliver instruction, counselor educators develop competence in the use of the technology.

F.7.c. Infusing Multicultural Issues/Diversity

Counselor educators infuse material related to multiculturalism/diversity into all courses and workshops for the development of professional counselors.

F.7.d. Integration of Study and Practice

In traditional, hybrid, and/or online formats, counselor educators establish education and training programs that integrate academic study and supervised practice.

F.7.e. Teaching Ethics

Throughout the program, counselor educators ensure that students are aware of the ethical responsibilities and standards of the profession and the ethical responsibilities of students to the profession. Counselor educators infuse ethical considerations throughout the curriculum.

F.7.f. Use of Case Examples

The use of client, student, or supervisee information for the purposes of case examples in a lecture or classroom setting is permissible only when (a) the client, student, or supervisee has reviewed the material and agreed to its presentation or (b) the information has been sufficiently modified to obscure identity.

F.7.g. Student-to-Student Supervision and Instruction

When students function in the role of counselor educators or supervisors, they understand that they have the same ethical obligations as counselor educators, trainers, and supervisors. Counselor educators make every effort to ensure that the rights of students are not compromised when their peers lead experiential counseling activities in traditional, hybrid, and/or online formats (e.g., counseling groups, skills classes, clinical supervision).

F.7.h. Innovative Theories and Techniques

Counselor educators promote the use of techniques/procedures/modalities that are grounded in theory and/or have an empirical or scientific foundation. When counselor educators discuss developing or innovative techniques/ procedures/modalities, they explain the potential risks, benefits, and ethical considerations of using such techniques/procedures/modalities.

F.7.i. Field Placements

Counselor educators develop clear policies and provide direct assistance within their training programs regarding appropriate field placement and other clinical experiences. Counselor educators provide clearly stated roles and responsibilities for the student or supervisee, the site supervisor, and the program supervisor. They confirm that site supervisors are qualified to provide supervision in the formats in which services are provided and inform site supervisors of their professional and ethical responsibilities in this role.

F.8. Student Welfare

F.8.a. Program Information and Orientation

Counselor educators recognize that program orientation is a developmental process that begins upon students' initial contact with the counselor education program and continues throughout the educational and clinical training of students. Counselor education faculty provide prospective and current students with information about the counselor education program's expectations, including

1. the values and ethical principles of the profession;
2. the type and level of skill and knowledge acquisition required for successful completion of the training;
3. technology requirements;
4. program training goals, objectives, and mission, and subject matter to be covered;
5. bases for evaluation;
6. training components that encourage self-growth or self-disclosure as part of the training process;
7. the type of supervision settings and requirements of the sites for required clinical field experiences;
8. student and supervisor evaluation and dismissal policies and procedures; and
9. up-to-date employment prospects for graduates.

F.8.b. Student Career Advising

Counselor educators provide career advisement for their students and make them aware of opportunities in the field.

F.8.c. Self-Growth Experiences

Self-growth is an expected component of counselor education. Counselor educators are mindful of ethical principles when they require students to engage in self-growth experiences. Counselor educators and supervisors inform students that they have a right to decide what information will be shared or withheld in class.

F.8.d. Addressing Personal Concerns

Counselor educators may require students to address any personal concerns that have the potential to affect professional competency.

F.9. Evaluation and Remediation

F.9.a. Evaluation of Students

Counselor educators clearly state to students, prior to and throughout the training program, the levels of competency expected, appraisal methods, and timing of evaluations for both didactic and clinical competencies. Counselor educators provide students with ongoing feedback regarding their performance throughout the training program.

F.9.b. Limitations

Counselor educators, through ongoing evaluation, are aware of and address the inability of some students to achieve counseling competencies. Counselor educators do the following:

1. assist students in securing remedial assistance when needed,

2. seek professional consultation and document their decision to dismiss or refer students for assistance, and

3. ensure that students have recourse in a timely manner to address decisions requiring them to seek assistance or to dismiss them and provide students with due process according to institutional policies and procedures.

F.9.c. Counseling for Students

If students request counseling, or if counseling services are suggested as part of a remediation process, counselor educators assist students in identifying appropriate services.

F.10. Roles and Relationships Between Counselor Educators and Students

F.10.a. Sexual or Romantic Relationships

Counselor educators are prohibited from sexual or romantic interactions or relationships with students currently enrolled in a counseling or related program and over whom they have power and authority. This prohibition applies to both in-person and electronic interactions or relationships.

F.10.b. Sexual Harassment

Counselor educators do not condone or subject students to sexual harassment.

F.10.c. Relationships With Former Students

Counselor educators are aware of the power differential in the relationship between faculty and students. Faculty members discuss with former students potential risks when they consider engaging in social, sexual, or other intimate relationships.

F.10.d. Nonacademic Relationships

Counselor educators avoid nonacademic relationships with students in which there is a risk of potential harm to the student or which may compromise the training experience or grades assigned. In addition, counselor educators do not accept any form of professional services, fees, commissions, reimbursement, or remuneration from a site for student or supervisor placement.

F.10.e. Counseling Services

Counselor educators do not serve as counselors to students currently enrolled in a counseling or related program and over whom they have power and authority.

F.10.f. Extending Educator–Student Boundaries

Counselor educators are aware of the power differential in the relationship between faculty and students. If they believe that a nonprofessional relationship with a student may be potentially beneficial to the student, they take precautions similar to those taken by counselors when working with clients. Examples of potentially beneficial interactions or relationships include, but are not limited to, attending a formal ceremony; conducting hospital visits; providing support during a stressful event; or maintaining mutual membership in a professional association, organization, or community. Counselor educators discuss with students the rationale for such interactions, the potential benefits and drawbacks, and the anticipated consequences for the student. Educators clarify the specific nature and limitations of the additional role(s) they will have with the student prior to engaging in a nonprofessional relationship. Nonprofessional relationships with students should be time limited and/or context specific and initiated with student consent.

F.11. Multicultural/Diversity Competence in Counselor Education and Training Programs

F.11.a. Faculty Diversity

Counselor educators are committed to recruiting and retaining a diverse faculty.

F.11.b. Student Diversity

Counselor educators actively attempt to recruit and retain a diverse student body. Counselor educators demonstrate commitment to multicultural/diversity competence by recognizing and valuing the diverse cultures and types of abilities that students bring to the training experience. Counselor educators provide appropriate accommodations that enhance and support diverse student well-being and academic performance.

F.11.c. Multicultural/Diversity Competence

Counselor educators actively infuse multicultural/diversity competency in their training and supervision practices. They actively train students to gain awareness, knowledge, and skills in the competencies of multicultural practice.

SECTION G
Research and Publication

Introduction

Counselors who conduct research are encouraged to contribute to the knowledge base of the profession and promote a clearer understanding of the conditions that lead to a healthy and more just society. Counselors support the efforts of researchers by participating fully and willingly whenever possible. Counselors minimize bias and respect diversity in designing and implementing research.

G.1. Research Responsibilities

G.1.a. Conducting Research

Counselors plan, design, conduct, and report research in a manner that is consistent with pertinent ethical principles, federal and state laws, host institutional regulations, and scientific standards governing research.

G.1.b. Confidentiality in Research

Counselors are responsible for understanding and adhering to state, federal, agency, or institutional policies or applicable guidelines regarding confidentiality in their research practices.

G.1.c. Independent Researchers

When counselors conduct independent research and do not have access to an institutional review board, they are bound to the same ethical principles and federal and state laws pertaining to the review of their plan, design, conduct, and reporting of research.

G.1.d. Deviation From Standard Practice

Counselors seek consultation and observe stringent safeguards to protect the rights of research participants when research indicates that a deviation from standard or acceptable practices may be necessary.

G.1.e. Precautions to Avoid Injury

Counselors who conduct research are responsible for their participants' welfare throughout the research process and should take reasonable precautions to avoid causing emotional, physical, or social harm to participants.

G.1.f. Principal Researcher Responsibility

The ultimate responsibility for ethical research practice lies with the principal researcher. All others involved in the research activities share ethical obligations and responsibility for their own actions.

G.2. Rights of Research Participants

G.2.a. Informed Consent in Research

Individuals have the right to decline requests to become research participants. In seeking consent, counselors use language that

1. accurately explains the purpose and procedures to be followed;
2. identifies any procedures that are experimental or relatively untried;
3. describes any attendant discomforts, risks, and potential power differentials between researchers and participants;
4. describes any benefits or changes in individuals or organizations that might reasonably be expected;
5. discloses appropriate alternative procedures that would be advantageous for participants;
6. offers to answer any inquiries concerning the procedures;
7. describes any limitations on confidentiality;
8. describes the format and potential target audiences for the dissemination of research findings; and
9. instructs participants that they are free to withdraw their consent and discontinue participation in the project at any time, without penalty.

G.2.b. Student/Supervisee Participation

Researchers who involve students or supervisees in research make clear to them that the decision regarding participation in research activities does not affect their academic standing or supervisory relationship. Students or supervisees who choose not to participate in research are provided with an appropriate alternative to fulfill their academic or clinical requirements.

G.2.c. Client Participation

Counselors conducting research involving clients make clear in the informed consent process that clients are free to choose whether to participate in research activities. Counselors take necessary precautions to protect clients from adverse consequences of declining or withdrawing from participation.

G.2.d. Confidentiality of Information

Information obtained about research participants during the course of research is confidential. Procedures are implemented to protect confidentiality.

G.2.e. Persons Not Capable of Giving Informed Consent

When a research participant is not capable of giving informed consent, counselors provide an appropriate explanation to, obtain agreement for participation from, and obtain the appropriate consent of a legally authorized person.

G.2.f. Commitments to Participants

Counselors take reasonable measures to honor all commitments to research participants.

G.2.g. Explanations After Data Collection

After data are collected, counselors provide participants with full clarification of the nature of the study to remove any misconceptions participants might have regarding the research. Where scientific or human values justify delaying or withholding information, counselors take reasonable measures to avoid causing harm.

G.2.h. Informing Sponsors

Counselors inform sponsors, institutions, and publication channels regarding research procedures and outcomes. Counselors ensure that appropriate bodies and authorities are given pertinent information and acknowledgment.

G.2.i. Research Records Custodian

As appropriate, researchers prepare and disseminate to an identified colleague or records custodian a plan for the transfer of research data in the case of their incapacitation, retirement, or death.

G.3. Managing and Maintaining Boundaries

G.3.a. Extending Researcher–Participant Boundaries

Researchers consider the risks and benefits of extending current research relationships beyond conventional parameters. When a nonresearch interaction between the researcher and the research participant may be potentially beneficial, the researcher must document, prior to the interaction (when feasible), the rationale for such an interaction, the potential benefit, and anticipated consequences for the research participant. Such interactions should be initiated with appropriate consent of the research participant. Where unintentional harm occurs to the research participant, the researcher must show evidence of an attempt to remedy such harm.

G.3.b. Relationships With Research Participants

Sexual or romantic counselor–research participant interactions or relationships with current research participants are prohibited. This prohibition applies to both in-person and electronic interactions or relationships.

G.3.c. Sexual Harassment and Research Participants

Researchers do not condone or subject research participants to sexual harassment.

G.4. Reporting Results

G.4.a. Accurate Results

Counselors plan, conduct, and report research accurately. Counselors do not engage in misleading or fraudulent research, distort data, misrepresent data, or deliberately bias their results. They describe the extent to which results are applicable for diverse populations.

G.4.b. Obligation to Report Unfavorable Results

Counselors report the results of any research of professional value. Results that reflect unfavorably on institutions, programs, services, prevailing opinions, or vested interests are not withheld.

G.4.c. Reporting Errors

If counselors discover significant errors in their published research, they take reasonable steps to correct such errors in a correction erratum or through other appropriate publication means.

G.4.d. Identity of Participants

Counselors who supply data, aid in the research of another person, report research results, or make original data available take due care to disguise the identity of respective participants in the absence of specific authorization from the participants to do otherwise. In situations where participants self-identify their involvement in research studies, researchers take active steps to ensure that data are adapted/ changed to protect the identity and welfare of all parties and that discussion of results does not cause harm to participants.

G.4.e. Replication Studies

Counselors are obligated to make available sufficient original research information to qualified professionals who may wish to replicate or extend the study.

G.5. Publications and Presentations

G.5.a. Use of Case Examples

The use of participants', clients', students', or supervisees' information for the purpose of case examples in a presentation or publication is permissible only when (a) participants, clients, students, or supervisees have reviewed the material and agreed to its presentation or publication or (b) the information has been sufficiently modified to obscure identity.

G.5.b. Plagiarism

Counselors do not plagiarize; that is, they do not present another person's work as their own.

G.5.c. Acknowledging Previous Work

In publications and presentations, counselors acknowledge and give recognition to previous work on the topic by others or self.

G.5.d. Contributors

Counselors give credit through joint authorship, acknowledgment, footnote statements, or other appropriate means to those who have contributed significantly to research or concept development in accordance with such contributions. The principal contributor is listed first, and minor technical or professional contributions are acknowledged in notes or introductory statements.

G.5.e. Agreement of Contributors

Counselors who conduct joint research with colleagues or students/supervisors establish agreements in advance regarding allocation of tasks, publication credit, and types of acknowledgment that will be received.

G.5.f. Student Research

Manuscripts or professional presentations in any medium that are substantially based on a student's course papers, projects, dissertations, or theses are used only with the student's permission and list the student as lead author.

G.5.g. Duplicate Submissions

Counselors submit manuscripts for consideration to only one journal at a time. Manuscripts that are published in whole or in substantial part in one journal or published work are not submitted for publication to another publisher without acknowledgment and permission from the original publisher.

G.5.h. Professional Review

Counselors who review material submitted for publication, research, or other scholarly purposes respect the confidentiality and proprietary rights of those who submitted it. Counselors make publication decisions based on valid and defensible standards. Counselors review article submissions in a timely manner and based on their scope and competency in research methodologies. Counselors who serve as reviewers at the request of editors or publishers make every effort to only review materials that are within their scope of competency and avoid personal biases.

SECTION H
Distance Counseling, Technology, and Social Media
Introduction

Counselors understand that the profession of counseling may no longer be limited to in-person, face-to-face interactions. Counselors actively attempt to understand the evolving nature of the profession with regard to distance counseling, technology, and social media and how such resources may be used to better serve their clients. Counselors strive to become knowledgeable about these resources. Counselors understand the additional concerns related to the use of distance counseling, technology, and social media and make every attempt to protect confidentiality and meet any legal and ethical requirements for the use of such resources.

H.1. Knowledge and Legal Considerations

H.1.a. Knowledge and Competency
Counselors who engage in the use of distance counseling, technology, and/ or social media develop knowledge and skills regarding related technical, ethical, and legal considerations (e.g., special certifications, additional course work).

H.1.b. Laws and Statutes
Counselors who engage in the use of distance counseling, technology, and social media within their counseling practice understand that they may be subject to laws and regulations of both the counselor's practicing location and the client's place of residence. Counselors ensure that their clients are aware of pertinent legal rights and limitations governing the practice of counseling across state lines or international boundaries.

H.2. Informed Consent and Security

H.2.a. Informed Consent and Disclosure
Clients have the freedom to choose whether to use distance counseling, social media, and/or technology within the counseling process. In addition to the usual and customary protocol of informed consent between counselor and client for face-to-face counseling, the following issues, unique to the use of distance counseling, technology, and/ or social media, are addressed in the informed consent process:

- distance counseling credentials, physical location of practice, and contact information;
- risks and benefits of engaging in the use of distance counseling, technology, and/or social media;
- possibility of technology failure and alternate methods of service delivery;
- anticipated response time;
- emergency procedures to follow when the counselor is not available;
- time zone differences;
- cultural and/or language differences that may affect delivery of services;
- possible denial of insurance benefits; and
- social media policy.

H.2.b. Confidentiality Maintained by the Counselor
Counselors acknowledge the limitations of maintaining the confidentiality of electronic records and transmissions. They inform clients that individuals might have authorized

or unauthorized access to such records or transmissions (e.g., colleagues, supervisors, employees, information technologists).

H.2.c. Acknowledgment of Limitations

Counselors inform clients about the inherent limits of confidentiality when using technology. Counselors urge clients to be aware of authorized and/or unauthorized access to information disclosed using this medium in the counseling process.

H.2.d. Security

Counselors use current encryption standards within their websites and/or technology-based communications that meet applicable legal requirements. Counselors take reasonable precautions to ensure the confidentiality of information transmitted through any electronic means.

H.3. Client Verification

Counselors who engage in the use of distance counseling, technology, and/ or social media to interact with clients take steps to verify the client's identity at the beginning and throughout the therapeutic process. Verification can include, but is not limited to, using code words, numbers, graphics, or other nondescript identifiers.

H.4. Distance Counseling Relationship

H.4.a. Benefits and Limitations

Counselors inform clients of the benefits and limitations of using technology applications in the provision of counseling services. Such technologies include, but are not limited to, computer hardware and/or software, telephones and applications, social media and Internet-based applications and other audio and/or video communication, or data storage devices or media.

H.4.b. Professional Boundaries in Distance Counseling

Counselors understand the necessity of maintaining a professional relationship with their clients. Counselors discuss and establish professional boundaries with clients regarding the appropriate use and/or application of technology and the limitations of its use within the counseling relationship (e.g., lack of confidentiality, times when not appropriate to use).

H.4.c. Technology-Assisted Services

When providing technology-assisted services, counselors make reasonable efforts to determine that clients are intellectually, emotionally, physically, linguistically, and functionally capable of using the application and that the application is appropriate for the needs of the client. Counselors verify that clients understand the purpose and operation of technology applications and follow up with clients to correct possible misconceptions, discover appropriate use, and assess subsequent steps.

H.4.d. Effectiveness of Services

When distance counseling services are deemed ineffective by the counselor or client, counselors consider delivering services face-to-face. If the counselor is not able to provide face-to-face services (e.g., lives in another state), the counselor assists the client in identifying appropriate services.

H.4.e. Access

Counselors provide information to clients regarding reasonable access to pertinent applications when providing technology-assisted services.

H.4.f. Communication Differences in Electronic Media

Counselors consider the differences between face-to-face and electronic communication (nonverbal and verbal cues) and how these may affect the counseling process. Counselors educate clients on how to prevent and address potential misunderstandings arising from the lack of visual cues and voice intonations when communicating electronically.

H.5. Records and Web Maintenance

H.5.a. Records

Counselors maintain electronic records in accordance with relevant laws and statutes. Counselors inform clients on how records are maintained electronically. This includes, but is not limited to, the type of encryption and security assigned to the records, and if/for how long archival storage of transaction records is maintained.

H.5.b. Client Rights

Counselors who offer distance counseling services and/or maintain a professional website provide electronic links to relevant licensure and professional certification boards to protect consumer and client rights and address ethical concerns.

H.5.c. Electronic Links

Counselors regularly ensure that electronic links are working and are professionally appropriate.

H.5.d. Multicultural and Disability Considerations

Counselors who maintain websites provide accessibility to persons with disabilities. They provide translation capabilities for clients who have a different primary language, when feasible. Counselors acknowledge the imperfect nature of such translations and accessibilities.

H.6. Social Media

H.6.a. Virtual Professional Presence

In cases where counselors wish to maintain a professional and personal presence for social media use, separate professional and personal web pages and profiles are created to clearly distinguish between the two kinds of virtual presence.

H.6.b. Social Media as Part of Informed Consent

Counselors clearly explain to their clients, as part of the informed consent procedure, the benefits, limitations, and boundaries of the use of social media.

H.6.c. Client Virtual Presence

Counselors respect the privacy of their clients' presence on social media unless given consent to view such information.

H.6.d. Use of Public Social Media

Counselors take precautions to avoid disclosing confidential information through public social media.

SECTION I
Resolving Ethical Issues

Introduction

Professional counselors behave in an ethical and legal manner. They are aware that client welfare and trust in the profession depend on a high level of professional conduct. They hold other counselors to the same standards and are willing to take appropriate action to ensure that standards are upheld. Counselors strive to resolve ethical dilemmas with direct and open communication among all parties involved and seek consultation with colleagues and supervisors when necessary. Counselors incorporate ethical practice into their daily professional work and engage in ongoing professional development regarding current topics in ethical and legal issues in counseling. Counselors become familiar with the ACA Policy and Procedures for Processing Complaints of Ethical Violations[1] and use it as a reference for assisting in the enforcement of the *ACA Code of Ethics*.

I.1. Standards and the Law

I.1.a. Knowledge

Counselors know and understand the *ACA Code of Ethics* and other applicable ethics codes from professional organizations or certification and licensure bodies of which they are members. Lack of knowledge or misunderstanding of an ethical responsibility is not a defense against a charge of unethical conduct.

I.1.b. Ethical Decision Making

When counselors are faced with an ethical dilemma, they use and document, as appropriate, an ethical decision-making model that may include, but is not limited to, consultation;

consideration of relevant ethical standards, principles, and laws; generation of potential courses of action; deliberation of risks and benefits; and selection of an objective decision based on the circumstances and welfare of all involved.

I.1.c. Conflicts Between Ethics and Laws

If ethical responsibilities conflict with the law, regulations, and/or other governing legal authority, counselors make known their commitment to the *ACA Code of Ethics* and take steps to resolve the conflict. If the conflict cannot be resolved using this approach, counselors, acting in the best interest of the client, may adhere to the requirements of the law, regulations, and/or other governing legal authority.

I.2. Suspected Violations

I.2.a. Informal Resolution

When counselors have reason to believe that another counselor is violating or has violated an ethical standard and substantial harm has not occurred, they attempt to first resolve the issue informally with the other counselor if feasible, provided such action does not violate confidentiality rights that may be involved.

I.2.b. Reporting Ethical Violations

If an apparent violation has substantially harmed or is likely to substantially harm a person or organization and is not appropriate for informal resolution or is not resolved properly, counselors take further action depending on the situation. Such action may include referral to state or national committees on professional ethics, voluntary national certification bodies, state licensing boards, or appropriate institutional authorities. The confidentiality rights of clients should be considered in all actions. This standard does not apply when counselors have been retained to review the work of another counselor whose professional conduct is in question (e.g., consultation, expert testimony).

I.2.c. Consultation

When uncertain about whether a particular situation or course of action may be in violation of the *ACA Code of Ethics*, counselors consult with other counselors who are knowledgeable about ethics and the *ACA Code of Ethics*, with colleagues, or with appropriate authorities, such as the ACA Ethics and Professional Standards Department.

I.2.d. Organizational Conflicts

If the demands of an organization with which counselors are affiliated pose a conflict with the *ACA Code of Ethics*, counselors specify the nature of such conflicts and express to their supervisors or other responsible officials their commitment to the *ACA Code of Ethics* and, when possible, work through the appropriate channels to address the situation.

I.2.e. Unwarranted Complaints

Counselors do not initiate, participate in, or encourage the filing of ethics complaints that are retaliatory in nature or are made with reckless disregard or willful ignorance of facts that would disprove the allegation.

I.2.f. Unfair Discrimination Against Complainants and Respondents

Counselors do not deny individuals employment, advancement, admission to academic or other programs, tenure, or promotion based solely on their having made or their being the subject of an ethics complaint. This does not preclude taking action based on the outcome of such proceedings or considering other appropriate information.

I.3. Cooperation With Ethics Committees

Counselors assist in the process of enforcing the *ACA Code of Ethics*. Counselors cooperate with investigations, proceedings, and requirements of the ACA Ethics Committee or ethics committees of other duly constituted associations or boards having jurisdiction over those charged with a violation.

[1]See the American Counseling Association web site at http://www.counseling.org/knowledge-center/ethics

GLOSSARY OF TERMS

Abandonment—the inappropriate ending or arbitrary termination of a counseling relationship that puts the client at risk.

Advocacy—promotion of the well-being of individuals, groups, and the counseling profession within systems and organizations. Advocacy seeks to remove barriers and obstacles that inhibit access, growth, and development.

Assent—to demonstrate agreement when a person is otherwise not capable or competent to give formal consent (e.g., informed consent) to a counseling service or plan.

Assessment—the process of collecting in-depth information about a person in order to develop a comprehensive plan that will guide the collaborative counseling and service provision process.

Bartering—accepting goods or services from clients in exchange for counseling services.

Client—an individual seeking or referred to the professional services of a counselor.

Confidentiality—the ethical duty of counselors to protect a client's identity, identifying characteristics, and private communications.

Consultation—a professional relationship that may include, but is not limited to, seeking advice, information, and/or testimony.

Counseling—a professional relationship that empowers diverse individuals, families, and groups to accomplish mental health, wellness, education, and career goals.

Counselor Educator—a professional counselor engaged primarily in developing, implementing, and supervising the educational preparation of professional counselors.

Counselor Supervisor—a professional counselor who engages in a formal relationship with a practicing counselor or counselor-in-training for the purpose of overseeing that individual's counseling work or clinical skill development.

Culture—membership in a socially constructed way of living, which incorporates collective values, beliefs, norms, boundaries, and lifestyles that are cocreated with others who share similar worldviews comprising biological, psychosocial, historical, psychological, and other factors.

Discrimination—the prejudicial treatment of an individual or group based on their actual or perceived membership in a particular group, class, or category.

Distance Counseling—The provision of counseling services by means other than face-to-face meetings, usually with the aid of technology.

Diversity—the similarities and differences that occur within and across cultures, and the intersection of cultural and social identities.

Documents—any written, digital, audio, visual, or artistic recording of the work within the counseling relationship between counselor and client.

Encryption—process of encoding information in such a way that limits access to authorized users.

Examinee—a recipient of any professional counseling service that includes educational, psychological, and career appraisal, using qualitative or quantitative techniques.

Exploitation—actions and/or behaviors that take advantage of another for one's own benefit or gain.

Fee Splitting—the payment or acceptance of fees for client referrals (e.g., percentage of fee paid for rent, referral fees).

Forensic Evaluation—the process of forming professional opinions for court or other legal proceedings, based on professional knowledge and expertise, and supported by appropriate data.

Gatekeeping—the initial and ongoing academic, skill, and dispositional assessment of students' competency for professional practice, including remediation and termination as appropriate.

Impairment—a significantly diminished capacity to perform professional functions.

Incapacitation—an inability to perform professional functions.

Informed Consent—a process of information sharing associated with possible actions clients may choose to take, aimed at assisting clients in acquiring a full appreciation and understanding of the facts and implications of a given action or actions.

Instrument—a tool, developed using accepted research practices, that measures the presence and strength of a specified construct or constructs.

Interdisciplinary Teams—teams of professionals serving clients that may include individuals who may not share counselors' responsibilities regarding confidentiality.

Minors—generally, persons under the age of 18 years, unless otherwise designated by statute or regulation. In some jurisdictions, minors may have the right to consent to counseling without consent of the parent or guardian.

Multicultural/Diversity Competence—counselors' cultural and diversity awareness and knowledge about self and others, and how this awareness and knowledge are applied effectively in practice with clients and client groups.

Multicultural/Diversity Counseling—counseling that recognizes diversity and embraces approaches that support the worth, dignity, potential, and uniqueness of individuals within their historical, cultural, economic, political, and psychosocial contexts.

Personal Virtual Relationship—engaging in a relationship via technology and/or social media that blurs the professional boundary (e.g., friending on social networking sites); using personal accounts as the connection point for the virtual relationship.

Privacy—the right of an individual to keep oneself and one's personal information free from unauthorized disclosure.

Privilege—a legal term denoting the protection of confidential information in a legal proceeding (e.g., subpoena, deposition, testimony).

Pro bono publico—contributing to society by devoting a portion of professional activities for little or no financial return (e.g., speaking to groups, sharing professional information, offering reduced fees).

Professional Virtual Relationship—using technology and/ or social media in a professional manner and maintaining appropriate professional boundaries; using business accounts that cannot be linked back to personal accounts as the connection point for the virtual relationship (e.g., a business page versus a personal profile).

Records—all information or documents, in any medium, that the counselor keeps about the client, excluding personal and psychotherapy notes.

Records of an Artistic Nature—products created by the client as part of the counseling process.

Records Custodian—a professional colleague who agrees to serve as the caretaker of client records for another mental health professional.

Self-Growth—a process of self-examination and challenging of a counselor's assumptions to enhance professional effectiveness.

Serious and Foreseeable—when a reasonable counselor can anticipate significant and harmful possible consequences.

Sexual Harassment—sexual solicitation, physical advances, or verbal/nonverbal conduct that is sexual in nature; occurs in connection with professional activities or roles; is unwelcome, offensive, or creates a hostile workplace or learning environment; and/or is sufficiently severe or intense to be perceived as harassment by a reasonable person.

Social Justice—the promotion of equity for all people and groups for the purpose of ending oppression and injustice affecting clients, students, counselors, families, communities, schools, workplaces, governments, and other social and institutional systems.

Social Media—technology-based forms of communication of ideas, beliefs, personal histories, etc. (e.g., social networking sites, blogs).

Student—an individual engaged in formal graduate-level counselor education.

Supervisee—a professional counselor or counselor-in-training whose counseling work or clinical skill development is being overseen in a formal supervisory relationship by a qualified trained professional.

Supervision—a process in which one individual, usually a senior member of a given profession designated as the supervisor, engages in a collaborative relationship with another individual or group, usually a junior member(s) of a given profession designated as the supervisee(s) in order to (a) promote the growth and development of the supervisee(s), (b) protect the welfare of the clients seen by the supervisee(s), and (c) evaluate the performance of the supervisee(s).

Supervisor—counselors who are trained to oversee the professional clinical work of counselors and counselors-in-training.

Teaching—all activities engaged in as part of a formal educational program that is designed to lead to a graduate degree in counseling.

Training—the instruction and practice of skills related to the counseling profession. Training contributes to the ongoing proficiency of students and professional counselors.

Virtual Relationship—a non–face-to-face relationship (e.g., through social media).

INDEX

CPSIA information can be obtained
at www.ICGtesting.com
Printed in the USA
BVHW020002010723
666614BV00007B/520

9 781516 510351